THE WOMEN'S CONVENT

THE WOMEN'S CONVENTION TURNED 30

Achievements, Setbacks, and Prospects

Edited by

Ingrid WESTENDORP

Cambridge – Antwerp – Portland

Intersentia Publishing Ltd.
Trinity House | Cambridge Business Park | Cowley Road
Cambridge | CB4 0WZ | United Kingdom
Tel.: +44 1223 393 753 | Email: mail@intersentia.co.uk

Distribution for the UK:
Hart Publishing Ltd.
16C Worcester Place
Oxford OX1 2JW
UK
Tel.: +44 1865 517 530
Email: mail@hartpub.co.uk

Distribution for the USA and Canada:
International Specialized Book Services
920 NE 58th Ave. Suite 300
Portland, OR 97213
USA
Tel.: +1 800 944 6190 (toll free)
Email: info@isbs.com

Distribution for Austria:
Neuer Wissenschaftlicher Verlag
Argentinierstraße 42/6
1040 Wien
Austria
Tel.: +43 1 535 61 03 24
Email: office@nwv.at

Distribution for other countries:
Intersentia Publishing nv
Groenstraat 31
2640 Mortsel
Belgium
Tel.: +32 3 680 15 50
Email: mail@intersentia.be

The Women's Convention Turned 30: Achievements, Setbacks, and Prospects
Ingrid Westendorp (ed.)

© 2012 Intersentia
Cambridge – Antwerp – Portland
www.intersentia.com | www.intersentia.co.uk

Cover illustration: Danny Juchtmans

ISBN 978-1-78068-085-9
D/2012/7849/104
NUR 828

British Library Cataloguing in Publication Data. A catalogue record for this book is available from the British Library.

No part of this book may be reproduced in any form, by print, photoprint, microfilm or any other means, without written permission from the publisher.

PREFACE

On 8 March 2010, International Women's Day, many of the authors of this book attended a one-day seminar organized by the Maastricht Centre for Human Rights of the Maastricht University. It was a most inspiring event on which new ideas were launched and thorough discussions were held. The seminar was not only attended by legal scholars from the Netherlands and abroad, but also by Non-Governmental Organisations' representatives, civil servants and students.

The 27 contributors of this book have different national and cultural backgrounds; some have just started their (academic) careers whilst others already are well-established in their particular field of work. They all had to write their particular contribution on top of a busy daytime job. As is not uncommon in projects such as this, some of the authors have managed to submit their Chapters in a very short period of time whilst others were facing unexpected challenges. It is never easy to get 27 individuals on the same page, but in the end every single chapter shows enthusiasm and dedication to the cause of equality for women. I am genuinely grateful to every single one of them.

I would also like to express my gratitude to the Maastricht Centre for Human Rights and the Faculty of Law's Research Fund for their (financial) support to organize this seminar, and to Intersentia for making the publication of this book possible.

Special thanks go to Chantal Kuypers who, on top of organizing the seminar, has always been my prop and stay with whatever problem I encountered during the compilation of this book.

Finally, my gratitude goes to three enthusiastic and hard-working student assistants who did research, looked up references and gave support to whoever needed it: Laura Visser, Samira Sakhi and Antonia Waltermann.

SUMMARY OF CONTENTS

Chapter 1. Introduction
    Ingrid Westendorp 1

Chapter 2. The United Nations and the Promotion and Protection of Women's Human Rights: A Work in Progress
    Fleur van Leeuwen 13

Chapter 3. The Essence of Discrimination Against Women: An Interpretation by CEDAW and the European Union
    Ingrid Westendorp and Antonia Waltermann 33

Chapter 4. The Principle of Equality
    Rolanda Oostland 67

Chapter 5. Temporary Special Measures under the Women's Convention and Positive Action under EU Law: Mutually Compatible or Irreconcilable?
    Lisa Waddington and Laura Visser 95

Chapter 6. Using Culture to Achieve Equality
    Ingrid Westendorp 111

Chapter 7. 'Because to me, a Woman Who Speaks in Public is a Public Woman': 30 Years Women's Convention and the Struggle to Eliminate Discrimination of Women in the Field of Trafficking and Prostitution
    Marjolein van den Brink and Marjan Wijers 135

Chapter 8. Articles 7 and 8: The Added Value of the Women's Convention and the Dutch Case of the Christian Party
    Margreet de Boer 163

Chapter 9. Equal Treatment of Women and Men in Nationality Law
    Gerard-René de Groot 187

Chapter 10. Barriers to Girls' Right to Education in Afghanistan
    Fons Coomans and Samira Sakhi 205

Summary of Contents

Chapter 11. Equal Employment Opportunities and Equal Pay: Measuring EU Law against the Standards of the Women's Convention
 Anja WIESBROCK 227

Chapter 12. Women's Right to Health and International Trade – Special Reference to the GATS and the TRIPS Agreement
 Jennifer SELLIN and Nishara MENDIS 249

Chapter 13. Eradicating Female Circumcision: Changing a Harmful Social Norm through the Women's Convention
 Phyllis LIVAHA 279

Chapter 14. Equality and Economic and Social Life Including Implications for the European Union
 Dagmar SCHIEK and Jule MULDER 303

Chapter 15. Rural Women's Right to Land and Housing in Times of Urbanization
 Ingrid WESTENDORP 325

Chapter 16. Equality of Men and Women before the Law: Towards a New Dutch Law on Names
 Tilly DRAAISMA 343

Chapter 17. Article 16 of the Women's Convention and the Status of Muslim Women at Divorce
 Pauline KRUINIGER 363

Chapter 18. CEDAW: A Full Human Rights Treaty Body?
 Cees FLINTERMAN 395

Chapter 19. Due Diligence Mania
 Menno T. KAMMINGA 407

Chapter 20. Reservations to the Women's Convention: A Muslim Problem Ill-addressed?
 Zoé LUCA 417

Chapter 21. The Optional Protocol to the Women's Convention: An Assessment of Its Effectiveness in Protecting Women's Rights
 Sille JANSEN 435

Chapter 22. Emerging from the Shadows: Violence Against Women and the Women's Convention
      Kate Rose-Sender 453

Chapter 23. The Impact of Corruption upon Women's Rights: A Neglected Area?
      Martine Boersma 467

Chapter 24. The Impact and Effectiveness of State Reporting under the Women's Convention: The Case of the Netherlands
      Jasper Krommendijk 487

CONTENTS

Preface v
Summary of Contents vii
List of Abbreviations xxiii
About the Contributors xxv

Chapter 1. Introduction
     Ingrid WESTENDORP 1

Chapter 2. The United Nations and the Promotion and Protection
of Women's Human Rights: A Work in Progress
     Fleur VAN LEEUWEN 13

1. Introduction 13
2. The First Step: Same Rights 15
   2.1. The UN Human Rights System 15
   2.2. The Commission on the Status of Women 18
3. The Second Step: Special Rights 21
4. The Third Step: Transformation of the Mainstream 24
5. Final Remarks 28

Chapter 3. The Essence of Discrimination Against Women:
An Interpretation by CEDAW and the European Union
     Ingrid WESTENDORP and Antonia WALTERMANN 33

1. Introduction 33
2. Defining Discrimination 35
   2.1. The Drafting History of Article 1 35
   2.2 A Comparison with other Definitions of Discrimination 36
3. CEDAW's Interpretation of Discrimination Against Women 39
   3.1. CEDAW's Concluding Observations and Article 1 39
   3.2. General Recommendations 41
   3.3. Decisions 44
   3.4. Inquiry 47
4. The Principle of Non-Discrimination under EU Law 48
   4.1. Primary Sources of EU Law 49
   4.2. Secondary Sources of EU Law 50

	4.3. Case Law.. 53
	4.4. Other Instruments 57
	4.4.1. The Daphne Programme: Violence Against Women 57
	4.4.2. Instruments Regarding Gender Equality and Gender Mainstreaming.. 58
	4.5. Limitations... 59
5.	Analysis.. 60
6.	Conclusion 63

Chapter 4. The Principle of Equality
Rolanda OOSTLAND 67

1. Introduction.. 67
2. The Principles of Equality and Non-Discrimiation 68
   2.1. Formal and Substantive Equality............................... 68
   2.2. Direct and Indirect Discrimination............................ 71
   2.3. The Relation Between the Principles of Equality and Non-Discrimination 73
3. Articles 2 and 3 of the Women's Convention 75
   3.1. Article 2 75
       3.1.1. General and Specific Obligations......................... 75
       3.1.2. Equality Clause in National Legislation 76
       3.1.3. Non-State Actors 78
       3.1.4. Modify Discriminatory Laws, Customs and Practices........ 80
   3.2. Article 3 82
       3.2.1. All Appropriate Measures................................ 82
       3.2.2. On a Basis of Equality with Men 84
       3.2.3. Not Temporary and in All Fields......................... 84
4. Article 3 ICCPR... 85
   4.1. General Comment No. 28 85
   4.2. Formal and Substantive Equality............................... 86
   4.3. Non-State Actors... 89
   4.4. Culture, Traditions and Religion 89
5. Conclusions 91

Chapter 5. Temporary Special Measures under the Women's Convention and Positive Action under EU Law: Mutually Compatible or Irreconcilable?
Lisa WADDINGTON and Laura VISSER 95

1. Introduction.. 95
2. Formal Equality, Substantive Equality and Temporary Special Measures/Positive Action... 97
3. Obligations to Adopt Temporary Special Measures under Article 4(1) of the Convention 98

4. Limitations to the Adoption of Positive Action Measures under EU Law. 101
5. A Comparison: The Obligation to Adopt Temporary Special Measures under the Convention and the Limits to Positive Action under EU Law.. 106

Chapter 6. Using Culture to Achieve Equality
Ingrid WESTENDORP.. 111

1. Introduction.. 111
2. Content and Meaning of Article 5: Introduction...................... 112
3. Implementation on the Domestic Level............................... 115
    3.1. Appropriate Measures According to CEDAW..................... 116
    3.2. Some Comments on CEDAW's Concluding Observations 120
4. The Two Faces of Culture... 122
    4.1. Culture as a Barrier.. 122
    4.2. Culture as an Instrument of Change........................... 126
    4.3. Relevant Actors.. 129
5. Conclusion 130

Chapter 7. 'Because to me, a Woman Who Speaks in Public is a Public Woman': 30 Years Women's Convention and the Struggle to Eliminate Discrimination of Women in the Field of Trafficking and Prostitution
Marjolein VAN DEN BRINK and Marjan WIJERS..................... 135

1. Introduction.. 135
2. International Legal Framework in a Historical Perspective............ 137
    2.1. From Regulation to Eradication of Prostitution 137
    2.2. The First Treaties.. 138
    2.3. Sex Workers Raise Their Voices 140
    2.4. The UN Trafficking Protocol.................................. 141
3. Drafting Article 6 142
4. CEDAW's Observations on Trafficking and Prostitution.............. 144
    4.1. Introduction... 144
    4.2. Trafficking 145
        4.2.1. Perception of the Problem............................. 145
        4.2.2. Causes of Trafficking................................. 146
        4.2.3. A Comprehensive Approach........................... 147
        4.2.4. The Legal Framework 148
    4.3. Exploitation of Prostitution................................... 151
        4.3.1. Defining the Problem................................. 151
        4.3.2. Causes... 152
        4.3.3. Measures 152
        4.3.4. Legal Measures 153

	4.3.4.1.	Measures to be taken in prohibitionist and abolitionist States 153
	4.3.4.2.	Measures to be taken in States which (partly) decriminalized the sex sector. 154

5. Analysis and Conclusion 155

Chapter 8. Articles 7 and 8: The Added Value of the Women's Convention and the Dutch Case of the Christian Party
Margreet DE BOER. 163

1. Introduction. 163
2. Historical Background 163
3. Political Participation and the Women's Convention 165
   3.1. General Recommendations. 165
   3.2. Decisions under the Optional Protocol. 167
   3.3. Concluding Comments 167
4. What Does the Women's Convention Add to Other Human Rights Obligations? 167
   4.1. The Scope 168
   4.2. Substansive Equality. 168
5. Measures. 169
   5.1. Measures in General Recommendation No. 23 170
   5.2. Measures in Concluding Observations. 171
   5.3. Temporary Special Measures: Quota, Numeric Goals and Time Frames 172
   5.4. Awareness Raising Campaigns. 173
   5.5. Training and Assisting Women Candidates. 173
   5.6. The Voice of Women. 174
   5.7. Participation of Women in NGOs and Associations Concerned with the Public and Political Life 174
   5.8. Measures and the Freedom of Political Parties and Associations. . . . 175
6. Case Study: The Case of the Dutch Christian Party that Excludes Women 175
   6.1. The SGP and 'The Women's Issue' 177
   6.2. Prologue to the Proceedings in the SGP-Case: CEDAW Concluding Observations 2001 178
   6.3. The Proceedings in the SGP-Case: The District Court. 178
   6.4. Intermezzo: CEDAW Concluding Observations 2007 179
   6.5. The Proceedings in the SGP-Case: The Appeal 179
   6.6. Intermezzo: CEDAW Concluding Observations 2010 180
   6.7. The Proceedings in the SGP-Case: The Verdict of the Supreme Court. 180

6.8. The Direct Effect of Article 7 Women's Convention and the Key Role of Political Parties in the Enforcement of the Right to Stand for Election.. 181
6.9. The Prohibition of Discrimination Regarding Political Rights in Relation to the Freedom of Religion and the Freedom of Association.. 182
6.10. The Role of the State: Responsibilities and Measures 183
7. Conclusion 183

Chapter 9. Equal Treatment of Women and Men in Nationality Law
Gerard-René DE GROOT... 187

1. Introduction.. 187
2. Treaty Provisions.. 187
3. Historical Background: From *Système Unitaire* to *Système Dualiste*...... 190
4. From *Ius Sanguinis a Patre* to *Ius Sanguinis a Patre et a Matre*.......... 195
5. Reservations to Article 9 of the Women's Convention 196
   5.1. Reservations to the Whole of Article 9 196
   5.2. Reservations to Article 9(2)................................... 198
5. Transitory Provisions 200
6. Conclusions 202

Chapter 10. Barriers to Girls' Right to Education in Afghanistan
Fons COOMANS and Samira SAKHI 205

1. Introduction.. 205
2. The Human Rights Framework.................................... 206
   2.1. The Purpose of Article 10 Women's Convention.................. 206
   2.2. Obligations Resulting from Article 10 Women's Convention....... 207
   2.3. Other Relevant International Instruments...................... 208
3. Gender Related Aspects of Education 209
4. Short Overview of Afghanistan's Educational Situation under Taliban Rule and after Transition to Democratic Governance.................. 212
5. Barriers to Girls' Right to Education in Afghanistan 214
   5.1. Insecurity... 214
   5.2. Poverty 215
   5.3. Early Marriages.. 216
   5.4. Other Barriers 217
6. Does Afghanistan Comply with Its Obligations Relating to the Right to Education for Girls? 218
7. Towards Universalising the Right to Education in Afghanistan? 219
   7.1. The Value of Education in Islamic Societies..................... 219
   7.2. Universalising the Right to Education 221
8. Concluding Remarks... 223

Chapter 11. Equal Employment Opportunities and Equal Pay: Measuring
EU Law against the Standards of the Women's Convention
  Anja WIESBROCK 227

1. Introduction 227
2. The Right to Equal Employment Opportunities and Equal Pay for
   Work of Equal Value 229
    2.1. Article 11 Women's Convention 229
    2.2. EU Law 231
3. Challenges in the Application of Employment Rights 233
    3.1. Non-Standard Forms of Employment 235
    3.2. Deep-Rooted Causes of Inequality and a Male Standard of Worker . 238
4. Implementation and Enforcement 242
5. Conclusion 244

Chapter 12. Women's Right to Health and International Trade – Special
Reference to the GATS and the TRIPS Agreement
  Jennifer SELLIN and Nishara MENDIS 249

1. Introduction 249
2. A Brief Background to the Right to Health 251
3. The Right to Health under the ICESCR and the Women's Convention . . . 254
4. TRIPS: Patents and Access to Medicines from the Perspective of
   a Woman's Right to Health 267
5. GATS: Liberalization of Health Services and a Women's Right to Health . 271
6. Conclusion 277

Chapter 13. Eradicating Female Circumcision: Changing a Harmful Social
Norm through the Women's Convention
  Phyllis LIVAHA 279

1. Introduction 279
2. FC Procedure 280
3. Cultural Relativism 282
4. Female Circumcision and Its Complications and Effects 285
5. CEDAW General Recommendation No. 14 and other International
   Instruments 286
6. Is Legislation Enough? The Enforcement of the Women's Convention . . . 289
7. Conclusion 298

Chapter 14. Equality and Economic and Social Life Including Implications for the European Union
      Dagmar SCHIEK and Jule MULDER............................... 303

1. Introduction.. 303
2. Broader Context of Article 13 within the UN....................... 304
3. Article 13 Analysed... 306
   3.1. Article 13(a) (Family Benefits) 306
   3.2. Article 13(b) (Financial Credit) 309
   3.3. Article 13(c) (Recreational Activities, Sports, Cultural Life)........ 315
4. EU Law and Article 13 316
   4.1. Article 13(a) (Family Benefits) 317
   4.2. Article 13(b) and (c) (Financial Services and Recreational and Cultural Activities)... 318
      4.2.1. Financial Services...................................... 318
      4.2.2. Recreational Activities and Cultural Life................ 320
5. Conclusion 321

Chapter 15. Rural Women's Right to Land and Housing in Times of Urbanization
      Ingrid WESTENDORP... 325

1. Introduction.. 325
2. Historical Development of Article 14.............................. 326
3. Urban vs. Rural 328
4. The Importance of Land... 330
   4.1. Barriers to Obtain and Control Land 331
   4.2. Consequences of Lack of Land 334
   4.3. CEDAW's Attention for Land in Article 14 335
5. Rural Women's Future 337
6. Concluding Remarks... 339

Chapter 16. Equality of Men and Women before the Law: Towards a New Dutch Law on Names
      Tilly DRAAISMA... 343

1. Introduction.. 343
2. Historical Context.. 343
   2.1. Charter of the United Nations 344
   2.2. Universal Declaration on Human Rights 344
   2.3. International Covenants on Human Rights...................... 344
   2.4. Declaration on the Elimination of Discrimination Against Women. 345

3. Drafting History of Article 15 345
   3.1. The Draft Proposals of the Working Group of the Commission
        on the Status of Women 345
   3.2. The Proposal of the Commission on the Status of Women 346
   3.3. Reviews of the Working Group of the Third Committee 347
   3.4. The Third Committee 348
   3.5. Plenary Meeting of the General Assembly of the United Nations ... 348
4. Significance of Article 15 348
5. Recommendations by CEDAW 349
6. Commentary 350
7. Towards a New Dutch Law on Names? 352
   7.1. The Law up till 1 January 1998 352
   7.2. Comments by the Committee 353
   7.3. The Fourth Periodic Report of the Netherlands and the
        Committee's Comments 353
   7.4. The Fifth Report of the Netherlands 354
   7.5. The Committee's Comments 357
   7.6. Concluding Observations 358
8. Conclusion 358

Chapter 17. Article 16 of the Women's Convention and the Status of
Muslim Women at Divorce
    Pauline KRUINIGER 363

1. Introduction 363
2. Article 16 Women's Convention 366
   2.1. Its Context 366
   2.2. Nature of Article 16 369
   2.3. Declarations and Reservations 370
3. 'Islamic' Divorce Laws and Practices 371
   3.1. 'Islamic' Law and Divorce 371
   3.2. Divorce in Morocco 373
        3.2.1. Introduction 373
        3.2.2. Divorce 374
        3.2.3. Assessment 377
   3.3. Divorce in Pakistan 379
        3.3.1. Introduction 379
        3.3.2. Divorce 381
        3.3.3. Assessment 384
4. Attitude of 'Islamic' States Towards the Women's Convention 385
5. Concluding Comments and Prospects 388

Chapter 18. CEDAW: A Full Human Rights Treaty Body?
Cees FLINTERMAN 395

1. Introduction 395
2. Composition of CEDAW 396
3. Mandate 398
4. Working Methods 399
5. CEDAW and NGOs. 401
6. Concluding Remarks. 403

Chapter 19. Due Diligence Mania
Menno T. KAMMINGA. 407

1. Introduction 407
2. International Law 409
3. Domestic Law. 410
4. Women's Rights 411
5. European Court of Human Rights 411
6. Conclusions 413

Chapter 20. Reservations to the Women's Convention: A Muslim Problem Ill-addressed?
Zoé LUCA 417

1. Introduction 417
2. Background 418
   2.1. Types of Reservations. 420
   2.2. The Evolving State of Reservations 421
3. CEDAW's Response Outside the Reporting Mechanism 423
4. CEDAW and Muslim States in the Reporting Mechanism. 427
   4.1. Assessing the Practice of Muslim States Since 2004 427
   4.2. CEDAW's Reaction within the Reporting Mechanism 430
5. Objections by States Parties. 432
6. Conclusions 433

Chapter 21. The Optional Protocol to the Women's Convention: An Assessment of Its Effectiveness in Protecting Women's Rights
Sille JANSEN 435

1. Introduction 435
2. The Evolution of the Procedures of the Protocol 436
3. The Terms of the Protocol and Its Case Law 438
   3.1. The Individual Complaints Procedure 438

		3.1.1.	Introduction 438
		3.1.2.	Admissibility.. 439
			3.1.2.1. Exhaustion of Domestic Remedies 439
			3.1.2.2. Admissibility *Ratione Materiae*................... 440
			3.1.2.3. Admissibility *Ratione Temporis*.................. 440
		3.1.3.	Justiciability and the Margin of Discretion 442
		3.1.4.	Interim Measures 444
		3.1.5.	Due Diligence 446
		3.1.6.	Follow-up... 448
	3.2.	Conclusion.. 449
4.	The Inquiry Procedure 450
5.	Conclusion 451

Chapter 22. Emerging from the Shadows: Violence Against Women and the Women's Convention
    Kate ROSE-SENDER 453

1. Introduction... 453
2. Formulation – The Drafting Process 454
3. Raising Awareness... 458
4. Function – The Work of the Committee 462
5. Summary and Conclusions 465

Chapter 23. The Impact of Corruption upon Women's Rights:
A Neglected Area?
    Martine BOERSMA... 467

1. Introduction... 467
  1.1. Background 467
  1.2. Structure and Methodology 468
2. Defining 'Corruption'.. 469
  2.1. Public vs. Private Sector Corruption 469
  2.2. Grand vs. Petty Corruption..................................... 471
  2.3. Taxonomy.. 471
      2.3.1. Bribery 471
      2.3.2. Trading in Influence 472
      2.3.3. Embezzlement.. 473
      2.3.4. Abuse of Functions...................................... 473
      2.3.5. Illicit Enrichment 474
3. Corruption as a Women's Rights Issue 474
  3.1. Introduction.. 474
  3.2. The Political Dimension: Access to Decision-Making Power 475
  3.3. The Law Enforcement Dimension: Protection of Women's Rights... 476

            3.3.1. The Justice System 476
            3.3.2. Human Trafficking..................................... 477
        3.4. The Socio-economic Dimension: Access to Resources............. 478
            3.4.1. Health.. 478
            3.4.2. Education... 480
    4. Practice of the UN Treaty Bodies 481
        4.1. CEDAW 482
        4.2. Other Treaty Bodies 483
    5. Conclusions and Recommendations 484

Chapter 24. The Impact and Effectiveness of State Reporting under the
Women's Convention: The Case of the Netherlands
        Jasper KROMMENDIJK.. 487

1. Introduction.. 487
2. Impact and Attention at the Domestic Level 488
    2.1. Governmental Informing of Parliament........................ 489
    2.2. National Reports and In-depth Studies......................... 490
    2.3. Parliamentary Scrutiny 492
    2.4. Media Coverage.. 495
    2.5. Courts and Legal Practice 496
3. Factors at the State Level 498
4. Factors Related to CEDAW 503
5. Differing Views about the Nature of the Obligations 505
6. Conclusion 508

LIST OF ABBREVIATIONS

CEDAW	Committee on the Elimination of Discrimination Against Women
CERD	Committee on the Elimination of Racial Discrimination
CESCR	Committee on Economic, Social and Cultural Rights
CHR	Commission on Human Rights
CMW	Committee on Migrant Workers
CO/COs	Concluding Observation(s)
CRC	Committee on the Rights of the Child
CSO/CSOs	Civil society organization(s)
CSW	Commission on the Status of Women
DEDAW	Declaration on the Elimination of Discrimination Against Women
ECJ	European Court of Justice
ECN	European Convention on Nationality
ECOSOC	Economic and Social Council of the United Nations
EU	European Union
FC	Female circumcision
GA	General Assembly of the United Nations
GATS	General Agreement on Trade in Services
HRC	Human Rights Committee
ICCPR	International Covenant on Civil and Political Rights
ICERD	International Convention on the Elimination of All Forms of Racial Discrimination
ICESCR	International Covenant on Economic, Social and Cultural Rights
ICMW	International Convention on the Protection of the Rights of All Migrant Workers and Members of Their Families
IGO/IGOs	Intergovernmental organization(s)
ILO	International Labour Organization
NGO/NGOs	Non-governmental organization(s)
UDHR	Universal Declaration on Human Rights
UN	United Nations
SRVAW	Special Rapporteur on Violence Against Women
TFEU	Treaty on the Functioning of the European Union
TRIPS	Agreement on Trade Related Aspects of Intellectual Property Rights
VAW	Violence Against Women
WHO	World Health Organization
WTO	World Trade Organization

ABOUT THE CONTRIBUTORS

Ms Margreet de Boer studied Dutch Law and Criminology (1982–1986). For her thesis she developed a complaint procedure on sexual harassment for the Free University. In 1989, Margreet de Boer started her career as a women's lawyer: she became partner in a law firm, and provided legal aid to women on family law, the legal position of victims of domestic and sexual violence, social security and equal treatment. She handled several cases on sex-discrimination for the equal treatment commission and the court.

In 2000, Margreet de Boer became a senior consultant with the Clara Wichmann Instituut, the expertise Centre for Women and Law, where she worked as senior consultant and director. Since 2004 she has her own consultancy firm on Women's Rights. In these positions she focussed on the analysis and research of the gender aspects of laws and their implementation. She was co-author of the Dutch Shadow Report on the implementation of CEDAW in the Netherlands (2006), and advisor for the Dutch Audit Committee on Gender mainstreaming (2005–2006). She developed several trainings, on gender aware legislation, on CEDAW and on the legal aspects of domestic violence. Margreet de Boer is partner in Rights 4 Change, a project organisation which focuses on human rights impact assessment.

Margreet de Boer is also an active member of the political party GroenLinks (GreenLeft). She was member of the local council in Amsterdam-West (from 2006–2011), and from June 2011 she is member of the Senate of the Dutch Parliament.

Ms Martine Boersma studied Law at Maastricht University (*cum laude*), where she specialized in company and commercial law, as well as in labour and health law. Subsequently, she started her PhD research in September 2007 with the Maastricht Centre for Human Rights. The dissertation addresses the possibilities for combating corruption in the public sector by making use of the systems of international human rights law and international criminal law. Martine also teaches various courses in the field of international and European law at Maastricht University. Since 2011 Martine Boersma works as a solicitor.

Dr Marjolein van den Brink has lectured at Utrecht Law School since 2000. Between 2001 and 2010 she combined this with a commissionership of the Dutch national Equality Body. Previously, she worked for the national advisory council to the government on matters of women's equality and empowerment, for a Dutch NGO focusing on international developments relevant to women in the Netherlands, and for the University of Leiden. In 2006 she defended her Ph.D. thesis, a gender analysis of the work of the UN Children's Rights Committee, focusing in particular on the effects of the Committee's recommendations on the position of parents in terms of gender. She has published on a variety of topics, ranging from human rights, and the (ir)relevance of sex as a legal category, to issues of multiculturalism, and gender bias in the international law concept of state sovereignty.

Prof. Dr Fons Coomans holds the UNESCO Chair in Human Rights and Peace. He is also the coordinator of the Maastricht Centre for Human Rights, and Senior Researcher at the Netherlands School of Human Rights Research. His fields of research include the international protection of economic, social and cultural rights in general and the right to education and food in particular, as well as international supervisory mechanisms in the field of human rights. He is the coordinator of the courses on economic, social and cultural rights of the Advanced European Masters Degree in Human Rights and Democratisation in Venice.

Dr M.C.E.M. (Tilly) Draaisma studied Dutch law (Utrecht University, 1980) and fiscal law (Tilburg University, 1991) and made her doctorate at the Free University, Amsterdam (2001). The title of her doctoral thesis was: *De stiefouder: stiefkind van het recht. Een onderzoek naar de juridische plaatsbepaling van de stiefouder* (*Stepparent: Stepchild of Law. A study into the Legal position of the stepparent*). She was a solicitor till 1985. Currently, she is senior lecturer international law in the department of law at the Dutch Open University, Heerlen.

Prof. Dr Cees Flinterman is honorary professor of human rights at Maastricht University and Utrecht University (the Netherlands). From 2003–2010 he was a member of the United Nations Committee on the Elimination of Discrimination Against Women. He is presently a member of the United Nations Human Rights Committee (2011–2014). In earlier years he was *inter alia* professor of constitutional and international law (Maastricht University, 1982–1998), professor of human rights, director of the Netherlands Institute of Human Rights (SIM) and director of the Netherlands School of Human Rights Research (Utrecht University, 1998–2007) and chair of the Netherlands delegation to the United Nations Commission on Human Rights (1993–1994) and the Second World Conference on Human Rights (19993); in 1993 he was elected as one of the Vice-Chairs of the United Nations Commission on Human Rights.

Prof. Dr Gerard René de Groot studied Law at the Rijksuniversiteit Groningen (the Netherlands) and at the Westfälische Wilhelmsuniversität Münster (Germany). In Groningen he obtained the degrees Magister iuris and

About the Contributors

Doctorandus iuris, and from 1974 until 1982, he taught Private and Comparative Law there. Since 1982 he has been teaching Private Law, Comparative Law and Private International Law at Maastricht University, where he obtained the degree of Doctor iuris. In 1988 he was appointed Professor of Comparative Law and Private International Law. He is also Professor at the University of Aruba (Dutch Caribbean) and the University Hasselt (Belgium). Gerard-René de Groot has published many books and articles on comparative nationality law.

Ms Sille Jansen graduated from University College Utrecht and Maastricht University. She is currently working as an advocacy officer for sexual and reproductive health and rights at Rutgers WPF, with women's rights as her particular focus. In her function as chair of CHOICE for youth and sexuality she advocates for youth participation in this field, as a lever for development.

Prof. Dr Menno T. Kamminga is Professor of International Law at Maastricht University and Director of the Maastricht Centre for Human Rights. He chairs the Netherlands' Government Advisory Committee on International Law and the Netherlands Human Rights Research School. He is co-editor (with Martin Scheinin) of The Impact of Human Rights Law on General International Law (Oxford: 2009).

Mr Jasper Krommendijk has been employed as a PhD researcher at the Maastricht Centre for Human Rights since 1st November 2009. His PhD research, under the supervision of Prof. Dr A.P.M. Coomans and Prof. Dr F. Grünfeld, deals with the impact and effectiveness of human rights state reporting under the main six UN human rights treaties and Concluding Observations at the domestic level. Jasper holds an LLM degree in International Law and Law of International Organisations from the University of Groningen Faculty of Law, The Netherlands (*cum laude*). He previously completed bachelor degrees in International Relations and International and European Law at the same university (both cum laude). After his studies, Jasper did an internship at the Dutch Ministry of Economic Affairs, working on issues relating to the EC Services Directive. In addition, he worked at the Ministry of Justice in the field of European criminal law and monitoring and evaluation mechanisms between May and October 2009.

Ms Pauline Kruiniger (LL.M Maastricht University, specialization in Islamic Law, Leiden University, the Netherlands) is currently working as PhD Researcher at the Maastricht Faculty of Law due to a grant from the Netherlands Organisation for Scientific Research (NWO). Her research which is entitled 'Repudiation or recognition of Islamic divorces in Europe?', focuses on the recognition of Islamic dissolutions of marriage in Europe from the perspective of the position of women.

About the Contributors

Dr Fleur van Leeuwen, LL.M., works as assistant professor at Yeditepe University in Istanbul, Turkey and conducts research on women's human rights. Fleur obtained her PhD in human rights law in 2009 at Utrecht University in the Netherlands. In that same year she published her dissertation: *Women's Rights are Human Rights – The Practice of the UN Human Rights Committee and the Committee on Economic, Social and Cultural Rights*. Fleur published articles on women's rights in various languages, books and journals. Besides her academic activities, she works as a consultant on human rights related issues in Turkey; conducts human rights projects on request; and is editor of the Dutch scientific *Tijdschrift voor Genderstudies* (Journal on Gender studies).

Ms Phyllis Livaha joined the Faculty of Law at Maastricht University in 2008, where she teaches both international law and international relations. She holds a Juris Doctor from Michigan State University College of Law and a B.A. (honours) in Political Science from Bennett College. Before joining the faculty at Maastricht, she was a volunteer researcher for International Rights Advocates, a litigation project of the International Labor Rights Fund that provides legal support to victims of human rights abuses around the world. She has also worked as a Client Support Specialist at EVE, Inc. (End Violent Encounters). She externed at Legal Services of South Central Michigan, volunteered as a Women's Program Assistant at Refugee Services, and interned at Amnesty International.

Ms Zoé Luca, who is of Belgian origin, completed her primary and secondary education in the DRC and South Africa. She holds a BA in Social Sciences from University College Maastricht and a LL.M. in international law from the Maastricht Law Faculty. In the framework of the latter, she was a member of the 2006/2007 Maastricht team for the Jessup International Law Moot Court Competition and studied for a year at the University of Salamanca. While completing a second LL.M., Zoé worked as research assistant, focusing inter alia on violence against women, and as assistant editor at the Maastricht Journal of European and Comparative Law (a post she maintained until March 2011). In October 2010, following her studies, Zoé took up the post of Assistant to the Women and War Advisor at the International Committee of the Red Cross. She has been replacing the Advisor ad interim since March 2011.

Ms Nishara Mendis is currently a PhD fellow at the Institute for Globalization and International Regulation and the Faculty of Law, Maastricht University. She obtained a degree in Law from the University of Colombo, Sri Lanka, with First Class Honours, and a Master of Laws from Yale Law School. She has worked as a lecturer in law at the University of Colombo and as a legal researcher and resource person for several Colombo-based NGOs.

About the Contributors

Ms Jule Mulder is a Ph.D. candidate at the University of Leeds, currently conducting research within European Non-Discrimination law and its national application. Her research interests are interdisciplinary Comparative Law and national, European and international Equality law.

Dr Rolanda Oostland wrote her PhD thesis Non-discrimination and Equality of Women, A Comparative Analysis of the Interpretation by the UN Human Rights Committee and the UN Committee on the Elimination of Discrimination against Women, at the Netherlands Institute of Human Rights (SIM), Utrecht University. In 2001 she undertook an internship at the United Nations Secretariat in New York at the UN Division for the Advancement of Women, assisting members of CEDAW during their 25th session. Between 2004 – 2009 she has been working as a lecturer in Public International Law at the Erasmus University Rotterdam. Currently she is working as a senior lawyer at the Ministry of the Interior and Kingdom Relations, Directorate for Constitutional Affairs and Legislation.

Dr Sarah (Kate) Rose-Sender earned her PhD from the University of Westminster in London in 2003. She graduated with Merit from the University of London LLM degree program in 1993. She received her undergraduate degree in Sociology from the University of Missouri (Kansas City) and completed her law degree (J.D.) at DePaul University College of Law (Chicago). Dr Rose Sender is a public international lawyer with experience in teaching and practicing in several international jurisdictions. She has worked with the Ministry of Justice, the Supreme Court and the Attorney General's Office in Kabul, Afghanistan to establish an independent national legal training centre. She has taught international law humanitarian law, constitutional law and human rights in Budapest, Cairo, Chicago, Kaunas, London and Pretoria. Dr Rose-Sender's most current research is in stabilization of States emerging from armed conflict. In 2009–2010, Dr Rose-Sender was the Executive Editor of the Maastricht Journal of European and Comparative Law and assistant professor with the International and European Law Department of Maastricht University. Currently, Dr Rose-Sender lives in Afghanistan where she advises the Afghan Government on human rights issues.

Ms Samira Sakhi was born in Kabul Afghanistan. At the age of nine she fled, with her family, to the Netherlands. She started her master globalization and law (human rights track) in February 2011. She is also active as country representative Afghanistan for Amnesty International and is working as a student- assistant international and European law for Maastricht University.

Prof. Dr Dagmar Schiek is Chair in European Law and Director of the Centre of European Law and Legal Studies at the University of Leeds, having held positions as associate professor at University of Oldenburg and as assistant professor at

University of Bremen previously. She has published extensively on European labour law and non-discrimination law. Her current research interests lie in the field of European Economic and Social constitutionalism, new forms of governance in the EU involving civil society and European and international equality law. She has been a visiting professor and guest lecturer at various universities, including London School of Economics and Maastricht University. She is on the editorial board of the Maastricht Journal for Comparative and European Law and of Kritische Justiz (Critical Legal Studies, Germany).

Ms Jennifer Sellin is a PhD candidate at the Maastricht Centre for Human Rights and the Faculty of Law, Maastricht University. She obtained a Bachelors degree European law and a Masters degree with honours in European and international law from Maastricht University. The topic of her PhD research is: The interface of intellectual property and human rights: Access to medicines for patients in developing countries.

Ms Laura Visser graduated cum laude from the Bachelor European Law School English Track. Currently she is enrolled in the Master International Laws at Maastricht University. In the academic year 2010–2011 she participated in the Women's Human Rights Clinic of Prof. C. Flinterman, which meant that she closely followed CEDAW's work for a year. In addition to her studies, she was the student assistant for the Maastricht Centre for Human Rights.

Prof. Dr Lisa Waddington is the Extraordinary Professor of European Disability Law at the Faculty of Law of Maastricht University. Professor Waddington is the disability coordinator of the EU Network of Legal Experts in the Non-Discrimination Field and joint editor (with Dagmar Schiek and Mark Bell) of Cases, Material and Text on National, Supranational and International Non-Discrimination Law, (Hart, 2007).

Ms Antonia Waltermann started her master Globalization and Law (specialization human rights) at Maastricht University in September 2011. Her focus is largely on legal philosophy, international human rights and humanitarian law, though her bachelolor gives her a background in European Law as well. During her master studies, she has partaken in the honour's research programme and worked as a student-assistant for the department of international and European law at Maastricht University. From September 2012 onwards, she will be working as a lecturer at the Constitutional Law Department at Maastricht University.

Dr Ingrid Westendorp is a senior lecturer/researcher in international law and woman and law at the Department of International and European Law of Maastricht University. She has studied Dutch law at the Netherlands Open

University. In 2007 she defended her doctoral thesis entitled Women and Housing: Gender Makes a Difference. Her teaching is focused on (optional) bachelor courses in international law and human rights of women. She has been a Visiting Lecturer at the Gadjah Mada University, Yogyakarta and at Udayana University, Denpasar, Indonesia where she taught courses in international law, problem based learning and gender and law.

Her research is focused on economic and social human rights, especially the right to adequate housing and the right to land. Within her research she takes a gender perspective into account.

Dr Anja Wiesbrock is an Assistant Professor in European Law at the Department of International and European Law of Maastricht University. She graduated (cum laude) in both European Studies (BA) and European Law (LLB, LLM) from Maastricht University. In 2009 she finalized her PhD thesis on the national implementation of EU legislation concerning regular migrants. For her doctoral and post-doctoral research, Anja has been a Visiting Researcher at Jawahrlal Nehru University and Harvard Law School. She has been a Visiting Lecturer at Dokuz Eylül University, teaching an introductory course on EU Law.

Anja's main research interests include EU substantive law, EU migration law, citizenship law, EU non-discrimination law and EU consumer law. She is currently involved in a Jean Monnet Multilateral Research Group as well as a research project on EU-India mobility.

Anja is a scholar of the Maastricht Centre for European Law and a member of the Ius Commune Research School.

Ms Marjan Wijers works as an independent researcher, consultant and trainer in the area of human rights, human trafficking and women's rights. From 2003 – 2007 she was President of the European Experts Group on Trafficking in Human Beings, established by the European Commission. Previously she worked at the Dutch Foundation against Trafficking in Women, the Clara Wichmann Institute, Dutch Expert Centre on Women & Law, a research institute and a children's hotline. At the Foundation against Trafficking in Women she was engaged in providing assistance to victims of trafficking, as well as in policy development, lobby and advocacy. Amongst others she was actively involved in the NGO lobby around the UN Trafficking Protocol. Over the past years she published a range of articles on trafficking in persons, sex work and human rights.

CHAPTER 1
INTRODUCTION

Ingrid WESTENDORP

It is the purpose of this book to give insight into the developments that have taken place in the three decades that the Convention on the Elimination of All forms of Discrimination Against Women (the Women's Convention) is already in existence. Central are the substantive provisions of the Convention, which are discussed in respect of their history, peculiarities, the difficulties in interpreting and implementing them, and the potential that they may have for future development. Each of these Chapters will be preceded by the text of the Article or Articles they examine.

In addition to the discussion of Articles contained in the Convention, in this book also various other issues are discussed that play a role as regards the achievement of women's equal rights. These additional issues concern gender mainstreaming, gender-based violence, the effect of corruption on women's rights, and the impact and effectiveness of State reporting under the Women's Convention. Furthermore, one Chapter assesses the effectiveness of the Optional Protocol to the Convention.

Some of the provisions in the Convention are very broad or can be approached from different angles. It goes without saying that within the confines of this book it was impossible to go into all different aspects and therefore authors had to make choices. Some have limited themselves to only one aspect contained in a provision; others have focused on a particular State party or a specific situation. Others still have made a comparison between the impact and implementation of a certain Article of the Women's Convention and a similar provision of European Union law.

All in all, the book gives a good impression of the shortcomings, the strengths and the potential of the Women's Convention for the furtherance of women's human rights and the role that has been and can be played by its monitoring body the Committee on the Elimination of All Forms of Discrimination Against Women (CEDAW).

In the next part, a short summary of the contents of each of the Chapters will be given.

CONTENTS OF THE CHAPTERS

In Chapter 2 Fleur van Leeuwen puts the Women's Convention into perspective by discussing the United Nations (UN) framework in which human rights are promoted and protected. It was clear from the outset, that the UN was of the opinion that *all* people are entitled to the same human rights for the simple reason that they are human beings. That is why discrimination of any kind, including on the basis of sex was forbidden. However, in practice the system was, and to some extent still is androcentric. In the past it was successfully shown that women's experiences and needs were not properly addressed and included. Fortunately, steps toward improvement were made.

In 1979 the Women's Convention was adopted: a Convention that focuses solely on the enjoyment of human rights by women. While the effect of this specific Convention was enhanced attention for women's life experiences and understanding of women's perspective, it did not lead to the desired result because women's rights were still not addressed in the *mainstream* human rights system. It was therefore argued that this strategy of specialization had led to the marginalization of women's human rights.

In order to counter the marginalization, the UN instigated a new strategy: a transformation of the mainstream system. Although this strategy has not yet led to the desired result either and more research is required, the author argues that when executed properly, this latest strategy, *together* with the previous strategies can lead to the effective promotion and protection of women's human rights in the UN human rights framework.

The central question in Chapter 3 on Article 1 by Antonia Waltermann and Ingrid Westendorp is whether and if so what CEDAW and the Court of Justice of the European Union (ECJ) can learn from each other as regards the implementation and interpretation of the prohibition of discrimination based on sex. More in particular it is studied how the concepts of direct and indirect discrimination are defined and used by CEDAW and under EU law, especially by the ECJ. Furthermore, it is examined whether the prohibition of discrimination based on sex – understood as the biological difference between women and men – is enough to work with or whether the concept should be broadened to include the idea of gender as the cultural understanding of women's and men's stereotypical roles in society.

The authors come to the conclusion that EU law is particularly clear and consistent as regards using the definitions of direct and indirect discrimination; this is something that CEDAW could improve. However, while the scope of the prohibition of sex discrimination under the Women's Convention is very broad, encompassing all human rights and even including, the prohibition of violence against women, discrimination based on sex has its limits under EU law. Within the EU there is hardly any specific focus on women because the term sex is used in a neutral manner and the concept only covers issues concerning employment, social policy and access to goods and services. Furthermore, the concept of gender is currently still lacking from EU legislation. This bears the danger that EU legislation and programmes will treat the symptoms instead of the root causes of discrimination against women.

In Chapter 4 on Articles 2 and 3, Rolanda Oostland takes a close look at the principle of equality. She starts by explaining that depending on the way in which equality is defined – only entailing formal equality or also including substantive equality – the scope of application of the concept of equality is much broader than the prohibition of discrimination and that is why the two principles should be distinguished. She continues by comparing the approach taken on the concept of equality by CEDAW with the interpretation that is given by the Human Rights Committee (HRC) of Article 3 of the International Covenant on Civil and Political Rights (ICCPR).

From the analysis of CEDAW's Concluding Observations (COs) and General Recommendations, it becomes clear that the Committee applies both the principles of formal and of substantive equality. Also States parties are urged to include both forms of equality of women in their national Constitutions or other legislation.

In General Comment No. 28 the HRC states that States parties should take positive measures to achieve the effective and equal empowerment of women. Although the HRC does not explicitly refer to the principle of substantive equality, these positive measures clearly fall within the scope of the principle of substantive equality. Nevertheless, the HRC's focus is more on formal equality. Furthermore, the HRC does not make a clear distinction between the principle of discrimination and the principle of equality. The Committee seems to regard these principles as more or less interchangeable.

From the comparison between the two monitoring bodies, the author concludes that CEDAW's interpretation of Articles 2 and 3 of the Women's Convention has an added value.

If the principle of equality is regarded to include both formal and substantive equality, it will not only regard the nature of the treatment, but also the result. The latter may actually entail differential treatment in order to reach an equal result. Compared to the principle of non-discrimination, the principle of equality – including substantive equality – has a more far reaching scope, as it entails that differential treatment is in fact regarded as an essential part of the principle of equality. The prohibition of discrimination as such does not oblige States parties to ensure substantive equality.

Lisa Waddington and Laura Visser compare in Chapter 5 the obligation to take 'temporary special measures' under Article 4 of the Women's Convention with the possibility to adopt 'positive action' measures under European Union (EU) law. All Member States of the EU are also parties to the Women's Convention and the question is whether the limitation that have been elaborated by the Court of Justice of the European Union (ECJ) on the possibility to take positive action for furthering women's equality in the field of employment may be in conflict with the obligations under the Women's Convention.

Positive action under EU law is allowed as long as the measures that are taken do not discriminate against men. Herein lies a potential conflict with the Women's Convention since EU States parties could be obliged to adopt temporary special measures in favour of women, but, at the same time, they may be limited in the kinds of measures they are allowed to take under EU law.

The authors come to the conclusion that many forms of temporary special measures, such as support programmes, the allocation of resources, and proactive measures to encourage more women to apply for high-ranking posts, seem to be compatible with EU law. However, conflict may arise when quota schemes are at issue. Quota schemes that automatically reserve a percentage of employment positions for women seem to be incompatible with EU law where they concern jobs.

From the study of CEDAW's Concluding Observations (COs) it becomes clear that the Committee assumes that EU Member States can and should use the full arsenal of temporary special measures, including employment quotas. However, EU Member States may be unable to act on the Committee's recommendations to impose quotas since this would entail a breach of EU law.

In Chapter 6, Article 5 is studied by Ingrid Westendorp. The Article is problematic in the sense that the obligation ensuing from it – abolition of gender stereotypes and customs that have a negative impact on women's human rights – is a legal obligation, but the measures that have to be taken to fulfil this obligation are of an extra-legal nature and involve influencing and changing societies' prejudices and conceptions about men's and women's proper role in society.

While sometimes the concepts of culture, custom and tradition suffer from the negative connotation of standing in the way between women and their right to equality and that especially in developing States women are their victims, the author focuses on the possibilities to use the dynamics of culture to bring about a change of mentality towards a society that is based on a culture of equality between women and men. It is the author's belief that harmful customs and stereotypes can only be abolished if they are replaced by new customs and traditions because belonging to a certain culture is important for all people as it gives a sense of identity, safety, and belonging.

As an international player, CEDAW can only play a modest and advisory role in this process since actual change will only happen if it is initiated at the national, local and community level by people who live the culture and who are able to convince both women and men that it is time to change course.

Chapter 7 deals with the very brief and very controversial Article 6 of the Convention: the only provision concerned with a form of gender-based violence. The – more than a century old – discussion on the contents of this Article focuses on the question whether prostitution is a human (women's?) rights violation *per se*, or that only coercion and humiliating, denigrating and abusive circumstances are to be regarded as human rights violations, and that otherwise people's (women's) agency should be respected. The authors, Marjolein van den Brink and Marjan Wijers have particularly studied CEDAW's Concluding Observations (COs) to find out which line of approach is taken by the Committee. From their study it has become clear that CEDAW does not take sides. Although initially, the COs were all in line with the abolitionist approach (prostitution should be eradicated, never accepted and accommodated) this was a reflection of the positions of the reporting State parties at the time, rather than an independent stance in the debate of the Committee itself.

In the course of time, the Committee has responded in a more or less similar way to situations of legalization of sex work on the one hand and further criminalization on the other. In either case, the Committee questions the impact of legislation (be it criminalizing or legalizing sex work) on the women involved in the sex industry, while the political choices are left to the discretion of the States parties. The authors think that this is an encouraging and sensible strategy that will maintain the Committee's authority. However, they also feel that it is disappointing that CEDAW barely addresses stereotypes and discrimination in the context of Article 6, and when it does, it focuses narrowly on the victims of trafficking and coercion. This means that the Committee misses the opportunity to point out the beneficial effects that getting rid of stereotypes in respect of sex workers could have on all women, including victims of trafficking, and sex workers, given the strong ties between these stereotypes and restrictive morals on how women should behave.

The authors conclude that CEDAW's work is primarily beneficial for victims of trafficking, and this fits with an abolitionist approach. The few, rather recent, COs on legalization of sex work, however, raise hope for the future and open opportunities for attention for non-abolitionist groups, among whom in the first place the group with the weakest position in the debate: the sex workers themselves. CEDAW's strategy to focus on the impact of legislation is a start, which it could refine by consistently and systematically ask States parties for the impact of anti-trafficking and prostitution legislation on the position of sex workers.

Margreet de Boer discusses Articles 7 and 8 in Chapter 8. While in most countries women are able to participate in politics, nowhere their actual participation in public and political life is on equal terms with men. The focus of this Chapter is whether the Articles in the Women's Convention can contribute to the realization of women's political rights, and whether the Convention is of added value compared to other international instruments containing the right to political participation.

In order to illustrate how the Women's Convention can be used to achieve equal political rights for women, the Dutch case on the exclusion of women by a small Christian party (SGP) is presented. In this case fundamental questions were raised on the direct effect of the Women's Convention, on the relation of the right not to be discriminated against on the one hand, and the freedom of religion and of association on the other, and on the responsibilities of the State: which measures should be taken?

In General Recommendation No. 23 and in Concluding Observations on various countries, CEDAW makes it very clear that, if necessary, it expects States to take temporary special measures – like numeric goals and quotas – to achieve *de facto* equal political rights.

In Chapter 9, Article 9 is studied by Gerard-René de Groot. Women's ability to retain their nationality upon marriage and to pass on their nationality to their children is a rather recent situation. Historically, a married woman's nationality depended completely on the nationality of her husband. Gradually, this developed into a situation where married women could keep their own nationality. The nationality of children developed in a similar way. At first the nationality of children depended principally on the nationality of their father and gradually this has changed into a system where both fathers and mothers can pass their nationality to their children.

Article 9 of the Women's Convention is the end station of all these developments. Originally, not all States parties endorsed the principles on nationality laid down in the Convention and a number of them made reservations. Luckily, however, several of them have meanwhile withdrawn their reservation while others are bringing their legislation in conformity with the Convention and therefore will soon be able to withdraw theirs. In conclusion it seems likely that in the near future all States parties will have implemented the Convention's nationality principles in their domestic legislation.

The authors of Chapter 10, Fons Coomans and Samira Sakhi, have focused on the situation in Afghanistan. Afghan girls and women have suffered from war and poverty for more than two decades and the provision on education in the Women's Convention has the potential of playing a key role in improving their situation. The current Government of Afghanistan is aware of this fact. Afghanistan is party to all treaties which provide for the right to education on a non-discriminatory basis. Article 10 of the Women's Convention stipulates, for example, that States parties shall take all appropriate measures to eliminate discrimination in the field of education. Education must be furthermore available, accessible, acceptable and adaptable in accordance with Article 13 of the International Covenant on Economic, Social, and Cultural Rights (ICESCR).

Chapter 1. Introduction

Since the collapse of the Taliban regime, efforts have been made to restore the country's educational system. The Government of Afghanistan has booked enormous successes in the field of education; today more Afghan children (in particular girls) are in school than at any other period in the country's history. However, insecurity, poverty, early marriages and non-existence of girls' schools are major barriers for the remaining 60% of the girls. A bottom-up process of universalizing the right to education, involving all relevant stake-holders, may help in strengthening real access to education for girls and women in Afghanistan. Such a process should take into account gender-related aspects of education.

While the UN human rights monitoring bodies have complimented the Government of Afghanistan for the major steps forward that have been made, there is also reason for concern because some obstacles and systematic problems are continuing.

In Chapter 11 Anja Wiesbrock examines the right to employment. Equality of opportunities and equal remuneration of men and women are key means to achieve gender equality in employment. At the same time, these two rights are characterized by immense challenges regarding implementation, in particular due to non-standard forms of employment, deep-rooted causes of inequality and a male standard of worker. When comparing the EU and the UN legislative framework, the rights to equal employment opportunities and equal pay guaranteed in the Women's Convention appear at times to be wider than those granted under EU law. Yet, the effective protection granted to individuals is much stronger in the context of EU law, due to the absence of effective enforcement mechanisms in the Women's Convention. The main role for the Women's Convention therefore seems to lie in steering the general direction of national employment policies.

The next two Chapters focus on Article 12. In Chapter 12 Nishara Mendis and Jennifer Sellin first give a general overview of the historical development of the right to health and they compare the contents of the provisions concerning this right as contained in the ICESCR and the Women's Convention. Next, they examine the relationship between international trade obligations – particularly those ensuing from the Agreement on Trade Related aspects of Intellectual Property Rights (TRIPS) and the General Agreement on Trade in Services (GATS) – and women's right to health. According to the authors a holistic approach to women's health rights and international trade in medicines and healthcare services is necessary because the impact of the trade rules on women's right to health and the influence on health policy-making is far reaching.

According to their research, in recent key discussions on trade and health, the language of human rights is either missing or diluted. Furthermore, the supposed flexibilities in trade agreements, such as TRIPS and GATS, with regard to protection of public health seem not to be as advantageous as is often argued. That is why the authors believe that there is a need for a continuous active engagement on trade and health issues, and specifically the use of a women's rights approach using the rights language as expressed in Article 12 of the Women's Convention.

In Chapter 13 Phyllis Livaha concentrates on the practice of Female Circumcision (FC) because this has very negative effects on the health of millions of women around the world. In 1990, CEDAW explicitly recognized the eradication of FC as a major objective on the United Nations agenda. The Women's Convention, however, has only limited potential to eradicate this culturally embedded practice. Though the instruments enable women, at least in theory, to contest FC on grounds of life, health, and gender equality, FC still escapes international intervention because it is protected under the guise of culture and religion.

CEDAW has highlighted the importance of educating communities and raising awareness about FC and other harmful practices. The implementation efforts should aim at gradually transforming public opinion about the practice through widespread education. The programmes should utilize the resources of local individuals from the communities practicing FC. They should also enlist leadership of people from the community, like healthcare providers, politicians and teachers. Most importantly, there should be sustained and coordinated long-term commitment by the campaigners which includes addressing the underlying factors concerning women's social and economic situation.

In Chapter 14 Dagmar Schiek and Jule Mulder discuss Article 13 in a broader international legal context, including its implications for European Union law. Article 13 aims at factual equality of women in relation to financial services (credit, insurance and similar) on markets, monetary benefits by public authorities and to leisure activities. It has been underused to date, and not been the subject of any specific activities of CEDAW. There is a variety of international and European data and case law demonstrating actual shortcomings of gender equality in this slightly disparate field. The Chapter argues that the Convention's substantive approach to equality requires a proactive approach of signatory States in ensuring that women are placed in a situation of factual equality, even if and when women might apply to different kinds or quantities of financial services, live in different family situations or enjoy different leisure activities. Moreover, the Article highlights the shortcomings of European Union Law within the field of equal access and supply of goods and services, which currently allow differentiations between the sexes, which are prohibited under Article 13 of the Convention.

Article 14 on rural women is discussed by Ingrid Westendorp in Chapter 15. In view of the fact that this provision consists of many different paragraphs, a choice was made to concentrate on the last two aspects and study access and right to land and adequate living conditions for rural women. There has always been a difference in the standard of living between urban and rural areas; the latter have always lagged behind as regards available facilities, services and possibilities for education and employment. At the moment, urbanization is one of the biggest problems in the world, especially in developing States, and it therefore receives a lot of attention. However, especially in poor States the majority of women live in rural areas where facilities and services are getting scarcer and employment possibilities drop even further when more people leave for the cities.

Rural women are discriminated against in various ways in respect to their land rights. Women's lack of land has severe consequences connected to, *inter alia*, their rights to food, adequate housing, access to credit and loans, decision-making, and the possibility to become economically independent. Not only for the benefit of rural women themselves, but also in the interest of the development of the State and the agricultural production as a whole, it is imperative that rural women get equal rights to and control over land.

In Chapter 16 Tilly Draaisma goes into the historical context and the drafting history of Article 15. This is followed by an indication of the significance of equality before the law and reference to CEDAW's relevant General Recommendation. In the last part of this Chapter, the significance of Article 15 is demonstrated in a concrete case: the (current) Dutch Law on Names. The conclusions of this Chapter are that it would be advisable in future judicial proceedings to make a subsidiary appeal on Article 15, and that the current Dutch Law on Names is *not* in accordance with the principle of equality as contained in the Convention.

In order to demonstrate the significance of Article 16 (1)(c) Women's Convention on gender equality at divorce for Muslim women, Pauline Kruiniger in Chapter 17 first highlights the importance of the 'persuasive power' of the Convention strengthened by – although being a soft law mechanism – its reporting procedure to CEDAW. As a result, the eagerness of States to create the image of being supportive of equality for women in the international community, as illustrated by Morocco and Pakistan, leads to corrosion of the legitimacy of their discriminating domestic divorce laws as it becomes more and more difficult for these States to justify their application; this process, as such, already indicates a transitional stage towards reform and thus compliance with the Convention. Moreover, these external pressure exerting powers are indispensable for and complementary to the domestic pressure for reforms by NGOs. Furthermore, an approach from a culturally nuanced perspective in order to further the implementation of Article 16 (1)(c) in Islamic States is advocated in this Chapter. It appears that the option of striving for substantive equality or equality of results is more feasible than to strive for the Convention's requirement of full equality. The latter is at odds with the fundamental Islamic legal principle that either spouse has his/her own modalities of divorce. Morocco is exemplary in this respect as its Government – under pressure of NGOs and CEDAW – has accomplished a balanced system of divorce modalities by introducing an independent accessible, judicial divorce modality for either or both spouses and submitting the repudiation-based divorces to judicial monitoring.

In Chapter 18 on Articles 17–22, Cees Flinterman gives an impression of how CEDAW has developed from a body that was on the margin of the UN supervisory system, meeting in Vienna for only two weeks annually, to a full human rights treaty body that has given a dynamic interpretation of its mandate and that nowadays has both an individual complaints procedure and an inquiry procedure at its disposal. For eight years, Flinterman was a member of CEDAW (2003–2010); one of the four male members that have served in the Committee until now. Particularly interesting are CEDAW's working methods since the Committee has played and is still playing a pioneering role in this regard.

In Chapter 19 Menno Kamminga comments on the view that has emerged among some experts and organs on Women's Rights, that the obligation to fully realize the rights recognized in the Convention as contained in Article 24, would amount to the exercise of due diligence. The standard of due diligence is not only applied in respect of abuses by State agents but also by non-State actors. According to Kamminga, the use of the due diligence standard is based on misconceptions since in general international law and in domestic law the due diligence standard is a weak standard; an obligation of conduct rather than an obligation of result. Its exercise is subject to available resources and a wide margin of appreciation is left to the States. That is why the due diligence standard is to the advantage of States and companies rather than to the advantage of the victims of human rights abuses and it should be dropped in favour of the positive obligations approach entailing that States have the duty to respect, protect, and fulfil the human rights of their citizens.

Zoé Luca discusses in Chapter 20 the possibility to make reservations as included in Article 28. Since the Women's Convention is an instrument aimed at altering fundamental inequalities in societies, many of which are built on patriarchal values, it has always been a controversial treaty. This evidently induced a large number of States to make reservations upon becoming a party to the Convention. Some of these States parties have been accused of compromising the integrity of the Convention by entering reservations that, to the Committee, other States and scholars, have been manifestly contrary to the object and purpose of the

Convention. In this Chapter CEDAW's efforts to narrow the scope and number of reservations to the Convention are assessed. Furthermore, the author examines whether reservations have become an essentially Muslim problem.

The author concludes that due to CEDAW's constant push for withdrawal of reservations, the proportion of reserving States has slowly diminished including a fair number of reserving Muslim States. Another positive step is that CEDAW has joined forces with the UN's other human rights monitoring bodies, presenting a united front on the question of competence for determining the impermissibility of reservations.

The Optional Protocol (OP) to the Women's Convention is examined by Sille Jansen in Chapter 21. The only monitoring mechanism contained in the Women's Convention is the reporting system. CEDAW's ability to contribute to the implementation of the Women's Convention was potentially improved by the entry into force of the OP in the year 2000, since two additional monitoring mechanisms came at the Committee's disposal: the individual complaint procedure and the inquiry procedure. The decisions of CEDAW under these procedures are, however, not legally binding. State parties are merely required to 'give due consideration to the views of the Committee' once it has presented its decision. Thus, the success of these mechanisms relies mainly on the good will of States to follow recommendations. The question that is raised in this Chapter is whether the OP has proven to be an effective tool to implement women's rights.

The author comes to the conclusion that overall, the procedures of the OP have not been as effective as was hoped for. While it is early days to assess the inquiry procedure (since it has been used only once), it is possible to assess CEDAW's approach to individual complaints. The Committee's approach shows some inconsistencies and ambiguities as regards questions about admissibility of complaints. Furthermore, when looking into the merits of the cases, there seems to be more eagerness to protect certain rights over others, in particular economic and social rights.

The non-binding character of the Committee's decisions also takes its toll since CEDAW's recommendations are given neither priority nor urgency by the States parties who have been involved in the complaints procedure so far.

Violence against women (VAW) is discussed by Kate Rose-Sender in Chapter 22. Gender-based violence is as old as humanity and has been tolerated, accepted and clothed in the protective cloak of tradition or religion across societies. It takes many forms, including sexual, physical or emotional abuse by a partner or other family member, sexual harassment, exploitation and abuse by authority figures, trafficking, forced marriage, dowry related violence, female genital mutilation, honour killing and systematic sexual abuse as part of armed conflict.

It is an often repeated proposition that at the time of the drafting of the Women's Convention VAW was considered an internal domestic problem and not on the international agenda. This may be true but, if so, it also reveals the need for both the Convention and the subsequent interpretation and application by its monitoring body, CEDAW. This Chapter addresses the Women's Convention in formulation and function with regard to VAW. It begins with a look at the history and drafting process. It then goes on to examine the role of civil society in awareness-raising before concluding with an assessment of the extent to which the Convention has succeeded in addressing the problem of violence.

In Chapter 23 Martine Boersma aims to identify the various ways in which corrupt practices in the public sector can have a particularly detrimental impact upon the lives of women, and can possibly constitute violations of women's rights, as enshrined in the Bill of Rights and the Women's Convention. The consequences of corruption for women can be felt in three areas: the political dimension, the law enforcement dimension, and the socio-economic dimension. In this analysis, attention will also be paid to the manner in which corruption is discussed by the UN treaty bodies, including CEDAW. This exercise results in a number of recommendations addressed to the treaty bodies, in order to combat the vicious phenomenon of corruption in a more systematic fashion.

Finally, Chapter 24 by Jasper Krommendijk focuses on the impact and effectiveness for the Netherlands of the process of State reporting under the Women's Convention and CEDAW's monitoring role in this regard. He examines in particular the impact of the Concluding Observations (COs) and the extent to which the COs are complied with by the Netherlands. His contribution shows that the COs for the Netherlands have hardly had any impact at the domestic level in terms of the attention that has been paid by domestic actors, such as Parliament, the media and courts. Furthermore, COs for the Netherlands have proved to be ineffective in terms of securing compliance. That is to say, COs hardly ever lead to policy changes that are directly the result of CEDAW's recommendations. In his contribution, Jasper Krommendijk highlights several important factors and reasons for the scarce attention paid at the domestic level and this low level of compliance. It appears that an active involvement of Parliament and media coverage are crucial for the attention paid and importance attached by Government (officials) to the process of State reporting, which is essential for compliance with COs.

CHAPTER 2
THE UNITED NATIONS AND THE PROMOTION AND PROTECTION OF WOMEN'S HUMAN RIGHTS: A WORK IN PROGRESS

Fleur van Leeuwen

'All human beings are born free and equal in dignity and rights'[1]

1. INTRODUCTION

All human beings, men *and* women, are equal in dignity and rights, thus reads Article 1 of the Universal Declaration of Human Rights (UDHR). It is clear that the international framework for the promotion and protection of human rights as set up by the United Nations (UN) shortly after the Second World War was intended to promote and protect the rights of all, men *and* women. Both the Charter of the UN of 1945, which provides the foundation of the international human rights system as we know it today, and the UDHR that was adopted three years later recognize that *all* human beings have human rights for the simple reason of being human.[2] The Charter forbids discrimination on the basis of race, *sex*, language, or religion.[3] Likewise, the UDHR lays down that everyone is entitled to all the rights and freedoms set forth in the Declaration, without distinction of any kind, including according to sex.[4]

But although the system aims to promote and protect the rights of *all*, in practice it does not. The system was, and to some extent still is androcentric. In

---

[1] Universal Declaration of Human Rights (UDHR), adopted by General Assembly (GA) Resolution 217 A (III) of 10 December 1948, Article 1.
[2] The Charter of the United Nations (UN) was signed on 26 June 1945, in San Francisco, at the conclusion of the UN Conference on International Organization, and came into force on 24 October 1945.
[3] UN Charter, Article 1, para. 3.
[4] UDHR, Article 2.

the past it was successfully argued by women's rights proponents that the international system addresses only degrading events commonly identified with the lives of men and not experiences common to the lives of women.[5] A recent study shows that steps of improvement have been made, but that also a lot still remains to be done.[6] Questions to be posed therefore are: what steps has the UN taken since its inception to promote and protect women's enjoyment of human rights within its human rights framework and why did these strategies not (yet) lead to the desired result?

This Chapter addresses these questions. It looks at the steps the UN has taken since its inception in 1945 to promote and protect women's rights within its human rights framework and it discusses the criticism voiced on these strategies for being inadequate and for arguably being even to the detriment of women's human rights. After this introduction, this Chapter starts by discussing the UN system for the promotion and protection of human rights as it was set up in 1945. As it was a time in which women often did not enjoy equal rights (many women did for example not have the right to vote or to hold public office), the first step of the UN was to grant women the same rights men had. But as will be

---

[5] See for example CHARLOTTE BUNCH, 'Transforming Human Rights from a Feminist Perspective', in: J. Peters and A. Wolper (eds.), *Women's Rights, Human Rights – International Feminist Perspectives*, Routledge, London, 1995, p. 13; URSULA O'HARE, 'Realizing Human Rights for Women', *Human Rights Quarterly*, vol. 21, 1999, no. 2, pp. 368 – 371; RHONDA COPELON, 'Intimate Terror: Understanding Domestic Violence as Torture', in: Rebecca J. Cook (ed.), *Human Rights of Women – National and International Perspectives*, University of Pennsylvania Press, Philadelphia, 1994, pp. 116 – 117; REBECCA COOK (ed.), *Human Rights of Women – National and International Perspectives*, University of Pennsylvania Press, Philadelphia, 1994, pp. 3 – 4; HILARY CHARLESWORTH, 'What Are Women's International Human Rights?', in: Rebecca J. Cook (ed.), *Human Rights of Women – National and International Perspectives*, University of Pennsylvania Press, Philadelphia, 1994, p. 59 – 60; V. SPIKE PETERSON and LAURA PARISI, 'Are Women Human? It's Not an Academic Question', in: T. Evans (ed.), *Human Rights Fifty Years On: A Reappraisal*, Manchester University Press, Manchester, 1998, p. 132; REBECCA COOK, 'Women's International Human Rights Law: The Way Forward', *Human Rights Quarterly*, vol. 15, 1993, no. 2, p. 231; CHARLOTTE BUNCH, 'Women's Rights as Human Rights: Toward a Re-Vision of Human Rights', *Human Rights Quarterly*, vol. 12, 1990, no. 4, p. 487; ANNE GALLAGHER, 'Ending the Marginalization: Strategies for Incorporating Women into the United Nations Human Rights System', *Human Rights Quarterly*, vol. 19, 1997, no. 2, p. 283; SUSAN MOLLER OKIN, 'Feminism, Women's Human Rights, and Cultural Differences', *Hypatia*, vol. 13, 1998, no. 2, pp. 34 – 35; DONNA SULLIVAN, 'The Public/Private Distinction in International Human Rights Law', in: J. Peters and A. Wolper (eds.), *Women's Rights, Human Rights – International Feminist Perspectives*, Routledge, London, 2005, p. 126; HILARY CHARLESWORTH, CHRISTINE CHINKIN and SHELLEY WRIGHT, 'Feminist Approaches to International Law', *The American Journal of International Law*, vol. 85, 1991, no. 4, p. 625; HILARY CHARLESWORTH, 'Human Rights as Men's Rights', in: J. Peters and A. Wolper (eds.), *Women's Rights, Human Rights – International Feminist Perspectives*, Routledge, London, 2005, p. 111; GAYLE BINION, 'Human Rights: A Feminist Perspective', *Human Rights Quarterly*, vol. 17, 1995, no. 3, p. 513 and p. 515.

[6] FLEUR VAN LEEUWEN, *Women's Rights are Human Rights – The Practice of the United Nations Human Rights Committee and the Committee on Economic, Social and Cultural Rights*, Intersentia, Antwerp. 2009, pp. 245 – 246.

shown, having the same rights as men did not necessarily mean that women's human rights were effectively promoted and protected. Abuses and constraints typical for women's lives around the world were not addressed by the international human rights system and discrimination against women persisted.

In order to remedy this deficiency of its human rights system, the UN adopted in 1979 the Convention on the Elimination of All Forms of Discrimination against Women (the Women's Convention): a Convention that focuses solely on the enjoyment of human rights by women. Section 3 of this Chapter, discusses this strategy of specialisation of women's rights by the UN and shows that also this second strategy of the UN did not lead to the desired result. For although women's rights were now expressly placed within the ambit of the international human rights framework, women's rights were still not addressed in the *mainstream* human rights system.[7] It was therefore argued that this strategy of specialisation had led to the marginalisation of women's human rights.

In order to address this problem of marginalisation of women's rights in the human rights framework, the UN instigated in 1993 its most recent strategy to promote and protect women's rights in its human rights framework: a transformation of the mainstream system. In Section 4, this current strategy is discussed. Although also this strategy of transformation has not yet led to the desired result and more research is required, it is argued that when executed properly, this latest strategy, together with the previous strategies, can lead to the effective promotion and protection of women's human rights in the UN human rights framework.

2. THE FIRST STEP: SAME RIGHTS

2.1. THE UN HUMAN RIGHTS SYSTEM

The Charter of the UN, which was adopted in 1945 by 51 States, provides the foundation of the international human rights system as we know it today. As noted previously, the Charter and the UDHR recognize that *all* human beings have human rights for the simple reason of being human.[8] The Declaration speaks purposefully of *all human beings,* when it holds in Article 1 that all human beings are born free and equal in dignity and rights. Although reference was made to *all men* in the original draft of the document, it is clear that all parties involved in the drafting process agreed that women were just as much entitled to the rights laid down in the Declaration as men. The original wording

---

[7] *Mainstream* refers in this context to those human rights treaties that do not focus specifically on the enjoyment of human rights *by women.*
[8] See UN Charter, Article 1, para. 3 and UDHR, Article 2.

was heavily contested during the negotiations. Some members of the drafting committee argued that since it was clear that both men and women should be able to enjoy human rights, the terminology of *all men* could be misleading. Mr Koretsky, the Russian delegate, for example, held that the assumption that *all men* included *all persons* implied a historical reflection on the mastery of men over women. He wanted the wording to be changed so as to make clear that *all human beings* were included. Agreement was found amongst the members on reference to *all human beings*.[9]

The notion that both men *and* women should be able to enjoy their human rights is part and parcel of all the main international human rights instruments. Not only the documents that compose the so-called Bill of Human Rights – the UDHR and the two Covenants: the International Covenant on Civil and Political Rights (ICCPR) and the International Covenant on Economic, Social and Cultural Rights (ICESCR) – refer explicitly to the principles of non-discrimination and equality, but also the more specialized human rights treaties lay down that States parties shall respect and ensure the rights as laid down therein without distinction of any kind.[10] These documents thus grant human rights to women on an equal basis with men; *i.e.* women should have the same rights men have.

This notion of formal equality of men and women as it was codified by the UN in its human rights treaties did not appear out of thin air. For it was this idea of formal equality that was the tenet of the women's rights movement in the period shortly after the Second World War; the period when the Charter and subsequently the UDHR were adopted. It was a time when only thirty of the original fifty-one UN Member States had given women equal voting rights or permitted them to hold public office. Hence, the most important precept of women's rights proponents at that time was that men and women were the same in rational ability and capacity for autonomy and self-determination. Their main goal was to achieve an equal status in law and hence for women to be accorded the same rights as men. Consequently, their position was focused on the concept of *sameness* of men and women, rather than on their *difference*.[11] This idea of

---

[9] JOHANNES MORSINK, 'Women's Rights in the Universal Declaration', *Human Rights Quarterly*, vol. 13, no. 2, 1991, pp. 233 – 236.

[10] See Article 2, para. 1 and Article 3 International Covenant on Civil and Political Rights (ICCPR); and Article 2, para. 2 and Article 3 International Covenant on Economic, Social and Cultural Rights (ICESCR). See with regard to the specialized treaties for example Article 2, para. 1 of the International Convention on the Rights of the Child; and Art. 1, para. 1 of the International Convention on the Rights of All Migrant Workers and Members of Their Families. See on the matter also MERJA PENTIKÄINEN, *The Applicability of the Human Rights Model to Address Concerns and the Status of Women*, The Erik Castrén Institute of International Law and Human Rights Research Reports, Publications of the Faculty of Law University of Helsinki, Helsinki, 1999, p. 17.

[11] LAURA PARISI, 'Feminist Praxis and Women's Human Rights', *Journal of Human Rights*, vol. 1, 2002, no. 4, p. 2.

sameness is reflected in the principles of non-discrimination and equality as laid down in the human rights documents that were drawn up after the inception of the UN.

The problem with this strategy lies in the fact that women and men are *de facto* not the same as they do not live similar lives. From the moment of birth, human beings are differentiated according to sex, being either a boy or a girl. Sex is the first factor that defines a human being in society, and it accordingly places a human being in a maze of expectations, customs, practices and constraints that stipulate his/her life. Since the biological and gender-related aspects of men and women differ, so do their lives and their experiences. Although no such thing as *the woman experience* or *the man experience* exists, and although social constructions of man and woman, and of masculinity and femininity, differ across places, cultures, and time, it is possible to draw parallels between the lives of women and the lives of men. The general picture of gender relations throughout the world portrays an asymmetry of power between men and women.[12] This asymmetry translates itself into certain issues which are characteristic of the lives of men, and those which are characteristic of the lives of women.

The concept of *sameness*, as expressed in the international human rights treaties in their reference to non-discrimination and equality, entailed that the UN human rights system did not take into account these differences and failed to tackle structures that perpetuate gender hierarchies. As noted, women were granted the same rights *as men*. The norms of the international human rights system reflected the lives and experiences of the (Western, white, heterosexual) male. It signified that when men had a right not to be arbitrarily detained, women had a right not to be arbitrarily detained. But although it is only fair that women should have this same right that men have, in practice it benefits their enjoyment of human rights less as it is not often arbitrary detention that affects women, but rather, for example, imprisonment in the family home or being only allowed to leave the house under male supervision.

Critics pointed out that degrading events commonly identified with the lives of men were addressed in the wording and interpretation of the provisions of the human rights instruments. Acts of torture and ill treatment, for example during incommunicado detention, and the use of excessive force by security forces were violations cited in both the wording and the interpretation of the human rights treaties, but experiences like rape and domestic violence, events common to the

---

[12] See for example CHARLOTTE BUNCH, 'Transforming Human Rights from a Feminist Perspective', in: J. Peters and A. Wolper (eds.), *Women's Rights, Human Rights – International Feminist Perspectives*, Routledge, London, 1995, p. 13; *The 1999 World Survey on the Role of Women in Development*, UN, New York, 1999, p. ix; and JILL MARSHALL, 'Feminist Jurisprudence: Keeping the Subject Alive', *Feminist Legal Studies*, vol. 14, 2006, no. 1, p. 42.

lives of many women, were not covered by the protection of these provisions.[13] In reality human rights were therefore men's rights: the *male* experience was accepted as the norm, or, as Parisi notes, as the *human* experience.[14] Abuses, exclusions and constraints that are more typical of women's lives were neither recognized nor addressed by the human rights instruments.

Although a first important step was made by granting women equal rights, such as the right to vote, the international human rights framework did not do what it was supposed to do: effectively promote and protect women's enjoyment of human rights.

2.2. THE COMMISSION ON THE STATUS OF WOMEN

The disadvantaged position of women worldwide was of concern to the UN and it intended to mend this situation. To that end, the Economic and Social Council of the UN (ECOSOC)[15] established in 1946, even prior to the adoption of the UDHR, a specialized body to deal with 'women's rights': the Commission on the Status of Women (CSW). Originally, the CSW functioned as a sub-commission to the former Commission on Human Rights (CHR).[16] This institutional structure, Parisi notes, 'was the result of a compromise between those feminists who pushed for full incorporation into the existing human rights framework and those who thought that the establishment of a separate body would be the best way to ensure attention for women's rights issues'.[17] Later that same year,

---

[13] See for example CHARLOTTE BUNCH, 'Transforming Human Rights from a Feminist Perspective', in: J. Peters and A. Wolper (eds.), *Women's Rights, Human Rights – International Feminist Perspectives*, Routledge, London, 1995, p. 13; URSULA O'HARE, 'Realizing Human Rights for Women', *Human Rights Quarterly*, vol. 21, 1999, no. 2, pp. 368 – 371; RHONDA COPELON, 'Intimate Terror: Understanding Domestic Violence as Torture', in: Rebecca J. Cook (ed.), *Human Rights of Women – National and International Perspectives*, University of Pennsylvania Press, Philadelphia, 1994, pp. 116 – 117.

[14] LAURA PARISI, 'Feminist Praxis and Women's Human Rights', *Journal of Human Rights*, vol. 1, 2002, no. 4, p. 7; See for example also V. SPIKE PETERSON NAD LAURA PARISI, 'Are Women Human? It's Not an Academic Question', in: T. Evans (ed.), *Human Rights Fifty Years On: A Reappraisal*, Manchester University Press, Manchester, 1998, p. 141; TITIA LOENEN, 'Rethinking Sex Equality as a Human Right', *Netherlands Quarterly of Human Rights*, vol. 12, 1994, no. 3, pp. 255 – 257; and JENNY GOLDSCHMIDT, *We Need Different Stories – Een Ander Verhaal in het Recht*, Tjeenk Willink, Zwolle, 1993, pp. 13 – 17.

[15] The Economic and Social Council (ECOSOC) is an authoritative body in the UN system that serves as the central forum for discussing international economic and social issues. ECOSOC formulates policy recommendations addressed to member States and the UN system. See www.un.org/en/ecosoc, accessed on 5 August 2010.

[16] Following the 2005 report 'In Larger Freedom', by former UN Secretary General Kofi Annan, the UN Commission on Human Rights (CHR) was replaced by the Human Rights Council. See UN doc. A/59/2005, para. 181 – 183; and UN doc. A/RES/60/251 of 2006, which establishes the Human Rights Council.

[17] LAURA PARISI, 'Feminist Praxis and Women's Human Rights', *Journal of Human Rights*, vol. 1, 2002, no. 4, p. 572.

however, the CSW received the status of full-fledged Commission so as to become an equal counterpart to the CHR. Amongst those that were against this shift in institutional structure was Eleanor Roosevelt, who at that time was chairperson of the CHR. Roosevelt and other opponents felt that the singling out of a group for *special* rights could lead to stigmatisation, backlash and marginalisation. For them, the preferable alternative was to seek inclusion in the primary UN human rights body rather than trying to establish 'separate but equal' human rights institutional mechanisms for women and men.[18] But proponents of the shift considered this promotion in status to be of crucial importance.

It was Bodil Begtrup, the first Chairperson of the sub-commission that requested ECOSOC in May 1946 to provide the CSW with full commission status. She noted that:

> 'Women's problems have now for the first time in history to be studied internationally as such and to be given the social importance they ought to have. And it would be, in the opinion of this Sub-Commission of experts in this field, a tragedy to spoil this unique opportunity by confusing the wish and the facts. Some situations can be changed by laws, education, and public opinion, and the time seems to have come for happy changes in conditions of women all over the world (…)'.[19]

In June 1946, the sub-commission formally became the CSW, a body functioning directly under the ECOSOC. Its original tasks were to prepare recommendations and reports to the ECOSOC on the promotion of women's rights in political, economic, social, and educational fields and to make recommendations to the Council on urgent problems that required immediate attention, but its mandate expanded over the years.[20] It is interesting to note that in its first years after coming into being, the CSW played an important role in the drafting process of the UDHR. It revised draft Articles that were sent to it for comments and gender-sensitive language, and would argue against references to *men* as a

---

[18] LAURA PARISI, 'Feminist Praxis and Women's Human Rights', *Journal of Human Rights*, vol. 1, 2002, no. 4, pp. 572 – 573.

[19] UN Division for the Advancement of Women (DAW), *Short History of the Commission on the Status of Women*, www.un.org/womenwatch/daw/CSW60YRS/CSWbriefhistory.pdf, pp. 1 – 2, accessed on 5 August 2010.

[20] See for example ECOSOC resolution 11 (II), UN doc. E/RES/11 (II), para. 1 and ECOSOC resolution 1987/22, UN doc. E/RES/1987/22, para. 1. See also a short history on the CSW on www.un.org/womenwatch/daw/CSW60YRS/CSWbriefhistory.pdf, accessed on 5 August 2010. At present the work of the CSW focuses on the implementation of the Platform for Action adopted at the Beijing Conference on Women in 1995 and the outcome of the twenty-third special session of the General Assembly (GA) held in this respect. DAW, Commission on the Status of Women, www.un.org/womenwatch/daw/csw/, accessed on 5 August 2010.

synonym for humanity and phrases like *men are brothers*.[21] Yet, in line with the tenet of the women's movement at the time, its focus was foremost on achieving equal rights for women and preventing sexist language in the Declaration.[22] The CSW did not argue in favour of inclusion of provisions in the Declaration that would more clearly reflect the lives of women by referring for example to domestic violence, rape, trafficking, maternal mortality or access to contraceptives. Rather it advocated full equality of civil rights, including the equal right to dissolution of marriage, the equal right to guardianship, the right to keep one's nationality, and the right to own property.[23] Naturally, in light of the status of women around the world at that time, this was an important first step.

In the years to follow, the CSW was involved in promoting women's rights and equality by setting standards and formulating international conventions, and it conducted research to assess the status of women worldwide. In that capacity it for example drafted the Convention on Political Rights of Women of 1952; the Convention on the Nationality of Married Women of 1957; and the Convention on Consent to Marriage, Minimum Age for Marriage and Registration of Marriages of 1962.[24] In 1963, the UN General Assembly (GA) requested the Commission to draft a declaration on the elimination of discrimination against women.[25] It was this Declaration that culminated sixteen years later in the Women's Convention, the text of which was prepared by working groups within the Commission.[26]

---

[21] Morsink argues that the lack of sexism in the Universal Declaration is primarily due to the aggressive lobbying of Begtrup and the steady pressure of the Soviet delegation. JOHANNES MORSINK, 'Women's rights in the Universal Declaration', *Human Rights Quarterly*, vol. 13, 1991, no. 2, p. 231. For a short history on the CSW see also DAW, www.un.org/womenwatch/daw/CSW60YRS/CSWbriefhistory.pdf, accessed on 5 August 2010. Gender refers here to the social construction of differences of men and women and ideas of masculinity and femininity: 'the excess cultural baggage associated with biological sex'. See HILARY CHARLESWORTH, 'Feminist Methods in International Law', *The American Journal of International Law*, vol. 93, 1999, no. 2, p. 379.

[22] JOHANNES MORSINK, 'Women's rights in the Universal Declaration', *Human Rights Quarterly*, vol. 13, 1991, no. 2, pp. 255 – 256.

[23] See UN doc. E/281/Rev.1 at 12.

[24] See also HANNA BEATE SCHÖPP-SCHILLING, 'The Nature and Scope of the Convention', in: Hanna Beate Schöpp-Schilling and Cees Flinterman (eds.), *The Circle of Empowerment – Twenty-Five Years of the UN Committee on the Elimination of Discrimination Against Women*, The Feminist Press, New York, 2007, pp. 11 – 12.

[25] Resolution 1921 of 5 December 1963.

[26] Declaration on the Elimination of Discrimination against Women, UN GA resolution 2263 (XXII), UN doc. A/RES/48/104. For a more elaborate overview of the work of the CSW see also a short history on the CSW on www.un.org/womenwatch/daw/CSW60YRS/CSWbriefhistory.pdf, accessed on 5 August 2010.

3. THE SECOND STEP: SPECIAL RIGHTS

> *'Noting however that in various fields there still remains,*
> *in fact if not in law, considerable discrimination against women.'*[27]

In 1963, the GA requested ECOSOC to invite the CSW to prepare a draft declaration on the elimination of discrimination against women, as it had noted that despite the efforts of the UN, discrimination against women persisted. The Declaration was adopted by the GA in 1967 and enumerates eleven provisions, which call upon States, for example, to take all appropriate measures to educate public opinion towards the eradication of prejudice and the abolition of customary and all other practices which are based on the idea of the inferiority of women, and, for example, asks to take all appropriate measures to combat all forms of traffic in women.[28] Yet, this Declaration proved not to be sufficient in eradicating discrimination against women. Despite the efforts of the GA and of various specialized agencies of the UN, it became clear in 1972 that discrimination against women could not be eliminated with the existing treaties alone. For that reason, the CSW recommended in that year to both ECOSOC and the GA that 1975 should become 'International Women's Year'. This initiative was meant to ensure that increased efforts were made to realize women's human rights.[29] Highlight of this 'International Women's Year' was the First UN World Conference on Women, held in Mexico City. It was here that a World Plan of Action was adopted, which laid down that high priority should be given to the preparation and adoption of the convention on the elimination of discrimination against women, with effective procedures for its implementation.[30]

It was the CSW that prepared the draft text of this convention. After lengthy negotiations in the CSW and within UN working groups of the Third Committee of the GA, the GA adopted the Women's Convention on 18 December 1979.[31] The Women's Convention, contrary to the other mainstream human rights treaties, focuses on the elimination of all forms of discrimination *against women*, and thus not, as is standard in the other human rights treaties, the elimination of

---

[27] GA Resolution 1921 of 5 December 1963, preamble.
[28] GA resolution 2263 (XXII), Articles 3 and 8.
[29] Hanna Beate Schöpp-Schilling, 'The Nature and Scope of the Convention', in: Hanna Beate Schöpp-Schilling and Cees Flinterman (eds.), *The Circle of Empowerment – Twenty-Five Years of the UN Committee on the Elimination of Discrimination Against Women*, The Feminist Press, New York, 2007, p. 11.
[30] Report of the World Conference of the International Women's Year, Mexico City, 19 June – 2 July 1975, UN doc. E/CONF.66/34, para. 198.
[31] Hanna Beate Schöpp-Schilling, 'The Nature and Scope of the Convention', in: Hanna Beate Schöpp-Schilling and Cees Flinterman (eds.), *The Circle of Empowerment – Twenty-Five Years of the UN Committee on the Elimination of Discrimination Against Women*, The Feminist Press, New York, 2007, p. 12.

discrimination on the ground of sex.³² Article 1 of the Convention lays down that discrimination is any distinction, exclusion or restriction made on the basis of sex which has the effect or purpose of impairing or nullifying the recognition, enjoyment, or exercise *by women*, irrespective of their marital status, on a basis of equality of men and women, of human rights and fundamental freedoms in the political, economic, social, cultural, civil, or any other field. In its substantive Articles, the Women's Convention addresses various issues that are characteristic of the lives of women and their enjoyment of human rights. Article 12(2) of the Convention, for example, lays down that:

> ' [...] States parties shall ensure to women appropriate services in connection with pregnancy, confinement and the post-natal period, granting free services where necessary, as well as adequate nutrition during pregnancy and lactation.'

The adoption of the Women's Convention meant that women's rights were for the first time expressly placed in the realm of the international human rights framework, be it in a specialized treaty. Hence, from then onwards, the UN human rights system aimed to promote and protect the enjoyment of human rights by women in two ways: through the principles of non-discrimination and equality in its mainstream human rights treaties and through these principles in a women-specific human rights treaty.

But although the Women's Convention was originally received as a big step forward in the promotion and protection of women's human rights, there was also criticism. It was argued that the creation of a specific mechanism to deal exclusively with the enjoyment of human rights of women led to the marginalisation of women's rights.³³ For example Charlesworth observes that the price of creating separate institutional mechanisms for women led to the

---

[32] See on this matter also RIKKI HOLTMAAT, *Toward Different Law and Public Policy – The Significance of Article 5 (a) CEDAW for the Elimination of Structural Gender Discrimination*, Dutch Ministry of Social Affairs and Employment, 2004, p. 7; and TITIA LOENEN, 'Rethinking Sex Equality as a Human Right', *Netherlands Quarterly of Human Rights*, vol. 12, 1994, no. 3, pp. 268 – 270.

[33] See for example ANDREW BYRNES, 'Women, Feminism and International Human Rights Law – Methodological Myopia, Fundamental Flaws or Meaningful Marginalisation? Some Current Issues', *Australian Yearbook of International Law*, vol. 12, 1992, pp. 205 – 206; ANNE GALLAGHER, 'Ending the Marginalization: Strategies for Incorporating Women into the United Nations Human Rights System', *Human Rights Quarterly*, vol. 19, 1997, no. 2, p. 285; RACHEL JOHNSTONE, 'Feminist Influences on the United Nations Human Rights Treaty Bodies', *Human Rights Quarterly*, vol. 28, 2006, no. 1, p. 151; HILARY CHARLESWORTH and CHRISTINE CHINKIN, *The Boundaries of International Law: A Feminist Analysis*, Manchester University Press, 2000, p. 218; HILARY CHARLESWORTH, 'Not Waving but Drowning: Gender Mainstreaming and Human Rights in the United Nations', *Harvard Human Rights Journal*, vol. 18, 2005, no.1, p. 1; LAURA REANDA, 'Human Rights and Women's Rights: The United Nations Approach', *Human Rights Quarterly*, vol. 3, 1981, no. 2, p. 12; HILARY CHARLESWORTH, 'Transforming the United Men's Club: Feminist Futures for the United Nations', *Transnational Law and Contemporary Problems*, vol. 4, 1994, no. 2, pp. 445 – 446.

building a *women's ghetto* with less power, resources, and priority than the mainstream human rights bodies.[34] Her arguments are exemplified by the fact that unlike the other human rights monitoring bodies, which meet in Geneva and are serviced by the Office of the High Commissioner for Human Rights (and previously by the former Centre for Human Rights), the Committee on the Elimination of Discrimination Against Women (CEDAW), the body that monitors the implementation of the Women's Convention, was until recently meeting in New York and was serviced by the UN Division for the Advancement of Women (DAW).[35] Although the adoption of the Women's Convention meant that women's rights were expressly placed in the ambit of international human rights, critics argued that the rights of women were still ignored by the mainstream human rights mechanisms. The claim was made that the monitoring bodies of the other human rights treaties did not address blatant violations of women's dignity as gross violations of human rights and left these issues up to the specialized CEDAW to deal with. Consequently, the adoption of the Women's Convention led to the marginalisation of human rights of women.[36] As Charlesworth notes, the existence of special women's institutions such as the Women's Convention and the CSW had allowed comparable but male-dominated forums such as the (former) Commission on Human Rights and the Human Rights Committee (HRC) to claim a general mandate that carried greater prestige and power. The effect of this was that women's interests were ghettoised: the creation of *women's institutions* meant that mainstream human rights bodies and institutions tended to downplay the application of human rights norms to women on the implicit assumption that women's rights were beyond their concern.[37]

As is clear from the above, the criticism was that the mainstream human rights instruments still did not pay attention to women's rights, or to phrase it differently, to situations that affect the enjoyment of human rights by women.

---

[34] HILARY CHARLESWORTH, 'Not Waving but Drowning: Gender Mainstreaming and Human Rights in the United Nations', *Harvard Human Rights Journal*, vol. 18, 2005, no.1, p. 1.

[35] Since January 2008 the CEDAW is serviced by the OHCHR and meets both in Geneva and New York. See UN doc. A/RES/62/218.

[36] ANDREW BYRNES, 'Women, Feminism and International Human Rights Law – Methodological Myopia, Fundamental Flaws or Meaningful Marginalisation? Some Current Issues', *Australian Yearbook of International Law*, vol. 12, 1992, pp. 205 – 206; Reanda moreover, speaks of a *ghettoisation* of questions relating to women; the concerns of women will be relegated to mechanisms with generally less resources and power than the mainstream human rights mechanisms. LAURA REANDA, 'Human Rights and Women Rights: the United Nations Approach', *Human Rights Quarterly*, vol. 3, 1981, no. 2, p.12.

[37] HILARY CHARLESWORTH, 'Transforming the United Nations Men's Club: Feminist Futures for the United Nations', *Transnational Law and Contemporary Problems*, vol. 4, 1994, no. 2, p. 446. See also URSULA O'HARE, 'Realizing Human Rights for Women', *Human Rights Quarterly*, vol. 21, 1999, no. 2, pp. 367 – 368; HILARY CHARLESWORTH, 'What are "Women's International Human Rights"?', in: Rebecca J. Cook (ed.), *Human Rights of Women – National and International Perspectives*, University of Pennsylvania Press, Philadelphia, 1994, p. 59.

And to that effect, women's human rights were still the poor cousins of the 'real' human rights. Thus although, or, as some say, because there was now a body in the UN human rights system that dealt exclusively with women's human rights, women's human rights were still not fully promoted and protected by the international system.

4. THE THIRD STEP: TRANSFORMATION OF THE MAINSTREAM

> *'The concept of human rights, like all vibrant visions, is not static or the property of any group; rather, its meaning expands as people reconceive of their needs and hopes in relation to it. In this spirit, feminists redefine human rights abuses to include the degradation and violation of women. The specific experiences of women must be added to traditional approaches to human rights in order to make women more visible and to transform the concept and practice of human rights in our culture so that it takes better account of women's lives.'*[38]

As mentioned, the first World Conference on Women was held in Mexico City in 1975. This Conference was followed-up by the second World Conference on Women five years later in Copenhagen. And then, in 1985, the world conference to review and appraise the achievements of the 'United Nations Decade for Women: equality, development, and peace' was held in Nairobi. At these conferences concerns were voiced about the effect of special development aid policies for women.[39] Charlesworth observes that the prevailing approach to women and development aid was criticized at these forums for being inadequate, as it identified women as a special interest group within the development sphere, needing particular accommodation. Hence, the specialisation of women's issues in regards to development aid was criticized. Strategies were proposed that encouraged the integration of women into the existing structures of development, *i.e.* so called *mainstreaming* of women's issues.[40] The Nairobi

---

[38] CHARLOTTE BUNCH, 'Women's Rights as Human Rights: Toward a Re-Vision of Human Rights', *Human Rights Quarterly*, vol. 12, 1990, no. 4, p. 487.

[39] For a more elaborate summary of the activities of the women's rights movement at these Conferences see for example ELISABETH FRIEDMAN, 'Women's Human Rights: The Emergence of a Movement', in: J. Peters and A. Wolper (eds.), *Women's Rights, Human Rights – International Feminist Perspectives*, Routledge, New York, 1995, pp. 18 – 35; JUDITH ZINSSER, 'From Mexico to Copenhagen to Nairobi: The United Nations Decade for Women, 1975 – 1985', *Journal of World History*, vol. 13, 2002, no. 1, pp. 139 – 168; and MARJOLEIN VAN DEN BRINK, *Moeders in de Mainstream – Een Genderanalyse van het Werk van het VN-Kinderrechtencomité*, 2006, Wolf Legal Publishers, Nijmegen, pp. 20 – 32.

[40] HILARY CHARLESWORTH, 'Not Waving but Drowning: Gender Mainstreaming and Human Rights in the United Nations', *Harvard Human Rights Journal*, vol. 18, 2005, no.1, p. 2.

Conference recognized that women's equality was not an isolated issue and that a woman's perspective and involvement was required on *all* issues.

The criticism voiced at these conferences regarding the specialisation of women's issues in development, also held true for the international human rights framework, for as shown, also here women's issues were only dealt with by a specialized women's treaty. It is therefore not surprising that this tenet in *mainstreaming women* was also brought forward by the women's movement at the World Conference on Human Rights held in Vienna in 1993. This Conference proved to be a landmark event in terms of public recognition of the lack of attention of the mainstream international human rights system for human rights of women. Although the focus of this World Conference was originally on human rights in general, especially on their universal character, and not on women's rights, a strong lobby of women's rights proponents managed to place the issue of women's human rights on the agenda of the Conference.[41] At the World Conference, the working group on *integration of women's rights into the human rights agenda* made it unequivocally clear to the participating States that much of what women experience as everyday abuse in their lives, in the family, in violation of their bodies, and in terms of economic and political deprivation was still largely kept outside the realm of the international human rights community. This despite the fact that it was common knowledge that women were regularly subjected to battering and torture, humiliation, starvation, sexual harassment and exploitation, forced marriages and pregnancy, compulsory heterosexuality, mutilation and even murder because of being female.[42]

The 171 States represented at the World Conference acknowledged this deficiency of the international system and stated in their final declaration and programme of action that the human rights of women and of the girl child were an inalienable, integral and indivisible part of universal human rights. They held that the human rights of women had to be integrated into the mainstream of United Nations system-wide activity and that these issues had to be regularly and systematically addressed throughout relevant United Nations bodies and mechanisms.[43] Moreover, in this Vienna Declaration and Programme of Action of 1993, the States call upon the monitoring bodies of the international human

---

[41] See for example ELISABETH FRIEDMAN, 'Gendering the Agenda: The Impact of the Transnational Women's Rights Movement at the UN Conferences of the 1990s', *Women's Studies International Forum*, vol. 26, 2003, no. 4, pp. 313 – 314.

[42] CHARLOTTE BUNCH, 'Strengthening Human Rights of Women', in: Manfred Nowak (ed.), *World Conference on Human Rights – The Contribution of NGOs Reports and Documents*, Manzsche Verlags- und Universitätsbuchhandlung, Vienna 1994, p. 33. See also KEVIN BOYLE, 'Stock-taking on Human Rights: The World Conference on Human Rights, Vienna 1993', *Political Studies*, vol. 43, 1995, no. 4, pp. 91 – 92.

[43] Vienna Declaration and Programme of Action, UN doc. A/CONF.157/23, part I, para. 18, and part II, para. 37. This call was a repetition of the statement made that same year by the CHR in its Resolution 1993/46 of 1993, UN doc. E/CN.4/RES/1993/46.

rights treaties to include the status and human rights of women in their deliberations and findings.[44]

The call made at the World Conference for integration of the status and human rights of women is one of transformation of the mainstream international human rights system. As research points out, the monitoring bodies were not only requested to pay attention to issues that affect women's enjoyment of human rights, but also to formulate obligations that effectively address these issues; to identify a possible link between these issues and discrimination of women and address this; and to do so in an integral manner, meaning in a manner that does not specialize these 'women's issues'.[45] As Bunch notes in this respect, the concept and practice of human rights needed to be transformed so as to take better account of women's lives.[46]

A study has recently been conducted to examine whether the mainstream international human rights bodies have, in the fifteen years after the Vienna Declaration and Programme of Action, complied with this call. The study consists of an analysis of the work of the HRC and the Committee on Economic, Social and Cultural Rights (CESCR) in regard to matters that affect women's physical integrity.[47] Its results point out that overall, the work of the HRC and the CESCR reflects compliance with three of the four necessary elements for transformation: the two Committees seem to make good use of the possibilities within their mandates to address issues that affect women's physical integrity; they formulate obligations for States parties that in general take into account the gender-specific form, circumstances and consequences of these human rights abuses; and, moreover, these matters are addressed in an integrated manner. But, safe a few exceptions, the HRC and the CESCR do not link specific experiences

---

[44] Vienna Declaration and Programme of Action, UN doc. A/CONF.157/23, part. II, para. 42.

[45] FLEUR VAN LEEUWEN, *Women's Rights are Human Rights – The Practice of the United Nations Human Rights Committee and the Committee on Economic, Social and Cultural Rights*, Intersentia, Antwerp, 2009, pp. 25 – 41. The call for transformation is sometimes understood as a call for *gendermainstreaming*. But gendermainstreaming and transformation, or integration of the status and human rights of women, as requested at the World Conference on Human Rights in 1993, are not one and the same. As Van den Brink notes in her dissertation of 2006 integration of human rights of women can be considered to be an important component of gender mainstreaming, but the concept of gender mainstreaming is broader and reaches beyond the scope of equal enjoyment of human rights: it requires, Van den Brink notes, the integration of gender in all areas of policy making and execution. See MARJOLEIN VAN DEN BRINK, *Moeders in de Mainstream – Een Genderanalyse van het Werk van het VN-Kinderrechtencomité*, Wolf Legal Publishers, Nijmegen, 2006, pp. 37 – 38. The policy of gendermainstreaming, reaching beyond the scope of promotion and protection of women's human rights, will not be discussed in this Chapter.

[46] CHARLOTTE BUNCH, 'Women's Rights as Human Rights: Toward a Re-Vision of Human Rights', *Human Rights Quarterly*, vol. 12, 1990, no. 4, p. 487.

[47] See for the study and its results: FLEUR VAN LEEUWEN, *Women's Rights are Human Rights – The Practice of the United Nations Human Rights Committee and the Committee on Economic, Social and Cultural Rights*, Intersentia, Antwerp, 2009.

of women to discrimination of women.[48] Hence, the HRC and the CESCR address the symptoms, but not the root cause of human rights abuses and constraints that typically affect women's enjoyment of human rights. The study thus shows that although the HRC and the CESCR are on the right track, more needs to be done for the international human rights system to effectively promote and protect women's human rights in the mainstream. The strategy of transformation has therefore not yet led to the desired result.

But this does not mean that the strategy of transformation has failed. After all, the HRC and the CESCR are now frequently addressing issues that characteristically affect the enjoyment of human rights by women and formulate obligations for States that effectively address these issues. What the results of the study on the work of the HRC and the CESCR signify is that steps need to be taken to improve the process of transformation.[49] In order to do so, more information is needed. It should first of all be noted that the study did not encompass the work of all mainstream human rights bodies. Further research is therefore required to determine whether the other monitoring bodies, like the Committee against Torture and the Committee on the Elimination of Racial Discrimination have also taken the call of the 1993 World Conference at heart. A second important question relates to the motivation of the Committees for addressing certain matters. Although there are strong signs that the work of NGOs is significant, it must, for example, also be examined whether the gender or nationality of individual Committee members plays a role in the attention that is paid by the human rights monitoring bodies to issues that affect women's enjoyment of human rights, and if so to what extent? Further research on this matter is required so as to discover the hitches in the process of including the status and human rights of women. And when these hitches and hurdles are known, it must be examined how these can be addressed and overcome. It is only when these and similar questions have been successfully dealt with that the process of transformation can be improved and effective promotion and protection of human rights of women in the mainstream be realized.

---

[48] FLEUR VAN LEEUWEN, *Women's Rights are Human Rights – The Practice of the United Nations Human Rights Committee and the Committee on Economic, Social and Cultural Rights*, Intersentia, Antwerp, 2009, pp. 235 – 251.

[49] Besides addressing the lack of attention of the HRC and the CESCR for discrimination against women as a root cause of human rights violations, also some other suggestions for improvement were made in the conclusions of the study on the work of the HRC and the CESCR. See FLEUR VAN LEEUWEN, *Women's Rights are Human Rights – The Practice of the United Nations Human Rights Committee and the Committee on Economic, Social and Cultural Rights*, Intersentia, Antwerp, 2009, pp. 235 – 246.

5. FINAL REMARKS

Since its inception in 1945, the UN has made considerable progress in the promotion and protection of women's human rights. Where it started in its early years with granting women equal rights, like the right to vote and the right to hold public office, but failed to address situations that characteristically hinder women in their enjoyment of human rights, it now recognizes, amongst other things, that women have a right to maternal health care, that States have the obligation to prosecute and punish all forms of violence against women, that women should have access to contraceptives, and that trafficking in women should be eliminated. But, as noted, sixty-five years after the UN laid down its aim to promote and protect the rights of all, there is also a lot of room for improvement as the system still does not fully and effectively promote and protect women's enjoyment of human rights.

As shown, the end of the transformation of the human rights mainstream is not in sight. Yet, it is clear that when implemented correctly, it can in theory certainly lead to an effective promotion and protection of women's human rights. The request of the 1993 World Conference on Human Rights is not a short-term assignment for the human rights monitoring bodies: it is *not* a matter of add and stir women's experiences into the big bowl of international human rights. Rather, it is a process that will be ongoing for as long as gender inequality exists. It is a process that requires the commitment of everyone involved in order to transform the international system so as to ensure that it fully accommodates and responds to human rights abuses and constraints that are typical of women's lives, now and in the future.

Next to this, the role CEDAW plays in the promotion and protection of women's human rights should not be disregarded. The strategy of transformation of the mainstream human rights system will likely only be successful if there is also attention for women's rights by a specialized committee. In this regard it should be noted that when the World Conference on Human Rights made a call for transformation in 1993, it also intended to strengthen the Women's Convention. The Declaration and Programme of Action of the World Conference on Human Rights lays down that:

> 'The United Nations should encourage the goal of universal ratification by all States of the Convention on the Elimination of All Forms of Discrimination against Women by the year 2000. Ways and means of addressing the particularly large number of reservations to the Convention should be encouraged.'[50]

The intention of the World Conference was clearly to follow a two-track approach in addressing human rights of women: by the mainstream *and* by a specialized

---

[50] Vienna Declaration and Programme of Action, UN doc. A/CONF.157/23, part II, para. 39.

monitoring body.[51] This position is supported by a widespread agreement amongst women's rights scholars and activists that human rights of women can best be promoted and protected, at the international legal level, through a combination of mainstream and specialist institutions and procedures.[52] In this regard it is pivotal that in the near future a study is conducted on the relation between the work of CEDAW and that of the mainstream human rights bodies in regards to the promotion and protection of women's human rights. Questions to be posed are for example: what is the added value of CEDAW?; and assuming that there is an added value: what can the mainstream human rights bodies learn from CEDAW?

It is clear that the story of the UN and the promotion and protection of women's human rights is not finished; it is a work in progress. But although we may not have achieved our goal, one thing is clear: in the last sixty-five years the system has, step by step, certainly come a long way.

---

[51] See also the report of the expert group meeting on the development of guidelines for the integration of a gender perspective into human rights activities and programmes, UN doc. E/CN.4/1996/105, para. 24.

[52] See for example ANNE GALLAGHER, 'Ending the Marginalization: Strategies for Incorporating Women into the United Nations Human Rights System', *Human Rights Quarterly*, vol. 19, 1997, no. 2, p. 331; and JULIE MERTUS and PAMELA GOLDBERG, 'A Perspective on Women and International Human Rights after the Vienna Declaration: The Inside/Outside Construct', *New York University Journal of International Law and Politics*, vol. 26, 1994, no. 2, p. 207.

ARTICLE 1

For the purposes of the present Convention, the term 'discrimination against women' shall mean any distinction, exclusion or restriction made on the basis of sex which has the effect or purpose of impairing or nullifying the recognition, enjoyment or exercise by women, irrespective of their marital status, on a basis of equality of men and women, of human rights and fundamental freedoms in the political, economic, social, cultural, civil or any other field.

CHAPTER 3

THE ESSENCE OF DISCRIMINATION AGAINST WOMEN: AN INTERPRETATION BY CEDAW AND THE EUROPEAN UNION

Ingrid WESTENDORP and Antonia WALTERMANN

1. INTRODUCTION

The Convention on the Elimination of All Forms of Discrimination Against Women (Women's Convention) is not concerned with discrimination in general, but only with discrimination based on sex. While the focus is clear, much of the meaning of the words is rather vague and, moreover, perceptions about what constitutes discrimination against women have changed over the years, which made it necessary for the Committee on the Elimination of Discrimination Against Women (CEDAW) to interpret and clarify Article 1.

The Treaty on the Functioning of the European Union (TFEU), the latest in a long line of EU treaties, contains as a general principle the prohibition of discrimination of which 'sex' is but one of the possible sources.[1] The combat of discrimination based on sex, or the advancement of women's rights did not feature high on the agenda when the European Economic Community was created in 1957. The first Article concerning women's equality and discrimination based on sex was Article 119 EEC.[2] However, the purpose of including this

---

[1] In Article 10 of the TFEU it is stipulated that: In defining and implementing its policies and activities, the Union shall aim to combat discrimination based on sex, racial or ethnic origin, religion or belief, disability, age or sexual orientation.

[2] Article 119 EEC read: Each Member State shall in the course of the first stage ensure and subsequently maintain the application of the principle of equal remuneration for equal work as between men and women workers.
For the purposes of this Article, remuneration shall mean the ordinary basic or minimum wage or salary and any additional emoluments whatsoever payable directly or indirectly, whether in cash or in kind, by the employer to the worker and arising out of the workers' employment.
Equal remuneration without discrimination based on sex means:

provision was not concern about discrimination against women, but rather based on economic considerations:[3] if men and women doing the same work would be paid the same wages in some countries, while in other Member States, men and women would receive unequal salaries – *i.e.*women doing the same job would earn less – this would create a disadvantage for the industries in those States that enacted equal pay for equal work.[4] Since those days, the focus of the EU has gradually broadened and perceptions about discrimination based on sex have changed particularly due to the interpretative work that has been done by the Court of Justice of the European Union (formerly known as the European Court of Justice, hereafter ECJ).

Since it is interesting to see how two so different bodies have dealt with discrimination based on sex, and how insights of discrimination against women have changed over the last few decades, the legal questions that will be investigated and answered in this Chapter concern what CEDAW and the ECJ can learn from each other about the principle of non-discrimination. More in particular, how are the concepts of direct and indirect discrimination defined and used by CEDAW and under EU law, especially by the ECJ? Is the prohibition of discrimination based on sex still valid, or should we move to the prohibition of discrimination based on gender and what are the limitations placed on the principle of non-discrimination by EU law?

Section 2 will start with the drafting history of Article 1 of the Women's Convention and the characteristics of this Article if compared to other provisions concerning the prohibition of discrimination based on sex. In section 3 the interpretative work that has been done by CEDAW will be under scrutiny. To this end the Committee's Concluding Observations (COs) on State reports, its General Recommendations, and its decisions on individual complaints and its findings concerning the sole inquiry procedure that was conducted will be examined. Section 4 will deal with the EU's approach to discrimination against women. First it will be determined how the concepts of direct and indirect discrimination against women are defined under EU law. Furthermore, the limitations placed on the principle of non-discrimination and its application under EU law will be analyzed. In section 5 an analysis will be made of the similarities and differences in the use and interpretation of sex discrimination under EU law and by CEDAW. At the end of the Chapter there will be a conclusion.

(a) that remuneration for the same work at piece-rates shall be calculated on the basis of the same unit of measurement; and
(b) that remuneration for work at time-rates shall be the same for the same job.
The text of Article 119 EEC has been modified slightly and can nowadays be found in Article 157 TFEU.

[3] NIGEL FOSTER, *EU law Directions*, 2nd ed. Oxford University Press, Oxford, 2010, p. 344.
[4] The original idea of equal pay for equal work has evolved into equal pay for work of equal value. The latter formulation can be found in Article 157 TFEU. Also see Chapter 11 in this book by Anja Wiesbrock.

2. DEFINING DISCRIMINATION

In this section first the *Travaux Préparatoires* for the Women's Convention will be examined with a view to determining how the wording of Article 1 came about. Next, the definition of discrimination in the Convention will be under scrutiny. The definition contains a few peculiarities that distinguish it from similar provisions in other human rights treaties. Moreover, CEDAW has broadened the scope of Article 1 considerably by including gender-based violence as a form of discrimination against women.

2.1. THE DRAFTING HISTORY OF ARTICLE 1

The first drafts of the definition of discrimination in the Women's Convention were submitted by the Philippines and the USSR. The Philippines' draft defined discrimination against women as '...] any distinction, exclusion, restriction or preference made on the basis of sex, which has the effect of or the purpose of nullifying or impairing the recognition, enjoyment or exercise, on an equal footing, of human rights and fundamental freedoms in the political, economic, social, cultural or any field of public life'.[5]

The USSR came up with the text: '...] the direct or indirect denial or the limitation of the equality of rights of women with men or the granting of direct or indirect advantages and preferences to men, thereby nullifying, or violating the principle of, equality of opportunities in all aspects of social and family life, is unjust and is incompatible with human dignity'.[6]

The discussion focused on whether the definition should concern discrimination against *women*, or discrimination on the *basis of sex*. Especially the representatives of Sweden, Denmark, Finland, Norway and the United States of America were more in favour of a convention that would focus on the elimination of discrimination based on sex in general, than on the abolition of discrimination against women. In the end, a compromise was formulated by the United Kingdom combining the two concepts.[7]

Further discussion ensued on the use of the term 'preference' in the draft version by the Philippines. It was felt by some representatives, that preference could also be explained in a favourable way, for instance preferential treatment,

---

[5] UN doc. E/CN.6/573, Text of the draft Convention on the Elimination of Discrimination Against Women Proposed by the Philippines, 6 November 1973. Also see, LARS ADAM REHOF, Guide to the *Travaux Préparatoires* of the United Nations Convention on the Elimination of All Forms of Discrimination Against Women, Martinus Nijhoff Publishers, Dordrecht/Boston/London, 1993, p. 43 and Annex I, p. 282.

[6] UN doc. E/CN.6/AC.1/L.2, Working paper submitted by the Union of Soviet Socialist Republics, 7 January 1974. REHOF, 1993, p. 43 and Annex I, p. 288.

[7] REHOF, 1993, p. 47.

and that forbidding preference on the basis of sex might turn out to be to women's disadvantage. Ultimately, the term preference was left out of the final text of Article 1 for fear that it would be too problematic.[8]

As regards equality between the sexes, the words 'on the basis of equality of men and women' were suggested by the Netherlands' representation and they were adopted by consensus as a substitute for the proposal to include the words 'on the basis of equality with men'.[9]

Finally, the scope of the Article was considered. While it was clear that the drafters wished the definition to apply to both the public and the private sphere, there was some discussion on the wording. In the end, suggestions to include the words 'family' or 'public life' were not accepted but instead it was agreed that the Article would cover women's human rights and fundamental freedoms 'in the political, economic, social, cultural, civil or any other field'.

2.2 A COMPARISON WITH OTHER DEFINITIONS OF DISCRIMINATION

If the definition of discrimination in the Women's Convention is compared to other international and regional human rights instruments[10] and the way in which discrimination is defined in the context of the European Union,[11] several characteristics stand out.

First of all, it is clear that the definition only covers the prohibition of discrimination against girls and women; boys and men are not protected by the provision.[12] In other instruments, discrimination is prohibited either as regards people in general[13] or for the benefit of specific groups,[14] but the formulation is

---

[8] REHOF, 1993, p. 48.
[9] REHOF, 1993, p. 49.
[10] The human rights instruments that were examined are: the Universal Declaration of Human Rights (Article 2); the International Covenant on Economic, Social, and Cultural Rights (Article 2(2)); the International Covenant on Civil and Political Rights (Articles 2(1) and 26); the International Convention on the Elimination of all Forms of Racial Discrimination (Article 1), the International Convention on the Rights of the Child (Article 2(1)); the European Convention for the Protection of Human Rights and Fundamental Freedoms (Article 14); the European Social Charter (1996) (Part V, Article E); the African Charter on Human and Peoples' Rights (Article 2); and the American Convention on Human Rights (Article 1(1)).
[11] Within the EU, a definition of non-discrimination may be found in the Treaty on the Functioning of the European Union (Article 10) and the Charter of Fundamental Rights of the European Union (Article 21(1)).
[12] The wording of Article 1 Women's Convention is rather similar to Article 1 of the International Convention on the Elimination of all Forms of Racial Discrimination (ICERD) in which the prohibition of discrimination is focused on and limited to 'race, colour, descent, or national or ethnic origin' and sex as a ground for discrimination is not mentioned at all.
[13] Discrimination in general is prohibited in the UDHR, ICESCR, ICCPR, ECHR, ESC, ACHPR, ACHR, the TFEU and the CFREU.
[14] Specific groups are protected against discrimination in the ICERD and the ICRC.

always gender-neutral and both men and women may benefit from the protection that is offered.

Secondly, the definition of discrimination in the Women's Convention is comprehensive and covers civil and political rights as well as economic, social, and cultural rights; it is based on the idea of indivisibility, interdependence, and interrelatedness of all human rights as is the case with the Universal Declaration on Human Rights.[15] Furthermore, as was already explained above, both public and private actions are covered, which means that protection is offered against discrimination by both State and non-State actors.[16]

An interesting feature is that discrimination based on marital status is explicitly prohibited; this is a ground for discrimination that is not mentioned anywhere else.[17]

With the adoption of General Recommendation No. 19 on Violence Against Women (VAW),[18] CEDAW considerably broadened the range of Article 1 by determining that gender-based violence should be considered as discrimination against women.[19]

Just like most other instruments that prohibit discrimination, the Women's Convention mentions 'on the basis of sex' as one of the sources of discrimination. The developments and growing insights of the last few decades have learned that 'on the basis of sex' may be too narrow to understand the complexity of discrimination against women and the underlying socio-economic perceptions, and that instead 'on the basis of sex and gender' would offer a better alternative. In this context, 'sex' is understood as a biological characteristic, in particular the difference between men's and women's reproductive abilities. The fact that only women menstruate, can become pregnant, give birth and can lactate their babies, may sometimes warrant a different treatment between men and women. This entails that differentiation based on sex may be justified and even welcomed under certain specified conditions.[20]

---

[15] The idea of comprehensiveness of the UDHR was lost during the Cold War with the result that civil and political rights were codified in one treaty and economic, social, and cultural rights in another.

[16] For women this is particularly important since many violations of girls' and women's human rights happen in the private sphere at the hands of private actors.

[17] According to Rehof, 'marital status' was inserted at a very late stage in the final version of Article 1. See REHOF, 1993, p. 47. It seems to be a highly valuable addition since in many countries matrimony may signify major changes in women's rights and legal capacity. Furthermore, Article 1 thus forms a prelude to Article 16.

[18] CEDAW has the authority to adopt General Recommendations under Article 21 of the Convention. Such Recommendations may contain an authoritative interpretation of one or more provisions of the Convention and will apply to all States parties.

[19] See CEDAW General Recommendation No. 19, 11th session, 1992, para. 6. For further information see section 3.2 on General Recommendations in this Chapter.

[20] Examples that come to mind are guarantees that women retain (part of) their salary while on pregnancy leave and guarantees that they can return to their jobs after confinement; special health care and facilities for menstruating and pregnant girls and women; or facilities for lactating mothers at their work place.

The concept of 'gender' is an artificial and culturally determined set of prejudices and stereotypes that are applied to men and women. Thus, gender is not based on actual biological differences between men and women, but is concerned with different characteristics and roles that are ascribed to the two sexes by society.[21] In this way, ideas about gender-appropriate roles have determined for centuries that men are to be found in the public sphere where they are the leaders and breadwinners for their families, while women are relegated to the private sphere of the home where they are to be the care-givers. While both sets of roles are intrinsically valuable and may complement each other, and families may live in peace and harmony based on this traditional role division,[22] nevertheless both men and women are restricted in their freedom and choices if they have to live up to society's expectations of them.[23] In addition, the part to be played by women is considered to be less important, is less appreciated and less paid which has a negative effect on the whole range of human rights that women are entitled to.

In the next section, CEDAW's interpretation of discrimination against women will be examined. An important point is to what extent CEDAW has moved from focusing on discrimination based on sex to including discrimination based on gender. It goes without saying that for the advancement of women's equality it is important that also other influential organs such as other human rights bodies and the EU understand that discrimination against women encompasses both sex and gender.[24] If the view remains focused on

---

[21] Gender is described by Lacey as 'the socially constructed meaning of sex', NICOLA LACEY, 'Feminist Legal Theory and the Rights of Women', in: Karen KNOP (ed.), *Gender and Human Rights*, Oxford University Press, Oxford, 2004, p. 15. Charlesworth and Chinkin describe gender as: '[...] the excess cultural baggage associated with biological sex. "Gender" draws attention to aspects of social relations that are culturally contingent and without foundation in biological necessity'. HILARY CHARLESWORTH and CHRISTINE CHINKIN, *The boundaries of international law; A feminist analysis*, Manchester University Press, Manchester, 2000, p. 3.

[22] In many societies, the traditional roles models for men and women are held in high esteem and are thought to bring harmony because they are complimentary. Sometimes the term equity between the sexes is used to indicate natural justice, evenness and fairness. However, equity is based on the idea that men and women have different roles and may therefore be treated differently. Women are thus referred to a subjugated position in the family, community and society at large. Women's lack of power and financial independence puts them in a vulnerable position that makes them susceptible to suppression and violence. They do not actually enjoy human rights because they are human beings, but they may have privileges based on their status in society – for instance as a wife and mother – if they behave in accordance to societal rules. See also CHARLESWORTH and CHINKIN, 2000, p. 80, who maintain that equity may be invoked to preserve the interests of the privileged.

[23] While men may generally benefit from the division in traditional gendered roles because they are on the receiving end of power, money, and property, they are also burdened with the responsibility to be the main or sole provider for their families. Even in modern societies, men will hardly ever get the chance to make a different choice in life and for instance become the prime care-takers of their children. This means that they will miss out on the chance to see their children grow up.

[24] In any case the HRC and the CESCR seem to make some headway in this regard. While the HRC already alludes in its General Comment No. 28 to the importance of understanding women's subordinate position in society by urging States parties not to accept any justifications for discrimination against women based on tradition, history, culture and

discrimination based on sex this may entail that the symptoms of discrimination against women are fought, but that the root causes remain intact.

3. CEDAW'S INTERPRETATION OF DISCRIMINATION AGAINST WOMEN

How CEDAW uses and interprets the contents of Article 1 may be observed from its various publications. In this section subsequently a selection of the Committee's Concluding Observations (COs) will be examined as well as relevant General Recommendations, and decisions that have been taken under Article 2 of the Optional Protocol. Finally the only inquiry procedure that has been conducted until today will be studied.

3.1. CEDAW'S CONCLUDING OBSERVATIONS AND ARTICLE 1[25]

From the COs that were investigated, it becomes clear that CEDAW does not always comment on the implementation or interpretation of

---

religious rules, the CESCR goes a step further by actually explaining in its General Comment No. 16 the concept of gender and how gender-based assumptions and expectations may disadvantage women. See UN doc. CCPR/C/21/Rev.1/Add.10, HRC General Comment No. 28, *Equality of rights between men and women* (Article 3), 2000, para. 5 and UN doc. E/C.12/2005/3, CESCR General Comment No. 16, *Article 3: the equal right of men and women to the enjoyment of all economic, social and cultural rights*, 2005, para. 14.

[25] For the purpose of this section, a selection was made of COs that were published by CEDAW between 2006 and 2011. The countries that were chosen represent a cross section of different geographical, cultural and development backgrounds. CEDAW's Concluding Observations on the following States parties were investigated: Albania (2010) UN doc. CEDAW/C/ALB/CO/3; Argentina (2010) UN doc. CEDAW/C/ARG/CO/6; Australia (2010) UN doc. CEDAW/C/AUL/CO/7; Bangladesh (2011) UN doc. CEDAW/C/BGD/CO/7; Belarus (2011) UN doc. CEDAW/C/BLR/CO/7; Botswana (2010) UN doc. CEDAW/C/BOT/CO/3; Burkina Faso (2010) UN doc. CEDAW/C/BFA/CO/6; China (2006) UN doc. CEDAW/C/CHN/CO/6; Cuba (2006) UN doc. CEDAW/C/CUB/CO/6; Denmark (2006) UN doc. CEDAW/C/DEN/CO/6; Egypt (2010) UN doc. EDAW/C/EGY/CO/7; Fiji (2010) UN doc. CEDAW/C/FJI/CO/4; Germany (2009) UN doc. CEDAW/C/DEU/CO/6; India (2007) UN doc. CEDAW/C/IND/CO/3; Indonesia (2007) UN doc. CEDAW/C/IDN/CO/5; Israel (2011) UN doc. CEDAW/C/ISR/CO/5; Kenya (2011) UN doc. CEDAW/C/KEN/CO/7; Liechtenstein (2011) UN doc. CEDAW/C/LIE/CO/4; Malawi (2010) UN doc. CEDAW/C/MWI/CO/6; Mexico (2006) UN doc. CEDAW/C/MEX/CO/6; The Netherlands (2010) UN doc. CEDAW/C/NLD/CO/5; Panama (2010) UN doc. CEDAW/C/PAN/CO/7; Papua New Guinea (2010) UN doc. CEDAW/C/PNG/CO/3; Russian Federation (2010) UN doc. CEDAW/C/USR/CO/7; Rwanda (2009) UN doc. CEDAW/C/RWA/CO/6; South Africa (2011) UN doc. CEDAW/C/ZAF/CO/4; Sri Lanka (2011) UN doc. CEDAW/C/LKA/CO/7; Sweden (2008) UN doc. CEDAW/C/SWE/CO/7; Tunisia (2010) UN doc. CEDAW/C/TUN/CO/6; Turkey (2010) UN doc. CEDAW/C/TUR/CO/6; Uganda (2010) UN doc. CEDAW/C/UGA/CO/7; Ukraine (2010) UN doc. CEDAW/C/UKR/CO/7; United Arab Emirates (2010) UN doc. CEDAW/C/ARE/CO/1; Uzbekistan (2010) UN doc. CEDAW/C/UZB/CO/4.

Article 1.[26] If the provision is mentioned in the CO, the Committee will either urge the State party to include a specific prohibition of discrimination based on sex in the constitution or basic law or other domestic legislation,[27] or it will commend a State for recently having included the prohibition on this ground in its legislation.[28]

CEDAW makes it clear that a definition on discrimination against women should encompass both direct and indirect discrimination.[29] While in the COs under scrutiny no definitions of direct or indirect discrimination could be found, some examples of these forms of discrimination were mentioned by the Committee that may be useful for a better understanding of what is expected of States parties.[30]

Unfortunately, the Committee is unclear as far as the distinction between discrimination based on sex and discrimination based on gender is concerned. Sometimes it treats the concepts of sex and gender as if they were synonymous,[31] while on other occasions, the Committee welcomes the fact that a State party has included the prohibition of both sex and gender as grounds of discrimination in

---

[26] In 22 out of the 34 COs that were examined, the Committee specifically mentioned or commented on the implementation of Article 1.

[27] This was the case with the COs on Belarus, 2011 (paras. 11 and 12); Botswana, 2010 (paras. 9 and 10); Burkina Faso, 2010 (paras. 9 and 10); China, 2006 (paras. 9 and 10); Cuba, 2006 (paras. 11 and 12); Indonesia, 2007 (paras. 15 and 16); Israel, 2011 (para. 18); Papua New Guinea, 2010 (para. 13); Russian Federation, 2010 (paras. 12 and 13); Rwanda, 2009 (paras. 15 and 16); South Africa, 2011 (paras. 14 and 15); Sri Lanka, 2011 (paras. 14 and 15); Tunisia, 2010 (paras. 14 and 15); Turkey, 2010 (paras. 10 and 11); United Arab Emirates, 2010 (paras. 14 and 15); Uzbekistan, 2010 (para. 9).

[28] This happened in the case of Albania, 2010 (para. 8); Panama, 2010 (para. 12);.

[29] This happened as regards Belarus, 2011 (para. 12); Botswana, 2010 (paras. 9 and 10); Burkina Faso, 2010 (paras. 9 and 10); China, 2006 (paras. 9 and 10); Cuba, 2006 (paras. 11 and 12); Israel, 2011 (paras. 10 and 18); Papua New Guinea, 2010 (para. 13); Russian Federation, 2010 (para.13); 2009 (paras. 15 and 16); South Africa, 2011 (para. 14); Sri Lanka, 2011 (para. 14); Ukraine, 2010 (paras. 16 and 17); Uzbekistan, 2010 (para. 9).
Germany was commended for including both direct and indirect discrimination in its 2006 General Equal Treatment Act, 2009 (para. 5).

[30] Direct discrimination was for instance found in the case of Indonesia where the Committee made it clear that the enactment of the 2007 Law on Natural Disaster Management is discriminatory against women heads of household, Indonesia, 2007 (para. 38). With regard to Malawi, the Committee uttered concern that both statutory and customary laws discriminate against women, Malawi, 2010 (para. 12).
Cases of indirect discrimination were pointed out as regards Hong Kong, in particular because of the electoral system, China, 2006 (para. 39); Botswana, 2010 (para. 39) where strategies for poverty reduction and income-generating activities indirectly discriminate against rural women who are left out because of their limited access to credit caused by lack of collateral.
In the CO on Rwanda, 2009 (para. 25) the Committee pointed out that some of the provisions in the Bill on the prevention and punishment of gender-based violence may directly or indirectly discriminate against women.

[31] Rwanda, 2009 (paras. 6 and 15).

its legislation,[32] or warns the State that discrimination based on sex and gender should be prohibited,[33] albeit without further explaining the difference.

In a few instances, the Committee stresses the scope of the provision and urges States to explicitly cover the domestic and private spheres in its legislation on discrimination against women.[34]

All in all it can be concluded that not much information of the meaning and interpretation of Article 1 may be gleaned from CEDAW's COs. Maybe that cannot be expected as COs are not the best forum for interpretative work. A better medium would be the General Recommendations since these are applicable to all States Parties and in them the Committee may give an authoritative interpretation and explanation of a provision in the Convention.

3.2. GENERAL RECOMMENDATIONS

Article 21 of the Women's Convention invites the Committee to adopt General Recommendations based on the examination of State reports and information that has been received from the States parties. Between 1986 and 2010, CEDAW has adopted 28 such General Recommendations.[35]

While the prohibition of discrimination is naturally one of the leading themes in the work of the Committee, it was not until General Recommendation No. 19, adopted in 1992, that CEDAW gave a first explanation and interpretation of how States parties should understand discrimination against women. With this Recommendation, the Committee wished to fill the lacuna that had been created by the drafters of the Convention by ignoring the issue of gender-based violence.[36] CEDAW repaired this gap by stating that:

> 'The Convention in article 1 defines discrimination against women. The definition of discrimination includes gender-based violence, that is, violence that is directed against a woman because she is a woman or that affects women disproportionately. It includes acts that inflict physical, mental or sexual harm or suffering, threats of such acts, coercion and other deprivations of liberty. Gender-based violence may breach

---

[32] Panama, 2010 (para. 6).
[33] In the case of Papua New Guinea, the Committee notes that the Constitution does not include the prohibition to discriminate on the basis of sex and continues by warning the State party that thereby discrimination on the ground or sex or gender are lawfully allowed. Papua New Guinea, 2010 (para. 13).
[34] See the COs on Bangladesh, 2011 (paras. 13 and 14); Germany, 2009 (paras. 17 and 18); Papua New Guinea, 2010 (para. 13); Israel, 2011 (para. 18); Russian Federation, 2010 (para. 13); Sri Lanka, 2011 (para. 15); Tunisia, 2010 (para. 15); United Arab Emirates, 2010 (para. 15); Uzbekistan, 2010 (para. 9).
[35] All General Recommendations may be found at: www2.ohchr.org/english/bodies/cedaw/comments.htm.
[36] For more information on this subject matter see Chapter 22 by Kate Rose-Sender in this book.

specific provisions of the Convention, regardless of whether those provisions expressly mention violence.'[37]

In the next paragraph, it continues with:

> 'Gender-based violence, [...] is discrimination within the meaning of article 1 of the Convention'.[38]

As a consequence, henceforward States parties have had to report on their actions as regards the elimination of VAW and the protection of the victims of such violence when they report on all measures they have taken under Article 1.[39]

In para. 9 of this Recommendation the Committee emphasizes that discrimination against women under the Convention is not restricted to actions by or on behalf of the State, but also encompasses discrimination by any person, organization or enterprise.[40]

The next General Recommendation that offers insight in CEDAW's understanding of the concept of discrimination against women is No. 25 on Article 4, paragraph 1 of the Women's Convention on temporary special measures, adopted in 2004. The Committee explains that the concept of discrimination used in the Convention goes beyond the prohibition of discrimination based on sex, and is concerned with the discrimination of women because they are women. According to the Committee this entails *inter alia* that States parties should focus on the elimination of both direct and indirect discrimination against women both in law and in practice.[41] In a footnote to paragraph 7 CEDAW explains that indirect discrimination against women:

> 'may occur when laws, policies and programmes are based on seemingly gender-neutral criteria which in their actual effect have a detrimental impact on women. Gender-neutral laws, policies and programmes unintentionally may perpetuate the consequences of past discrimination. They may be inadvertently modelled on male lifestyles and thus fail to take into account aspects of women's life experiences which may differ from those of men. These differences may exist because of stereotypical expectations, attitudes and behaviour directed towards women which are based on the biological differences between women and men. They may also exist because of the generally existing subordination of women by men.'

---

[37] CEDAW General Recommendation No. 19 on Violence against women, 11th session, 1992, para. 6.
[38] *Ibid.*, para. 7.
[39] The duty to submit reports to the Committee on a regular basis can be found in Article 18 of the Convention.
[40] CEDAW General Recommendation No. 19, 1992, para. 9.
[41] CEDAW General Recommendation No. 25, on Article 4, paragraph 1 of the Convention on the Elimination of all Forms of Discrimination Against Women, on temporary special measures, 2004, paras. 5–7.

The Committee continues by urging the States parties to address prevailing gender relations and gender stereotypes that affect women and that exist both in the law and in societal constructions. The meaning of gender is again explained in a footnote as:[42]

> 'Gender is defined as the social meanings given to biological sex differences. It is an ideological and cultural construct, but is also reproduced within the realm of material practices; in turn it influences the outcomes of such practices. It affects the distribution of resources, wealth, work, decision-making and political power, and enjoyment of rights and entitlements within the family as well as public life. Despite variations across cultures and over time, gender relations throughout the world entail asymmetry of power between men and women as a pervasive trait. Thus, gender is a social stratifier, and in this sense it is similar to other stratifiers such as race, class, ethnicity, sexuality, and age. It helps us understand the social construction of gender identities and the unequal structure of power that underlies the relationship between the sexes.'[43]

The Committee reiterates that States should protect women from discrimination both in the public and in the private sphere against State actors and private actors, and that next to legislation concrete and effective policies and programmes should be adopted.[44]

Finally, General Recommendation No. 28 on Article 2 of the Convention, adopted in 2010, also sheds light on CEDAW's interpretation of Article 1. A definition of direct discrimination is given in paragraph 16 reading:

> 'Direct discrimination against women constitutes different treatment explicitly based on grounds of sex and gender differences.'

In the same paragraph also indirect discrimination is defined as:

> 'Indirect discrimination against women occurs when a law, policy, programme or practice appears to be neutral in so far as it relates to men and women, but has a discriminatory effect in practice on women because pre-existing inequalities are not addressed by the apparently neutral measure. Moreover, indirect discrimination can exacerbate existing inequalities owing to a failure to recognize structural and historical patterns of discrimination and unequal power relationships between women and men.'[45]

---

[42] It seems strange that the Committee would explain in two footnotes to para. 7 what is meant with indirect discrimination and gender. For a better understanding of States parties and more emphasis, it might have been more appropriate to include such valuable explanations in the main body of the text.

[43] This description of gender was quoted by CEDAW from the World Survey on the Role of Women in Development, United Nations, New York, 1999, page ix.

[44] General Recommendation No. 25, 2004, para. 7.

[45] General Recommendation No. 28, on the core obligations of States parties under Article 2 of the Convention on the Elimination of All Forms of Discrimination Against Women,

In paragraph 5 of the same General Recommendation the Committee states that although the text of the Convention only mentions discrimination based on sex, in fact, the interpretation of Article 1, read together with Articles 2(f) and 5, indicates that gender-based discrimination against women is covered. In this Recommendation, CEDAW defines 'gender' as:

> 'socially constructed identities, attributes and roles for women and men and society's social and cultural meaning for these biological differences resulting in hierarchical relationships between women and men and in the distribution of power and rights favouring men and disadvantaging women'.[46]

States parties' obligation to protect women from discrimination against all kinds of actors is repeated in this General Recommendation as well:

> 'States parties also have an obligation to ensure that women are protected against discrimination committed by public authorities, the judiciary, organizations, enterprises or private individuals, in the public and private spheres.'[47]

In conclusion it can be said that it took the Committee a long time before it included its explanation and interpretation of the concept of discrimination against women in its General Recommendations. Particularly Recommendations Nos. 19, 25 and 28 have been used by the Committee for the clarification of the concept. The most important aspects of CEDAW's interpretation concern that discrimination based on sex should be understood as covering the concept of gender. Furthermore, that discrimination may exist in the forms of direct and indirect discrimination. From Recommendation No. 19 it has become clear that gender-based violence should be considered as a form of discrimination against women and, finally, the Committee has made it clear that States parties are under an obligation to protect women against discrimination both in the public and private spheres against State- and non-State actors.

3.3. DECISIONS

With the entry into force of the Optional Protocol (OP) to the Women's Convention in 2000, CEDAW has next to the reporting procedure, two additional monitoring mechanisms at its disposal: an individual or group's complaint procedure, and an inquiry procedure.[48] Obviously, CEDAW will only

---

16 December 2010, para. 16.
[46] *Ibid.*, para. 5.
[47] *Ibid.*, para. 17.
[48] The individual complaints procedure can be found in Article 2 of the OP, while the inquiry procedure is contained in Article 8. For more information on the OP see Chapter 21 by Sille

have the authority to hear complaints, or conduct an inquiry in relation to States parties that have ratified the OP.[49] While the decisions that CEDAW takes under these procedures are not legally binding, they are highly authoritative and they may offer information on the interpretative work of the Committee.

Of the 23 decisions that have been made public,[50] only 12 were deemed admissible. Since the Committee will not go into the merits of a case if it is held inadmissible, obviously no official information on Article 1 or non-discrimination can be found in these views.

In ten of the admissible cases, Article 1 or discrimination based on sex and/or gender is dealt with. Seven of these complaints are about gender-based violence. Of these seven, five concern cases of domestic violence, one concerns rape by a private actor, and one is about sexual harassment by prison personnel.

The first complaint concerning domestic violence was Communication No. 2 about a Hungarian woman who was abused on a regular basis by her partner, but who could not leave the apartment she co-owned with the abuser since one of her children is severely handicapped and none of the shelters in Hungary was at the time equipped to house this child. While the Committee recalled that it has determined in its General Recommendation No. 19 that the definition of discrimination includes gender-based violence, it did not state in its final decision that Hungary had violated Article 1 or Recommendation No. 19, but only the violation of Article 2(a), (b) and (e) and Article 5(a) in conjunction with Article 16 was mentioned.[51]

Article 1 is specifically mentioned as regards Communications No. 5 and No. 6 both dealing with the deaths of women of Turkish descent who were killed by their partners in Austria. In both cases, CEDAW held that Austria had *inter alia* violated Article 1 in conjunction with General Recommendation No. 19 since the State party had not done enough to protect these women against gender-based violence – *i.c.* domestic violence – which is to be understood as a form of discrimination against women.[52] Also in Case No. 20, concerning a victim of domestic violence in Bulgaria who did not receive effective protection, the Committee recalled that gender-based violence constitutes discrimination within the meaning of Article 2, read in conjunction with Article 1, of the Convention and General Recommendation No. 19.[53]

Jansen in this book.
[49] In July 2012 the number of States parties that had ratified the OP was 104.
[50] At the time that this Chapter was written (July 2012) only 23 decisions by CEDAW had been published.
[51] UN doc. CEDAW/C/36/D/2/2003, Ms A.T. vs. Hungary, 26 January 2005, paras. 9.2 and 9.6.
[52] See UN doc. CEDAW/C/39/D/5/2005, Communication No. 5/2005, Şahide Goecke vs. Austria, 6 August 2007, paras. 12.1.6 and 12.2 and UN doc. CEDAW/C/39/D/6/2005, Communication No. 6/2005, Fatma Yildirim vs. Austria, 1 October 2007, paras. 12.1.6 and 12.2.
[53] UN doc. CEDAW/C/49/D/20/2008, Ms. V.K. vs. Bulgaria, 27 September 2011, paras. 9.8 and 9.15.

In Communication No. 19 concerning Canada, Article 1 was brought up by an aboriginal woman victim of domestic violence who was evicted from her home while seeking protection from domestic violence in a battered women's shelter, and who was tricked out of her property rights. The combination of facts led to the Committee's decision that the complainant was the victim of discrimination based on sex and gender. Canada was held to have violated her rights under Article 2, paragraphs (d) and (e), and 16, paragraph 1(h), read in conjunction with Article 1.[54] This time the connection with General Recommendation No. 19 was not made, however, nor was any explanation given why the violation constituted discrimination based both on sex and on gender.

In case No. 18 concerning a Philippine woman who had been raped by an acquaintance who had offered her a ride home, the Committee decided that the Philippines had violated Article 1 and General Recommendation No. 19 because the State had failed to adequately protect against rape, which according to CEDAW is a crime that 'constitutes a violation of women's right to personal security and bodily integrity'.[55]

In the last Communication concerning VAW, No. 23 concerning Belarus, the complainant had been detained in a temporary detention facility for five days in poor, unhygienic and degrading conditions. The detention facility was staffed exclusively by male prison guards who sexually harassed and humiliated her. In its decision the Committee states that the fact that there were no specific facilities for female prisoners already constitutes a violation of Article 1 on itself. In addition, the inappropriate treatment by the male prison staff constituted sexual harassment and discrimination based on sex. Belarus was found to have violated Articles 1 and 5(a) of the Convention and General Recommendation No. 19.[56]

Two cases deal primarily with discrimination based on sex in relation to the access to health care. Communication No. 17 concerned the death of a pregnant Brazilian woman who had not received adequate obstetric care. According to the Committee the failure of the State party to provide appropriate maternal health services constitutes a violation of Articles 12 in conjunction with Article 1. The link with Article 1 was made because 'measures to eliminate discrimination against women are considered to be inappropriate in a health-care system which lacks services to prevent, detect and treat illnesses specific to women'.[57]

In Communication No. 22 against Peru the victim L.C. became pregnant at the age of 13 years as a result of repeated sexual abuse. Because abortion on the ground of rape or sexual abuse is legally not possible in Peru, she was desperate

---

[54] UN doc. CEDAW/C/51/D/19/2008, Communication No. 19/2008, Cecilia Kell vs. Canada, 26 April 2012, paras. 10.2 and 11.
[55] UN doc. CEDAW/C/46/D/18/2008, Communication No. 18/2008, Karen Tayag Vertido vs. The Philippines, 1 September 2010, paras. 8.7 and 8.9.
[56] UN doc. CEDAW/C/49/D/23/2009, Inga Abramova vs. Belarus, 27 September 2011, paras. 7.2, 7.4, 7.5 and 7.7.
[57] UN doc. CEDAW/C/49/D/17/2008, Communication No. 17/2008, Alyne da Silva Pimentel Teixeira (deceased) vs. Brazil, 27 September 2011, paras. 7.3 and 8.

and attempted suicide by jumping from a building. She severely injured her back, but when she explained that she had tried to commit suicide because of her unwanted pregnancy, surgery was delayed for fear of harming the foetus. After L.C. had a spontaneous miscarriage, she underwent surgery for her spinal injuries, almost three and one half months after it had been decided that an operation was necessary. Currently she is paralyzed from the neck down. The Committee considered that the State party had not complied with its obligations and had therefore violated the rights of L.C. established in Articles 2(c) and (f), 3, 5 and 12, together with Article 1, of the Convention.[58]

Finally, in communication No. 28 concerning Turkey, discrimination based on sex and gender in combination with the right to employment in Article 11 was considered. The complainant worked at a hairdresser's shop in Kocaeli when after 6 years her contract was terminated because allegedly she was having an extramarital relationship with one of her male colleagues, which supposedly would harm the good name of the shop, although it was generally known that several male employees were having extramarital relationships. One of the managers of the shop put pressure on the complainant to sign a document saying that she had benefited from all her rights by threatening her that he would spread rumours that she had relationships with other men if she would not sign. Since the complainant is a married woman, she was very scared that the threat would be carried out, but nevertheless she refused to sign. The Committee found that the author was dismissed on account of gender discrimination under Article 1. The Committee emphasized that implementation of the Convention requires steps to eliminate direct and indirect discrimination and the modification and transformation of gender stereotypes and the elimination of wrongful gender stereotyping.[59]

From these decisions it seems that Article 1 plays a modest but important role. In the cases dealing with VAW, the Committee makes a connection between gender-based violence and discrimination based on sex as contained in Article 1. In the cases concerning health care and employment, the Committee determines *inter alia* that the behaviour of the respective States parties is in violation of Article 1: lack of women specific legislation and the existence of stereotypes and/or traditional role models are taken into account to determine discrimination based on sex and gender.

3.4. INQUIRY

The Committee may conduct an inquiry based on general reports concerning gross and systematic violations that have been received from Civil Society Organizations (CSOs) or Non-Governmental Organizations (NGOs).[60] In view

---

[58] UN doc. CEDAW/C/50/D/22/2009, L.C. vs. Peru, 25 November 2011, paras. 8.7 and 9.
[59] UN doc. CEDAW/C/51/D/28/2010, R.K.B. vs. Turkey, 13 April 2010, paras. 8.5 – 8.10.
[60] See Article 8 of the Optional Protocol to the Women's Convention.

of the concept of State sovereignty, fact-finding missions on the territory of the State under scrutiny are only allowed with the express permission of the State. The Committee decided to start an inquiry procedure after it had received CSO and NGO reports claiming that in and around Ciudad Juárez in the north of Mexico at least 230 women had been abducted, raped and murdered. Since Mexico offered its full cooperation to the inquiry, two CEDAW members conducted a fact-finding mission on Mexican territory in 2003.[61]

In its report, CEDAW reminds the State party of Article 1 of the Convention by repeating the text of the provision and recalling that:

> 'gender-based violence constitutes an exclusion and restriction which impedes the enjoyment of their fundamental rights. This is confirmed in the Committee's Recommendation No. 19, which states that "the definition of discrimination includes gender-based violence, that is, violence that is directed against a woman because she is a woman…" and that "gender-based violence is a form of discrimination that seriously inhibits women's ability to enjoy rights and freedoms…".'[62]

While the Committee does not take a decision based on an inquiry, some conclusions are drawn and recommendations are made to the State party. In this case, the Committee recommended Mexico to comply with all obligations assumed under the Women's Convention and reminded the State party:

> 'that the obligation to eliminate discrimination against women refers not only to actions or omissions by the State at all levels, but also to the need to take all appropriate measures to eliminate discrimination against women by any person, organization or enterprise'.[63]

As was to be expected, also in its report on Mexico, the Committee clearly determines gender-based violence as a form of discrimination against women as included in Article 1, and reminds the State party that it is under an obligation to eradicate discrimination based on sex both in the public and the private sphere.

4. THE PRINCIPLE OF NON-DISCRIMINATION UNDER EU LAW

The European Union (EU) is generally described as a legal system *sui generis*. It has undergone considerable development since the conclusion of the European Coal

---

[61] UN doc. CEDAW/C/2005/OP.8/MEXICO, Report on Mexico produced by the Committee on the Elimination of Discrimination against Women under article 8 of the Optional Protocol to the Convention, and Reply from the Government of Mexico, 27 January 2005.
[62] Report on Mexico, para. 51.
[63] Report on Mexico, para. 264.

and Steel Community Treaty in 1951. The main immediate goal was economic welfare, with political integration intended as a long-term result as well.[64]

The legal framework of the EU can be divided into primary sources, namely the Treaties, secondary sources, such as directives and regulations, that is, secondary legislation adopted in accordance with the provisions of a Treaty, and case law. In the following, these three sources of EU law will be analyzed as regards the anti-discrimination law on grounds of sex within the EU. Other, non-legislative or non-binding instruments of the EU, will also briefly be considered.

4.1. PRIMARY SOURCES OF EU LAW

What is now the European Union started out as the European Coal and Steel Community (ECSC) which together with the European Economic Community (EEC) and the European Atomic Energy Community (EURATOM) constituted the European Communities (EC). It was not until 1992 with the signing of the Maastricht Treaty that the European Union was created and the ECSC and the EC were combined into the European Community. With the entry of the Lisbon Treaty in 2009, the primary sources of EU law became the Treaty on European Union (TEU) and the Treaty on the Functioning of the European Union (TFEU).

Article 119 of the Treaty of Rome – the treaty founding the EEC which was later renamed EC – was the first, and for a long time only, mention of sex equality in this economically-focused and -driven community: It referred to the principle of equal pay for equal work between men and women.[65] However, this Article did not give a legal basis for secondary legislation until the amendment by the Amsterdam Treaty which was signed in 1997 and entered into force in 1999.[66] This amendment inserted a paragraph which allowed for the adoption of measures ensuring the application of the principle of equal opportunities and equal treatment of men and women in matters of employment and occupation, including – but no longer limited to – the principle of equal pay.[67] The Amsterdam Treaty furthermore created a general provision providing a legal basis for secondary legislation to combat discrimination based on a number of grounds, one of which was sex.

At the time of writing, the TEU names the principle of non-discrimination on grounds of sex as one of the fundamental principles of the EU. It is named as a value prevailing among the Member States.[68] Article 3 of the TEU lists the promotion of equality between men and women as one of the fundamental aims

---

[64] E. Ellis, *Sex Equality Law*, Clarendon Press, Oxford, 1998, p. 1 f.
[65] Article 119 EC, today Article 157 TFEU.
[66] Ellis, 1998, p. 4 f.
[67] This provision is today Article 19 TFEU.
[68] Treaty on European Union, OJ 2008 C115/13 (TEU), Article 2.

of the EU and pledges to combat discrimination.[69] Article 8 TFEU states that 'in all its activities, the Union shall aim to eliminate inequalities, and to promote equality, between men and women'[70] and Article 10 TFEU further holds that the EU shall aim to combat discrimination on the grounds of, *inter alia*, sex.[71] This places the equality between men and women and the fight to eliminate discrimination against women at the heart of the Union's values. However, these more general provisions leave open the definition of the concepts of equality and non-discrimination.

A number of secondary legislative instruments clarify the concepts and provide for their application in more detail. These will be considered in the following section.

The Charter of Fundamental Rights of the European Union, originally drawn up in 1999 to give greater visibility to the fundamental rights applicable at EU level, was given binding legal effect equal to that of the Treaties with the entry into force of the Lisbon Treaty.[72] It prohibits 'any discrimination based on any ground such as sex, race, colour, ethnic or social origin, genetic features, language, religion or belief, political or any other opinion, membership of a national minority, property, birth, disability, age or sexual orientation'[73] and holds that 'equality between women and men must be ensured in all areas, including employment, work and pay. The principle of equality shall not prevent the maintenance or adoption of measures providing for specific advantages in favour of the under-represented sex.'[74] The Charter is addressed to the institutions, bodies, offices and agencies of the Union, and to the Member States only when they are implementing Union law.[75]

4.2. SECONDARY SOURCES OF EU LAW

There are various types of secondary legislation under EU law: regulations, directives and decisions. Article 288 TFEU defines these as follows:

> 'A regulation shall have general application. It shall be binding in its entirety and directly applicable in all Member States.

---

[69] TEU, Article 3(2) and (3).
[70] Treaty on the Functioning of the European Union, OJ 2008 C115/47, Article 8.
[71] *Ibid.*, Article 10.
[72] Summaries of EU legislation, Fundamental rights within the European Union, available at: http://europa.eu/legislation-summaries/human-rights/fundamental-rights-within-european-union/l33501-en.htm [accessed 20 July 2012].
[73] Charter of Fundamental Rights of the European Union, OJ [2010] C 83/389, Article 21.
[74] *Ibid.*, Article 23.
[75] *Ibid.*, Article 51.

A directive shall be binding, as to the result to be achieved, upon each Member State to which it is addressed, but shall leave to the national authorities the choice of form and methods.
A decision shall be binding in its entirety. A decision which specifies those to whom it is addressed shall be binding only on them.'[76]

Article 19 TFEU gives a legal basis for the adoption of secondary legislation for the combating of discrimination based on sex, racial or ethnic origin, religion or belief, disability, age or sexual orientation, though where a more specific provision provides a legal basis, this should be used. In the case of discrimination on the ground of sex, this is Article 157 TFEU.

A number of directives have been enacted, concerning non-discrimination on the ground of sex and sex equality, non-discrimination on the ground of race, and non-discrimination on the other grounds named in Article 19 TFEU.[77] These directives are: Council Directive 75/117 on the approximation of the laws of the Member States relating to the application of the principle of equal pay for men and women ('Equal Pay Directive'), Council Directive 76/207/EEC on the implementation of the principle of equal treatment for men and women as regards access to employment, vocational training and promotion, and working conditions ('Equal Treatment Directive') – amended by Directive 2002/73, Council Directive 2000/43/EC implementing the principle of equal treatment between persons irrespective of racial or ethnic origin, ('Racial Equality Directive'), Council Directive 2000/78/EC establishing a general framework for equal treatment in employment and occupation, ('Framework Directive') and Council Directive 2004/113/EC implementing the principle of equal treatment between men and women in the access to and supply of goods and services, ('Equal Access Directive').[78]

Within the directives dealing with anti-discrimination, the definitions of the concepts of direct and indirect discrimination are used consistently.[79] This usage of a common definition leads to a coherent framework of anti-discrimination law within the *acquis communautaire* of the EU.

Direct discrimination on grounds of sex in the directives is defined as applying 'where one person is treated less favourably, on grounds of sex, than

---

[76] Article 288 TFEU.
[77] E. ELLIS, *EU Anti-Discrimination Law*, Oxford University Press, Oxford, 2005, p. 18.
[78] Council Directive 75/117, OJ [1975] L45/19; Council Directive 76/207, OJ [1976] L39/40; Council Directive 2000/43, OJ [2000] L180/22; Council Directive 2000/78, OJ [2000] L303/16; Council Directive 2002/73, OJ [2002] L269/15, Council Directive 2004/113, OJ [2004] L373/37.
[79] This excludes the Equal Pay Directive and the Equal Treatment Directive, which do not define the concepts of direct and indirect discrimination specifically. However, the Equal Treatment Directive, by virtue of its amendment in 2002, has been brought in line with the other anti-discrimination directives, including the definition of direct and indirect discrimination.

another is, has been or would be treated in a comparable situation.'[80] Indirect discrimination applies:

> 'where an apparently neutral provision, criterion or practice would put persons of one sex at a particular disadvantage compared with persons of the other sex, unless that provision, criterion or practice is objectively justified by a legitimate aim and the means of achieving that aim are appropriate and necessary.'[81]

The Equal Pay Directive obliges Member States to introduce all measures necessary to ensure enforcement possibilities for equal pay,[82] protect employees from unfair wage agreements[83] and dismissal where the employee attempts to enforce the principle of equal pay.[84] It seeks the abolition of 'all discrimination between men and women arising from laws, regulations or administrative provisions which is contrary to the principle of equal pay'[85] and the full application of the principle of equal pay in both vertical (between the individual and the State) and horizontal (between two private actors, here the employee and the employer) relations.[86]

The Equal Treatment Directive seeks to put into effect the principle of equal treatment for men and women regarding access to employment. This includes promotions and vocational training as well as working conditions and, under certain conditions, social security. The principle of equal treatment means that:

> 'there shall be no discrimination whatsoever on grounds of sex either directly or indirectly by reference in particular to martial or family status.'[87]

The scope of this directive is confined to the workplace.[88]

The Racial Equality Directive and the Framework Directive will not be discussed here, as they do not concern themselves with discrimination on grounds of sex. The Equal Access Directive, however, seeks to:

> 'lay down a framework for combating discrimination based on sex in access to and supply of goods and services, with a view to putting into effect in the Member States the principle of equal treatment between men and women.'[89]

---

[80] *E.g.* Access Directive, Article 2(a).
[81] Access Directive, Article 2(b).
[82] Equal Pay Directive, Article 2.
[83] *Ibid.*, Article 4.
[84] *Ibid.*, Article 5.
[85] *Ibid.*, Article 3.
[86] *Ibid.*, Article 3 & Article 7.
[87] Equal Treatment Directive, Article 2(1).
[88] ELLIS, 2005, p. 214.
[89] Equal Access Directive, Article 1.

It applies to all persons who provide goods and services available to the public, whether the provider is active in the public or the private sector, including public bodies. It excludes the area of private and family life and does not apply to the content of media, advertising or education. It furthermore does not apply to matters of employment and occupation, nor self-employment in as far as this is covered by other legislative acts.[90] It prohibits direct and indirect discrimination as well as harassment in its field of application,[91] and obliges Member States to ensure remedies and enforcement possibilities.[92]

The secondary legislation started out as confined to the principle of equal pay and equal treatment regarding employment and has since broadened its scope, particularly since the adoption of the Equal Access Directive. However, the principles of direct and indirect discrimination are not without limitations.

While there is no possibility for justification of a discriminatory measure mentioned in the definition of direct discrimination and it may thus be understood as absolute, the directives hold that there shall be no 'prejudice to more favourable provisions concerning the protection of women as regards pregnancy and maternity.'[93] Similarly, there are recurring provisions concerned with positive action.[94] The prohibition on direct discrimination on grounds of sex can thus be limited by explicit legislative provisions which exclude certain measures from its scope of application.

As regards indirect discrimination, the definition of the concept already contains a limitation in that indirectly discriminatory measures can be objectively justified, given that the aim of the measure and the chosen means of achieving it are both appropriate and necessary. The test for objective justification has been subject of a number of cases and was originally developed through case law.

4.3. CASE LAW

The case law of the Court of Justice of the European Union (ECJ) has played a significant role in shaping the legal framework of the EU. In landmark cases such as *Van Gend en Loos*[95] and *Costa vs. ENEL*,[96] the ECJ has developed the fundamental characteristics of the EU, such as supremacy over national law and its enforceability by individuals bringing proceedings before national courts. National courts have the power and, in a number of situations, the obligation to

---

[90] *Ibid.*, Article 3.
[91] *Ibid.*, Article 4.
[92] *Ibid.*, Chapter II.
[93] *Ibid.*, Article 4(2); Equal Treatment Directive, Article 2(7).
[94] Equal Access Directive, Article 6; Equal Treatment Directive, Article 2(6).
[95] Case 26/62 [1963] ECR 1.
[96] Case 6/64 [1964] ECR 585.

refer questions to the ECJ for preliminary rulings, where cases before them concern issues of EU law.[97]

The ECJ has, by means of preliminary rulings, played a considerable role in shaping the anti-discrimination law of the EU, especially where 'vital concepts, words, and phrases have either been left undefined in the relevant legislation, or have been defined only broadly.'[98]

The ECJ has considered over 120 cases concerning direct discrimination on ground of sex and over 40 cases concerning indirect discrimination on ground of sex.[99]

In *Defrenne II*, the ECJ considered the concepts of direct and indirect discrimination on ground of sex for the first time. This case concerned an air hostess bringing a claim for compensation of loss on the grounds that male and female flight attendants performing equal work did not receive equal pay. The ECJ considered that a distinction must be made between:

> 'direct and overt discrimination which may be identified solely with the aid of the criteria based on equal work and equal pay referred to by the Article in question and, secondly, indirect and disguised discrimination which can only be identified by reference to more explicit implementing provisions of a Community or national character.'[100]

This use of the concepts can be described as confusing.[101] However, this case also confirmed that Article 119 and the prohibition on discrimination contained therein, applied:

> 'not only to the actions of public authorities, but also to all agreements which were intended to regulate paid labour collectively, as well as to contracts between individuals.'[102]

In *Jenkins vs. Kingsgate (Clothing Productions)*, the ECJ considered indirect discrimination as:

> 'any practice which, although not founded on any discriminatory motives, nevertheless has a discriminatory effect.'[103]

---

[97] Article 267 TFEU.
[98] ELLIS, 2005, p. 18 f. It also bears mentioning that the General Court (formerly: the Court of First Instance, CFI) has not been influential regarding the development of anti-discrimination law, which was largely driven by preliminary rulings.
[99] Numbers are based on EUROPEAN COMMISSION, *Compilation of case law on the equality of treatment between women and men and on non-discrimination in the European Union*, 3rd edition, 2009. The covered time frame is 1971 until 2009.
[100] Case 43/75 [1976] ECR 455, at 473.
[101] ELLIS, 2005, p. 89.
[102] EUROPEAN COMMISSION, *Compilation of case law on the equality of treatment between women and men and on non-discrimination in the European Union*, 3rd edition, 2009, p. 34.
[103] Case 96/80 [1981] ECR 911, at 918.

It furthermore equated indirect discrimination with adverse impact.[104] This case concerned a measure by a clothing company which entailed that part-time workers received 10% less hourly pay than full-time workers. This did not, in the view of the ECJ, constitute discrimination *per se*, but if it would be shown that a considerably smaller number of women than men worked full-time and received the higher payment rate, this would nevertheless be in violation of Article 119 EC.

In *Bilka-Kaufhaus*, the issue of indirect discrimination was further elaborated upon by the ECJ.[105] In this case, a group of department stores granted a pension scheme to full-time workers but not to part-time workers unless they had worked full-time for at least 15 years over a period of 20 years in total. Mrs Weber, the complainant in this case, had not worked full-time for 15 years and was thus not paid an occupational pension under Bilka's pension scheme. In this case, it was already considered as given that indirect discrimination existed where a measure affected a 'far greater number of women than men.'[106] The ECJ furthermore held that the exclusion of part-time workers from the pension scheme could be justified:

> 'where it is found that the means chosen for achieving that objective corresponds to a real need on the part of the undertaking, are appropriate with a view to achieving the objective in question and are necessary to that end.'[107]

This test for an objective justification is now contained in the secondary anti-discrimination legislation of the EU.

The final decision regarding justification technically lies with the national court and is considered a question of fact, though the ECJ frequently gives an indicative ruling regarding the justifiability of the policy in question.[108] Whether the means of achieving the aims are appropriate and necessary depends, in the case law of the ECJ, to some extent on the subject matter in question. In employment matters, the ECJ has adopted a 'robust proportionality test,' while there is broad discretion for Member States when it comes to social policies.[109] As described above, in *Bilka-Kaufhaus*, the ECJ first laid down the test that a *prima facie* indirectly discriminatory measure can be objectively justified where there is (1) a legitimate aim, and the means to achieving this aim are both (2) appropriate and (3) necessary.[110] The case law of the ECJ regarding social policy, however, appears to have developed towards a reasonableness test rather than the

---

[104] *Ibid.*
[105] Case 170/84 [1986] ECR 1607.
[106] *Ibid.*, para. 24.
[107] *Ibid.*, para. 37.
[108] T. Hervey, 'Thirty Years of EU Sex Equality Law: Looking Backwards, Looking Forwards', in: *Maastricht Journal for European & Comparative Law*, Vol.12, 2005, p. 315.
[109] *Ibid.*
[110] Case 170/84, *Bilka-Kaufhaus v. Weber von Hartz*, [1986] ECR 1607, at 37.

three-fold test that is now reflected in the anti-discrimination directives: In a number of cases concerning social policy rather than employment, *i.e.* particularly where a State measure rather than a contract between employer and employee is at stake, the ECJ qualified the test for objective justification. By stating that 'in exercising its competence, the national legislature was reasonably entitled to consider that the legislation in question was necessary', Member States were granted a broad margin of discretion due to the consideration that 'social policy is a matter for the Member States who can choose the measures capable of achieving the aim of their social and employment policy.'[111]

In *R v. Secretary of State for Employment, ex parte Seymour-Smith*, the question of the degree of adverse impact required for the existence of indirect discrimination was raised.[112] Two employees alleged that a rule under UK law requiring a period of two years' employment with an employer before a complaint of unfair dismissal could be brought was indirectly discriminatory because fewer women than men were able to comply with this two year rule. The ECJ held that:

> 'in order to establish whether a measure adopted by a Member State has disparate effect as between men and women to such a degree as to amount to indirect discrimination for the purpose of Article 119 of the Treaty, the national court must verify whether the statistics available indicate that a considerably smaller percentage of women than men is able to fulfil the requirement imposed by that measure. If that is the case, there is indirect sex discrimination, unless that measure is justified by objective factors unrelated to any discrimination based on sex.'[113]

Both direct and indirect discrimination can only be established by reference to a comparator. This comparator, *i.e.* the person in a comparable situation, need not necessarily exist, a hypothetical establishment of favourable treatment on grounds of sex is sufficient to trigger direct discrimination. While this test appears straightforward, it must be noted that much depends on this comparator and that it is up to the court to construct and define who would be in a comparable situation. In the case of *Lisa Grant v. South West Trains Ltd.*, for example, the ECJ constructed the comparator in such a way that a woman in a same-sex relationship must be compared to a man in a same-sex situation rather than a man in a heterosexual relationship.[114] Holzleithner holds that this comparison of 'two different, yet in their discrimination similarly situated, members of a certain group' subverts the very point of anti-discrimination law.[115]

---

[111] C. BARNARD & B. HEPPLE, 'Indirect Discrimination: Interpreting *Seymour-Smith*', in: *The Cambridge Law Journal*, Vol. 58, 1999, p. 409.
[112] Case C-167/97 [1999] ECR I-623.
[113] *Ibid.*, Ruling under 4.
[114] Case C-249/96, *Lisa Grant v. South West Trains Ltd.*, [1998] ECR I-00621.
[115] E. HOLZLEITHNER, 'Mainstreaming Equality: Dis/Entangling Grounds of Discrimination', in: *Transnational Law & Contemporary Problems*, Vol. 14, 2005, p. 934 f.

The ECJ has held that, the provisions regarding non-discrimination on grounds of sex apply to the situation of transsexuals,[116] but do not extend to grounds of sexuality.[117] This explains the situation criticized by Holzleithner regarding direct discrimination where the comparator was constructed accordingly.

4.4. OTHER INSTRUMENTS

Outside of primary and secondary sources of EU legislation, the concept of non-discrimination and gender equality features in other instruments such as strategies, action plans or communications. Some of these non-binding instruments will be considered in this section.

4.4.1. *The Daphne Programme: Violence Against Women*

The EU anti-discrimination framework does not cover violence against women *per se*. However, 'harassment and sexual harassment within the meaning of this Directive shall be deemed to be discrimination on the grounds of sex and therefore prohibited.'[118] Harassment is defined as unwanted conduct related to the sex of a person which occurs with 'the purpose or effect of violating the dignity of a person and of creating an intimidating, hostile, degrading, humiliating or offensive environment' while sexual harassment is the same where the conduct is of a sexual nature.[119] However, this prohibition of harassment extends only as far as the scope of the Directives in which it is included, which means it does not cover VAW in general.

The Daphne programme is geared towards violence specifically; it is currently in its third phase and 'aims to prevent and combat all forms of violence, especially of a physical, sexual or psychological nature, against children, young people and women.'[120] The first phase of the programme covered the time from 2000 to 2003,[121] the second phase that from 2004 to 2008.[122] The current phase covers the time from 2007 to 2012.[123] It seeks to achieve its objectives by, *inter alia*, assisting and encouraging NGOs, developing and implementing awareness-raising actions, setting up and supporting multidisciplinary networks to

---

[116] Case C-13/94, *P v. S and Cornwall County Council*, [1996] ECR I-2143; Case C-117/01, *KB v. National Health Service Agency, Secretary of State for Health*, [2004] ECR I-541.
[117] Case C-249/96, *Lisa Grant v. South West Trains Ltd.*, [1998] ECR I-00621.
[118] Equal Treatment Directive, Article 4(3).
[119] *Ibid.*, Article 2(c) and (d).
[120] Summaries of EU legislation, Combating violence towards children, adolescents and women: Daphne III programme (2007–2013), http://europa.eu/legislation-summaries/human-rights/fundamental-rights-within-european-union/l33600-en.htm [accessed 20 July 2012].
[121] Decision No 293/2000/EC, OJ [2000] L34/1, Article 1.
[122] Decision No 803/2004/EC, OJ [2004] L143/1, Article 1.
[123] Decision No 779/2007/EC, OJ [2007] L173/19, Article 1.

strengthen cooperation between NGOs and other organizations, building a knowledge base, designing and testing awareness-raising and educational materials to prevent violence and studying phenomena related to it as well as developing and implementing support programmes.[124] For this purpose, the programme is funded with an amount of € 116.85 million.[125] As the description of this programme already reveals, it is concerned solely with violence against women, though the preamble states that 'violence against women takes many forms ranging from domestic violence, which is prevalent at all levels of society, to harmful traditional practices associated with the exercise of physical violence against women, such as genital mutilation and honour-related crimes, which constitute a particular form of violence against women.'[126] It takes a holistic approach to the issue of violence, seeking to address the root-causes of it and developing preventive measures.[127]

4.4.2. Instruments Regarding Gender Equality and Gender Mainstreaming

The European Commission[128] has developed a Strategy for gender mainstreaming which is concerned with issues of equal economic independence, equal pay for equal work and work of equal value, equality in decision-making, dignity, integrity and an end to gender-based violence, gender equality in external actions and with horizontal issues.[129] The purpose of this strategy is to address remaining gender gaps and to translate the objectives of the Women's Charter which the Commission adopted in 2010 into reality.

The Women's Charter was adopted in commemoration of the 15th anniversary of the adoption of a Declaration and Platform for Action at the Beijing UN World Conference on Women and of the 30th anniversary of the Women's Convention.[130] While both the Women's Charter and the Strategy for gender mainstreaming speak about gender equality, neither of the two defines the term 'gender', nor is the concept of discrimination, either direct or indirect, widely used. Gender mainstreaming is defined as:

> 'the integration of the gender perspective into every stage of policy process – design, implementation, monitoring and evaluation – *and into all policies of the Union*, with a view to promoting equality between women and men. It means assessing how policies impact on the life and position of both women and men – and taking

---

[124] *Ibid.*, Article 3.
[125] *Ibid.*, Article 12.
[126] *Ibid.*, preamble at (12).
[127] *Ibid.*, preamble at (15).
[128] The European Commission represents the interests of the European Union as a whole. It is one of three main institutions involved in EU legislation.
[129] European Commission, Strategy for equality between women and men 2010–2015, European Union, 2011.
[130] COM(2010) 78.

responsibility to re-address them if necessary. This is the way to make gender equality a concrete reality in the lives of women and men: creating space for everyone within the organizations as well as in communities – to contribute to the process of articulating a shared vision of sustainable human development and translating it into reality.'[131]

The Council of the European Union[132] meanwhile has adopted the European Pact for Gender Equality (2011 – 2020) which aims at closing the gender gaps in employment and social protection, promoting better work-life balance for women and men and enhancing gender equality, increasing women's participation in the labour market and at combating all forms of violence against women.[133] This pact urges action at Member State and, where appropriate, also at Union level in the above-mentioned fields; it furthermore seeks to keep gender equality on the agenda of the EU.[134]

The inclusion of gender perspectives in the activities and policies of the European Union as a whole certainly constitutes an important step forward. Though it is unclear in how far a distinction is made between the terms gender equality and equality between men and women, the switch in terminology towards gender hints at a broader and more inclusive understanding of the situation of women.

4.5. LIMITATIONS

While EU law has developed the concepts of direct and indirect discrimination, first through case law and then by codifying it in the anti-discrimination directives where a common definition is used for the concepts which coincides with the case law of the ECJ, a number of limitations nevertheless apply to the concept of non-discrimination within the framework of the EU.

First of all, any and all conclusions drawn from studying the legal framework of the EU, the treaties, directives and corresponding case law, apply to the reality of discrimination against women only in as far as Member States to the EU have implemented the concepts and obligations as defined under EU law and considered in this Chapter. Member States have a duty to do so under Article 4 TEU, but especially in the case of newer Member States, the legal reality of women in a Member State and the existing legal framework on European level may be two different things. Nevertheless, it must be mentioned here that this distinction is likely less pronounced regarding EU law than it is international

---

[131] *Ibid.*, p. 35.
[132] The Council is the legislative institution of the European Union which represents the executives of the Member States.
[133] 7370/11 SOC 205, Annex.
[134] *Ibid.*

law, due to the systematic differences between the two when it comes to *e.g.* issues of enforcement and the mandatory jurisdiction of the supervising bodies.

Secondly, the application of the principle of non-discrimination against women under EU law was originally restricted exclusively to matters of employment and social policy. While this has changed to some extent, the application of the principle under EU law remains more limited in scope than under international law.[135] Indeed, the definitions of the concept already show that the principle of non-discrimination under EU law does not so much prohibit discrimination against women as it prohibits discrimination on the grounds of sex. More specifically, this means that at times, positive measures designed to combat discrimination against women specifically will violate the principle of non-discrimination on the grounds of sex.[136]

The definition of indirect discrimination on the grounds of sex itself already entails a limitation in that indirect discrimination can be objectively justified. The ECJ has, at times, offered Member States a broad margin of discretion in determining what constitutes an objective justification.[137]

5. ANALYSIS

In this section a comparison between CEDAW's and the EU's interpretation of discrimination against women will be made by looking into the various elements that determine contents and scope of this concept. Subsequently, discrimination against women, direct and indirect discrimination, discrimination based on sex and gender, the scope and possible actors of discrimination, and enforcement possibilities will be discussed.

Discrimination against women is exclusively used as a form of discrimination in the framework of the Women's Convention. The effect is that only girls' and women' human rights are protected by the Convention. In EU law, there is no specific legislation focused on the discrimination of women. Anti-discrimination laws and policies are formulated in a neutral manner and both men and women benefit equally from any protection that is offered.

Direct discrimination was only recently defined by CEDAW in General Recommendation No. 28 as constituting different treatment explicitly based on grounds of sex and gender. The EU definition is older and understands the concept as less favourable treatment of a person on the grounds of sex, than another who is in a comparable situation. The similarity between the two

---

[135] *Cf.* Access Directive.
[136] *Cf.* Case C-450/93, *Kalanke v Freie Hansestadt Bremen*, [1995] ECR I/3069, though also C-409/97, *Marshall v Land Nordrhein-Westfalen*, [1997] ECR I-6363. An in-depth discussion of the issue of positive action under EU law can be found in Chapter 5 of this book.
[137] Case C-317/93, *Nolte v. Landesversicherungsanstalt Hannover*, [1995] ECR I/4625; Case C-444/93, *Megner & Scheffel v. Innungskrankenkasse Vorderpfalz*, [1995] ECR I-4741.

Chapter 3. The Essence of Discrimination Against Women:
An Interpretation by CEDAW and the European Union

definitions is that they are focused on 'treatment' and that in principle the concept is absolute, but that legal exceptions that are favourable for women – in particular in connection to pregnancy and maternity – may be allowed.

The differences comprise that CEDAW is only concerned with different treatment of women, while EU law uses 'on the grounds of sex' in a neutral way that encompasses, men, women, and transsexuals. Furthermore, CEDAW explicitly includes 'gender', while it is unclear to what extent 'gender' is included in EU law, and – if it is included – what exactly is meant by the term. Finally, determining whether there is indeed different treatment based on sex requires a comparator under EU law, while this is not the case in the context of the Women's Convention.

In the EU the concept of *indirect discrimination* was first developed in case law and later a definition was laid down in secondary legislation. The definition entails that apparently neutral provisions, criteria or practices disadvantage persons of one sex if compared with persons of the other sex. However, provisions, criteria or practices that have such an effect are not always prohibited because if there is a legitimate aim and the means of achieving that aim are appropriate and necessary, they may be justified.

While the concept of indirect discrimination was already mentioned by CEDAW in earlier publications, the best definition can be found in General Recommendation No. 28 describing this form of discrimination as legislation, policies, programmes or practices that appear to be neutral as regards men and women, but in practice have a discriminatory effect on women because already existing socio-economic inequalities are not taken into account.

An obvious similarity between the two definitions is that the starting point is an apparently neutral provision or situation that works out to the disadvantage of one of the sexes. While CEDAW is only concerned with effects that have an adverse impact on women, the EU is concerned with negative effects on either men or women. CEDAW fears that indirect discrimination against women may occur or even exacerbate existing inequalities when structural and historical patterns of discrimination and unequal power relations between women and men are not taken into account. This is not a concern that is expressed in EU (case)law. Another difference concerns the possibility to justify indirect discrimination. While such a justification is not possible under the Women's Convention, it seems that EU Member States can make use of an escape if they can prove that there is a legitimate aim to take a measure and that the means of achieving that aim are appropriate and necessary. This begs the question what kind of aim is superior to the interest of abolishing discrimination based on sex?

As has become clear already from the definition of direct discrimination, *discrimination based on sex* is used in the EU as a broad and gender neutral concept; it is prohibited both against men and women. CEDAW, however, understands 'sex' as the biological difference between women and men and as such it is a limited concept.

Discrimination based on gender is understood by CEDAW as discrimination that goes beyond actual biological differences, and concerns prejudices and stereotypes that result in hierarchical and unequal power relationships between women and men that disadvantage women and favour men. In the course of the last few decades, CEDAW has come to understand discrimination based on sex and on gender as included in Article 1.

Within EU legislation no definition or inclusion of 'gender' in the sense as described above can be found. However, policy instruments and programmes focused on the advancement of women's equality, seem to take gender into account without explicitly defining the phenomenon.

CEDAW understands the *scope* of the prohibition of discrimination as very broad and inclusive, encompassing all human rights women may have. In the course of the years, it has even explicitly included gender-based violence as falling under the definition of discrimination in Article 1.

Meanwhile, the scope of non-discrimination based on sex in the framework of the EU is limited. It started as applying only to matters of employment and social policy and now includes access to goods and services. Even so it does not take the full spectrum of human rights of women into account, and does not go into all areas of life. For instance, (sexual) harassment is prohibited only in as far as the individual legislation in which it is included extends, such as the workplace. However, policy programmes have been developed to prevent and combat violence, including violence against women.

Regarding possible *actors* of discrimination based on sex, CEDAW time and again has explained that women may suffer discrimination both at the hands of public and private actors, and that Article 1 applies to the public and the private sphere.

Similarly, under EU law the prohibition of sex discrimination applies both to State measures and to discrimination between private parties, in as far as it is applicable since its scope is more limited.

As far as *enforcement* is concerned, it is possible to invoke provisions of the Women's Convention before national courts when they have direct effect. In addition, in States which are parties to the Optional Protocol to the Convention, it is possible to lodge individual complaints to CEDAW. However, the decisions that are taken by the Committee do not have binding force: they are recommendations that have political and moral weight.

Within the framework of the EU, all national courts are considered European courts tasked with applying EU provisions. Where there is a lack of clarity regarding such a provision, the ECJ can give a preliminary ruling.

6. CONCLUSION

The main question of this Chapter has been whether and if so what CEDAW and the ECJ can learn from each other about the principle of non-discrimination. As can be seen from the above analysis, both the Women's Convention and EU law explicitly prohibit discrimination, however the understanding of the concepts varies. Where the EU consistently applies the same definitions of direct and indirect discrimination, CEDAW is not always clear or explicit on what these concepts signify. Conversely, the EU could learn from the Committee regarding the inclusion and meaning of gender. If women's socio-economic position is not taken into account within the context of the prohibition of discrimination based on sex, EU legislation and programmes will only treat the symptoms rather than the root causes of discrimination against women.

Furthermore, attention has to be paid to the fact that EU Member States may fall short of their obligations ensuing from the Women's Convention if they apply non-discrimination in the limited manner EU law requires.

ARTICLE 2

States parties condemn discrimination against women in all its forms, agree to pursue by all appropriate means and without delay a policy of eliminating discrimination against women and, to this end, undertake:

(a) To embody the principle of the equality of men and women in their national constitutions or other appropriate legislation if not yet incorporated therein and to ensure, through law and other appropriate means, the practical realization of this principle;
(b) To adopt appropriate legislative and other measures, including sanctions where appropriate, prohibiting all discrimination against women;
(c) To establish legal protection of the rights of women on an equal basis with men and to ensure through competent national tribunals and other public institutions the effective protection of women against any act of discrimination;
(d) To refrain from engaging in any act or practice of discrimination against women and to ensure that public authorities and institutions shall act in conformity with this obligation;
(e) To take all appropriate measures to eliminate discrimination against women by any person, organization or enterprise;
(f) To take all appropriate measures, including legislation, to modify or abolish existing laws, regulations, customs and practices which constitute discrimination against women;
(g) To repeal all national penal provisions which constitute discrimination against women.

ARTICLE 3

States parties shall take in all fields, in particular in the political, social, economic and cultural fields, all appropriate measures, including legislation, to ensure the full development and advancement of women, for the purpose of guaranteeing them the exercise and enjoyment of human rights and fundamental freedoms on a basis of equality with men.

CHAPTER 4

THE PRINCIPLE OF EQUALITY

Rolanda Oostland

1. INTRODUCTION

The main aim of the Convention on the Elimination of All Forms of Discrimination Against Women is, as the name of this treaty indicates, eliminating discrimination against women.[1] Clearly, there is a close relation between the prohibition of discrimination against women, on the one hand, and equality of men and women, on the other hand. Several authors merely regard non-discrimination to be the negative statement of the principle of equality.[2] However, this approach is too simple, as this Chapter will show. Depending on how the principle of equality is interpreted, only entailing formal equality or also including substantive equality, it can have a much broader scope of application than the prohibition of discrimination. These different theoretical principles of equality and how these principles of equality are related to the principles of non-discrimination will be addressed in Section 2 of this Chapter.

In Section 3 it will be analysed which theoretical principles of equality CEDAW applies in relation to Articles 2 and 3 of the Women's Convention that provide for, *inter alia*, equal rights for women. Does CEDAW regard that men and women have to be treated the same, as they have equal rights? Or should they be treated differently, if they are in a different situation? In other words, does CEDAW regard the principle of equality to entail only formal equality or

---

[1] This chapter is based on my PhD-thesis: *Non-discrimination and Equality of Women, A Comparative Analysis of the Interpretation by the UN Human Rights Committee and the UN Committee on the Elimination of Discrimination against Women*, Utrecht University, 2006 (see: http://igitur-archive.library.uu.nl/search/search.php?language=nl&qry=non-discrimination and equality).

[2] See *e.g.* J.E.S. Fawcett, *The Application of the European Convention on Human Rights*, Clarendon Press, Oxford, 1987, p. 299; Y. Dinstein, 'Discrimination and International Human Rights', in: *Israel Yearbook on Human Rights*, Vol. 15, 1985, p. 19; A. Bayesfsky, 'The Principle of Equality or Non-discrimination in International Law', *Human Rights Law Journal*, Vol. 11, No. 1–2, 1990, pp. 1, 2; B.G. Ramcharan, 'Equality and Nondiscrimination', in: L. Henkin (ed.), *The International Bill of Rights*, Columbia University Press, New York, 1981, p. 252.

also substantive equality? Although affirmative action also falls within the scope of substantive equality, affirmative action will only shortly be addressed in relation to the aforementioned principles, as affirmative action is the topic of the next Chapter.

In Section 3 also some clauses of Article 2 that regard discrimination of women will be addressed. This is due to the close relation between non-discrimination and equality, which is also exemplified by Article 2 of the Women's Convention that regards both non-discrimination as well as equality. Issues that specifically will be addressed are eliminating discrimination by non-State actors and modifying or abolishing discriminatory customs and traditions.

The interpretation by CEDAW of Articles 2 and 3 of the Women's Convention will be compared to the interpretation the Human Rights Committee gives to Article 3 of the ICCPR that provides for the equal right of men and women to the enjoyment of their civil and political human rights. Hence, in Section 4 the interpretation by the Human Rights Committee of the principle of equality and how this relates to the principle of non-discrimination will be addressed in relation to Article 3 of the ICCPR. Specific issues, such as non-discrimination by non-State actors and discriminatory traditions, will also be addressed in this context. The reason that a comparison is made with an overlapping provision of the ICCPR is that it is also explicitly acknowledged in the preamble to the Women's Convention, after having referred to among other instruments the ICCPR, that 'despite these various instruments extensive discrimination against women continues to exist', and that such discrimination 'violates the principles of equality of rights and respect for human dignity'. Hence, it was generally acknowledged in 1979 that there was a need for a special instrument to eliminate discrimination against women. In Section 5 it will be concluded whether CEDAW's interpretation of Articles 2 and 3 of the Women's Convention has indeed an added value, compared to the interpretation by the Human Rights Committee of Article 3 of the ICCPR.

2. THE PRINCIPLES OF EQUALITY AND NON-DISCRIMIATION

In this section the different theoretical principles of equality and how these principles of equality are related to the principles of non-discrimination will be addressed.

2.1. FORMAL AND SUBSTANTIVE EQUALITY

Equality entails that persons should in principle be treated equally, if they can be considered to be in an equal situation. This is referred to as formal equality, which implies having equal rights and being treated equally. Whereas formal equality implies being treated equally, substantive equality deals with the result of the treatment that should be equal. Hence, the difference between the two forms of equality is that formal equality concerns the *nature* of the treatment, while substantive equality deals with the *result* of a certain treatment.[3] An example of formal equality is that in most countries women were granted the right to vote in the 20th century, which was a right formerly only granted to men. Thus granting the right to vote equally to women means that women are treated the same when it comes to having the right to vote.

The limitation of the principle of formal equality is that although persons are granted the same rights, this does not ensure that these rights have the same impact on everyone, since not everybody will be in the same situation. In other words, formal equality puts a strong emphasis on the primacy of the individual and does not take the social and economical background of particular groups in society into account.[4] This can be illustrated with the following example. Granting girls officially equal access to education might still not lead to similar enrolment rates for girls as for boys, when parents cannot afford to send all their children to school.[5] Formal equality is therefore criticised for assuming an ideal world, in which all human beings are on an equal footing.[6] Or as Gallagher has stated, this prevents the recognition of the fact that equal treatment of persons in unequal situations will invariably operate to perpetuate, rather than to eradicate injustices.[7]

We can conclude that formal equality thus calls for the equal treatment of men and women, since they should, as such, regarded to be equal. However, when men and women should be regarded as being in a different situation, the principle of formal equality might actually perpetuate this difference.[8] In these situations the principle of substantive equality, which focuses on an equal result, is of more use. An example of a situation in which the principle of substantive equality should therefore be applied concerns pregnant employees. If a woman employee is pregnant she is in a different situation than a male employee, who

---

[3] E.W. VIERDAG, *The Concept of Non-Discrimination in International Law*, Martinus Nijhoff, The Hague, 1973, p. 14.
[4] M. KIRILOVA ERIKSSON, *Reproductive Freedom: In the Context of International Human Rights and Humanitarian Law*, Martinus Nijhoff, The Hague, 2000, p. 29; S. FREDMAN, 'Combating Racism with Human Rights: The Right to Equality', in: S. Fredman (ed.), *Discrimination and Human Rights: The Case of Racism*, Oxford University Press, Oxford, 2001, p. 17.
[5] See *e.g.* UNESCO, 'Education for All Global Monitoring Report 2007', *Strong Foundations: Early Childhood Care and Education*, UNESCO, Paris, 2007, Table 2.9, p. 29, p. 33.
[6] M. KIRILOVA ERIKSSON, *Reproductive Freedom: In the Context of International Human Rights and Humanitarian Law*, Martinus Nijhoff, The Hague, 2000, p. 30.
[7] A. GALLAGER, 'Ending the Marginalization: Strategies for Incorporating Women into the United Nations Human Rights System', *Human Rights Quarterly*, Vol. 19, 1997, p. 290.
[8] S. FREDMAN, 'Combating Racism with Human Rights: The Right to Equality', in: S. Fredman (ed.), *Discrimination and Human Rights: The Case of Racism*, Oxford University Press, Oxford, 2001, p. 17.

obviously can never become pregnant. According to the principle of substantive equality they should be treated differently so that an equal result is reached. This can mean, for example, that the female worker is entitled to a pregnancy leave, which allows her to give birth to her baby and, subsequently, to return to her job. In order to achieve substantive equality, unequal treatment can thus be necessary to achieve an equal result. Although it might seem a paradox, as Vierdag and Alexy have stated, that the principle of equality also calls for unequal treatment, according to the principle of substantive equality it is required that unequal factual patterns are treated unequally in order to attain an equal result.[9]

In the Women's Convention it is provided that in order to achieve equality, affirmative action – or temporary special measures as it is called in Article 4(1) of the Women's Convention[10]- should be permitted. The term 'affirmative action' can be defined differently; I will regard it to entail *different treatment* by taking specific measures for women with the aim to create the same result or opportunities for them as for men. In general, affirmative action programmes can be found in employment, political participation and education. An example of affirmative action with respect to employment is when a man and a woman are both suitable candidates for a particular job, but preference is given to employing the woman if women are underrepresented in that segment or level of the labour market.

According to Article 4(1) of the Women's Convention, affirmative action is only allowed if it is temporary.[11] It has to stop when the objective aimed at – to establish *de facto* equality – has been achieved. That affirmative action is only allowed when it is temporary, is related to the fact that affirmative action should be ended when members of a certain group can no longer be regarded as being in a disadvantaged position. If affirmative action measures would not end after the situation of disadvantage ceases to exist, it could constitute a violation of the prohibition to discriminate. It would also not be in line with the principle of substantive equality, since if we can consider persons to be in an equal situation, this would call for equal and not unequal treatment.

We can conclude that using the principle of substantive equality is especially relevant for groups who have a different or disadvantaged position in society, since unequal factual patterns are treated unequally to attain an equal result. In this way these groups are better protected by the principle of substantive equality than by formal equality, since the latter sustains the *status quo* of the different or

---

[9] R. ALEXY, *Theorie der Grundrechte*, Nomos Verlagsgesellschaft, Baden-Baden, 1985, p. 379; E.W. VIERDAG, *The Concept of Non-Discrimination in International Law*, Martinus Nijhoff, The Hague, 1973, p. 13.

[10] See also BOSSUYT, 'The concept of affirmative action is generally referred to in international law as "special measures"', in: M. Bossuyt, *Comprehensive Examination of Thematic Issues relating to Racial Discrimination: The Concept and Practice of Affirmative Action*, UN doc. E/CN.4/Sub.2/2000/11, 19 June 2000, para. 4.

[11] See Article 4(1) of the Women's Convention and Article 1(4) of ICERD.

disadvantaged position of certain groups in society, because it does not aim to attain an equal result. Substantive equality can thus contribute to the inclusion of these groups in society.[12]

2.2. DIRECT AND INDIRECT DISCRIMINATION

The verb to discriminate has two meanings: 'to be able to see the difference between two things or people' and 'to treat a person or particular group of persons differently, especially in a worse way from the way in which you treat other people, because of their skin colour, religion, sex, etc'.[13] In international law, the prohibition of discrimination is commonly used in the latter sense.[14] We can distinguish between direct and indirect discrimination. Direct discrimination occurs when persons who should be treated equally are explicitly treated unequally. If, for example, women are not allowed to vote because they are women, this constitutes direct discrimination. In the case of direct discrimination the principle of formal equality, which implies that equals should be treated equally, is violated. The prohibition of direct discrimination thus protects the formal equality of, for instance, men and women.

A symmetrical definition of discrimination focuses on the individual, without taking the social context of this individual into account. Contrary, an asymmetrical approach of discrimination, which is primarily aimed at the protection of structurally disadvantaged groups in society and not at members of dominant groups in society, protects disadvantaged groups in society against discrimination. Consequently, affirmative action is in an asymmetrical approach of non-discrimination in principle allowed if it temporarily benefits disadvantaged groups in society, even though affirmative action measures may violate the prohibition of direct discrimination with respect to the members of dominant groups in society. The definition of discrimination that is provided for in Article 1 of the Women's Convention is in fact an asymmetrical definition; it only prohibits discrimination against women and not against men. Hence, this definition allows for affirmative action measures to improve the situation of women, without this being regarded to constitute direct discrimination of men.

---

[12] Nevertheless, it should not be forgotten that even when people belong to a certain group in society, this does not mean that the interests of all group members are always the same. See also J. GOLDSCHMIDT, 'Back to the Future – An Agenda for a More Equal Future', in: T. Loenen and P. Rodrigues (eds.), *Non-discrimination Law: Comparative Perspectives*, Kluwer Law International, The Hague [etc.], 1999, p. 440; T. LOENEN, *Het gelijkheidsbeginsel* [= *The equality principle*], Ars Aequi Libri, Nijmegen, 1998, p. 56.

[13] Cambridge Dictionaries online, Cambridge Advanced Learner's Dictionary: http://dictionary.cambridge.org/search/british/?q=discriminate.

[14] N. LERNER, *Group Rights and Discrimination in International Law*, Martinus Nijhoff, The Hague, 2003, p. 31; W. MCKEAN, *Equality and Discrimination under International Law*, Clarendon Press, Oxford, 1983, pp. 10–11.

Indirect discrimination, also sometimes referred to as disparate impact,[15] occurs when a neutral regulation that applies equally to all persons has a discriminatory effect and there exists no objective justification for this result.[16] An example of indirect discrimination is the famous case of Bilka-Kaufhaus.[17] The European Court of Justice decided in this case that the exclusion of part-time workers from a supplementary retirement pension scheme constituted indirect discrimination against women, as (a) a far greater number of women than men were affected by this exclusion due to the fact that most part-time workers were women and, (b) no objective justification existed for this result.[18]

The advantage of the principle of indirect discrimination is that it can draw attention to the underlying values of certain measures or regulations which at first sight seem to be neutral, but in effect disadvantage or exclude members of less powerful groups.[19] However, the limitation of the principle is that the underlying inequalities themselves are not necessarily addressed.[20] Thus the principle of indirect discrimination can challenge dominant standards in society, but it will not necessarily change those standards.[21] Substantive equality, which requires more than eradicating indirect discrimination,[22] is in that respect more suitable for changing dominant standards, since it calls for differential treatment. Another limitation of the principle of indirect discrimination is that indirect discrimination can be justified by an objective justification.[23] It will depend on whether an objective justification is interpreted in a wide or narrow sense, what kind of impact the principle of indirect discrimination can have on improving the position of the disadvantaged members of society.

It can be concluded that although the principle of indirect discrimination has its limitations, it has the important advantage that, contrary to the principle of

---

[15] Disparate impact is the American equivalent of indirect discrimination, see: T. LOENEN, 'Indirect Discrimination: Oscillating Between Containment and Revolution', in: T. Loenen and P. Rodrigues (eds.), *Non-discrimination Law: Comparative Perspectives*, Kluwer Law International, The Hague [etc.], 1999, pp. 196, 197.

[16] See also CEDAW General Recommendation No. 28 (2010), 'The core obligations of States parties under Article 2', para. 16.

[17] ECJ 13 May 1986, *Bilka-Kaufhaus GmbH v. Karin Weber Von Hartz* (case 170/84), European Court Reports 1986, p. 01607.

[18] *Ibid.*, para. 31.

[19] T. LOENEN, 'Indirect Discrimination: Oscillating Between Containment and Revolution', in: T. Loenen and P. Rodrigues (eds.), *Non-discrimination Law: Comparative Perspectives*, Kluwer Law International, The Hague [etc.], 1999, p. 199; CEDAW General Recommendation No. 28 (2010), The core obligations of States parties under Article 2, para. 16.

[20] *Ibid.*, p. 204; T. LOENEN, 'Rethinking Sex Equality as a Human Right', *Netherlands Quarterly of Human Rights*, No. 3, 1994, p. 266.

[21] T. LOENEN, Indirect Discrimination: Oscillating Between Containment and Revolution. in: T. Loenen and P. Rodrigues (eds.), *Non-discrimination Law: Comparative Perspectives*, Kluwer Law International, The Hague [etc.], 1999, p. 204.

[22] *Ibid.*

[23] *Ibid.*, p. 208; T. LOENEN, 'Rethinking Sex Equality as a Human Right', *Netherlands Quarterly of Human Rights*, No. 3, 1994, p. 265.

direct discrimination, it can draw attention to the underlying values of certain measures or regulations which at first sight seem to be neutral, but in effect tend to disadvantage or exclude members of less powerful groups.

2.3. THE RELATION BETWEEN THE PRINCIPLES OF EQUALITY AND NON-DISCRIMINATION

Clearly, there is a relation between the principles of equality and non-discrimination. But how are they related? Could it be said that non-discrimination and equality are content-wise equivalent principles? Or should the principle of equality be regarded as being a broader principle than the principle of non-discrimination? Those who consider the principle of non-discrimination to entail only direct discrimination and the principle of equality to entail only formal equality, would regard these principles as equivalent.[24] They generally consider equal treatment and non-discrimination as merely positive and negative statements of the same principle. Other authors are of the opinion that the principle of equality is broader than the principle of non-discrimination.[25] According to Craven, the principle of non-discrimination is only a limited means by which to pursue equality. He argues that non-discrimination is merely a procedural principle or an obligation of conduct to treat persons equally, which may be conditioned by the wider principle of equality that may take factual social inequalities into account.[26] In other words, Craven seems to regard the principle of equality as not only entailing formal equality, but also substantive equality. However, in relation to the principle of discrimination, Craven does not seem to take the principle of indirect discrimination into account. This principle prohibits a neutral regulation from having a discriminatory result; consequently different treatment is necessary to come to an equal result. But the principle of indirect discrimination does not cover the whole scope of the principle of substantive equality. The latter is indeed

---

[24] See *e.g.* J.E.S. FAWCETT, *The Application of the European Convention on Human Rights*, Clarendon Press, Oxford, 1987, p. 299; Y. DINSTEIN, 'Discrimination and International Human Rights', in: *Israel Yearbook on Human Rights*, Vol. 15, 1985, p. 19; A. BAYEFSKY, 'The Principle of Equality or Non-discrimination in International Law', *Human Rights Law Journal*, Vol. 11, No. 1–2, 1990, pp. 1, 2; B.G. RAMCHARAN, 'Equality and Nondiscrimination', in: L. Henkin (ed.), *The International Bill of Rights*, Columbia University Press, New York, 1981, p. 252.

[25] T. MERON, 'The Meaning and Reach of the International Convention on the Elimination of All Forms of Racial Discrimination', *American Journal of International Law*, Vol. 79, 1985, p. 286; M. CRAVEN, *The International Covenant on Economic, Social and Cultural Rights: A Perspective on its Development*, Clarendon Press, Oxford, 1995, pp. 155, 156.

[26] M. CRAVEN, *The International Covenant on Economic, Social and Cultural Rights: A Perspective on its Development*, Clarendon Press, Oxford, 1995, pp. 155, 156.

a much broader principle. On this basis Loenen also concludes that the principle of equality is wider than the principle of non-discrimination.[27]

It should be pointed out that it is also possible to define the prohibition of discrimination to include both the principle of formal equality and of substantive equality. In this regard Vierdag defines discrimination as 'wrongly equal, or wrongly unequal treatment'.[28] Vierdag explains that discrimination thus 'occurs, for example, through equal treatment of cases that must be considered as essentially unequal'.[29] In other words, Vierdag has defined non-discrimination to include the prohibition of unequal treatment of equal cases and the prohibition of equal treatment of unequal cases. If we use this definition of non-discrimination, it also includes the principle of substantive equality. However, the definition of Vierdag is not the definition of non-discrimination which is normally used. In general, definitions of non-discrimination only protect formal equality.

It could be asked whether it makes any difference that the principle of equality entails a positive duty, whereas the principle of non-discrimination concerns a prohibition, a negative duty. In this regard Craven explains that non-discrimination tends to concentrate on the prohibition of differential treatment, rather than identifying those forms of action that are necessary to achieve substantive equality.[30] Fredman also underlines that non-discrimination entails a reactive and negative approach, which is better replaced by proactive equality laws, which include a substantive equality approach, that entail positive duties to promote equality.[31] Indeed, if the focus is on the prohibition to discriminate, differential treatment will often be considered to be suspect, as it might be deemed to violate the prohibition to discriminate. If, however, we take equality as a starting point, this entails a positive duty to advance equality. When the principle of equality includes substantive equality, then this would entail that differential treatment is regarded as an essential part of the principle of equality. Fredman adds, moreover, that a substantive equality approach moves beyond the individual focus of non-discrimination.[32] The latter applies if an individual can show that he/she is a victim of an act of discrimination, whereas substantive equality entails a recognition that discrimination moves beyond individual cases by drawing attention to the exclusion of certain non-dominant groups in society.

---

[27] T. LOENEN, *Het gelijkheidsbeginsel* [= *The Equality Principle*], Ars Aequi Libri, Nijmegen, 1998, p. 42.

[28] E.W. VIERDAG, *The Concept of Non-Discrimination in International Law*, Martinus Nijhoff, The Hague, 1973, p. 23, p. 60.

[29] *Ibid.*, p. 23.

[30] M. CRAVEN, *The International Covenant on Economic, Social and Cultural Rights: A Perspective on its Development*, Clarendon Press, Oxford, 1995, p. 156.

[31] S. FREDMAN, 'Combating Racism with Human Rights: The Right to Equality', in: S. Fredman (ed.), *Discrimination and Human Rights: The Case of Racism*, Oxford University Press, Oxford, 2001, p. 27.

[32] *Ibid.*, p. 26.

3. ARTICLES 2 AND 3 OF THE WOMEN'S CONVENTION

In Section 3 it will be analysed which theoretical principles of equality CEDAW applies in relation to Articles 2 and 3 of the Women's Convention that provide for equal rights for women. Also some clauses of Article 2 that regard discrimination of women will be addressed, due to the close relation between non-discrimination and equality. Some issues that specifically will be addressed in this regard are: eliminating discrimination by non-State actors and modifying or abolishing discriminatory customs and traditions.

3.1. ARTICLE 2

3.1.1. *General and Specific Obligations*

Article 2 focuses on what States parties have to undertake in order to eliminate discrimination against women. This makes it a very crucial provision, as CEDAW also states in its in 2010 adopted elaborate General Recommendation No. 28 'on the core obligations of States parties under Article 2'.[33] Article 2 is sometimes also referred to as the heart of the Women's Convention.[34] It is both a general and a concrete provision.[35] It contains the general obligation for States parties to condemn discrimination in all its forms. According to CEDAW 'in all its forms' means that 'the Convention anticipates the emergence of new forms of discrimination that had not been identified at the time of its drafting'.[36] Article 2 continues with the obligation that States parties have to undertake a policy to eliminate discrimination against women by using all appropriate means.[37] According to Article 2, States parties are obliged to undertake a policy of eliminating discrimination against women 'without delay'. As CEDAW indicates in General Recommendation No. 28, this means that as soon as they have ratified

---

[33] CEDAW General Recommendation No. 28 (2010), 'The core obligations of States parties under Article 2', paras. 6 and 41.
[34] See E.A. ALKEMA, B. ZAAIJER, 'De reikwijdte van het Vrouwenverdrag', in: Aalt Willem Heringa, Joyce Hes en Liesbeth Lijnzaad (eds.), *Het Vrouwenverdrag: een beeld van een verdrag*, MAKLU Publishers, Antwerp, 1994, p. 15; MARGARETA WADSTEIN, 'Implementation of the UN Convention on the Elimination of All Forms of Discrimination against Women', *Netherlands Quarterly of Human Rights*, No. 4, 1988, p. 10.
[35] See E.A. ALKEMA, B. ZAAIJER, 'De reikwijdte van het Vrouwenverdrag', in: Aalt Willem Heringa, Joyce Hes en Liesbeth Lijnzaad (eds.), *Het Vrouwenverdrag: een beeld van een verdrag*, MAKLU Publishers, Antwerp, 1994, p. 16.
[36] CEDAW General Recommendation No. 28 (2010), 'The core obligations of States parties under Article 2', para. 8.
[37] In General Recommendation No. 28 (2010), 'The core obligations of States parties under Article 2', CEDAW addresses in paras. 37 and 38 which measures can be regarded to be appropriate measures.

the Women's Convention they have to start implementing the Convention.[38] But it does not stop there. It continues by indicating in paragraphs (a) to (g) rather precisely what States parties should undertake to achieve the aforementioned objectives. States parties are thus also obliged to undertake concrete steps to end discrimination against women. These measures are elaborated in paragraphs (a) to (g).

Article 2 (a) provides that ratifying States must embody the principle of equality in their national constitutions or other laws. They also have to adopt legislative and other measures, including sanctions, as appropriate (Article 2(b)). States parties must establish legal protection against discrimination through national tribunals and other public institutions to ensure the effective protection of women against acts of discrimination (Article 2(c)). Public authorities and institutions in States parties are to refrain from discriminatory practices (Article 2(d)). States are also obliged to take appropriate measures to eliminate discrimination against women by any person, organization or enterprise (Article 2(e)). States parties must modify or abolish existing laws, customs and practices that discriminate against women, as well as penal provisions that amount to discrimination against women (Article 2(f)). They also have to repeal all national penal provisions that constitute discrimination against women (Article 2(g)).

We can conclude that the focus of most paragraphs is on creating legal protection or amending legislation; paragraphs (a), (b), (c), (f) and (g) all provide for these kinds of actions to be undertaken by the States parties. Paragraphs (d) and (e) focus upon eliminating discriminatory acts by providing that the public authorities have to refrain from discriminatory acts, and that they have to take measures to eliminate discrimination by any person, organization or enterprise. Finally, paragraph (f) does not only concern amending legislation, but also the modification of customs and practices that constitute discrimination against women.

3.1.2. Equality Clause in National Legislation

Paragraph (a) provides that the principle of the equality of men and women has to be embodied in the national constitution or other appropriate legislation. In its older concluding observations, CEDAW often recommended States parties to include the definition of discrimination given in Article 1 of the Women's Convention in their national constitution.[39] CEDAW has made it clear in its concluding observations that it regards Article 1 as referring to both direct and

---

[38] CEDAW General Recommendation No. 28 (2010), 'The core obligations of States parties under Article 2', paras. 24 and 29.
[39] See *e.g.* concluding observations on Guinea 31 July 2001, paras. 118 and 119; concluding observations on Morocco 15 July 2003, paras. 160 and 161; concluding observations on Samoa, 24 January 2005, paras. 46 and 47.

indirect discrimination.[40] Regarding Article 2(a), CEDAW has clarified in its concluding observations that the principle of equality entails both formal and substantive equality.[41] In addition, CEDAW recommends in more recent concluding observations that States parties should also include a clause on the equality of men and women in their constitution or other appropriate legislation in relation to Article 2(a).[42] In General Recommendation No. 25, which was adopted in 2003, CEDAW indirectly acknowledges that Article 2(a) also includes substantive equality. In this General Recommendation CEDAW recommends States parties to report under Article 2 on the legal basis of temporary special measures and whether such legislation provides for the mandatory or voluntary nature of temporary special measures.[43] CEDAW also states in General Recommendation No. 25, though not in relation to Article 2, that States parties should include in their constitution or in their national legislation provisions that allow for the adoption of temporary special measures.[44] CEDAW does not specify how this should be done, but there are two possibilities in this regard. The first option is to include substantive equality in relevant national laws or the constitution providing for the equality of men and women. This will allow the use of temporary special measures which provide for favourable treatment of women in order to achieve substantive equality between men and women. The second option is that States parties should ensure that the constitution or anti-discrimination legislation contains a similar clause as Article 4(1) of the Women's Convention. This provision provides that temporary special measures aimed at accelerating *de facto* equality between men and women are not discriminatory. In General Recommendation No. 28, that was recently adopted, CEDAW explicitly states that 'States parties must ensure that, through constitutional amendments or by other appropriate legislative means, the principle of equality between women and men *and* of non-discrimination is enshrined in domestic law' (emphasis added).[45] Hence, it can be concluded that CEDAW makes a distinction between the principle of non-discrimination and the principle of equality.

---

[40] See *e.g.* concluding observations on the United Kingdom 1 July 1999, paras. 300 and 301; concluding observations on Estonia 7 May 2002, paras. 87 and 88; concluding observations on Bhutan 30 January 2004, paras. 15 and 16; concluding observations on United Republic of Tanzania 2008, paras. 109 and 110.

[41] See *e.g.* concluding observations on Bolivia 2008, para. 82; concluding observations on Lebanon 2008, para. 174.

[42] See *e.g.* concluding observations on Morocco 2008, paras 221 and 222; observations on Yemen 2008, paras. 359 and 360.

[43] CEDAW General Recommendation No. 25 (2004), Temporary special measures (Article 4(1)), para. 30.

[44] *Ibid.*, para. 31.

[45] CEDAW General Recommendation No. 28 (2010), 'The core obligations of States parties under Article 2', para. 31.

In this regard it is also relevant to note that in its concluding observations on Belgium CEDAW 'urges the State party to frame its gender policy in both the elimination of discrimination and the promotion of equality, which are *two different but equally important goals* in the quest for women's empowerment' (emphasis added).[46] In a few other recent concluding observations CEDAW sometimes also recommended States parties to adopt a definition of discrimination in accordance with Article 1 and with the principle of equality of men and women provided by Article 2(a).[47] Overall we can conclude that CEDAW recognizes that the principle of equality, entailing also substantive equality, has a more far reaching scope than the principle of non-discrimination.

3.1.3. Non-State Actors

Although this Chapter focuses on equality, it is relevant to also pay attention to paragraph (e) of Article 2. Due to this paragraph the Women's Convention does not solely address discrimination by the State or by actors that represent the State. According to Article 2(e), States are also obliged 'to take all appropriate measures to eliminate discrimination against women by any person, organization or enterprise'. Hence, this provision obliges States parties specifically to take appropriate measures to eliminate discrimination against women by non-State actors. This is quite unique, since most international human rights treaties do not contain a provision that specifically regards the acts by non-State actors. Under Article 2(e) a State party is accountable for discrimination by a private actor, unless the State has taken appropriate measures to prevent or address a violation of this prohibition. This is especially relevant in the context of the elimination of discrimination against women, since many women suffer from discrimination within their private environment by their family, community, employer or others.

Regarding violence against women, which is also often perpetrated by private actors, CEDAW has indicated in two General Recommendations what States parties should undertake in order to eliminate this form of discrimination. In General Recommendation No. 12 CEDAW recommends that States parties should include in their periodic reports information about the 'legislation in force to protect women against the incidence of all kinds of violence in everyday life (including sexual violence, abuses in the family, sexual harassment at the workplace, etc.)' and the 'existence of support services for women who are the victims of aggression or abuses'.[48] In General Recommendation No. 19 CEDAW indicates, among other things, that 'States may also be responsible for private

---

[46] Concluding observations on Belgium 10 June 2002, para. 146.
[47] See *e.g.* concluding observations on Latvia 14 July 2004, paras. 45 and 46; concluding observations on Algeria 11 January 2005, paras. 139 and 140.
[48] CEDAW General Recommendation No. 12 (1989), Violence against women, paras. 1 and 2.

acts of discrimination if they fail to act with due diligence to prevent violations or to investigate and punish acts of violence, and for providing compensation'.[49] CEDAW also repeats this in more general terms by recommending that States parties 'should take appropriate and effective measures to overcome all forms of gender-based violence, whether by public or private act'.[50] In General Recommendation No. 28 CEDAW refers with respect to violence against women, *inter alia* in the family and domestic unit, also to General Recommendation No. 19 and repeats the due diligence obligation of States parties to prevent, investigate and punish such acts, while adding the obligation to also prosecute these acts.[51] In its views on individual complaints regarding domestic violence, CEDAW has held States parties responsible for the violation of, *inter alia*, Article 2(e) when a State party had not acted with due diligence to prevent or to investigate and punish acts of domestic violence by non-State actors.[52] We can therefore conclude that if States parties do not take appropriate measures to prevent or address violence against women or other forms of discrimination against women by private actors, States parties violate their obligation under Article 2(e).

With respect to migrant women, CEDAW pays much attention in General Recommendation No. 26 to possible human rights violations by different non-State actors, such as recruitment agencies and employers. In this regard CEDAW indicates, amongst other things, that States parties should adopt regulations and design monitoring systems to ensure that recruiting and employment agencies respect the rights of women migrant workers, States parties should ensure that employers do not confiscate or destroy travel documents and States parties should monitor and prosecute recruitment agencies for acts of violence, coercion, deception or exploitation.[53]

More general, CEDAW indicates in General Comment No. 28 that the appropriate measures States parties are obliged to take to ensure that private actors do not discriminate against women 'include the regulation of the activities of private actors with regard to education, employment and health policies and practices, working conditions and work standards, and other areas in which

---

[49] CEDAW General Recommendation No. 19 (1992), Violence against women, para. 9.
[50] *Ibid.*, para. 24 (a).
[51] CEDAW General Recommendation No. 20 (2010), The core obligations of States parties under Article 2, para. 19.
[52] CEDAW Communication No. 2/2003, *Ms. A.T. versus Hungary*; CEDAW Communication No. 5/2005, *The Vienna Intervention Centre against Domestic Violence and the Association for Women's Access to Justice on behalf of Hakan Goekce, Handan Goekce, and Guelue Goekce (descendants of the deceased) versus Austria*; CEDAW Communication No. 6/2005, *The Vienna Intervention Centre against Domestic Violence and the Association for Women's Access to Justice on behalf of Banu Akbak, Gülen Khan and Melissa Özdemir (descendants of the deceased) versus Austria*.
[53] CEDAW General Recommendation No. 26 (2009), Women migrant workers, paras. 24(c), 26(d) and 26(h).

private actors provide services or facilities, such as banking and housing.'[54] Hence, it can be concluded that Article 2(e) makes the scope of Article 2 very far reaching.

3.1.4. Modify Discriminatory Laws, Customs and Practices

Article 2(f) makes the scope of application of the Women's Convention significantly wider, as this provision goes beyond law reform and requires that States parties ensure that also customs and practices that discriminate against women are abolished. This seems to be rather crucial in the elimination of discrimination against women, since discrimination against women is often also embedded in customs and practices. Generally, this will regard direct discrimination of women, which is a violation of the principle of formal equality. Due to this conceptual overlap and the importance of abolishing discriminatory practices and customs, which are some of the more persistent forms of discrimination that are deeply entrenched in many societies, Article 2(f) will be specifically addressed in this section.

Between Article 2(f) and Article 5(a) an overlap exists. Article 5(a) concerns, amongst other obligations, the elimination of customary and other practices that are based on inferiority or stereotyping of women and men. In its more recent concluding observations CEDAW also often refers to Articles 2(f) and 5 together.[55] In addition, it is also relevant to note that these customs and practices often entail discrimination by private actors, which shows the strong interconnection between Article 2(e) and Article 2(f).

As CEDAW states in General Recommendation No. 19, while referring to Articles 2(f), 5 and 10(c): 'Traditional attitudes by which women are regarded as subordinate to men or as having stereotyped roles perpetuate widespread practices involving violence or coercion, such as family violence and abuse, forced marriage, dowry deaths, acid attacks and female circumcision'.[56] CEDAW adds that 'Such prejudices and practices may justify gender-based violence as a form of protection or control of women'.[57] In individual complaints regarding domestic violence CEDAW also states that there are linkages between traditional attitudes by which women are regarded as subordinate to men and violence against women.[58] In General Recommendation No. 19 CEDAW

---

[54] CEDAW General Recommendation No. 28 (2010), The core obligations of States parties under Article 2, para. 13. More specific appropriate measures are listed in para. 36.
[55] See *e.g.* concluding observations on Angola 12 July 2004, para. 147; concluding observations on Equatorial Guinea 8 July 2001, para. 196; concluding observations on Samoa 24 January 2005, para. 53; concluding observations on Turkey 20 January 2005, para. 368.
[56] CEDAW General Recommendation No. 19 (1992), Violence against women, para. 11.
[57] *Ibid.*, para. 11.
[58] CEDAW Communication No. 2/2003, *Ms. A.T. versus Hungary*, para. 9.4; CEDAW Communication No. 5/2005, *The Vienna Intervention Centre against Domestic Violence and the Association for Women's Access to Justice on behalf of Hakan Goekce, Handan Goekce, and*

furthermore underlines that the 'effect of such violence on the physical and mental integrity of women is to deprive them of the equal enjoyment and exercise and knowledge of human rights and fundamental freedoms'.[59] CEDAW thus clearly underlines the importance of the modification of these practices in order to ensure that women are not deprived of the enjoyment of their human rights. In this regard CEDAW states that States parties 'should identify the nature and the extent of attitudes, customs and practices that perpetuate violence against women'.[60] CEDAW adds that States parties should also take effective measures to overcome these attitudes and practices. Furthermore, 'States should introduce education and public information programmes to help eliminate prejudices which hinder women's equality'.[61]

In General Recommendation No. 21 CEDAW refers in many paragraphs to the fact that customs and practices can discriminate against women in marriage and family relations.[62] This regards the role of customs and practices in relation to, amongst other things, women's restricted right to litigate, unequal status within the family, forced marriages, an unequal division of property at the end of a marriage or with respect to inheritance. Consequently, CEDAW concludes that 'States parties should introduce measures directed at encouraging full compliance with the principles of the Convention, particularly where religious or private law or custom conflict with those principles'.[63]

In General Recommendation No. 26, regarding migrant women workers, CEDAW states, while referring to Article 2(f), that States parties 'should lift restrictions that require women to get permission from their spouse or male guardian to obtain a passport or to travel'.[64] Furthermore, CEDAW underlines that 'women migrant workers are entitled to the protection of their human rights, which include[s]… the right to personal liberty'.[65] As CEDAW indicates, apart from risks, migration may also create 'new opportunities for women and may be a means for their economic empowerment'.[66]

Guelue Goekce (descendants of the deceased) versus Austria, para. 12.2; CEDAW Communication No. 6/2005, *The Vienna Intervention Centre against Domestic Violence and the Association for Women's Access to Justice on behalf of Banu Akbak, Gülen Khan and Melissa Özdemir (descendants of the deceased) versus Austria*, para. 12.2.
[59] *Ibid.*, para. 11.
[60] *Ibid.*, para. 24(e).
[61] *Ibid.*, para. 24(f).
[62] CEDAW General Recommendation No. 21 (1994), Equality in marriage and family relations, paras. 8, 12, 13, 16, 28, 33, 35 and 36.
[63] *Ibid.*, para. 50.
[64] CEDAW General Recommendation No. 26 (2009), Women migrant workers, para. 24(a).
[65] *Ibid.*, para. 6.
[66] *Ibid.*, para. 2.

3.2. ARTICLE 3

3.2.1. All Appropriate Measures

Like Article 2, Article 3 contains a general obligation of what States parties have to undertake. Whereas Article 2 also specifies what in particular needs to be undertaken by States parties, Article 3 contains a very general aim: to ensure the full development and advancement of women. In this regard Article 3 states that *all* appropriate measures to ensure the full development and advancement of women should be taken by the States parties. But which measures can be regarded as falling within the scope of application of Article 3?

Unfortunately General Recommendation No. 25, which deals with temporary special measures as provided for by Article 4(1), does not address the relationship between Articles 3 and 4(1).[67] However, CEDAW does state in this General Recommendation that States parties should clearly distinguish between temporary special measures under Article 4(1) and other general social policies to improve the situation of women.[68] CEDAW explains that 'Not all measures that potentially are, or will be, favourable to women are temporary special measures'.[69] CEDAW adds that providing general conditions in order to guarantee the human rights of women to ensure them a life of dignity and non-discrimination, are not regarded as being temporary special measures.[70] Although CEDAW tries to clarify what it considers as falling under general social policy, the aforementioned explanation given in General Recommendation No. 25 is rather general and vague. It seems that CEDAW wants to distinguish between affirmative action measures and other measures that should lead to substantive equality. However, it is difficult to draw a line between these measures, as affirmative action measures also fall within the category of measures that aim to ensure substantive equality. CEDAW indicates this too by underlining in General Comment No. 28 that achieving substantive equality includes also, where appropriate, the adoption of temporary special measures.[71] Hence, it can be concluded that affirmative action measures can also be regarded as falling under the category of measures provided by Article 3 to ensure the full development and advancement of women.

The fact that Article 4(1) allows specifically for affirmative action, probably explains why CEDAW does not often refer to the very generally phrased Article 3

---

[67] Although reference is made in para. 34 what CEDAW regards as relevant in relation to Article 3, CEDAW does not explain how Article 3 relates to Article 4(1).
[68] CEDAW General Recommendation No. 25 (2003), Temporary special measures (Article 4(1)), para. 19.
[69] Ibid., para. 19.
[70] Ibid., para. 19.
[71] CEDAW General Recommendation No. 28 (2010), The core obligations of States parties under Article 2, para. 20.

Chapter 4. The Principle of Equality

in its General Recommendations, with the exception of the recently adopted General Recommendation No. 26. Moreover, only in five General Recommendations can a reference to Article 3 in isolation be found. The most recent reference, that can be found in General Comment No. 28, will be addresses in Section 3.2.3. In General Recommendation No. 6 CEDAW recommends States parties, among other things, to establish or strengthen national machinery with adequate resources to advise on the impact of government policies, to monitor the situation of women and to help formulate new policies and carry out strategies and measures to eliminate discrimination against women.[72] The existence of effective national machinery is also often addressed by CEDAW in its concluding observations.[73] In General Recommendation No. 18, concerning disabled women, CEDAW recommends that information on special measures for disabled women is provided by States parties. However, this General Recommendation does not clarify what kind of measures States parties should take. In General Recommendation No. 25 CEDAW asks States to report under Article 3 about institutions that are responsible for the implementation and supervision of temporary special measures.[74] In General Recommendation No. 26, which regards women migrant workers, many references are being made to Article 3 in combination with other provisions and several to Article 3 in isolation. The latter are being made, *inter alia*, in relation to indicating that States parties should formulate policies and programmes for women migrant workers regarding, for example, awareness-raising programmes in respect of the rights of migrant women workers and gender sensitive training for State employees.[75] In addition, General Recommendation No. 26 also indicates that States parties who are sending or receiving countries should enter into bilateral and regional agreements or memorandums of understanding protecting the rights of women migrant workers and share best practices to promote the full protection of the rights of women migrant workers.[76] It is interesting that according to this General Recommendation, Article 3 also obliges States parties to facilitate the right of women migrant workers to return to their country of origin and to oblige States parties to train and supervise their consular and diplomatic staff to ensure that they also protect the rights of these women when they are abroad.[77] The aforementioned measures show that CEDAW gives a broad scope to the

---

[72] CEDAW General Recommendation No. 6 (1988), Effective national machinery and publicity, para. 1.
[73] See *e.g.* concluding observations on Slovakia 30 June 1998, para. 71; concluding observations on Myanmar 28 January 2000, para. 104; concluding observations on Albania 16 January 2003, paras. 66 and 67; concluding observations on Democratic People's Republic of Korea 18 July 2005, paras. 47 and 48.
[74] General Recommendation No. 25 (2003), Temporary special measures (Article 4(1)), para. 34.
[75] CEDAW General Recommendation No. 26 (2009), Women migrant workers, para. 26(g).
[76] *Ibid.*, para. 27(a) and (b)(i).
[77] *Ibid.*, para 24(b): (h) and (i).

application of Article 3 regarding the rights of migrant women and also indicates which kind of measures CEDAW regards to fall under Article 3.

3.2.2. On a Basis of Equality with Men

Although Article 3 provides that measures have to be taken to ensure the full development and advancement of women, Article 3 also provides that these measures have to be taken to ensure women the exercise and enjoyment of their human rights on a basis of equality with men. If we would conclude that the latter clause in Article 3 would only encompass formal equality, Article 3 could not provide that States parties should take specific measures for women. But according to Article 3, the measures to ensure the full development and advancement of women should be undertaken 'for the purpose of guaranteeing them [women] the exercise and enjoyment of human rights and fundamental freedoms on a basis of equality with men'. Thus, in order to ensure that women can equally exercise and enjoy their human rights like men, measures should be taken to ensure the full development and advancement of women. Hence, Article 3 recognises implicitly that the *de facto* situation between men and women is not equal and that measures should therefore be taken to correct this situation. This means that Article 3 provides for substantive equality of men and women, by means of all appropriate measures.

3.2.3. Not Temporary and in All Fields

Whereas temporary special measures should be discontinued when, according to Article 4(1) of the Women's Convention, the objectives of equality of opportunity and treatment have been achieved, a time-limit is not provided for in Article 3. Taking these differences into account and the fact that Article 3 provides that all appropriate measures should be taken, we can conclude that Article 3 has a broader scope of application than Article 4(1). In this regard, it is somewhat surprising that CEDAW does not often refer to Article 3 in its concluding observations. The reason for this lack of application could be that Article 3 is phrased in such general terms that it could be argued that it lacks specification.

According to Article 3, these measures have to be taken in all fields, in particular in the political, social, economic and cultural fields. This gives Article 3 a very broad scope of application. In that regard, CEDAW recommends States parties in General Recommendation No. 18 to provide information on measures taken for disabled women, 'including special measures to ensure that they have equal access to education and employment, health services and social security, and to ensure that they can participate in all areas of social and cultural life'.[78]

---

[78] CEDAW General Recommendation No. 18 (1991), Disabled women.

General Comment No. 28 further clarifies that by referring to all fields in Article 3 'the emergence of new forms of discrimination that had not been identified at the time of its drafting' is anticipated.[79] Finally, it should be noted that the words 'shall' and 'ensure' that are used in Article 3, indicate that States parties are obliged to take measures to ensure women's full development and advancement in all fields. Hence, Article 3 is of a mandatory nature.

4. ARTICLE 3 ICCPR

> 'The States Parties to the present Covenant undertake to ensure the equal right of men and women to the enjoyment of all civil and political rights set forth in the present Covenant.'

The interpretation by CEDAW of Articles 2 and 3 of the Women's Convention will be compared to the interpretation the Human Rights Committee gives to Article 3 of the ICCPR. Hence, in this section the interpretation by the Human Rights Committee of the principle of equality and how this relates to the principle of non-discrimination will be addressed in relation to Article 3 of the ICCPR. Specific issues, such as non-discrimination by non-State actors and discriminatory traditions, will also be addressed in this context.

4.1. GENERAL COMMENT NO. 28

In March 2000 the Human Rights Committee adopted General Comment No. 28 on the equality of rights between men and women, as provided for by Article 3 of the ICCPR. This elaborate General Comment of 32 paragraphs is a good example of gender mainstreaming.[80] The Committee spells out, for almost all human rights provisions of the Covenant, on which specific issues affecting women information should be provided and/or measures should be taken by the States parties.[81] Or, in other words, the implications of what the accessory Article 3 provides for in relation to the other provisions of the Covenant is clarified in General Comment No. 28. It deals with issues like clandestine abortions (Article 6), the burning of widows (Article 6), domestic violence (Article 7), genital mutilation (Article 7), trafficking in women (Article 8), regulations concerning

---

[79] CEDAW General Recommendation No. 28 (2010), The core obligations of States parties under Article 2, para. 8.
[80] T. LOENEN, 'General Comment No. 28 en de voorbeeldfunctie van het mensenrechtencomité inzake sekse-gelijkheid' [= General Comment No. 28 and the exemplary practice of the Human Rights Committee regarding sex equality], *NJCM-Bulletin*, Vol. 26, No. 4, 2001, pp. 498, 507.
[81] The Human Rights Committee does not address Articles 1, 11, 20, 21 and 22.

clothing to be worn by women in public (Articles 7, 9, 12, 17, 18, 19, 26 and 27), female guards for women prisoners (Articles 7 and 10), requirements which prevent women from travelling (Article 12), direct and autonomous access to the courts for women (Article 14), legal capacity to own property (Article 16), obligatory pregnancy tests (Article 17), pornographic material (Article 19), minimum age for marriage (Article 23), polygamy (Article 23), inheritance rights (Article 23), equal treatment of boys and girls in relation to education (Article 24), women in publicly elected office (Article 25) and so-called 'honour crimes' (Articles 6, 14 and 26). It is clear from these examples that women can find themselves in different situations compared to men. In order to ensure the equal enjoyment of the Covenant rights by women, these issues need to be taken into account when the Human Rights Committee evaluates the implementation of the Covenant rights by States parties.

In the concluding observations of the Human Rights Committee we can also find some references to General Comment No. 28.[82] This indicates the importance which the Committee attaches to this General Comment, since it is relatively rare for the Committee to make references to General Comments in its concluding observations.

4.2. FORMAL AND SUBSTANTIVE EQUALITY

General Comment No. 28 spells out many different measures which States parties should take to ensure the enjoyment by women of the rights provided by the ICCPR. States parties are required to take all necessary steps to enable every person to enjoy these rights, which includes 'the removal of obstacles to the equal enjoyment of such rights, the education of the population and of State officials in human rights, and the adjustment of domestic legislation'.[83] The Committee adds that 'States parties must provide information regarding the actual role of women in society so that the Committee may ascertain what measures, in addition to legislative provisions, have been or should be taken'.[84] General Comment No. 28 furthermore provides that 'The State party must not only adopt measures of protection, but also positive measures in all areas so as to achieve the effective and equal empowerment of women'.[85] Hence, the measures which States parties should take do not only refer to adopting or amending legislation, but also to taking positive measures that should lead to the effective and equal

---

[82] See *e.g.* concluding observations on Kuwait 27 July 2000, para. 8; concluding observations on the Syrian Arab Republic 24 April 2001, para. 18; concluding observations on El Salvador 22 July 2003, para. 14; concluding observations on Benin 1 December 2004, para. 10.
[83] CCPR General Comment No. 28 (2000), Equality of rights between men and women (Article 3), para. 3.
[84] *Ibid.*, para. 3.
[85] *Ibid.*, para. 3.

empowerment of women. These positive measures clearly fall within the scope of the principle of substantive equality, whereas legislative measures would often concern formal equality.

The Committee also concretely indicates in General Comment No. 28 which issues should be addressed in relation to different provisions of the ICCPR. These mainly concern issues of formal equality, such as: requirements preventing women from travelling (Article 12), access to justice on equal terms with men (Article 14), the capacity of women to own property (Article 16), the right to enter into marriage with free and full consent (Article 23), equal grounds for divorce for men and women (Article 23), that girls are treated equally to boys in education (Article 24), etc.[86] However, also some examples regarding substantive equality can be found. This regards measures such as to ensure that women do not have to undergo life-threatening clandestine abortions (Article 6), measures taken to eliminate the trafficking of women and forced prostitution (Article 8) and effective and positive measures to promote and ensure women's participation in the conduct of public affairs and in public office, including appropriate affirmative action (Article 25).[87]

Overall, we can conclude that the Committee interprets Article 3 not only as providing for formal equality, but also for substantive equality. The Committee underlines that States parties should take positive measures which lead to the empowerment of women, but no explicit reference is made in that context to affirmative action. Only in relation to Article 25, does the Human Rights Committee not only refer to positive measures, but also to appropriate affirmative action. Consequently, it is not clear whether the Committee interprets Article 3 to include in its general scope of application affirmative action, or whether affirmative action should only be applied in relation to Article 25. No other reference to affirmative action can be found in General Comment No. 28. This is remarkable, as in General Comment No. 4 the Committee states explicitly that affirmative action should also be taken to ensure the positive enjoyment of the rights set forth in the ICCPR.[88] However, this General Comment is replaced by General Comment No. 28, according to paragraph 1 of General Comment No. 28. In General Comment No. 28 the Committee only underlines that States parties must take positive measures in all areas to achieve the effective and equal empowerment of women.[89] Hence, in this General Comment the Committee seems to leave it up to the States parties to determine which measures they should use to fulfil their obligations with respect to the equal enjoyment by women of their rights under the ICCPR. However, in General Comment No. 18 on non-discrimination the Human Rights Committee

---

[86] *Ibid.*, paras. 16, 18, 23, 26 and 28.
[87] *Ibid.*, paras. 10, 11, 12 and 29.
[88] CCPR General Comment No. 4 (1981), Equality between the sexes (Article 3), para. 2.
[89] CCPR General Comment No. 28 (2000), Equality of rights between men and women (Article 3), para. 3.

reaffirms that the principle of equality sometimes requires States parties to take affirmative action in order to diminish or eliminate conditions which cause or help to perpetuate discrimination.[90] According to the Committee such action may involve granting for a time to the part of the population concerned preferential treatment in specific matters.[91] Furthermore, the Committee indicates that as long as such action is needed to correct discrimination in fact, it is a case of legitimate differentiation.[92] However, the approach taken by the Human Rights Committee in General Comment No. 28, that specifically addresses the equal right of men and women to the enjoyment of their rights, is more limited.

It should be noted that in the concluding observations in general more references are made by the Human Rights Committee to discrimination against women than to the unequal enjoyment by women of their rights.[93] However, quite often the Committee refers to both non-discrimination and unequal treatment within the same concluding observation.[94] Throughout General Comment No. 28, the Committee also does not make a clear distinction between the principle of discrimination and the principle of equality.[95] The Committee seems to regard these principles as more or less interchangeable. According to the Committee:

> 'States parties are responsible for ensuring the equal enjoyment of rights without any discrimination. Articles 2 and 3 mandate States parties to take all steps necessary, including the prohibition of discrimination on the ground of sex, to put an end to discriminatory actions, both in the public and the private sector, which impair the equal enjoyment of rights.'[96]

Although the principles of equality and discrimination are closely related, a distinction can be made. The prohibition of discrimination as such does not oblige States parties to ensure substantive equality. However, the aforementioned interpretation of the Committee also explains its general focus on formal equality.

---

[90] CCPR General Comment No. 18 (1989), Non-discrimination, para. 10.
[91] *Ibid.*, para. 10.
[92] *Ibid.*, para. 10.
[93] See *e.g.* concluding observations on Zambia 3 April 1996, para. 9; concluding observations on Armenia 19 November 1998, para. 15; concluding observations on Egypt 28 November 2002, para. 9.
[94] See *e.g.* concluding observations on Poland 29 July 1999, para. 12; concluding observations on the Syrian Arab Republic 24 April 2001, para. 18; concluding observations on Yemen 9 August 2005, para. 9.
[95] CCPR General Comment No. 28 (2000), Equality of rights between men and women (Article 3), paras. 7, 13, 19, 21, 24, 25, 29 and 30.
[96] *Ibid.*, para. 4.

4.3. NON-STATE ACTORS

The Human Rights Committee attaches great importance in General Comment No. 28 to the elimination of discrimination by non-State actors. The Committee underlines that States parties should take all necessary steps to put an end to discriminatory actions, both in the public and the private sector, which impair the equal enjoyment of rights.[97] In addition, the Committee makes many references to non-State actors with respect to specific provisions of the ICCPR. This concerns, for example, violations of women's privacy (Article 17) by employers who request a pregnancy test before hiring a woman.[98] The Committee also refers to constraints on the freedom of religion for women (Article 18) by rules requiring permission from third parties, or by interference from fathers, husbands or brothers.[99] And the Committee addresses the issue of a guardian consenting to a marriage (Article 23) instead of the woman herself.[100] With respect to Article 26 the Committee underlines that States have to act against discrimination by public and private agencies in all fields.[101] Furthermore, States should prohibit discrimination by non-State actors in areas such as employment, education, political activities and the provision of accommodation, goods and services.[102]

In its concluding observations the Human Rights Committee does not often pay attention to certain acts of discrimination by private actors, with the exception of discrimination by private actors in relation to domestic violence. In this regard, the Human Rights Committee often refers to measures that should be taken to address domestic violence by stating, *inter alia*, that the population should be sensitised, police officers should be trained and perpetrators should be prosecuted.[103]

4.4. CULTURE, TRADITIONS AND RELIGION

The influence of religion, traditions and culture on equal treatment of women is a very important issue, since this can seriously impair the equal enjoyment by women of their rights. The Human Rights Committee recognises in General Comment No. 28 that:

---

[97] *Ibid.*, para. 4.
[98] *Ibid.*, para. 20.
[99] *Ibid.*, para. 21.
[100] *Ibid.*, para. 23.
[101] *Ibid.*, para. 31.
[102] *Ibid.*, para. 31.
[103] See *e.g.* concluding observations on Ukraine 2002, para. 10; concluding observations on Benin 2005, para. 9; concluding observations on Algeria 2008, para. 21.

'Inequality in the enjoyment of rights by women throughout the world is deeply embedded in tradition, history and culture, including religious attitudes. [...] States parties should ensure that traditional, historical, religious or cultural attitudes are not used to justify violations of women's equal right to equality before the law and to equal enjoyment of all Covenant rights.'[104]

Hence, according to the Committee tradition, culture and religion cannot be used to validate discrimination against women. In addition, the Committee states explicitly with respect to Article 18 that this provision – regarding freedom of thought, conscience and religion – may not be relied upon to justify discrimination against women.[105] Furthermore, the Committee underlines that the rights enjoyed by persons belonging to minorities under Article 27, regarding their culture and religion, do not authorise violations of the equal enjoyment by women of their rights. Hence, when there is a clash between the rights protected under Article 3 and those under Article 18 or 27, the rights protected under Article 3 will prevail according to the Committee.

The Committee also gives concrete examples, in relation to specific provisions of the ICCPR, of unequal treatment of women based on culture, tradition or religion. This includes practices that prevent the marriage between a woman of a particular religion and a man who professes no religion or a different religion (Article 23),[106] cultural or religious practices which jeopardise the freedom and well-being of female children (Article 24),[107] customs and traditions that discriminate against women particularly with regard to access to better paid employment and to equal pay for work of equal value (Article 26),[108] and cultural or religious practices within minority communities that affect women's rights (Article 27).[109] Reference is also made to practices such as burning of widows and dowry killings (Article 6),[110] genital mutilation (Article 7),[111] polygamy (Article 23)[112] and so-called 'honour crimes' (Article 26).[113]

In the case of *Müller and Engelhard versus Namibia* the Committee was confronted with a complaint that concerned traditions being used to justify unequal treatment of women.[114] After their marriage, Mr Müller wanted to assume the surname of his wife Ms Engelhard. However, according to Namibian laws this was not possible. The Committee stated in that respect:

---

[104] CCPR General Comment No. 28 (2000), Equality of rights between men and women (Article 3), para. 5.
[105] *Ibid.*, para. 21.
[106] *Ibid.*, para. 24.
[107] *Ibid.*, para. 28.
[108] *Ibid.*, para. 31.
[109] *Ibid.*, para. 32.
[110] *Ibid.*, para. 10.
[111] *Ibid.*, para. 11.
[112] *Ibid.*, para. 24.
[113] *Ibid.*, para. 31.
[114] CCPR Communication No. 919/2000, *Müller and Engelhard versus Namibia*.

> 'In view of the importance of the principle of equality between men and women, the argument of a long-standing tradition cannot be maintained as a general justification for different treatment of men and women, which is contrary to the Covenant.'[115]

It can be concluded, based on the aforementioned decision and on General Comment No. 28, that according to the Committee in case of a clash between the equal enjoyment by women of their rights and religious norms, traditions and culture, preference will be given to the equal enjoyment by women of their rights, as protected by Article 3 of the ICCPR.

5. CONCLUSIONS

If the principle of equality is regarded to include both formal and substantive equality, it will not only regard the nature of the treatment, but also the result. The latter may actually entail differential treatment in order to reach an equal result. This is also referred to as the paradox of the principle of equality. Compared to the principle of non-discrimination, the principle of equality – when including substantive equality – has a more far reaching scope, as it entails that differential treatment is in fact regarded as an essential part of the principle of equality. The prohibition of discrimination as such does not oblige States parties to ensure substantive equality.

In relation to Articles 2 and 3 of the Women's Convention, CEDAW applies both the principles of formal and of substantive equality. CEDAW indicates in relation to incorporating the principle of the equality of men and women in the national constitutions or other legislation, that this should include both formal and substantive equality. Furthermore, CEDAW underlines in relation to Article 3 of the Women's Convention that there needs to be national machinery to monitor the situation of women and to help formulate new policies. More generally, CEDAW has stated in its General Recommendations and concluding observations, that governments should develop policies and programmes specifically for women.

In General Comment No. 28 the Human Rights Committee states in paragraph 3 that States parties should also take positive measures to achieve the effective and equal empowerment of women. Although the Human Rights Committee does not explicitly refer to the principle of substantive equality, these positive measures clearly fall within the scope of the principle of substantive equality. Nevertheless, the Human Rights Committee's focus is more on formal equality, as the Committee refers in General Comment No. 28 to many specific issues that should be addressed in relation to the different provisions of the ICCPR that regard formal equality. Furthermore, the Human Rights Committee

---

[115] *Ibid.*, para. 6.8.

does not make a clear distinction between the principle of discrimination and the principle of equality. The Committee seems to regard these principles as more or less interchangeable.

Although there are differences between the principles of non-discrimination and equality, there is also a close relation between these two principles, *inter alia*, because direct discrimination is the negative statement of formal equality. Regarding (direct) discrimination by non-State actors, CEDAW has clarified in its General Recommendations that if States parties do not take appropriate measures to prevent or address *e.g.* violence against women or violations of the rights of migrant women, this will result in a violation of Article 2(e) of the Women's Convention. With respect to discriminatory customs and practices, that should be eliminated according to Article 2(f) of the Women's Convention, CEDAW underlines the importance of the modification of these practices in order to ensure that women are not deprived of the enjoyment of their human rights. Also the Human Rights Committee attaches great importance to the elimination of discrimination by non-State actors. The Committee underlines in General Comment No. 28 that States parties should take all necessary steps to put an end to discriminatory actions in the private sector, which impair the equal enjoyment of rights by women. Furthermore, the Committee states clearly in General Comment No. 28 that traditions, culture and religion cannot be used to validate discrimination against women.

Based on the aforementioned it can be concluded that, especially with the adoption by the Human Rights Committee of General Comment No. 28 in 2000, there is clearly an overlap in the interpretation of the equality provisions of the Women's Convention and of the ICCPR. Although there is an overlap, the added value of CEDAW's interpretation is its focus on substantive equality, and the distinction it makes in this regard between the principles of non-discrimination and of equality. More generally, it is important to keep in mind that due to the different mandates of CEDAW (a specialized treaty body addressing human rights of women) and the Human Rights Committee (with a general mandate regarding civil and political human rights), CEDAW pays more attention in General Recommendations, views and concluding observations to women's rights and the principle of equality. Hence, as it was in general pre-supposed with the adoption of the Women's Convention in 1979, it can be concluded in relation to the principle of equality that CEDAW's interpretation of Articles 2 and 3 of the Women's Convention has indeed an added value, compared to the interpretation by the Human Rights Committee of Article 3 of the ICCPR.

ARTICLE 4

1. Adoption by States parties of temporary special measures aimed at accelerating *de facto* equality between men and women shall not be considered discrimination as defined in the present Convention, but shall in no way entail as a consequence the maintenance of unequal or separate standards; these measures shall be discontinued when the objectives of equality of opportunity and treatment have been achieved.
2. Adoption by States parties of special measures, including those measures contained in the present Convention, aimed at protecting maternity shall not be considered discriminatory.

CHAPTER 5
TEMPORARY SPECIAL MEASURES UNDER THE WOMEN'S CONVENTION AND POSITIVE ACTION UNDER EU LAW: MUTUALLY COMPATIBLE OR IRRECONCILABLE?

Lisa WADDINGTON* and Laura VISSER

1. INTRODUCTION

A 2004 General Recommendation of the Committee on the Elimination of Discrimination against Women[1] elaborates on Article 4 and identifies the purpose of the Article as 'to accelerate the improvement of the position of women to achieve their *de facto* substantive equality with men, and to effect the structural, social and cultural changes necessary to correct past and current forms and effects of discrimination against women'.[2] The General Recommendation makes it clear that, in certain circumstances, States parties are under an obligation to take 'temporary special measures', and that the Convention does not merely grant States parties the possibility to adopt such measures. In contrast, EU law, which has a long history of addressing sex discrimination, has never done more than allow Member States the possibility to adopt 'measures providing for specific advantages … for the under-represented sex'[3] in the context of vocational activities. Such measures, which are generally labelled positive action under EU law, do not breach the principle of non-discrimination (against men), as long as they meet certain criteria that have been developed by the Court of Justice. However, positive action which oversteps the

---

* The author is grateful to Tom Theuns, graduate of University College Maastricht, Maastricht University, for his research assistance.
[1] CEDAW General Recommendation No. 25, on Article 4, paragraph 1, of the Convention on the Elimination of All Forms of Discrimination against Women, on temporary special measures.
[2] General Recommendation No. 25, para. 15.
[3] Article 157(4) Treaty on the Functioning of the European Union (TFEU).

limits imposed by the Court is regarded as discriminating against men, and is therefore incompatible with EU law.

This Chapter seeks to examine the compatibility of the requirement, at times, to adopt temporary special measures under the Convention, with the obligation not to adopt positive action measures which discriminate against men under EU law. Herein lies a potential conflict, as all EU Member States are also parties to the Convention on the Elimination of All Forms of Discrimination Against Women (Women's Convention). This means that potentially they could be obliged to adopt temporary special measures in favour of women under the Convention, but, at the same time, be limited in the kinds of measures they can adopt under EU law.

The focus of this Chapter is on temporary special measures/positive action relating to employment, since it is in this field that the Court of Justice has elaborated limitations on the possibility to adopt measures. In those fields that fall outside of the scope of EU law, EU Member States face no restrictions with regard to meeting their obligations under the Convention.[4]

The Chapter begins by elaborating briefly on the purpose of positive action, and its relationship to formal and substantive equality (Section 2). The Chapter then proceeds to examine the nature of the obligation to adopt temporary special measures under the Convention (Section 3) and the limitations imposed on the adoption of positive action measures under EU law (Section 4). The Chapter concludes by reflecting on whether there is a potential conflict between the Convention (duty to adopt temporary special measures) and EU law (obligation not to adopt positive action measures which are regarded as discriminating against men) (Section 5).

---

[4] However, determining which areas fall outside the scope of EU law, and the status of EU law with regard to positive action measures that do not obviously address employment, is not an easy matter, and will not be considered further in this short article. For example, as noted in PANOS KAPOTAS, 'Gender Quotas in Politics: The Greek System on the Light of EU Law', *European Law Journal*, Vol. 16, Nr. 1, January 2010, 29, 'the dominant position in the literature appears to be that candidature for political office does not constitute "employment" in the sense of EU law' at 29–30, implying that such provisions fall outside the scope of EU law. However, Kapotas expresses some doubt as to whether such provisions do indeed fall outside the scope of EU law. Kapotas argues '… at least the Court of Human Rights has a clear mandate to determine whether a compulsory quota system in political candidature violates the right of citizens to freely choose their representatives through democratic elections. Since the Convention has a special status as a source of EU fundamental rights law, as confirmed by the case-law on a number of occasions, it is also plausible to suggest that the ECJ as well is in principle vested with the authority to decide on the matter. It is, therefore, a mistake to claim that positive action in elected office falls outside the regulatory scope of EU law altogether. Even if Article 141(4) is inapplicable in this case, a legal challenge on the basis of EU law is still possible', at 39.

2. FORMAL EQUALITY, SUBSTANTIVE EQUALITY AND TEMPORARY SPECIAL MEASURES/ POSITIVE ACTION

Non-discrimination laws are grounded on different notions of equality. These differences reflect various concepts of equality, most of which centre on the distinction between formal equality and substantive equality.[5]

Formal equality is concerned with guaranteeing equality of treatment. Formal equality requires that people who are similarly situated are treated in the same way. According to this model, individual and societal differences, as a result of which people find themselves differently situated, are ignored. In an employment context, the application of this model implies that requiring job applicants to meet a number of work-related criteria, such as height, physical strength, years of experience and ability to work unsocial hours, would not raise questions of equality and discrimination. In contrast, substantive equality is concerned with the construction of social conditions needed to ensure that people are treated equally, in terms of equal opportunities or equality of results. This model acknowledges the importance of differences and takes account of individual and environmental barriers that inhibit societal participation. Under this model, requiring job applicants to meet the aforementioned criteria can raise questions of equality and discrimination, once it becomes clear that these criteria have an adverse impact on the employment opportunities of (members of) a particular group, such as women.

Since the goal of substantive equality is equality of opportunity or equality of results,[6] this model of equality also embraces the idea that equality not only imposes an obligation not to discriminate or treat people unequally, but also entails the obligation to 'effectively put an end to discriminatory practices and disadvantaged positions of women'.[7] This model of equality therefore has particular implications with regard to positive (or affirmative) action. In this respect Julia O'Brien has argued:

---

[5] For further comment on this see, for example, BOB HEPPLE and CATHERINE BARNARD, 'Substantive Equality', *Cambridge Law Journal*, Vol. 59, 2000, 562 at 562–567 and CHRISTOPHER MCCRUDDEN, 'Theorizing European Equality Law', in: Cathryn Costello and Eilis Barry (eds.), *Equality in Diversity, The New Equality Directives*, Irish Centre for European Law, 2003, 1.

[6] It is recognized that equality of opportunity and equality of results are not equivalent. However, for the purposes of this paper, this distinction will not be explored further. However, note the position of the Court of Justice described below on this matter.

[7] INEKE BOEREFIJN, FONS COOMANS, JENNY GOLDSCHMIDT, RIKKI HOLTMAAT and RIA WOLLESWINKEL (eds.), *Temporary Special Measures, Accelerating de facto Equality of Women under Article 4(1) UN Convention on the Elimination of All Forms of Discrimination Against Women*, Intersentia, Antwerp, 2003, 'Introduction' at 4.

'Implicit in the concept of affirmative action is the notion that substantive equality requires more than simple termination of discriminatory practices. It requires programs to correct or compensate for past or present discrimination, or to prevent discrimination from recurring in the future.'[8]

Similarly Maria Herminia Graterol[9] has argued, in the context of the Women's Convention, that as 'measures aimed at accelerating *de facto* equality', temporary special measures may depart from the formal equality model in order to achieve substantive equality between men and women. She argues that while formal equality promotes equal treatment, substantive equality recognizes that the neutral gender-blind character of formal equality masks structural discrimination and privilege that are embedded or built into institutions as a result of past discrimination. It is this embedded structure of discrimination that temporary special measures aim to address. Maria Herminia Graterol concludes that substantive equality differs from formal equality in three ways:

- it requires States to ensure equality of results between men and women
- it acknowledges that States may need to treat men and women differently for this purpose
- it recognizes the need for enabling conditions to achieve this.[10]

In conclusion, temporary special measures/positive action are based on the substantive concept of equality. This recognizes that, in some circumstances, it is necessary to confer advantages on (members of) disadvantaged groups, such as women, and that this does not breach the principle of equality where it leads to members of other groups (men) being denied equivalent advantages or opportunities.

3. OBLIGATIONS TO ADOPT TEMPORARY SPECIAL MEASURES UNDER ARTICLE 4(1) OF THE CONVENTION

> 'The scope and meaning of Article 4, paragraph 1, must be determined in the context of the overall object and purpose of the Convention, which is to eliminate all forms of discrimination against women with a view to achieving women's de jure and de facto equality with men in the enjoyment of their human rights and fundamental freedoms.'[11]

---

[8] JULIE O'BRIEN, 'Affirmative Action, Special Measures and the Sex Discrimination Act', *University of New South Wales Law Journal*, Vol. 27, Nr. 3, 2004, 840.

[9] MARIA HERMINIA GRATEROL, *Addressing Intersectional Discrimination with Temporary Special Measures*, IWRAW Asia Pacific Occasional Papers Series No. 8, 2006, at 4.

[10] *Ibid.*, 8–9.

[11] General Recommendation No. 25, para. 4.

Chapter 5. Temporary Special Measures under the Women's Convention and
Positive Action under EU Law: Mutually Compatible or Irreconcilable?

As noted above, Article 4(1) of the Convention addresses temporary special measures. The concept of temporary special measures was already familiar within the field of international human rights law prior to the adoption of the Convention on the Elimination of All Forms of Discrimination Against Women. A provision similar to Article 4(1) was included in the Convention on the Elimination of All Forms of Racial Discrimination,[12] which was adopted in 1965, almost 15 years before the Women's Convention. That Article includes the elements found in Article 4(1): namely the requirements that special measures are to be temporary in nature, are not to be considered discriminatory, and should not lead to 'the maintenance of separate rights for different racial groups'.[13]

Whilst the term 'temporary special measures' is not defined in the Convention itself, it is submitted that the concept is not complicated. The temporary nature of the measure is referred to in Article 4(1), which requires that 'these measures shall be discontinued when the objectives of equality of opportunity and treatment have been achieved'. This implies that the measures will not include a predetermined time-frame. The measures are 'special' in that they are intended to serve a 'specific goal', as explained in General Recommendation No. 25.[14] The General Recommendation also makes it clear that the adoption of such measures is not meant to portray women as vulnerable or weak and therefore in need of 'special' measures.[15]

Whilst at first glance Article 4(1) merely seems to grant States parties the possibility to adopt temporary special measures, and not to impose an obligation to act in this way, an examination of the Convention as a whole, as well as General Recommendation No. 25, reveals that the taking of temporary special measures can be a duty that flows from the commitments States parties undertake when ratifying the Convention. This has been noted by Maria Herminia Graterol who, in a paper written for the International Women's Rights Action Watch Asia Pacific, has argued that 'when taken together, Articles 2, 3 and 5 imply an obligation on the part of States parties to employ temporary special measures when necessary, to end discrimination and gender stereotypes, as well as to ensure the development and advancement of women'.[16] In Article 2 of the Convention States parties condemn discrimination against women 'in all its forms' and agree to pursue a policy of eliminating discrimination against women; Article 3 directs States to undertake in all areas 'all appropriate measures […] to ensure the full development and advancement of women, for the purpose of guaranteeing them the exercise and enjoyment of human rights

---

[12] Convention on the Elimination of All Forms of Racial Discrimination, Article 1(4).
[13] Idem.
[14] General Recommendation No. 25, para. 21.
[15] Idem.
[16] MARIA HERMINIA GRATEROL, *Addressing Intersectional Discrimination with Temporary Special Measures*, IWRAW Asia Pacific Occasional Papers Series No. 8, 2006, at 3.

and fundamental freedoms on a basis of equality with men'; while Article 5 requires States parties to adopt 'all appropriate measures' to eliminate prejudicial gender stereotypes. Moreover, the General Recommendation itself refers to a 'joint reading of Articles 1 to 5 and 24'.[17] The latter Article calls on States parties to adopt the measures necessary to ensure the full realization of all the rights in the Convention. The General Recommendation also notes that Article 4(1) needs to be applied to Articles 6–16 of the Convention, meaning that temporary special measures fall within the definition of 'all appropriate measures' which States parties are obliged to take under these Articles.[18]

It can be concluded that it is the opinion of the UN Committee on the Elimination of Discrimination against Women, as expressed in the General Recommendation, that equality between men and women cannot be achieved when women are only guaranteed equal treatment to men, in line with the formal model of equality. The Convention 'targets discriminatory dimensions of past and current societal and cultural contexts which impede women's enjoyment of their human rights and fundamental freedoms' and aims at the 'elimination of the causes and consequences of their [women's LW] *de facto* and substantive inequality'.[19] The Committee concludes that temporary special measures may be required to address these inequalities[20] and that the adoption of temporary special measures does not amount to discrimination against men, but is rather a means to achieve *de facto* equality of women with men.[21]

The General Recommendation gives a few examples of 'measures' that may fall within Article 4(1). In general, such measures can be legislative, executive, administrative and other regulatory policies and practices. Examples of specific temporary special measures include preferential treatment, targeted recruitment, numerical goals with timeframes and quotas.[22] The choice and appropriateness of particular measures is dependent on the situation in which Article 4(1) is applied, and on the specific goal that is meant to be achieved.[23]

The Committee has commented on measures implemented in the field of employment by States parties to the Convention through their Concluding Observations. The Committee often makes the general statement that the States parties need to take temporary special measures in the field of employment, not specifying what these measures should be. Sometimes, however, the Committee goes into detail and recommends that the State party adopt quota systems, often combined with time-bound goals or timetables. It did so for example with

---

[17] General Recommendation No. 25, para. 6.
[18] *Ibid.*, para. 24.
[19] *Ibid.*, para 14.
[20] *Ibid.*, para. 8.
[21] *Ibid.*, paras. 14 and 18.
[22] *Ibid.*, para. 22.
[23] *Idem.*

Spain[24] and Germany[25] in 2009 and the United Kingdom[26] and Sweden[27] in 2008.

Nevertheless, it is worth noting that the Concluding Observations of the Committee, and indeed the General Recommendations issued by the Committee, are not binding under international law. However, these measures can be seen as soft law instruments and the Committee is the sole body that has the authority to interpret the Convention, meaning that its opinions do have a certain status.[28]

In conclusion, the adoption of temporary special measures is, at times, regarded as an obligation under the Convention when this is necessary to meet the substantive obligations which States parties have accepted by ratifying the Convention.

4. LIMITATIONS TO THE ADOPTION OF POSITIVE ACTION MEASURES UNDER EU LAW[29]

Unlike the Convention, EU law is 'gender-neutral' in requiring equality and combating discrimination. As a consequence, measures that disadvantage or discriminate against women are not particularly suspect or specifically targeted.

---

[24] UN doc. CEDAW/C/ESP/CO/6, *Concluding Observations of the Committee on the Elimination of Discrimination of Women, Spain*, 7 August 2009, para. 16.

[25] UN doc. CEDAW/C/DEU/CO/6, *Concluding Observations of the Committee on the Elimination of Discrimination of Women, Germany*, 12 February 2009, para. 26.

[26] UN doc. CEDAW/C/UK/CO/6, *Concluding Observations of the Committee on the Elimination of Discrimination of Women, United Kingdom of Great Britain and Northern Ireland*, 10 July 2008, para. 269.

[27] UN doc. CEDAW/C/SWE/CO/7, *Concluding Observations of the Committee on the Elimination of Discrimination of Women, Sweden*, 8 April 2008, para. 25.

[28] H.B. SCHÖPP-SCHILLING, 'Reflections on a General Recommendation on Article 4(1) of the Convention on the Elimination of All Forms of Discrimination Against Women', in: I. Boerefijn, F. Coomans, J. Goldschmidt, R. Holtmaat and R. Wolleswinkel (eds.), *Temporary Special Measures. Accelerating de facto Equality of Women under Article 4(1) UN Convention on the Elimination of All Forms of Discrimination Against Women*, Intersentia, Antwerp, 2003, 16.

[29] A large number of academic publications address the issue of the scope for positive action under EU law. For further and more detailed commentary see, for example, ANNE PETERS, 'The Many Meanings of Equality and Positive Action in Favour of Women under European Community Law – A Conceptual Analysis', *European Law Journal*, Vol. 2, No. 2, 1996, 177; SANDRA FREDMAN, 'Affirmative Action and the European Court of Justice: A Critical Analysis', in: Jo Shaw (ed.) *Social Law and Policy in an Evolving European Union*, Hart, 2000, 171; DAGMAR SCHIEK, 'Positive Action before the European Court of Justice – New Conceptions of Equality in Community Law? From *Kalanke* and *Marschall* to *Badeck*', *The International Journal of Comparative Labour Law and Industrial Relations*, Vol. 16, Nr. 3, 2000, 251; CHRISTA TOBLER, *Positive Action under the revised Second Equal Treatment Directive*, Paper presented to the European Congress on Gender Equality and Professional Life – Current Developments in Europe, organized by the Association Française des Femmes Juristes and the European Women Lawyers Association, Paris, 20 and 21 September 2002.

Instead, the goal of EU law is to prohibit and combat discrimination based on sex, irrespective of whether the victim is male or female. As a result, any measure that is designed to advantage, or address the discrimination experienced by women, can be regarded as suspect, and as potentially discriminating against men. Nevertheless, in recognition of the fact that some groups can be particularly disadvantaged, EU law does allow for positive action in some circumstances. However, even the EU law provision allowing for positive action is framed in a gender-neutral way. These aspects of EU equality law are explored further below.

The basic legal framework with regard to positive action is established by a number of Council directives and the Treaty on the Functioning of the European Union (TFEU), as well as related case law of the Court of Justice. In essence, these instruments allow Member States to permit positive action in favour of either women or men within certain limits. However, EU Member States cannot allow positive action which exceeds the limits established by EU law; but, there is also no obligation on them to allow the maximum scope for positive action as provided for under EU law, and it is compatible with EU law to impose further restrictions on positive action which are not required under EU law.

Positive action was first addressed in the original Gender Equal Treatment Directive,[30] which prohibited employment discrimination, and provided an exception from the prohibition of discrimination for positive action measures in Article 2(4): 'this Directive shall be without prejudice to measures to promote equal opportunity for men and women, in particular by removing existing inequalities which affect women's opportunities ...'. This early provision reveals the already mentioned essential element of the EU's approach to positive action: there is no obligation on Member States, or other parties, to permit or adopt positive action measures. Instead, as De Vos has noted: 'The Community's [now EU's LW] positive action provisions provide Member States with a policy option which, within the general limits [established by EU law, LW], is essentially used at their discretion.'[31]

The Court of Justice (henceforth: Court) has had various opportunities to consider the meaning of Article 2(4) of the Equal Treatment Directive.[32] In its first decision on the issue, *Kalanke*, the Court stressed that 'as a derogation from an individual right laid down in the Directive, Article 2(4) must be interpreted

---

[30] Council Directive 76/207/EEC on the Implementation of the Principle of Equal Treatment for Men and Women as Regards Access to Employment, Vocational Training and Promotion, and Working Conditions, [1976] OJ L.39/40.

[31] MARC DE VOS, *Beyond Formal Equality: Positive Action under Directives 2000/43/EC and 200/78/EC*, Directorate General for Employment, Social Affairs, and Equal Opportunities, 2007 at 38.

[32] See C-450/93, *Kalanke v Freie Hansestadt Bremen*, [1995] ECR I-3069; C-409/97, *Marschall v Land Nordrhein-Westfalen*, [1997] ECR I-6363; C-158/97, *Badeck v Hessischer Ministerpräsident*, [2000] ECR I-1875; C-407/98, *Abrahamsson and Anderson v Fogelqvist*, [2000] ECR I-5539; Case C-476/99, *Lommers v Ministerie van Landbouw, Natuurbeheer en Visserij*, [2002] ECR I-2891. All these cases are discussed below.

strictly.'[33] *Kalanke* concerned a local law[34] which provided that, in cases where women were under-represented within certain functions within the public sector,[35] female applicants who were equally qualified to male applicants were to be given automatic priority in the allocation of jobs. This did not provide for a system of strict quotas in favour of women, but for a 'system of quotas dependent on candidates' abilities. Women enjoy[ed] no priority unless the candidates of both sexes [we]re equally qualified.'[36] In deciding the case, the Court first concluded that '[a] national rule that, when men and women who are candidates for the same promotion are equally qualified, women are automatically to be given priority in sectors where they are under-represented, involves discrimination on grounds of sex.'[37] The Court then considered whether the measure was nevertheless 'saved' by Article 2(4) of the Directive, and therefore permitted. The Court noted that '[t]hat provision is specifically and exclusively designed to allow measures which, although discriminatory in appearance, are in fact intended to eliminate or reduce actual instances of inequality which may exist in the reality of social life'.[38] National measures which give 'a specific advantage to women with a view to improving their ability to compete on the labour market and to pursue a career on an equal footing with men'[39] are therefore permitted; however '[n]ational rules which guarantee absolute and unconditional priority for appointment or promotion go beyond promoting equal opportunities and overstep the limits of the exception in Article 2(4) of the Directive'.[40] Moreover, 'such a system substitutes for equality of opportunity as envisaged in Article 2(4) the result which is only to be arrived at by providing such equality of opportunity'.[41] As a consequence, the Court found the relevant law to be incompatible with the Directive on the ground that it discriminated against men.

Two years later, in the *Marshall* judgment, the Court elaborated on its position. The *Marshall* case concerned a challenge to a similar local law. However, unlike in *Kalanke*, the relevant law provided that, in situations of under-representation, women were to be given priority for appointment or promotion over equally qualified men, 'unless reasons specific to an individual [male] candidate tilt the balance in his favour.'[42] The Court found that the inclusion of this 'saving clause' rendered the provision compatible with the

---

[33] *Kalanke*, ibid., p. 3078.
[34] Bremen Law on Equal Treatment for Men and Women in the Public Service.
[35] Under-representation was deemed to exist when women did not make up at least half of the staff in the individual pay brackets in the relevant personnel group or in the functions levels.
[36] *Kalanke*, para. 8.
[37] *Kalanke*, para. 16.
[38] *Kalanke*, para. 18.
[39] *Kalanke*, para. 19.
[40] *Kalanke*, para. 22.
[41] *Kalanke*, para. 23.
[42] *Marschall*, para. 3.

Directive. The Court did not find that the provision exceeded the limits of Article 2(4) of the Directive since, 'in each individual case, it provides for male candidates who are equally as qualified as female candidates a guarantee that the candidatures will be the subject of an objective assessment which will take account of all criteria specific to the individual candidates and will override the priority accorded to female candidates where one or more of those criteria tilt the balance in favour of the male candidate.'[43]

Whilst the Court has consistently maintained since *Kalanke* that it will not accept positive action schemes based on gender that produce 'equal results' through automatic mechanisms at the selection stage, it has been willing to permit a range of positive action measures, including strict quotas, prior to the point of employment selection. For example, in the later case of *Badeck* the Court was prepared to accept measures which imposed a strict quota reserving at least 50% of training places for women, and requiring at least 50% of all candidates invited to interview to be women.[44]

The Court has also addressed positive action in the context of working conditions. In *Lommers*, which concerned a provision which offered female staff access to childcare facilities, but only allowed male staff such access in situations of 'emergency', the Court held that 'it is not places of employment which are reserved for women but enjoyment of certain working conditions designed to facilitate their pursuit of, and progression in, their careers …'.[45] The Court regarded this measure as forming 'part of the restricted concept of equality of opportunity',[46] which was allowed under Article 2(4). Again, the fact that men were not automatically excluded from accessing the benefit, but could do so in situations of 'emergency', was regarded as important in finding that the scheme was compatible with the Directive.

The original Equal Treatment Directive, which contained Article 2(4), has now been replaced by the 'Recast' Directive,[47] which codifies all of the older gender equality employment directives. Article 2(4) has been deleted, and instead all gender based employment positive action schemes now find their legal foundation in Article 157(4) TFEU.[48] This latter Article was inserted into the EC (now TFEU) Treaty as a result of the Treaty of Amsterdam, and was originally numbered Article 141(4) EC. The Article provides: 'with a view to ensuring full equality in practice between men and women in working life, the principle of equal treatment shall not prevent any Member State from

---

[43] *Marschall*, para. 33.
[44] *Badeck*, paras. 55 and 63.
[45] *Lommers*, para. 38.
[46] Ibid.
[47] Directive 2006/54/EC on the implementation of the principle of equal opportunities and equal treatment of men and women in matters of employment and occupation (recast), [2006] OJ L 204/23.
[48] See Article 3 of the 'Recast' Directive.

maintaining or adopting measures providing for specific advantages in order to make it easier for the under-represented sex to pursue a vocational activity or to prevent or compensate for disadvantages in professional careers.' Although this provides a more positive formulation than that found in Article 2(4), the Court's interpretation of Article 141(4) EC (now Art. 157(4) TFEU) suggests it does not significantly increase the scope for positive action. In *Abrahamsson*, which was decided on the basis of Article 141(4) as well as Article 2(4) of the Equal Treatment Directive, the Court ruled as impermissible a positive action scheme that provided automatic priority for women who possessed 'sufficient qualifications for the post'[49] in the case of appointments where women were under-represented in the relevant section (*in casu* university professors at a Swedish university). Notably, this ruling also applied to posts which had been created as part of a specific programme allowing for the application of positive action measures.

In conclusion, EU law allows Member States a fair amount of scope to adopt positive action measures in favour of women with regard to employment; however, the scope is not unlimited. Quota schemes, which automatically reserve a percentage of employment positions for women seem to be incompatible with EU law where they concern jobs, although the Court has taken a more relaxed attitude to quotas for training positions. Moreover, again in the context of (permanent) jobs,[50] schemes that automatically favour female applicants over equally qualified male applicants breach EU law. In short, schemes that provide for positive action at the point of selection must be *flexible* in nature and guarantee an *objective and individual* assessment of all candidates.[51] The case law suggests that the Court is prepared to accept measures which are designed to facilitate equality of opportunity, within limits, but measures designed to achieve equality of results fall outside the scope for action permitted under EU law.

---

[49] Notably, this was not a scheme which only required that women be appointed in case of equal qualification, but also in case of 'sufficient' qualification, meaning that, as part of a positive action programme, a less qualified female candidate could be appointed in preference to a better qualified male candidate. However, the provision in question required that positive action must not be applied where the difference in the candidates' qualification was so great that such application would give rise to a breach of the requirement of objectivity in the making of appointments (para. 14).

[50] In *Badeck* binding targets (or quotas), for temporary posts in the academic service and for academic assistants, which were based on the percentage of women among graduates, holders of higher degrees and students within each discipline were regarded as acceptable. This amounted to 'using an actual fact as a quantitative criterion for giving preference to women'. Para. 42.

[51] *Marschall*, para. 35.

5. A COMPARISON: THE OBLIGATION TO ADOPT TEMPORARY SPECIAL MEASURES UNDER THE CONVENTION AND THE LIMITS TO POSITIVE ACTION UNDER EU LAW

The above analysis has revealed that the adoption of temporary special measures is an obligation under the Convention, when this is necessary to meet the substantive obligations which States parties have accepted by ratifying the Convention, including with regard to employment,[52] and that the adoption of positive action 'with a view to ensuring full equality in practice' is permitted under EU law, subject to limitations as established by the Court of Justice. To be compatible with EU law, positive action measures with regard to recruitment must guarantee an objective and individual assessment of all candidates, and not discriminate against men (or women). Many forms of temporary special measures, such as outreach and support programmes, the allocation of resources, and proactive measures to encourage more women to apply for high-ranking posts seem to be fully compatible with EU law, and in that respect no potential conflicts arise between the Convention and the EU law obligations which EU Member States are subject to.

The issue becomes more vexed when quota schemes are at issue. As revealed by the analysis of EU legislation and case law, quota schemes that automatically reserve a percentage of employment positions for women seem to be incompatible with EU law where they concern jobs, although the Court has taken a more relaxed attitude to quotas for training positions. However, this limitation on the competence of EU Member States to adopt or sanction positive action in the form of an employment quota, may sit uneasily with obligations those same States have accepted under the Convention, or at least with the expectations of the Committee on the Elimination of Discrimination against Women. The Committee, in its Concluding Observations on individual States, has recommended to a number of EU Member States that they consider adopting quota schemes in the context of employment. For example, in 2009 the Committee 'recommended' that Spain gave 'consideration to the further implementation of temporary special measures, including [...] the setting of time-bound goals and quota, in areas where women are underrepresented or disadvantaged'.[53] A similar recommendation had already been made to the United Kingdom in 2008.[54] In 2009, the Committee also 'urged' Germany 'to

---

[52] See Article 11 of the Convention.
[53] UN doc. CEDAW/C/ESP/CO/6, *Concluding Observations of the Committee on the Elimination of Discrimination of Women, Spain*, 7 August 2009, para. 16.
[54] UN doc. CEDAW/C/UK/CO/6, *Concluding Observations of the Committee on the Elimination of Discrimination of Women, United Kingdom of Great Britain and Northern Ireland*, 10 July 2008, para. 269.

establish concrete goals, such as quotas and timetables, to accelerate the achievement of substantive equality between women and men in relevant areas in the Convention'.[55] Meanwhile, in 2008, the Committee 'recommended' to Sweden that it 'further include in its gender equality legislation provisions to mandate the use of temporary special measures, including goals or quotas, enhanced by a system of incentives, in both the public and the private sector'.[56] The Committee clearly assumes that EU Member States, which are also States parties to the Convention, have available to them the full arsenal of temporary special measures or positive action measures, and that all such measures, including employment quotas, can and should be used where necessary. However, as revealed, EU Member States may not have the freedom to adopt all forms of positive action and to follow up in full on the recommendations of the Committee. In conclusion, with regard to one narrow form of positive action, namely employment quotas, EU Member States may find themselves unable to act on the Committee's recommendations with a view to implementing the Convention without breaching EU law. However, a wide range of 'milder' positive action or temporary special measures remain available to EU Member States, and no potential conflict between the Convention and EU law arises with regard to such instruments.

---

[55] UN doc. CEDAW/C/DEU/CO/6, *Concluding Observations of the Committee on the Elimination of Discrimination of Women, Germany*, 12 February 2009, para. 26.

[56] UN doc. CEDAW/C/SWE/CO/7, *Concluding Observations of the Committee on the Elimination of Discrimination of Women, Sweden*, 8 April 2008, para. 25.

ARTICLE 5

States parties shall take all appropriate measures:

(a) To modify the social and cultural patterns of conduct of men and women, with a view to achieving the elimination of prejudices and customary and all other practices which are based on the idea of the inferiority or the superiority of either of the sexes or on stereotyped roles for men and women;
(b) To ensure that family education includes a proper understanding of maternity as a social function and the recognition of the common responsibility of men and women in the upbringing and development of their children, it being understood that the interest of the children is the primordial consideration in all cases.

CHAPTER 6
USING CULTURE TO ACHIEVE EQUALITY

Ingrid WESTENDORP

1. INTRODUCTION

Although the extent and seriousness may vary, worldwide women face discrimination because of their gender irrespective of whether they live in developed or developing States.[1] Almost everywhere this form of discrimination and lack of equality is characterized by a huge contrast between the formal, legal situation and the actual situation in practice. International, regional and national laws and regulations have been adopted and on paper women seem to have become men's equals. Authorities think that their work is done and they leave it to the individual woman to realize the rights that she is entitled to. The crux of the matter is, however, that the barrier that stands between theory and practice is to be found in people's perception; the existing image of how women and men should behave in society, which roles they should play and which characteristics befit either gender. As long as this barrier has not been demolished, women will fight an uphill battle. They are caught between their own and their family's/community's prejudices and expectations on the one hand and their human needs, entitlements, ambitions and capacities on the other. That is why Article 5 of the Women's Convention plays a vital part. As long as harmful traditions and stereotyped gender patterns are not replaced by new customs and traditions that are based on the idea of gender equality, women's human rights will remain a dead letter.

---

[1] The term gender is understood as a set of supposed differences society uses in order to distinguish between women and men. These supposed differences find their basis in the fact that certain characteristics, roles, and abilities are ascribed to either of the sexes as if they were general, inherent, and unchangeable. It is remarkable to notice that irrespective of cultural differences or geographic locations, similar patterns and stereotypical ideas about men and women have developed all over the world. Also see RIKKI HOLTMAAT and JONNEKE NABER, *Women's Human Rights and Culture: From Deadlock to Dialogue*, Intersentia, Antwerp, 2011, p. 31.

However, culture, tradition and custom should not be regarded as negative powers that by definition victimize girls and women. Being part of a group's culture may give a sense of safety and belonging, while some customs may be to women's advantage and should be preserved. Furthermore, while the current culture may appear to be fixed and uncompromising, in fact culture is by nature flexible and dynamic and can and will change over time due to all kinds of influences. Individual women as well as national and international women's organizations and organs such as CEDAW that are bent on achieving equality, should make use of this natural progress to turn culture and custom in such a way that harmful traditions are replaced by beneficial practices. That is why the central question of this Chapter is how culture could be used as an instrument to achieve equality for women and who should be the actors.

First, the content and unique meaning of Article 5 will be discussed by having a look at the *travaux préparatoires* and the connection with Article 2(f) of the Convention. In Section 3 the implementation of Article 5 on the national level will be explored. CEDAW plays an important role in advising States on the measures that could be taken. Recent advice given in Concluding Observations on State reports will be examined and analyzed. In Section 4 the different sides to culture will be central. First the reasons why culture may form a barrier to the realization of women's human rights will be examined and next suggestions will be given for further measures that may bend culture in the direction of gender equality. The last sub-section will go into the actors that should be recruited to bring this change of direction about. The Chapter will end with a brief conclusion.

2. CONTENT AND MEANING OF ARTICLE 5: INTRODUCTION

The idea that prejudice and harmful practices need to be eradicated in order to achieve equality between men and women was already included in the Declaration on the Elimination of Discrimination against Women, drafted by the UN Commission on the Status of Women and adopted by the UN General Assembly in 1967.[2] The text of Article 3 of this Declaration reads: 'All appropriate measures shall be taken to educate public opinion and to direct national aspirations towards the eradication of prejudice and the abolition of customary and all other practices which are based on the idea of the inferiority of women.'

From the *travaux préparatoires* of the Women's Convention it becomes clear that the first paragraph of Article 5 of the Women's Convention was met with

---

[2] UN doc. A/RES/2263, XXII, 7 November 1967.

much assent. In the first draft, which was proposed by the Philippines,[3] already the basis was laid for the final text. The original proposal read: 'State parties undertake to adopt immediate, effective appropriate measures, particularly in the fields of teaching, education, culture and information, with a view to educating public opinion and to directing national aspirations towards the eradication of prejudice and the abolition of customary and all other practices which are based on the idea of inferiority of women.'

More discussion was needed as regards the second paragraph of Article 5 since some States wanted to stress the social value of motherhood, while others felt that this would maintain women and men in complementary roles which might work to women's disadvantage because of their association with caregiving work. Finally, consensus could be achieved over the text that the upbringing and development of children is the responsibility of both fathers and mothers.[4]

Article 5 does not stand on its own; it is a logical sequence of Article 2(f) of the Women's Convention in which it is stipulated that equality of women should be achieved both *de iure* and *de facto*.[5] In indicating that *de facto* equality must be one of the two goals and that to achieve this goal all appropriate measures have to be taken, Article 2(f) forms the basis for the legal and extra-legal measures that must be taken in order to realize the obligations ensuing from Article 5.[6] That is why State parties that have made a reservation to Article 5, but not to Article 2(f) are not exempted from abolishing discriminatory cultural rules, for if they do not tackle customs that have a negative impact on women's equality, they will violate their obligation to achieve *de facto* equality.

Up till now, CEDAW has not yet adopted a specific General Recommendation on Article 5. The composition of the Committee, with members from different cultural backgrounds, makes the subject matter of Article 5 a delicate topic about which it may be difficult to reach consensus. Article 5 and its importance

---

[3] UN doc. E/CN.6/573 of 6 November 1973.
[4] LARS ADAM REHOF, *Guide to the Travaux Préparatoires of the United Nations Convention on the Elimination of All Forms of Discrimination Against Women*, Martinus Nijhoff Publishers, Dordrecht, 1993, pp. 77–88.
[5] The exact text of Article 2(f) reads: 'State parties condemn discrimination against women in all its forms, agree to pursue by all appropriate means and without delay a policy of eliminating discrimination against women and, to this end, undertake: [...] (f) To take all appropriate measures, including legislation, to modify or abolish existing laws, regulations, customs and practices which constitute discrimination against women'.
[6] This is also the opinion of Rebecca Cook who states that Articles 2(f) and 5(a) combined 'strongly reinforce the commitment to eliminate all forms of discrimination, since many pervasive forms of discrimination against women rest not on law as such but on legally tolerated customs and practices of national institutions'. She explicitly mentions personal law systems and religious institutions. REBECCA COOK, 'State Accountability Under the Convention on the Elimination of All Forms of Discrimination Against Women', in: Rebecca J. Cook (ed.), *Human Rights of Women, National and International Perspectives*, University of Pennsylvania Press, Philadelphia, 1994, pp. 239–240.

are mentioned, however, in several General Recommendations and the last few years CEDAW pays explicit attention to Article 5 in the majority of the Concluding Observations on individual State reports.[7]

Another human rights provision that explicitly calls upon States to interfere in cultural patterns, albeit under particular and restricted circumstances, is Article 24(3) of the Convention of the Rights of the Child.[8] In the relevant paragraph it is stipulated that: 'State parties shall take all effective and appropriate measures with a view to abolishing traditional practices prejudicial to the health of children'. Since virtually all States in the world are party to this Convention,[9] and no explicit reservations have been made as to this specific paragraph of Article 24,[10] it may be assumed that there is a worldwide consensus that under certain conditions it is acceptable to forego tradition, as part of culture, in the interest of a person's human rights. From the *travaux préparatoires* it becomes clear that 'health' is to be interpreted rather broadly. It would include, for instance, the traditional practice of son preference.[11] The phrase 'all effective and appropriate measures' to achieve this goal seems to be more focused on a change of mentality than on justiciable rules.[12]

An important soft law provision giving precedence to human rights to cultural patterns in case of a possible clash may be found in Article 4 of the Declaration on the Elimination of Violence against Women, which reads in part: 'States should condemn violence against women and should not invoke any custom, tradition or religious consideration to avoid their obligations with respect to its elimination.'[13]

---

[7] See sub-section 3.1 of this Chapter.

[8] Although the CRC has not (yet) adopted a specific General Comment on Article 24, this provision is one of the subjects under scrutiny in General Comment No. 4, Adolescent health and development in the context of the Convention on the Rights of the Child, UN doc. CRC/GC/2003/4, 1 July 2003. Particularly relevant is para. 24 of this document which reads: In light of Articles 3, 6, 12, 19 and 24(3) of the Convention, State parties should take all effective measures to eliminate all acts and activities which threaten the right to life of adolescents, including honour killings. The Committee strongly urges State parties to develop and implement awareness-raising campaign, education programmes and legislation aimed at changing prevailing attitudes, and address gender roles and stereotypes that contribute to harmful traditional practices. [...]'.

[9] In October 2011 193 States had ratified the Convention on the Rights of the Child. Only two States have only signed and not ratified the Convention. These are the United States of America and Somalia. See Status of ratification of the Convention on the Rights of the Child at www.treaties.un.org/Pages/ViewDetails.aspx?src=TREATY&mtdsg_no=IV-11&chapter=4&lang=en, consulted on 13 October 2011.

[10] See overview of Declarations and reservations to the Convention on the Rights of the Child, www.treaties.un.org/Pages/ViewDetails.aspx?src=TREATY&mtdsg_no=IV-11&chapter=4&lang=en, consulted on 13 October 2011.

[11] SHARON DETRICK, *A Commentary on the United Nations Convention on the Rights of the Child*, Kluwer Law International, The Hague, 1999, pp. 414–419.

[12] JAN WILLEMS, *Wie zal de Opvoeders Opvoeden? Kindermishandeling en het Recht van het Kind op* Persoonsworking, T.M.C. Asser Press, The Hague, 1998, p. 950.

[13] UN doc. A/RES/48/104, Declaration on the Elimination of Violence against Women, 20 December 1993.

More general human rights provisions may also entail an obligation to dispose of harmful traditions should these prevent the realization of a person's human rights. The Human Rights Committee for one interprets Article 3 ICCPR on equality rights between women and men in this sense. In General Comment No. 28 the HRC points out that the inequality of women is embedded in tradition, history, and culture including religion. States parties have the obligation to ensure that tradition, and religious or cultural rules are not used as justifications for violations of women's right to equality before the law or of the equal enjoyment of the rights contained in the Covenant. States parties should specifically mention in their reports to the Committee which measures they have taken to eradicate such practices.[14] Thus the HRC clearly puts the universal human right principle of equality as contained in Article 3 of the ICCPR above cultural prescriptions. This seems a logical choice since the object and purpose of the provision is to achieve *de iure* and *de facto* equality and the latter is impossible if cultural patterns are maintained that refer women to a subordinate position in society and that deny them the full realization of the rights they are entitled to under the Covenant.

The CESCR is not as explicit in its General Comment No. 16 on Article 3 of the ICESCR. Although it is admitted that women are often denied equal enjoyment of economic, social and cultural rights because of tradition and custom, and it is stressed that the mandate of Article 3 is to achieve *de facto* equality in addition to *de iure* equality, there is no clear requirement to eradicate harmful traditional practices. That abolition of such practices may be warranted may be inferred from the statement that in order to achieve substantive equality, States parties are expected to concern themselves with the effects of laws, policies, and *practices*, and to ensure that they do not uphold, but rather alleviate, the inherent disadvantage that particular groups experience.[15]

In conclusion it may be said that Article 5 of the Women's Convention, albeit the most explicit and comprehensive, is not the only legally binding treaty provision that demands the abolition of cultural patterns if these inhibit the enjoyment of universal human rights and in particular the right to equality.

3. IMPLEMENTATION ON THE DOMESTIC LEVEL

In order to implement Article 5 on the domestic level States are under the obligation to take 'all appropriate measures'. Obviously, States are already under an obligation to take legal measures to promote and guarantee equality between

---

[14] CCPR General Comment No. 28, Equality of Rights between Men and Women (art. 3), 2000, para. 5.
[15] CESCR General Comment No. 16, Article 3: the equal right of men and women to the enjoyment of all economic, social and cultural rights, 13 May 2005, paras. 5–8.

men and women since this ensues from Article 2, but it is rather vague which other, extra-legal measures have to be taken especially since these should be measures that are appropriate to modify social and cultural patterns of conduct. From the draft versions of the Article it appears that the drafters were thinking of public education and information. In the next sub-section it will be explored which kind of measures CEDAW advises States parties to take.[16]

3.1. APPROPRIATE MEASURES ACCORDING TO CEDAW

Which 'appropriate' measures are recommended by CEDAW may be gleaned from examining the Committee's Concluding Observations.[17] In many comments, Article 5 is discussed under the heading of 'stereotypes and practices that are harmful for women'. It is clear that CEDAW is acutely aware of the fact that the fulfilment of Article 5 is crucial for the realization of many if not all substantive human rights that are contained in the Women's Convention since the necessity to eradication harmful practices is also frequently discussed in sections that concern the right to education (not only as regards girls' and women's access to education,[18] but also in respect of the importance to eradicate educational segregation that keeps women in traditional fields of education and vocational training);[19] the right to employment (in particular the horizontal and vertical segregation of the labour market that finds women in low paid and part-time jobs and the omnipresent and persistent gender wage-gap between men and women);[20] political participation, including decision-making on the local level;[21]

---

[16] For the purpose of this section Concluding Observations by CEDAW between 2006 and 2011 have been studied. The author has chosen a mix of States in all continents of the world, with different cultures and different stages of development: Albania (2010), Argentina (2010), Australia (2010), Bangladesh (2011), Belarus (2011), Botswana (2010), Burkina Faso (2010), China (2006), Cuba (2006), Denmark (2006), Egypt (2010), Fiji (2010), Germany (2009), India (2007), Indonesia (2007), Israel (2011), Kenya (2011), Liechtenstein (2011), Malawi (2010), Mexico (2006), The Netherlands (2010), Panama (2010), Papua New Guinea (2010), Russian Federation (2010), Rwanda (2009), South Africa (2011), Sri Lanka (2011), Sweden (2008), Tunisia (2010), Turkey (2010), Uganda (2010), Ukraine (2010), United Arab Emirates (2010), Uzbekistan (2010).

[17] Since 2008 the Concluding Observations are neatly arranged which makes it easier to find the Committee's comments and advice in respect of combating traditional gender roles.

[18] For instance as regards Albania, Burkina Faso, Egypt, Kenya, and Uganda.

[19] For instance with regard to Argentina, Belarus, Germany, Liechtenstein, The Netherlands, Russian Federation, and Sri Lanka.

[20] For instance in the Concluding Observations on Australia, Belarus, Denmark, Germany, Israel, Liechtenstein, The Netherlands, Russian Federation, Sri Lanka, and Sweden.

[21] In Liechtenstein women are underrepresented in all political organs. None of the current mayors is female. The State party's explanation for this fact is that women are often too burdened with professional and family duties to take part in political life. UN doc. CEDAW/C/LIE/CO/4, Concluding Observations, Liechtenstein, 5 April 2011, paras. 28 and 29. Also see the comments on Belarus, Russian Federation, and Sri Lanka.

rights in respect of marriage and family life;[22] and women's right to land and property, in particular traditional practices that deny women ownership of land and refuse them a part of the inheritance.[23] Furthermore, in many comments CEDAW points out the connection between stereotypes and traditional gender roles and the occurrence of violence against women, in particular domestic violence.[24]

In many cases, CEDAW expresses its concern 'about the persistence of patriarchal attitudes and deep-rooted stereotypes concerning women's roles and responsibilities that discriminate against women and perpetuate their subordination within the family and society. It notes that such discriminatory attitudes and stereotypes constitute serious obstacles to women's enjoyment of their human rights and the fulfilment of the rights enshrined in the convention.'[25] Usually, CEDAW will subsequently call upon the State party to adopt a comprehensive plan or strategy that is in conformity with the obligations under Articles 2(f) and 5(a).[26] Occasionally, it is explicitly mentioned that such an approach encompasses the abolition or modification of discriminatory legislation or adoption of new legislation explicitly giving equal right to

---

[22] Harmful practices that discriminate against women both during marriage and at the dissolution of marriage exist in abundance. Polygamy, bride price, early marriages, forced and arranged marriages all undermine women's human rights. Furthermore, men are still regarded as the breadwinners and heads of the family, while women are expected to stay at home to do the household chores and raise the children which prevents them to develop and use all their capacities. See *e.g.* the comments on Indonesia, Papua New Guinea, and the Russian Federation. In Israel, traditional religious laws govern all marriages and divorces. For the Jewish part of the population (which is everyone of Jewish descent both religious and not religious) the rule that men have the unilateral power to divorce (grant the 'get') is applied without exception. UN doc. CEDAW/C/ISR/CO/5, Concluding Observations, Israel, 5 April 2011, paras. 48 and 49.

[23] See for example the comments on Bangladesh, Botswana, Burkina Faso, Fiji, India, Kenya, Malawi, Papua New Guinea, South Africa, Sri Lanka and Uganda. A very interesting example is that CEDAW emphasizes that one of the causes of witch-hunting in India would be control over land by men. UN doc. CEDAW/C/IND/CO/3, Concluding Comments, India, 2 February 2007, para. 27.

[24] Concern that patriarchal attitudes and deep-rooted stereotypes form a root cause for the persistence of violence against women in general and domestic violence in particular is for instance expressed by CEDAW in its Concluding Observations on Cuba, Egypt, Fiji, Kenya, Malawi, Mexico, Russian Federation, and Uzbekistan.

[25] This particular quote has been taken from the Concluding Observations on Botswana, UN doc. CEDAW/C/BOT/CO/3, Concluding Observations, Botswana, 26 March 2010, para. 23.

[26] *E.g.*: UN doc. CEDAW/C/ARG/CO/6, Concluding Observations, Argentina, 16 August 2010, para. 18; UN doc. CEDAW/C/BOT/CO/3, Concluding Observations, Botswana, 26 March 2010, para. 24; UN doc. CEDAW/C/BFA/CO/6, Concluding Observations, Burkina Faso, 5 November 2010, para. 20; UN doc. CEDAW/C/CUB/CO/6, Concluding Observations, Cuba, 25 August 2006, para. 18; UN doc. CEDAW/C/KEN/CO/7, Concluding Observation, Kenya, 5 April 2011, para. 18; UN doc. CEDAW/C/MWI/CO/6, Concluding Observations, Malawi, 5 February 2010, para. 20; UN doc. CEDAW/C/NLD/CO/5, Concluding Observations, The Netherlands, 5 February 2010, para. 25.

women.[27] In a few cases the Committee has recommended multi-cultural societies to intervene and change the customary laws and/or personal laws for certain societal groups and bring them in conformity with the obligations under the Convention. This was for instance done in the case of India even though the State party has made a reservation to Article 5.[28]

It is clear, however, that the main legal obligation under Article 5 pertains to the taking of extra-legal measures that target the existing inequality in practice. In conformity with the ideas that were already expressed during the drafting of the provision, CEDAW advises States parties to focus on teaching, both formal and informal education, and public information with the purpose of bringing about a change in mentality by creating awareness of, and developing understanding for, the equality between women and men and the need to eradicate gender stereotypes. According to the Committee, these educational and awareness-raising programmes should target a broad public covering children and adults of both sexes. In some cases, States parties are recommended to give specific training to teachers, the judiciary, the police, and local authorities including chiefs and other traditional or religious community leaders.[29] States may also be advised to conduct such programmes in collaboration with Civil Society Organizations (CSOs).[30] Sometimes, the State party is urged to revise the contents of textbooks for school children with the purpose of eradicating traditional role patterns and stereotypical images.[31]

---

[27] *E.g.*: UN doc. CEDAW/C/EGY/CO/7, Concluding Observations, Egypt, 5 February 2010, para. 22; UN doc. CEDAW/C/MWI/CO/6, Concluding Observations, Malawi, 5 February 2010, para. 20; UN doc. CEDAW/C/UGA/CO/7, Concluding Observations, Uganda, 5 November 2010, para. 20; UN doc. CEDAW/C/UZB/CO/4, Concluding Observations, Uzbekistan, 26 January 2010, para. 20.

[28] 'The Committee urges the State party to withdraw its reservations to Articles 5(a) and 16(1) and to proactively initiate and encourage debate within the relevant communities on gender equality and the human rights of women and in particular work with and support women's groups as members of these communities so as to [...] b) review and reform personal laws of different ethnic and religious groups to ensure *de iure* gender equality and compliance with the Convention.', UN doc. CEDAW/C/IND/CO/3, Concluding Comments, India, 2 February 2007, para. 11.

[29] *E.g.*: UN doc. CEDAW/C/ALB/CO/3, Concluding Observations, Albania, 16 September 2010, para. 25; UN doc. CEDAW/C/KEN/CO/7, Concluding Observation, Kenya, 5 April 2011, para. 18(a); UN doc. CEDAW/C/MWI/CO/6, Concluding Observations, Malawi, 5 February 2010, para. 2; UN doc. CEDAW/C/PNG/CO/3, Concluding Observations, Papua New Guinea, 30 July 2010, para. 24; UN doc. CEDAW/C/RWA/CO/6*, Concluding Observations, Rwanda, 8 September 2009, para. 22.

[30] *E.g.* in the case of Albania, Botswana, Egypt, Fiji, Liechtenstein, Papua New Guinea, Russian Federation, South Africa, Sri Lanka, Turkey, and Uganda.

[31] *E.g.*: UN doc. CEDAW/C/CHN/CO/6, Concluding Comments, China, 25 August 2006, para. 18; UN doc. CEDAW/C/ISR/CO/5, Concluding Observations Israel, 5 April 2011, para. 34; UN doc. CEDAW/C/UKR/CO/7, Concluding Observations, Ukraine, 28 January 2010, para. 24.

Much emphasis is put on the role of the media. States parties are requested to work with the media,[32] influence the media,[33] or use the media themselves[34] to abolish stereotypes and/or degrading images of women and instead portray girls and women in a positive, non-stereotypical, and non-discriminatory way.[35]

It is interesting to note that CEDAW only sporadically comments on the division of care-taking work between women and men. Some States parties are advised to enhance the role of fathers by adopting legislation and promoting the possibilities of taking parental leave for fathers and getting them more involved in the raising of their children.[36]

---

[32] *E.g.* UN doc. CEDAW/C/BGD/CO/7, Concluding Observations, Bangladesh, 22 March 2011, para. 18(b); UN doc. CEDAW/C/BLR/CO/7, Concluding Observations, Belarus, 6 April 2011, para. 18; UN doc. CEDAW/C/BOT/CO/3, Concluding Observations, Botswana, 26 March 2010, para. 24; UN doc. CEDAW/C/EGY/CO/7, Concluding Observations, Egypt, 5 February 2010, para. 22; UN doc. CEDAW/C/FJI/CO/4, Concluding Observations, Fiji, 16 September 2010, para. 21; UN doc. CEDAW/C/KEN/CO/7, Concluding Observation, Kenya, 5 April 2011, para. 18(c); UN doc. CEDAW/C/LIE/CO/4, Concluding Observations, Liechtenstein, 5 April 2011, para. 19(b).

[33] For instance in the case of Albania: While respecting the independence of the media and the right to freedom of expression, the media should be encouraged to project positive non-stereotypes images of women and of their equal status and role in the private and public spheres. UN doc. CEDAW/C/ALB/CO/3, Concluding Observations, Albania, 16 September 2010, para. 25; Or with regard to Sweden: The Committee calls upon the State party to strengthen its strategies to combat sexualisation of the public sphere and to take proactive measures to ensure that media production and coverage are non-discriminatory and increase awareness of these issues among media proprietors and other relevant actors in the industry. UN doc. CEDAW/C/SWE/CO/7, Concluding Observations, Sweden, 8 April 2008, para. 23.

[34] *E.g.*: UN doc. CEDAW/C/CHN/CO/6, Concluding Comments, China, 25 August 2006, para. 18; UN doc. CEDAW/C/CUB/CO/6, Concluding Comments, Cuba, 25 August 2006, para. 18.

[35] *E.g.*: UN doc. CEDAW/C/BOT/CO/3, Concluding Observations, Botswana, 26 March 2010, para. 24; UN doc. CEDAW/C/KEN/CO/7, Concluding Observation, Kenya, 5 April 2011, para. 18(c); UN doc. CEDAW/C/PNG/CO/3, Concluding Observations, Papua New Guinea, 30 July 2010, para. 26; UN doc. CEDAW/C/USR/CO/7, Concluding Observations, Russian Federation, 16 August 2010, para. 21; UN doc. CEDAW/C/ZAF/CO/4, Concluding Observations, South Africa, 5 April 2011, para. 21.

[36] *E.g.*: In the case of Albania: The Committee recommends '[…] promotion of sharing domestic and family responsibilities between women and men, *inter alia* through awareness-raising and education initiatives for both women and men on the adequate sharing of care of children and other dependent family members and domestic tasks.', UN doc. CEDAW/C/ALB/CO/3, Concluding Observations, Albania, 16 September 2010, para. 33; with regard to Sweden: 'The Committee recommends that the State party continue its efforts to ensure reconciliation of family and professional responsibilities and for the promotion of equal sharing of domestic and family tasks between women and men.', UN doc. CEDAW/C/SWE/CO/7, Concluding Observations, Sweden, 8 April 2008, para. 27; and on Tunisia: 'The Committee encourages the State party to step up its efforts to assist women and men in striking a balance between family and employment responsibilities through, *inter alia*, further awareness-raising and education initiatives for both women and men on adequate sharing of care of children and domestic tasks, as well as by providing men with the possibility and incentives, to take up part-time employment.', UN doc. CEDAW/C/TUN/CO/6, Concluding Observations, Tunisia, 5 November 2010, para. 45.

Particularly with regard to developing States, CEDAW occasionally takes the stance that culture should be treated as a dynamic concept. States parties should not hide behind cultural justifications treating tradition as fixed but instead they should move on, discarding or modifying practices that stand in the way of the realization of women's human rights.[37] States are strongly advised to enlist non-State actors such as CSOs, local authorities, and religious leaders to bring about such a change in culture.

3.2. SOME COMMENTS ON CEDAW'S CONCLUDING OBSERVATIONS

From the analysis of CEDAW's Concluding Observations both positive and negative aspects come to mind.

To this author it seems to be highly positive that attention to stereotypes and harmful practices is paid in a separate section of the Concluding Observations. This emphasizes the importance of Article 5 and stresses the legal obligation that is included in the provision. It is therefore a pity that the Committee is not consistent in devoting a separate section to Article 5. For instance, in the Concluding Observations concerning Australia (2010) and Israel (2011) such a section is lacking while at the same time it becomes obvious from the comments in sections on violence against women and on employment that stereotypes and traditional role patterns are pervasive in both countries and cause violations of women's human rights and in particular their right to equality.

While it is commendable that the Committee urges States to regard culture as a dynamic concept that is subject to change, it is difficult to understand why such an approach is only impressed upon a few developing States instead of on all States parties. Sadly not one State in the world can boast a culture that is based on gender equality which implies that culture needs to be changed everywhere. CEDAW's emphasis on developing States may give cause to friction and give the impression that harmful practices are only to be found in non-Western States. In fact, harmful stereotypes are also so ingrained in Western States that while at the

---

[37] On Botswana: 'The Committee urges the SP to view culture as a dynamic dimension of the country's life and social fabric, subject to many influences over time and therefore subject to change.', UN doc. CEDAW/C/BOT/CO/3, Concluding Observations, Botswana, 26 March 2010, para. 24; on Malawi: 'The Committee urges the State party to view culture as a dynamic dimension of the country's life and social fabric, subject to many influences over time and therefore to change', UN doc. CEDAW/C/MWI/CO/6, Concluding Observations, Malawi, 5 February 2010, para. 21; and on Papua New Guinea: 'The Committee invites the SP to view culture and tradition as dynamic aspects of the country's life and social fabric and therefore as subject to change.', UN doc. CEDAW/C/PNG/CO/3, Concluding Observations, Papua New Guinea, 30 July 2010, para. 26.

surface it may seem as if women are equal to men, the root causes of inequality between the sexes have not yet been adequately tackled let alone eradicated.[38]

It is a good thing that CEDAW takes a holistic approach and requests States parties to adopt a comprehensive plan or strategy that is in conformity with Articles 5 and 2(f). While it is clear that States have do draw up such strategies themselves since they know best which strategy is suitable in view of the particular national and cultural context, it is still a pity that the Committee remains unclear about the contents of such a plan or strategy and does not give any concrete suggestions. CEDAW calls upon States to come up with innovative measures to change attitudes, but fails to think beyond the beaten track of legislation, education and information.

The focus on the media seems justified. Television, radio, newspapers and internet to a great extent influence the way in which people perceive the world. The media can transmit traditional gender roles, but may also introduce new societal patterns and depict women and men in non-traditional ways. In addition to more 'modern' methods of information spreading, people's view of the world is also influenced by (traditional) stories,[39] plays, dances and songs.[40] States should not only be mindful of stereotyped television programmes, advertisements and commercials,[41] but also of the power of more traditional ways to convey and imprint gender stereotypical images.

---

[38] If the Special Rapporteur on violence against women, Radhika Coomaraswamy was right, and the main cause of gender-based violence is the unequal power relation between men and women, not much has changed in the Western world if the pervasiveness of violence against women, including domestic violence, is taken into consideration. See UN doc. E/CN.4/1995/42, Preliminary report by the Special Rapporteur on violence against women, its causes and consequences, 22 November 1994, paras. 49–57.
In addition, the huge income gap between men and women, the segregation in the labour market, and the large amount of part-time working mothers, pay witness to the unequal socio-economic position of women in the developed world.

[39] For instance Hindu epics like the Ramayana about Lord Rama and his wife Sita, and the story of the God Siva and his consort Sati, both depict the ideal woman as chaste, obedient and self-sacrificing – even to the extent that she is prepared to self-immolate in order to save the honour of her husband – while the ideal man is presented as a warrior. See COURTNEY W. HOWLAND, 'The Challenge of Religious fundamentalism to the Liberty and Equality Rights of Women: An Analysis Under the United Nations Charter', in: Susan Deller Ross (ed.), *Women's Human Rights: The International and Comparative Law Casebook*, University of Pennsylvania Press, Philadelphia, 2008, pp. 124–125.

[40] While traditional songs may surely perpetuate stereotypical behaviour, it is perhaps more worrisome that in some contemporary pop music such as hip hop and rap, denigrating terms for girls and women are used and violence against women is accepted or sometimes even glorified.

[41] In August 2011, one of my students, Benedicta Deogratias, conducted a short empirical research in respect of gender stereotyping in TV commercials. For a period of three days she watched all commercials that were shown between 20.30 and 22.30 hrs on one specific channel in the Netherlands. The outcome shows that more than 75% of the commercials contained stereotypical elements.

The fact that only sporadically attention is drawn to the role of fathers seems to be a missed chance. Only when household responsibilities including raising children are equally shared between women and men, and the perception of such tasks as inferior and women's work is abolished, will women get the chance to fully develop themselves and enjoy their human rights.

4. THE TWO FACES OF CULTURE[42]

Culture, in the sense of a comprehensive set of rules of acceptable societal behaviour, plays an important role in people's lives. The culture of the group in which a person is born will not only have a huge impact on the possibilities and chances that a person will get to develop her or himself, culture also gives people a sense of belonging, security, and of identity.[43] In this section, first the reasons are studied why culture may be a barrier that keeps women from realizing their right to equality. Next, the makeability of culture will be examined and the possibilities to introduce new customs and practices that are based on the idea of gender equality. In the last sub-section attention will be paid to the actors that may play a role in bending current unequal gender patterns in a new direction.

4.1. CULTURE AS A BARRIER

For many girls and women all over the world customs and traditional gender stereotypes form a barrier between their legal right to equality and the chances that they get to bring this right into practice. Their choices in life are limited because their families and communities already make certain choices for them in line with society's culturally determined expectations of women's role in the community. Girls' parents may consciously or unconsciously show that they favour their brothers because it has become custom that sons will take (financially) care of their parents in old age, or religious rules demand that only sons perform burial or cremation rituals, or simply because they have the feeling

---

[42] The term culture is very broad. In the Oxford Dictionary it is defined as: the arts and other manifestations of human intellectual achievement, but also as the ideas, customs and social behaviour of a particular people or society. Afkhami distinguishes 'the best in the arts, manners, literature, music, philosophy, science and all the other refined attributes that a civilization has achieved' and 'the concepts, habits, skills, instruments, institutions, etc. of a given people in a given period'. MAHNAZ AFKHAMI, 'Cultural Relativism and Women's Human Rights', in: Kelly D. Askin and Dorean M. Koenig (eds), *Women and International Human Rights Law*, Vol. 2, 1998, Transnational Publishers Inc., Ardsley, New York, p. 482.

[43] RIKKI HOLTMAAT and JONNEKE NABER, 2011, p. 33. Also ABDULLAHI AHMED AN-NA'IM and JEFFREY HAMMOND, 'Cultural Transformation and Human Rights in African Societies', in: Abdullahi A. An-Na'im (ed.), *Cultural Transformation and Human Rights in Africa*, Zed Books, London, 2002, p. 21.

that boys are worth more than girls because they are the future bread winners and leaders. Son preference may be expressed by better food, better health care and better schooling for boys.[44] Parents may also expect different behaviour from sons and daughters when they are children. Many girls are brought up with the idea that they should be modest, polite and obedient,[45] while boys may be encouraged to assert themselves and take command, and it may be tolerated that they show boisterous behaviour in games and sports. Both girls and boys are prompted to play gender appropriate games or play with gender appropriate toys, training them for their future roles in society.[46]

When girls approach adolescence, their sexuality may be viewed as potentially dangerous. In many societies girls are supposed to remain virgins till they marry, and married women must be chaste because the family's honour depends on their behaviour.[47] Boys' and men's sexuality is not seen as a problem, but they may have the task to control the sexuality of their female relatives.[48]

This gender stereotypical upbringing diminishes girls' equal chances to access education, or predestines them for certain types of vocational training. Furthermore, girls grow up with the notion that if they want a family, it will be their task to take care of the household and raise the children, and if they also wish to pursue a career, it is their problem as 'working' mothers to find a solution how to combine their manifold tasks.

Obviously, boys are also steered in a gender-specific direction. From an early age on, it is imprinted on them that they are to be the future breadwinners of their families. They have to enter the public sphere and make a career and it is not regarded as an acceptable option for them to stay at home to raise the children.

---

[44] For the effect of son preference on girls and women see *e.g.* CHRISTINA M. CERNA and JENNIFER C. WALLACE, 'Women and Culture', in: Kelly D. Askin and Dorean M. Koenig (eds.), *Women and International Human Rights Law*, Vol. 1, Transnational Publishers Inc., Ardsley, New York, 1999, pp. 630–634.

[45] Howland sees the obedience rule as a fundamental religious rule that has a severe impact on women's access to education and employment. COURTNEY W. HOWLAND, 2008, pp. 117–118.

[46] In Western countries it is striking to see that even the toy industry may apply sex segregation in respect of advertising their toys. Boys are encouraged to play with building blocks, cars and airplanes. For girls there are dolls, miniature kitchens, and pink vacuum cleaners and if they should have any ambition in the direction of building with bricks, special boxes for girls are provided – some of them even with pink bricks – around themes like playing house or taking care of animals.

[47] In some cultures the fear that a girl will lose her virginity and thus will become unmarriageable, will lead to the practice of early marriage with detrimental effects on a girl's right to education, employment and health due to early pregnancies. See *e.g.* CHRISTINA M. CERNA and JENNIFER C. WALLACE, 1999, p. 636.

[48] The burden is particularly heavy on the shoulders of under-age brothers or other male relatives who may be coerced into honour killings. KATHRYN CHRISTINE ARNOLD, 'Are the Perpetrators of Honor Killings Getting Away With Murder? Article 340 of the Jordanian Penal Code Analyzed Under the Convention on the Elimination of All Forms of Discrimination Against Women', *American University International Law Review* Vol. 16, no. 5, 2001, p. 1347.

Men are supposed to be suited for all kinds of professions that are thought to be unfitting or less suitable for women. Both women and men are prejudiced as regards which kind of work is 'female' or 'masculine' and on average, masculine work is valued more than female work.[49] As a result, work that is regarded as female is not as well paid or sometimes not paid at all,[50] and women will not become economically independent, but instead they will remain dependent on their fathers, partners or on welfare their whole life.[51] Similar patterns can be found in all States of the world in all kinds of communities, irrespective of their cultural or religious backgrounds. Obviously, there are gradations and differences in the ways in which women are discriminated against, but the patriarchal roots and stereotypes basically are the same and their effect is that stereotypical ideas are perpetuated irrespective of the existence of equal rights on paper.

For people who belong to a certain community, it may be very difficult to break with customs and traditions and to behave in a way that is different from what is expected of them. For girls and women it is many times more difficult not to behave in a culturally appropriate way than for boys and men, since girls and women are to a large extent dependent on their families or communities and in addition they may also have been taught that they have to uphold the family honour – they are regarded as the 'bearers' of culture – or that it is their divine duty to bear their lot. Indeed, if girls and women choose to turn their backs on cultural prescriptions and claim their human rights, they may be accused of betraying their family, community, religion or culture.[52] The ultimate result may be that they are ostracized which means that they can no longer fall back on the safety net of their family or community.[53]

---

[49] Especially low skilled or labour-intensive work that requires a lot of patience and manual dexterity is stereotypically viewed as 'women's work'. VALERIE L. OOSTERVELD, 'Women and Employment', in: Kelly D. Askin and Dorean M. Koenig (eds.), *Women and International Human Rights Law*, Vol. 1, Transnational Publishers Inc., Ardsley, New York, 1999, pp. 389–390.

[50] In addition to the unremunerated work women may do in their own household, many women are not paid for the work they do in the family business. See *e.g.* J.E. BIESHEUVEL-VERMEIJDEN, 'Loon naar Werken' (*To get what you deserve*)', in: A.W. Heringa, J. Hes, L. Lijnzaad (eds.), *Het Vrouwenverdrag: een beeld van een verdrag… (The Women's Convention: a picture of a treaty…)*, MAKLU Uitgevers, Antwerpen-Apeldoorn, 1994, p. 202.

[51] Typically, women will earn an 'individual' income, while men will earn a 'family' income since they are supposed to be the family's provider. OOSTERVELD, 1999, p. 389. SANDRA FREDMAN, *Discrimination Law*, Clarendon Law Series, Oxford University Press, Oxford, 2002, pp. 29–30.

[52] AYELET SHACHAR, *Multicultural Jurisdictions; Cultural Differences and Women's Rights*, Cambridge University Press, Cambridge, 2001, p. 39.

[53] Corinne Packer states that Sub-Saharan African women who are aware of their lower social status have no other option but to accept the *status quo* including harmful traditional practices since their low economic, financial and educational status makes it impossible for them to leave. CORINNE PACKER, *Using Human Rights to Change Tradition: Traditional Practices Harmful to Women's Reproductive Health in sub-Saharan Africa*, Intersentia, Antwerp, 2002, p. 48.

It is important to understand the motives why there is such a strong urge to cling to traditional practices and customs and to penalize those who wish to opt out because such understanding is essential for the possibilities of change. First of all, certain groups in society will have a vested interest to maintain the *status quo*. Men who take leadership positions, who traditionally are the land owners, the income generators and the ones who will receive the inheritance, may not wish to give up their privileged position and they may fear that their masculinity is under attack when women are claiming equal positions in society.[54] This also brings up the issue of who can rightfully claim that certain cultural practices should be maintained. Those who stake such claims may have vested interests in upholding them and they may not represent the sentiment of the cultural group as a whole.[55]

But it is not only men or the elite of a certain group that may oppose cultural change. Also women may be very hesitant to change cultural ways and especially religious customs. Many women derive their identity and security from being part of a cultural group.[56] They may be afraid of change or of taking financial responsibility, and some women also have an interest to maintain traditional practices such as circumcisers or wedding arrangers.[57] For groups that form a cultural, ethnic or religious community within a multicultural State, as well as for former colonies, the urge to stick to the old ways and traditions becomes like a sacred duty.[58] Also women, who understand that they are discriminated against within their own group, will defend their culture for fear of losing their identity and sense of belonging.

The interests of the State to maintain the *status quo* should also not be underestimated. Many States fail to understand the long term benefits of women participating equally in society, but only see the short term obstacles and costs for society. States may wish to be identified by their unique cultural identity even

---

54 RIKKI HOLTMAAT and JONNEKE NABER, 2011, pp. 72–73. FREDMAN, 2002, p. 30.
55 As Chanock puts it: 'There is a wide gap between those who speak for cultures and those who live the culture. The voices of the elites overwhelm the others. Culture tends to privilege some voices and patterns of acts while ignoring and marginalizing others.' MARTIN CHANOCK, 'Human Rights and Cultural Branding: Who Speaks and How', in: Abdullahi A. An-Na'im (ed.), *Cultural Transformation and Human Rights in Africa*, Zed Books Ltd, London, 2002, pp. 38–39. Also see RIKKI HOLTMAAT and JONNEKE NABER, 2011, p. 45.
56 FLORENCE BUTEGWA, 'Mediating Culture and Human Rights in Favour of Land Rights for Women in Africa: A Framework for Community-level Action', in: Abdullahi A. An-Na'im (ed.), *Cultural Transformation and Human Rights in Africa*, Zed Books, London, 2002, p. 109.
57 ISABELLE R. GUNNING, 'Women and Traditional Practices: Female Genital Surgery', in: Kelly D. Askin and Dorean M. Koenig (eds.), *Women and International Human Rights Law*, Vol. 1, Transnational Publishers Inc., Ardsley, New York, 1999, p. 659.
58 'Particularly formerly oppressed and colonized cultures demand that their own historical experiences and cultural differences be respected. It is this demand for parity of respect which underpins the stress on preservation of cultural differentiation, the invention of tradition and the imagining of communities.' CHANOCK, 2002, p. 53. For groups in multicultural societies see SHACHAR, 2001, p. 46.

if this entails maintaining an unequal position for women in their culture.[59] Moreover, women take a lot of important work on their shoulders that is unpaid such as taking care of children, the elderly and the sick. Work of great social value and necessity in every community, and it would cost an enormous amount of money if society would have to pay for it. What is forgotten, however, is that women as part of the workforce and as independent human beings who can take care of themselves and their family are of much more value to society and will actually contribute to a country's development and welfare.[60]

4.2. CULTURE AS AN INSTRUMENT OF CHANGE

While the current culture may seem to be permanent and rigid, in essence it is dynamic and it will change over time due to all kinds of influences.[61] Fredman suggests that what we need is transformative equality; a radical restructuring of society before true equality can be achieved.[62] This would not only involve the abolition of traditional practices and customs that negatively affect women's equality, but would also mean the introduction of completely new ideas, practices and customs that are based on gender equality.

It is a fallacy to suppose that gender equality already exists in the West or that it would be based on a Western tradition. In my opinion it is also a mistake to think that cultures are so diverse that universal agreement about women's rights would be impossible to achieve. What can be perceived at the moment is that irrespective of cultural diversity, worldwide a culture of discrimination against women has developed based on universal gender stereotypes and gender roles that deny women the right to develop themselves and use their full potential. What is needed is a strong promotion of a universal culture of gender equality until it becomes part of customary law and is regarded as so valuable and important that the prohibition of gender discrimination is accepted by States as a rule of *ius cogens*.

---

[59] RIKKI HOLTMAAT and JONNEKE NABER, 2011, p. 74.
[60] See *e.g.* UNDP, 'Human Development Indicators', in: *Human Development Report 2007–2008*, UNDP, New York, 2007, pp. 326–346.
[61] Cultural norms and habits will be discarded and replaced in response to changing socio-economic circumstances. FLORENCE BUTEGWA, 2002, p. 122.
[62] 'Instead of attempting to adapt members of under-represented groups better to fit in with the existing framework, it is crucial to transform the existing framework in order to reflect the norms of the excluded "other"'. SANDRA FREDMAN, 2002, pp. 193–194. Also SANDRA FREDMAN, 'Beyond the dichotomy of formal and substantive equality. Towards new definitions of equal rights', in: I. Boerefijn, F. Coomans, J. Goldschmidt, R. Holtmaat and Ria Wolleswinkel (eds.), *Temporary special measures. Accelerating de facto equality of women under Article 4(1) UN Convention on the Elimination of All Forms of Discrimination Against Women*, Intersentia, Antwerp, 2003, pp. 111–118, and RIKKI HOLTMAAT and JONNEKE NABER, *Women's Human Rights and Culture: From Deadlock to Dialogue*, Intersentia, Antwerp, 2011, pp. 26–27.

An-Na'im rightly claims that all States have to start by critically evaluating their own culture and determining to what extent they need to change it in order to bring it in conformity with human rights. To this end he recommends the use of internal discourse – implying that everybody in society should be involved in assessing cultural rules and traditions – and of cross-cultural dialogue since all cultures may learn from each other's experiences, and good practices in one State may be an inspiration to act along similar lines in another State.[63] While An-Na'im's theory may have some imperfections that make it difficult to put it to practice,[64] his point of departure that cultural assessment is necessary in every State is certainly a valuable notion and signifies that as far as the socio-economic position of women is concerned, no culture should feel superior or inferior to another.

Breaking through gendered patterns will necessitate the rearrangement of society and the development of a more flexible social structure. For instance, at the moment many Western societies rely on the traditional family model where men are the breadwinners who will leave the house in the morning for their remunerated employment only to return in the evening. Women predominantly stay at home to take care of the household, the children, the sick and the elderly and in addition struggle to combine all this with some income generating work. More flexibility in working hours and more and differently organized childcare services would facilitate the combination of raising children and remunerated employment for *all* parents.[65] If women participate as equals on the labour market and are able to contribute substantively to the financial costs of the family, this will make it possible for men to spend less hours on remunerated employment and instead get the chance to see their children grow up. Men should realize that they are missing out on a great part of their family life at the moment and thus they stand to gain a lot when tasks are more equally divided between men and women.

---

[63] ABDULLAHI AHMED AN-NA'IM, 'State Responsibility Under International Human Rights Law to Change Religious and Customary Laws', in: Rebecca J. Cook (ed.), *Human Rights of Women, National and International Perspectives*, University of Pennsylvania Press, Philadelphia, 1994, p. 174. Also see ABDULLAHI A. AN-NA'IM and JEFFREY HAMMOND, 'Cultural Transformation and Human Rights in African Societies', in: Abdullahi A. An-Na'im (ed.), *Cultural Transformation and Human Rights in Africa*, Zed Books, London, 2002, pp. 13–37.

[64] For example, internal discourse about gender equality will depend on the input of women. However, the most oppressive societies are characterised by the fact that women are not involved in decision-making which makes it difficult to hear their voices. Particularly former colonies may resent Western States and their ideas to such an extent that they do not wish to be influenced by them, but on the contrary want to fall back on traditions that pre-date colonialism.

[65] Fredman suggests that the tradition of long working hours should be replaced by a flexible system that makes it easier to attain a balance between home and work both for male and female workers. FREDMAN, 2002, p. 193..

In order to change people's mindset about gender appropriate behaviour, new measures should be introduced. For instance, as regards the education of school children it is not enough to delete gender stereotypes from school books. In addition, schools should introduce new subjects and learning methods that teach children that irrespective of their sex they have to become autonomous, responsible citizens who are able to take care of themselves and their families. Learning about hygiene, food processing, and childcare, both in theory and in practice, is important for all human beings next to cognitive development, and making it part of the curriculum is bound to change the low appreciation that momentarily exists for care-giving work. Parents should be convinced that girls too will be expected to bear the financial burden of their families once they are adults which should have consequences for their education, job training and status.

States should become actively involved in all kinds of information providing means and methods that can be used to influence and change people's stereotypical ideas. Next to banning negative stereotypes from the media, advertising, language, and songs, new television and radio programmes, shows, plays, songs, dances, proverbs or other culturally appropriate activities and expressions should be developed that break with traditional patterns and inferior images of women. Some good examples may be found as regards the methods that were used to eradicate traditional practices such as foot binding,[66] sati,[67] and – in some communities – female genital mutilation.[68]

It may be a task for international organs, such as CEDAW to make it clear to States, and ethnic groups, that there is no need to fear the loss of cultural identity if they live up to human rights obligations. Multiculturalism is interesting and variety is a positive thing. However, diversity should be found in such things as the fine arts, language, architecture or business mores, and not in the way in which, or the extent to which women are discriminated against. Surely cultural diversity and identity can survive if girls and women become boys' and men's equals both before the law and in practice.

---

[66] When laws against foot binding were largely ignored, new innovative arguments and measures were used that did have the desired effect. Several actors played a role: male reformers argued that it in order to strengthen the nation, it was necessary to improve the status of women; anti-foot binding societies, encouraged parents to let their sons only marry with girls who had normal feet; missionary schools promoted natural feet by offering scholarships only to girls with unbound feet, etc. KATHRYN SIKKINK, 'Historical Precursors to Modern Campaigns for Women's Human Rights: Campaigns Against Footbinding and Female Circumcision', in: Susan Deller Ross (ed.), *Women's Human Rights: The International and Comparative Law Casebook*, University of Pennsylvania Press, Philadelphia, 2008, pp. 482–486.

[67] A pivotal role in the campaign against sati – the burning of Hindu widows – was played by a Bengali Brahmin who argued that sati was contrary to Hinduism and who gave an alternative interpretation of religious texts. CORINNE PACKER, 2002, pp. 162–164.

[68] Rites of passage for girls that entail information and education on hygiene and childcare instead of cutting make becoming a woman a festive occasion rather than a painful and traumatic experience. Also see Chapter 13 by Phyllis Livaha in this book.

4.3. RELEVANT ACTORS

Cultural changes may be initiated and supported at different levels. CEDAW can be of invaluable assistance especially when good practices of State behaviour are noted and published so that other States parties can benefit from them. However, the international level is of minor importance with regard to changing attitudes and mentalities; it can only promote and advise. The actual change must come from within and must happen at the domestic, community, and family level. That is why the actors on these levels are the most important.

To start with at the domestic level it is important that all kinds of authorities are well aware of the rights and obligations contained in the Women's Convention and particularly of women's right to equality and the implications this may have for customs, traditions and stereotypes. That is why States parties should give specific training in this regard to all kinds of officials, especially the judiciary and the police. In Court cases judges should not give precedence to discriminatory traditional rules and habits over women's legal right to equality. The fact that a woman belongs to a certain ethnic or religious group, does not imply that she has given up her right to equality.[69] Especially in cases of gender based violence such as rape, female genital mutilation and domestic violence, the police should be aware of the illegality of such acts and not pass them off as a private matter or, worse, put the blame on the female victim because apparently she did not obey her husband.[70]

In order to come up with innovative extra legal measures that will significantly change society, States should not only seek advice of human rights experts, but also depend on authorities in other disciplines – such as psychologists, sociologists and anthropologists – because they will understand which measures will work to change the population's gender biased mindset.

At the community level, besides local authorities, Civil Society Organisations – in particular grassroots NGOs that know the culture and speak the language, religious leaders and teachers have a great deal of influence. If States succeed in enlisting these actors, and in giving them a gender sensitive training the battle will be half won since they are better equipped to change people's way of thinking than national authorities.

---

[69] Public authorities are sometimes under the impression that women have made a conscious choice to belong to a certain group and that they can easily sever all connections when they feel that they are discriminated against. This 'right of exit' argument is invalid, however, because for women who lack education and income and who have emotional ties to their family and community cannot simply opt out. AYELET SHACHAR, *Multicultural Jurisdictions; Cultural Differences and Women's Rights*, Cambridge University Press, Cambridge, 2001, p. 41.

[70] See *e.g.* INGRID WESTENDORP, 'If home is no haven: women's right to adequate housing in cases of domestic violence', in: Ingrid Westendorp and Ria Wolleswinkel (eds.), *Violence in the Domestic Sphere*, Intersentia, Antwerp, 2005, p. 132.

The most difficult bastion to tackle in the struggle towards gender equality will be religious institutions. Considering the role that religion plays in most cultures – even in secular States – it is imperative that religious leaders can be convinced of the necessity that discriminatory attitudes against girls and women have to be remodelled. While all religions preach human dignity and respect for human beings, they are invariably based on traditional views that date back to times when gender roles were dictated by men's physical strength and women's unbridled pregnancy. Times have changed, however, and it should be possible to abolish religious customs that discriminate against women without affecting or harming the core of people's religious beliefs. Without the help and support of religious leaders, it will be almost impossible to change certain deep rooted customs and traditions. Particularly ideas that girls and women should behave in a certain way because it is their divine duty carry so much weight that secular authorities or other actors will be unable to alter or abolish them.[71]

Finally, the real change must take place at the family level. This is the level where discrimination against girls begins and will leave an imprint that determines the rest of a woman's life. Many women grow up with the idea that they have a certain predestined role to play in society and they are not aware of any other options that they may have. They abide by certain practices and traditions without realizing that these make them powerless and subjugated in relation to men.[72] Many men, too, are not aware of women's right to equality and they play their stereotyped role without thinking twice about it. Awareness raising and formal and informal education, both general literacy and human rights education are therefore of the utmost importance. When parents are well informed and aware of the harm in certain practices and stereotypes, while at the same time they realize that adequate alternatives are available, chances are that they will raise their sons and daughters in a different way, breaking with traditional patterns.

5. CONCLUSION

Culture should not be regarded as working against women, but on the contrary, it should be embraced as instrumental in achieving a change of mentality and taking women's equality to the next level. It seems clear that equality cannot be achieved without a radical change in societies all over the world. The right way to implement Article 5 is not only to abolish or modify gender stereotypes and harmful practices, but also to introduce new customs and practices that will become generally accepted.

---

[71] In the fight against female genital mutilation it has been particularly helpful that several Islamic religious leaders have publicly explained that the Qur'an does not contain a duty to circumcise girls. In the struggle to abolish sati the alternative interpretation of Hindu religious texts was a deciding factor.

[72] Christina M. Cerna and Jennifer C. Wallace, 1999, pp. 644–645.

Examination of CEDAW's Concluding Observations shows that the Committee may be ready to adopt a General Recommendation on Article 5 that is not offensive or too controversial, but may be useful to guide the States parties. Such a Recommendation would make CEDAW's advice more consistent and applicable to all States.

The General Recommendation should be based on the notion that culture is a dynamic concept that changes over time. States parties should be requested to look into the national situation and make an inventory of all existing traditional customs and stereotypes and assess whether and if so to what extent such practices have harmful effects on the human rights of girls and women. Such a catalogue is important because awareness is the first step towards change. Simultaneously, all legislation and policies that may support or perpetuate discriminatory practices should be abolished.

While the obligations under Article 5 are legal obligations, the appropriate measures that have to be taken to achieve a culture of equality are of an extra legal character. That is why States parties should be advised to draw up a comprehensive plan not just with the help of human rights lawyers, but also after consultation with and the assistance of sociologists, psychologists, and anthropologists because these experts will have better insights to determine which measures would appeal to people and would have the desired impact.

It should be made clear that the national authorities themselves are unable and unsuited to bring about a change of mentality. That is why they must enlist the cooperation of all kinds of actors, particularly NGOs, teachers, and religious leaders. While it will be non-State actors who actually inform and educate the public, it should be the States parties that finance training, performances and campaigns.

Innovative new programmes for education of children should be introduced that are aimed at raising autonomous persons who can take care of themselves and their dependents both financially and otherwise. This new way of teaching implies that teachers receive a special training in which they learn to recognize stereotypical patterns and know how to convey gender equality on the children and, indirectly, on their parents.

The media and any other way of informing the public in general should be used that is adequate and suitable in a certain society. This may entail that with the help of religious leaders, artists, and performers, new ceremonies, plays, songs, dances etcetera may have to be created that are based on equality if that is the best way in which new customs can be introduced.

In order to make a General Recommendation on Article 5 more concrete, it would be useful if CEDAW would refer to good practices that have resulted in a change of mentality or the abolition of harmful traditions.

A cultural change will only be successful if it is accepted by the people who live the culture and acceptance becomes viable when new alternatives are offered that leave the sense of identity, security and belonging intact.

ARTICLE 6

States parties shall take all appropriate measures, including legislation, to suppress all forms of traffic in women and exploitation of prostitution of women.

CHAPTER 7
'BECAUSE TO ME, A WOMAN WHO SPEAKS IN PUBLIC IS A PUBLIC WOMAN'*

30 Years Women's Convention and the Struggle to Eliminate Discrimination of Women in the Field of Trafficking and Prostitution

Marjolein VAN DEN BRINK and Marjan WIJERS

1. INTRODUCTION

The Women's Convention has turned 30 and so did Article 6, the Convention's provision that urges States parties to combat trafficking in women (and girls) and the exploitation of prostitution. This Chapter focuses on the contribution of the Convention and its monitoring body CEDAW to the improvement of the position of women and the elimination of all forms of discrimination against them in the field covered by the provision.

While some Articles of the Women's Convention are quite lengthy, Article 6 is remarkably short: 'States parties shall take appropriate measures, including legislation, to suppress all forms of traffic in women and exploitation of prostitution of women.' Not only is it the shortest Article, it is perhaps also one of the most difficult provisions to interpret. It is certainly one of the most controversial. Significantly, it does not give a definition of 'traffic in women' nor of 'exploitation of the prostitution of others'. This is by no means accidental. The question of precisely what practices should be suppressed has been controversial

---

* In the early days of the UN, the chair of the 'Third Committee' (social issues) opened a meeting by remarking that he would not give the floor to women for the reason quoted. See BOB REINALDA and NATASCHA VERHAAREN, *Vrouwenbeweging en internationale organisatie 1868–1986. Een vergeten hoofdstuk uit de geschiedenis van de internationale betrekkingen*, Ariadne, De Knipe, 1989, p. 129.

from the very beginning, starting with the first treaties on trafficking and the exploitation of prostitution at the beginning of the 20th century and continuing up till today. Whereas for a long time there was no international consensus on what should be understood by 'trafficking' – all prostitution or only prostitution under force, only (forced) prostitution or also, for example, forced domestic work or forced marriage – the adoption of the UN Protocol on trafficking in 2000 brought some clarity.[1] According to the Protocol, trafficking means the recruitment or transportation of human beings with the use of coercion, deceit or abuse of authority for the purpose of (sexual or other) exploitation, again, by the way, without defining 'sexual exploitation'.[2] Although the definition is complex and there is still much debate on its interpretation, at least there is general consensus on a number of core elements: the presence of coercion or deceit, the fact that trafficking can occur for all types of work or services, and that it can take place both within and across borders. The main controversies revolve around the question how to deal with prostitution: is prostitution *per se* a violation of human rights, or should only coercive or abusive recruitment and/or working conditions be combated? Another question that keeps causing confusion is whether only 'innocent' women, as opposed to prostitutes, can be trafficked.

In Section 2 the historical development of the international legal framework is sketched. The next section discusses the drafting process of Article 6 Women's Convention and its predecessor, the Declaration on the Elimination of Discrimination Against Women (DEDAW).[3] In Section 4 the work of CEDAW is explored, in particular its Concluding Observations on Article 6. CEDAW's observations regarding trafficking and prostitution, issued between 1999 and 2010 (sessions 21 – 45), have been examined. The outcomes of this exploration are discussed in Section 5. The impact of the Committee's recommendations on the position of women is analysed with the help of the threefold purpose of the Convention, as explained by the Committee in its General Recommendation on temporary special measures: to ensure legal equality as well as protection against discrimination, to improve women's *de facto* position, and to combat prejudice,

---

[1] UN doc. GA RES. 55/25, *Protocol to Prevent, Suppress and Punish Trafficking in Persons, Especially Women and Children, Supplementing the United Nations Convention against Transnational Organized Crime*, 15 November 2000.

[2] The full text of Article 6(a) reads: Trafficking in persons shall mean the recruitment, transportation, transfer, harbouring or receipt of persons by means of the threat or use of force or other forms of coercion, of abduction, of fraud, of deception, of the abuse of power or of a position of vulnerability or of the giving or receiving of payments or benefits to achieve the consent of a person having control over another person for the purpose of exploitation. Exploitation shall include, at a minimum, the exploitation of the prostitution of others or other forms of sexual exploitation, forced labour or services, slavery or practices similar to slavery, servitude or the removal of organs.

[3] UN doc. GA RES. 2263 (XXII), 7 November 1967.

harmful customs and sex and gender-based stereotypes.[4] Throughout the Chapter, the underlying focus is on two related issues: CEDAW's position in the debate on trafficking and on prostitution in particular and secondly, the consequences thereof for the potential impact of the Convention on the position of women. Our primary concern is with the impact on women working in prostitution – by consent or by force.

2. INTERNATIONAL LEGAL FRAMEWORK IN A HISTORICAL PERSPECTIVE

2.1. FROM REGULATION TO ERADICATION OF PROSTITUTION

The movement to suppress trafficking in women for the purpose of prostitution has a long history.[5] Its beginning is most often located in 19th century Victorian society, when feminists and moral purists joined forces to repress prostitution. By that time a system of State-controlled prostitution had been put in place in large parts of Europe, driven by fear for the spread of venereal diseases, in particular among the military. Brothels were brought under surveillance by a system of licensing and prostitutes were compelled to undergo regular health checks.

Immediate cause for the beginning of what later became the anti-trafficking movement was the adoption in 1869 by the British Parliament of the last of the Contagious Diseases Acts, which gave the police the power to – in principle – arrest any woman walking alone in the streets at night and subject her to a genital examination for symptoms of venereal diseases. In practice, of course, predominantly working class women were targeted, who had little choice than to walk on the streets late at night, going to and from their jobs. In reaction, Josephine Butler, a 19th century British feminist and social reformer, founded the Ladies National Association for the Repeal of the Contagious Diseases Acts as a protest against State control and the abuse of working class women, including

---

[4] UN doc. A/59/38(SUPP) ANNEX I, *General Recommendation No. 25, on Article 4, paragraph 1, of the Convention on the Elimination of All Forms of Discrimination against Women, on temporary special measures*, 18 March 2004, paras. 6–7.

[5] For an extensive discussion of the history of this movement see PETRA DE VRIES, *Kuisheid voor mannen, vrijheid voor vrouwen. De reglementering en bestrijding van prostitutie in Nederland, 1850–1911*, Verloren, Hilversum, 1997, pp. 79–81. For a discussion of the international legal framework regarding trafficking and prostitution see: ANNE T. GALLAGHER, *The International Law of Human Trafficking*, Cambridge University Press, Cambridge, 2010; and MARJAN WIJERS and LIN LAP-CHEW, *Trafficking in Women. Forced Labour and Slavery-like Practices in Marriage, Domestic Labour and Prostitution*, STV & GAATW, Utrecht-Bangkok, 1999 (2nd ed.).

the abuse of prostitutes. In her view, State brothels made the State an accessory to the abusive conditions that prevailed in brothels.

In the following years the movement expanded to other European countries and became largely superseded by a purity movement in favour of the eradication of prostitution *per se*.[6] Some feminists thereupon left this coalition of Christian purists and feminists because of the negative consequences they anticipated for the women concerned.[7]

Just like the original abolitionists fought for the abolition of slavery, this new generation of abolitionists fought (and fights) for the abolition of prostitution as 'sexual slavery', or 'white slavery' as it was initially called. Prostitution became synonymous with slavery and prostitutes became slaves in need of rescue. However, unlike the original concept of slavery, the idea of 'sexual slavery' is not linked to the abolishment of a certain type of relationship, notably the ownership of one person over another person, but to the eradication of the activity as such. Prostitution is by its very nature considered to be a form of violence against women and a violation of women's human rights. Any reference to the will or the consent of the woman is rejected. Prostitutes need to be 'rescued', if necessary against their will. Today this view is represented by the French Abolitionist Movement and the American Coalition Against Trafficking (CATW). A similar view is held by the European Women's Lobby (EWL).[8]

2.2. THE FIRST TREATIES

Prompted by alarm at reports of European women being tricked into brothels far from home with offers of other employment or marriage,[9] the first international agreement against 'white slavery' was adopted in 1904.[10] Underlying concern was the protection of 'innocent' women from being lured into brothels. This treaty was followed by a number of others, each gradually extending the legal scope, first in 1910 to traffic within borders and to non-compulsive forms of

---

[6] GAIL PHETERSON, *The Prostitution Prism*, Amsterdam University Press, Amsterdam 1996, p. 138; ROELOF HAVEMAN and MARJAN WIJERS, 'Een paradijs voor pooiers', in: *De Gids*, No. 7–8 July/August 1997, p. 498; PETRA DE VRIES, *Kuisheid voor mannen, vrijheid voor vrouwen. De reglementering en bestrijding van prostitutie in Nederland, 1850–1911*, Verloren, Hilversum, 1997, pp. 79–81.

[7] MICHAEL MUSHENO and KATHRYN SEELY, 'Prostitution policy and the women's movement. Historical Analysis of feminist thought and organisation', in: *Contemporary Crises*, vol. 10, 1986, p. 238.

[8] See their campaign 'Together for a Europe free from prostitution!' at www.womenlobby.org/spip.php?rubrique187 [accessed 25 October 2011].

[9] J. BINDMAN and J. DOEZEMA, *Redefining Prostitution as Sex Work on the International Agenda*, Anti-Slavery International, London, 1997.

[10] League of Nations, *Treaty Series*, Vol. 9, p. 415, *International Agreement for the Suppression of the White Slave Trade*, Paris, 18 May 1904.

procurement in the case of minor females,[11] then in 1921 to boys.[12] In 1933 the scope was broadened even further to the recruitment of adult women 'for immoral purposes' in another country *'even with her consent'*.[13] With regard to the traffic in women within borders, the requirement of constraint was left intact. A State could thus tolerate on a national level what it condemned on an international level.[14]

In 1949 all previous international conventions were integrated in one new convention.[15] The Convention for the Suppression of the Traffic in Persons and of the Exploitation of the Prostitution of Others links, for the first time, trafficking as procurement with prostitution as exploitation. Article 1 requires States parties to punish any person who 'to gratify the passions of another procures, entices or leads away, for purposes of prostitution, another person, even with the consent of that person', thus erasing the previous distinction between international and national trafficking: any recruitment for prostitution is punishable now, even if the woman concerned consents. Subsequent provisions broaden the scope of the treaty to include 'the exploitation of prostitution'. The distinction between trafficking and prostitution has more or less disappeared.

Although the Convention has been ratified by a limited number of States, prostitution laws of the majority of countries are based on an abolitionist view, as expressed in the 1949 Convention.[16] Central feature is that prostitution in itself is not an offence, but any 'exploitation of the prostitution of another person' is criminalised, that is, any involvement of a third party. Prostitutes are considered to be victims, rather than deviants or criminals.

---

[11] Great Britain, *Treaty Series*, No. 20 (1912), *International Agreement for the Suppression of the White Slave Trade*, Paris, 4 May 1910.

[12] League of Nations, *Treaty Series*, Vol. 9, p. 415, *International Convention for the Suppression of the Traffic in Women and Children*, Geneva, 30 September 1921.

[13] League of Nations, *Treaty Series*, Vol. 150, p. 431, *International Convention for the Suppression of the Traffic in Women*, Geneva, 11 October 1933.

[14] MARJAN WIJERS and LIN LAP-CHEW, *Trafficking in Women. Forced Labour and Slavery-like Practices in Marriage, Domestic Labour and Prostitution*, STV & GAATW, Utrecht-Bangkok, 1999 (2nd ed.), ch. 2; R. HAVEMAN and J.C. HES, 'Vrouwenhandel en de exploitatie van prostitutie', in: A.W. HERINGA, J. HES and L. LIJNZAAD (eds.), *Het Vrouwenverdrag, een beeld van een verdrag…*, Maklu Uitgevers, Antwerp, 1994, pp. 59–74 and pp. 67–68.

[15] UN GA Res. 317 (IV), *Convention for the Suppression of the Traffic in Persons and of the Exploitation of the Prostitution of Others*, 2 December 1949.

[16] MARJAN WIJERS, 'Delincuente, víctima, mal social o mujer trabajadora: perspectivas legales sobre la prostitución', in: Raquel Osborne (ed.), *Trabajadoras del sexo, Derechos, migraciones y tráfico en el siglo XXI*, serie General Universitaria, Edicions Bellaterra, Barcelona, 2004, pp. 209–222, p. 210.

2.3. SEX WORKERS RAISE THEIR VOICES

During the sixties and the seventies of the twentieth century, however, prostitutes started to organize and to challenge traditional approaches. They argued that it is not prostitution itself that is the problem, but the clandestine and illegal nature of prostitution and the resulting marginalization, stigmatization and criminalization that forces them into an illegal circuit without protection against violence and exploitation. They advocated the recognition of sex work as legitimate work and the decriminalization of prostitution businesses, so that the sex industry could be regulated under civil and labour laws instead of criminal law.[17] Resistance to this development was fierce. In Ireland, for example, a prostitute, trying to organize her colleagues, was burned to death when her house was set on fire.[18]

Within this perspective, the focus of the debate shifted from moral positions to working conditions and workers' rights. Doubts were raised as to the appropriateness of the existing anti-trafficking framework and anti-trafficking laws to promote the rights of women and the prosecution of their violators.[19] As stated by the NSWP (Network of Sex work Projects): 'Historically, anti-trafficking measures have been more concerned with protecting women's "purity" than with ensuring the human rights of those in the sex industry. This approach limits the protection afforded by these instruments to those who can prove that they did not consent to work in the sex industry. It also ignores the abusive conditions within the sex industry, often facilitated by national laws that place (migrant) sex workers outside of the range of rights granted to others as citizens and workers.'[20]

The concept of 'trafficking' was questioned as outmoded and the development of new language was advocated to describe abuses in labour migration and abusive conditions in the sex-industry. The issue was separated from national and State interests in protecting borders and controlling female sexuality. Obligations, such as those in the 1949 Convention, to take measures to rehabilitate victims of prostitution were denounced. Instead, enforcement of

---

[17] MARJAN WIJERS, 'Delincuente, víctima, mal social o mujer trabajadora: perspectivas legales sobre la prostitución', in: Raquel Osborne (ed.), *Trabajadoras del sexo, Derechos, migraciones y tráfico en el siglo XXI*, serie General Universitaria, Edicions Bellaterra, Barcelona, 2004, pp. 209–222, pp.217–218.

[18] GAIL PHETERSON, 'Not repeating history', in: Gail Pheterson (ed.), *A Vindication of the Rights of Whores*, Seal Press, Seattle, 1989, pp. 3–30, p. 7.

[19] JO DOEZEMA, 'Sex worker rights, abolitionism, and the possibilities for a rights-based approach to trafficking', *Alliance News, A Rights Based Approach to Trafficking*, Issue 22, December 2004, pp. 15–22.

[20] THE NETWORK OF SEX PROJECTS, *Commentary On The Draft Protocol To Combat International Trafficking In Women And Children Supplementary To The Draft Convention On Transnational Organized Crime*, January 1999, available at: www.nswp.org/resource/commentary-the-draft-protocol-combat-international-trafficking-women-and-children-supplemen [accessed 29 July 2011].

existing gender-neutral instruments was advocated, such as the ILO conventions on forced labour, the conventions on slavery and slavery-like practices, the migrant workers conventions and provisions prohibiting debt-bondage.[21]

An important reason for (some) feminists to join the decriminalization camp was that abolitionist laws tended to deteriorate the position of prostitutes instead of improving it. Even improvement of working conditions (such as good sanitary equipment or the supplying of condoms) could be considered as 'promoting' prostitution, as exemplified by a number of court rulings in Germany in the nineties of the last century.[22] Prohibitions on living off the earnings of prostitution reinforced the social isolation of prostitutes by making it difficult for them to live and share an income with other persons, including partners and (adult) children, as the latter ran the risk of being charged with pimping or living off the earnings of prostitution.[23] A second reason was the recognition of women's agency: in an utterly gender-biased labour market, sex work could be a good or even the best option. Moreover, prostitution was certainly not the only risky business for women.

2.4. THE UN TRAFFICKING PROTOCOL

Both abolitionists and decriminalizers were strongly represented in the negotiations in the 1990s on a new instrument on trafficking.[24] The result was a political compromise: the 2000 UN Trafficking Protocol contains a broad definition, covering trafficking into all sectors.[25] At the same time, however, it makes a distinction between trafficking for 'the exploitation of the prostitution of others or other forms of sexual exploitation' and trafficking for 'forced labour

---

[21] MARJAN WIJERS and MARIEKE VAN DOORNINCK, *Only rights can stop wrongs. A critical assessment of anti-trafficking strategies*, paper IOM conference on trafficking, 2002, available at: www.walnet.org/csis/papers/wijers-rights.html [accessed 6 September 2011]. The title of the paper is the slogan of the Millennium Milan Mela ('large gathering') in 2001 in Calcutta, where 25.000 sex workers from India and other South Asian countries came together to stand up for their rights and to protest against stigmatisation, bad working conditions, exploitation and abuse. See for a discussion of the Mela, JYOTI SANGHERA, *Only rights can stop wrongs*, available at: www.hrsolidarity.net/mainfile.php/2001vol11no4/52/[accessed 19 October 2011].

[22] EUROPAP, *Final Report Europap (European Intervention Projects Aids Prevention for Prostitutes*, Ghent, Belgium, 1995, p. 103.

[23] MARJAN WIJERS, 'Delincuente, víctima, mal social o mujer trabajadora: perspectivas legales sobre la prostitución', in: Raquel Osborne (ed.), *Trabajadoras del sexo, Derechos, migraciones y tráfico en el siglo XXI*, serie General Universitaria, Edicions Bellaterra, Barcelona, 2004, p. 214.

[24] See for a discussion of the negotiations on this issue, *e.g.* MARJAN WIJERS and MELISSA DITMORE, 'The negotiations on the UN Protocol on Trafficking in Persons. Moving the focus from morality to actual conditions', in: *Nemesis*, no. 4, 2003, pp. 79–88, available at: www.bayswan.org/traffick/NEMESIS_Ditmore.PDF [accessed 19 October 2011].

[25] The parent convention on transnational organised crime came into force on 29 September 2003; the Trafficking Protocol came into force on 25 December 2003 (see Section 1).

or services, slavery or practices similar to slavery and servitude', while intentionally leaving the terms 'exploitation of the prostitution of others' and 'sexual exploitation' undefined. The latter was done in order to allow all States, independent of their domestic policies on prostitution, to ratify the Protocol.

By treating trafficking for prostitution and trafficking for forced labour as separate issues,[26] the Protocol reinstated the old debate between the abolitionist and the decriminalization movements, representing two diametrically opposed views on sex work and their corresponding strategies to combat trafficking. One sees prostitution *per se* as slavery and therefore equivalent to trafficking. Combating trafficking is combating prostitution. The other sees sex work as work and trafficking as forced labour, whether inside or outside the sex industry, which should be combated with the same instruments as forced labour in other industries. Starting point of the latter position is that adult women (and men) have the right – and the agency – to make their own decisions to work in prostitution. Not prostitution *per se*, but the conditions of exploitation, coercion and abuse make it a violation of human rights: the right that needs to be protected is the right to self determination.

3. DRAFTING ARTICLE 6

Compared to the decades of fierce debates on trafficking and prostitution preceding the Women's Convention, the drafting process of Article 6 was remarkably short.[27] The Philippines, that drafted the first proposal for a text, felt that the subject of prostitution and trafficking in women was already adequately covered by the Convention for the Suppression of the Traffic in Persons and of the Exploitation of the Prostitution of Others of 1949. It proposed therefore to repeat the wording used in DEDAW (1967), the forerunner of the Women's Convention. And after some discussion this was exactly what happened.[28]

The provision in DEDAW (Article 8) had at the time been included because it was held that a declaration on women's rights that did not contain a reference to the necessity to eliminate manifestations of trafficking in women was

---

[26] The ILO Committee of Experts, for example, has always treated forced prostitution as a form of forced labour. See: ILO, *The Cost of Coercion, Global report under the follow-up to the ILO Declaration on Fundamental Principles and Right at Work*, 2009, p. 6, para. 26, available at: www.ilo.org/wcmsp5/groups/public/---ed_norm/---declaration/documents/publication/wcms_106268.pdf [accessed 1 September 2011].

[27] This section is, unless indicated otherwise, largely based on LARS ADAM REHOF, *Guide to the Travaux Préparatoires of the United Nations Convention on the Elimination of All Forms of Discrimination against Women*, Martinus Nijhoff Publishers, Dordrecht, 1993, pp. 89–92.

[28] Only the order of the words used in Articles 8 DEDAW and 6 Women's Convention differs slightly: Article 8 DEDAW reads: 'All appropriate measures, including legislation, shall be taken to combat all forms of traffic in women and exploitation of prostitution of women.'

incomplete, although not everybody agreed that a declaration on discrimination of women was the appropriate instrument to deal with such issues, prostitution in particular.[29] The Iraqi delegate, for instance, remarked that prostitution was a matter for criminal law, and did not seem relevant to a declaration on discrimination of women. Nigeria agreed and stated that prostitution was 'in no wise a form of discrimination'. It was a 'social plague' and its causes economic in origin. Therefore, it could not be combated through legislation. Tanzania did see the issue as a human rights issue, but a general one, and not one of particular importance in the context of discrimination of women. Those in favour of the inclusion of a provision argued optimistically that this declaration might achieve what previous documents had failed to deliver. They also emphasized the deplorable character of these practices. However, they did not explain why trafficking and prostitution should be dealt with in a document on women's discrimination. In the end the provision was adopted with 80 votes in favour, 4 against and 11 abstentions; quite a remarkable result given the discussions.

Debate on the draft provision for the Women's Convention was, as mentioned above, even shorter. Denmark proposed to qualify traffic as 'illicit traffic'. This wording was taken from the Platform for Action of the first World Conference on Women in Mexico (1975).[30] The proposal was dropped because of lack of support. In a similar vein, but possibly with a slightly different purpose, Norway suggested focusing the Article on combating 'prostitution and the illicit traffic in women'. This can be understood as an (unsuccessful) attempt to outlaw all forms of prostitution, as opposed to 'merely' trafficking that should be 'illicit'. At a later stage a similar attempt to reject not only trafficking and exploitation but also prostitution as such, was rejected with 48 votes against, 19 in favour and 46 abstentions. The Netherlands proposed at some point to replace the words 'exploitation of prostitution of women' by 'exploitation of women, in particular through prostitution'. This amendment was important because it shifted the focus from 'sexual exploitation' to harmful exploitation as such. However, it was not accepted.

Proposals for extra elements to be added to the provision include a Portuguese suggestion to extend protection to 'those forms of commercial advertisement and exploitation which use the female body in a way contrary to human dignity'. Belgium proposed to add protection of the 'physical integrity of

---

[29] See MARJOLEIN VAN DEN BRINK, *Aan den Lijve. Over het Vrouwenverdrag en lichamelijke integriteit*, Utrecht Papers on International, Social and Economic Law, No. 16, Utrecht University, Utrecht, 1993, pp. 34–35, available at: www.iiav.nl/epublications//IAV_B00043634.pdf [accessed 29 July 2011]. The quotes included in the text are taken from this source, which contains references to the relevant UN documents.

[30] UN doc. E/CONF.66/34, *Report of the World Conference of the International Women's Year*, Mexico City, 19 June – 2 July 1975, para. 159.

women',[31] and Romania wanted media exploitation to be taken into account. None of these proposals survived. Article 6 of the Women's Convention thus replicates Article 8 DEDAW, with only a slight difference in the order of the words.

If anything, this brief overview shows that Article 6 of the Women's Convention does fit the international legal framework, in the sense that both sides in the debate may feel at home. The dual meaning of the notion of exploitation – signifying both use and misuse – leaves room for plural interpretations and diverging national practices concerning prostitution. The question exactly which practices should be suppressed is left undecided.

Haveman & Hes have argued that the merit of Article 6 is that it has bundled and summarized the contents of a large number or earlier treaties.[32] The responsibility of States for actions of private parties involved in trafficking and exploitation of prostitution has added value, according to these authors.

Still, the fact that a provision on the issue was included at all is somewhat intriguing, now that several of the representatives felt that trafficking and prostitution was not a problem of law, human rights or (sex)discrimination. Arguably, it was included because its drafters felt that an instrument regarding the position of women, that did not deal with an issue that was so strongly connected to the female sex, simply seemed incomplete, just like the drafters of DEDAW before them. Certainly, the *travaux préparatoires* of the Women's Convention do not indicate that the then existing policies and legal framework regarding trafficking and prostitution were ever subjected to a gender analysis. Inclusion was mainly a confirmation of what was already there.

4. CEDAW'S OBSERVATIONS ON TRAFFICKING AND PROSTITUTION

4.1. INTRODUCTION

In this section CEDAW's comments on trafficking and on prostitution are dealt with separately. Although the two are historically and up till today systematically

---

[31] With this proposal, the Belgian delegation wanted a public condemnation of female circumcision, a practice that was not very well known at the time, but about which a few articles had just been published, that had shocked if not the world, at least the Belgians. The proposal didn't make it, basically because the countries concerned felt offended by it. See MARJOLEIN VAN DEN BRINK, *Aan den Lijve. Over het Vrouwenverdrag en lichamelijke integriteit*, Utrecht Papers on International, Social and Economic Law, No. 16, Utrecht University, Utrecht, 1993, pp. 31–32, available at: www.iiav.nl/epublications//IAV_B00043634.pdf [accessed 29 July 2011].

[32] R. HAVEMAN and J.C. HES, 'Vrouwenhandel en exploitatie van prostitutie', in A.W. Heringa, J. Hes and L. Lijnzaad (eds.), *Het Vrouwenverdrag: een beeld van een verdrag...*, Maklu Uitgevers, Antwerp, 1994, pp. 59–74, on p. 73.

linked both in the Convention and elsewhere, that link is far from self-evident.[33] The coerced or deceitful recruitment and transportation of people to exploit them under forced labour or slavery-like conditions, be it in the sex industry or elsewhere, violates all kinds of (human) rights and is therefore generally rejected, although disagreements exist on the exact scope of the concept. The main discussion topics regard the best ways to prevent and trace it, as well as the best ways to deal with its victims.

Prostitution, on the other hand, is a boiling moral potato, on which also feminist groups are utterly divided. Common ground is limited to the rejection of forced prostitution. There is not even a beginning of a consensus on non-coerced adult sex work, the very notion being impossible for abolitionists.

4.2. TRAFFICKING

4.2.1. Perception of the Problem

The position held by several of the Convention's drafters, that trafficking as such is not a human rights issue, is still visible in the approach of many States parties, which predominantly deal with trafficking as a criminal law issue. Starting point for CEDAW, however, is that trafficking must be understood as a human rights violation, and not, for instance, as a crime against public decency.[34] A human rights perspective on trafficking implies that victims should be provided with assistance and protection and not be penalized, not even for violation of migration laws or for engaging in prostitution in countries where prostitutes are criminalized.[35]

CEDAW used to focus on trafficking for prostitution or 'sexual exploitation', as the Committee tended to call it. However, at the end of the nineties it started to widen its approach, drawing attention to cross-border trafficking of young girls for marriage purposes, to the dependent position of migrant spouses and to forced marriages among migrant and minority communities.[36] Since the adoption of the Trafficking Protocol in 2000, States that have not yet ratified the UN Protocol are called upon to do so.[37] The Committee regularly urges

---

[33] Unless of course one equates the two and considers all prostitution to be trafficking, regardless conditions of consent or force.
[34] Switzerland 28 (2003), Suriname 27 (2002). To prevent too lengthy footnotes, references to Concluding Observations in the footnotes are abridged (country, session, year).
[35] Albania 28 (2003), Kyrgyzstan 30 (2004), Cambodia 34 (2006), Malaysia 35 (2006), Uzbekistan 36 (2006), Syrian Arab Republic 38 (2007).
[36] Nepal 21 (1999), Germany 22 (2000), and Germany 30 (2004).
[37] China 36 (2006), Hong Kong 36 (2006), Macao 36 (2006), Mexico 36 (2006), Poland 37 (2007), Bhutan 44 (2009), Guinea Bissau 44 (2009). In addition, European States are asked to ratify the Council of Europe *Convention on Action Against Trafficking in Human Beings*, Council of Europe Treaty Series No. 197, Warsaw, 16 May 2005.

governments to broaden their definitions of trafficking so as to include trafficking for other forms of exploitation than prostitution, including fake arranged marriages, using women as mules for drug trafficking, sex tourism, exploitation of domestic workers, and 'labour exploitation'.[38] The Committee asked the Governments of China, Hong Kong and Macao to review the situation of North Korean women refugees and asylum-seekers and 'to ensure that they do not become victims of trafficking and marriage enslavement because of their status as illegal aliens'.[39]

4.2.2. Causes of Trafficking

Combating trafficking requires attention for its causes. Initially CEDAW focused in particular on poverty and economic hardship as major causes of both trafficking and prostitution.[40] Improving women's social and economic situation was and is seen as an important strategy to prevent both prostitution and trafficking, because it reduces their vulnerability.[41] Education opportunities, in particular for vulnerable groups such as teenage girls,[42] and raising awareness about trafficking are other elements of this approach.[43]

More recently, also other concerns have been raised by the Committee, such as the increase in female labour migration, because it enhances women's vulnerability to trafficking.[44] Other groups identified as especially vulnerable, are minority women, in particular Roma and Sinti, women in rural areas, and 'migrant, asylum-seeking and refugee women who, falling victim to

---

[38] Israel 33 (2005), Bosnia Herzegovina 35 (2006), Columbia 37 (2007), Germany 43 (2009).

[39] China 36 (2006), Hong Kong 36 (2006), Macau 36 (2006).

[40] E.g. Georgia 21 (1999), Nepal 21 (1999), Democratic Republic of Congo 22 (2000), Cameroon 23 (2000), Fiji 26 (2002), Angola 31 (2004), Guatemala 35 (2006), Philippines 36 (2006), Madagascar 42 (2008), Armenia 43 (2009), Liberia 44 (2009), Spain 44 (2009).

[41] Cuba 23 (2000), Cameroon 23 (2000), Republic of Moldova 23 (2000), Romania 23 (2000), Kazakhstan 24 (2001), Viet Nam 25 (2001), Ukraine 27 (2002), Armenia 27b (2002), Czech Republic 27b (2002), Uganda 27b (2002), Albania 28 (2003), Belarus 30 (2004), Kyrgyzstan 30 (2004), Nigeria 30 (2004), Bangladesh 31 (2004), Latvia 31 (2004), Paraguay 32 (2005), Burkina Faso 33 (2005), Democratic People's Republic of Korea 33 (2005), Gambia 33 (2005), Cambodia 34 (2006), Mali 34 (2006), Thailand 34 (2006), Bosnia & Herzegovina 35 (2006), Malaysia 35 (2006), Cuba 36 (2006), Georgia 36 (2006), Philippines 36 (2006), Republic of Moldova 36 (2006), Azerbaijan 37 (2007), Colombia 37 (2007), Kazakhstan 37 (2007), Nicaragua 37 (2007) Peru 37 (2007), Tajikistan 37 (2007), Viet Nam 37 (2007), Ecuador 42 (2008), Madagascar 42 (2008), Armenia 43 (2009), Cameroon 43 (2009), Timor-Leste 44 (2009), Guinea Bissau 44 (2009), Japan 44 (2009), Liberia 44 (2009), Egypt 45 (2010).

[42] Ukraine 27 (2002), Armenia 27b (2002), Czech Republic 27b (2002).

[43] E.g. Costa Rica 29 (2003), Democratic People's Republic of Korea 33 (2005), Cyprus 35 (2006), Mexico 36 (2006), Colombia 37 (2007), Ecuador 42 (2008), El Salvador 42 (2008), Kyrgyzstan 42 (2008), Uruguay 42 (2008), Cameroon 43 (2009), Guatemala 43 (2009), Panama 45 (2010).

[44] E.g. Mexico 27b (2002), Ecuador 29 (2003), Ethiopia 30 (2004), Cambodia 34 (2006), Philippines 36 (2006), Kyrgyzstan 42 (2008), Myanmar 42 (2008), Tuvalu 44 (2009).

discrimination, are pushed into the informal economy, including sex work, and become vulnerable to sexual exploitation'.[45]

Other causes identified by CEDAW include tourism as a factor for trafficking, sex-selective abortions and female infanticide, and discrimination and social exclusion.[46]

In a few cases reference is made to the prevalence of stereotypical gender roles and gender inequality as a root cause.[47] CEDAW asked Switzerland to 'take appropriate measures to protect the women concerned from all forms of exploitation and to take action aimed at changing men's and society's perception of women as sex objects.'[48] Finland was urged 'to encourage a positive change of atmosphere regarding sex phone lines as they run counter to the efforts made to portray women positively, and not as "sex objects" in the media'.[49]

In just one case the Committee mentioned the involvement of police officers in trafficking and the sexual exploitation of women.[50]

4.2.3. A Comprehensive Approach

Whereas in the first years CEDAW addressed trafficking rather selectively, from its 23rd session in 2000 on it consistently stressed the need for a comprehensive or holistic approach, in accordance with Article 6 and the Committee's General Recommendation No. 19 on Violence against Women.[51]

Such approaches should include both legal (see Section 4.2.4) and non-legal measures. Cooperation and information exchange between countries of origin, transit and destination was encouraged,[52] and in a number of cases CEDAW

---

[45] Germany 30 (2004), Madagascar 42 (2008), Malawi 35 (2006) and Ecuador 42 (2008).
[46] Saint Kitts and Nevis 27 (2002), China 36 (2006) and Macau 36 (2006), Ecuador 42 (2008).
[47] Armenia 43 (2009).
[48] Switzerland 28 (2003).
[49] Finland 24 (2001).
[50] Brazil 29 (2003).
[51] CEDAW General Recommendation No. 19, *Violence against Women*, 1992.
[52] E.g. Nepal 21 (1999), Belarus 22 (2000), Lithuania 23 (2000), Republic of Moldova 23 (2000), Romania 23 (2000), Finland 24 (2001), Kazakhstan 24 (2001), Viet Nam 25 (2001), Estonia 26 (2002), Iceland 26 (2002), Portugal 26 (2002), Russian Federation 26 (2002), Belgium 27 (2002), Norway 28 (2003), Switzerland 28 (2003), Bhutan 30 (2004), Nigeria 30 (2004), Bangladesh 31 (2004), Latvia 31 (2004), Malta 31 (2004), Spain 31 (2004), Paraguay 32 (2005), Democratic People's Republic of Korea 33 (2005), Israel 33 (2005), Cambodia 34 (2006), Malawi 35 (2006), Malaysia 35 (2006), Romania 35 (2006), Saint Lucia 35 (2006), Cape Verde 36 (2006), Republic of Moldova 36 (2006), Uzbekistan 36 (2006), Austria 37 (2007), Colombia 37 (2007), Maldives 37 (2007), Tajikistan 37 (2007), Viet Nam 37 (2007), Syrian Arab Republic 38 (2007), Honduras 39 (2007), Republic of Korea 39 (2007), Saudi Arabia 40 (2008), Iceland 41 (2008), Yemen 41 (2008), Belgium 42 (2008), El Salvador 42 (2008), Mongolia 42 (2008), Slovenia 42 (2008), Bahrain 42 (2008), Guatemala 43 (2009), Haiti 43 (2009), Libyan Arab Jamahiriya 43 (2009), Denmark 44 (2009), Guinea Bissau 44 2009), Switzerland 44 (2009), Egypt 45 (2010), Panama 45 (2010), Ukraine 45 (2010), United Arab Emirates 45 (2010), Uzbekistan 45 (2010).

emphasized the need to cooperate with NGOs.[53] Attention should also be paid to witness protection and assistance to victims and to preventive measures. Professionals such as law enforcement officers and border police, but also the judiciary, lawyers, social workers, and health care providers should be trained 'to recognise victims of trafficking and provide them with support'.[54] Sometimes the allocation of sufficient human and financial resources was mentioned.[55] Provision of social support, rehabilitation and integration programmes should include the provision of shelter, counselling and medical care.[56] In later sessions free legal aid, psycho-social support, financial support, adequate housing, opportunities for further training, and the creation of livelihood options when necessary were added.[57]

Sometimes the Committee referred to 'rehabilitation' and 'integration', at other times it used more neutral terms, like specialized support services, assistance and support, support and protection, or protection and recovery.

4.2.4. The Legal Framework

Prosecution of traffickers requires an adequate legal framework: trafficking should be penalized and sanctions should be appropriate to the gravity of the crime. At various occasions the Committee expressed its concern that trafficking was not explicitly defined as a crime or that there was no specific legislation on

---

[53] Georgia 21 (1999), Lithuania 23 (2000), Costa Rica 29 (2003), United Arab Emirates 45 (2010).

[54] E.g. Germany 22 (2000), Portugal 26 (2002), Ukraine 27 (2002), Armenia 27b (2002), Czech Republic 27b (2002), Albania 28 (2003), Norway 28 (2003), Switzerland 28 (2003), Bangladesh 31 (2004), Democratic People's Republic of Korea 33 (2005), Ireland 33 (2005), Mexico 36 (2006), Austria 37 (2007), Colombia 37 (2007), Ecuador 42 (2008), El Salvador 42 (2008), Madagascar 42 (2008), Myanmar 42 (2008), Slovenia 42 (2008), Uruguay 42 (2008), Guatemala 43 (2009), Rwanda 43 (2009), Lao People's Democratic Republic 44 (2009), Egypt 45 (2010), Panama 45 (2010), Uzbekistan 45 (2010).

[55] E.g. Madagascar 42 (2008), Myanmar 42 (2008), Armenia 43 (2009), Guatemala 43 (2009), Rwanda 43 (2009), Switzerland 44 (2009), Ukraine 45 (2010).

[56] Latvia 31 (2004), Paraguay 32 (2005), Ireland 33 (2005), Burkina Faso 33 (2005), Democratic People's Republic of Korea 33 (2005), Gambia 33 (2005), Israel 33 (2005), Cambodia 34 (2006), Thailand 34 (2006), The Former Yugoslav Republic of Macedonia 34 (2006), Bosnia & Herzegovina 35 (2006), Malaysia 35 (2006), Romania 35 (2006), China 36 (2006), Chile 36 (2006), China 36 (2006), Georgia 36 (2006), Hong Kong 36 (2006), Macau 36 (2006), Republic of Moldova 36 (2006), Uzbekistan 36 (2006), Azerbaijan 37 (2007), Colombia 37 (2007), Kazakhstan 37 (2007), Nicaragua 37 (2007), Suriname 37 (2007), Viet Nam 37 (2007), Syrian Arab Republic 38 (2007), Honduras 39 (2007), Republic of Korea 39 (2007), Saudi Arabia 40 (2008), Iceland 41 (2008), United Kingdom 41 (2008), Yemen 41 (2008), Belgium 42 (2008), El Salvador 42 (2008), Madagascar 42 (2008), Mongolia 42 (2008), Myanmar 42 (2008), Portugal 42 (2008), Uruguay 42 (2008), Bahrain 42 (2008), Cameroon 43 (2009), Guatemala 43 (2009), Rwanda 43 (2009), Azerbaijan 44 (2009), Bhutan 44 (2009), Timor-Leste 44 (2009), Guinea Bissau 44 (2009), Japan 44 (2009), Liberia 44 (2009), Egypt 45 (2010), Malawi 45 (2010), Panama 45 (2010), Ukraine 45 (2010), United Arab Emirates 45 (2010), Uzbekistan 45 (2010).

[57] Austria 37 2007), Mongolia 42 (2008), Myanmar 42 (2008), Lao People's Democratic Republic 44 (2009), Uzbekistan 45 (2010).

trafficking,[58] that sanctions were too lenient to deter traffickers,[59] or more recently, that legislation was not in line with the UN Trafficking Protocol, despite ratification.[60] Another concern was the insufficient enforcement of criminal law against trafficking and the low rates of prosecution and conviction.[61]

A serious concern of a completely different nature was the accusation implicit in a recommendation to Myanmar to 'ensure that the anti-trafficking legislation and directives are not misused by authorities to impose increased restrictions on communities or falsely arrest and charge innocent people, particularly women of ethnic groups'.[62]

CEDAW asked Switzerland to reconsider its special visa regulations for foreign cabaret dancers. Six years later it commended Switzerland for the various measures taken, such as the provision of briefings and informational materials in consulates and embassies. It encouraged the Government to continue to regularly review the visa and other regulations for cabaret dancers, and 'to consider including provisions that would allow women to change to a different sector of work'.[63] A similar issue played in Japan.[64]

Germany was recommended to review 'its procedures for issuance of visas to dependent spouses, taking into consideration their vulnerability for sexual exploitation'.[65] Concerns were also expressed with regard to live-in migrant domestic workers in Canada, but without connecting the issue to trafficking.[66] However, in the case of Saudi Arabia, CEDAW did link the two, and it expressed its concern 'about the persistence of trafficking and the economic and sexual exploitation and ill-treatment of young migrant girls employed as domestic servants'. It called upon the Government 'to grant in law and practice female domestic migrant workers [sic], including their children, the rights provided for in the Convention and to implement measures aimed at informing them about these rights. It also urged the State party to adopt a labour law concerning domestic workers as a priority.'[67]

Initially, CEDAW linked the obligation of States to provide protection and support to enabling victims giving testimony against their traffickers: victims

---

[58] E.g. Estonia 26 (2002), Norway 28 (2003), Ecuador 29 (2003), Ireland 33 (2005), Syrian Arab Republic 38 (2007), Honduras 39 (2007), Saudi Arabia 40 (2008), Haiti 43 (2009).
[59] E.g. Belgium 27 (2002), Suriname 27 (2002), Japan 29 (2003).
[60] Paraguay 32 (2005), Israel 33 (2005).
[61] E.g. Singapore 25 (2001), Viet Nam 25 (2001), Russian Federation 26 (2002), Cambodia 34 (2006), The Former Yugoslav Republic of Macedonia 34 (2006), Philippines 36 (2006), Republic of Moldova 36 (2006), Greece 37 (2007), Tajikistan 37 (2007), Republic of Korea 39 (2007), El Salvador 42 (2008), Mongolia 42 (2008), Slovenia 42 (2008), Timor-Leste 44 (2009).
[62] Myanmar 42 (2008).
[63] Switzerland 28 (2003) and 44 (2009), Cyprus 35 (2006).
[64] Japan 44 (2009).
[65] Germany 22 (2000).
[66] Canada 28 (2003), see also Germany 30 (2004).
[67] Saudi Arabia 40 (2008).

should receive support 'so they can provide testimony'.[68] This might include residence permits.[69] That touched a sensitive issue. Even so, CEDAW quickly took things a step further and expressed concern about 'the inadequacy of protective measures for trafficked women, especially foreign women and girls, who do not testify against their traffickers. The Committee recommended that State parties consider issuing residence permits to victims of trafficking whether or not they testify against their traffickers, and whether or not the perpetrators are punished.'[70] The Netherlands were urged to ensure that trafficked women are not, in any circumstances, held in immigration detention or other forms of custody.[71]

By 2006, following an EU Directive,[72] many EU States had introduced a so-called 'reflection period', aimed at providing victims time to recover and decide whether or not they wanted to act as witnesses. CEDAW, however, was concerned that the period granted often was too short for victims to recover and prepare for their return to their country of origin. In reaction to these concerns, Denmark extended the reflection period from 30 days to 100 days and offered trafficking victims legal, medical and psychological assistance 'if they agree to be repatriated and cooperate in investigations'. The Committee welcomed the change although it regretted that the emphasis still was on repatriation instead of the recovery and rehabilitation of the victims.[73] The Committee encouraged Denmark to continue working closely with countries of origin to ensure safe repatriation of victims and their access to adequate care and rehabilitation.

In earlier sessions the Committee had already commented on the issue of victims who, for various reasons, cannot or dare not return to their home country after conclusion of the criminal proceedings. In such cases States should either ensure that trafficked women are provided with full protection in their countries of origin or grant them asylum or refugee status under the 1951 Geneva Convention on Refugees on grounds of gender-based persecution.[74] At

---

[68] Germany 22 (2000), Portugal 26 (2002), Belgium 27 (2002), Ukraine 27 (2002), Armenia 27b (2002), Czech Republic 27b (2002), Albania 28 (2003), Belarus 30 (2004), Bangladesh 31 (2004), Spain 31 (2004), Guatemala 43 (2009), Libyan Arab Jamahiriya 43 (2009), Panama 45 (2010).

[69] Switzerland 28 (2003).

[70] France 29 (2003). Independent residence permits became an important focus of NGO campaigns, now endorsed by CEDAW. See the Netherlands 25 (2001) & 37 2007), Australia 34 (2006), United Kingdom 41 (2008), Belgium 42 (2008), Denmark 44 (2009), Switzerland 44 (2009).

[71] The Netherlands 45 (2010).

[72] Council Directive 2004/81/EC of 29 April 2004 *on the residence permit issued to third-country nationals who are victims of trafficking in human beings or who have been the subject of an action to facilitate illegal immigration, who cooperate with the competent authorities*. The Directive leaves the duration of the permit to the discretion of the State.

[73] Resp. Denmark 36 (2006) and Denmark 44 (2009).

[74] *E.g.* the Netherlands 25 (2001), Spain 31 (2004) & 44 (2009), see also United Kingdom 41 (2008).

the same time States of origin were urged to provide support to victims and protect them from traffickers and agents.[75]

4.3. EXPLOITATION OF PROSTITUTION

4.3.1. Defining the Problem

As with trafficking, the Committee emphasizes the need to approach exploitation of prostitution as a human rights issue.[76] Despite the great number of recommendations on 'sexual exploitation', it is unclear whether 'exploitation' only refers to coerced exploitation, or also includes non-coerced adult sex work. Many recommendations are in line with the abolitionist view in that they emphasize the need to develop policies to discourage exploitation by criminalizing procurement and more and more also the demand for prostitutes, meaning clients.[77] Simultaneously, CEDAW urges States not to punish prostitutes, but to protect and rehabilitate them, which coincides with the abolitionist view of prostitutes as victims. It condemns policies that seem to exacerbate their situation instead of improving it. In regard to China, Hong Kong and Macau it expressed concern that 'the continued criminalization of prostitution disproportionately impacts on prostitutes rather than on the prosecution and punishment of pimps and traffickers.'[78] The concern about the Tunisian situation where there are authorized places for prostitution, despite it being legally prohibited, also suggested an abolitionist perspective.[79] Nevertheless, in particular in more recent concluding observations on countries that have legalized sex work, the Committee does not appear to condemn prostitution *per se*, but continues to focus on the impact of laws and policies on the situation of the women concerned.

---

[75] Lao People's Democratic Republic 44 (2009). See also Myanmar 42 (2008), Uzbekistan 45 (2010).
[76] E.g. Surinam 27 (2002).
[77] E.g. Angola 31 (2004), Croatia 32 (2005), Lao People's Democratic Republic 32 (2005), Paraguay 32 (2005), Israel 33 (2005), Australia 34 (2006), Venezuela 34 (2006), Malawi 35 (2006), Saint Lucia 35 (2006), Cuba 36 (2006), Denmark 36 (2006), Mauritius 36 (2006), Mexico 36 (2006), Philippines 36 (2006), Uzbekistan 36 (2006), Syrian Arab Republic 38 (2007), Honduras 39 (2007), Armenia 43 (2009), Libyan Arab Jamahiriya 43 (2009), Denmark 44 (2009), Japan 44 (2009), Lao People's Democratic Republic 44 (2009), Botswana 45 (2010).
[78] China 36 (2006), Hong Kong 36 (2006), Macau 36 (2006).
[79] Tunisia 27 (2002); a similar concern was expressed regarding the 'zones of tolerance and of protection' in Hungary, Hungary 27b (2002).

4.3.2. Causes

CEDAW has identified a variety of factors as causing or intensifying sexual exploitation. Among these are both sex tourism and the impact of tourism on (the increase of) prostitution,[80] traditional practices and beliefs,[81] low minimum ages of sexual consent,[82] the presence of peace-keeping forces,[83] and increased vulnerability due to factors such as legal regulations regarding residence and/or working permits, and lack of access to the labour market.

In Denmark the number of women involved in prostitution 'increased during the reporting period and is expected to further increase as a result of the ban on the purchase of sexual services in other Scandinavian countries'.[84] The Committee urged Denmark to address the demand for prostitution. Discouraging demand for prostitution is now a recurring aspect of the Committee's approach to the exploitation of prostitution.[85]

4.3.3. Measures

Prostitutes should be protected, rather than punished and States must take appropriate measures for the rehabilitation and reintegration into society of women and girls 'who wish to discontinue their lives in prostitution',[86] provide for educational and economic alternatives,[87] and 'educate women and girls on

---

[80] E.g. Jamaica 24 (2001), Nicaragua 25 (2001), Barbados 27b (2002), Gambia 33 (2005), Thailand 34 (2006), Saint Lucia 35 (2006), Cape Verde 36 (2006), Mauritius 36 (2006), Madagascar 42 (2008).

[81] E.g. the practice of 'temple prostitutes', Nepal 21 (1999).

[82] Guyana 33 (2005).

[83] Germany 43 (2009).

[84] Denmark 44 (2009).

[85] Angola 31 (2004), Dominican Republic 31 (2004), Equatorial Guinea 31 (2004), Latvia 31 (2004), Spain 31 (2004), Croatia 32 (2005), Lao People's Democratic Republic 32 (2005), Paraguay 32 (2005), Israel 33 (2005), Australia 34 (2006), Venezuela 34 (2006), Malawi 35 (2006), Saint Lucia 35 (2006), Cuba 36 (2006), Denmark 36 (2006), Mauritius 36 (2006), Mexico 36 (2006), Philippines 36 (2006), Uzbekistan 36 (2006), Syrian Arab Republic 38 (2007), Honduras 39 (2007), Armenia 43 (2009), Libyan Arab Jamahiriya 43 (2009), Japan 44 (2009), Lao People's Democratic Republic 44 (2009), Botswana 45 (2010).

[86] Australia 34 (2006), Denmark 36 (2006), Armenia 43 (2009), Azerbaijan 44 (2009), Denmark 44 (2009), Lao People's Democratic Republic 44 (2009).

[87] E.g. Democratic Republic of Congo 22 (2000), Cameroon 23 (2000), Lithuania 23 (2000), Nicaragua 25 (2001), Portugal 26 (2002), Suriname 27 (2002), Kenya 28 (2003), Switzerland 28 (2003), Angola 31 (2004), Latvia 31 (2004), Croatia 32 (2005), Samoa 32 (2005), Australia 34 (2006), Mali 34 (2006), Venezuela 34 (2006), Malawi 35 (2006), Saint Lucia 35 (2006), Turkmenistan 35 (2006), China 36 (2006), Hong Kong 36 (2006), Macau 36 (2006), Mauritius 36 (2006), Mexico 36 (2006), Philippines 36 (2006), Maldives 37 (2007), Suriname 37 (2007), Tajikistan 37 (2007), Syrian Arab Republic 38 (2007), Republic of Korea 39 (2007), Ecuador 42 (2008), Germany 43 (2009), Rwanda 43 (2009), Japan 44 (2009), Botswana 45 (2010), Egypt 45 (2010).

career options in order to eliminate prostitution as the only option'.[88] A few times CEDAW mentioned stigma as a barrier to reintegration, but without calling on States to combat the stigma on prostitutes.[89] However, it did call on Viet Nam to prevent (further) stigma following reports 'that rehabilitation measures, such as administrative camps, may stigmatize girls and young women victims of prostitution and deny them due process rights.'[90]

States should ensure access to health services for prostitutes, especially in light of growing concerns about HIV/AIDS.[91] However, it rejected mandatory testing of 'women and girls exploited in prostitution and trafficking'.[92] In a number of cases CEDAW directly linked prostitution with the spread of HIV/AIDS: 'the transmission of sexually transmitted diseases and HIV/AIDS is further exacerbated by sexual exploitation'.[93]

In a few cases the Committee pointed out that measures to combat trafficking may have a negative impact.

4.3.4. Legal Measures

4.3.4.1. Measures to be taken in prohibitionist and abolitionist States

The Committee regularly expresses its concern that prostitutes are penalized while procurers and/or clients are not.[94] In regard to Lithuania, for example, it 'draws attention to Article 6 of the Convention and notes that criminal penalties imposed only on prostitutes entrench sexual exploitation of women'.[95] In regard to Ecuador, it explicitly noted that the fact that current legislation fails to penalize pimps for managing premises for this type of exploitation is incompatible with Article 6 of the Convention.[96] Sanctions should be commensurate with the gravity of the offences, in particular regarding child prostitution.[97]

The Committee welcomed the criminalization by Sweden of the purchase of sexual services, but at the same time expressed concern that this may have increased the incidence of clandestine prostitution, thereby rendering prostitutes more vulnerable. It encouraged the Government to 'evaluate the effect of the

---

[88] Cameroon 43 (2009).
[89] Azerbaijan 44 (2009).
[90] Viet Nam 37 (2007).
[91] Democratic Republic of Congo 22 (2000), Myanmar 22 (2000), Cameroon 23 (2000), Guinea 25 (2001), Guyana 25 (2001), Uganda 27b (2002), Hungary 27b (2002).
[92] India 22 (2000).
[93] Nigeria 30 (2004), see also Cambodia 34 (2006).
[94] E.g. Egypt 24 (2001), Guyana 25 (2001), Albania 28 (2003), Mauritius 36 (2006), Armenia 43 (2009), Rwanda 43 (2009), Japan 44 (2009), Egypt 45 (2010).
[95] Lithuania 23 (2000), see also Guinea 25 (2001), Armenia 43 (2009), Egypt 45 (2010).
[96] Ecuador 29 (2003), see also Georgia 21 (1999), Belgium 27 (2002).
[97] Guatemala 27b (2002).

current policy of criminalizing the purchase of sexual services, especially in view of the complete lack of data on clandestine prostitution which may have incidental effects on the trafficking of women and girls'.[98] In regard to China, Hong Kong and Macau the Committee was concerned that 'prostitutes may be kept in administrative detention without due process of law'.[99]

An issue that is barely addressed – by NGOs and the Committee – is violence and discrimination against sex workers. An exception was the shadow report of Tais Plus, a sex workers organization in Kyrgyzstan.[100] The most outstanding issues they addressed are systematic harassment of sex workers by law enforcement officers, including physical violence, extortion of money as well as illegal arrests and threats, and the impossibility of obtaining identification documents for sex workers who have lost their documents in one way or another – mostly to their employers or to law enforcement officers. Under the heading 'vulnerable groups' the Committee expressed its concern about the harassment against women in prostitution by police officials, and urged the Government to 'take all appropriate measures to ensure that the Convention applies to all women without discrimination and to further take all necessary steps to protect them from all forms of discrimination and violence by public and private individuals'.[101]

4.3.4.2. Measures to be taken in States which (partly) decriminalized the sex sector

A slowly growing number of States chooses to decriminalize (aspects of) prostitution, among them New Zealand, the Netherlands, Iceland and Germany. This is generally ascribed to increasing organization of sex workers, who claim civil and workers rights and demand that sex work be recognized as work. The Committee does not take the stand that decriminalization violates the Convention, but raises concerns that decriminalization by merely repealing some offences will not as such stop the risks of exploitation and violence faced by prostitutes.[102]

It urged the Netherlands to 'conduct an impact assessment of the intended as well as unintended effects of the law abolishing the ban on brothels. Such an assessment should also cover violence and health risks, in particular for women without residence permits who are engaged in prostitution.'[103] Compulsory registration for monitoring purposes is considered a risk. The Committee fears

---

[98] Sweden 25 (2001).
[99] China 36 (2006), Hong Kong 36 (2006), Macao 36 (2006).
[100] TAIS PLUS, *Shadow report to the Third Periodic Report of Kyrgyzstan to the Committee on the Elimination of Discrimination Against Women*, Kyrgyz Republic, 2008.
[101] Kyrgyzstan 42 (2008).
[102] New Zealand 29 (2003); see also Iceland 41 (2008).
[103] The Netherlands 37 (2007), see also the Netherlands 25 (2001).

that 'the law, rather than improving the situation of prostitutes, might on the contrary undermine efforts to combat the sexual exploitation of women and increase the vulnerability of prostitutes who are not able or not willing to register by worsening their working conditions and exacerbating their social exclusion. The Committee expresses concern that this new legislation may also create serious risks for registered prostitutes' privacy and safety.'[104] Just like Sweden, albeit in a completely different legal climate, it urged the Netherlands to conduct a risk assessment of the proposed law, in consultation with relevant organizations and groups before adopting it.

Regarding Germany, CEDAW raised the concern that prostitutes 'although they are legally obliged to pay taxes [...] still do not enjoy the protection of labour and social law'.[105] In 2002 Germany changed its prostitution policies to allow prostitutes to conclude legal contracts and access social security schemes. The Committee was however concerned that 'the Act has only succeeded in realizing the intended goals to a very limited extent. In particular, the Committee regrets that the Act has not been able to improve the social security of prostitutes nor the working conditions in terms of health and hygiene, nor to reduce prostitution-related crime.'[106] The Committee, however, did not require Germany to take measures to improve the social position of sex workers, but encouraged the Government to continue developing programmes to prevent women from entering prostitution and to establish programmes of rehabilitation and support for women and girls who wish to leave prostitution.

5. ANALYSIS AND CONCLUSION

As the previous sections have shown, discussions on the exact purposes of international action directed at trafficking abound, but to date there is little consensus to speak of. The terse wording of Article 6 of the Women's Convention is remarkably vague on the precise purpose of the provision, and the Convention's drafting history does not shed more light on its scope or goals. Moreover – rather atypical given the predilection of many States parties to make reservations to the Women's Convention – neither reservations nor interpretative declarations have been made to Article 6 that might elucidate the (perceived) purport of the provision.

So far CEDAW did not issue a General Comment on Article 6. It refers to trafficking and exploitation in other General Comments, notably the Comment

---

[104] The Netherlands 45 (2010).
[105] Germany 22 (2000).
[106] Germany 43 (2009).

on violence and the Comment on the right to health.[107] Prostitutes are identified as one of the groups that are particularly vulnerable to violence, disease, and discrimination. However, in the Comments on older women and on Article 2, prostitutes are not among the groups identified as especially vulnerable.[108] Despite the clear link between migration and trafficking, CEDAW also refrains from discussing issues related to trafficking and prostitution in its General Comment on women migrant workers, although the Comment repeatedly refers to sexual abuse and similar problems.[109] In a footnote, the Committee explains that the Comment only deals with 'work-related situations of women migrants', and that it feels that the phenomenon of trafficking may be more comprehensively addressed through Article 6.

From the picture emerging from the inventory in the preceding section, it can be concluded that States' obligations regarding trafficking are clear, as opposed to the obligations regarding prostitution, that are significantly less so. Generally, CEDAW seems inclined to 'go with the flow', not speaking out on the (un)desirability of sex work as such, but leaving that to the discretion of the States parties. This is understandable, given the huge controversies surrounding the topic. As a solution, CEDAW seems to manoeuvre between the different poles by focusing on the impact of prostitution regimes on the position of sex workers. However, because sex work is illegal in many countries, recommendations in this regard tend to stress the importance to exempt them from prosecution, (immediate) deportation and so on. Very few recommendations actually focus on improving the position of women who are willingly engaged in sex work, but face deplorable and abusive working conditions. The 2010 recommendation on the Netherlands is an exception (see Section 4.3.4.2). Nevertheless, such exceptions show that CEDAW is not averse to exploring possibilities to improve women's position other than those offered by abolitionist approaches. For those advocating strengthening women's agency, including the ability to actually choose to do sex work if that seems the better option, it seems a good idea to make use of CEDAW's susceptibility by drawing the Committee's attention to violations of women's rights in the sphere of working conditions and abuse by State agencies. Unfortunately, many NGOs involved in shadow reports to CEDAW are inclined to include only sex workers' voices that do support an abolitionist approach. Given the time, money and expertise required for the drafting and 'plugging' of

---

[107] CEDAW General Recommendation No. 19, *Violence against Women*, 1992, and CEDAW General Recommendation No. 24, *Article 12: Women and Health*, 1999.
[108] UN doc. CEDAW/C/GC/27, *General Recommendation on older women and protection of their human rights*, 16 December 2010, and UN doc. CEDAW/C/2010/47/GC.2, *General Recommendation No. 28 on the Core Obligations of States Parties under Article 2 of the Convention on the Elimination of All Forms of Discrimination against Women*, 19 October 2010.
[109] UN doc. CEDAW/C/2009/WP.1/R, *General recommendation No. 26 on women migrant workers*, 5 December 2008.

shadow reports, it is a serious obstacle for sex workers to make their voices heard. To improve the relevance of CEDAW's observations for the position of sex workers, the Committee should systematically question reporting States about the impact of domestic legislation on sex workers. In order to help sex workers overcome their deeply rooted distrust in the State and State institutions, CEDAW should make sure that sex workers who do raise their voices, even if not very loud, are heard and acknowledged. In light of the oft-found unwillingness of many women's and human rights' NGOs to co-operate with sex workers who do not adhere to abolitionist views, CEDAW might also ask NGO representatives about the participation of sex workers groups in the drafting of their shadow reports.

In terms of the threefold purpose of the Convention, as explained by the Committee in its General Comment No. 25, the Concluding Observations show the following picture.

At the level of ensuring legal equality, the Committee firmly rejects the criminalization of sex workers and continuously points at the imbalance in the legislation in many States, where only prostitutes but not their pimps or clients are criminalized and/or actually prosecuted. However, it is not really equality that is at stake here. In the Committee's interpretation, the Convention requires States parties not to punish prostitutes at all, as opposed to procurers and clients. The Committee consistently holds this (abolitionist) position, apparently even regarding prostitutes who voluntarily engage in prostitution in countries where prostitution is forbidden. Discrimination and violence against sex workers is rarely mentioned, as the focus of the Committee seems to be directed predominantly at the 'rehabilitation' of sex workers and the issue of forced prostitution. Thus, it is mostly support that is required, and not so much the elimination of discriminatory laws and attitudes against prostitutes. However, regarding countries where prostitution has been decriminalized, the Committee has occasionally pointed at the necessity to offer sex workers labour law protection and such, on an equal footing with other workers, albeit not in very explicit words. There are no references to other forms of discrimination of those involved in sex work, although sex workers, given the stigma, must suffer from all sorts of discrimination, also or maybe even more, outside the immediate context of their activities. But no mention at all is made of discrimination against prostitutes regarding issues unrelated to their activities as such, for example the possibility to share their lives with a partner of their choice, to raise their children, or to have their privacy respected.

Most remarkable, and worrying, is the almost complete lack of attention to harassment, intimidation, blackmail and violence by government officials such as the police, despite the fact that this is a huge and persistent problem in almost all countries.[110] This is an area that CEDAW ought to look into, because such

---

[110] See *e.g.* SEX WORKERS' RIGHTS ADVOCACY NETWORK, *Arrest the violence. Human rights abuses against sex workers in Central and Eastern Europe and Central Asia. A Community-*

harassment and violence constitute a 'first degree' violation of the Convention, given the fact that it is committed by the State itself. Moreover, there is no doubt at all about its despicability.

The improvement of the position of women, the second purpose of the Convention, is clearly the starting point for the Committee, and visible throughout the Concluding Observations. However, there seems to be a big difference in the kind of improvement envisaged. In abolitionist and prohibitionist countries, the improvement seems to be restricted to 'saving' women. Of course, rescue will be appreciated by those who are helpless against abusive exploitation. However, addressing people as helpless victims tends to deny their agency instead of empowering them. This seems contrary to the purpose of the Convention. In countries that have decriminalized prostitution, the Committee's recommendations, aimed at providing access to social security schemes for instance, seem more appropriate to empower sex workers. However, such recommendations are rare exceptions, given the limited number of countries where sex work is legal. Nevertheless, it is encouraging that the Committee is prepared to consider different kinds of approaches to the problem of exploitation of prostitution, including non-abolitionist approaches. Moreover, it seems equally critical and aware of the possibility of adverse effects of abolitionist and other policies.

A very small number of recommendations seem directed at fulfilling the third purpose of the Convention that is to change gender relations and combat prejudice, harmful customs and sex and gender-based stereotypes. In so far as this is addressed, it is mostly in the form of 'ending the (male) demand for prostitution' by criminalizing clients, which in fact reinforces existing attitudes on prostitution and – thus inevitably also – prostitutes as morally reprehensible. The Committee's few references to the stigma pertaining to prostitution, seem primarily focused at the harmful consequences thereof for those women who wish to leave sex work and 're-enter' society, and not to efforts to combat the stigma as such. Nor does it address the relation between stigma and the idea that prostitutes can be abused with impunity. Arguably, the Committee may be reluctant to do so, as encouraging States to combat the prejudice against prostitution may be (and probably rightfully so) understood as an attempt to 'normalize' prostitution, and that is definitely something that most States parties are not prepared to consider for now. It is nonetheless to be deplored, because the negative stigma of prostitution is directly related to ideas on 'sexual purity' of women and their 'deserving' protection against violence and abuse, and women's

---

Based Research Project of the Sex Workers' Rights Advocacy Network in Central and Eastern Europe and Central Asia, November 2009, available at: www.swannet.org/files/swannet/File/Documents/Arrest_the_Violence_SWAN_Report_Nov2009_eng.pdf [accessed 6 September 2011].

sexuality generally.[111] Thus, CEDAW's silence is not merely detrimental for women working in the sex industry, but for all women.

All in all, the emerging picture shows that the work of CEDAW may have positive effects on the position of women who have been coerced into prostitution – the 'classic victims', given the comprehensive approach and support encouraged by the Committee. However, also women who agree to working in the sex industry but resent their employment conditions or are subject to force in the course of their work, may benefit from CEDAW's work if the Committee continues to consistently take as its starting point the impact of laws and policies on the position of the women involved. However, according to the present authors – positive effects on the position of women will necessarily remain limited, as long as abolitionist approaches prevail and are not denounced. Their detrimental effects on sex workers are well-known, but either accepted because of moralistic notions of chastity, family values and the like, or legitimized by radical feminist theories of sex work as inherently degrading and sex workers as victims in need of rescue. However, the fact that the Committee leaves States a 'margin of appreciation' and is prepared to consider situations of legal sex work is certainly to be preferred over the endorsement of an abolitionist approach. Given the resurging dominance of the abolitionists in the global debate on prostitution, this position is certainly to be cherished. Hopefully, in the next thirty years, the Committee will seize the opportunity to hammer out in more detail the dangers for sex workers of the wrong kind of legislation, regardless whether it concerns criminal law or laws that intend to regulate the sex industry. By ignoring the specificities and long history of the branch, such legislation will achieve nothing but a turn for the worse for the women (and men) working in the sex industry, including victims of trafficking. And that is definitely not in accordance with the general goals of the Convention's drafters over thirty years ago.

---

[111] The close link between prostitution and women's sexual conduct more generally, speaks clearly from the situation in the Maldives: there is a risk that women and girls, who have been exploited in prostitution, could be re-victimized by the authorities because of the criminalization of extramarital relations; Maldives 37 (2007). See also: Jo DOEZEMA, 'Loose women or lost women. The re-emergence of the Myth of White Slavery in Contemporary Discourses of Trafficking in Women', in: *Gender Issues,* Vol. 18, no. 1, Winter 2000, pp. 23–50, available at: www.walnet.org/csis/papers/doezema-loose.html.

ARTICLE 7

States parties shall take all appropriate measures to eliminate discrimination against women in the political and public life of the country and, in particular, shall ensure to women, on equal terms with men, the right:

(a) To vote in all elections and public referenda and to be eligible for election to all publicly elected bodies;
(b) To participate in the formulation of government policy and the implementation thereof and to hold public office and perform all public functions at all levels of government;
(c) To participate in non-governmental organizations and associations concerned with the public and political life of the country.

ARTICLE 8

States parties shall take all appropriate measures to ensure to women, on equal terms with men and without any discrimination, the opportunity to represent their Governments at the international level and to participate in the work of international organizations.

CHAPTER 8

ARTICLES 7 AND 8: THE ADDED VALUE OF THE WOMEN'S CONVENTION AND THE DUTCH CASE OF THE CHRISTIAN PARTY

Margreet DE BOER

1. INTRODUCTION

In most countries, women have the right to vote, and the right to be eligible for election, but nowhere women actually participate in public and political life on equal terms with men.

This Chapter tries to answer the question whether the Women's Convention can contribute to the actual fulfilment of women's political rights. After a brief description of the historical background, the focus will be on what the Women's Convention and the CEDAW Committee (CEDAW) state about political participation. The added value of the Women's Convention will be looked into regarding the scope and regarding the level of equality that should be achieved. Next, it will be examined which measures State parties should take to ensure women's political rights.

To illustrate how the Women's Convention can be used to achieve equal political rights for women, the Dutch case on the exclusion of women by a small Christian party will be presented. In this case fundamental questions are raised (and answered) on the direct effect of the Women's Convention, on the relation of the right not to be discriminated against on the one hand and the freedom of religion and of association on the other, and on the responsibilities of the State: which measures should be taken?

The Chapter will end with a brief conclusion.

2. HISTORICAL BACKGROUND

The realization of political rights for women was one of the key issues for the feminist movements in the late nineteenth/early twentieth century (the so called first wave). All over the world women claimed their right to vote. We all remember the pictures of the Suffragettes in England. This fight was successful: the number of States in which women had the right to vote in national elections rose from three in 1914 (New Zealand, Australia and Norway), to 36 in 1945, and 58 in 1952.[1]

Within the United Nations, political participation has always been an issue. Although not explicitly, the Universal Declaration of Human Rights of 1945 gives women the right to political participation as Article 21 states that 'Everyone has the right to take part in the government of his country, directly or through freely chosen representatives', while Article 2 states that 'Everyone is entitled to all rights and freedoms set forth in this declaration without distinction of any kind such as race, colour, sex, language, religion.'

This general right was elaborated in the International Covenant on Civil and Political Rights (ICCPR) of 1966, which states in Article 25:

'Every citizen shall have the right and the opportunity, without any of the distinctions mentioned in Article 2 and without unreasonable restrictions:

(a) To take part in the conduct of public affairs, directly or through freely chosen representatives;
(b) To vote and to be elected at genuine periodic elections which shall be by universal and equal suffrage and shall be held by secret ballot, guaranteeing the free expression of the will of the electors;
(c) To have access, on general terms of equality, to public service in his country.'

Article 2 contains a non-discrimination provision, while Article 3 of the ICCPR explicitly focuses on the equality between men and women: 'The States parties to the present Covenant undertake to ensure the equal right of men and women to the enjoyment of all civil and political rights set forth in the present Covenant.'

THE RIGHT TO POLITICAL PARTICIPATION OF WOMEN

Right from the beginning, the UN not only paid attention to political rights in general, but also to the political rights of women in particular. In 1953 the UN adopted the Convention on the Political Rights of Women. The main Articles of this Convention are:

---

[1] In 1952, women had no right to vote in fifteen countries (among which Switzerland), and a limited right (compared to men) in eight countries. Figures from: *The road to equality, Political Rights of Women*, United Nations, Department of Social Affairs, Division of Human rights, New York 1953. United Nations Publication 1953.IV.4.

1. Women shall be entitled to vote in all elections on equal terms with men, without any discrimination.
2. Women shall be eligible for election to all publicly elected bodies, established by national law, on equal terms with men, without any discrimination.
3. Women shall be entitled to hold public office and to exercise all public functions, established by national law, on equal terms with men, without any discrimination.

The Declaration on the Elimination of Discrimination against Women (1967) sees to the political participation of women in Article 4:

'All appropriate measures shall be taken to ensure to women on equal terms with men, without any discrimination:

a. the right to vote in all elections and be eligible for election to all publicly elected bodies;
b. the right to vote in all public referenda;
c. the right to hold public office and to exercise all public functions.

Such rights shall be guaranteed by legislation.'

3. POLITICAL PARTICIPATION AND THE WOMEN'S CONVENTION

In the Convention on the Elimination of all Forms of Discrimination Against Women of 1979 (hereafter the Women's Convention or the Convention) the participation of women in political and public life is addressed in Article 7, while Article 8 focuses on equal representation of women in the international representation. Besides the right to vote, the right to be eligible and the right to exercise all public functions, Article 7 includes the right to participate in the formulation of government policy and the implementation thereof and the right to participate in non-governmental organizations and associations concerned with the public and political life of the country.

3.1. GENERAL RECOMMENDATIONS

CEDAW issued several General Recommendations on Articles 7 and 8, starting with the very brief General Recommendation No. 8 on Article 8 (1988), in which the Committee (only) recommends that States parties take further measures in accordance with Article 4 of the Convention to ensure the full implementation of Article 8 of the Convention.

In 1997 this brief recommendation was followed by the extensive General Recommendation No. 23 on both Article 7 and Article 8.[2] In General Recommendation No. 25 (temporary special measures)[3] and No. 26 (Women migrant workers)[4] the Committee mentions political participation.[5] In General Recommendation No. 23 the Committee elaborates on the background of the Articles and comments on the existing situation regarding the political participation of women. It describes that women have always been assigned to the private sphere, while men dominate the public sphere, and have exercised the power to confine and subordinate women to the private sphere. In all nations cultural traditions, religious beliefs and stereotyping (including by the media) have played and still play a role in confining women to the private, domestic spheres, excluding them from active participation in public life.[6] The Committee also gives an overview of factors which impede the exercising of political rights by women, such as the (lack of) access to information, illiteracy, lack of knowledge and understanding of political rights and systems, women's double burden of work, financial constraints, traditions and cultural stereotypes, restrictions on the freedom to move, and obstacles which derive from the electoral systems.[7]

In its General Recommendations the Committee mentions possible measures, sometimes formulated as good practices, sometimes as recommendations. These measures will be discussed below.

In addition to possible measures, the Committee determines what States should report under Articles 7 and 8. States should *inter alia* describe the legal measures that give effect to the rights contained in Article 7; provide details on any restrictions to those rights, whether arising from legal provisions or from any practice; describe the measures to overcome the barriers; include statistical data, disaggregated by sex, showing the percentage of women relative to men enjoying rights and actual participating in a wide range of functions and organizations as ensured by Articles 7 and 8, describe the extent to which women participate in (women's) NGOs and analyse the extent to which the State ensures that these organizations are consulted.[8]

---

[2] General Recommendation No. 23 (16th session, 1997), HRI/GEN/1/Rev.9 (Vol. II).
[3] General Recommendation No. 25, on Article 4, para. 1, of the Convention on the Elimination of All Forms of Discrimination Against Women, on temporary special measures, CEDAW, 2004.
[4] General Recommendation No. 26, on women migrant workers: CEDAW/C/2009/WP.1/R.
[5] General Recommendation No. 26, para. 23 (b): Active involvement of women migrant workers and relevant non-governmental organizations: States parties should seek the active involvement of women migrant workers and relevant non-governmental organizations in policy formulation, implementation, monitoring and evaluation (article 7 (b)).
[6] General Recommendation No. 23, under 8, 10 and 12.
[7] General Recommendation No. 23, under 20–23.
[8] General Recommendation No. 23, paras. 48 and 50.

3.2. DECISIONS UNDER THE OPTIONAL PROTOCOL

Until now, there have been no decisions of the Committee on Articles 7 or 8 under the Optional Protocol.[9]

3.3. CONCLUDING COMMENTS

In most Concluding Comments on State Reports the Committee pays attention to the implementation of Articles 7 and 8 by States parties.

In 1994 Goldschmidt and Verhage studied the Concluding Comments of the Committee in the second CEDAW session (1983), de seventh session (1988) de ninth (1990) and the eleventh session (1992) regarding Articles 7 and 8.[10] They found that the Committee frequently asked for (more specific) statistics on the political participation of women. Besides that, they found the Committee very much interested in the influence of women on public decision making, which showed in two ways: by asking for statistics on the public functions, and by asking about the measures the governments had taken to facilitate women's access to decision making.

In addition to the research of Goldschmidt and Verhage, the present author studied the Concluding Observations of the 45th session (2010). It seems that nowadays the Committee hardly ever asks for more statistics on the political participation of women. Most questions and comments are aimed at the (lack of) measures, with a focus on temporary special measures.

The measures that are suggested by CEDAW will be examined after a short discussion on the added value of the Women's Convention in the next section.

4. WHAT DOES THE WOMEN'S CONVENTION ADD TO OTHER HUMAN RIGHTS OBLIGATIONS?

The question is whether the provisions in the Women's Convention on political participation have an added value when compared to other human rights conventions. This added value could have various dimensions. In this Chapter the focus is on the scope and on the level or kind of equality that is required.

---

[9] For the text of the Optional Protocol see Annex II to this book.
[10] J.E. GOLDSCHMIDT and B. VERHAGE, 'Participatie in binnen- en buitenlands beleid', in: A.W. Heringa, J. Hes and L. Lijnzaad (eds.), *Het Vrouwenverdrag: een beeld van een verdrag...*, Maklu uitgevers, Apeldoorn, 1994, pp. 75–88.

4.1. THE SCOPE

The political rights as formulated in earlier conventions are included in the Women's Convention. However, in addition to the right to vote, to be elected, to hold public office and to exercise all public functions, Articles 7 and 8 contain additional rights:

- the participation in the formulation and implementation of government policy;
- the participation in non-governmental organizations and associations concerned with the public and political life;
- the equal opportunity to represent the government on the international level and to participate in international organizations.

In the General Recommendations and Concluding Comments of the Committee the added value of this broader scope becomes clear. Only part of the questions and recommendations of the Committee address the right to vote and the right to be elected as such. The Committee obviously sees political participation as a much broader topic, which is about the influence of women in decision making, and their actual participation on all levels of public life. In General Recommendation No. 23 the Committee states that the scope is even broader: The obligation specified in Article 7 extends to all areas of public and political life and is not limited to those areas specified in subparagraphs (a), (b) and (c). The political and public life of a country is a broad concept. It refers to the exercise of political power, in particular the exercise of legislative, judicial, executive and administrative powers. The term covers all aspects of public administration and the formulation and implementation of policy at the international, national, regional and local levels. The concept also includes many aspects of civil society, including public boards and local councils and the activities of organizations such as political parties, trade unions, professional or industry associations, women's organizations, community-based organizations and other organizations concerned with public and political life.[11]

4.2. SUBSTANSIVE EQUALITY

Where the 1953 Convention is mainly about formal (*de iure*) equality, the wording of both the Declaration of 1967 and the Women's Convention make it clear that equality before the law is not sufficient. Women's political rights have to be ensured, which means that women can really enjoy these rights in practice. Some authors have argued that the wording 'on equal terms with men' confirms that

---

[11] General Recommendation No. 23, para. 5.

Articles 7 and 8 mainly ask for formal equality.[12] I do not agree with this opinion. Almost all Articles of the Women's Convention contain the phrase 'on equal terms with men'. This does not mean that all provisions of the Convention are limited to formal equality. On the contrary, both the preamble and Articles 2 and 3 of the Women's Convention make it very clear that the Convention is not only concerned with *de iure* equality, but also (and maybe even more so) with *de facto*, or substantive equality.[13] This is also apparent when General Recommendation No. 23 and the Concluding Comments of the Committee are examined: the obligations of States parties do not stop at creating the same formal rights for women and men; they have to ensure the full and equal participation of women in decision-making. In General Recommendation No. 23 the Committee states: The concept of democracy will have real and dynamic meaning and lasting effect only when political decision-making is shared by women and men and takes equal account of the interests of both.[14] And very specific: While removal of *de iure* barriers is necessary, it is not sufficient. Failure to achieve full and equal participation of women can be unintentional and the result of outmoded practices and procedures which inadvertently promote men.[15] The Committee refers to the Beijing Platform for Action,[16] addressing the gap between the *de iure* and *de facto* situation, or the right on paper as against the reality of women's participation in politics and public life generally as the critical issue.[17]

5. MEASURES

To ensure *de iure* equality regarding political participation it is rather clear what measures States should take: States should adapt their legislation in such a manner that women have the same rights as men. But the question which measures States should take to fulfil their obligations regarding the *de facto* participation of women in public and political life is not easy to answer. The Convention itself does not mention any measures; it speaks of 'all appropriate measures'. States have a lot of freedom to choose what measures they take, as long as they do take measures, and as long as measures are appropriate and effective. Nevertheless, over the years CEDAW mentioned some measures; both in General Recommendation No. 23 and in Concluding Observations on individual States.

---

[12] See J.E. GOLDSCHMIDT and B. VERHAGE, 'Participatie in binnen- en buitenlands beleid', in: A.W. Heringa, J. Hes and L. Lijnzaad (eds.), *Het Vrouwenverdrag: een beeld van een verdrag...* Maklu uitgevers, Apeldoorn, 1994, p. 76.
[13] On substantive equality see Chapter 4 in this book by Rolanda Oostland.
[14] General Recommendation No. 23, para. 14.
[15] General Recommendation No. 23, para. 15.
[16] Beijing Declaration and Platform for Action, Fourth World Conference on Women, 15 September 1995, A/CONF.177/20 (1995) and A/CONF.177/20/Add.1 (1995).
[17] General Recommendation No. 23, para. 16.

In the next sub-sections a general description of what is said about measures in General Recommendation No. 23 and in (some) Concluding Observations will be given. After that, a thematically ordered overview of the measures that are mentioned will be provided, and some words will be spent on topics that are poorly off when it comes to concrete recommendations. This section will end with a brief discussion of the role of political parties as regards measures to ensure the rights of women to political participation.

5.1. MEASURES IN GENERAL RECOMMENDATION NO. 23

In General Recommendation No. 23 CEDAW does not recommend many concrete measures but gives examples of measures that have been taken by certain States. While CEDAW does not literally recommend these measures to all States, it is clear that the Committee refers to them with appreciation. These measures will be discussed in the next sub-sections. In addition, the Committee sums up in which fields measures should be taken, and what the goal and purpose of these measures should be. To some extent it is merely a repetition of the goals already mentioned in the Article of the Convention; in other respects it gives some more grip on what measures should be about.

CEDAW recommends that in order to ensure the right to women to vote and to be eligible for elections, States should take measures designed to:

- achieve a balance between women and men holding publicly elected positions;
- ensure that women understand their right to vote, the importance of this right and how to exercise it;
- ensure that barriers to equality are overcome, including those resulting from illiteracy, language, poverty and impediments to women's freedom of movement;
- assist women experiencing such disadvantages to exercise their right to vote and to be elected.[18]

In order to ensure women the right to participate in the formulation and implementation of government policy and to perform all public functions at all levels of government States should take measures designed to:

- ensure equality of representation of women in the formulation of government policy;
- ensure women's enjoyment in practice of the equal right to hold public office;
- ensure recruiting processes directed at women that are open and subject to appeal.[19]

---

[18] General Recommendation No. 23, para. 45.
[19] General Recommendation No. 23, para. 46.

With the purpose of ensuring women's right to participate in non-governmental organizations States should take measures designed to:

- ensure that effective legislation is enacted prohibiting discrimination against women;
- encourage non-governmental organizations and public and political associations to adopt strategies that encourage women's representation and participation in their work.[20]

When it comes to Article 8, CEDAW gives no concrete recommendations which measures States should take to ensure women, on equal terms with men and without any discrimination, the opportunity to represent their governments at the international level and to participate in the work of international organizations. What CEDAW does do is specifying the international organizations: States should take measures designed to ensure a better gender balance in membership of all United Nations bodies, including the Main Committees of the General Assembly, the Economic and Social Council and expert bodies, including treaty bodies, and in appointments to independent working groups or as country or thematic Special Rapporteurs.[21]

In General Recommendation No. 23 CEDAW explicitly recommends temporary special measures in accordance with Article 4 of the Convention (see further: Section 5.3).

5.2. MEASURES IN CONCLUDING OBSERVATIONS

The research of Goldschmidt and Verhage[22] shows that in the period they studied (1983–1992), the suggestion to take certain measures was often made implicitly: CEDAW asked individual States whether certain measures were taken or considered. From the questions asked States could infer what the Committee recommended. Explicit recommendations were also made, but not as often as they are nowadays. In 2010 CEDAW formulated most of its recommendations rather concrete, and with referral to General Recommendation No. 23 (which did not yet exist in the period 1983–1992).

The topics on which questions are asked and recommendations were given in 2010 are slightly different from those in 1983–1992. In both periods CEDAW is very much interested in quota, numeric goals, time frames and other temporary special measures. However, the special interest the Committee had in 1983–1992 in the question how the input by women is ensured in the process of decision

---

[20] General Recommendation No. 23, para. 47.
[21] General Recommendation No. 23, para. 49.
[22] Ibid., 12, pp. 78–84.

making did not show in the Concluding Observations of the 45th session in 2010. On the other hand: while in 1983–1992 questions on campaigns and training were scarce, these topics received a lot of attention in 2010.

5.3. TEMPORARY SPECIAL MEASURES: QUOTA, NUMERIC GOALS AND TIME FRAMES

In General Recommendation No. 23 CEDAW explicitly recommends to take temporary special measures: 'Under article 4, the Convention encourages the use of temporary special measures in order to give full effect to articles 7 and 8. The formal removal of barriers and the introduction of temporary special measures to encourage the equal participation of both men and women in the public life of their societies are essential prerequisites to true equality in political life. [...] In order, however, to overcome centuries of male domination of the public sphere, women also require the encouragement and support of all sectors of society to achieve full and effective participation, encouragement and support which must be given by States parties to the Convention, as well as by political parties and public officials. States parties have an obligation to ensure that temporary special measures are clearly designed to support the principle of equality and therefore comply with constitutional principles which guarantee equality to all citizens. Those countries that have developed effective temporary strategies in order to achieve equality of participation, have implemented a wide range of measures, including setting numerical goals and quotas.'[23]

In the Concluding Observations in the years 1983–1992 CEDAW asked several States whether political parties used a quota-system for women. CEDAW highly recommended the quota-system to Tanzania. The Committee also asked the Government of this State whether numeric goals for increasing the number of women members of farmer organizations had been set.[24]

In the 45th session of 2010, the Concluding Observations of CEDAW contain a standard phrase reading that the State party should introduce temporary special measures, in accordance with Article 4, paragraph 1, of the Convention and the Committee's General Recommendation No. 25 on temporary special measures. For some countries, the recommendations were more specific. Botswana and the United Arab Emirates were recommended to establish concrete goals and timetables to accelerate women's equal participation in public and political life. The Committee called upon all the governments of the Netherlands, including those of the Netherlands Antilles and local and provincial authorities, to accelerate their efforts to achieve equal representation in their elected bodies and, with that aim, to adopt temporary special measures,

---

[23] General Recommendation No. 23, para. 15.
[24] *Ibid.*, 12, p. 81.

in particular quotas, numerical goals and measurable targets aimed at increasing the participation of women, including migrant and minority women, in political and public decision-making at all levels. Both Panama and Ukraine were recommended to increase the effort to adapt and implement already drafted/ adapted laws which established – *inter alia* – a 30% quota for both genders in elected bodies. CEDAW expressed serious concerns at the limited scope of a newly established quota in Egypt (a quota of 64 additional seats reserved for women in the People's Assembly (lower house).

5.4. AWARENESS RAISING CAMPAIGNS

Campaigns directed at equal participation are mentioned in General Recommendation No. 23 as an example of a measure which has been implemented where countries have developed effective temporary strategies in an attempt to achieve equality of participation.[25]

In the period studied by Goldschmidt and Verhage the Committee suggested to Barbados to start programmes to increase women's political awareness. To Ghana one of the members of CEDAW mentioned changes in attitude through education. New Zealand was asked which measures the Government had taken to erase prejudices against the participation of women in public and political life.[26]

In 2010 CEDAW urged and called on most States[27] to implement awareness raising programmes, not only to encourage women to participate in public life and politics, but also to highlight the importance to society as a whole of women's full and equal participation in leadership positions at all levels of decision-making for the development of the country. CEDAW's recommendations to Panama and Ukraine on awareness raising are even broader. The Committee urges these States to intensify their efforts aimed at modifying stereotypical attitudes and cultural norms on the responsibilities and roles of women and men in the family, workplace, political life and society, including through awareness raising campaigns.

5.5. TRAINING AND ASSISTING WOMEN CANDIDATES

In General Recommendation No. 23 CEDAW indicates that financially assisting and training women candidates are measures that have been implemented in

---

[25] General Recommendation No. 23, para. 15.
[26] *Ibid.*,12, pp. 80–82.
[27] Botswana, Egypt, Panama, United Arab Emirates, Uzbekistan.

countries that have developed effective temporary strategies to achieve equality of participation. Alas without concrete examples.

Goldschmidt and Verhage note that CEDAW asked Uruguay whether women representatives receive financial compensation.[28]

In 2010 the Committee recommended several States to develop targeted training and mentoring programmes for women candidates and women elected to public office, as well as programmes on leadership and negotiation skills for current and future women leaders.[29]

5.6. THE VOICE OF WOMEN

Goldschmidt and Verhage describe that in the period 1983–1992 CEDAW is not only interested in the actual political participation of women in elected bodies, but is also very much interested in the influence women, and women's organizations have on decision making. For example, Uruguay is asked how, with very few female MPs, opinions and interests of women are reported to decision makers, and how they are weighed.

In session 45 of 2010 no concrete recommendations were made on ensuring that the voice of women is heard in formulating all policies. Consulting women's NGOs is mentioned, but always in relation to specific topics (like violence against women), or to the implementation of the Convention and achieving gender equality. For example, the Committee encourages Ukraine to cooperate with women's organizations, in order to formulate and adopt a new national plan of action which should provide a comprehensive approach to gender equality. The Committee reminds the public authorities of the Netherlands that a constructive dialogue with civil society is imperative for the effective protection and promotion of women's rights. The Committee calls upon them to ensure systematic consultation with NGOs in the elaboration and evaluation of policies aimed at achieving gender equality.

5.7. PARTICIPATION OF WOMEN IN NGOS AND ASSOCIATIONS CONCERNED WITH THE PUBLIC AND POLITICAL LIFE

Goldschmidt and Verhage mention that CEDAW asked Tanzania which percentage of members of the Farmers' Organization was female, and whether the Government had set numeric goals to increase this percentage.

---

[28] *Ibid.*, 12, p. 80.
[29] See Concluding Observations on Egypt, Panama and Uzbekistan.

In 2010, the only reference to participation in NGOs and associations was made in the Concluding Observations on the Netherlands. CEDAW urged the Netherlands to make efforts to implement previous recommendations on the discrimination against women by a political party that continues to exclude women from the party's posts.[30] CEDAW makes it clear that it is the State party's obligation to adopt measures against discrimination, including discrimination within the political party SGP.[31]

5.8. MEASURES AND THE FREEDOM OF POLITICAL PARTIES AND ASSOCIATIONS

With that last recommendation, an important question is raised: do the obligations under the Women's Convention apply to political parties and associations, and if so, what does this mean for the party or organization? What measures can and should a government take? What about the principle that it is up to political parties to make up their ballots and that associations have the freedom to choose their own board members and representatives, and that the State should not interfere with this?

Exactly these questions are key in the case of the Dutch Christian party, which will be discussed in section 6.

Besides the observations on the Netherlands, CEDAW does not say much on the role of political parties and associations in its General Recommendations, nor in its Concluding Observations. In General Recommendation No. 23 the Committee only emphasizes that the encouragement for women to enter into politics must be led by States parties to the Convention as well as by political parties and public officials. In the years 1983–1992 CEDAW asked several States whether political parties used a quota-system for women.

But what measures should be taken? This question will be discussed after the next section which will examine the case of the Dutch Christian party SGP.

6. CASE STUDY: THE CASE OF THE DUTCH CHRISTIAN PARTY THAT EXCLUDES WOMEN

Why bother that a small Christian party in the Netherlands is excluding women from membership and from being elected? Is this not their freedom of religion? Is it not a cultural tradition that should be acknowledged? Why should the State take measures?

---

[30] The previous recommendations (2007) held that the State should take measures to end this discrimination.
[31] See footnote 34.

The fact that these questions were (and are) asked, shows that discrimination against women is still accepted, even today, even in the Netherlands. One of the women who initiated the legal proceedings in this case put it this way: 'everybody knows that would it have been Jews or ethnic minorities that were excluded from the membership of a political party, the State would have intervened'.[32]

In 2003 the test case fund 'Clara Wichmann' and around ten other NGOs started proceedings against the SGP,[33] an orthodox Christian party that excluded women from its membership, and against the State, which allowed this exclusion, did not take any measures to end it, and even subsidized the party. As I see it, the three main goals of these test cases were to end the discrimination against women by the SGP, to make it clear that the State has a positive obligation to take measures to end this discrimination; and to get a verdict that acknowledges that some provisions of the Women's Convention have direct effect in the Dutch legal system.

Between 2003 and 2010, several courts heard the case. The final decision was made by the Supreme Court on April 9th 2010. In this section some background information on the SGP and its 'opinion upon women' will be given. After that the case and the court decisions will be described. In accordance with the decision of the Supreme Court, the three aspects of the case will be briefly discussed. Does the exclusion of women – from membership or from the ballot – by a political party fall within the scope of Article 7(c)? If so: does this Article – in this case – have direct effect before a Dutch Court? And what measures should the party and/or the State take to end the discrimination? Of course there are a lot of other interesting aspects to the case, like the question how the prohibition of discrimination against women is related to the freedom of association and the freedom of religion. What the courts have said in this respect will be summarized, but it will not be discussed in depth.[34] Nor will this section go into the discussion whether a court case on human rights is the most desirable or effective way to achieve social change within an orthodox religious community.[35]

---

[32] Elsbeth Boor, in her speech on 2 December 2005, on the occasion of the awards of the Harriet Freezer ring to herself and the test case fund Clara Wichmann. A shortened version of the speech is published in: Margreet de Boer en Marjan Wijers, *Vrouw en Recht: De beweging, de mensen, de issues*, Pallas Publications, 2009, pp. 111–115.

[33] SGP stands for *Staatkundig Gereformeerde Partij*, which can be translated as Political Reformed Party.

[34] See for a discussion on this topic: Titia Loenen, *Geloof in het geding: Juridische grenzen van religieus pluralisme in het perspectief van de mensenrechten*, 2006, SDU, The Hague.

[35] For this discussion see: Barbara M. Oomen, Joost Guijt, and Mattias Ploeg, 'CEDAW, the Bible and the State of the Netherlands: The Struggle Over Orthodox Women's Political Participation and Their Responses (June 2010)', *Utrecht Law Review*, Vol. 6, No. 2, pp. 158–174, June 2010. Available at SSRN: www.ssrn.com/abstract=1625682.

6.1. THE SGP AND 'THE WOMEN'S ISSUE'

The point of view that women's destiny is at home, and not in the public sphere, is one of the main reasons of existence of the SGP. The party was founded in 1918 as a reaction to the fact that the main Reformed Party supported the universal suffragette.[36] For decades, the discussion within the party on the political participation of women focused on the question whether they were allowed to vote. The principled members argued that voting was against the women's destination, while the pragmatists wanted as many votes for the party as possible and therefore wished to allow women to vote. It was not until the early 1980s, when several women from the SGP-community had become members of some local sections of the party, that the SGP started to formulate an official position on political participation of women. In 1989 the programme of principles of the party was amended with two articles on the political participation of women. Article 7 states: 'Each striving for emancipation that misjudges the destiny and place of men and women as given by God is revolutionary and should be challenged forcefully'. Article 10 adds: 'The notion of women's suffrage, based upon a revolutionary striving for emancipation, conflicts with women's destiny. This also applies to women taking a place in political bodies, both representative and administrative. A woman's conscience will guide her in deciding whether to vote, taking into account the place given to her by the Lord.'

As long as the opinion of the party was (only) expressed in the principles, there was no official obstacle for women to become a member, and some of them did. This lead to a new discussion within the party, and eventually in 1996 to new provisions in the Statutes which read that members of the party are men, and that special members can be both men and women. Special members are excluded from board-functions and representation within the party, the right to vote within the party, and a place on the ballot for elections.[37] By including these provisions in the Statutes, the SGP no longer only was of the *opinion* that women should not participate in politics, but also in reality *made a distinction* between the rights of men and women to participate.

In 2007 – so during the procedures that are discussed below – the Statutes of the SGP were changed again: both men and women can be full members of the party. But only (and this was not the case before 1996) when they subscribe the principles of the party, including article 10, which excludes women from taking a seat in political bodies and being eligible for election.[38]

---

[36] This Party, the ARP, did so in exchange for State support for religious schools.
[37] Statutes of the SGP 1996, Articles 5 and 5a; in 1997 renumbered into Articles 4 and 5.
[38] Statutes of the SGP 2007, Article 4.

6.2. PROLOGUE TO THE PROCEEDINGS IN THE SGP-CASE: CEDAW CONCLUDING OBSERVATIONS 2001

'The Committee notes with concern that, in the Netherlands, there is a political party represented in the Parliament that excludes women from membership, which is a violation of article 7 of the Convention. The Committee recommends that the State party take urgent measures to address this situation, including through the adoption of legislation that brings the membership of political parties into conformity with its obligations under article 7'.[39]

6.3. THE PROCEEDINGS IN THE SGP-CASE: THE DISTRICT COURT

In 2003 the test case fund 'Clara Wichmann' and around ten other NGOs started civil proceedings against both the SGP and the State. In the case against the party, the SGP was summoned to end their discrimination against women and to adapt the Statutes and other rules of the party in order to make it possible that women become members of the party on equal terms with men. In the case against the State, the plaintiffs asked the judge for a declaratory judgment that the Dutch State was acting unlawfully by tolerating and even supporting the discrimination against women by the SGP. The judge was also requested to condemn the State for not taking measures to end the discrimination by the SGP.

In September 2005 the District Court of The Hague gave a verdict in both cases.[40] In the case against the SGP the verdict was that the changing of the Statutes of the party is not of general interest for which the test fund and the other plaintiffs can come up in court, but only of interest to women who want to be a member of the SGP. As no SGP-women were involved in the case, the judge declared the case against the SGP inadmissible. As the case failed on the admissibility, the judge gave no judgment on the merits. In the case against the State, the court judged that under the Women's Convention the State is obliged to take appropriate measures to eliminate discrimination against women in political and public life. The State did not meet these obligations, because not only did it take no action to end the discrimination against women by the SGP, but it even supported the party by giving it financial support.[41] The Court ordered that the State should terminate the financial support to the SGP given that the party would not allow women to become members of the party on equal terms with men. The State appealed against this verdict; the SGP joined the appeal as an interested party.

---

[39] CEDAW/A/56/38, paras. 219 and 220.
[40] Rechtbank 's-Gravenhage 7 September 2005, HA ZA 03/3396, LJN: AU2091, and Rechtbank 's-Gravenhage 7 September 2005, HA ZA 03/3395, LJN: AU2088.
[41] In the Netherlands all political parties which are represented in parliament receive financial support from the State.

6.4. INTERMEZZO: CEDAW CONCLUDING OBSERVATIONS 2007

> 'The Committee notes with concern that a political party continues to discriminate against women and exclude them from party posts, which is a violation of articles 1, 2 and 7 of the Convention. The Committee notes with concern that the State party has appealed a decision by the District Court of The Hague [...], which gave direct effect to article 7 of the Convention in national law and which held that the State's funding, under the Political Parties (Funding) Act, of a political party that excludes women from membership was in violation of its obligations under the Convention. The Committee recommends that the State party adopt legislation to bring the qualification for seeking political office into conformity with its obligations under articles 1, 2 and 7 of the Convention, as well as to consider withdrawing its appeal and acknowledging the direct effect of the Convention in the domestic legal order.'[42]

6.5. THE PROCEEDINGS IN THE SGP-CASE: THE APPEAL

The State did not withdraw its appeal. But while the (civil) appeal proceedings were pending with the higher court in The Hague, the State terminated the financial support of the SGP. The SGP challenged this decision in an administrative procedure with the Council of State. In December 2007 the Council of State judged in the administrative procedure that terminating the financial support to the SGP was incorrect.[43]

Two weeks later the judgment of the Council of State is followed by the judgment of the Court of Appeal in the civil case of the NGOs against the State.[44] Like the District Court, the Court of Appeal judged that the distinction made by the SGP between men and women is forbidden under – inter alia – the Women's Convention, which obliges the State to ensure women their right to stand for election on the same terms with men. Not acting on this discrimination against women by the State would be unlawful. The State must take measures which lead to providing the right to be elected by the SGP to women. The measure has to be effective, but at the same time be the least intrusive in respect of the SGP members' rights. It is the discretion of the State to choose the measure. Because a legal measure is required, it cannot be ordered by the court. Other than the District Court, the Court of Appeal states that it cannot judge on the termination of the financing; that is up to the Administrative Court. Besides that, the Court of Appeal considers that the termination of the subsidy is not an appropriate measure, because the Court does not think it is reasonable that ending the financial means

---

[42] CEDAW/C/NLD/CO/4, paras. 25 and 26.
[43] Raad van State 5 december 2007, 200609224/1, LJN: BB9493.
[44] Gerechtshof 's-Gravenhage 20 december 2007, 05/1725, LJN: BC0619.

will lead to the SGP accepting women to stand for election. The State decides to lodge an appeal with the Court of Cassation (the Dutch Supreme Court).

6.6. INTERMEZZO: CEDAW CONCLUDING OBSERVATIONS 2010

> *'The Committee acknowledges the relatively short time between the adoption of the previous concluding observations and the examination of their implementation. It regrets, however, that some of the concerns it expressed and the recommendations it adopted after the consideration of the fourth periodic report of the Netherlands [...] in 2007 have been insufficiently addressed. These include, for instance, those regarding the status of the Convention in the domestic legal system, discrimination against women by a political party that continues to exclude women from the party's posts, [...]. The Committee urges the Netherlands to make every effort to address the previous recommendations that have not yet been fully implemented, as well as the concerns contained in the present concluding observations. The Committee reiterates its call on the State party to reconsider its position and to ensure that substantive provisions of the Convention are fully applicable in the domestic legal order, in compliance with the obligation of the State party to adopt measures against discrimination (including within the political party SGP) and to provide for domestic remedies for alleged violations of any rights guaranteed to individuals by the Convention.'*[45]

6.7. THE PROCEEDINGS IN THE SGP-CASE: THE VERDICT OF THE SUPREME COURT

On 9 April 2010 the Supreme Court issued the final decision in the case.[46] The appeal was rejected, and the decisions of the Court of Appeal were confirmed. The considerations of the Supreme Court were brief, but clear. They cover the admissibility of the plaintiffs (not being SGP-women but organizations which serve the general interest), the direct applicability of Articles 7a and 7c of the Convention in court, the question whether the State can and should interfere in political parties, the relation and balance between the prohibition of discrimination and other fundamental rights, and the measures the State should take. The question of admissibility will not be explored any further; the other issues will be discussed in the next sections.

---

[45] CEDAW/C/NLD/CO/5, paras. 10, 11 and 13.
[46] Hoge Raad 9 April 2010, 08/01354, LJN: BK4547.

6.8. THE DIRECT EFFECT OF ARTICLE 7 WOMEN'S CONVENTION AND THE KEY ROLE OF POLITICAL PARTIES IN THE ENFORCEMENT OF THE RIGHT TO STAND FOR ELECTION

In the Dutch legal order, provisions of treaties have direct effect (are self executing) if they are binding on all persons by virtue of their contents.[47] Provisions of international law which are binding on all persons prevail over conflicting Dutch law.[48] It is up to the courts to decide whether a provision is binding on all persons, and therefore has direct effect.

In this case, the Supreme Court is very clear that both Article 7a and 7c of the Women's Convention have direct effect. The Supreme Court starts its reasoning with the remark that under Article 7 of the Women's Convention, States should not only take all appropriate measures to eliminate discrimination against women in political and public life, but also to ensure the right to (a) vote in all elections and public referenda and to be eligible for election to all publicly elected bodies and (c) to participate in non-governmental organizations and associations concerned with the public and political life of the country. The Supreme Court goes on: 'That the provisions under (a) have direct effect is – correctly – presumed by the government at the consideration of the ratification of the Women's Convention, on the grounds that the right to equal treatment regarding the right to vote and to be elected is already included in other treaties, of which the direct effect was accepted in court. The government left it to the courts to decide whether the provisions under (c) have direct effect.' The Supreme Court decides that also Article 7c has direct effect, because of the close relationship between Article 7a and 7c. 'In our system, like in many other democratic electoral systems, political parties do play a key role in the elections of public elected bodies, because the enforcement of the right to stand for election by a person depends on his nomination by a political party, while this nomination usually depends on the membership of the party. Through this role, there is no doubt that the direct effect of the provisions under (a) do bring along the direct effect of the provisions under (c), insofar the active participation in a political party is a condition for the effective enforcement of the right to stand for election as ensured under a.'[49]

---

[47] Article 93 of the Constitution of the Netherlands.
[48] Article 94 of the Constitution of the Netherlands.
[49] Hoge Raad 9 April 2010, consideration 4.4.2., translation MdB.

6.9. THE PROHIBITION OF DISCRIMINATION REGARDING POLITICAL RIGHTS IN RELATION TO THE FREEDOM OF RELIGION AND THE FREEDOM OF ASSOCIATION

The Supreme Court considers that in a specific case, the right to equal treatment of women, as laid down in – *inter alia* – Article 7 of the Women's Convention, can conflict with other fundamental rights, such as the freedom of religion and the freedom of association. In that case, the court has to weigh which right has to prevail. Other than the plaintiffs argue this weighing has not been made on forehand within Article 7. The question rises whether an exception to the equal rights of women regarding the right to stand for election, as guaranteed by Article 7 can be accepted in a case like this, in which a political party, the political aim of which is based upon its religious beliefs and as a result of these beliefs, excludes women from the ballot for publicly elected bodies. The Supreme Court answers this question in the negative. The freedom of religion and the freedom of association guarantee that people can organize themselves in a political party on the grounds of a religious or ideological belief, and can express the political principles and programmes based upon these beliefs. In a democratic State, however, these principles and programmes can only be practiced within the limits set by laws and conventions. The representative bodies represent the entire population of the State. They are at the heart of the democracy. The right to vote and the right to stand for election are fundamental in order to guarantee the democratic value of these bodies. Because the possibility to be able to practice the right to stand for election is key for the democratic State, it is not acceptable that a political group acts against the fundamental right that guarantees the political rights of all citizens, even when this acting is based on a principle rooting in the religious or ideological beliefs. Here, the prohibition of discrimination prevails. Subsequently, the conclusion must be drawn that the violation by the SGP of the fundamental rights of women to stand for elections on equal terms with men, as guaranteed in the Constitution and the international conventions, is not justified because the opinion of the party regarding the destination and role of women in society is rooted in its religious beliefs. Although the party cannot be denied to hold this opinion, it is not up to the civil court to judge upon the importance of the opinion within the religious beliefs of the members of the party, and a democratic State requires tolerance on opinions grounded on religious or ideological beliefs, the court can and does judge that the way in which the SGP brings its opinion into practice regarding the balloting for general elections cannot be accepted.[50]

---

[50] Hoge Raad 9 April 2010, consideration 4.5.2–4.5.5.

6.10. THE ROLE OF THE STATE: RESPONSIBILITIES AND MEASURES

Because of the direct effect of Article 7(c) of the Women's Convention the State is obliged to guarantee its citizens that political parties not only accept women as members, as far as membership is a condition to be balloted, but also accept women to the ballot itself. Only then the State can effectively guarantee the right to be elected for women, as required by the Convention. On this point, the Convention leaves no freedom of policy to the State.[51]

The Court held that the opinion of the State that it was justified not to take any measures against the exclusion of women from the ballot is not correct. The State is obliged to take measures which actually achieve that the SGP grants women the right to be on the ballot. This measure should be effective but should harm the fundamental rights of (members of) the SGP in the least possible way. However, the Court cannot order the State to take specific measures. The Court does not have the power to oblige the State to issue formal legislation. Nor can the Court prescribe specific other measures, because the choice of the measures taken by the State requires a weighing of interests which touches a political weighing to such an extent that it cannot be asked from the Court. The same is true for the termination of the financing by the State, which is not possible under the current laws.

Until now – six months after the decision of the Supreme Court – the Dutch Government has not taken any measures.

7. CONCLUSION

My conclusion is that the Women's Convention has an added value when it comes to the realization of political rights of women. Its scope is broader than that of other conventions, and it requires not only equality before the law, but substantive equality. The measures States can take to achieve this equality are described rather detailed, both in General Recommendation No. 23 and in Concluding Observations on various countries. CEDAW makes it very clear that it expects States to take temporary special measures like numeric goals and quotas to achieve *de facto* equal political rights.

The Dutch case of the exclusion of women by a small Christian party shows us that the Convention can be useful in cases where the equal participation of women is at stake. The considerations and decisions of the Dutch Supreme Court are well founded, and might be of use for cases in other countries as well. The

---

[51] Hoge Raad, 9 April 2010, consideration 4.5.1.

consideration that not only Article 7(a) has direct effect, but Article 7(c) as well, at least 'insofar the active participation in a political party is a condition for the effective enforcement of the right to stand for election' is important for all countries where provisions of international conventions can have direct effect. It means that women can call upon the State to guarantee their participation in political parties. The line of arguing in the weighing of equal political rights against the freedom of religion can be of even broader importance. The Supreme Court states that because the possibility to be able to practice the right to stand for election is key for the democratic State, it is not acceptable that a political group acts against this fundamental right that guarantees the political rights of all citizens, even when this acting is based on a principle rooted in the religious or ideological beliefs; as a result the prohibition of discrimination prevails. The Supreme Court also makes it very clear that the State is obliged to take measures which actually achieve that political parties accept women to the ballot. Which measures are taken is up to the Government, as long as they are effective. Not taking any measures, however, is not an option.

ARTICLE 9

1. States parties shall grant women equal rights with men to acquire, change or retain their nationality. They shall ensure in particular that neither marriage to an alien nor change of nationality by the husband during marriage shall automatically change the nationality of the wife, render her stateless or force upon her the nationality of the husband.
2. States parties shall grant women equal rights with men with respect to the nationality of their children.

CHAPTER 9
EQUAL TREATMENT OF WOMEN AND MEN IN NATIONALITY LAW

Gerard-René DE GROOT

1. INTRODUCTION

In this contribution first of all the relationship of Article 9 Women's Convention to provisions in other treaties will be described (Section 2). Then the historical development from a system where the nationality position of a married woman depended completely on the nationality of her husband to a system where married women have a nationality of their own will be explained (Section 3). Also the development of a system where the nationality of children depended principally on the nationality of their father to a system where father and mother can pass their nationality to their children under equal terms will be sketched (Section 4). Article 9 Women's Convention is the end station of these developments. However, not all States endorsed the principles enshrined in this Article completely. Therefore, it will be examined which countries made a reservation to Article 9 at the occasion of becoming a party to the Women's Convention (Section 5). Finally, some attention is paid to transitory provisions enacted by countries in the legislation implementing the principles of Article 9 in their national laws (Section 6).

2. TREATY PROVISIONS

The content of paragraph 1 of Article 9 of the Convention on the Elimination of All Forms of Discrimination Against Women (hereinafter: Women's Convention) is repeated by Article 4(d) European Convention on Nationality of 1997[1] (hereinafter: ECN) which states that neither marriage nor the dissolution

---

[1] CETS (Council of Europe Treaty Series) 166.

of a marriage between a national of a State party and an alien, nor the change of nationality by one of the spouses during marriage, shall automatically affect the nationality of the other spouse. It has to be underpinned that the ECN does not allow making a reservation on the Articles 3–5.

Some elements of this rule could already be found in older conventions. The Hague Treaty on Nationality of 1930 initiated by the League of Nations already aimed at avoiding that women became stateless because of the fact that they followed the nationality status of their husbands.[2] The convention provided *inter alia*:

> 'Article 8. If the national law of the wife causes her to lose her nationality on marriage with a foreigner, this consequence shall be conditional on her acquiring the nationality of the husband.
> Article 9. If the national law of the wife causes her to lose her nationality upon a change in the nationality of her husband occurring during marriage, this consequence shall be conditional on her acquiring her husband's new nationality.
> Article 10. Naturalisation of the husband during marriage shall not involve a change in the nationality of the wife except with her consent.
> Article 11. The wife who, under the law of her country, lost her nationality on marriage shall not recover it after the dissolution of the marriage except on her own application and in accordance with the law of that country. If she does recover it, she shall lose the nationality which she acquired by reason of the marriage.'[3]

That women should not become stateless by marriage or as a consequence of being married, is also stressed by Articles 5 and 6 of the United Nations Convention on the reduction of statelessness 1961:[4]

> 'Article 5(1). If the law of a Contracting State entails loss of nationality as a consequence of any change in the personal status of a person such as marriage, termination of marriage, legitimation, recognition or adoption, such loss shall be conditional upon possession or acquisition of another nationality.'
> Article 6. If the law of a Contracting State provides for loss of its nationality by a person's spouse or children as a consequence of that person losing or being deprived of that nationality, such loss shall be conditional upon their possession or acquisition of another nationality.'

---

[2] UNTS 179, 89; LNTS Bd. 179, 89. Compare Article 2 of the Convention on the nationality of women concluded in Montevideo on 26 December 1933: 'There shall be no distinction based on sex as regards nationality, in their legislation or in their practice.'

[3] These articles were at the time of their codification in the 1930 Convention obviously very controversial. H.Ch.G.J. van der Mandere, *Vijftien jaren arbeid van den Volkenbond 1919–1935*, Brand, Hilversum, 1935, p. 486, writes that the poor ratification status of the 1930 Convention is caused by hesitations on the Articles 8–11. It should be mentioned that the Netherlands ratified the 1930 Convention with a reservation on the Articles 8, 9 and 10.

[4] UNTS 989, 175.

But four years earlier another, more important step was taken by an international convention initiated by the United Nations. The 1957 Convention on the nationality of married women gave to women an independent position in nationality matters.[5] However, they could acquire the nationality of their husband by privileged naturalisation procedure or by making a special declaration of option. In other words, the acquisition of the nationality of the husband was not a general rule anymore, but the convention nevertheless tried to promote one single nationality in a family by giving women the right to acquire the nationality of their husbands under very privileged conditions. The treaty contained *inter alia* the following provisions:

> 'Article 1. Each Contracting State agrees that neither the celebration nor the dissolution of a marriage between one of its nationals and an alien, nor the change of nationality by the husband during marriage, shall automatically affect the nationality of the wife.
> Article 2. Each Contracting State agrees that neither the voluntary acquisition of the nationality of another State nor the renunciation of its nationality by one of its nationals shall prevent the retention of its nationality by the wife of such national.
> Article 3(1). Each Contracting State agrees that the alien wife of one of its nationals may, at her request, acquire the nationality of her husband through specially privileged naturalization procedures; the grant of such nationality may be subject to such limitations as may be imposed in the interests of national security or public policy.
> Article 3(2). Each Contracting State agrees that the present Convention shall not be construed as affecting any legislation or judicial practice by which the alien wife of one of its nationals may, at her request, acquire her husband's nationality as a matter of right.'

It has to be underpinned that there is a conflict between the 1957 Treaty and the Women's Convention. The fact that a woman should – according the rules of this treaty – be able to easily obtain the nationality of her husband, but the man could not obtain the nationality of his wife in the same way, could, when carefully observed, lead to discrimination against women. Spouses often think it practical for all kinds of reasons to have the same nationality. Under the rules of the 1957 Treaty it is usually the woman who has to give up her nationality if the couple wishes to possess a common nationality, since it is a lot harder for the man to change his nationality. For that reason, the Netherlands denounced the

---

[5] UNTS 309, 65; on this Convention see MARIE-HELENE MARESCAUX, 'Nationalité et statut personnel dans les instruments des Nations Unies', in: Michel Verwilghen (ed.), *Nationalité et statut personnel*, Bruylant, Brussels, 1984, pp. 57-62. See furthermore: *Nationality of Married Women*, Report submitted by the Secretary-General, United Nations, Commission on the Status of Women, New York, 1950 and *Convention on the nationality of married women, historical backgrounds*, United Nations, Department of Economic and Social Affairs, New York, 1962.

1957 Treaty on 16 January 1992; only a few months after the Netherlands ratified the Women's Convention, in order to avoid conflicting obligations.[6] The 1957 Convention was also denounced by Luxembourg (2007) and the United Kingdom (1981).

In this light it is remarkable that even today States ratify the outdated 1957 Treaty, including three of the new Member States of the European Union.[7] The United Nations should stimulate the denunciation of the 1957 Convention by those States which have ratified the Women's Convention.

The content of the second paragraph of Article 9 is also enshrined in Article 6(1) ECN:

> 'Each State Party shall provide in its internal law for its nationality to be acquired *ex lege* by the following persons: a) children one of whose parents possesses, at the time of the birth of these children, the nationality of that State Party, subject to any exceptions which may be provided for by its internal law as regards children born abroad. With respect to children whose parenthood is established by recognition, court order or similar procedures, each State Party may provide that the child acquires its nationality following the procedure determined by its internal law; ...'

It follows from this treaty provision that States are not allowed to treat women less favourable than men in respect of the possibility to transmit their nationality to the next generation. Although the ECN allows making a reservation on this Article, none of the 20 States which have ratified the Convention have made any reservation related to this provision.

3. HISTORICAL BACKGROUND: FROM *SYSTÈME UNITAIRE* TO *SYSTÈME DUALISTE*

In the past, all jurisdictions provided that husband and wife had the same nationality. In fact, women were treated in nationality law as an 'appendix' of their husbands. A foreign woman who married a national generally would acquire the nationality of her husband. By marrying a foreigner a woman would

---

[6] Article 2 Rijkswet of 3 July 1991, Stb. 355 'tot goedkeuring van het Verdrag inzake de uitbanning van alle vormen van discriminatie van vrouwen' (New York, 18 December 1979). *Cf.* also *Hoge Raad* (Supreme Court of the Netherlands) 4 March 1988, *NJ* 1989, 626, annotated by G.R. de Groot.

[7] After the Women's Convention came in force in 1981, the following States ratified the 1957 convention: Antigua and Barbados 1988, Armenia 1994, Azerbaijan 1996, Bosnia and Herzegovina 1993, Côte d'Ivoire 1999, Croatia 1992, Czech Republic 1993, Kazakhstan 2000, Kyrgyzstan 1997, Latvia 1992, Liberia 2005, Libya 1989, The former Yugoslav Republic of Macedonia 1994, Montenegro 2006, Nicaragua 1986, Rwanda 2003, Serbia 2001, Slovakia 1993, St Lucia 1991, St Vincent and the Grenadines 1999, South Africa 2002, Venezuela 1986, Zimbabwe 1998. Remarkably, all these States did also ratify the Women's Convention.

lose her original nationality.⁸ Therefore, husband and wife possessed one and the same nationality, which was, in *ius sanguinis* countries, also transferred to their children. If a man would acquire another nationality during the marriage and therefore would lose his original nationality, his wife (and in most cases their children) would also follow this new nationality position.

This can be illustrated with a description of the position of women in the Netherlands Nationality Act of 1892. According to this statute a wife would follow the nationality of her husband in all circumstances. A foreign woman who married a Netherlands citizen would acquire Netherlands citizenship automatically (Article 5 Nationality Act 1892). A Netherlands woman who married a foreigner or a stateless person, would lose her Netherlands nationality automatically (Articles 5 and 7(2) Nationality Act 1892). If a foreigner would acquire Netherlands citizenship, his wife would acquire this citizenship as well (Article 5 Nationality Act 1892). If a man would lose his Netherlands nationality, his wife would lose this status too (Articles 5 and 7(1) Nationality Act 1892). Legitimate children of a Netherlands father (and his Netherlands wife) would acquire the nationality of the father (Articles 1(a) and (b) Nationality Act 1892). An illegitimate child of a Netherlands mother would acquire her citizenship provided that the child was recognized (only) by her (Article 1(c) Nationality Act 1892). If the child later on was recognized by a foreigner, it would lose the nationality of its mother (Articles 1(a) and (c) Nationality Act 1892).

This system, which did more or less also exist in other States, is often described as a 'unitary system' (*système unitaire*).⁹ A huge disadvantage of this system was that in most countries women also used to lose their nationality if they married a stateless person or if their husband became stateless during the marriage. In order to avoid this disadvantage, some States provided that women would only lose their nationality, if they acquired the nationality of their husbands.¹⁰ This policy was encouraged later on by the already mentioned

---

8   See for examples around 1900: Austria (para. 32 ABGB), Belgium (Article 17 sub 3 Cc), Denmark, Germany (Article 13 Act 1870), Greece (Article 25 Cc), Luxembourg (Article 17 sub 3 Cc), Netherlands (Article 5 Act 1892), Spain (Article 22 Cc), Sweden (Article 6 Act 1894), Switzerland, Turkey (compare: Article 7 Act 1869), United Kingdom (Sect. 10 sub 1 Act 1870).

9   This expression was used by BERNARD DUTOIT, *La nationalité de la femme mariée*, Band I: Europa, Droz, Genève, 1973; Band II: Afrique, Droz, Genève, 1976; Band III: Amérique, Asie, Océanie, Droz, Genève, 1980; compare as well BERNARD DUTOIT, 'Nationalité et mariage: leur interaction dans le droit comparé de la nationalité', in: Michel Verwilghen (ed.), *Nationalité et statut personnel*, Bruylant, Brussels, 1984, pp. 443–474.

10 The first country to do this was – as far as we know – Bulgaria (Article 25; this provision was very liberal; no loss *ex lege*, but marriage was a ground for renunciation on initiative of the woman involved, see MATJAZ TRATNIK, *Het nationaliteitsrecht in de Oosteuropese landen*, Kluwer, Deventer, 1989, p. 125). See furthermore: France (Article 19), Italy (Article 14), Norway, Portugal (Article 22 sub 4); see ANDRÉ WEISS, *Traité théorique et pratique de droit international privé*, vol. I (La nationalité), 2nd edition, Sirey, Paris, 1907, 24. Austria (since 1925); Denmark (since 1925), Finland (since 1927), Greece (since 1926), Iceland (only loss if

Articles 8 – 11 of the Hague 1930 Convention on nationality. These provisions were *inter alia* a reaction to the fact that after the revolutions of 1918 the number of stateless persons had increased considerably.

Already during the twenties, some countries had made an additional step and had granted women an even more independent position by providing that marriage would not influence their nationality. The Soviet Union, Bulgaria and France were the first European States to do this.[11] Some other States made it possible for women to retain their own nationality after marriage by making a declaration.[12]

In the Netherlands the unitary system was revised in 1936 as a consequence of the ratification of the Hague convention on nationality of 1930.[13] A foreign woman, who married a Netherlands citizen, would still acquire Netherlands citizenship automatically, but a Netherlands wife of a foreigner or a stateless person would not automatically lose her Netherlands nationality in all cases (Article 5 Nationality Act 1892 (1936)). She would retain her Netherlands nationality, if she did not acquire and could not acquire (*niet deelachtig worden noch kunnen worden*) the citizenship of her husband by marriage.[14] Moreover, a child of a Netherlands mother and a stateless father would acquire the Netherlands nationality of its mother if it was born in the Netherlands (Article 2(c) Nationality Act 1892 (1936)). But in principle, a married woman would still follow the nationality of her husband. If her husband would acquire Netherlands citizenship, she would also acquire this status; if her husband would lose his Netherlands nationality, she would as well except in case this would entail that she would become a stateless person; then she would keep her Netherlands nationality (Article 5 Nationality Act 1892 (1936)).

An important revision of Netherlands nationality law was realized in 1963 as a consequence of the ratification of the New York Convention on the nationality of married women.[15] As already mentioned, this treaty prescribed an independent status for a married woman in nationality law. As a result of the revision of

---

residence abroad), Netherlands (since 1937, but with retroactivity to 1893), Norway, Sweden (since 1924), United Kingdom (since 1934).

[11] Soviet Union in 1918. Bulgaria: see previous footnote. Since 1927 until 1938 loss of nationality by a French woman marrying a foreigner occurred exclusively, if the spouses were living abroad and the nationality of the husband was acquired; since 1938 no longer any loss by marriage.

[12] Austria (since 1947); Belgium (since 1926); Greece (since 1955); Luxembourg (since 1934); Switzerland (since 1941), United Kingdom (since 1934).

[13] Act of 21 December 1936, *Staatsblad* 209, entered into force on 1 July 1937. According to a judgment of the *Hoge Raad* (Supreme Court) of 13 April 1948, *NJ* 1948, nr. 647 this revision had retroactivity from 1 July 1893!

[14] See on the practical consequences of this formulation including the burden of proof, an instruction of the Ministry of Foreign Affairs of 1948: Circulaire van de Minister van Buitenlandse Zaken van 20 October 1948, dir. jur. en adm. Zaken nr. 113100 aan de hoofden der Nederlandse vertegenwoordigingen in het buitenland.

[15] Act of 14 November 1963, Stbl. 467, entered into force on 1 March 1964.

Netherlands nationality law, a foreign wife of a Netherlands national would not automatically acquire the Netherlands nationality of her husband anymore. She was given the choice to acquire this status by a declaration of option (Article 8 Nationality Act 1892 (1963)). A Netherlands woman who married a foreigner or a stateless person would keep her citizenship (Article 8a Nationality Act 1892 (1963)). The regulation of the acquisition of the nationality of legitimate children *iure sanguinis* was not modified. A legitimate child could still exclusively acquire the Netherlands nationality of the father; only an illegitimate child not recognized by a foreign father, would acquire the nationality of the mother.

The position of women in nationality law was completely changed by a new Nationality Act, which entered into force on 1 January 1985. Since then, the Netherlands law of nationality is based on a system of *ius sanguinis a patre et a matre*. A child will acquire the Netherlands nationality if the father or the mother is a Netherlands national at the time of its birth or is a Netherlands national who died before the birth of the child (Article 3 section 1 Nationality Act 1984).

Another consequence of the equality of the parents regarding the nationality of their children is that a minor will never lose his/her Netherlands nationality if and for as long as one parent still possesses the Netherlands nationality (Article 16 Nationality Act 1984). For instance, if a parent is naturalized abroad and the minor child is included in that naturalization, the parent will often lose his/her Netherlands nationality because of voluntary acquisition of a foreign nationality (Article 15(1)(a) Nationality Act 1984).[16] However, the child will have dual nationality if the other parent still possesses the Netherlands nationality.

Equal treatment of men and women has also been realized in respect of the possibility for foreigners to acquire the nationality of their Netherlands spouse. The foreign spouse of a Netherlands national neither acquires the Netherlands nationality automatically nor has an option right to this nationality. Nevertheless, he or she can be naturalized in the Netherlands after having been married for at least three years (Article 8(2) Nationality Act 1984). For this naturalization of a foreign spouse or a foreign registered partner it is not necessary that the normal condition of at least five years habitual residence in the Netherlands prior to the application has been fulfilled (Article 8(1)(c)). It is remarkable, that the condition of a five years residence prior to the application is also shortened to a three years habitual residence in the case of unmarried persons who have lived together with an unmarried Netherlands nationals for at least three years in a permanent relationship other than marriage or registered partnership.[17]

---

[16] Exceptions in Article 15(2) Netherlands Nationality Act.
[17] This provision does not only apply to a heterosexual relationship but to a homosexual relationship as well.

A consequence of this gradual development is that in almost all countries provisions dealing with the nationality position of women after marriage, or the loss of the nationality involved by their husbands, are lacking because these consequences no longer exist.

Nevertheless, in some countries some provisions still deal with the position of married women. In France Article 21–1 Code civil underscores that a marriage does not affect the acquisition or loss of French citizenship. In Ireland even two provisions deal with this issue. Sect. 22 Irish Nationality and Citizenship Act provides:

> '1. The death of an Irish citizen shall not affect the citizenship of his or her surviving spouse or children.
> 2. Loss of Irish citizenship by a person shall not of itself affect the citizenship of his or her spouse or children.'

Section 23 underscores:

> 'A person who marries an alien shall not, merely by virtue of the marriage, cease to be an Irish citizen, whether or not he or she acquires the nationality of the alien.'

Also Article 4 of the Lithuanian Citizenship Act underpins, that a marriage between a citizen of the Republic of Lithuania and a person who is a citizen of another State or a stateless person, or a dissolution of such marriage does not change the citizenship of either spouse.

These provisions can be understood as a reaction to the previous legal situation, but are – strictly speaking – superfluous.

The trend is obvious. In the recent Euro-citizenship project in which the grounds for acquisition and loss of nationality of 33 European countries (all Member States of the European Union, Croatia, Iceland, Moldova, Norway, Switzerland and Turkey) were analyzed, marriage with a foreigner has disappeared as a ground for loss of nationality.[18] In none of these countries marriage has as a consequence the acquisition of the nationality of the spouse.[19] All countries provide for a facilitation of the acquisition of the nationality of the spouse, but strictly on a gender-neutral manner.[20]

---

[18] GERARD-RENÉ DE GROOT/MAARTEN P. VINK, *Loss of citizenship, Trends and regulations in Europe*, June 2010, available on: www.eudo-citizenship.eu.

[19] MAARTEN P. VINK and GERARD-RENÉ DE GROOT, 'Citizenship attribution in Western Europe: International framework and domestic trends', *Journal of Ethnic and Migration Studies*, 2010, pp. 713–734.

[20] GERARD-RENÉ DE GROOT, 'The access to European citizenship for third country spouses of a European citizen', in: Christine Biquet-Mathieu *et al.* (ed.), *Liber amicorum Paul Delnoy*, Larcier, Brussels, 2005, pp. 93–133.

4. FROM *IUS SANGUINIS A PATRE* TO *IUS SANGUINIS A PATRE ET A MATRE*

The next obvious step was to allow women to transmit their own nationality to their children. Before Word War II exclusively the Soviet Union provided for that possibility in all cases.[21] Since 1927 the French nationality act provided for the transmission of the French nationality of a French mother to all her children born on French territory. After World War II gradually several countries in Eastern Europe also recognized a completely independent position of women in nationality matters and also allowed the transmission of the nationality to the next generation under the same conditions as men, following the example of the Soviet Union.[22]

An important development was a resolution of the Committee of Ministers of the Council of Europe on the nationality of children born in wedlock adopted in 1977 which recommended:[23]

> 'to grant their nationality at birth to children born in wedlock if their father or mother possesses such nationality; alternatively, to provide for these children up to the age of 22 facilities to acquire that nationality.'

The dominance of *ius sanguinis a patre* has nearly in all European States been replaced by a *ius sanguinis a patre et a matre*.[24] Some countries make exceptions on the *ius sanguinis* principle in case of birth abroad (Belgium, Germany, Ireland, Portugal, United Kingdom, moreover – in case of nationality-mixed marriages – Latvia, Slovenia, compare also Lithuania and FYR Macedonia).[25] These exceptions are in accordance with Article 6(1) ECN, but should never lead to statelessness.[26]

It is odd, that now men are discriminated against in some countries in respect of transmission of their nationality to children born out of wedlock.[27]

---

[21] Already since 1918/1924, see TRATNIK, pp. 59–68.
[22] Albania 1946, Bulgaria 1948, German Democratic Republic 1954, Hungary 1957, Yugoslavia 1945, Poland 1951, Romania 1948, Czechoslovakia 1949.
[23] Resolution 77/13 of 27 May 1977.
[24] All the States included in the Euro-citizenship-project did introduce a *ius sanguinis a matre et a patre*.
[25] MAARTEN P. VINK and GERARD-RENÉ DE GROOT, 'Citizenship attribution in Western Europe: International framework and domestic trends', *Journal of Ethnic and Migration Studies*, 2010, pp. 713–734.
[26] Recommendation R 99 (18) of the Committee of Ministers of the Council of Europe, repeated in Recommendation 2009/13. Also see GERARD-RENÉ DE GROOT and ERIK P.J. VRINDS, *The position of children in respect of decisions made by their parents regarding their nationality*, Report for the 3rd European conference on nationality, Strasbourg, 2004.
[27] MAARTEN P. VINK and GERARD-RENÉ DE GROOT, 'Citizenship attribution in Western Europe: International framework and domestic trends', *Journal of Ethnic and Migration Studies*, 2010, pp. 713–734.

In some non-European countries discrimination against women still exists, in particular in Islamic countries. But even in those States a tendency towards equal treatment of men and women can be perceived.[28]

5. RESERVATIONS TO ARTICLE 9 OF THE WOMEN'S CONVENTION

In order to be able to assess the acceptance of the rules codified in Article 9 Women's Convention it is of course necessary to study the number and the content of reservations made regarding Article 9.[29]

5.1. RESERVATIONS TO THE WHOLE OF ARTICLE 9

On the occasion of becoming a party to the Women's Convention, seven States made reservations pertaining to the whole of Article 9: Fiji (28 August 1995), Iraq (13 August 1986), (South) Korea (27 December 1984), Malaysia (5 July 1995/6 February 1998), Monaco (18 March 2005), Singapore (5 October 1995), United Arab Emirates (6 October 2004) and the United Kingdom (7 April 1986). Three of these States indicated their grounds for this reservation.

The United Arab Emirates simply underpinned the autonomy of States in nationality matters:

> 'The United Arab Emirates, considering the acquisition of nationality an internal matter which is governed, and the conditions and controls of which are established, by national legislation makes a reservation to this article and does not consider itself bound by the provisions thereof.'[30]

The United Kingdom accepted the equal treatment of women and men in nationality as such, but made a reservation for transitory situations:

> 'The British Nationality Act 1981, which was brought into force with effect from January 1983, is based on principles which do not allow of any discrimination against women within the meaning of Article 1 as regards acquisition, change or retention of

---

[28] GIANLUCA PAROLIN, *Citizenship in the Arab world*, Amsterdam University Press, Amsterdam, 2009, p. 98.

[29] Reservations may be made at the time of ratification or accession to the Women's Convention. See Article 28(1). On reservations to the Women's Convention also see Chapter 20 in this book by Zoé Luca.

[30] Compare also the argumentation of Iraq, where only is referred to the fact that Article 9(1) is contrary to Iraqi nationality law. See the Combined second and third periodic reports on Iraq submitted 19 October 1999, UN Doc. CEDAW/C/IRQ/2–3, p. 13.

their nationality or as regards the nationality of their children. The United Kingdom's acceptance of Article 9 shall not, however, be taken to invalidate the continuation of certain temporary or transitional provisions which will continue'

Remarkable was – to put it politely – the argumentation of Singapore:

'Singapore is geographically one of the smallest independent countries in the world and one of the most densely populated. The Republic of Singapore accordingly reserves the right to apply such laws and conditions governing the entry into, stay in, employment of and departure from its territory of those who do not have the right under the laws of Singapore to enter and remain indefinitely in Singapore and to the conferment, acquisition and loss of citizenship of women who have acquired such citizenship by marriage and of children born outside Singapore.'

Furthermore, it has to be mentioned, that Turkey (20 December 1985) made the following *declaration*:

'Article 9, paragraph 1 of the Convention is not in conflict with the provisions of article 5, paragraph 1, and article 15 and 17 of the Turkish Law on Nationality, relating to the acquisition of citizenship, since the intent of those provisions regulating acquisition of citizenship through marriage is to prevent statelessness.'

However, this declaration was withdrawn on 29 January 2008.

Malaysia originally made a reservation to the whole of Article 9, but restricted this reservation to Article 9(2) on 6 February 1998.

Fiji withdrew its reservation on Article 9 on 24 January 2000. Of the other countries, the nationality regulations of Iraq, South-Korea and Singapore have in the meantime been brought in conformity with the principles prescribed by the Women's Convention. Article 18(2) of the Constitution of Iraq provides since 2005 for a *ius sanguinis a patre et a matre*. In Korea Article 2(1) (1) of the Nationality Act provides also for *ius sanguinis a patre et a matre* since the modification of 29 October 1987. Article 6 of the Korean Nationality Act provides on a sex-neutral manner for facilitated naturalization of the spouses of Korean nationals. In Singapore Article 122(1) (b) of the Constitution provides since 2004 for a *ius sanguinis a patre et a matre*. Therefore, all these countries could withdraw their reservations.

In Monaco Act 1276 of 22 December 2003 modified Act 1155 of 18 December 1992: in main lines *ius sanguinis a patre et a matre* was introduced, but some restrictions still exist in respect of the transmission of nationality *iure sanguinis* by mothers who have acquired the nationality of Monaco by marriage.[31] This is still an evident discrimination.[32]

In respect of the nationality law in the United Arab Emirates as yet there are no developments towards a more equal treatment of women and men.

5.2. RESERVATIONS TO ARTICLE 9(2)

Considerably more countries made a reservation to Article 9(2) of the Women's Convention obliging for the equal transmission of nationality *iure sanguinis* from mothers and fathers to their children.

Algeria (22 May 1996), Bahamas (10 July 1995), Bahrain (18 June 2006), Brunei Darussalam (24 May 2006), Egypt (18 September 1981), Jordan (1 July 1992), Kuwait (2 September 1994), Lebanon (16 April 1997), Liechtenstein (22 December 1995), Malaysia (5 July 1995/6 February 1998), Morocco (21 June 1993), Democratic People's Republic of Korea (7 February 2001), Oman (7 February 2006), Saudi-Arabia (7 September 2000), Syria (28 March 2003), Thailand (9 August 1985), Tunisia (20 September 1985).

Some of these States have stated the reasons, why they made a reservation.

Algeria simply referred to the content of their national Nationality Law:

'The Government of the People's Democratic Republic of Algeria wishes to express its reservations concerning the provisions of article 9, paragraph 2, which are incompatible with the provisions of the Algerian Nationality code and the Algerian Family Code.

The Algerian Nationality code allows a child to take the nationality of the mother only when:

– the father is either unknown or stateless;
– the child is born in Algeria to an Algerian mother and a foreign father who was born in Algeria;

---

[31] Article 1 of the Nationality Act of Monaco provides since 2003: 'Est monégasque:
1°- Toute personne née d'un père monégasque.
2°- Toute personne née d'une mère née monégasque qui possédait encore cette nationalité au jour de la naissance.
3°- Toute personne née d'une mère monégasque et dont l'un des ascendants de la même branche est né monégasque.
4°- Toute personne née d'une mère monégasque ayant acquis la nationalité monégasque par naturalisation, par réintégration ou par application des dispositions du second alinéa de l'article 6 ou du quatrième alinéa de l'article 7 de la présente loi.
5°- Toute personne née d'une mère ayant acquis la nationalité monégasque par déclaration suite à une adoption simple.
6°- Toute personne née à Monaco de parents inconnus.
La nationalité de l'enfant qui a fait l'objet d'une adoption légitimante est déterminée selon les distinctions établies à l'alinéa précédent.'
[32] Until 2006 the Swiss legislation contained a similar discriminatory regulation.

- moreover, a child born in Algeria to an Algerian mother and a foreign father who was not born on Algerian territory may, under Article 26 of the Algerian Nationality Code, acquire the nationality of the mother providing the Ministry of Justice does not object.

Egypt argued:

'This is in order to prevent a child's acquisition of two nationalities where his parents are of different nationalities, since this may be prejudicial to his future. It is clear that the child's acquisition of his father's nationality is the procedure most suitable for the child and that this does not infringe upon the principle of equality between men and women, since it is customary for a woman to agree, upon marrying an alien, that her children shall be of the father's nationality.'

Like Egypt also Morocco only referred to the fact that national law differed from the content of the treaty:

'The Government of the Kingdom of Morocco makes a reservation with regard to this article in view of the fact that the Law of Moroccan Nationality permits a child to bear the nationality of its mother only in the cases where it is born to an unknown father, regardless of place of birth, or to a stateless father, when born in Morocco, and it does so in order to guarantee to each child its right to a nationality. Further, a child born in Morocco of a Moroccan mother and a foreign father may acquire the nationality of its mother by declaring, within two years of reaching the age of majority, its desire to acquire that nationality, provided that, on making such declaration, its customary and regular residence is in Morocco.'

It has to be mentioned that several States objected to these reservations as incompatible with the object and purpose of the Convention.[33]

Several States withdrew their reservation to Article 9(2) after they introduced *ius sanguinis a patre et a matre* in their nationality law: Algeria 15 July 2009, Egypt 4 January 2008, Liechtenstein 3 October 1996, Thailand 26 October 1992.

In the meantime, also some other countries would be able to withdraw their reservations, because the national rules of their countries are – anno 2010 – already in accordance with Article 9(2) after they introduced a *ius sanguinis a patre et a matre*. This would apply to Tunisia (1993),[34] North Korea (1999),[35] and Morocco (2007).[36]

---

[33] Against the Algerian reservations: Sweden (4 August 1997), Portugal (14 August 1997), Denmark (24 March 1998); against the reservation by Jordan: Sweden (5 February 1993); against the reservation by Kuwait: Denmark (12 February 1997); against the reservation by Lebanon: Denmark (26 June 1998).
[34] Law 62/1993. See PAROLIN, p. 98.
[35] Article 5 Nationality Act.
[36] Decree 80/2007.

However, in a number of States the rules on the transmission of nationality to children still discriminate against women. This is the case in the Bahamas (Articles 8 and 9 Constitution),[37] Bahrain (Article 4 Nationality Act 1989), Brunei (Article 4 Nationality Act), Jordan (Article 3 Nationality Act), Lebanon (Article 1 Nationality Act), Kuwait (Article 2 Nationality Act), Malaysia (Article 6 Nationality Act), Oman (Article 1 Nationality Act), Saudi-Arabia (Article 7 Nationality Act) and Syria (Article 3 Nationality Act).[38]

But even in some of these States the introduction of a *ius sanguinis a matre* is under discussion. This is the case in Bahrain, Jordan, Lebanon and Kuwait.[39]

It is appropriate to underpin, that none of the Islamic countries which made a reservation to Article 9(2) declared that this provision would violate the *shari'a*. The aim of these reservation is obviously the preservation of discriminatory provisions of the national law.[40] It is therefore likely, that in the next future all Islamic countries will implement the rules of Article 9.

5. TRANSITORY PROVISIONS

It has already been mentioned that the United Kingdom made a reservation in order to maintain some 'certain temporary or transitional provisions'. In many countries the equal treatment of men and women was introduced *ex nunc*. However, in some countries children who had already been born as child of a mother who was a national and a foreign father before the equal treatment rule was introduced, nevertheless acquired the nationality of their mother if they had not yet reached a certain age (*e.g.* in Belgium: 18 years). In some other countries they could acquire their mother's nationality by way of registration or by lodging a declaration of option. Often, this registration or declaration had to take place within a rather short period of time (Germany: two years; Netherlands: three

---

[37] However since 2002 a Committee on revision of the constitution also raised the question whether *i.e.* Articles 8 and 9 should be revised: see The Bahamas Constitution: options for change, prepared by the secretariat of the Bahamas Constitutional Commission, Nassau (Bahamas) 2003, p. 9–15, available on: www.lexbahamas.com/Constitutional%20reform%20optizons%20for%20change.PDF (last visited on 4 September 2010).

[38] Furthermore, it has to be mentioned that the nationality rules of Iran, which did not ratify the Women's Convention, violates Article 9, Section 1 and 2. See Civil code of Iran: Article 976 sub 2 (*ius sanguinis a patre*) and sub 6: automatic acquisition of citizenship by foreign woman marrying an Iranian man.

[39] PAROLIN, p. 98.

[40] EKATERINA YAHYAOUIKRIVENKO, *Women, Islam and International Law, Within the context of the Convention on the elimination of all forms of discrimination against women*, Martinus Nijhoff Publishers, Leiden/Boston, 2009, p. 160.

years). In the past few years, a new discussion on the question whether these temporal restrictions were reasonable could be witnessed.[41]

In the Netherlands the consequence of this discussion was, that the possibility to acquire the nationality of the mother by declaration of option was reopened without any temporal limitation for the children of a Netherlands mother and a foreign father born before 1985 (the year of introduction of *ius sanguinis a patre et a matre* in the Netherlands). Also the grandchildren were granted this possibility of lodging a declaration of option provided that their parent had used the option or had already passed away. This modification was realized recently by Act of 17 June 2010 and entered into force on 1 October 2010.[42]

However, this transitory regulation still is not perfect since it is conditional upon the circumstance that the mother still was in possession of the Netherlands nationality at the moment of birth of her child. For children born within wedlock, this causes a difficulty. As we have seen above, in principle Netherlands women used to lose their nationality by marriage with a foreigner until 1 March 1964. If the Netherlands mother married before that date, she only kept her nationality if she did not acquire the nationality of her husband and could not easily acquire this nationality. The access to Netherlands nationality of the (grand)children of women who married with a foreigner before 1 March 1964, therefore depends on the answer to the question how discriminatory the nationality rules in the country of the husband were. If the country of the husband discriminated against women, the access to Netherlands nationality of the children born within such a marriage is thwarted. A country like Argentina did neither provide for an automatic acquisition of nationality by a foreign wife of an Argentinean man nor for an easy possibility to register as such since 1897. A country like Belgium abolished the automatic acquisition of Belgian nationality only in 1985. The chances of becoming Netherlands nationals of children whose Netherlands mother married a foreigner before 1st March 1964, therefore depend on the degree of equal treatment of men and women in a foreign country. That is – to put it mildly – remarkable. Without a doubt, this issue will be next on the agenda of advocates of equal treatment in the field of nationality. And this should not only happen in the Netherlands. Also the transitory measures in other countries should be revisited and – if necessary – revised.

---

[41] STAN GOUDSMIT, BETTY DE HART and HERMIE DE VOER, 'Latente Nederlanders: Discriminatie van kinderen van Nederlandse moeders in het nationaliteitsrecht', *Nederlands Juristenblad* 2006, pp. 932–939 and STAN GOUDSMIT, 'Latente Nederlanders wachten op hun paspoort', *Migrantenrecht* 2007, pp. 97–100 with further references.

[42] *Staatsblad* 2010, p. 242. See on the new option procedure GERARD-RENÉ DE GROOT, Een optierecht voor latente Nederlanders: beschouwingen over de nationaliteitsrechtelijke positie van voor 1985 geboren (klein)kinderen van een Nederlandse moeder en een niet-Nederlandse vader', *Asiel- en Migratierecht* 2010, October-issue.

6. CONCLUSIONS

In the foregoing we witnessed that there is no automatic influence of marriage on the nationality position of married women anymore. The rule prescribed by Article 9(1) Women's Convention is implemented in all States which are contracting parties to the Convention. Furthermore, we could observe that – in accordance with Article 9(2) Women's Convention – States increasingly introduced a *ius sanguinis a patre et a matre*.

However, in respect of children born out of wedlock in some States men are nowadays discriminated against in respect of the transmission of their nationality to these children.

Regarding the transmission of nationality to children a number of States made reservations to Article 9 Women's Convention, but increasingly these reservations are withdrawn. Moreover, several States which made reservations already fulfil in their nationality law the rules prescribed by Article 9 and therefore could withdraw their reservations. Therefore, we can be confident that the principles enshrined in Article 9 Women's Convention will be implemented in the nationality legislation all over the world within the next future.

Finally we have seen, that there is a growing attention to re-open possibilities to acquire the nationality *a matre* for children born before a State provided for *ius sanguinis a patre et a matre*. This remarkable development is – of course – completely in line with the spirit of the Convention. It would be desirable, if in the next future also regarding other treaty obligation attention to the transitory situations would be paid. Of course, in respect of several obligations the unjust treatment of women in the past cannot be repaired or compensated. But in respect of some obligations elegant transitory solutions would be welcome.

ARTICLE 10

State parties shall take all appropriate measures to eliminate discrimination against women in order to ensure to them equal rights with men in the field of education and in particular to ensure, on a basis of equality of men and women:

a) The same conditions for career and vocational guidance, for access to studies and for the achievement of diplomas in educational establishments of all categories in rural as well as in urban areas; this equality shall be ensured in pre-school, general, technical, professional and higher technical education, as well as in all types of vocational training;
b) Access to the same curricula, the same examinations, teaching staff with qualifications of the same standard and school premises and equipment of the same quality;
c) The elimination of any stereotyped concept of the roles of men and women at all levels and in all forms of education by encouraging coeducation and other types of education which will help to achieve this aim and, in particular, by the revision of textbooks and school programmes and the adaptation of teaching methods;
d) The same opportunities to benefit from scholarships and other study grants;
e) The same opportunities for access to programmes of continuing education, including adult and functional literacy programmes, particularly those aimed at reducing, at the earliest possible time, any gap in education existing between men and women;
f) The reduction of female student drop-out rates and the organization of programmes for girls and women who have left school prematurely;
g) The same opportunities to participate actively in sports and physical education;
h) Access to specific educational information to help to ensure the health and well-being of families, including information and advice on family planning.

CHAPTER 10
BARRIERS TO GIRLS' RIGHT TO EDUCATION IN AFGHANISTAN

Fons COOMANS and Samira SAKHI

1. INTRODUCTION

Afghanistan has been very much in the news recently, and not always in a positive sense. Violence, human rights violations and a Government that is unable to exercise full control over part of its territory because of Taliban armed actions. However, one should not forget that the current Government is trying to establish democratic governance, the rule of law and respect for human rights. The latter includes strengthening the position of women in a country that is predominantly Islamic. Education can play a key role in empowering women in social and public life. The present authors have chosen Afghanistan as a country where the Women's Convention, and in particular its provision on education, can make a difference. Afghanistan is a State party to the Women's Convention, but also to the International Covenant on Economic, Social and Cultural Rights (ICESCR), the Convention on the Rights of the Child (ICRC) and the UNESCO Convention against Discrimination in Education. These treaties all provide for the right to education on a non-discriminatory basis. The questions we would like to address in this Chapter are threefold. First, which obstacles do girls face in Afghanistan if they want to exercise their right to education? Secondly, how do these barriers relate to the human rights obligations of Afghanistan that emanate from the right to education? Relevant in this regard are also the gender related aspects of education. Thirdly, if one would depart from the notion of the universality of human rights, what steps should be taken to eliminate barriers and strengthen the practical significance of the right to education for girls in Afghanistan? The approach applied in this Chapter will be the following. We will start with the human rights framework on education and in particular the obligations emanating from Article 10 Women's Convention. Next, gender related aspects of education will be dealt with. In section 4 a description of the background of the present educational situation in Afghanistan will be given, followed by a more normative section which will explain how the right to education for girls in Afghanistan can be strengthened by using the concept of universalisation of human rights.

2. THE HUMAN RIGHTS FRAMEWORK

This section will deal with those parts of international human rights law that are particularly relevant for a proper understanding of the right to education for girls.

2.1. THE PURPOSE OF ARTICLE 10 WOMEN'S CONVENTION

Article 10 is a comprehensive and lengthy provision. It contains many elements aimed at ensuring equal rights of women with men in the area of education. Article 10 should be read and interpreted in conjunction with Articles 2 and 5 of the Convention. The broader goal of Article 10 may be characterized as achieving changes in social and cultural patterns in and through education, catching up educational deprivation and an improvement of the general social position of girls and women. This wider goal of Article 10 is clear from a number of its paragraphs. For example, paragraph a) talks about the obligation of States parties to ensure the same conditions for career development and vocational guidance, for access to studies and for the achievement of diplomas in educational institutions in both urban and rural areas. Very relevant is also paragraph c) which deals with the obligation to eliminate stereotyped concepts of the roles of men and women at all levels and in all forms of education. This is key to raising awareness and changing views about the roles of men and women in society. There is a clear link here with Article 5(a) which deals with the need to modify social and cultural patterns. If biased, stereotyped cultural views and patterns are maintained in education, this may have an effect on all women in society, because the values and ideas conveyed to children at an early age usually tend to have a big impact on their way of thinking and behaviour at a later age.[1] Alternatively, education is an appropriate means to achieve the purposes of Article 5.

---

[1] INGRID WESTENDORP, *Women and Housing: Gender Makes a Difference*, Intersentia, Antwerp, 2007, p. 251.

2.2. OBLIGATIONS RESULTING FROM ARTICLE 10 WOMEN'S CONVENTION

Article 10 stipulates that States parties shall take all appropriate measures to eliminate discrimination in the field of education. Pursuant to Article 2(f), States have an obligation to take steps, without delay, to modify or abolish existing laws, regulations, customs and practices which constitute discrimination against women.[2] Human rights give rise to obligations to respect, to protect and to fulfil.[3] For example, a breach of the obligation to respect the right to education of girls in Afghanistan would imply that the State interferes with or denies, *de iure* or *de facto*, the enjoyment of the right to education of girls by refusing access to educational institutions or limiting girls to education of an inferior standard.[4] For present purposes the obligation to protect the right to education is particularly relevant, because its aim is to protect women against discrimination by private actors, such as school boards, teachers, religious leaders and parents who may discriminate girls or channel them to classes or curricula of a biased or inferior nature. The obligation to protect also entails a duty to engage in an active policy aimed at eliminating customary and other practices that prejudice and perpetuate the notion of inferiority or superiority of either women or men and of stereotyped roles.[5] The obligation to fulfil, finally, requires the State to take action, both at the short and the long term, to make educational facilities for girls and women available, accessible, acceptable and adaptable to their needs. Implementing this obligation may call for a wide variety of measures and discretion for the State. An example could be temporary special measures as provided for in Article 4(1) Women's Convention, such as temporary quotas to ensure that women are represented in school management committees, or a temporary programme commissioned by the State which would invite popular singers to write and sing songs which hail educated girls, or alternatively, criticize the practice of forcing pregnant girls to leave school.[6]

---

[2] UN doc. CEDAW/C/2010/47/GC.28, *General Recommendation No. 28 on the Core Obligations of States Parties under Article 2 of the Convention on the Elimination of All Forms of Discrimination against Women*, 19 October 2010, para. 31.

[3] For an extensive discussion see MAGDALENA SEPÚLVEDA, *The Nature of the Obligations under the International Covenant on Economic, Social and Cultural Rights*, Intersentia, Antwerp, 2003, Chapter V.

[4] Compare Article 1(1) UNESCO Convention against Discrimination in Education.

[5] CEDAW, General Comment No. 28, para. 9.

[6] Both examples are drawn from CORINNE PACKER, 'Rights-Based Education to Gender Equality', in: I. Boerefijn, F. Coomans, J. Goldschmidt, R. Holtmaat and R. Wolleswinkel (eds.), *Temporary Special Measures*, Intersentia, Antwerp, 2003, pp. 173–179, at 176, 178.

2.3. OTHER RELEVANT INTERNATIONAL INSTRUMENTS

There are other international human rights treaties that include obligations on non-discrimination and education. One example is Article 13 of the ICESCR, a treaty which is comprehensive, because it covers various levels and dimensions of education. The right to education as laid down in the ICESCR has four features, which have been labelled as the 'four A's'.[7] This means that education must be available, accessible, acceptable and adaptable. All of these four key features are important and relevant for the situation of girls in Afghanistan in matters of education. Availability means that schools for girls, teachers and school facilities have to be available. For Afghanistan this could also mean separate schools for girls. Accessibility has three different dimensions: non-discrimination in law and fact; physical accessibility and economic accessibility. Non-discrimination implies for Afghanistan that public schools may not discriminate pupils, meaning denying access, or offering education of an inferior standard, because of their sex, ethnic or social status or religion. Physical accessibility means that schools have to be available and accessible both in urban and rural areas, that schools should be within safe geographical reach and also that schools must be safe havens.[8] Economic accessibility means that attending school must be affordable; fees may not act as a barrier preventing parents from sending their children to school. Acceptability implies that education, including curricula and teaching methods, must be of good quality and culturally appropriate, which means, for example, respecting the wish of parents to have separate schools for boys and girls. Finally, education has to adaptable, which implies the need to take into account the special situation of girls in the curriculum and in textbooks, the need to have female teachers and to actively contribute to eliminating stereotypes and prejudice about the roles of girls and women in society.

Particularly relevant for Afghanistan is the issue of separate schools for girls; the question arises whether this is a sensible alternative for mixed schools and whether it would guarantee quality education for girls. Article 10(c) provides for the elimination of stereotyped concepts of men and women by encouraging co-education. The idea is that when boys and girls mix at school this will have a positive effect on achieving *de facto* equality between men and women. Since January 2010 Afghanistan is also a State party to the UNESCO Convention

---

[7] See UN doc. E/C.12/1999/10, *General Comment No. 13 on the Right to Education*, CESCR, 2 December 1999, para. 6. See also FONS COOMANS, 'Content and Scope of the Right to Education as a Human Right and Obstacles to Its Realization', Donders and Volodin (eds.), *Human Rights in Education, Science and Culture – Legal Developments and Challenges*, UNESCO/Ashgate, Paris/Aldershot, 2007, pp. 183–229, at 189.

[8] In June 2010, the UN Human Rights Council adopted a resolution condemning attacks by non-State actors on school children, particularly girls, in Afghanistan. See UN doc. A/HRC/14/L.7, *Addressing attacks on school children in Afghanistan*, 14 June 2010.

against Discrimination in Education.[9] According to Article 2(a) of this Convention 'the establishment or maintenance of separate educational systems or institutions for pupils of the two sexes, if these systems or institutions offer equivalent access to education, provide a teaching staff with qualifications of the same standard as well as school premises and equipment of the same quality, and afford the opportunity to take the same or equivalent courses or study' shall not be deemed a situation of discrimination as prohibited by this Convention. Note that the Women's Convention in Article 10 requires almost everywhere the *same* standards, opportunities and programmes for girls as those open to boys, while the UNESCO Convention refers to *equivalent* access to education for girls when offered in separate institutions. One may argue that the term 'equivalent' is a permissive concept open to interpretation. It would give more discretion to the State, while the term 'the same' is unequivocal. Burrows has argued in this respect that the UNESCO Convention 'does not meet the problem of sex-role stereotyping in education',[10] while Shelton is of the view that 'since it has been shown that segregation on the basis of sex, like racial segregation, invariably leads to inequality of education, the inclusion of this provision and the continuation of this practice is regrettable'.[11] However, it may be argued that separate educational institutions for girls and boys may be acceptable for a transitional period of time, provided quality standards are met, and could be an option for a country, such as Afghanistan, to offer a safe place to girls and protect them from a cultural environment which has not yet accepted girls' education.

3. GENDER RELATED ASPECTS OF EDUCATION

Gender related aspects of education may refer to two different concepts. *Gender parity* is a quantitative concept; it refers to the equal enrolment and participation of both girls and boys in different levels of education. *Gender equality* is a qualitative concept. It refers to equal educational outcomes for boys and girls. This latter concept takes into account that girls and boys usually have a different starting position and face different obstacles. Equality in educational outcomes relates to the number of school years attended, learning performance and achievements, academic qualifications and the opportunity to find a job after completing education.[12] Both gender parity and gender equality may be studied by using a distinction between rights *to* education, rights *within* education and

---

[9] 15 December 1960; entered into force 22 May 1962. Text available at www.unesco.org, last visited 1 March 2011.
[10] NOREEN BURROWS, 'The 1979 Convention on the Elimination of All Forms of Discrimination against Women', *Netherlands International Law Review*, 1985, pp. 419–460, at 435.
[11] DINAH SHELTON, 'Women and the Right to Education', *Revue des Droits de l'Homme*, Vol. 8, 1975, pp. 51–70, at 63.
[12] EFA Global Monitoring Report 2003/2004, p. 116.

rights *through* education.¹³ This idea has been proposed by the late Katarina Tomaševski. She argued that 'the indivisibility of human rights should inform the entire education strategy. The orientation and purpose of education substantively shape the scope for the enjoyment of the right to education and all other human rights through education'.¹⁴ In other words, the approach to influence gender-based inequality in education should be the promotion of all human rights. Too much emphasis on promoting the opportunities for girls to access and attend school masks systemic forms of discrimination of girls inspired by cultural, social and religious factors.¹⁵ This is well illustrated by Packer who wrote:

> '[S]o long as girls' other rights, such as to freely enter into marriage, decide the number and timing of her pregnancies, or obtain gainful employment are not secured then efforts to promote a girl's right to education through increased access to schooling will prove hollow. And these rights will likely be unsecured so long as the stereotypes, norms and traditions which uphold the low status of women remain unchallenged.'¹⁶

Rights *to* education relate to equal access for boys and girl to educational institutions. Rights *within* education relate to the possibility to enjoy basic human rights while children are in school. As far as gender is concerned, this dimension concerns situations and instances in which both girls and boys are victims of violence at school, sexism, sexual harassment, intolerance and discrimination. The central issue is here whether more girls tend to be the victim of such practices than boys. Rights *through* education deal with the opportunities pupils have to enjoy other human rights after school completion, such as the right to employment, to an adequate standard of living, to take part in cultural life, to the freedom of expression and the right to political participation. An additional aspect is to measure progress in equality *of* both women and men, rather than merely equality *between* women and men.¹⁷ This refers, for example to differences between urban and rural girls in access to education, or differences in drop-out rates between boys from poor families compared to boys from rich families.

---

¹³ EFA Global Monitoring Report 2003/2004, p. 116–117; KATARINA TOMAŠEVSKI, *Human Rights in Education as Prerequisite for Human Rights Education*, Right to Education Primers No. 4, Lund/Gothenburg, 2001, available at www.right-to-education.org (last visited 1 March 2011) and DUNCAN WILSON, *Human Rights: Promoting Gender Equality in and through education*, 2003, Background Paper for the EFA Global Monitoring Report 2003/2004.
¹⁴ KATARINA TOMAŠEVSKI, 'Rights-Based Education as Pathway to Gender Equality', in: I. Boerefijn, F. Coomans, J. Goldschmidt, R. Holtmaat and R. Wolleswinkel (eds.), *Temporary Special Measures*, Intersentia, Antwerp, 2003, pp. 151–171, at 151.
¹⁵ CORINNE PACKER, 'Rights-Based Education to Gender Equality', in: I. Boerefijn, F. Coomans, J. Goldschmidt, R. Holtmaat and R. Wolleswinkel (eds.), *Temporary Special Measures*, Intersentia, Antwerp, 2003, pp. 173–179, at 174.
¹⁶ *Ibid.*
¹⁷ UN doc. E/CN.4/2004/45, Report of the UN Special Rapporteur on the right to education, Katarina Tomaševski, para. 31.

Obstacles for girls in exercising their right *to* education deal with school facilities of a lower standard (such as less resources for girls' schools in countries with single-sex schooling), fewer or less qualified teachers and sometimes forms of overt discrimination of girls, such as the practice in a number of countries to suspend pregnant girls from school. Also restrictions on the courses girls are allowed to take negatively affect their right to education.[18] There is information that income inequalities between families also exacerbate gender inequalities. This implies, *inter alia*, that girls will not be enrolled in school when a family gets poorer. In many cases, boys will be given preference to girls to attend schools.[19]

As far as rights *within* education are concerned, girls are often the victims of discrimination, sexual abuse, punishment and intolerance by other pupils and by teachers, compared to boys. This may lead to high drop-out rates and underachievement of girls, compared to boys. In other words, schools may not be safe havens for girls.[20] Other obstacles that girls may face within schools include stereotypes and sexism in textbooks and curricula, a curriculum giving more weight to non-academic subjects such as vocational and home-making skills and science and math courses of a lower level, compared to those for boys.[21]

As for rights *through* education, the overall picture is that as education systems gradually achieve gender parity and improved quality, girls are likely to perform better than boys.[22] However, that does not mean that girls are in a better position to benefit from these qualifications in other spheres of life. Achieving gender equality through education is often still far away. As the UN Special Rapporteur on the right to education put it:

> 'Getting girls into schools often founders because education as a single sector does not, on its own, generate sufficiently attractive incentives for girls' parents and the girls themselves if educated girls cannot apply their education to sustaining themselves and/or helping their families. Years of attending school appear wasted when women do not have access to employment and/or are precluded from becoming self-employed, do not have a choice as to whether to marry and bear children, or their opportunities for political representation are foreclosed.'[23]

---

[18] AUDREY CHAPMAN and SAGE RUSSELL, *Violations of the right to education*, UN doc. E/C.12/1998/19, para. 24.
[19] KEVIN WATKINS, *Break the Cycle of Poverty*, Oxfam, London, 1999, p. 100; EFA Global Monitoring Report 2003/2004, p. 135.
[20] EFA Global Monitoring Report 2003/2004, pp. 143–144.
[21] AUDREY CHAPMAN and SAGE RUSSELL, *Violations of the right to education*, UN doc. E/C.12/1998/19, para. 24.
[22] EFA Global Monitoring Report 2003/2004, p. 150.
[23] UN doc. E/CN.4/2002/60, *Annual report of the Special Rapporteur on the right to education*, para. 40.

4. SHORT OVERVIEW OF AFGHANISTAN'S EDUCATIONAL SITUATION UNDER TALIBAN RULE AND AFTER TRANSITION TO DEMOCRATIC GOVERNANCE

In 1996 the Taliban took control of Afghanistan. Their regime lasted until 2001. At the start of their occupation the Taliban introduced a rigid gender policy as they wanted to 'clean' public space of women. This gender policy had the following elements: to ban women from employment and education, to impose a dress code for women and to impose strict control of women's freedom of movement.[24] The Taliban took their gender policy very seriously and soon after their arrival they closed all girls' schools in the country. Women and girls were not allowed to go to school or work.[25]

The UN Special Rapporteur, Mr. Choong-Hyun Paik, visited Afghanistan during the Taliban regime in January 1997. When he met the chairman of the Council of Religious Scholars he raised the issue of female education and employment, the Special Rapporteur pointed out that separate schools could be established for boys and girls in accordance with Islam and the local cultures. The chairman of the Council of Religious Scholars stated that: 'If we ask them to come out for work, then this is a violation of women's rights. God has limited their right to staying at home'. He explained further that: 'If education is required by women, then women can get this education from their brothers and fathers'.[26]

After the ban on female education, underground schools were set up by, for example, former female teachers, who risked their lives in order to teach their studious students. In other cases, educated parents taught girls in their homes. However, these home schooling initiatives did not have the expertise and means to replace the compulsory schooling system. Thus, at the beginning of 2001 the school enrolment of girls was 3%. Most of these girls lived in the northern provinces of Afghanistan (which were not controlled by the Taliban) or attended the above mentioned home schooling systems.[27]

After the fall of the Taliban regime in November 2001 efforts have been made to restore the educational system in Afghanistan. The Afghan Constitution of 2004 devotes six articles to the right to education.[28] The right to education is for

---

[24] PETER MARSDEN, *The Taliban: war, religion and the new order in Afghanistan*, Zed Books Ltd, New York, 1998, p. 88.
[25] UN doc. E/CN.4/2000/68/Add.4, *Report of the Special Rapporteur on violence against women, its causes and consequences*, Ms Radhika Coomaraswamy, 13 March 2000, para. 23.
[26] UN doc. E/CN.4/1997/59, *Report of the Special Rapporteur on the situation of human rights in Afghanistan*, Mr. Choong-Hyun Paik, 20 February 1997, para. 88..
[27] UN doc. E/CN.4/1997/59, *Report of the Special Rapporteur on the situation of human rights in Afghanistan*, Mr. Choong-Hyun Paik, 20 February 1997, para. 81.
[28] Articles 17, 43, 44, 45, 46 and 47 of the Afghan Constitution, 2004.

example guaranteed in Article 43 of the Afghan Constitution, which states that: 'Education is the right of all citizens of Afghanistan, which shall be offered up to the B.A. level in the State educational institutes free of charge by the State. To expand balanced education as well as to provide mandatory intermediate education throughout Afghanistan, the State shall design and implement effective programmes and prepare the ground for teaching mother tongues in areas where they are spoken'.

Article 44 of the Afghan Constitution obliges the State to pay special attention to particular groups of inhabitants, such as women and nomads, by stating that: 'The State shall devise and implement effective programmes to create and foster balanced education for women, improve education of nomads as well as eliminate illiteracy in the country.' Furthermore, the Education Law of 2008 also contains a few articles which are extremely important for the right of women and girls to education. Article 3 of the Education Law requires that: 'The nationals of the Islamic Republic of Afghanistan shall have an equal right to education without any forms of discrimination.'

The Government of the Islamic Republic of Afghanistan started, with the assistance of NGOs and aid agencies, a 'Back-to-School' campaign in 2002. Between 2001 and 2008 the school enrolment in Afghanistan increased from 900.000 to 6.5 million in 2008. During the Taliban regime the percentage of women and girls attending school was 3%, today the percentage of girls in the school populations is 37%. Thus, the Afghan Government has booked enormous successes in the field of education; today more Afghan children are in school than at any other period in the country's history.[29] In addition to the formal schooling system, community based education developed further. This is an informal form of education, usually organized as home education. These schools are small and often based in rural areas where there are no public schools. Relatively many girls attend this type of schooling, because it is culturally more acceptable, closer to home, more informal and teachers often come from the local community.[30]

There have been reports recently that the Taliban have become more tolerant towards education for girls. They now seem to accept that schools for girls are allowed, provided that teaching is in accordance with Islam and not inspired by Western ideas. This announcement has been seen primarily as a political statement in light of a possible process of reconciliation with the Taliban.[31] However, in the province of Ghazni, an area under Taliban control, small schools

---

[29] UNESCO, *Focusing on opportunities* (UNESCO Kabul Newsletter- Issue No. 4), 4 January 2010, p. 6.

[30] Netherlands Ministry of Foreign Affairs, *Thematisch ambtsbericht schoolgaande kinderen (in het bijzonder meisjes) in Afghanistan*, (Thematic Country Report on school going children in Afghanistan, especially girls), 29 March 2011, p. 2, www.minbuza.nl, last visited 30 March 2011.

[31] 'Taliban Ready to Lift Ban on Girls' Schools, Says Minister', *The Guardian*, 13 January 2011.

for girls have reopened after pressure from the local population.[32] The fact that nation-wide 37% of girls attend school is of course very welcome, however we should also pay attention to the remaining 63%, which is a huge number, of Afghan girls who do not or cannot attend school. Why does this group of girls not attend school? What are the current barriers to girls' education in Afghanistan?

5. BARRIERS TO GIRLS' RIGHT TO EDUCATION IN AFGHANISTAN

The UN Special Rapporteur on violence against women, Yakin Ertürk, mentioned the following barriers to girls' education in today's Afghanistan: attacks on girls' schools, poverty and early marriages.[33] A resent research of Afghanistan's Independent Human Rights Commission introduces a few other barriers to girls' education, such as distance and in some cases non existence of girls' schools, which are also very important to mention.[34]

5.1. INSECURITY

Insecurity is one of the most important barriers to girls' education in Afghanistan. In 2006 more than three hundred schools were shut down because of fear for attacks by Taliban and Al-Qaeda. Attacks against teachers and students are also common in various parts of the country.[35] Many of these attacks are directed at girls and girls' schools due to the Taliban's belief that girls should not attend school or work outside their homes. In November 2008 two sisters, Shamsia and Atifa, were attacked by the Taliban on the way to school in Kandahar. The Taliban first asked the girls: 'Will you be going to school anymore?' and then threw acid on both of the girls. Both sisters were burned

---

[32] See BETTE DAM, 'Meisjes mogen wel biologie leren, binnen Allah's wetten' ('Girls may learn about biology, however only within the framework of Allah's laws'), *NRC Handelsblad*, 24 March 2011, pp. 12–13.
[33] UN doc. A/58/421, *Situation of women and girls in Afghanistan*, Yakin Ertürk, 6 October 2003, p. 8.
[34] Afghanistan's Independent Human Rights Commission (AIHRC), www.aihrc.org.af/2010_eng/Eng_pages/Reports/Thematic/research_Access_f_Children_Education_n_Afghanistan_12_sep_09.pdf, last visited 9 March 2011.
[35] Human Rights Watch, 'Lessons in terror: attacks on education in Afghanistan', Vol. 18 Number 6 (C), July 2006, p. 31. Netherlands Ministry of Foreign Affairs, *Thematisch ambtsbericht schoolgaande kinderen (in het bijzonder meisjes) in Afghanistan*, (Thematic Country Report on school going children in Afghanistan, especially girls), 29 March 2011, pp. 5–7, www.minbuza.nl, last visited 30 March 2011.

really badly.³⁶ Attacks like this are very common in Afghanistan today. Due to current insecurity in Afghanistan young girls are also subjected to (sexual) harassment on their way to school. As a result of this kind of attacks parents are often afraid to send their children, especially daughters, to school.³⁷

5.2. POVERTY

Another crucial barrier to girls' education in Afghanistan is poverty. Due to the conflicts of the last three decades, today one-third of the Afghans live in extreme poverty and another 37% of the population is hovering on the edge of extreme poverty.³⁸ Despite the fact that the citizens of Afghanistan have the chance to be educated up to B.A. level free of cost, there are still costs associated with education (costs of school supplies, uniforms, sometimes transport and food). The poor people of Afghanistan cannot cope with these costs and are forced to take decisions which affect their children's education. In such an economically hard situation Afghan parent prefer to give their sons, instead of their daughters, the benefit of getting an education. As a result of these kind of practices poverty is an important barrier to girls' education.³⁹

Children from these poor families are also engaged in child labour. The conflicts of the last thirty years have left many Afghan children without a guardian and families without a breadwinner. Consequently, these children have to work in order to take care of themselves and their family members. The Afghan Research and Evaluation Unit surveyed 50 households in 2006, 50% of these households contained one or more working children. The number of boys and girls engaged in child labour is equal (especially at a young age).⁴⁰ The money that these young children earn from selling food in the marketplace, carrying loads, weaving carpets, working in restaurants etc. often goes to the primary needs of their families like shelter and food. After paying their primary needs they usually do not have money left to pay for their school supplies. These children also do not have time to attend school because of their work responsibilities.

---

36   *Afghan Girls, Scarred by Acid, Defy Terror, Embracing School*, www.nytimes.com/2009/01/14/world/asia/14kandahar.html, last visited 9 March 2011.
37   See Human Rights Watch, *'We Have the Promises of the World'* – Women's Rights in Afghanistan, New York, 2009, p. 81.
38   OHCHR, 'Human Rights Dimension of Poverty in Afghanistan', March 2010.
39   Save the Children, 'Barriers to accessing education in conflict-affected fragile states', Case Study: Afghanistan, 2010, pp. 16–17.
40   PAMELA HUNTE, 'Looking beyond the school walls: Household decision-making and school enrolment in Afghanistan', *AREU briefing paper,* March 2006, p. 5.

5.3. EARLY MARRIAGES

Another major barrier for girls' education, especially teenage girls, which is also mentioned by the Special Rapporteur is the barrier of early marriages. The legal marriageable age is sixteen in Afghanistan, girls between fifteen and sixteen can marry through their father or competent court (after it is found that a man is appropriate for a girl). The marriage of girls below fifteen is in no case admissible.[41] However, in practice, child marriages are very common in Afghanistan as a result of customs and national poverty. A survey held by the Afghanistan Independent Human Rights Commission showed that 57% of the girls in Afghanistan are forced to marry before the age of eighteen.[42] Poor families prefer to marry their daughters at a young age in order to benefit from the financial profits of the traditional practice of bride price. Young girls are sometimes also 'given away' as a compensation for a crime committed by a male family member, this practice is called '*baad*'.

For example, if a father commits a murder then he has to give his daughter in marriage to a family member of the victim in order to settle the dispute in a peaceful manner. In such cases, young girls have to pay for the faults of their male relatives.[43] When a girl moves into her husband's house, she is not allowed to attend school according to the local customs. These girls are after their marriage, most of the time, also engaged in other responsibilities (household or responsibilities for their children) which prevent them from attending school. In the summer of 2010 one of the authors of the present Chapter went to Afghanistan to visit her family. At that time she was 22 years old. Her cousin, who is 3 years younger, was already married. When she met her and her mother in-law, she asked her how she combined her school responsibilities with marriage. Her mother-in-law, instead of the cousin herself, answered the question. She said that her daughter-in-law was not attending school anymore. 'Why would she go to school', she said. 'What is it good for? She has other responsibilities now, which need her full attention'.

The views on girls' education differ a lot in Afghanistan. They depend on various factors – such as the background of the head of the family – and are in general formed in the family sphere. Elders, such as grandparents, parents and parents in-law have a great influence on the lives of their children and grandchildren. When the mother-in-law of the cousin decided that she could not go to school anymore that was the end of the story. The cousin could not disagree with her, that would have been disrespectful and it could bring her into trouble. Once these girls become members of their husband's family, there is a good chance that they can no longer be engaged in remunerated employment, because

---

[41] Articles 70 and 71 of the Afghan Civil Code, 1977.
[42] AIHRC, 'Situations of human rights Afghanistan during the year of 1386', 2007.
[43] Women and Children Legal Research Foundation, 'Early Marriage in Afghanistan', 2008.

they have to look after the children and in-laws. Often pressure is put on them to adjust to traditional cultural and social norms.[44] Even within one family the views on girls' education are not always the same. In rural, remote areas in particular, girls are kept indoors by their conservative parents. The family often plays a crucial role in decisions about school attendance of girls. Such decisions are influenced by the broader social and institutional framework of custom and opportunity.[45]

5.4. OTHER BARRIERS

In general, girls who live in the cities, like Kabul, have more chance to attend school. Others who live in the rural parts of the country face other barriers which are rare in the urban parts of Afghanistan. A long distance between home and school is a major barrier in the rural parts of the country. More than 50% of the rural communities had no primary school at the beginning of 2003. The shortage of secondary level girls' schools is another matter of concern, especially in the rural part of the country. This means that girls drop out, because appropriate secondary schools are not available for them. Drop-out rates for girls are higher than those for boys.[46] The above mentioned distance becomes even more of a problem in parts of the country where security is in danger. A ten minute walk to school becomes 'too far' when parents know that their children are exposed to various dangers such as the risk of being kidnapped or harassed. This barrier affects girls in particular, because they are more vulnerable in Afghanistan.[47]

Lack of female teachers is also a great obstacle to girls' education, especially older girls, in Afghanistan. Most of the current female teachers work in Kabul, and as a result other parts of the country face a shortage of female teachers which is detrimental for the organization of secondary education for girls. Female teachers prefer to work in the urban parts of the country because of safety reasons.[48] The Government has built a system of teacher training colleges but these are mainly concentrated in urban areas, especially in Kabul. The

---

[44] Netherlands Ministry of Foreign Affairs, *Thematisch ambtsbericht schoolgaande kinderen (in het bijzonder meisjes) in Afghanistan*, (Thematic Country Report on school going children in Afghanistan, especially girls), 29 March 2011, p. 8, www.minbuza.nl, last visited 30 March 2011.
[45] Education for All (EFA) Global Monitoring Report 2003/2004, *Gender and Education for All – The Leap to Equality*, UNESCO, Paris, 2003, p. 118.
[46] See Human Rights Watch, *'We Have the Promises of the World' – Women's Rights in Afghanistan*, New York, 2009, p. 77.
[47] See Human Rights Watch, *'We Have the Promises of the World' – Women's Rights in Afghanistan*, New York, 2009, pp. 79–80.
[48] Human Rights Watch, 'Lessons in Terror: Attacks on Education in Afghanistan', Vol. 18 Number 6 (C), July 2006, pp. 84–91.

Government has responded to the existing imbalance by integrating rural community schools into the Government system and bringing the local teachers onto the Government payroll. This should make the teaching profession more attractive.[49]

6. DOES AFGHANISTAN COMPLY WITH ITS OBLIGATIONS RELATING TO THE RIGHT TO EDUCATION FOR GIRLS?

It is beyond doubt that major headway has been made over recent years as regards the accessibility of education for girls and women in Afghanistan. The UN human rights monitoring bodies have complimented the Government for these major steps forward.[50] However, treaty bodies are also concerned about ongoing obstacles and systemic problems. For example, the CESCR, when examining the Afghan State report dealing with the implementation of the ICESCR stated:

> 'while noticing the efforts deployed by the State party to improve and promote the access to education and reducing gender disparities, notes with concern and in particular that the right to education is not guaranteed in the State party without discrimination, and at the poor situation of the education in Afghanistan. In particular, the Committee is deeply concerned about the increase in the number of child victims of attacks against schools by insurgents and the throwing of acid to prevent girls and female teachers from going to school. (Articles 13 and 14).
>
> The Committee recommends that the State party, in implementing its National Education Strategy Plan, take into account the Committee's general comments No. 11 and 13 (1999) and establish an effective monitoring mechanism for the plan. In particular, the Committee recommends that the State party take adequate steps to encourage the school enrolment of girls, including by providing facilities in schools (*e.g.* separated toilets for girls), and by training and recruiting female teachers, in particular in rural areas. The State party should improve security for children in school as well as on their way to and from school, and increase the awareness of the value of girls' education.'[51]

In many cases the full realization of the right to education can only be achieved over time. This does not mean that a government can remain passive. On the contrary, it must take deliberate, concrete and targeted measures aimed at the

---

[49] EFA Global Monitoring Report 2009, *Overcoming Inequality: Why Governance Matters*, Summary, UNESCO, Paris, 2008, p. 29.
[50] See UN doc. CRC/C/AFG/1, *Concluding Observations on Afghanistan*, CRC, 4 February 2011, para. 59.
[51] UN doc. E/C.12/AFG/CO/2-4, Concluding Observations on Afghanistan, CESCR, 21 May 2010, para. 43.

progressive realization of the right. It requires a State party to move as expeditiously and effectively as possible towards that end.[52] Governments have latitude in selecting and implementing those measures that are most appropriate in the specific domestic situation. In the opinion of treaty bodies there is no room for discretion and progressiveness when it comes to the prohibition and elimination of discrimination in matters of education.[53] States have an immediate obligation to tackle these problems, however it should be taken into account that eliminating deeply rooted ideas, perceptions, customs and practices about the traditional role of women (and men) in society cannot be realized overnight. Countering these systemic phenomena requires measures that may only turn out to be effective after many years, if not generations. Conducive to such a change of perception and mentality would be several suggestions made by the CRC when it examined Afghanistan's State report on the Children's Rights Convention. These included setting up social mobilization campaigns, increasing the number of adequately trained female teachers, promoting the quality of education through revising curricula and introducing interactive learning methods.[54] Such measures would help in strengthening girls' rights *in* and *through* education. All in all one could say that Afghanistan is certainly on the right track in complying with its obligations to realize the right to education for all, but that more specific measures are needed to eliminate systemic, cultural and religion-based forms of discrimination of girls which negatively affect their full participation in education and social life.

7. TOWARDS UNIVERSALISING THE RIGHT TO EDUCATION IN AFGHANISTAN?

7.1. THE VALUE OF EDUCATION IN ISLAMIC SOCIETIES

The right to education as a universal human right can be studied from three different angles.[55] The first one is the legal dimension. Has the right to education been legally accepted by a State, for example in its Constitution, or by becoming a State party to a human rights treaty. In addition, has the right to education an inclusive nature, which entails the question whether all people in a given society can enjoy the right to education, such as girls and women, members of ethnic

---

[52] UN doc. E/C.12/1999/10, General Comment No. 13 on the Right to Education, CESCR, 2 December 1999, paras 43–44.

[53] See for example, UN doc. E/C.12/1999/10, General Comment No. 13 on the Right to Education, CESCR, 2 December 1999, para. 31.

[54] UN doc. CRC/C/AFG/1, Concluding Observations on Afghanistan, CRC, 4 February 2011, para. 61 d) and e).

[55] See CHRISTIAN TOMUSCHAT, *Human Rights Between Idealism and Realism*, Oxford University Press, Oxford, 2008, pp. 69–96.

groups and migrants. As far as Afghanistan is concerned, the right to education is part of the Constitution and the country is a State party to a number of human rights treaties that provide for the right to education. The inclusive nature of the right in Afghanistan is guaranteed in theory; no one who is eligible to access education is excluded, the scope of the right is comprehensive. The second dimension is the empirical situation in each country: is the right to education enjoyed in practice by all. This is certainly not the case in Afghanistan, as many practical obstacles exist as has been explained above. There is thus a gap between theory and practice, between the standard or the norm and everyday reality. Finally, the value dimension reflects the idea whether a given society embraces the underlying values that have inspired the Universal Declaration of Human Rights.[56] One could argue that raising and teaching children in order to develop intellectually and socially is a value shared by all societies. In many countries and societies, in addition to family education, a formal or a non-formal education system has been established in order to translate that value into practical arrangements. For our discussion this would imply the acceptance of education as a key value of Afghan society and also that all members of society, men and women, have equal opportunity to enjoy that right. Islamic sources and authors present different views about the value of education and the right of girls/women to access education.

In 1947, one Islamic author, by way of input for the drafting of the Universal Declaration, argued that the right to education is a basic right, because education is 'necessary for developing the latent faculties and enabling the individual to function as an effective member of society'.[57] In 1965 another author maintained that according to the Qur'an each individual has an obligation to learn whatever is necessary for practicing his or her religion and the conduct of one's affairs.[58] According to the Prophet, 'to seek knowledge is the duty of every Muslim, both man and woman'.[59] This author was of the view that according to Islam it is the duty of a woman to learn and study 'when she needs such knowledge for the practice of her religion and the fulfilment of her role in life'.[60]

From the analysis of obstacles girls face in enjoying their right to education presented above, it has become clear that in some respects practice is quite different from religious doctrine. In a critical article about cultural and religious bars girls and women face in Islamic societies, Elizabeth Chamblee argued that private Islamic customs very much shape the lives of Muslim women in general and in particular their educational opportunities. The basis for these customs

---

[56] TOMUSCHAT, p. 73.
[57] HUMAYUN KABIR, 'Human Rights: Islamic Tradition and the Problems of the World Today', 1947, reproduced in: *Human Rights Teaching* (UNESCO) Vol. IV, 1985, p. 18.
[58] ALI ABDEL WAHID WAFI, 'The Problems of Human Rights in the Islamic Tradition', 1965, reproduced in: *Human Rights Teaching* (UNESCO) Vol. IV, 1985, p. 40.
[59] Quoted by ALI ABDEL WAHID WAFI, p. 40.
[60] *Ibid.*

and beliefs lies in a restrictive interpretation of the Qur'an. In an attempt to preserve their leading position in interpreting the Islamic belief, fundamentalists deny educational opportunities for women, because acquired knowledge may empower women. In addition, many conservative Islamic families view (early) marriage as a higher priority than the education of their daughters. Domestic work and staying at home are considered to be a better and more appropriate way of life for girls than attending school which, it is argued, leads to nothing useful. Education should take place at home and is restricted to learning how to become a good housewife, wife and mother.[61] These practices, customs and beliefs are supported and promoted by conservative religious leaders and institutions that exert a major influence on policy-making in matters of education.[62] Consequently, it can be argued that religious and cultural ideas, customs and practices may have a serious impact on the educational opportunities of girls in orthodox Islamic societies.

7.2. UNIVERSALISING THE RIGHT TO EDUCATION

The idea that all human rights have a number of core elements which should be interpreted uniformly and guaranteed under all circumstances is a helpful way of understanding and applying the notion of the universal nature of human rights. Beyond the core elements of a right, which may be called the periphery, there is more room for diversity and States have discretion in implementing these peripheral elements.[63] The CESCR has applied this notion to the right to education in its General Comment No. 13. It confirmed that:

> 'States parties have "a minimum core obligation to ensure the satisfaction of, at the very least, minimum essential levels" of each of the rights enunciated in the Covenant, including "the most basic forms of education". In the context of Article 13, this core includes an obligation: to ensure the right of access to public educational institutions and programmes on a non-discriminatory basis; to ensure that education conforms to the objectives set out in Article 13 (1); to provide primary education for all in accordance with Article 13 (2) (a); to adopt and implement a national educational strategy which includes provision for secondary, higher and fundamental education; and to ensure free choice of education without interference from the State

---

[61] ELISABETH CHAMBLEE, 'Rhetoric or Rights?: When Culture and Religion Bar Girls' Right to Education', *Virginia Journal of International Law*, Vol. 44, 2003–2004, pp. 1073–1138, at 1106–1107, 1118–1119.
[62] EFA Global Monitoring Report 2003/2004, p. 143.
[63] See for the core-periphery notion in relationship to human rights, FONS COOMANS, 'Exploring the Normative Content of the Right to Education as a Human Right: Recent Approaches', *Persona y Derecho*, Vol. 50, 2004, pp. 61–100; Netherlands Advisory Council on International Affairs, *Universality of Human Rights – Principles, Practice and Prospects*, Report No. 63, November 2008, p. 23.

or third parties, subject to conformity with "minimum educational standards" (Articles 13 (3) and (4)).[64]'

Being a State party to the ICESCR this interpretation of Article 13 would imply that Afghanistan is obliged to make all forms of public education accessible for both girls and boys on a non-discriminatory basis. This should be done according to the standards of Article 10 Women's Convention. However, taking into account the specific features of the situation in Afghanistan one could maintain that the aim of promoting girls' attendance at schools may require separate schools for girls, the staffing of these schools by female teachers only, while providing the same quality criteria as those that apply to schools for boys. In addition, the quality level of schools for girls should be monitored by an independent School Inspectorate. This would mean that the features of this particular country situation may justify a margin of discretion for the authorities in implementing the core content of the right to education.

Cultural exceptions that challenge values underlying the universality of human rights are often put forward by local communities, and stake-holders or political and religious leaders who fear losing their leading position in society.[65] With respect to Afghanistan the role of the parents and the family is crucial. From research conducted by Human Rights Watch in Afghanistan it has become clear that parents do not object to sending their daughters to school if a number of conditions are met. These include having sex-segregated classrooms, female teachers, schools at a reasonable and safe distance from home, being affordable and meeting basic quality standards.[66] These measures would make education for girl acceptable. If the achievement of access to quality education for girls in Afghanistan is really to be taken seriously in order to bridge the gap between principle and practice, then a process of universalizing the right to education in Afghan society should be developed by using a bottom-up approach. Universalisation entails increasing knowledge and awareness of human rights and their acceptance among different stake-holders and mobilizing human rights in addressing social concerns.[67] As An-Na'im and Hammond put it:

> 'The project of the universality of human rights is to be realized through a confluence of internal societal responses to injustice and oppression, instead of attempting to transplant a fully developed and conclusive concept and its implementation mechanism from one society to another. The way to get a universal idea accepted

---

[64] UN doc. E/C.12/1999/10, *General Comment No. 13 on the Right to Education*, CESCR, 2 December 1999, para. 57.
[65] Compare Netherlands Advisory Council on International Affairs, *Universality of Human Rights – Principles, Practice and Prospects*; Report No. 63, November 2008, pp. 32–33.
[66] See Human Rights Watch, *'We Have the Promises of the World'* – Women's Rights in Afghanistan, New York, 2009, p. 78.
[67] Netherlands Advisory Council on International Affairs, *Universality of Human Rights – Principles, Practice and Prospects*; Report No. 63, November 2008, p. 35.

locally is to present it in local terms, which can best be done by local people. Conversely, local acceptance enriches the universal idea by giving it meaning and relevance to people's lives.'[68]

An appropriate way to achieve this with respect to the right to education for girls in Afghanistan seems to be human rights education for girls and women (mothers) which departs from more modern interpretations of the Qur'an. This could first be framed as rights-based education outside the school system, for example organized by community-based organizations, in order to promote awareness about human rights and literacy among girls and women. Secondly, human rights education should take place within schools through, for example, a revision of curricula and textbooks in order to counter stereotypes and prejudice about the traditional roles of women and men in society.[69] Such a strategy not only aims at promoting the right *to* education for girls, but also at fostering rights *in* education and rights *through* education. These goals require an active involvement of all relevant stake-holders, such as central and local governmental authorities, religious leaders, school authorities, teachers, parents, community-based organizations and finally the children themselves.

8. CONCLUDING REMARKS

Article 10 Women's Convention gives important guidance to State parties what to do in order to achieve non-discrimination and substantive equality between girls and boys in matters of education. It is important, however, that when designing measures due regard is given to the particularities of the local situation and the practical obstacles girls are facing. Tailor-made measures are required, such as a clear and concrete plan to make secondary education accessible to girls in rural and remote areas, for example by establishing small community based schools and guaranteeing safe routes to schools.[70] For Afghanistan the early involvement of parents, other family members and community leaders is important in order to create awareness about the value of education and find a social basis for sending girls to school. By applying such an approach a compromise may be reached between the cultural and religious characteristics of a multi-ethnic Afghan society and the universal nature of the right to education as a human right.

---

[68] ABDULLAHI A. AN-NA'IM and JEFFREY HAMMOND, 'Cultural Transformation and Human Rights in African Societies', in A.A. An-Na'im (ed.), *Cultural Transformation and Human Rights in Africa*, Zed Books, London, 2002, p. 16.

[69] ELISABETH CHAMBLEE, 'Rhetoric or Rights?: When Culture and Religion Bar Girls' Right to Education', *Virginia Journal of International Law*, Vol. 44, 2003–2004, pp. 1134–1135.

[70] As proposed in Human Rights Watch Report, *'We Have the Promises of the World'* – *Women's Rights in Afghanistan*, New York, 2009, p. 82.

ARTICLE 11

1. States parties shall take all appropriate measures to eliminate discrimination against women in the field of employment in order to ensure, on a basis of equality of men and women, the same rights, in particular:
   a) The right to work as an inalienable right of all human beings;
   b) The right to the same employment opportunities, including the application of the same criteria for selection in matters of employment;
   c) The right to free choice of profession and employment, the right to promotion, job security and all benefits and conditions of service and the right to receive vocational training and retraining, including apprenticeships, advanced vocational training and recurrent training;
   d) The right to equal remuneration, including benefits, and to equal treatment in respect of work of equal value, as well as equality of treatment in the evaluation of the quality of work;
   e) The right to social security, particularly in cases of retirement, unemployment, sickness, invalidity and old age and other incapacity to work, as well as the right to paid leave;
   f) The right to protection of health and to safety in working conditions, including the safeguarding of the function of reproduction.

2. In order to prevent discrimination against women on the grounds of marriage or maternity and to ensure their effective right to work, States parties shall take appropriate measures:
   a) To prohibit, subject to the imposition of sanctions, dismissal on the grounds of pregnancy or of maternity leave and discrimination in dismissals on the basis of marital status;
   b) To introduce maternity leave with pay or with pay or with comparable social benefits without loss of former employment, seniority or social allowances;
   c) To encourage the provision of the necessary supporting social services to enable parents to combine family obligations with work responsibilities and participation in public life, in particular through promoting the establishment and development of a network of child-care facilities;
   d) To provide special protection to women during pregnancy in types of work proved to be harmful to them.

3. Protective legislation relating to matters covered in this Article shall be reviewed periodically in the light of scientific and technological knowledge and shall be revised, repealed or extended as necessary.

CHAPTER 11
EQUAL EMPLOYMENT OPPORTUNITIES AND EQUAL PAY: MEASURING EU LAW AGAINST THE STANDARDS OF THE WOMEN'S CONVENTION

Anja WIESBROCK

1. INTRODUCTION

The right to work is not only a socio-economic but also as a fundamental right.[1] According to the Committee on Economic, Social and Cultural Rights (CESCR), the fundamental right to work 'is essential for realizing other human rights and forms an inseparable and inherent part of human dignity'.[2] Employment is considered to be more than just a means of earning a livelihood, but an essential component of developing an individual's identity and self-esteem as well as his/her role and social status in society.[3] The Committee on the Elimination of Discrimination Against Women (CEDAW) has underlined the importance of the right to work in respect of other Convention rights. It has stated that the situation of working women is of special concern under the Convention, as it shows the 'extent of women's independent status as individuals'.[4]

Article 11 of the Convention on the Elimination of All Forms of Discrimination against Women (hereinafter Women's Convention) requires States parties to 'take all appropriate measures to eliminate discrimination against women in the field of employment'. Inspiration regarding the interpretation and scope of the 'right to work as an inalienable right of all human

---

[1] K. DRZEWICKI, 'The right to work and rights in work', in A. Eide, C. Krause and A. Rosas, *Economic, Social and Cultural Rights*, Martinus Nijhoff Publishers, The Hague, 2001, pp. 223–243.
[2] UN doc. E/C.12/GC/18, CESCR, *General Comment no. 18. The right to work*, 7–25 November 2005, p. 2.
[3] See the preamble to ILO Convention No. 168 (1988); see also S. TURNELL, 'The Right to Employment: Extending the Core Labour Standards and Trade Debate', *Macquarie Economics Research Papers* 1/2001, 2001, pp. 4, 5.
[4] UN doc. CEDAW/C/1994/7, CEDAW, *Contribution of the Committee to International Conferences*, 17 January-4 February 1994, para. 14.

beings'[5] can be drawn from other international instruments, such as Article 23 of the Universal Declaration of Human Rights (UDHR) and Article 6 of the International Covenant on Economic, Social and Cultural Rights (ICESCR). Whereas, in principle States parties have an obligation to ensure the 'progressive realization' of the exercise of the right to work, they are also subject to certain immediate obligations, including the obligation to guarantee that the right to work will be exercised without discrimination.[6]

The right to work in Article 11 Women's Convention is complemented by similar rights contained in various human rights treaties[7] and international labour legislation. The International Labour Organization (ILO) has adopted numerous Conventions and Recommendations that deal specifically with the rights of women[8] or are of particular relevance to the situation of women.[9] In terms of policy documents, attention must be paid to the 1995 'Beijing Declaration and Platform for Action, adopted at the Fourth UN World Conference in Beijing. Moreover, at the regional level, employment-related rights of a varying scope and intensity have been established.[10] In particular within the context of the European Union, a comprehensive body of directly effective primary and secondary legislation has consolidated the rights of female employees.

This Chapter focuses on the right to equal employment opportunities and the right to equal pay for work of equal value. Equality of opportunities and equal remuneration of men and women are key means to achieve gender equality in employment. At the same time, these two rights are characterized by immense challenges regarding implementation. There is a large discrepancy between the existence of the right to equal employment opportunities and the right to equal pay for work of equal value in the legislation of the States parties and the enjoyment of such rights in practice. This Chapter seeks to illuminate the

---

[5] Article 11(1)(a) Women's Convention.
[6] UN doc. E/C.12/GC/18, CESCR, *General Comment No. 18. The right to work*, 7–25 November 2005, p. 2.
[7] The right to work is contained in Article 23 of the Universal Declaration of Human Rights (UDHR) and Article 6 of the International Covenant on Economic, Social and Cultural Rights (ICESCR). Both legal instruments refer to the enjoyment of the rights guaranteed without distinction on grounds of *inter alia* sex (Article 2 UDHR and Article 2 ICESCR). In addition, Article 3 ICESCR obliges States parties explicitly to ensure the equal right of men and women to the enjoyment of all rights contained in the Covenant.
[8] See for instance the Underground Work (Women) Convention No. 45 (1935), the Night Work (Women) Convention (Revised) No. 89 (1948) and the Maternity Protection Convention No. 183 (2000).
[9] For instance due to the high percentage of women engaged in part-time and home work. See the Discrimination (Employment and Occupation) Convention No. 111 (1958), the Workers with Family Responsibilities Convention No. 156 (1981), the Part-Time Work Convention No. 175 (1994) and the Home Work Convention No. 177 (1996).
[10] Regional legal instruments that embody employment-related rights include the African Charter on Human and Peoples' Rights (Article 15) and the European Social Charter (Article 1).

persisting key challenges in respect of implementing these rights in practice. The following major problems in respect of the two rights under scrutiny will be identified and discussed: non-standard forms of employment, deep-rooted causes of inequality and a male standard of worker.

The question arises in how far the rights to equal employment opportunities and equal remuneration can be guaranteed in practice and what kind of responsibilities and restrictions apply to national governments in this respect. For this purpose, the recommendations and measures proposed by CEDAW and other human rights committees will be compared with the case law of the Court of Justice of the European Union (CJEU) and the responsibilities of Member States under EU law. This will lead to conclusions on the extent to which inspiration can be drawn from the Women's Convention when applying women's employment rights under EU law and vice versa. After discussing the extent and scope of the right to equal employment opportunities and equal remuneration under the Women's Convention and under EU Law, this Chapter highlights the existing limitations to the exercise of these rights, followed by an analysis on how these problems have been addressed by CEDAW and the CJEU respectively. Particular attention will be paid to the implementation and enforcement of EU and Convention rights in practice.

2. THE RIGHT TO EQUAL EMPLOYMENT OPPORTUNITIES AND EQUAL PAY FOR WORK OF EQUAL VALUE

2.1. ARTICLE 11 WOMEN'S CONVENTION

Article 11 Women's Convention covers three main issues: employment rights of women, the prohibition of discrimination on grounds of marriage or maternity and protective legislation. The first paragraph deals with the right to equal employment opportunities and equal pay for work of equal value, the right to free choice of profession[11] and the right to social security benefits.[12] It also covers the right to protection of health and to safety in working conditions.[13] The second paragraph of Article 11 calls upon States parties to take appropriate measures to prevent discrimination against women on the grounds of marriage or maternity and to ensure their effective right to work.[14] The third paragraph

---

[11] Article 11(1)(c) Women's Convention.
[12] Article 11(1)(e) Women's Convention.
[13] Article 11(1)(f) Women's Convention.
[14] This includes the prohibition of dismissal on grounds of pregnancy, maternity or marital status, the introduction of maternity leave with pay or comparable social benefits as well as the development of child-care facilities and other supporting social services, enabling parents to combine work and family obligations. Moreover, States parties must grant special

foresees a periodical review of protective legislation in light of new scientific and technological knowledge. This Chapter focuses on the rights to the same employment opportunities and the right to equal remuneration, contained in Articles 11(1)(b) and (d) Women's Convention.

Article 11(1)(b) guarantees the right to the same employment opportunities, including the application of identical selection criteria. Whereas the right to employment as such is not an absolute, justiciable right, there exists a clear duty of governments to create an environment, where all individuals, irrespective of gender, have the same employment opportunities. Thus, whereas individuals cannot rely on the right to employment as such, they can rely on the right of equal treatment in respect of employment opportunities.[15] When interpreting this right under the Women's Convention, identical or similar rights in other international instruments must be taken into account. Article 3 ICESCR has been interpreted by the Committee on Economic, Social and Cultural Rights in a way that requires States parties to ensure equal opportunities and treatment between men and women in relation to their right to work.[16] Moreover, Article 2 of ILO Convention No. 111 obliges States parties to apply a policy that is designed to promote equality of opportunities and treatment in respect of employment and occupation, in order to eliminate any discrimination in this respect. It follows from Articles 2(b) and 2(f) of the Women's Convention that governments must take legislative action in order to ensure that equality of opportunity is guaranteed. The Beijing Platform for Action requests 'strong commitment' from the governments to equal opportunities and the equal participation of women and men, including an adequate mobilization of resources.[17]

Article 11(1)(d) Women's Convention embodies the right to equal remuneration, including benefits, and to equal treatment in respect of work of equal value, as well as equality of treatment in the evaluation of the quality of work. The right to equal pay for work of equal value is equally contained in ILO Convention No. 100 and has been read into Article 3 ICESCR by the CESCR.[18] CEDAW has in its General Recommendation No. 13 (eighth session, 1989) commented on the application and interpretation of Article 11(1)(d). The Committee underlined that even though the

---

protection of pregnant women from potentially harmful types of employment. For more details see H. SCHNEIDER, 'Zwangerschapsverlof-ouderschapsverlof-kinderopvang: geen makkelijke bevalling!', in: A.W. Heringa, J. Hes and L. Lijnzaad, *Het Vrouwenverdrag: een beeld van een verdrag...*, Maklu, Antwerpen/Apeldoorn, 1994, pp. 149–162; M. MONSTER, E. CREMERS and L. WILLEMS, *Vrouwenverdrag, moederschap, ouderschap en arbeid*, Ministerie van Sociale Zaken en Werkgelegenheid, The Hague, 1998.

[15] H. VAN VOSS, 'Vrouwenverdrag en de arbeid', in: A.W. Heringa, J. Hes and L. Lijnzaad, *Het Vrouwenverdrag: een beeld van een verdrag...*, 1994, Antwerpen/Apeldoorn, Maklu, pp. 123–134.

[16] UN doc. E/C.12/2005/4, CESCR, *General Comment no. 16. The equal right of men and women to the enjoyment of all economic, social and cultural rights*, 11 August 2005, paras. 23–25.

[17] Beijing Platform for Action, Fourth World Conference on Women, 15 September 1995, para. 5.

[18] UN doc. E/C.12/2005/4, CESCR, *General Comment No. 16. The equal right of men and women to the enjoyment of all economic, social and cultural rights*, 11 August 2005, paras. 23–25.

principle of equal pay for work of equal value has been incorporated in the legislation of many countries, more action is needed in order to implement this principle in practice and to 'overcome the gender-segregation in the labour market'. The Committee encourages States to ratify the 1951 ILO Convention No. 100 concerning Equal Remuneration for Men and Women Workers for Work of Equal Value. It also calls upon States to adopt a job evaluation system based on gender-neutral criteria, comparing the value of jobs in which women predominate with jobs in which men predominate. The Committee would like to be informed on this data by way of reports submitted by the States parties. The last paragraph of the Recommendation subscribes the development of implementation mechanisms. Whenever possible, States should apply the principle of equal remuneration for work of equal value in the drafting of collective agreements. Also in concluding observations on State reports CEDAW has underlined the importance of enacting measures to ensure that women receive equal pay for equal work and work of equal value. Moreover, it has encouraged the establishment of sanctions for discrimination against women in private and public sector employment and the creation of effective enforcement and monitoring mechanisms.[19]

2.2. EU LAW

In the EU, the right to equal employment opportunities and the right to equal pay for work of equal value is covered by a body of primary and secondary legislation. As regards primary law, Article 157 TFEU (ex Article 141 TEC) embodies the principle of equal pay for work of equal value for male and female workers. The Court emphasized in *Roberts v Birds Eye Walls*[20] that the principle of equal pay for men and women must be seen as an embodiment of the general principle of non-discrimination. Article 157(3) contains a legal basis for the European Parliament and the Council to adopt legislation on the application of the principle of equal opportunities and equal treatment of men and women in matters of employment and occupation. Moreover, the fourth paragraph of Article 157 allows Member States to undertake or maintain positive action 'providing for specific advantages in order to make it easier for the underrepresented sex to pursue a vocational activity or to prevent or compensate for disadvantages in professional careers.' A further provision of primary law is Article 19 TFEU (ex Article 13 TEC), introduced by the Treaty of Amsterdam in 1997. Article 19 TFEU grants the Union competence to take action to combat discrimination on a number of grounds, including sex.

---

[19] UN doc. CEDAW/C/KHM/CO/3, CEDAW, *Concluding comments: Cambodia*, 25 January 2006, paras. 27 and 28.
[20] Case C-132/92 *Roberts* [1993] ECR I-5579], para. 17.

Regarding secondary legislation, starting in the mid-1970s, the EU legislator has adopted a number of legal instruments with the objective of establishing equal treatment of men and women in employment matters.[21] The very first Directive adopted in 1975 was the Equal Pay Directive, incorporating the concept of equal pay for work of equal value.[22] Only one year later the Council adopted the so-called 'Equal Treatment Directive', establishing equal treatment in other aspects of employment, such as hiring, promotions and dismissals.[23] Furthermore, the Council adopted Directives on the burden of proof in sex discrimination cases[24] and the implementation of the principle of equal treatment for men and women in occupational security schemes.[25] All these Directives have since been repealed by the recast Directive 2006/54/EC of 5 July 2006 on the implementation of the principle of equal opportunities and equal treatment of men and women in matters of employment and occupation.[26] On the basis of Article 19 TFEU, the Union legislator has adopted a 'General Framework Directive', covering equal treatment in employment and occupation.[27] The Directive has the objective of establishing a general framework for combating discrimination on grounds of *inter alia* sex as regards employment and occupation.[28]

---

[21] See C. HOSKYNS, *Integrating Gender: Women, Law and Politics in the European Union*, 1996, London, Verso.

[22] Council Directive 75/117/EEC of 10 February 1975 on the approximation of the laws of the Member States relating to the application of the principle of equal pay for men and women, OJ L45/19, 19 February 1975.

[23] Council Directive 76/207/EEC of 9 February 1976 on the implementation of the principle of equal treatment for men and women as regards access to employment, vocational training and promotion, and working conditions, OJ L39/40, 14 February 1976. This Directive was amended by Directive 2002/73/EC of 23 September 2002, OJ L 269/15, 5 October 2002.

[24] Council Directive 97/80/EC of 15 December 1997 on the burden of proof in cases of discrimination based on sex [1998] OJ L14/6, 20 January 1998, as amended by Directive 98/52/EC, OJ L 205/66, 22 July 1998.

[25] Council Directive 86/378/EEC of 24 July 1986 on the implementation of the principle of equal treatment for men and women in occupational social security schemes, OJ L 225/40, 12 August 1986, as amended by Directive 96/97/EC, OJ L 46/20, 17February 1997.

[26] Directive 2006/54/EC of the European Parliament and of the Council of 5 July 2006 on the implementation of the principle of equal opportunities and equal treatment of men and women in matters of employment and occupation (recast), OJ L 204/23, 26 July 2006. The period of implementation for this Directive expired on 15 August 2008 and the Directives mentioned above were repealed on 15 August 2009 (see Articles 33 and 34 of the Directive).

[27] Council Directive 2000/78/EC of 27 November 2000, establishing a general framework for equal treatment in employment and occupation, OJ L 303/16, 2 December 2000. On 2 July 2008 the European Commission put forward a draft directive prohibiting discrimination on grounds of religion, belief, disability, age or sexual orientation in areas outside employment, see European Commission, Proposal for a Council Directive on implementing the principle of equal treatment between persons irrespective of religion or belief, disability, age or sexual orientation, COM(2008) 426 final, 2 July 2008.

[28] Article 1 of the Directive. See R. WHITTLE, 'The Framework Directive for equal treatment in employment and occupation: an analysis from a disability rights perspective', 27 *European Law Review*, pp. 303–326.

Next to the Treaties and secondary legislation, female employees in the EU can rely on the right to non-discrimination as a 'fundamental principle of EU law'.[29] Even though initially economic considerations played a key role in adopting equal treatment provisions,[30] the Court established as early as 1976 that the principle of equal treatment of women and men constitutes a fundamental principle of EU law.[31] A crucial legislative instrument in this respect is the Charter of Fundamental Rights, which acquired legally binding force with the entry into force of the Treaty of Lisbon. According to Article 23 of the Charter, 'equality between men and women must be ensured in all areas, including employment, work and pay.' Moreover, the second paragraph of the Article provides for positive action by the Member States (measures providing for specific advantages in favour of the under-represented sex). A general non-discrimination clause, prohibiting discrimination based on various grounds can be found in Article 21 of the Charter.

3. CHALLENGES IN THE APPLICATION OF EMPLOYMENT RIGHTS

A persistent challenge in the implementation of Article 11 Women's Convention as well as primary and secondary EU law is to ensure that legislative employment rights of women are also guaranteed in practice. This difficulty applies in particular to the rights of equal employment opportunities and equal pay. Both rights are easily adopted into national legal settings, but are difficult to evaluate and to guarantee in practice. There is thus a gap between formal (*de iure*) and real (*de facto*) progress in respect of equal employment opportunities and equality of pay. This is exemplified by two persisting major problems: the gender wage gap and occupational segregation. CEDAW has stressed that female labour market participation continues to be characterized by a wage gap, low representation of women in high managerial positions and significant occupational segregation.[32] Thus, the practical limitations to the right contained in Article 11 become apparent in the persistent phenomena of a gender wage gap and labour market segregation.[33]

Recent data from the ILO confirm the difficulties in guaranteeing equal employment opportunities and equal pay in practice. As regards access to

---

[29] Case C-555/07 *Kücükdeveci v Swedex* [2010] ECR I-0000.
[30] C. BARNARD, 'The Economic Objectives of Article 119', in T. Hervey and D. O'Keefe, *Sex Equality Law of the European Union*, Wiley 1996, pp. 321–334.
[31] Case C-43/75 *Defrenne II* [1976] ECR 455.
[32] UN doc. CEDAW/C/DEN/CO/6, *Concluding comments: Denmark*, 25 August 2006, paras 14 and 15.
[33] UN Development Fund for Women (UNIFEM), *Briefing Paper: Human Rights Protections Applicable to Women Migrant Workers*, 2003, p. 19.

employment and labour market segregation, the ILO has noted in its 2010 report on women in labour markets[34] that the gender gap in labour force participation narrowed slightly between 1980 and 2008. Yet, women continue to feature labour market participation rates that are significantly lower than those of men (51.7 per cent for women as opposed to 77.7 per cent for men in 2008). Similarly, the female employment-to-population ratio (the share of women above working age who are employed) in 2009 was still around 2/3 that of men,[35] even though men saw a higher decrease of the employment-to-population ratio than women over the last decade. In spite of the fact that the financial crisis has had an equally detrimental effect on women and men, the ILO stressed that the crisis has lead to a further deterioration in the labour market position of particularly vulnerable groups, such as women and young people.[36] Due to different behaviour patterns in the face of a crisis, it can be expected that male and female employees will benefit to a different extent from economic recovery. Experience from previous economic crises shows, that female job-losers are slower to return to work and more likely to accept part-time and flexible jobs, which bears the danger of an increasing marginalization of female labour.[37]

According to the ILO,[38] there is still a clear labour market segregation of men and women. Female employees dominate in sectors that are characterized by low pay, long hours and informal working arrangements. Moreover, female employees continue to dominate in part-time work, with the consequences of lower pay, restricted benefits and diminished career opportunities. Women continue to be primarily engaged in household work, classified as a non-economic activity. Thus, one main factor behind the overall difference in earnings between women and men is the fact that women are conducting most of the non-paid work at home. As a consequence, they are more frequently engaged in part-time work, receiving lower wages than their male counterparts.[39] The wage-gap between full time and part time employment also has implications for women's practical right to maternity and pregnancy leave (Article 11(2)).[40] Women are also much more frequently engaged in unconventional forms of

---

[34] ILO, *Women in labour markets: measuring progress and identifying challenges*, ILO, Geneva, 2010, pp. 3–5.
[35] In 2009 the female employment-to-population ratio was 48.4 per cent, compared to a ratio of 22.3 per cent for men.
[36] ILO, *Global Employment Trends*, 2010, Geneva, p. 42.
[37] ILO, *Women in labour markets: measuring progress and identifying challenges*, ILO, Geneva, 2010, pp. 3–5.
[38] ILO, *Women in labour markets: measuring progress and identifying challenges*, ILO, Geneva, 2010, pp. 3–5.
[39] In respect of rights of part-time employees, see ILO Convention No. 175 concerning Part-Time Work (1994).
[40] M. MONSTER, E. CREMERS and L. WILLEMS, *Vrouwenverdrag, moederschap, ouderschap en arbeid*, Ministerie van Sociale Zaken en Werkgelegenheid, The Hague, 1998.

employment, including family enterprises, which means that they receive low wages or are conducting non-remunerated work.

In its Global Wage Report 2008/2009[41] the ILO concluded that there is still a large difference in earnings between men and women and that the gender wage gap is only closing slowly. Even though a slight increase in the ratio of female to male average wages could be observed in the majority of countries between 1995 and 2007, these changes were mostly small if not negligible. Indeed, the ILO considers the narrowing of the wage gap 'disappointing', considering the closing of the gender gap in terms of educational achievements and work experience. Moreover, the ILO highlights the persistent problems regarding the pay gap between men and women doing different work of equal value or even doing similar work, in particular in the area of skilled trade and highly skilled employment. Differences in wages between men and women can be observed in all occupations and at all skills bases, including employees with a university degree.[42]

The difficulties in guaranteeing the right to equal employment opportunities and equal pay in practice can be traced back to three major difficulties in the implementation of these rights: the dominance of women in non-standard forms of employment, deep-rooted causes of inequality and the adoption of a male standard of worker and instance of multiple discrimination. The following section discusses these three problems in guaranteeing effective equal treatment rights in respect of access to employment and remuneration and evaluates the way in which these problems have been addressed within the context of Article 11 Women's Convention and EU law.

3.1. NON-STANDARD FORMS OF EMPLOYMENT

A first major challenge in respect of the practical application of the right of equal employment opportunities and the right to equal pay for work of equal value is the dominance of women in non-standard forms of employment, which may fall outside the scope of the relevant legislative provisions. Due to the frequent engagement of women in employment that falls outside the formal sectors of employment, they are faced with both a lack of promotion opportunities and limited or absent level of remuneration. Due to the fact that a large proportion of women are engaged in atypical forms of employment, they are in a disadvantaged position, in particular with regard to access to promotion and better paid employment. In order to reach full equality of opportunities and remuneration

---

[41] ILO, Global Wage Report 2008/09, *Minimum wages and collective bargaining. Towards policy coherence*, Geneva, 2008, pp. 29 ff.
[42] ILO, *Women in labour markets: measuring progress and identifying challenges*, ILO, Geneva, 2010, pp. 3–5.

of men and women, it is crucial to include such non-standard forms of employment into the scope of non-discrimination provisions. In this respect, it appears that the Women's Convention has a broader personal scope than the relevant provisions of EU law.

The text of Article 11 of the Women's Convention does not indicate clearly whether the provision is merely applicable to employment in the commercial sector. However, it appears from the preparatory documents to the Convention that Article 11 has to be interpreted widely, encompassing all types of employment, including employment in the public and non-profit sector as well as household and domestic work.[43] Also in more general terms, the scope of the provision should be interpreted broadly, including not only women in employment, but also in self-employment or in other employment relationships than a formal employment contract.

As regards persons who do not hold a permanent position, but have a less steady employment situation, it can be inferred from the wording of Article 11 in conjunction with Article 5 that such persons fall under the scope of the Convention. Article 5 aims in general terms at the elimination of prejudices and stereotypes.[44] As a consequence, not only the classical employment relationship, but also different, more flexible forms of works, which are most frequently conducted by women, must be considered to fall under the scope of the Convention.

In its tenth session (General Recommendation No. 16, 1991),[45] CEDAW increased the attention paid to the situation of women who are employed as family members of a family business. It seems that in a large part of States parties to the Convention, women do not receive a salary and do not enjoy social security when working in a family business. According to the Committee 'unpaid work constitutes a form of women's exploitation that is contrary to the Convention'. States parties are advised to draft reports and collect statistical information on the legal and social situation of women, who are carrying out unpaid work in family businesses. Moreover, the necessary measures must be taken in order to guarantee payment and a right to social security of such women.

In the past it was arguable that the scope of the non-discrimination provisions under EU law was not as broad as under the Women's Convention. Article 157 TFEU as well as the non-discrimination Directives refer to 'employment' and/or the concept of 'worker'. Their application is thus limited to a formal employment context. For instance, the Framework Directive 2000/78/EC is restricted to discrimination in the context of employment and occupation.

---

[43] L.A. REHOF, *Guide to the Travaux Préparatoires of the United Nations Convention on the Elimination of All forms of Discrimination Against Women*, Martinus Nijhoff Publishers, The Hague, 1993, pp. 122–134.

[44] For more details see Chapter 6 of this book by Ingrid Westendorp.

[45] UN doc. A/46/38, CEDAW, *General Recommendation No. 16: Unpaid women workers in rural and urban family enterprises*, 1991, paras. 1–2.

Even though the number of aspects listed as falling within the concept of employment and occupation in Article 3 of the Directive is rather extensive, covering the public and the private sector, as well as employment and self-employment, there must be some kind of formal employment relationship for Directive 2000/78/EC to apply. Article 19 TFEU contains an open-ended non-discrimination clause, but does not directly grant any rights to female employees. It merely provides a legal basis for adopting legislation in this area.

Yet, the situation has changed with the entry into force of the Treaty of Lisbon in December 2009 and the consequent legally binding force of the Charter of Fundamental Rights. Article 23 thereof grants a right of equal treatment between men and women in *all areas*, including employment and work. This Article must be considered to equally cover non-standard forms of employment. The same applies to the general right to non-discrimination contained in Article 21 of the Charter. Moreover, the Court has made clear in the recent judgment of *Kücükdeveci*[46] that the Directives are merely emanations of the fundamental principle of non-discrimination under EU law. Thus, it is not inconceivable that a situation that falls outside the personal or material scope of one of the non-discrimination Directives is nevertheless covered by the general principle of non-discrimination.[47] Moreover, whereas the first directives on equal treatment between men and women were confined to equal treatment in standard forms of employment, more recent legal instruments encompass also non-standard, atypical forms of employment, such as part-time and temporary work.[48]

Thus, it seems that the scope of EU law has widened to encompass also situations that fall outside a formal employment relationship. Yet, there continues to be one major requirement for a situation to be covered by EU non-discrimination provision: the situation must fall within the scope of EU law. It is unlikely that reliance on a provision of the Charter will suffice in order to argue that the situation at hand falls within the scope of EU law. This is due to the fact that the Charter only applies when Member States are implementing Union law.[49] Thus, even though the scope of application of EU law has widened, the Convention applies in certain situations where EU law fails to grasp. Apart from the basic fundamental rights contained in the Charter, the personal scope of EU legislative provisions is still more restricted, covering employment and self-employment. This means that due to its broad personal scope, Article 11 of the Women's Convention also covers women who are prone to fall outside the scope of EU law, as they are not considered workers due to the absence of a formal employment relationship, such as house workers and domestic workers.

---

[46] Case C-555/07 *Kücükdeveci v Swedex* [2010] ECR I-0000.
[47] A. WIESBROCK, 'Case Note – Case C-555/07, Kücükdeveci v. Swedex, Judgment of the Court (Grand Chamber) of 19 January 2010', *German Law Journal*, Vol. 11, No. 5, 2010, pp. 539–550.
[48] J. PILLINGER, *Feminising the Market: Women's Pay and Employment in the European Community*, Macmillan, Basingstoke, 1992.
[49] Article 51 of the Charter.

3.2. DEEP-ROOTED CAUSES OF INEQUALITY AND A MALE STANDARD OF WORKER

A second major problem in addressing differences in terms of treatment as far as employment opportunities and remuneration is concerned, is the general objective of eradicating any difference in treatment between men and women in a similar situation. By adopting a male pattern of life as the standard, such an approach does not tackle the deep-rooted causes of inequality. Prevailing customs and traditions in many countries are strong and lead to *de facto* discrimination against women, in particular with regards to promotion and remuneration. For instance, at times where full-time employment remains the standard for achieving advancement and promotion, equal treatment in respect of employment opportunities between men and women, who are much more frequently engaged in part-time work, can hardly be achieved. The presumably gender-neutral concept of employment becomes ambiguous when taking into account that women continue to be dominant in under-paid work, such as part-time work, temporary work, and domestic work. The fact that a 'male worker' is generally used as a standard against whom the female worker is compared renders it problematic to apply the equality principle in case a 'comparable male' is missing. The continued segregation of labour markets is a case in point, demonstrating how the employment opportunities of men and women are still dominated by public perceptions and role models. Therefore, it has been suggested to replace the concept of formal equality with a 'test of disadvantage', which considers discrimination as a legislation or practice which reinforces disadvantages of a certain group in society.[50] A legal framework guaranteeing equality in treatment in respect of employment opportunities and wages can only be effective if it addresses the root causes of gender inequality, including the gender division of labour. Such root causes form part of national mindsets, institutions, policies and practises related to the family, the society and the socio-economic order.[51]

In the context of the Women's Convention, Article 5 requires States parties to eradicate social and cultural norms and stereotypes that reinforce the perceived inferiority of women. Thus by virtue of Article 5 Women's Convention States parties are obliged to address existing prejudices, social and cultural patterns as root causes of differential treatment between women and men. For instance in respect of the right to equal pay for work of equal value, the requirement to address the root causes of inequality implies that it is not sufficient to incorporate such a right into national law. States parties are required on the basis of Article 5

---

[50] K. FROSTELL AND M. SCHEININ, 'Women', in: A. Eide, C. Krause and A. Rosas, *Economic, Social and Cultural Rights*, Martinus Nijhoff, 2001, pp. 331–351.

[51] E. RUMINSKA-ZIMNY, 'Gender Architecture in the European Union: Achievements, Challenges and the Future', in: A. Grzybek, *Gender in the EU. The Future of the Gender Policies in the European Union*, Warsaw, 2009, p. 15.

to investigate and address the phenomenon of women being employed in positions that pay less, including part time work, and the social and cultural practices and perceptions that underlie such a division of work. Thus, addressing the root causes of inequality equally requires the recognition of a link between paid and non paid work.

CEDAW has expressed its concerns regarding the root causes of inequalities in respect of employment opportunities and pay in a General Recommendation as well as in State reports. Recommendation No. 17 (tenth session, 1991)[52] deals with unpaid house work. CEDAW proposed to conduct a study on the value of unpaid house work in relation to the brut national product. States were encouraged to include unpaid house work into the calculation of their brut national product. According to the Committee 'the measurement and quantification of the unremunerated domestic activities of women ... will help to reveal the de facto economic role of women.' Also in its concluding observations addressed at States parties the Committee has expressed concerns regarding the root causes of the disadvantaged position of women in the labour market, being traditional practices and stereotypical attitudes about the roles and responsibilities of women and men in family and society.[53]

Within the context of EU law, the concept of 'substantive equality' has been used to describe a legal framework that not only guarantees a right to non-discrimination but that also addresses the problem of underlying stereotypes and a division between public roles and domestic responsibilities of men and women.[54] Critics have argued that EU equal treatment law does not tackle the root causes of inequality but applies gender biases by adopting a male standard of worker, for instance in the Directives on maternity rights and parental leave. Therefore, it has been contended that the EU legal framework focuses on formal rights, rather than encouraging a more comprehensive approach addressing the persistence of stereotypes and the construction of gender roles.[55] However, since the adoption of the first Directives on gender equality in the 1970s, the EU legislator and the Court have gone a long way in guaranteeing *de facto* equality and taking a broader approach, addressing not only formal but also substantive equality. For instance in the Case *Webb v EMO Air Cargo*, which concerned the dismissal of a female worker on account of pregnancy, the Court recognized the flaws of adopting a 'male standard of worker' in order to determine an incident of discrimination by emphasizing that the situation of a pregnant women is in no way comparable with the situation of a man with a pathological condition or

---

[52] UN doc. CEDAW/A/46/38, *General Recommendation No. 17: Measurement and quantification of the unremunerated domestic activities of women and their recognition in the gross national product*, 1991, pp. 1–2.
[53] UN doc. CEDAW/C/ICE/CO/6, *Concluding observations: Iceland*, 18 July 2008, para. 29.
[54] See, for example, C. BARNARD, *EC Employment Law* (3rd ed.), 2006, pp. 333–338.
[55] R. GUERINNA, 'Mothering in Europe: Feminist Critique of European Policies on Motherhood and Employment', *European Journal of Women's Studies*, Vol. 9(1), 2002, pp. 49–68.

unavailability for work on non-medical ground.[56] Moreover, the very objective of the Gender Equal Treatment Directive is to arrive at 'real equality of opportunity for men and women'. This objective was confirmed by the Court in cases such as *Marshall*[57] and *Belinda*.[58]

In EU law the notion of substantive equality is intrinsically linked to the concept of 'positive action'. Article 2(4) of the Second Equal Treatment Directive (in its original version) allows Member States to take positive action. Article 3 of Directive 2006/54/EC permits Member States to maintain or adopt measures which are aimed at ensuring 'full equality in practice between men and women in working life'. Thus, Member States may take measures, which, although discriminatory in appearance, are in fact intended to eliminate or reduce actual instances of inequality which may exist in the reality of social life. It authorizes measures relating to access to employment, including promotion, which give a specific advantage to women with a view to improving their ability to compete on the labour market and to pursue a career on an equal footing with men.[59] In this context the Court has accepted the validity of a public service scheme under which, in trained occupations in which women are under-represented and for which the State does not have a monopoly of training, at least half of the training places are allocated to women. The scheme was seen to form part of a 'restricted concept of equality of opportunity', as it did not reserve places in employment but places in training for women, therefore improving their chances of obtaining employment in the public sector. The scheme was therefore seen as a means designed to eliminate the causes of women's reduced opportunities of access to employment and careers.[60] Similarly, in *Lommers*, the Court held that a subsidized nursery scheme, which reserves places to female employees, forms part of the restricted concept of equality of opportunity, as it does not reserve *places of employment* for women but guarantees enjoyment of certain working conditions designed to facilitate their pursuit of their career. This falls in principle into the category of measures designed to eliminate the causes of women's reduced opportunities for access to employment and careers and improves their ability to compete on the labour market and to pursue a career on an equal footing with men.[61] Thus, due the fact that the employment situation in the relevant Ministry was characterized by a significant under-representation of women and the female employees were more likely to give up their jobs due to an insufficiency of suitable nursery facilities, the measure was not in violation of EU law, even though a difference of treatment on the grounds of gender had been created.

---

[56] Case C-32/93 *Webb* [1993] ECR I-5199].
[57] Case C-409/95 *Marschall* [1997] ECR I-6363, para. 24.
[58] Case C-185/97 *Belinda* [1998] ECR I-5199, para. 27.
[59] Case C-476/99 *Lommers* [2002] ECR I-2891, para. 32; Case C-158/97 *Badeck and Others* [2000] ECR I-1875, para. 19.
[60] Case C-158/97 *Badeck and Others* [2000] ECR I-1875, paras 52 to 55.
[61] Case C-476/99 *Lommers* [2002] ECR I-2891, para. 38.

Yet, the Court's approach has been criticized for perceiving positive action in favour of women as a form of (*prima facie*) discrimination against men.[62] In cases such as *Badeck*[63] and *Abrahamsson*,[64] the Court has stressed that even if positive action measures are formulated in terms that are neutral as regards sex and are thus capable of benefiting men too, in general they favour women. Such criteria are according to the Court intended to lead to substantive, rather than formal equality, by reducing inequalities which may occur in practice in social life. Substantive equality is thus presented as an exception to the rule of formal equality, with the implication that such an exception to the general principle of non-discrimination must be interpreted strictly.[65]

In any case, affirmative action cannot be a substitute of addressing deep-rooted causes of inequality. The current approach of EU policies is still subject to criticism. It has been maintained that EU policies do not address the root causes of gender inequality embedded in the traditional model of market economy. Gender policies are dominated by traditional assumptions, according to which economic growth prevails and gender equality forms a constraint from an economic perspective. Moreover, gender issues are mainly addressed within the context of social policies and little efforts are undertaken to mainstream gender issues into other policy areas, such as economic policies, science and research.[66] Also little has been done to address the root causes of gender inequality in terms of recognizing the link between paid and non-paid work.

Thus, whereas Article 5 Women's Convention requires a firm commitment of States parties to take action counteracting stereotypes and addressing the root causes of gender inequalities in respect of employment opportunities and pay, the scope for positive action under EU law is more limited. Being considered by the CJEU as an exception to the general principle of non-discrimination (rather than an embodiment thereof), positive action measures are subject to significant limitations and a restrictive interpretation by the Court.[67]

---

[62] C. TOBLER, *Indirect Discrimination. A Case Study into the Development of the Legal Concept of Indirect Discrimination under EC Law*, Intersentia, Antwerp, 2005, pp. 70, 71.
[63] Case C-158/97 *Badeck and Others* [2000] ECR I-1875, para. 32.
[64] Case C-407/98 *Abrahamsson and Anderson* [2000] ECR I-5539, para. 47.
[65] As opposed to this general approach, Advocate General Saggio in *Badeck* has put forward the opinion that positive action and the general principle of non-discrimination actually pursue the same objective, see points 26 and 27 of the Advocate General's opinion.
[66] E. RUMINSKA-ZIMNY, 'Gender Architecture in the European Union: Achievements, Challenges and the Future', in: A. Grzybek, *Gender in the EU. The Future of the Gender Policies in the European Union*, Warsaw, 2009, p. 15.
[67] See Chapter 5 by Lisa Waddington and Laura Visser in this book.

4. IMPLEMENTATION AND ENFORCEMENT

It appears from the comparison above that women's rights to equal employment opportunities and equal remuneration under the Women's Convention go further than those under EU law. As a consequence, it could be perceived that the Convention is a highly suitable instrument to address the persisting shortcomings in women's employment opportunities and wage equality. Yet, even though the Women's Convention can potentially be a powerful tool to promote gender equality, critics have pointed to the fragmented and inaccurate implementation of the Articles of the Convention by many States parties.[68] Moreover, it is underlined that the extensive conditions attached to ratification by several countries practically undermine the rights and protections contained in the Convention.[69] The broad reservations adopted by some countries call into question the States parties' commitment to the objective of the Convention and bear the danger of rendering the Convention in these countries largely ineffective.

This holds particularly true for the right to equal employment opportunities and the right to equal pay for work of equal value. In spite of the fact that women's right to equal employment opportunity is globally recognized, the implementation of this basic right remains problematic.[70] Regarding the right to equal treatment in respect of work of equal value, several States, such as Micronesia and Mauritius have indicated that they are not able to fully apply this provision. Some other governments, such as that of Finland, Germany and Mexico have expressed their concern about the reservations made, claiming that such broad reservations are in contradiction with the object and purpose of the Convention.[71]

Even apart from reservations and inadequate implementation, the enforcement of employment rights and the lack of effective sanctions for non-compliance are problematic. The Committee on the Elimination of Discrimination against Women[72] has underlined the importance of enacting measures to ensure that women receive equal pay for equal work and work of equal value. Moreover, it has encouraged the establishment of sanctions for

---

[68] E. Evatt, 'Finding a Voice for Women's Rights: The Early Days of CEDAW', *George Washington International Law Review*, Vol. 34, 2002, p. 515; L. Keller, 'Discrimination against women: evolution and (non)implementation worldwide', *Thomas Jefferson Law Review*, Vol. 27, 2004, p. 35.

[69] B. Clark, 'The Vienna Convention Reservations Regime and the Convention on Discrimination Against Women', *American Journal of International Law*, Vol. 85, 1991, p. 281.

[70] J. Andrews, 'National and International Sources of Women's Right to Equal Employment Opportunities: Equality in Law Versus Equality in Fact', *Northwestern Journal of International Law & Business*, Vol. 14, 1993/1994, p. 14.

[71] 7 September 2005; the Finnish Government also recalled that reservations incompatible with the object and purpose of the Convention are prohibited on the basis of Article 29 thereof.

[72] UN doc. CEDAW/C/KHM/CO/3, CEDAW, Concluding observations, 2006, paras. 27 and 28.

discrimination against women in private and public sector employment and the creation of effective enforcement and monitoring mechanisms. In terms of enforcing the right to equal treatment under the Convention, Article 2 condemns discrimination against women in all its forms and requires States to pursue by all appropriate means and without delay a policy of eliminating discrimination against women by enacting constitutional, legislative and administrative measures. State parties are obliged on the basis of Article 2 Women's Convention to eliminate and take steps to prevent not only governmental discrimination, but also private sector discrimination by any person, organization or enterprise. Article 11 states that States parties shall take *all appropriate measures* to eliminate discrimination against women in the field of employment.

Regarding the possibilities of individuals to directly rely on Article 11 CEDAW, it is crucial to have a look at the interpretation of Article 11 CEDAW by national courts. It cannot be derived neither from the text of the Convention nor from the legislative history that the States parties intended to grant direct effect to certain provisions. In fact, it seems that the possible direct effect of the provisions of the Women's Convention in countries where this is possible was not discussed during the negotiations of the Treaty.[73] It has been consistently held for example by Dutch courts that Article 11 does not have direct effect, but merely imposes obligations on the government to act. The fact that Member States are obliged to reconsider protective legislation in the light of recent scientific and technological knowledge and the lack of a clear standard for the implementation of this provision, have led the courts to conclude that Article 11 cannot be directly relied upon.[74] Other voices have argued that at least certain provisions of Article 11, such as Article 11(2)(b) and Article 11(2)(c) are sufficiently concrete to impose a duty on the legislator to ensure income during pregnancy and maternity leave and to make child-care facilities available.[75]

An individual complaint procedure was introduced by an Optional Protocol of 1999 that entered into force in December 2000. The Protocol allows individuals to petition the Committee concerning States parties' violation of the Convention provided that a number of criteria, including the exhaustion of all domestic remedies, have been met.[76] States ratifying the Protocol have the option to declare that they do not accept the inquiry procedure but no reservations may be made (Article 17 of the Protocol). As of August 2011 the Protocol has been

---

[73] Memorie van Toelichting bij de Goedkeuringswet, Tweede Kamer, vergaderjaar 1984–1985, 18950 (R 1281), nrs. 1–3, p. 8.
[74] Centrale Raad van Beroep, 4 januari 2000, RSV 2000/79 and CRvB, 25 april 2003, RSV 2003, 193; Rechtbank 's-Gravenhage, zaaknummer 257427, 25 juli 2007.
[75] S.D. Burri, *Gelijke behandeling: oordelen en commentaar 2004*, Kluwer, 2005, p. 46.
[76] See for more details F. Gomez Isa, 'The Optional Protocol for the Convention on the Elimination of All Forms of Discrimination against Women: Strengthening the Protection Mechanisms of Women's Human Rights', *Arizona Journal of International and Comparative Law*, Vol. 20, 2003, p. 291.

ratified by 102 States, 4 of which have made such a declaration. Yet, even in those States where the Protocol applies, individual applicants have to exhaust all domestic remedies and may only submit their complaint to the Committee, rather than relying directly on Article 11 Women's Convention before a national court.

The situation is entirely different under EU law. The CJEU has established early in the landmark rulings of *Costa/ENEL*[77] and *Van Gend en Loos*[78] the supremacy and direct effect of EU law. As a consequence, the non-discrimination provisions enshrined in the Treaties and secondary legislation must take precedence over national law and some of them can be invoked directly in proceedings before national courts. Even in cases where direct effect cannot be established, national courts are obliged to interpret national law in light of the wording and purpose of the provision of EU law.[79] In recent non-discrimination cases the Court has stressed the responsibility of national courts to dis-apply provisions of national law that are in conflict with the general principle of non-discrimination.[80] The vast number of non-discrimination cases that have arisen before the CJEU illustrate the crucial role of the Court in effectively guaranteeing equal treatment for men and women in employment matters. In cases such as *Paquay*[81] the Court has stressed the importance of real and effective procedural guarantees, concluding that the objective of real equality of opportunity 'cannot be attained in the absence of measures appropriate to restore such equality when it has not been observed'. To that end the Court has constantly called for effective, proportionate and dissuasive sanctions for non-observance of employment-related equal treatment rights.[82]

5. CONCLUSION

It is beyond doubt that some progress has been achieved in raising the level of female participation in the labour market *inter alia* by adopting measures allowing women and men to reconcile work and family through maternity and parental leave schemes. However, women are struggling with employment discrimination and *de facto* equal opportunities and equal remuneration of men and women at all levels still needs to be achieved. When looking at the

---

[77] Case 6/64 *Costa v ENEL* [1964] ECR 585.
[78] Case 26/62 *Van Gend en Loos* [1963] ECR 1.
[79] Case 14/83 *von Colson and Kamann* [1984] ECR 1891.
[80] Case C-144/04 *Mangold* [2005] ECR I-9981; Case C-555/07 *Kücükdeveci v Swedex* [2010] ECR I-0000.
[81] Case C-460/06 *Paquay* [2007] ECR I-8511, para. 45.
[82] See for instance Case 68/88 *Commission v Greece* [1989] ECR 2965, para. 23 and 24; see, more recently, Joined Cases C-387/02, C-391/02 and C-403/02 *Berlusconi and Others* [2005] ECR I-3565, para. 65, Joined Cases C-378/07 to C-380/07 *Angelidaki and Others* [2009] ECR I-3071, para. 93.

legislation-practice divide it is evident that in spite of the existence of far-reaching non-discrimination provisions, in practice little has changed. Areas of concerns are in particular occupational segregation and concentration of women in the low-skilled sector. There is still a large gap between equality in law and equality in fact as far as equal employment opportunities are concerned. The wide number of legal instruments covering equal employment opportunities, including UN treaties and EU Directives can only be effective if they are correctly implemented by the States parties/Member States. Yet, national legislation on discrimination at the workplace, including working conditions as well as recruitment and promotion processes still features numerous gaps.

When comparing the EU and UN legislative framework, the rights to equal employment opportunities and equal pay guaranteed in the Women's Convention appear at times to be wider than those granted under EU law. Yet, the effective protection granted to individuals is much stronger in the context of EU law, due to the absence of effective enforcement mechanisms in the Women's Convention. Even after the entry into force of the Optional Protocol, enforcement of the Women's Convention remains problematic, as individuals cannot rely on Article 11 of the Convention in proceedings before national courts. This is contrary to the directly effective provisions of EU law, which may be directly relied upon before national courts.

The main role for the Women's Convention therefore seems to lie in steering the general direction of national employment policies. The concluding observations drawn up by CEDAW in response to State reports can point to difficulties in the implementation of the principle of equal treatment in employment matters at the national level. The more concrete EU norms lead to a review of violation of the principle of non-discrimination by the courts, but they are less apt to a review of structural problems. Thus, the concluding observations offer the opportunity to address and rectify in particular structural gender-related problems of national labour market policies. The reporting procedure may take a while and may not lead to binding judgments, but it can be useful in order to stimulate discussions of the actual effects of national policies and to steer long-term policy decisions. Being of only limited use for individual applicants, the value of the Women's Convention therefore lies in guiding policy decisions and emphasizing remaining problems in respect of implementing women's employment rights.

ARTICLE 12

1. State parties shall take all appropriate measures to eliminate discrimination against women in the field of health care in order to ensure, on a basis of equality of men and women, access to health care services, including those related to family planning.
2. Notwithstanding the provisions of paragraph 1 of this Article, States parties shall ensure to women appropriate services in connection with pregnancy, confinement and the post-natal period, granting free services where necessary, as well as adequate nutrition during pregnancy and lactation.

CHAPTER 12
WOMEN'S RIGHT TO HEALTH AND INTERNATIONAL TRADE
Special Reference to the GATS and the TRIPS Agreement

Jennifer SELLIN and Nishara MENDIS

1. INTRODUCTION

Rules and principles of international economic and trade law are probably not the first problems that spring to mind when most of us think about women's right to health. However, under the World Trade Organization (WTO), an international trading system is in the process of being created and consolidated and promoters of international human rights are arguing that international trade obligations may hamper some of the efforts to expand and deepen human rights commitments of States. The WTO system of trade rules consists of many trade agreements, including the much debated Agreement on Trade Related aspects of Intellectual Property Rights (TRIPS) and the General Agreement on Trade in Services (GATS). These two agreements will be focused on for the purposes of this Chapter,[1] due to their controversial nature with regard to

---

[1] This is not to say that other aspects of international trade law are not relevant – it should be pointed out that trade in goods also has health-related consequences for women. Trade in goods is dealt with under the General Agreement on Tariffs and Trade (GATT 1994 of the WTO), and related Agreements, which we will not be discussing for the purposes of this Chapter. The GATT is also at times read with the SPS Agreement (Agreement on Sanitary and Phytosanitary Measures) of the WTO, which prescribes rules requiring a scientific basis for measures that restrict imports on the basis of health or safety concerns. Issues relevant to women's health and trade in goods include the increased targeting of women as an emerging consumer market for cigarettes (see World Health Report 2003, 'Shaping the Future', at paras. 52 and 54) and premature sexual development of girls and increased risks of breast and reproductive cancers in menopausal women that has been linked to the use of hormones in beef production. These issues were referred to, albeit marginally, under the former GATT system in *Thailand-Cigarettes (GATT)* (*Thailand – Restrictions on Importation of and Internal Taxes on Cigarettes (GATT)*, DS10/R – 37S/200) and the ongoing *EC-Hormones* cases

limitation of the access to medicines and access to healthcare services: medicines and healthcare services being a key part of women's right to health, as will be discussed further in the Chapter. Thus the Women's Convention cannot be looked at in isolation to these developments regarding trade rules. However, in the course of research for this Chapter, the authors noticed that there is insufficient discussion of this relationship between trade and women's right to health. For example, in a recent World Health Organization (WHO) publication titled *Women's Health and Human Rights: Monitoring the Implementation of CEDAW* there is not a single mention of the international trade regime.[2] A holistic approach to women's health rights and international trade in medicines and healthcare services is necessary because the impact of the trade rules on women's right to health and the influence on health policy-making is far reaching.[3] The Women's Convention can be and should be used to play a part in directing the processes of change, for the benefit of the right to health of women across the world, now and in the future.

The right to health of women is not only a question of gender equality (equal access to healthcare as men) but also the right of a human being to receive adequate healthcare in the first place. Poor women and rich women both have the right to health, but poor women are often at greater risk of suffering the negative consequences of high healthcare costs and more likely to face inadequate or insufficient health services. Existing gender inequality in income and lesser autonomy with regard to participation in economic opportunities also means that women are more likely to be poor – a situation that is being described as the 'feminization of poverty'.[4] Furthermore, women usually bear a disproportionate responsibility of care-giving in families and in many cultural contexts, also a low prioritization of their own health needs. Thus, in situations of ill-health in the family, the burden of increased healthcare costs in terms of labour and healthcare cost-cutting is usually also borne by women.[5] Furthermore, the added physical vulnerability of women and girls due to their

---

concerning beef hormones in the WTO dispute settlement (*European Communities – Measures Concerning Meat and Meat Products* WT/DS26 and WT/DS48).

[2] World Health Organization, Department of Reproductive Health and Research, 2007.
[3] The WTO currently consists of 153 members and 30 observers, covering almost the entire volume of international trade.
[4] See *Review and Appraisal of the Implementation of the Beijing Platform for Action: Report of the Secretary-General*, UN doc. E/CN.6/2000/PC/2. Also see VALENTINE M. MOGHADAM, *The 'Feminization Of Poverty' and Women's Human Rights*, Gender Equality and Development Section, UNESCO, July 2005 and; SAKIKO FUKUDA-PARR, 'What Does Feminization of Poverty Mean? It Isn't Just Lack of Income, Feminist Economics', Volume 5, Number 2, July 1999, pp. 99 – 103.
[5] See LORRAINE CORNER AND SARAH RAPUCCI (authors), NOHA EL-MIKAWY and L.S. SENFTOVA (eds.), *UNIFEM – A users guide to measuring gender sensitive basic services delivery* (2009).

reproductive role adds another dimension to the women's health issue.[6] It is argued that the economic liberalization processes promoted by the WTO does nothing to help and much to hinder the achievement of women's right to health worldwide, by increasing health costs and further limiting the already limited access to health.

In this context, it becomes more and more important to realize that the objectives of the Women's Convention cannot be achieved without tackling the implications of the WTO regimes, especially TRIPS and GATS. The objective of this Chapter is to present the challenge of interpreting the TRIPS and GATS Agreements in light of women's right to health and hopefully to inspire further research and action in this area.

This Chapter is structured into four main sections. The first part presents a historical background to both a woman's right to health and the WTO system. The second part analyses the content of the right to health under Article 12 of the International Covenant on Economic, Social and Cultural Rights (ICESCR) and the expert commentaries on the content of the State obligations under this Article in General Comment No. 14 of the Committee on Economic, Social and Cultural Rights (CESCR) (2000), which refers specifically to the right to health of women. The second part then analyses Article 12 of the Women's Convention, together with General Recommendation No. 24 of the Committee on the Elimination of Discrimination Against Women (CEDAW) on Women and Health (1999). The discussion of the State's obligation towards respecting, protecting and fulfilling the right to health in the General Comment No. 14 of the CESCR to Article 12 of the ICESCR will be used to define the area of *access* to the right to health and this will be linked with the specific obligations under the Women's Convention. The third and fourth parts discuss the TRIPS Agreement and the GATS, highlighting the need to take women's rights into account in the debates on the future of medicines and health services. In the conclusion, some thoughts on the direction of future research and activism in the area will be presented.

2. A BRIEF BACKGROUND TO THE RIGHT TO HEALTH

The historical antecedents to the right to health developed hand-in-hand with the international law on non-discrimination against women. In the post-World War II period, following the establishment of the United Nations Organization (1945), core standards of human rights have become universally accepted through the deliberations, declarations and treaties agreed upon by most

---

[6] See *e.g.* Resolution during the 11th Human Rights Council on Preventable maternal mortality and morbidity and human rights, UN doc. A/HRC/RES/11/8, dated 17 June 2009.

countries in the world acting collectively. The right to health and the non-discrimination of women as human rights originates from the Charter of the United Nations and the Universal Declaration of Human Rights (UDHR, 1948).

The World Health Organization (WHO), a specialized agency of the UN established in 1948, defined the vision of ideal health in the preamble to its constitution as:

> 'Health is a state of complete physical, mental and social well-being and not merely the absence of disease or infirmity.'[7]

The preamble further states that:

> 'The enjoyment of the highest attainable standard of health is one of the *fundamental rights of every human being* without distinction of race, religion, political belief, economic or social condition.' (emphasis added).[8]

The WHO has been for the past six decades, the co-ordinating authority on health within the UN system.

The legal enforceability of the principles of human rights expressed in the UDHR was achieved only by 1976, when the International Covenant on Civil and Political rights (ICCPR) and the International Covenant on Economic and Social rights (ICESCR) came into force. The separation of rights into Civil and Political Rights and Economic, Social and Cultural Rights – a historical divide which reflects the differing ideologies of the Cold War period – affects the justiciability and full realization of economic, social and cultural rights to this day.[9] The right to health is expressed in Article 12 of the ICESCR. The ICCPR

---

[7] WHO, The WHO Constitution, adopted by the representatives of 61 States during the International Health Conference, New York, 22 July 1946, entered into force on 7 April 1948. Amendments adopted by the Twenty-sixth (1977), Twenty-ninth (1984), Thirty-ninth (1994) and Fifty-first (2005) World Health Assemblies are incorporated in the present text.

[8] *Ibid.*

[9] However, it is now stated that this division should no longer be considered as a hierarchy of rights. See Article 5 of the Vienna Declaration and Programme of Action (1993):
'All human rights are universal, indivisible and interdependent and interrelated. The international community must treat human rights globally in a fair and equal manner, on the same footing, and with the same emphasis. While the significance of national and regional particularities and various historical, cultural and religious backgrounds must be borne in mind, it is the duty of States, regardless of their political, economic and cultural systems, to promote and protect all human rights and fundamental freedoms.'
It is also stated that economic and social rights must be 'progressively realized' and cannot be guaranteed immediately, and therefore cannot get the same level of protection as civil and political rights – ICESCR Article 2(1): 'Each State Party to the present Covenant undertakes to take steps, individually and through international assistance and co-operation, especially economic and technical, to the maximum of its available resources, with a view to achieving progressively the full realization of the rights recognized in the present Covenant by all appropriate means, including particularly the adoption of legislative measures.'

only refers to health in relation to public health measures being an allowable *restriction* to the freedoms of speech, movement, assembly, association and the freedom to manifest one's religion – and not in the context of a *right*.

Meanwhile, a parallel set of developments were also occurring. The Bretton Woods Conference at the close of World War II resulted in the creation of the World Bank, The International Monetary Fund (IMF) and the General Agreement for Tariffs and Trade (GATT 1947)[10] – the new foundations for 'free market' economic policy and the liberalization of international trade. The Tokyo and Uruguay Round negotiations of the former GATT system led to the establishment of the WTO in 1995.[11]

While the areas of health rights and women's rights are showing some convergence, the relationship between implementing the rules of the WTO system and the realization of human rights continues to be problematic and even described by some experts as 'a veritable nightmare'.[12] There has been no use of human rights language in any of the WTO texts or in the findings of the dispute settlement system, and human rights concerns have made inroads into the WTO only via the terminology of 'public health' used in *e.g.* the TRIPS-related Doha Declaration on Public Health.[13]

There is also at times insufficient incorporation of the impacts of the WTO on health at the highest levels in the human rights-related regimes. In 2002, the WTO and the WHO published a joint study on WTO agreements and public

---

[10] The proposal for an International Trade Organization did not succeed without the support of the United States and the final agreement was limited to the GATT 1947.

[11] The Marrakesh Agreement establishing the WTO and the covered agreements including the GATT 1994, GATS and TRIPS came into force on January 1st 1995.

[12] '[the]WTO has been described as the 'practical manifestation of globalization in its trade and commercial aspects'. A closer examination of the organization will reveal that while trade and commerce are indeed its principle focus, the organization has extended its purview to encompass additional areas beyond what could justifiably be described as within its mandate. Furthermore, even its purely trade and commerce activities have serious human rights implications. This is compounded by the fact that the founding instruments of WTO make scant (indeed only oblique) reference to the principles of human rights. The net result is that for certain sectors of humanity – particularly the developing countries of the South – the WTO is a veritable nightmare'- The Realization Of Economic, Social And Cultural Rights: Globalization and its impact on the full enjoyment of human rights – Preliminary report submitted by J. OLOKA-ONYANGO and DEEPIKA UDAGAMA, in accordance with Sub-Commission resolution 1999/8, para. 15 UN doc. E/CN.4/Sub.2/2000/13, 15 June 2000.

[13] The WTO Ministerial Declaration on the TRIPS agreement and public health, WT/MIN(01)/DEC/2, adopted on 14 November 2001 during the Doha Ministerial Conference. Paragraph 4 states – 'We agree that the TRIPS Agreement does not and should not prevent members from taking measures to protect public health. Accordingly, while reiterating our commitment to the TRIPS Agreement, we affirm that the Agreement can and should be interpreted and implemented in a manner supportive of WTO members' right to protect public health and, in particular, to promote access to medicines for all.' The general exceptions provisions to the GATS includes Article XIV(b) -measures 'necessary to protect human, animal or plant life or health', which has not yet been used successfully. These issues will be discussed further later in this Chapter.

health[14] – this report does not use a human rights approach to health nor does it mention human rights at any point in the text. It follows the approach of the WTO, which refers to 'public health' as a legitimate policy interest in the context of trade disputes, yet avoids any allusion to the language of legal rights. The World Health Report 2003, *Shaping the Future*, mentions both the TRIPS agreement and trade in health services as having 'an obvious and direct impact on health'. But these impacts are not elaborated or discussed further. The most recent World Health Report (2008), which focuses on *Primary Health Care* makes passing reference to TRIPS and the Doha Declaration but makes no mention at all of the implications of the GATS.[15]

Furthermore, another disturbing development in the WHO is seen in the 2005 report by the WHO Secretariat titled *International Trade and Health*.[16] This Report uses the phrase 'highest attainable standard of health for all persons' but without once mentioning human rights or the *right* to health. The fundamental human right to health cannot be forfeited or justified on the basis of conformity with trade rules, but the abovementioned report speaks of 'policy coherence' in international trade and health without reference to rights language. These subtle but fundamental shifts are exactly what cause the fear of proponents of the right to health that human rights have already largely given way to the primacy of trade rules. The authors of this Chapter believe that the importance of the promotion of an uncompromised *human rights approach to health* in dealing with the impacts of the trade regime should not be under-estimated.

3. THE RIGHT TO HEALTH UNDER THE ICESCR AND THE WOMEN'S CONVENTION

In this section we will discuss women's right to health as protected under the Women's Convention and the International Covenant on Economic, Social and Cultural Rights (ICESCR). The area of the right to health is rich in international and regional legal standards, political commitments and commentaries on State

---

[14] WTO Secretariat and WHO, *WTO Agreements and Public Health: A Joint Study by The WHO and The WTO Secretariat*, World Health Organization and World Trade Organization, 2002, full text available online at www.who.int/trade/resource/wtoagreements/en/index.html, last accessed 24 June 2010.

[15] The neglect of GATS is surprising as reforms that ensure universal coverage, improved service delivery, cross sector public policy reforms and leadership reforms that 'replace … laissez-faire disengagement of the state' are encouraged under the theme of 'people centred' health care (at p.18 of the above Report).

[16] *The WHO, International Trade and Health: Report of the Secretariat*, EB116/4, 28 April 2005, available at www.apps.who.int/gb/ebwha/pdf_files/EB116/B116_4-en.pdf, last accessed 30 June 2010.

obligations.[17] We will first discuss the right to health in more general terms under the ICESCR, before turning to the protection of the right to health specifically for women under the Women's Convention.

The right to health is codified in Article 12 of the ICESCR. It is a fundamental human right[18] recognizing 'the right of everyone to the enjoyment of the highest attainable standard of physical and mental health.'[19] In addition, paragraph 2 of Article 12 ICESCR explicitly lists a number of elements which are included in the international right to health:

> 'The steps to be taken by the States parties to the present Covenant to achieve the full realization of this right shall include those necessary for:
>
> a) The provision for the reduction of the stillbirth-rate and of infant mortality and for the healthy development of the child;
> b) The improvement of all aspects of environmental and industrial hygiene;
> c) The prevention, treatment and control of epidemic, endemic, occupational and other diseases;
> d) The creation of conditions which would assure to all medical service and medical attention in the event of sickness.'[20]

---

[17] For example: *International Convention on the Elimination of All Forms of Racial Discrimination,* Article 5 – In compliance with the fundamental obligations laid down in article 2 of this Convention, States Parties undertake to prohibit and to eliminate racial discrimination in all its forms and to guarantee the right of everyone...The right to public health, medical care, social security and social services...'; *African [Banjul] Charter on Human and Peoples' Rights* 1981, Article 16 – ... States parties to the present Charter shall take the necessary measures to protect the health of their people and to ensure that they receive medical attention when they are sick.'; The *Copenhagen Declaration* (Report of the World Summit for Social Development, 1986) Commitment 6 – 'We commit ourselves to... attaining... universal and equitable access to... the highest attainable standard of physical and mental health, and... access of all to primary health care...'; *The Cairo Declaration on Human Rights in Islam* (World Conference on Human Rights, 1990), Article 17 – 'Everyone shall have the right to medical and social care, and to all public amenities provided by society and the State within the limits of their available resources... The States shall ensure the right of the individual to a decent living that may enable him to meet his requirements and those of his dependents, including food, clothing, housing, education, medical care and all other basic needs...'; *Declaration of Alma-Ata* (International Conference on Primary Health Care,1978) Article 1 – 'The Conference strongly reaffirms that health...is a fundamental human right and that the attainment of the highest possible level of health is a most important world-wide social goal...'; *Additional Protocol to the American Convention on Human Rights (Protocol of San Salvador)* Article 10 – '...In order to ensure the exercise of the right to health, the States Parties agree to recognize health as a public good ... There is also the international political commitment on women's health rights – the Beijing Declaration and Platform for Action of the Fourth World Conference on Women of 1995, wherein Strategic Objective (C) focuses on the area of Women and Health.
[18] CESCR, General Comment No. 14, para. 1; Preamble to the WHO Constitution.
[19] Article 12(1) ICESCR.
[20] Article 12(2). *Ibid.*

The wording of Article 12 ICESCR is extremely broad. Although it gives a non-exhaustive list of steps States parties should take, defining the term 'health' is difficult because of the term's subjective nature.[21]

An important element of the right to health and the other rights found in the ICESCR is the principle of non-discrimination as stated in Article 2(2) of the ICESCR.[22] Furthermore, Article 3 of the ICESCR confirms that both men and women have equal rights to the enjoyment of the rights under the Covenant.[23] Both Articles clearly entail that any discrimination with respect to access to health care and underlying determinants of health on the abovementioned grounds is prohibited, as corroborated by the CESCR. Non-discrimination and equal treatment are one of the essential components of the right to health.[24] The CESCR has, furthermore, stressed that measures intended to eliminate health-related discrimination can be taken with few costs, and can even be adopted in times of serious resource constraints.[25]

Thus, as stated above the international right to health does not entail a right for individuals to be healthy, but encompasses a number of freedoms and entitlements so that individuals are able to attain the highest possible standard of health. In more general terms the right to health comprises two broad components: health care and underlying determinants of health. In that regard the right to health is inextricably linked to other human rights, such as the right to life, adequate housing, an adequate standard of living, education etc.

The CESCR has further elaborated the right to health in its General Comment No. 14. Similarly CEDAW has also issued a number of documents, called General Recommendations, further elaborating the rights protected under the Women's Convention, those of which that are relevant for the right to health will be discussed below. These General Comments and General Recommendations function as explanatory documents for States parties aiding them with the implementation of the obligations found in a particular human

---

[21] BIRGIT C.A. TOEBES, *The Right to Health as a Human Right in International Law* (School of Human Rights Research Series, Vol. 1), Intersentia, Antwerp, 1999, p. 20 *et seq*. When is a person considered to be 'healthy'? Does 'health' include only physical, or physical and mental well-being, or maybe even include social well-being? Moreover, descriptions vary from health being the 'absence of disease' to the 'ability to function in society' to the total package of 'well-being'.

[22] Article 2(2) of the ICESCR reads as following: The States Parties to the present Covenant undertake to guarantee that the rights enunciated in the present Covenant will be exercised without discrimination of any kind as to race, colour, sex, language, religion, political or other opinion, national or social origin, property, birth or other status.

[23] See specifically for the right to health, CESCR, General Comment No. 14, paras. 20–21.

[24] UN Commission on Human Rights, *Report of the Special Rapporteur, Paul Hunt, on the Right of Everyone to the Enjoyment of the Highest Attainable Standard of Physical and Mental Health*, UN doc. E/CN.4/2003/58, para. 26.

[25] CESCR, General Comment No. 14, para. 18.

rights treaty.²⁶ Although General Comments adopted by a treaty monitoring body are authoritative interpretations of the obligations laid down in the relevant human rights treaty, they are, as the wording clearly states, 'comments' or 'recommendations' and, therefore, not binding on States parties to the relevant international human rights treaty.²⁷

In General Comment No. 14 the CESCR states that the right to health has four interrelated and essential elements, the application of which will depend on the specific situation within a State party.²⁸ These elements include:

Availability. According to the CESCR availability entails that '[f]unctioning public health and health care facilities, goods and services, as well as programmes, have to be available in sufficient quantity within the State party', the precise nature of which depends on various factors within that State party, including its developmental level. Such facilities, though, will include underlying determinants of health such as safe drinking water, adequate sanitation facilities, hospitals, clinics, trained medical and profession personnel and also essential drugs as defined by the WHO Action Programme on Essential Drugs.²⁹

Accessibility. 'Health facilities, goods and services have to be accessible to everyone without discrimination, within the jurisdiction of the State party.' Accessibility, according to the CESCR, has four overlapping dimensions: firstly, accessibility must be ensured on the principle of non-discrimination; secondly, accessibility includes physical accessibility, meaning that both health facilities, goods and services and underlying determinants of health must be within in safe physical reach, also for rural areas; thirdly, accessibility also entails economic accessibility, or affordability, requiring that health facilities, goods and services must be affordable for all; and, fourthly, accessibility entitles everyone to seek, receive and impart information and ideas with regard to health issues.³⁰

Acceptability. 'All health facilities, goods and services must be respectful of medical ethics and culturally appropriate'.³¹

Quality. Finally, 'health facilities, goods and services must also be scientifically and medically appropriate and of good quality.'³²

Furthermore, the analysis of ICESCR Article 12 highlights access to sexual and reproductive health services, family planning and pre- and post-natal care, emergency obstetric services³³ as well as basic preventive, curative and

---

[26] CHRISTIAN TOMUSCHAT, *Human Rights: Between Idealism and Realism*, eds. Marise Cremona et al. (second edn., The Collected Courses of the Academy of European Law), Oxford University Press, New York, 2008, pp. 156–158.
[27] See further TOMUSCHAT, *Human Rights*, pp. 190–191.
[28] CESCR, General Comment No. 14, para. 12.
[29] *Ibid.*, para. 12(a).
[30] *Ibid.*, para. 12(b).
[31] *Ibid.*, para. 12(c).
[32] *Ibid.*, para. 12(d).
[33] Para. 14: the right to maternal, child and reproductive health.

rehabilitative heath services for all.[34] With regard to the right to health services under Article 12(2)(d), the participation of the population in the organization of the health sector, the health insurance system and political decision-making relating to the right to health is highlighted.[35] Whatever the power imbalances in the WTO system of trade negotiations may be, the General Comment reminds that it remains the responsibility of States to have an inclusive, democratic process from community to parliamentary level with regard to the development of the health sector.

The CESCR goes on setting out States parties' obligations with regard to the right to health where it has made use of the tripartite typology of obligations.[36] Just as with other human rights, the right to health has three levels of State obligations: firstly, States parties have the obligation to *respect*, that is to abstain from interfering directly or indirectly with individuals' enjoyment of the right to health; secondly, States parties have the obligation to *protect* by preventing third parties from interfering with the right to health; and, thirdly, States parties have the obligation to *fulfil* the right to health requiring the State to adopt appropriate measures, whether legislative, administrative, budgetary or judicial, towards the full realization of the right to health.[37] Moreover, States parties are required to progressively realize the rights protected under the Covenant by taking steps, individually and through international assistance and co-operation to the maximum of their available resources using all appropriate means.[38] The concept of progressive realization, however, complicates monitoring States parties' compliance with their obligations under the ICESCR.[39] In that regard, the Committee has found that there is a strong presumption that retrogressive measures, measures which take a step back in fulfilling the ICESCR's rights, are not permissible under the ICESCR.[40] If any such retrogressive measures, for example regarding the right to health, are deliberately taken, the State party is strictly obliged to prove that any alternatives have been carefully considered, and such retrogressive measures are duly justified by reference to the other rights under the Covenant and the full use of the State party's maximum available resources.[41] For example, the Report of the High Commissioner for Human Rights on Liberalization of Trade in Services has commented on the need of a human rights approach to continuously assess the real and potential impacts of

---

[34] Para. 17: the right to health facilities, goods and services.
[35] *Ibid.*
[36] CESCR, General Comment No. 14, para. 33.
[37] *Ibid.*
[38] Article 2(1) ICESCR.
[39] AUDREY CHAPMAN and SAGE RUSSELL (eds.), *Core Obligations: Building a Framework for Economic, Social and Cultural Rights*, Intersentia, Antwerp, 2002, p. 5.
[40] CESCR, General Comment No. 14, para. 32.
[41] *Ibid.*

trade law and policies to avoid retrogressive measures: this being one of the criticisms of the impacts of WTO rules.[42]

The CESCR has also developed the concept of 'core obligations', which are those obligations without which the Covenant's rights would be devoid of any meaning and relevance. Thus, the State party must at the very least ensure the satisfaction of a minimum essential level with regard to the right to health. Guided by the Alma-Ata Declaration,[43] the CESCR finds that State parties' core obligations with regard to the right to health include the obligation to: ensure the right of access to health facilities, goods and services without any form of discrimination, especially regarding vulnerable and marginalised groups, such as for example women; ensure access to the minimum essential level of food necessary to ensure freedom from hunger; ensure access to basic shelter, housing and sanitation and adequate supply of safe drinking water; to ensure equitable distribution of health facilities, goods and services; to adopt and implement a national public health strategy and plan of action; and to ensure the provision of essential medicines as defined by the WHO Action Programme on Essential Drugs.[44]

Regarding the final point, accessibility of medicines, we clearly see how the international trading system impacts States' ability to realize the right to health. The WHO considers sufficient access to medicines as a priority health issue.[45] It estimates that although the share of people lacking access to medicines has fallen since 1975 from half of the world's population to a third of the world's population in 1999, the absolute number still totals at around 1.7 billion.[46] From that total number of patients who lack access to medicines 1.3 billion, that is around 80%, live in low-income countries.[47] There are many reasons why patients in developing countries lack adequate access to medicines.[48] One significant reason is the price of a medicine. Especially in countries without a well-organized, well-functioning health care system where the majority of patients have to pay for their medication privately, the cost of medicines can easily become too burdensome and, therefore, unaffordable.[49] Moreover, developing countries with limited (financial) resources struggle with the same problem, in that having to

---

[42] Commission on Human Rights, *Liberalization of Trade in Services* (Report of the High Commissioner), UN doc. E/CN.4/Sub.2/2002/9, 25 June 2002, para. 12.
[43] WHO (1978), *Declaration of Alma-Ata*, Alma-Ata, USSR: International Conference on Primary Health Care.
[44] CESCR, General Comment No. 14, para. 43.
[45] WHO, 'Equitable Access to Essential Medicines: A Framework for Collective Action', *Policy Perspectives on Medicines*, 8, 2004.
[46] WHO, *The World Medicines Situation*, WHO, Geneva, 2004, p. 61.
[47] *Ibid.*, 2004, p. 63.
[48] HOLGER HESTERMEYER, *Human Rights and the WTO: The Case of Patents and Access to Medicines*, Oxford University Press, Oxford, 2007, p. 151.
[49] Of course having to assess the 'affordability' of a medicine is problematic and as such will depend on the national context.

provide patients throughout their jurisdiction with affordable medicines places a considerable burden on their health care budget.

It has been argued that patents play a role why medicine prices are often high and thus unaffordable for a large part of the world's population.[50] For example, with respect to the HIV/AIDS pandemic which disproportionately affects developing countries, we see that when antiretroviral medicines were introduced their treatment costs reached over US$ 10.000 per patient per year.[51] These medicines were mostly protected by patents, which are time-bound monopoly rights granting the right holder a number of exclusive rights. However, in 2001 the Indian generic manufacturer Cipla announced that it would produce and supply a generic version of the antiretroviral triple therapy which would be marketed at the cost of about US$ 350 per patient per year.[52] This was partly due to the fact that India until 2005, when the transition period for the implementation of the TRIPS Agreement expired, did not grant product patents for pharmaceuticals.[53] The TRIPS Agreement was the first agreement to require that all WTO members provide for the possibility to patent pharmaceutical products and processes.

In that regard, the CESCR also notes that States parties must ensure that the right to health is given due account in international agreements and in their actions as members of international organizations, for example the WTO.[54] With regard to access to medicines and health services, the right to health under the ICESCR obliges States parties to take the right to health into account when implementing the obligations under the TRIPS and the GATS as part of the WTO framework. For example, this could entail that countries must take due account of the TRIPS and GATS' flexibilities to respect, protect and fulfil the right to health as required by the ICESCR when implementing the obligations of these agreements. However, the prevailing attitude of many trade lawyers as expressed by Petersmann, who writes extensively on the trade and human rights debate, seems to be that:

> 'Trade experts fear that a 'human rights approach' will unduly complicate WTO negotiations in view of the fact that, for example, the [ICESCR] has not been ratified by more than 30 WTO member countries including the United States.'[55]

---

[50] See for an extensive discussion on the link between medicine prices and patent protection HESTERMEYER, *Human Rights and the WTO: The Case of Patents and Access to Medicines*, p. 138 *et seq*.

[51] WHO, 'Access to Medicines', *WHO Drug Information*, 19/3, 2005, pp. 236–241.

[52] SUDIP CHAUDHURI, *The WTO and India's Pharmaceutical Industry. Patent Protection, TRIPS and Developing Countries*, Oxford University Press, New Delhi, 2005, p. 8.

[53] *Ibid.*

[54] WHO, 'Access to Medicines', *WHO Drug Information*, 19/3, 2005, pp. 236–241.

[55] ERNST-ULRICH PETERSMANN, 'The 'Human Rights Approach' advocated by the UN High Commissioner For Human Rights and by the International Labour Organization: is it

Furthermore, the Committee recognizes that in the spirit of Article 56 of the UN Charter, the provisions of the ICESCR (particularly Articles 2(1), 12, 22[56] and 23)[57] and the Alma-Ata Declaration[58] States parties should recognize the important role of international cooperation, and observe their commitment to take joint and separate action to fulfil the realization of the right to health.[59] Further, the CESCR makes it clear that, for States parties to fulfil their international obligations with respect to the right to health, they must respect individuals' enjoyment of the right to health in other countries, and, to the extent possible, prevent third parties from violating the right to health in other countries.[60]

Finally, it can be concluded that under the ICESCR States parties have to comply with obligations that are twofold:[61] firstly, States parties to the Covenant have the obligation to *progressively* realize the fulfilment of the Covenant's rights; secondly, States parties also have *immediate* obligations under the Covenant, such as for example the prohibition of discrimination (as can be found in Articles 2.2 and 3 ICESCR)[62] or the obligation to take deliberate, concrete and targeted steps towards fulfilling the right to health.[63] Monitoring States parties' compliance with the first obligation, that of progressively realizing the right to health, is difficult though, since under this concept States parties' obligations are neither uniform nor universal, and dependent on the State party's level of

---

relevant for WTO law and policy?', *J. Int. Economic Law* 2004 7, pp. 605–627, *J. Int. Economic Law* 2004 7, pp. 585–603 at p. 607.

[56] Article 22 ICESCR: The Economic and Social Council may bring to the attention of other organs of the United Nations, their subsidiary organs and specialized agencies concerned with furnishing technical assistance any matters arising out of the reports referred to in this part of the present Covenant which may assist such bodies in deciding, each within its field of competence, on the advisability of international measures likely to contribute to the effective progressive implementation of the present Covenant.

[57] The States parties to the present Covenant agree that international action for the achievement of the rights recognized in the present Covenant includes such methods as the conclusion of conventions, the adoption of recommendations, the furnishing of technical assistance and the holding of regional meetings and technical meetings for the purpose of consultation and study organized in conjunction with the Governments concerned.

[58] WHO, Declaration of Alma-Ata.

[59] CESCR, General Comment No. 14, para. 38.

[60] *Ibid.*, para. 39.

[61] While States are the primary duty bearers with regard to human rights, the Special Rapporteur on the Right to Health, Paul Hunt, has noted that all actors, individuals, local communities, inter-governmental and non-governmental organizations, health professional, private enterprises etc., have responsibilities regarding the realization of the right to health. UN Commission on Human Rights, Report of the Special Rapporteur, Paul Hunt, on the Right of Everyone to the Enjoyment of the Highest Attainable Standard of Physical and Mental Health, UN doc. E/CN.4/2003/58, para. 30.

[62] AUDREY CHAPMAN and SAGE RUSSELL (eds.), *Core Obligations: Building a Framework for Economic, Social and Cultural Rights*, pp. 5–6.

[63] CESCR, General Comment No. 14, para. 30; UN Commission on Human Rights, Report of the Special Rapporteur, Paul Hunt, on the Right of Everyone to the Enjoyment of the Highest Attainable Standard of Physical and Mental Health, UN doc. E/CN.4/2003/58, para. 27.

development and availability of resources.[64] The CESCR noted, in its General Comment No. 14, that when determining whether a State has violated the right to health, one must distinguish between a State party's inability from its unwillingness to comply with its obligations under the ICESCR.[65] Moreover, the CESCR stressed that regardless of the circumstances a State party has a non-derogable obligation to comply with the aforementioned core obligations; non-compliance with these core obligations, including the provision of essential medicines, cannot be justified under any circumstances.[66] Consequently, it has been argued that the core obligation to make essential medicines accessible and available throughout a State party's jurisdiction is an obligation of immediate effect not subject to progressive realization.[67] If a State does violate the right to health it is essential for the individual harmed by the State's actions or omissions to be able to bring his or her claim before a judicial or quasi-judicial body to be reviewed.[68]

The CESCR has also addressed women's position regarding the right to health and although it only compasses two paragraphs of the 65 paragraph long General Comment, it recommends States parties to include a gender perspective in their health-related policies, planning, programmes and research.[69] 'A gender-based approach recognizes that biological and socio-cultural factors play a significant role in influencing the health of men and women.'[70] Furthermore, that to be able to identify and remedy inequalities in health States parties should disaggregate health and socio-economic data according to sex.[71] It goes on stating that:

> 'To eliminate discrimination against women, there is a need to develop and implement a comprehensive national strategy for promoting women's right to health throughout their life span. Such a strategy should include interventions aimed at the prevention and treatment of diseases affecting women, as well as policies to provide access to a full range of high quality and affordable health care, including sexual and reproductive services. A major goal should be reducing women's health risks, particularly lowering rates of maternal mortality and protecting women from domestic violence. The realization of women's right to health requires the removal of all barriers interfering with access to health services, education and information, including in the area of sexual and reproductive health. It is also important to undertake preventive, promotive and remedial action to shield women from the

---

[64] CHAPMAN and RUSSELL (eds.), *Core Obligations: Building a Framework for Economic, Social and Cultural Rights*, p. 5.
[65] CESCR, General Comment No. 14, para. 47.
[66] Ibid.
[67] PAUL HUNT and RAJAT KHOSLA, 'The Human Right to Medicines', 5/8 *SUR – International Journal on Human Rights*, 2008, p. 104.
[68] CESCR, General Comment No. 14, paras. 59–61.
[69] CESCR, General Comment No. 14, para. 20.
[70] Ibid.
[71] Ibid.

impact of harmful traditional cultural practices and norms that deny them their full reproductive rights.'[72]

The right to health specifically for women is further protected in Article 12 of the Convention on the Elimination of Discrimination Against Women which reads as follows:

> '1. States Parties shall take all appropriate measures to eliminate discrimination against women in the field of health care in order to ensure, on a basis of equality of men and women, access to health care services, including those related to family planning.
> 2. Notwithstanding the provisions of paragraph 1 of this Article, States Parties shall ensure to women appropriate services in connection with pregnancy, confinement and the post-natal period, granting free services where necessary, as well as adequate nutrition during pregnancy and lactation.'

The right to health is also mentioned in Article 11 of the Women's Convention which states that all States parties should take all appropriate measures to eliminate discrimination against women in the field of employment in order to ensure, on a basis of equality of men and women, the same rights, including 'the right to protection of health and to safety in working conditions, including the safeguarding of the function of reproduction.' Furthermore, Article 14 of the Women's Convention requires that States parties take particular account of the problems faced by rural women, and should take all appropriate measures to ensure the application of the rights protected under the Convention to women in rural areas, including the right to have access to adequate health care facilities, including information, counselling and services in family planning.

Firstly, as stated above the Convention intends to eliminate all forms of discrimination against women and as such defines discrimination in its Article 1 as:

> 'any distinction, exclusion or restriction made on the basis of sex which has the effect or purpose of impairing or nullifying the recognition, enjoyment or exercise by women, irrespective of their marital status, on a basis of equality of men and women, of human rights and fundamental freedoms in the political, economic, social, cultural, civil or any other field.'

To fulfil this end the Women's Convention obliges all States parties to 'condemn discrimination against women in all its forms' and 'agree to pursue by all appropriate means and without delay a policy of eliminating discrimination against women'.[73] To achieve this end Article 2 goes on to state a number of

---

[72] CESCR, General Comment No. 14, para. 21.
[73] Article 2 Women's Convention.

actions a State party is required to take, such as to embody the principle of equality in their national legislative framework; adopt appropriate legislative or other measures; establish a system of legal protection of the rights of women on the basis of equality; to refrain from any act or practice of discrimination against women; to take all appropriate measures to eliminate discrimination against women by any person, organization or enterprise; to take all appropriate measures to modify or abolish existing laws, regulations, customs and practices which constitute discrimination against women; and, finally, to repeal all national penal provisions which constitute discrimination against women.

CEDAW has further outlined the right to health under the Women's Convention in its General Recommendation No. 24, where it has confirmed that women's right of access to health care, including reproductive health is a basic, fundamental right under the Convention.[74] Although the Committee's Recommendations are non-binding instruments, they carry authoritative weight on the manner in which to interpret the Convention's provisions and States parties' obligations under it.

Just as the CESCR did, the Committee acknowledges the importance of using reliable data disaggregated by sex on the incidence and severity of diseases and conditions affecting women and on the availability and cost-effectiveness of preventative and curative measures when evaluating States parties measures' appropriateness to eliminate discrimination in the field of health care.[75] It went on to state that for State measures to be *appropriate* a national health care system must include services to prevent, detect and treat illnesses specific to women.[76] Thus, it would be discriminatory for a State party to refuse to legally provide for the performance of certain reproductive health services for women.[77] Moreover, State measures on health care should address health rights from the perspective of women's needs and interests, and take into account factors and features which differ for women in comparison to men, such as:

> 'Biological factors which differ for women in comparison with men, such as their menstrual cycle, their reproductive function and menopause. Another example is the higher risk of exposure to sexually transmitted diseases which women face;
> Socio-economic factors, such as unequal power relationships between women and men in the home and workplace, domestic violence, sexual abuse and cultural or traditional practices such as female genital mutilation;
> Psychosocial factors vary between women and men and include depression in general and post-partum depression in particular; and
> Respect for the confidentiality of patients, even though this affects both men and women, it may deter women from seeking advice and treatment, for example with

---

[74] CEDAW, General Recommendation No. 24, para. 1.
[75] CEDAW, General Recommendation No. 24, para. 9.
[76] CEDAW, General Recommendation No. 24, para. 11.
[77] *Ibid.*

respect to diseases of the genital area, contraception, abortions and in case they suffered sexual or physical abuse, and as result may adversely affect their health and well-being.'[78]

The Committee here also makes use of the tripartite typology of obligations for States parties to *ensure, on a basis of equality between men and women, access to health care* services, information and education, which implies an obligation to respect, protect and fulfil women's rights to health care.[79] The obligation to *respect* rights requires States parties to refrain from obstructing action taken by women in pursuit of their health goals.[80] For example, States parties should not restrict women's access to health services or to the clinics that provide those services on the ground that women do not have the authorization of husbands, partners, parents or health authorities, because they are unmarried or because they are women.[81] The obligation to *protect* rights relating to women's health requires States parties to take action to prevent and impose sanctions for violations of rights by third parties.[82] This is especially important when it comes to gender-related violence.[83] The duty to *fulfil* rights places an obligation on States parties to take appropriate legislative, judicial, administrative, budgetary, economic and other measures to the maximum extent of their available resources to ensure that women realize their rights to health care.[84] Furthermore, States parties must also put in place a system which ensures effective judicial action.[85]

The Committee requires States parties to report on measures taken to eliminate barriers that women face in gaining access to health care services and ensuring that women have timely and affordable access to such services.[86] It has clarified that barriers include requirements or conditions that prejudice women's access, such as high fees for health care services, the requirement for preliminary authorization by a spouse, parent or hospital authorities, distance from health facilities and absence of convenient and affordable public transport.[87]

---

[78] CEDAW, General Recommendation No. 24, para. 12.
[79] CEDAW, General Recommendation No. 24, para. 13.
[80] CEDAW, General Recommendation No. 24, para. 14.
[81] *Ibid.*
[82] CEDAW, General Recommendation No. 24, para. 15.
[83] *Ibid.*
[84] CEDAW, General Recommendation No. 24, para. 17.
[85] CEDAW, General Recommendation No. 24, para. 13.
[86] CEDAW, General Recommendation No. 24, para. 21.
[87] Gender sensitive service delivery includes taking into account distance and mode of transportation from households to the service delivery point. Cultural restrictions on travelling alone, lack of public transport, lack of financial independence and fear of gender violence (e.g. due to lack of safe modes of transportation) can be easily overlooked, but are crucial issues for women's access to health services. See LORRAINE CORNER and SARAH RAPUCCI (authors), NOHA EL-MIKAWY and L.S. SENFTOVA (eds.), *UNIFEM – A users guide to*

Additionally, States parties must also report on measures adopted to ensure access to quality health care services, for example, by making them acceptable to women, and on measures taken with respect to family planning, in particular and sexual and reproductive health in general.[88]

In that respect the issues of HIV/AIDS and other sexually transmitted diseases are central to the rights of women and adolescent girls to sexual health.[89] In many countries adolescent girls and women lack adequate access to information and services necessary to ensure sexual health.[90] But also unequal power relations based on gender and harmful traditional practices may result in increased risk of contracting HIV/AIDS or other STDs, which is especially true for women in prostitution.[91] The expanding HIV/AIDS pandemic and its adverse effects on women and children in particular have led the Committee, already in 1990, to adopt a General Recommendation on the avoidance of discrimination against women in national strategies for the prevention and control of AIDS.[92] Here it recommends that in combating HIV/AIDS special attention should be given to the rights and needs of women, and to their reproductive role and, in some societies, subordinate position.[93]

Article 12(2) of the Women's Convention obliges States parties to ensure women have access to appropriate services *in connection with pregnancy, labour and the post-natal period*, to reduce maternal mortality and morbidity. Here the Committee acknowledges the importance of ensuring such services are sufficiently accessible to women.[94] Where necessary free services should be provided to ensure safe pregnancies, childbirth and post-partum periods for women.[95] The Committee notes that it is the duty of States parties to ensure women's right to safe motherhood and emergency obstetric services and they should allocate to these services the maximum extent of available resources.[96]

Finally, the Committee makes a number of recommendations for State action which encompasses implementing a comprehensive national strategy to promote women's health throughout their life, including interventions to prevent and treat diseases and conditions affecting women, responding to violence against

---

measuring gender sensitive basic services delivery, 2009. This highlights that planning and implementation of health services delivery cannot thus be left solely in the hands of private entrepreneurship, where the profit motive would decide basics such as location of the service delivery point and the other issues would be irrelevant. However, with planning for gender sensitive *public* health services or even public-private partnerships, the obligations of the State are clear.

[88] CEDAW, General Recommendation No. 24, paras. 22–23.
[89] CEDAW, General Recommendation No. 24, para. 18.
[90] Ibid.
[91] Ibid.
[92] CEDAW, General Recommendation No. 15.
[93] Ibid.
[94] CEDAW, General Recommendation No. 24, para. 27.
[95] Ibid.
[96] Ibid.

women and ensuring universal access to a wide range of high quality affordable health care services.[97] To this end, States parties must allocate adequate budgetary, human and administrative resources so as to ensure that women's health needs take an equal share to that of men's needs of the overall budget.[98]

Although less clearly set out, here we see that the key elements as determined by the CESCR namely that all health facilities, services and goods should be available, accessible, acceptable and of quality, are also elements of women's right to health recognized under the Women's Convention. The context of having a right to health under the Women's Convention highlights the special health needs of women and can thus be used to further enhance the understanding of the gender dimension of the right to health as expressed in the ICESCR. As long as gender inequality continues to affect the lives and the health of women, the right to health provisions of the Women's Convention focuses attention on this issue so it can be flagged by policymakers – and, it is hoped, lead to concrete steps and results.

4. TRIPS: PATENTS AND ACCESS TO MEDICINES FROM THE PERSPECTIVE OF A WOMAN'S RIGHT TO HEALTH

As we have seen, the right to health both under the ICESCR and the Women's Convention entails a number of elements: availability, accessibility, including affordability, acceptability and quality. Moreover, the CESCR explicitly considers the provision of essential medicines to be a non-derogable core obligation of States parties to the ICESCR and stressed that non-compliance with these core obligations cannot be justified under any circumstances.[99] Unfortunately there is no such similar statement within a General Recommendation of CEDAW. However, it would be most logical and useful to look at the more recent CESCR Comment when interpreting the right to health under Article 12 CEDAW.

Lack of access to medicines affects both men and women. However, where medicines are costly and patients have to pay for these out of their own pocket, women are disproportionately affected. Gender inequality regarding income and economic opportunities results in the higher likelihood of women being poorer and thus not being able to afford medication for themselves and family members.[100] The HIV/AIDS pandemic is an illustration of this. The incidence and spread of HIV/AIDS are disproportionately high among certain populations,

---

[97] CEDAW, General Recommendation No. 24, para. 29.
[98] CEDAW, General Recommendation No. 24, para. 30.
[99] *Ibid*.
[100] OHCHR & WHO, Factsheet 31, p. 22.

including women.[101] Factors that play a significant role here are gender inequality and failure to respect the rights of girls and women.[102] The Special Rapporteur on violence against women, its causes and consequences has recognized that 'poverty, illiteracy and gender power imbalances within families and communities limit women's access to preventative care, drugs and treatment.'[103] In many situations women and girls have less access to available treatment and adequate information.[104] Moreover, regarding HIV/AIDS she has stressed that 'feminized poverty poses a barrier to treatment given the high cost of antiretrovirals.'[105]

As stated above, there is a strong indication of a link between high medicine prices and patent protection of those medicines. This issue came to the forefront internationally in the 1990s with the adoption of the TRIPS Agreement within the WTO context: the first agreement to oblige WTO members to allow for the granting of patent protection for pharmaceutical products and processes, a major achievement of TRIPS.[106] The TRIPS Agreement provides minimum standards of Intellectual Property (IP) protection, also in the field of patents. In addition to these minimum standards TRIPS also covers enforcement, acquisition and maintenance of Intellectual Property Rights (IPRs), dispute prevention and settlement, transitional arrangements and institutional arrangements. These obligations set out within the TRIPS Agreement are important for the issue of access to essential medicines for a number of reasons. First, the TRIPS Agreement is an agreement concluded within the framework of the WTO, which entails that it has widespread membership throughout the world.[107] Secondly, as opposed to previous conventions dealing with intellectual property, the agreements concluded within the WTO framework are subject to the effective WTO dispute settlement mechanism. Thirdly, the TRIPS Agreement is the first international instrument to set out minimum standards of protection of IP, which all WTO members are obliged to incorporate within their own domestic legal system. As such, the minimum standards required by TRIPS must be incorporated within the national laws of the WTO members and have, thus, a very real effect on (developing) members' ability to manage their public health problems.

Article 27 TRIPS sets out that all members must make patent protection available for inventions within all fields of technology, as long as the invention is

---

[101] Women today are more vulnerable to infection than men. See Joint United Nations Programme on HIV/AIDS, *Report on the global AIDS epidemic*, Geneva, 2006.
[102] OHCHR & WHO, Factsheet 31, p. 22.
[103] UN doc. E/CN.4/2005/72, para. 21.
[104] *Ibid.*
[105] UN doc. E/CN.4/2005/72, para.75.
[106] Article 27 TRIPS.
[107] On July 23rd, 2008 the WTO consisted of 153 Member States. See www.wto.org/english/thewto_e/whatis_e/tif_e/org6_e.htm.

novel, involves an inventive step and is capable of industrial application. Article 28 TRIPS grants the right holder of a product patent a set of exclusive rights to prevent third parties without his consent from making, using, offering for sale, selling, or importing for these purposes the patented product. Before the adoption of TRIPS a number of countries, notably India, did not provide for product patent protection for pharmaceuticals. This allowed the Indian pharmaceutical industry to market cheaper generic versions of many originator pharmaceuticals both for the Indian market and for export to many developing countries.[108] However, now that the transition period for implementing TRIPS has lapsed (in 2005 – though Least Developed Countries still have until 2016) developing WTO members must introduce a full-fledged patent system restricting any existing freedom to limit patent protection for pharmaceutical products.

That there may be tension between protecting intellectual property and guaranteeing access to IP protected products is also recognized within TRIPS which tries to balance both objectives. As such it states that the protection and enforcement of IPRs should contribute to the promotion of technological innovation and to the transfer and dissemination of technology, to the mutual advantage of producers and users of technological knowledge and in a manner conducive to social and economic welfare, and to a balance of rights and obligations.[109] Moreover, members are free to adopt measures necessary to protect public health as long as such measures are consistent with TRIPS.[110] In addition to these provisions stating TRIPS' objectives and principles, TRIPS also provides exceptions to the exclusive rights granted under a patent, the so-called flexibilities such as parallel importation and compulsory licensing.[111] However, it seems that developing countries are not able (or willing) to use the flexibilities to the full extent to guarantee access to affordable medicines. A logical explanation is that there still exists ambiguity regarding members' exact obligations under TRIPS and that developing States are probably hesitant to make use of these ambiguities for fear of a complaint against them under the WTO Dispute Settlement Mechanism.

In recent years, there has been much debate on the topic of patents and access to medicines, and also on the underlying debate regarding the relationship of IP and human rights. Not only activists[112] but also international organizations

---

[108] SUDIP CHAUDHURI, *The WTO and India's Pharmaceutical Industry. Patent Protection, TRIPS and Developing Countries*, p. 53 et seq.
[109] Article 7 TRIPS.
[110] Article 8 TRIPS.
[111] See Articles 6 (parallel importation), 30 (general exception) and 31 (compulsory licensing) TRIPS.
[112] The following NGOs have been active campaigning for adequate access to essential medicines for all patients: Essential Action's Access to Medicines Project: (www.essentialaction.org/access/); Health Action International:

within the UN (human rights) framework have been active within this field.[113] Unfortunately though there has been little attention for this issue from the perspective of women's rights. In its Resolution 53/2 (2009) on Women, the Girl Child and HIV/AIDS the Commission on the Status of Women (CSW) urged governments to prioritize and expand access to treatment, and promote access to affordable, high quality, safe and effective medicines, particularly for women and girls.[114] Although the CSW did not explicitly link the protection of IP through the TRIPS Agreement with the availability of affordable medicines, it did remind

---

(www.haiweb.org/02_focus.htm); Médecins Sans Frontières' Access to Essential Medicines Campaign: (www.accessmed-msf.org/); Oxfam International: (www.oxfam.org/) and specifically Oxfam America: www.oxfamamerica.org/whatwedo/campaigns/access_to_medicines); and the Consumer Project on Technology: (www.cptech.org/ip/health/). In addition there have also been regional campaigns, see for example the Treatment Action Campaign in South Africa: (www.tac.org.za/community/) and India's Peoples Health Movement: (www.phm-india.org/index.php?option=com_content&view=frontpage&Itemid=14).

[113] See for example for documents relating to the World Health Organization: WHO, 'Globalization, TRIPS and Access to Pharmaceuticals' 3 *Policy Perspectives on Medicines* (March 2001); WHA (2003), *Intellectual Property Rights, Innovation and Public Health*, WHA56.27; WHO, 'Equitable Access to Essential Medicines: A Framework for Collective Action', 8 *Policy Perspectives on Medicines*, March 2004; WHO, 'Access to Medicines', 19 *WHO Drug Information*, 2005:3, pp. 236–41; WHA (2008), *Global Strategy and Plan of Action on Public Health, Innovation and Intellectual Property*, WHA61.21; WHO Executive Board (2002), *Ensuring Accessibility of Essential Medicines*, EB109.R17.
For documents from UN bodies, like the General Assembly and the Commission on Human Rights, see: UN Commission on Human Rights (2001), Access to Medication in the Context of Pandemics Such as HIV/AIDS, UN doc. E/CN.4/RES/2001/33; UN Sub-Commission on the Promotion and Protection of Human Rights (2001), Globalization and Its Impact on the Full Enjoyment of Human Rights, UN doc. E/CN.4/Sub.2/2001/10; UN Sub-Commission on the Promotion and Protection of Human Rights (2001), Economic, Social and Cultural Rights. The Impact of the Agreement on Trade-Related Aspects on Intellectual Property Rights on Human Rights, UN doc. E/CN.4/Sub.2/2001/13; UN Commission on Human Rights (2002), Access to Medication in the Context of Pandemics Such as HIV/AIDS, UN doc. E/CN.4/RES/2002/32; UN Commission on Human Rights (2003), Economic, Social and Cultural Rights. The Right of Everyone to the Enjoyment of the Highest Attainable Standard of Physical and Mental Health. Report of the Special Rapporteur, Paul Hunt, Submitted in Accordance with Commission Resolution 2002/31, UN doc. E/CN.4/2003/58; UN Commission on Human Rights (2004a), Access to Medication in the Context of Pandemics Such as HIV/AIDS, Tuberculosis and Malaria, UN doc. E/CN.4/RES/2004/26; UN General Assembly (2004), Access to Medication in the Context of Pandemics Such as HIV/AIDS, Tuberculosis and Malaria, UN doc. A/RES/58/179; UN Commission on Human Rights (2004c), Economic, Social and Cultural Rights. The Right of Everyone to the Enjoyment of the Highest Attainable Standard of Physical and Mental Health. Report of the Special Rapporteur, Paul Hunt. Addendum, Mission to the WTO, UN doc. E/CN.4/2004/49/add.1; UN Commission on Human Rights (2005), Access to Medication in the Context of Pandemics Such as HIV/AIDS, Tuberculosis and Malaria, UN doc. E/CN.4/RES/2005/23; UN General Assembly (2006), Report of the Special Rapporteur on the Right of Everyone to the Enjoyment of the Highest Attainable Standard of Physical and Mental Health, UN doc. A/61/338.

[114] Commission on the Status of Women (2009), Resolution 53/2 on Women, the girl child and HIV/AIDS, para. 16.

Chapter 12. Women's Right to Health and International Trade

States of the flexibilities within trade-related intellectual property rights to be used to protect public health.[115]

Activism within civil society, and also perfect timing, led the Ministerial Conference of the WTO to adopt the Doha Declaration on TRIPS and Public Health in November 2001.[116] The Doha Declaration recognizes the gravity of the public health problems afflicting many developing and least developed countries.[117] Furthermore, it states that the TRIPS Agreement does not and should not prevent Members from taking measures to protect public health, and affirms that the Agreement can and should be interpreted and implemented in a manner supportive of WTO members' right to protect public health and, particularly, promote access to medicines for all.[118] In that regard it reaffirms the right of WTO members to use, to the full, the provisions in the TRIPS Agreement, which provide flexibility for this purpose.[119] The Doha Declaration eventually led to an amendment of the TRIPS Agreement to make it possible for States to export pharmaceuticals under compulsory license.[120]

These developments are promising. Although the Doha Declaration does not explicitly make use of the human rights language it does clearly confirm that developing countries have a right to use the TRIPS flexibilities to the full extent in dealing with public health issues. However, access to medicines from a women's rights perspective has not yet entered the debate on the relationship of IP and public health. Therefore, it is essential that the women's rights community step forward while this debate is still ongoing in order to ensure that sufficient attention is given to women's right to health.

5. GATS: LIBERALIZATION OF HEALTH SERVICES AND A WOMEN'S RIGHT TO HEALTH

As discussed earlier, there is an obligation under the ICESCR and the Women's Convention to achieve at least the minimum standard of women's right to health

---

[115] Commission on the Status of Women (2009), Resolution 53/2 on Women, the girl child and HIV/AIDS, para. 13.
[116] WTO Ministerial Conference (2001), Declaration on the TRIPS Agreement and Public Health. Adopted on 14 November 2001, Ministerial Conference, Fourth Session, Doha, 9–14 November 2001, WT/MIN(01)/DEC/2.
[117] WTO Ministerial Conference, Doha Declaration on the TRIPS Agreement and Public Health, para. 1.
[118] *Ibid.*, para. 4.
[119] *Ibid.*
[120] WTO General Council (2003) *Implementation of Paragraph 6 of the Doha Declaration on the TRIPS Agreement and Public Health. Decision of 30 August 2003*, WT/L/540. This decision was then formalized in an amendment to the TRIPS Agreement, which has not yet entered into force since not all required ratifications are in. WTO General Council (2005) *Amendment of the TRIPS Agreement. Decision of 6 December 2005*, WT/L/641.

through the provision of access to adequate, equitable and effective health services. For this, the importance of the provision of *public* health services – and of gender-sensitive service delivery – needs to be taken into account. Consequently, assessing the possible impact the GATS may have on public health services is vital. However, the linkage between trade and rights is often unfortunately missing in the context of health services and the right to health of women. For example, the WHO in a recent publication titled *Women's Health and Human Rights: Monitoring the Implementation of CEDAW* presented a questionnaire for WHO Headquarters and regional and country offices and for United Nations country teams for use in preparation of technical contributions and reports to CEDAW, in which questions are asked about financing of public health services and whether women are included in waivers and exceptions to fee-for-service schemes for the poor.[121] These issues are directly related to the concerns about the GATS, yet there is no reference in this publication to the impact on public services of the commodification of health services via trade liberalization.[122]

The clarification and interpretation of what is sometimes referred to as the 'public services exemption' of the GATS is thus very important. Furthermore, GATS members should be able to use the flexibilities available in the negotiating and scheduling of commitments and in the exceptions in the GATS to the fullest possible extent in order to implement measures to promote, protect and fulfil the right to health and women's health.[123]

The issue of the supposed exemption of public services is a problematical one in the GATS context as the relevant provisions – Article I:3(b) and I:3(c) of the GATS[124] – have not yet been interpreted authoritatively by WTO dispute settlement and remain unclear.[125] It is also likely that the provisions will be interpreted more narrowly within the trade regime than expected by supporters of

---

[121] World Health Organization, Department of Reproductive Health and Research, 2007, p. 34.
[122] Some observers have linked the lack of improvement or deterioration in public health service delivery and the increase in healthcare costs on the implementation of a market-based approach to services via the GATS with a corresponding neglect by the State of its human rights obligations.
[123] *Ibid.* The Report of the High Commissioner of Human Rights on the Liberalization of Trade in Services and Human Rights encourages interpretations of GATS that are human rights-compatible and ensure the flexibility for governments' right and duty to regulate for national developmental needs.
[124] Article I:3(b) – 'services' includes any service in any sector except services supplied in the exercise of governmental authority: Article I:3(c): 'a service supplied in the exercise of governmental authority' means any service which is supplied neither on a commercial basis, nor in competition with one or more service suppliers.'
[125] See further, M. KRAJEWSKI, 'Public Services and Trade Liberalization: Mapping the Legal Framework', *Journal of International Economic Law* 6(2), 2003, pp. 341–367; R. ADLUNG, 'Public Services and the GATS', *Journal of International Economic Law* 9(2), 2006, pp. 455–485; R. CHANDRA, *GATS and its Implications for Developing Countries: Key Issues and Concerns*, DESA Discussion Paper 25, November 2002, pp.16–19.

public services.¹²⁶ For many of those whose approach to health services is human rights-based, this is very troubling and some even see in this the groundwork for the gradual and insidious privatization of health services.¹²⁷ Liberalization is *not necessarily* privatization of existing public services, but this impression has been created due to the promotion of public-private partnerships by international financial institutions¹²⁸ combined with possible withdrawal of the possibility of preferential State benefits for public services under the GATS and the playing down of the right to health obligations of the State within the trade in services context. Exacerbating these fears are the uncertainties regarding the likelihood of the development of new, stringent WTO disciplines in the areas of domestic regulatory autonomy, subsidies, foreign investment and government procurement that will impact on public health services and national health policy-making.

Moreover, the GATS is aimed only at achieving progressively higher levels of liberalization of trade in services and this is not necessarily linked with improvement of national health systems as a whole.¹²⁹ This process of liberalization is to be conducted either through successive rounds of trade negotiations – or autonomously by the members, and it is important to understand this process to assess the implications of the GATS for the right to health. The trade negotiations in the WTO are carried out on parallel multilateral or bilateral tracks. The multilateral negotiations are focused on establishing rules and disciplines and the bilateral negotiations in GATS are related to creating market access opportunities. The obligations concerning market access and extension of national treatment¹³⁰ to foreign services and service suppliers

---

126 See WTO Council for Trade in Services. Report of the meeting held on 14 October 1998, S/C/M/30, 12 November 1998 (98-4478), which suggested that the Articles abovementioned should be interpreted narrowly.

127 See *e.g.* ALLYSON POLLACK and DAVID PRICE, 'Rewriting the regulations: How the World Trade Organization could accelerate privatization in health-care systems', *The Lancet*, Volume 356, Issue 9246, 9, December 2000, pp. 1995–2000. Some research argues that increased privatization of the health sector increases overall quality of service provision, but usually these studies do not take into account equity and access rights. It can be pointed out that overall efficiency of the health system can be calculated without considering the inequity of a two-tier health system that is created through profit-oriented high quality service delivery for those who can afford it and declining expenditure on public services for the disadvantaged. Case studies do not show improvement in public services alongside the increase in private services delivery, but rather the contrary: *e.g.* see J. KAUFMAN J. and F. JING, 'Privatisation of Health Services and the Reproductive Health of Rural Chinese Women', *Reproductive Health Matters*, Vol. 10, Issue 20, November 2002, pp. 108–116.

128 See, World Bank, IRINA A. NIKOLIC and HARALD MAIKISCH, *Health, Nutrition and Population (HNP)*, Discussion Paper, Public-Private Partnerships and Collaboration in the Health Sector: An Overview with Case Studies from Recent European Experience, 2006.

129 Progressive liberalization is referred to on the WTO official website as one of the 'pillars' of the GATS, along with the principle of transparency (of services information and data). See The GATS – A General Introduction, WTO, 29 March 2006 (3776.4), available online at www.wto.org/english/tratop_e/serv_e/gsintr_e.doc, accessed 19 May 2010.

130 The principle of 'National Treatment' in the WTO basically means that foreign companies must be treated the same as domestic firms. With regard to the GATS, this is not an obligation

depend on the commitments undertaken by GATS members either autonomously or pursuant to bilateral negotiations with other members.[131] There is a lot of comment on how flexible and non-coercive GATS obligations are, as members decide on whether or not to schedule commitments – but the availability of policy space and real choice in this process of liberalization needs to be looked at critically and realistically.

Health services under the GATS are spread across a classification system comprised of 12 core service sectors which are further subdivided into a total of some 160 sub-sectors. It is a positive list approach wherein any service sector may be included in a member's schedule of commitments with specific market access and national treatment obligations. Each WTO member has submitted such a schedule under the GATS. This classification itself already causes a problem of overlap or fracturing for health services. CESCR General Comment No. 14 highlights the need for a *comprehensive national strategy* for promoting women's right to health throughout their lifespan', including 'policies to provide access to a full range of high quality and affordable healthcare'.[132] It can be argued that the possibility of developing a holistic policy for health as a social service and human right is already undermined by this classification in GATS where health services are already partly divided up into at least three of the core sectors – profit oriented social services (health services), business services (health workers) and financial services (health insurance). Currently, the health sector remains one of the least committed areas in WTO member's services schedules, due to the perceived need on retaining these areas as areas of national policy competence.

In addition to the possibility of scheduling GATS commitments under this sectoral classification, there is another additional 'flexibility' to commit a sector (to liberalize) only according to certain modes of delivery.[133] Even trade experts have noted that that liberalization of services may lead to marginalization of the poor[134]

---

automatically arising from WTO membership itself, but taken on by Members in the autonomous or bilateral negotiations described above.

[131] Due to the 'Most Favoured Nation' principle of the WTO, any privilege accorded to one WTO member is applicable to all WTO members unless it falls within specified exemptions in WTO law *e.g.* economic integration agreements.

[132] Para. 21: Women and the right to health.

[133] This other method of classification of services in the GATS is based on the physical location of the supplier and consumer and pursuant to Article I:2 of the GATS, covers services supplied in the following 'modes' or means of delivering services: Mode 1 – Cross-border trade ('telemedicine'); Mode 2 – Consumption abroad ('health tourism'); Mode 3 – Commercial presence (establishment foreign-owned health services supplier (or a subsidiary or affiliate) such as a hospital or clinic; and Mode 4 – Presence of natural persons(e.g. migration of health service personnel).

[134] MARY E. FOOTER and CAROL GEORGE, 'The General Agreement on Trade in Services', in: Patrick F.J. MACRORY, ARTHUR E. APPLETON and MICHAEL G. PLUMMER (eds.), *The World Trade Organization: Legal, Economic and Political Analysis*, Vol. I., Springer, 2005, p. 727, referring to the reports of the UN High Commission for Human Rights.

and that with regard to health services '... different gender issues may arise depending on the mode of services involved'.[135] It has been further noted that:

> 'Poor women who depend on public health systems for reproductive care and medical care of children would be particularly affected under this scenario'.[136]

Countering the criticism that economic policy is dictated by the WTO, the system of scheduling of commitments has led to the GATS being regularly described as being the most flexible agreement in the WTO system as members supposedly can assume or avoid obligations to liberalize according to national policy and even when undertaken, the extent of commitments can vary widely from member to member. In reality, when a sector is scheduled, it is considered as without restrictions unless national treatment and market access restrictions are specified. Therefore although disputes could theoretically be avoided by intelligent scheduling, there will be situations where errors and oversights or differences in interpretation in dispute settlement context could still happen.

Furthermore, even if the schedule correctly reflects the policy position as intended, no policy is set in stone and there could be subsequent position changes. The 'lock-in' of national policy into one type of GATS-controlled liberalization is another major criticism of the international trading system. Considering the difficulty of changing the commitments once made and the obligation of compensating those countries whose trade interests are harmed by the change of commitments, implementing measures that appeal to evolving social values and do not reflect what is in the schedule of commitments, could result in recourse to exceptions to the GATS obligations rather than changes to the schedule.

Furthermore, it is often only the trade and commerce sections of government that are involved in the preparation and negotiation processes under the GATS and other relevant bodies, such as *e.g.* Ministries of Health with regard to health services issues, are usually insufficiently involved, if at all. It is questionable to what extent the marginalized sections of society, who would suffer most if essential health services are cut down, withdrawn or left undeveloped, have a voice in the negotiating process. Taking into account the lack of women's representation in governance and policy-making in many societies, a gender sensitive negotiating position that takes into account the special health needs of women is to be seen even rarer, if at all. Women's Affairs Ministries or Departments are even less likely to be included in developing trade policy positions on health services than Health Ministries, and civil society groups working on women's issues, even less so.

---

[135] *Ibid.*
[136] *Ibid.*

Liberalization per se suggests no gains for the health of women, especially poor women, without policies to redistribute the benefits to the disadvantaged. If governments do draft such measures, the GATS compliance of such redistribution schemes is something that they must additionally spend time and resources upon, if such resources are available. Another suggested strategy is for a member to indefinitely postpone liberalization by choosing not to make commitments in a particular sector – or that in the alternative, a member can make and indefinitely retain bindings below existing status quo for sectors they wish to protect, such as health. It is often stated that nothing in the Agreement itself prevents such a position being held as long as they wish; however this is counterbalanced by the obligation to 'progressively liberalize'[137] and realistically speaking, the pressures from stronger trading partners upon weaker countries (particularly developing and least developed members) to liberalize their economies further should also not be discounted. It has been commented that the process of liberalization of services has been historically driven by US and European corporate interests in search of access to markets, and as long as this agenda is sustained, the real-world political pressures also remain.[138]

A WTO member may have to ultimately rely on exceptions in the GATS.[139] However, to what extent these exceptions translate into real and effective policy space for such members to take measures in their national interest remains unclear. Article XIV(b) of the GATS allows for a general exception to GATS obligations for measures 'necessary to protect human, animal or plant life or health'. While measures taken in furtherance of obligations relating to the right to health can easily fall under this provision, the identification of a measure as within the scope of Article XIV is not the problem. The cases relating to exceptions to WTO rules usually revolve around the conditions under which such a measure can be justified according to WTO law. A measure must not constitute *arbitrary and unjustifiable discrimination*, which is a requirement of

---

[137] See Article XIX of GATS – Negotiation of Specific Commitments is under Part IV of the Agreement, which is titled 'Progressive Liberalization'.

[138] BERNARD HOEKMAN, AADITYA MATTOO and ANDRÉ SAPIR, 'The Political Economy of Services Trade Liberalization: A Case For International Regulatory Cooperation?', *Oxford Review of Economic Policy* 2007 23(3):367, p. 1. Also see MARY E. FOOTER and CAROL GEORGE, 'The General Agreement on Trade in Services', in: Patrick F.J. MACRORY, ARTHUR E. APPLETON, and MICHAEL G. PLUMMER (eds.), *The World Trade Organization: Legal, Economic and Political Analysis*, Vol. I., Springer, 2005, pp. 804–805 on the role of the United States, EC, Japan, Canada, the Nordic Countries and the OECD in general in proposing and supporting the inclusion of a services round.

[139] Article XIV is the general exceptions clause of the GATS. There is also a possibility to use Articles V and V*bis* (economic integration and labour market integration) and Article XII (restrictions to safeguard the balance of payments) and the as yet undetermined procedures on emergency safeguard measures provided for by Article X of the GATS. In addition to the specific Articles, the special concern for developing or least developed members in the GATS Preamble and several other articles.

the chapeau of Article XIV.[140] The requirement of proving the *necessity* of a disputed measure and that it is carried out in good faith and is not an arbitrary or unjustifiable discrimination or disguised restriction on trade, is often the stumbling block, even if the measure falls within the scope of the exception.[141] Thus the much vaunted flexibilities and possibilities for balancing the right to health in the context of the GATS obligations may become quicksand as opposed to firm ground – unless the interpretation and application of the rules can escape the rigidity of a purely market-based, trade liberalization approach to respect social objectives and the human right to health.

6. CONCLUSION

In this Chapter we have given a general overview of women's right to health as protected under the ICESCR and the Women's Convention. According to the authors one of the issues regarding women's right to health is the problematic lack of engagement of the women's rights community with the international trading system. It is important to promote and make use of the human rights language to strengthen the rights and obligations of States with regard to the right to health in order to balance these with the rules of the international trading system. Therefore, it is unfortunate that in recent key discussions on trade and health, the language of human rights is strangely missing or diluted. Furthermore, as has been discussed above, the supposed flexibilities in trade agreements, such as TRIPS and GATS, with regard to protection of public health are not as advantageous as is often argued.

The authors of this Chapter believe that there is a need for a continuous active engagement on trade and health issues, and specifically the use of a women's rights approach using the rights language as expressed in Article 12 of the Women's Convention. As the WTO rules and Dispute Settlement System become more firmly established the window of opportunity to take women's right to health into the debate on trade and human rights diminishes.

'It is the common fate of the indolent to see their rights become prey to the active'.[142] Let this not be the result in the ongoing struggle for primacy between trade rules and the right to health.

---

[140] 'Subject to the requirement that such measures are not applied in a manner which would constitute a means of arbitrary or unjustifiable discrimination between countries where like conditions prevail, or a disguised restriction on trade in services, nothing in this Agreement shall be construed to prevent the adoption or enforcement by any Member of measures…'.

[141] See further CAREN GROWN, ELISSA BRAUNSTEIN and ANJU MALHOTRA (eds.), *Trading Women's Health and Rights: Trade Liberalization and Reproductive Health in Developing Economies*, Zed Books, London, 2006.

[142] THOMAS DAVIS (ed.), *The Speeches of John Philpot Curran*, On the election of the Lord Mayor of Dublin, 10 July 1790, London, 1847, p. 94.

CHAPTER 13
ERADICATING FEMALE CIRCUMCISION: CHANGING A HARMFUL SOCIAL NORM THROUGH THE WOMEN'S CONVENTION

Phyllis LIVAHA

1. INTRODUCTION

Female Genital Mutilation (FGM) – also known as Female Genital Cutting (FGC), Female Circumcision (hereafter referred to as FC)[1] or simply 'cutting' – a word which conveys the raw pain its prepubescent victims suffer[2] – is an ancient procedure involving the partial or total removal of the external female genitalia.[3]

---

[1] The term female circumcision (FC) will be used in this Chapter. The term was used under CEDAW General Recommendation No. 14. Some scholars believe that using this term 'still connotes the severity of the practice, while allowing respect to the cultures in which it is practiced.' See AMANDA CARDENAS, 'Female Circumcision: The Road to Change', *Syracuse Journal of International Law and Commerce* (26 SYRJILC), Spring 1999, p. 293. See also JESSICA HORN, 'Not Culture But Gender: Reconceptualizing Female Genital Mutilation /Cutting', in: Wendy Chavkin and Ellen Chesler (eds.), *Where Human Rights Begin: Health, Sexuality, and Women in the New Millenium*, Rutgers University Press, United States, 2005, p. 38. In 1993, the 46th World Health Assembly of the World Health Organization passed a resolution supporting the use of the term 'female genital mutilation' to describe clitoridectomy, infibulation, and other related practices. JAIMEE K. WELLERSTEIN, 'In the Name of Tradition: Eradicating the Harmful Practice of Female Genital Mutilation', *Loyola of Los Angeles International and Comparative Law Review* (22 loy. L.a. Int'l & comp. L. Rev.) 1999, p. 99, p. 105.

[2] JO-ANN GOODMAN and DAVID JONES, *The unspeakable practice of female circumcision that's destroying young women's lives in Britain*, Mail Online, 3 January 2008, available at www.dailymail.co.uk/femail/article-505796/The-unspeakable-practice-female-circumcision-thats-destroying-young-womens-lives-Britain.html#ixzz0ivdq6rZK (last visited 10 June 2010). See also LYNN HARRIS, *Female Genital Mutilation in the US; No Compromise*, Violence Against Women, available at www.salon.com/life/feature/2010/06/02/fgm_genital_nick; 'In a revision published on April 26, the AAP – primarily out of stated "respect" for the "experience of the many women who have had their genitals altered and who do not perceive themselves as 'mutilated'" – replaced the term "mutilation" with the more "neutral," less "inflammatory" and, they suggest, dialogue-stifling term "cutting" (or FGC).' (last visited 1 July 2010).

[3] QASSIM KHIDIR, *Women in Kurdistan – Female Circumcision Ban Urged*, Global Arab Network, 11 February 2010, available at www.english.globalarabnetwork.com/201002114764/

By some accounts, the clitoris of a girl/woman is sliced off and ash is applied to the incision to ease the pain.[4] It is commonly performed under unsanitary conditions by women with no formal medical training.[5] 'Globally, at least 2 million girls a year are at risk of [FC]. Overall, an estimated 85 to 114 million girls and women in the world are [circumcised].'[6]

The custom of FC poses complex challenges in international attempts to address and eradicate the practice. In 1990, the Committee on the Elimination of Discrimination Against Women (CEDAW), which was created by the Convention on the Elimination of All Forms of Discrimination Against Women (the Women's Convention), explicitly recognized the eradication of FC as a major objective on the United Nations (hereinafter UN) agenda.[7] The Women's Convention, however, has only limited potential to eradicate this culturally embedded practice, as do other international instruments. Even though the instruments enable women, at least in theory, to contest FC on grounds of life, health, and gender equality, they might not help much in the international campaign to eradicate the practice. This Chapter will explore how FC still escapes international intervention because it is protected under the guise of culture and religion, even with the health hazards associated with the practice, as well as international and national instruments in place. It also discusses ways in which these provisions, in particular the Women's Convention, have been inefficient to effectuate substantial change in the practice of FC. Finally, a framework for the effective implementation as an establishment of the means to eradicate the practice is recommended. This can be an integrated approach that makes use of both the legal measures, as well as educational and outreach programmes.

2. FC PROCEDURE

FC takes various forms, the least severe of which is ritual circumcision or the 'pricking of the clitoral hood prepuce to release a drop of blood.'[8] Another mild form and most medically non-threatening is *Sunna*, which means tradition and

---

Related-news-from-Iraq/women-in-kurdistan-female-circumcision-ban-urged.html (last visited 10 June 2010).

[4] *Ibid.* See also KHADIJA F. SHARIF, 'Female Genital Mutilation, What does the New Federal Law Really Mean?', *Fordham Urban Law Journal*, (24 *FDMUJ* 409), Winter 1997, p. 413.

[5] *Ibid.*

[6] This approximation was given in 1995, and is still used currently, NAHID TOUBIA, 'Female Genital Mutilation, Women's Rights, Human Rights', in: Julia Peters and Andrea Wolper (eds.), *International Feminist Perspectives*, Routledge, New York 1995, p. 224.

[7] See UN GAOR Supp., 34th Sess., No. 221 (A/34/46) at 193, UN Doc. A/RES/34/180 (entered into force 3 September 1981).

[8] LOIS S. BIBBLINGS, 'Female Circumcision: Mutilation or Modification?', in: Jo Bridgeman and Susan Millns (eds.), *Law and Body Politics Female Circumcision*, Dartmouth Publishing Company, Vermont, 1995, p. 151.

entails the excision of the clitoral prepuce or 'hood of clitoris.'[9] Clitoridectomy or excision is a 'more radical form'[10] of the surgeries and entails the complete removal of the clitoris.[11] This includes the removal of the 'clitoral glands' and some of the *nympha* or labia minora, the narrow lip-like enclosures of the vagina.

Infibulation is the most severe of the surgeries, requiring the removal of the *mons veneris* – the removal or scraping of the labia majora which is the 'two rounded folds of tissue that control the external boundaries of the vulva,'[12] – and removal of the labia minora.[13] Infibulation is the surgery that has the most significant risks and hazards during and after surgery.[14] Immediately following infibulation, the wounds are sewn together by the operator, leaving a small opening the size of a fingertip[15] for urination and menstruation.[16] Deinfibulation is the 'cutting apart' of the 'healed wound' from a female circumcision in order to enable childbirth, while reinfibulation is the 're-closing' of the deinfibulation wound.[17]

HISTORY OF FEMALE CIRCUMCISION

The origins of the practice are unclear. It predates the rise of Christianity and Islam.[18] The history of FC has been traced back as far as the 2nd century BC, when a geographer, Agatharchides of Cnidus, wrote about female circumcision as it occurred among tribes residing on the western coast of the Red Sea (now modern-day Egypt).[19] There is mention made of Egyptian mummies that display characteristics of FC.[20] Historians such as Herodotus claim that in the fifth century BC the Phoenicians, the Hittites and the Ethiopians practised FC.[21] It is also reported that FC rites were practised in tropical zones of Africa, in the

---

[9] Ibid.
[10] LESLYE AMEDE OBIORA, 'Bridges and Barricades: Rethinking Polemics and Intransigence in the Campaign against Female Circumcision', in: Adrien Katherine Wing (ed.), *Global Critical Race Feminism: An International Reader*, New York University Press, New York, 2000.
[11] BIBBLINGS, *supra* note 8, p. 151.
[12] OBIORA, *supra* note 10, p. 262.
[13] BIBBLINGS, *supra* note 8, p. 151.
[14] OBIORA, *supra* note 10, p. 262. Also known as pharaonic circumcision. See also KHADIJA F. SHARIF, 'Female Genital Mutilation, What does the New Federal Law Really Mean?', *Fordham Urban Law Journal* (24 FDMUJ 409), Winter 1997.
[15] JAIMEE K. WELLERSTEIN, 'In the Name of Tradition: Eradicating the Harmful Practice of Female Genital Mutilation', 22 *loy. L.a. Int'l & comp. L. Rev.*, 1999, p. 105.
[16] BIBBLINGS, *supra* note 8, p. 151.
[17] Ibid.
[18] GOODMAN and JONES, *supra*, note 2.
[19] Available at www.mtholyoke.edu/~ehtoddch/politics/historyfgm.html.
[20] GOODMAN and JONES, *supra*, note 2.
[21] Ibid.

Philippines, by certain tribes in the Upper Amazon, and in Australia by women of the Arunta tribe and also occurred among the early Romans and Arabs.[22]

As recently as the 1950s, clitoridectomy, a type of FC, was practised in Western Europe and the United States to treat 'ailments' in women as diverse as hysteria, epilepsy, mental disorders, masturbation, nymphomania, melancholia and lesbianism.[23] In other words, the practice of FC has been followed by many different peoples and societies across the ages and the continents.[24] Research shows that FC has been practiced traditionally for centuries. It has been followed by many different peoples and societies across the ages and the continents.[25]

Predominantly found in various communities in Africa, FC is also prevalent in parts of Southeast Asia and the Middle East.[26] It is also practiced by indigenous groups in Mexico, Brazil, Peru and Columbia.[27] 'Moreover, through immigration, the practice has moved into countries where the practice is stringently opposed.'[28] There have been reports of FC among certain immigrant communities in Europe, Australia, Canada and the United States.[29]

3. CULTURAL RELATIVISM

When one studies traditional practices, in particular FC, it must be noted from the outset that these practices are rooted in a whole set of beliefs, values and cultural and social behaviour patterns which govern the lives of the societies concerned.[30] Muslims who practice the ritual believe that it is an Islamic custom

---

[22] *Ibid.*
[23] *Ibid.*
[24] *Ibid.*
[25] SINI SANUMAN, *Healthy Tomorrow*, available at www.stopexcision.net/about_fgm.htm (viewed 11 June 2010).
[26] GOODMAN and JONES, *supra*, note 2.
[27] EFUA DORKENOO, *Cutting the Rose: Female Genital Mutilation, the Practice and its Prevention*, Minority Rights Publication, London, 1994. pp. viii-xi.
[28] CARDENAS, *supra* note 1, p. 291.
[29] UNFPA, 'Promoting Gender Equality', available at www.unfpa.org/gender/practices2.htm#21.
[30] Final Report Special Rapporteur on Harmful Traditional Practices, UN doc. E/CN.4/Sub.2/2005/36, 11 July 2005. While many international human rights activists argue that the practice is a violation of women's human rights (ALLISON T. SLACK, 'Female Circumcision: A Critical Appraisal', 10 *Hum. Rts. Q.*, 1988, pp. 437, 439), others assert cultural and religious defenses as a reason to respect the practice (*Ibid.*). This debate exemplifies the struggle between cultural relativism and universal human rights. Cultural relativists oppose conforming to 'universal' norms, arguing that majority preference should not dictate what is moral. *Ibid.*, p. 463. According to theorists, cultural relativism is complex, and seeks to question how much we can actually understand of other culturally based realities, while it simultaneously prescribes appreciation for those diversities. Conversely, universal human rights activists argue that those practices that have neither factual, historical validity nor contemporary legitimacy in terms of societal values, and that furthermore inflict harm and injury on their adherents, must be abandoned (SANDRA D. LANE and ROBERT A. RUBINSTEIN, 'Judging the Other: Responding to Traditional Female Genital Surgeries', *Hastings Center*

encouraged by Prophet Muhammad, even though there is no major Islamic citation making the practice a religious requirement.[31] 'The power of beliefs, respect for family structures, poverty, lack of education and social constraints and – a factor which should not be overlooked – colonialism have, especially in developing countries, helped to keep alive FC as a tradition. Societies engage wholeheartedly and faithfully in the practice because it has always formed part of their everyday lives.'[32] Among many cultural and ethnic groups, FC is inseparable from views of women's social and sexual identity.

FC assumes varying degrees of prevalence, according to culture and region, despite all the health risks involved.[33] This is evidenced through the continuation of the practice regardless of the reported deaths and health problems attributable to the procedure.[34] 'One of the most difficult justifications to address is social acceptance. [FC] occurs most frequently in societies where women have a one-dimensional presence and purpose.'[35] In a society where girls are brought up to fulfill the role of wife and mother, [FC] can become a prerequisite for achieving this goal. If a girl does not undergo some form of circumcision, she is deemed unfit for this role and has no other societal role. In areas where FC is practiced, most men will not marry uncircumcised women, and other women will not associate with them.[36] 'They are considered social outcasts, sometimes perceived as dirty, different, and even dangerous.'[37]

Report, May-June 1996, p. 31. SHELLEY SIMMS, 'What's Culture Got to Do With It? Excising the Harmful Tradition of Female Circumcision',106 Harv. L. Rev., 1993, pp. 1944, 1960).

[31] KHADIJA F. SHARIF, 'Female Genital Mutilation, What does the New Federal Law Really Mean?', Fordham Urban Law Journal (24 FDMUJ 409), Winter 1997. Some scholars say that texts on FGM/FGC exist in some authoritative interpretations, RENÉE KOOL, 'Female Genital Mutilation: A Matter for Criminal Justice?', in: Ingrid Westendorp en Ria Wolleswinkel (eds.), Violence in the Domestic Sphere, Intersentia, Antwerp, 2005, p. 103. See also ROSEMARY SKAINE, Female Genital Mutilation: Legal, Cultural and Medical Issues, McFarland & Company, UK, 2005, pp. 119, 121–122, while others say that neither the Quran nor the 'hadith' (collections of the sayings of Prophet Mohammed) includes a direct call for FGM/FGC. TOUBIA, supra note 6.

[32] Ibid. 'The fear of losing the psychological, moral, and material benefits of "belonging" is one of the greatest motivations to conformity.' TOUBIA, supra note 6, p. 232.

[33] SANUMAN, supra, note 25.

[34] DORKENOO, supra note 27, p. 31.

[35] CATHERINE L. ANNAS, 'Irreversible Error: The Power and Prejudice of Female Genital Mutilation', Journal of Contemporary Health Law and Policy (12 JCHLP 325), Spring 1996, p. 332. See also TONI Y. JOSEPH, 'Scarring Ritual; Ancient African Custom of Female Circumcision Destines Women to Life of Subservience, Critics Say', Dallas Morning News, 18 April 1993.

[36] Ibid. See also FRAN HOSKEN, 'The Hosken Report: 'Genital and Sexual Mutilation of Females', 4th ed., Win News, Massachusetts, 1994, p. 34.

[37] Ibid. See HOPE LEWIS, 'Between Irua and "Female Genital Mutilation": Feminist Human Rights Discourse and the Cultural Divide', 8 Harv. Hum. Rts. J. 1, 1995, pp. 20–21, p. 23 (commenting that women who have not endured FC are considered unclean and are barred from social and economic aid); 'These prejudices will not likely change until the practice of [FC] is abolished.' HOSKEN, Ibid., p. 40. See also KAY BOULWARE-MILLER, 'Female

One theory states that female circumcision originated as a way to control women's sexuality. It was thought that the practice would control a woman's desire for sex and thus prevent premarital relations and keep the woman faithful to her husband after marriage.[38] It went to the extent that female circumcision made men masters over female sexual function, thus, it historically reinforced the idea that wives are their husband's private property.[39]

Most girls are circumcised between the ages of four and ten.[40] However, depending on the culture, the procedure may be done at a wide range of ages from infants to just before marriage or even after the woman's first child.[41] The Ethiopian Jewish Falashas (now living in Israel) and Sudanese Nomads have reported the performance of circumcision upon females that are only a few days old.[42] Some of the communities in the Northern African countries, including Egypt, perform the circumcision on girls around the age of seven, while others like Nigeria perform the procedure on girls in their adolescence.[43] What makes it more difficult to eradicate FC is that the practitioners believe that eradication of the practice would mean loss of prestige for the women and girls and loss of money or some sort of payment for the people who perform the circumcision.[44] To further legitimize and preserve the practice, the argument given is not only that the ritual serves important values (like adolescent initiation rites to adulthood), but also that 'the few traditional practices that remain after colonialism must be preserved.'[45]

Circumcision: Challenges to the Practice as a Human Rights Violation', 8 *Harv. Women's L.J.*, 1985, pp. 155, 157–58.

[38] BIBBLINGS, *supra*, note 8, p. 151.

[39] *Ibid.* See also Report of the Fourth World Conference on Women, Beijing Declaration and Platform for Action, UN Doc. A/Conf. 177/20, 1995. This document was introduced and adopted at the United Nations Fourth World Conference on Women in Beijing, China. The document provides 'Violence against women is a manifestation of the historically unequal power relations between men and women, which have led to domination over and discrimination against women by men and to the prevention of women's full advancement.' The author of this Comment was present at the conference and worked on the document.

[40] NAHID TOUBIA, 'Female Circumcision as a Public Health Issue', 331 *New Eng. J. Med.* 712, 1994, pp. 712–716.

[41] *Ibid.*

[42] DORKENOO, *supra* note 27, pp. 10–12.

[43] *Ibid.*

[44] TOUBIA, *supra*, note 6, pp. 230–33.

[45] *Ibid.*, p. 231. 'Africans who love and cherish the positive aspects of their cultures and have been wounded by colonialism (colonial governments passed legislation forbidding various cultures, and looked upon the indigenous culture with disdain) fear that actions against female circumcision will be used as another excuse to invade and humiliate them.' *Ibid.*, pp. 232 and 234.

4. FEMALE CIRCUMCISION AND ITS COMPLICATIONS AND EFFECTS

The practice of FC carries with it potential health risks and consequences. These health risks vary according to the type of female circumcision performed. 'Immediate health consequences may include shock, gangrene, and accidental damage to the urethra.'[46] More long-term effects include scarring, urinary tract infection, and infertility.[47] Complications with childbirth are almost unavoidable for infibulated women.[48] To give birth, the scar, caused by infibulation, must be reopened, resulting in increased blood loss and extreme pain.[49]

Long term complications are most common among infibulated females because of the interference the surgery has with the drainage of urine and menstrual blood.[50] Sometimes, the closing of the labia majora leads to a hole that is too small for menstruation and urine. This often leads to chronic pelvic infection which causes pelvic and back pain, *dysmenorrhea* (painful menstruation), and infertility, while in other cases, chronic urinary tract infections occur which can often lead to urinary stones and severe kidney damage.[51]

Psychologically, the sexuality of the woman is denied by shaving off the sensitive tissue and removal of the clitoris, thus taking away the specialized female sexual organ dedicated to pleasure.[52] 'Where the "protective hood" is allowed to be cut open or dilated only to permit the husband his lawful access to the vagina'[53] reduces the woman to a sexual object and reproductive vehicle for the man.[54]

Death is also one of the harmful outcomes of FC. It is difficult to find out how many girls and women die because the majority of circumcisions take place in rural areas and unsuccessful attempts are concealed from strangers and health authorities.[55] 'The ones who perform the circumcisions are protected by the community and, when death or consequences ensue, it is usually blamed on

---

[46] ALI DIRIE MAHID, *Female Circumcision In Somalia: Medical and Social Implications*, Somali National University, Mogadishu, 1985.
[47] *Ibid.*
[48] SCILLA MCLEAN and STELLA EFUA GRAHAM, 'Female Circumcision, Excision, and Infibulation: The Facts and Proposals For Change', *Minority Rights Group, Report No. 47*, London, 1980, p. 3.
[49] *Ibid.*
[50] CARDENAS, *supra* note 1, pp. 295–296.
[51] *Ibid.*, p. 296.
[52] TOUBIA, *supra* note 6, p. 229.
[53] *Ibid.*
[54] *Ibid.* Attention is usually given to the health problems associated with the physical aspect, and little attention is given to the psychological problems, especially since they appear later in life. These psychological symptoms are usually interpreted as the work of evil spirits and traditional rituals are used to cure them.
[55] CARDENAS, *supra* note 1, p. 296. See also DORKENOO, *supra* note 27, p. 14.

witchcraft or the "evil eye."'[56] A country's unstructured health care system also results in inaccurate or unreported deaths. Due to the lack of recorded documentation, information regarding the number of infections and fatalities during childbirth for both the infibulated women and the newborn child is unavailable.[57]

5. CEDAW GENERAL RECOMMENDATION NO. 14 AND OTHER INTERNATIONAL INSTRUMENTS

Although many States have publicly denounced the practice of FC and provided laws denouncing it, implementation and enforcement of the adopted legislation is still a problem. International standards applicable to the issue of FC are already in place. Most of the affected countries have ratified, among other treaties, the United Nations' Women's Convention[58] as well as the Convention on the Rights of the Child (CRC).[59]

'Recent efforts at the official international level, particularly by the United Nations agencies, have successfully put FC on women's health and human rights agendas as a health hazard and a form of violence against women.'[60] The

---

[56] *Ibid.*
[57] McLean, *supra* note 48, p. 3.
[58] Convention on the Elimination of All Forms of Discrimination Against Women (hereinafter Women's Convention), G.A. Res. 180, UN GAOR, 34th Sess., Supp. No. 46, at 194, UN Doc. A/34/830 (1979) (entered into force 3 September 1981) (hereinafter Women's Convention). The Women's Convention has been ratified by 187 countries. It requires signatory members to institute affirmative steps to modify cultural patterns that impair the enjoyment of the rights of women. Specifically, Article 5(a) requires member States 'to modify the social and cultural patterns of conduct… with a view to achieving the elimination of prejudices and customary and all other practices which are based on the idea of the inferiority or the superiority of either of the sexes or on stereotyped roles for men and women.' The international community views this Article of the Women's Convention as specifically applying to the practice of female circumcision. *Ibid.*, Article 5(a).
[59] Toubia, *supra* note 6, p. 234; see Convention on the Rights of the Child (hereinafter CRC), adopted 20 November 1989, Article 24, para. 3, G.A. Res. 44/25, Annex, UN GAOR, 44th Session, Supp. No. 49, at 167, UN Doc. A/44/736 (entered into force 2 September 1990), reprinted in 28 I.L.M. 1448, 1448 (stating that '[S]tate [p]arties shall take all effective and appropriate measures with a view to abolishing traditional practices prejudicial to the health of children.'). Article 19 proscribing child abuse, Article 16 providing children with privacy, and Article 37 prohibiting the torture or cruel, inhuman, or degrading treatment of children.
[60] *Ibid.*, p. 225. On health, CEDAW General Recommendation No. 24 recommends that governments device health policies that take into account the needs of girls and adolescents who may be vulnerable to traditional practices such as female circumcision. Anika Rahman and Nahid Toubia, *Female Genital Mutilation: A Guide to Worldwide Laws and Policies*, Zed Books Ltd., London, 2000, p. 27. CEDAW, General Recommendation No. 24, 1999: Women and Health (General Comments) para. 12(b); 'On violence against women, it is important to note that the definition of such violence in the Declaration on the Elimination of Violence Against Women does not require intent to harm.', Rahman and Toubia, *supra*, p. 25; see also United Nations General Assembly, Declaration on the Elimination of Violence Against

observations and recommendations of the various UN treaty monitoring committees, such as the one established under the Women's Convention, are of particular value since they 'monitor national compliance with international human rights treaties'.[61] 'Nations that are parties to these committees are required to submit reports on a periodic basis to document their compliance'... [on] statements issued by the committees interpreting human rights instruments to prohibit female circumcision.[62]

In addition, 'The UN General Assembly has issued a Declaration on the Elimination of Violence Against Women, which characterizes [FC].'[63] The Women's Convention is another human rights instrument that is vital to the international campaign against FC.[64] CEDAW General Recommendation No. 14 puts substantive provisions on FC as a form of gender-based discrimination within the meaning of the Women's Convention.[65] The Convention imposes a definitive duty on the participating States to reevaluate their cultural traditions and determine whether these traditions discriminate against women and, if so, to abolish them.[66]

Further, calls to eliminate FC are found in documents adopted at regional and international conferences, like the Cairo Conference, and the Beijing Declaration and Platform of Action.[67] The European Council also designated FC

Women Article 1 (85th Plenary Meeting, 1993), A/RES/48/104; General Assembly Resolution adopting the Declaration on the Elimination of Violence against Women, A/RES.48/104, December 20, 1993, Article 2(a); CEDAW, General Recommendation No. 19, Eleventh Session, 1992, Violence Against Women, A/47/38 (General Comments). CEDAW General Recommendation No. 14, under General Comments supports the fact that FC is indeed a matter of gender discrimination, A/45/38 (General Comments).

[61] RAHMAN and TOUBIA, *supra* note 60, p. 12. Other committees have been established under, *e.g.*, the Covenant on Civil and Political Rights (ICCPR), the Convention on the Rights of the Child (CRC).

[62] *Ibid.*, p. 19. See CEDAW, General Recommendation No. 14, Female Circumcision, A/45/38 (General Comments); Committee on the Rights of the Child (CRC), Concluding Observations of the Committee on the Rights of the Child: Togo (Fifteenth Session, 1997), CRC/C/15/Add. 83; Human Rights Committee, Concluding Observations of the Human Rights Committee: Sudan (Sixty-first Session, 1997) CCPR/C/79/Add. 85.

[63] Such declarations, even though not binding, may be considered evidence of international custom or general principles of law, and even the basis for formulation of a future treaty. *Ibid.*, para. 2.

[64] The WOMEN'S CONVENTION, *supra* note 58.

[65] CEDAW, General Recommendation No. 14. See also WELLERSTEIN, *supra* note 15, p. 117, '[The Women's Convention] calls for an end to all forms of gender-based discrimination and establishes international machinery for the implementation of proclamations such as the Universal Declaration of Human Rights and the International Covenant on Civil and Political Rights.'

[66] *Ibid.*, Article 5.

[67] RAHMAN and TOUBIA, *supra* note 60, p. 19. See also Program of Action of the International Conference on Population and Development, Cairo, Egypt, 5–13 September 1994, in Report of the International Conference on Population and Development, UN Doc. A/CONF. 171/13/Rev.I, UN Sales No. 95XIII.18, 1995 (paras. 4.22, 5.5, 7.6, 7.40); Beijing Declaration and Platform for Action, Fourth World Conference on Women, Beijing, China, 4–15 September

as an 'inhumane procedure.'[68] The African Charter on Human Rights prevents this same kind of torture or inhumane or degrading treatment while also referring to the protection of the rights of women and children as outlined in international declarations and conventions.[69] 'The African Charter on the Rights and Welfare of the Child states in Article 21, "appropriate measures can be taken in order to eradicate traditional practices and customs which are prejudicial to the child."'[70] These Charters have been signed and ratified by many African countries where FC still takes place.

'Many European countries, including Belgium, the Netherlands, Norway, Sweden and Switzerland, have passed laws making [FC] an independent crime [assault] or have specifically included it in the definition of criminal child abuse.'[71] The United Kingdom passed the Prohibition of Female Circumcision Act in 1985, outlawing the two more severe forms of mutilation.[72] In 1994, the Canadian Deputy Prime Minister announced that Canadian criminal laws would condemn FC, regardless of the fact that Canadian laws made no specific reference to it.[73] The United States outlawed FC in the Federal Prohibition of Female Genital Mutilation of 1995.[74] Some African countries have implemented laws banning FC to put force behind the international prohibition.[75]

While it is important to draft international legal documents that specifically prohibit the practice of FC, like Recommendation No. 14 above, it is not

---

1995, 1 UN Doc. DPI/1766/Wom, 1996 (paras. 107, 113, 124, 232, 277). Both articles explicitly urge governments to take action to eliminate female circumcision in the 'context of calls to improve women's status, reduce violence against women, and improve women's health'. *Ibid.*, para. 3.

[68] Article 3 European Convention on Human Rights and Fundamental Freedoms (ECHR).

[69] African Charter on the Human and Peoples' Rights, 27 June 1981, 21 *I.L.M.* 58, Articles 5 and 18(3), reprinted in Basic Documents Supplement to International Law, p. 509, p. 511, p. 514.

[70] NAHID TOUBIA, *Female Genital Mutilation: A Call for Global Action*, 2nd Edition, Rainbo, New York, 1995, p. 57.

[71] NATALIE J. FRIEDENTHAL, 'It's Not All Mutilation: Distinguishing Between Female Genital Mutilation and Female Circumcision', *New York International Law Review* (19 *NYILR* 111), Winter 2006, pp. 126–127. Combating Female Genital Mutilation in the EU, Texts adopted, European Parliament, EU 2008/2071(INI), available at www.europarl.europa.eu/sides/getDoc.do?pubRef=-//EP//TEXT+TA+20090324+ITEMS+DOC+XML+V0//EN&language=EN#sdocta16.

[72] HARP, *Female Genital Mutilation/Female Circumcision*, available at www.harpweb.org.uk/content.php?section=women&sub=w9 (last visited 25 August 2010). See also BBC NEWS ONLINE: HEALTH, *Female Circumcision Clampdown Call*, November 22, 2000, available at www.news.bbc.co.uk/1/low/health/1033732.stm (last visited 25 August 2010).

[73] ANNAS, *supra* note 35, p. 334.

[74] See Federal Prohibition of Female Genital Mutilation Act of 1995, 18 U.S.C. §116(a) (2005) (asserting that any person who assists the infibulation of another will face legal consequences), available at www.fgmnetwork.org/legisl/US/federal.html (last visited 26 August 2010).

[75] Benin, Burkina Faso, Central African Republic, Chad, Cote d'Ivoire, Djibouti, Egypt (Ministerial decree), Ghana, Guinea, Kenya, Niger, Nigeria (multiple States), Senegal, Tanzania, Togo. In Sudan only the most severe form of FGM/FGC is forbidden by law. Available at www.unfpa.org/gender/practices2.htm#21 (last visited 12 May 2010).

enough.[76] Some scholars argue that the creation of these international laws impose no punishment for disobedience, and are therefore ineffective.[77] They propose that individual countries must enforce criminal laws prohibiting FC and punish those who practice it, thereby making an unequivocal statement that the practice will not be tolerated.[78]

Even though the practice is usually punishable under assault or child abuse laws as provided by some States, cases are never taken before the courts.[79] France is the only State where FC cases have been actively prosecuted.[80] Therefore, even though the passage of the various national provisions or criminal laws in the cases of FC are timely, as noted at the beginning of Recommendation No. 14 above,[81] the implementation of the provisions is usually non existent. This is mainly because both victims and perpetrators of the practice are insulated within their communities, and often do not report it.[82] Another reason given for the non-implementation is that FC is practised in remote places where governments have no easy access.[83]

6. IS LEGISLATION ENOUGH? THE ENFORCEMENT OF THE WOMEN'S CONVENTION

Under the scope of several international human rights treaties and conventions, FC can be seen as a human rights violation.[84] While some of these instruments are of a more universal and non-gender-specific nature, the Women's Convention

---

[76] See also WELLERSTEIN, *supra* note 15, p. 102.
[77] *Ibid.*
[78] *Ibid.*
[79] KOOL, *supra* note 31, p. 100.
[80] *Ibid.* Female genital mutilation is a crime in France, but judges usually choose suspended sentences subject to probation over incarceration even though France estimates that 4,000 girls undergo female genital mutilation within its borders every year. See A. DOROZYNSKI, 'French Court Rules in Female Circumcision Case', 309 *brit. Med. J.*, 1994, pp. 831–32, available at: www.bmj.bmjjournals.com/cgi/content/full/309/6958/831/a (last visited on August 25, 2010). Although it seems like legislation is effective toward the prevention of FC where only a small minority are practitioners (for example western countries with immigrants from Africa or Asia), the laws are not usually implemented. See also Texts adopted, European Parliament, *supra* note 71.
[81] Recommendation No.14; 'Noting with satisfaction that Governments where such practices exist ... remain seized of the issue having particularly recognized that such traditional practices as female circumcision have serious health and other consequences for women and children.'
[82] See also WELLERSTEIN, *supra* note 15, p. 102.
[83] *Ibid.* See also Recommendation No. 14 above; 'Noting with grave concern that there are continuing cultural, traditional and economic pressures which help to perpetuate harmful practices, such as female circumcision.'
[84] BARRET BREITUNG, 'Interpretation and Eradication: National and International Responses to Female Circumcision', *Emory International Law Review (10 EMORY Int'l L. Rev. 657)*, Winter 1996, p. 678.

addresses gender-related issues and special needs of women.[85] The Convention calls for States to end gender discrimination by modifying social and cultural patterns.[86] In particular, the Convention creates an obligation to protect women from FC by calling on ratifying States to reexamine traditional practices that can be harmful to women.[87] The progress of the Convention's implementation is monitored through the efforts of CEDAW which reports annually to the UN General Assembly.[88]

'Unfortunately, [the Women's Convention] suffers from a predicament that many human rights instruments face. It cannot be strictly enforced since most states remain unwilling to accord international jurisdiction to those entities which could mandate compliance with the terms of human rights treaties.'[89] A high number of reservations to the Convention have been put forward under the guise of cultural relativism, making the Convention subject to fewer restrictions, thus, weaker implementation obligations and procedures.[90] Some States have even asserted that the Convention 'should be afforded a lesser status than other treaties because its subject matter is culturally sensitive.'[91] Furthermore, CEDAW, as a monitoring body, has been provided fewer resources and given a lesser mandate, making it difficult to supply an enforcement mechanism for the investing and adjudication of complaints arising under the terms of the Convention.[92]

CEDAW has been set up to monitor treaty compliance and investigate allegations that states are not living up to their treaty obligations. Signatories to the treaty submit reports every four years after which CEDAW releases its Concluding Observations, stating what more the country should do to be in compliance. From the observations, there is little evidence that governments are attempting to monitor the effectiveness of their laws and policies and to strengthen enforcement mechanisms and implement all actions necessary to ensure *de facto* equality for women.[93] For example, even though States are obligated to submit reports every four years, if they fall behind in their reporting,

---

[85] Ibid.
[86] Women's Convention, *supra* note 58, Articles 2(f), 5(a), 10 and 12.
[87] BREITUNG, *supra* note 84, p. 683.
[88] G.A. Res. 180, UN Doc. A/34/180, 1980, Article 17.
[89] JULIE DIMAURO, 'Toward a More Effective Guarantee of Women's Human Rights: A Multicultural Dialogue in International Law', *Women's Rights Law Reporter*, Summer 1996, p. 342.
[90] BREITUNG, *supra* note 84, p. 683. See also Ontario Women's Justice Network (OWJN), 'Legal Information on Issues Related to Violence Against Women,' available at www.owjn.org/owjn_2009/index.php?option=com_content&view=article&id=281%Acedaw-background-information&catid=59&Itemid=108 (last visited 7 March 2011).
[91] NANCY KIM, 'Toward a Feminist Theory of Human Rights: Straddling the Fence Between Western Imperialism and Uncritical Absolutism', *Columbia Human Rights Law Review* (25 COLUM. Hum. Rts. Rev. 69), p. 81.
[92] Ibid. See also OWJN, *supra* note 90.
[93] SHANTHI DAIRIAM, 'The Status of CEDAW Implementation in the ASEAN Countries and Selected Muslim Countries', 2003, *Presented at the Round Table Discussion on Rights and Obligations Under CEDAW*, Kuala Lumpur, Malaysia, p. 17.

they are not reprimanded, but encouraged to present consolidated reports.[94] This shows that the failure of States to maintain their obligation to the Convention is less vigilantly pursued. For example, The Gambia, a State where FC is still widely practised, provided the last report in 2005. In their concluding comments, CEDAW only expressed concern at the high incidence of FC, and lack of mechanisms aimed at eradicating the practice.[95] It then urged the State to 'adopt and adequately implement legislation prohibiting [FC], and to ensure that offenders are adequately prosecuted and punished,'[96] as well as develop a plan of action to eliminate the practice.[97] Today, no action has been taken by the State of Gambia where FC eradication is concerned. Communities are working together, without the support of the government to end the practice.[98]

CEDAW encourages governments to include Non Governmental Organizations (hereinafter NGOs) in preparing their reports, and these NGOs are further invited to give direct input in the form of independent or 'shadow' reports, which play a big role in the Concluding Observations.[99] However, even though CEDAW issues general recommendations in the Concluding Observations, they do not have authority to issue sanctions.[100]

Under the terms of the Optional Protocol to the Women's Convention, women gained the right to take complaints directly to the UN in the form of individual complaints.[101] Although the Protocol has gained widespread international acceptance, the number of complaints dealt with by CEDAW has been limited. An assessment of the Protocol found that it had rarely been used as expected, and thus had no impact on policy-making.[102] The assessment found that even though there had been some limited access in highlighting the importance of effective policies to protect women from domestic violence and sterilization, the Protocol 'has not led to a breakthrough in advancing women's

---

[94] International Women's Rights Action Watch, *Producing Shadow Reports to the CEDAW Committee: A Procedural Guide, January*, 2009, available at www.1.umn.edu/humanrts/wraw/proceduralguide-08.html (last visited 1 March 2011).
[95] CEDAW, 'Concluding Comments: Gambia,' 33rd Session, 22 July 2005, available at www2.ohchr.org/english/bodies/cedaw/docs/CEDAW.C.GMB.CO.1-3_en.pdf, p. 4.
[96] *Ibid.*, p. 5.
[97] *Ibid.*
[98] JULIA LALLA-MAHARAJH, 'How the Gambia is Fighting FGC,' *World News*, 5 February 2011, available at www.thedailybeast.com/blogs-and-stories/2011-02-05/female-genital-cutting-how-the-gambia-is-fighting-it/ (last visited 6 March 2011).
[99] International Women's Rights Action, *supra* note 94.
[100] OWJN, *supra* note 90.
[101] See Optional Protocol to the Women's Convention, available at www.un.org/womenwatch/daw/cedaw/protocol. This is an international treaty which establishes complaint and inquiry mechanisms for the Women's Convention. Parties to the Protocol allow CEDAW to hear complaints from individuals or inquire into 'grave or systematic violations' of the Convention. On the Optional Protocol also see Chapter 21 by Sille Jansen.
[102] JIM MURDOCH, 'The Optional Protocol to the United Nations Women's Convention. The Experience of the United Kingdom', available at www.justice.gov.uk/publications/docs/un-optional-protocol-women.pdf, pp. 12–17.

rights.'[103] The complaints mechanisms of the Protocol are lengthy and lack transparency, while the recommendations given by CEDAW are not legally binding. All of these factors are seen by critics as key limits to effectiveness.[104]

Traditional attitudes by which women are regarded as subordinate to men or as having stereotyped roles perpetuate widespread practices involving violence or coercion, among which FC is just one. The excuse for the continuing practice of FC is that 'girls who have not experienced the procedure may suffer emotionally from certain social consequences, such as difficulty in finding a spouse or in gaining acceptance among peers.'[105] 'However, the adverse social consequences faced by some girls and women, must, of course, be viewed in light of the negative health effects of [FC], as well as the implications of the procedure on women's subordinate status.'[106] The Women's Convention addresses the issue of discrimination and the specific obligations for States.[107] However, these Articles are rarely addressed by State parties in their reports, since many discriminatory practices are specifically grounded in custom. States rarely acknowledge that ratification of the Women's Convention requires them to abandon the defence of custom and to promote new attitudes.[108]

States are required by the Women's Convention to take measures to ensure equal access to healthcare.[109] FC as a form of violence puts girls' and women's health at risk. The complications associated with FC can have devastating effects upon a woman's and child's physical and psychological (emotional) health, thus this procedure can be viewed as an infringement of the right to health, and not just as being prejudicial to the health and well-being of women and children.[110]

---

[103] Ibid.
[104] See CATHERINE MACKINNON, 'CEDAW's Optional Protocol Procedures', Interights Bulletin 14(4), 2004, pp. 173–174. See also BAL SOKHI-BALLEY, 'The Optional Protocol to CEDAW: First Steps,' Human Rights Law Review 6 (1), 2006, p. 157.
[105] RAHMAN and TOUBIA, supra note 60, p. 30. See also KAY L. LEVINE, 'Negotiating the Boundaries of Crime and Culture: A Sociolegal Perspective on Cultural Defense Strategies', 28 Law & Soc. Inquiry 39, 2003, p. 63 (noting that parents force their children to undergo [FC] in order to prevent them from becoming social outcasts); LORI ANN LARSON, 'Female Genital Mutilation in the United States: Child Abuse or Constitutional Freedom?', 17 Women's Rts. L. Rep. 237, 1996, pp. 246–47 (claiming that it is usually women who have undergone genital mutilation who subject their daughters to the same procedure).
[106] RAHMAN and TOUBIA, supra note 60, p. 27.
[107] Women's Convention, supra note 58, Articles 2(f), 5 and 10(c). See also DEUTSCHES INSTITUT FÜR MENSCHENRECHTE, 'The Optional Protocol to CEDAW: Mitigating Violations of Women's Human Rights', International Seminar for NGOs and Women's Rights Activists, Berlin, Germany, 13–15 March 2003, available at www.institut-fuer-menschenrechte.de/uploads/tx_commerce/documentation_the_optional_protocol_to_cedaw.pdf (last visited 3 March 2011), p. 4. These Articles refer to a set of actions that States must undertake to comply with specific obligations.
[108] Ibid., DEUTSCHES INSTITUT FÜR MENSCHENRECHTE, p. 7.
[109] Women's Convention, supra note 58, Article 12.
[110] RAHMAN and TOUBIA, supra note 60, p. 27. See also Recommendation No. 14.

Even in the absence of such complications, FC comprises a violation of the right to health. 'Any invasive procedure – no matter how "safely" performed – entails risks to the health of the person who undergoes it. Subjecting a person to health risks in the absence of medical necessity should be viewed as a violation of that person's right to health.'[111] Further, where the practice results in the removal of bodily tissue necessary for the enjoyment of a satisfying and safe sex life, a woman's right to the 'highest attainable' standard of physical and mental health has been compromised.[112] Practical application by States still remains a problem, because most of the women and girls who undergo FC do not have access to the healthcare system in case of complications.[113] In addition, many of the States do not have preventive measures in place, thus little effort is expended on preventing the procedure from taking place.[114]

Although the rights under The Universal Declaration of Human Rights (hereinafter Universal Declaration) are directly relevant to the practice of FC, the traditional interpretation of these rights has generally failed to include violence against women. 'This [oversight] arises from a common misconception that States are not responsible for human rights abuses committed within the home or the community.[115] Violence against women was not initially included in the Women's Convention, but was later directly addressed in Recommendations Nos. 12 and 19.[116] Recommendation No. 14 specifically brings to the forefront that the practice of FC violates internationally recognized human rights, such as the right to health,[117] the right to be free from Torture and other Cruel, Inhumane or Degrading Treatment or Punishment (hereinafter CATCID)[118] the

---

[111] *Ibid.*, pp. 27–28.
[112] *Ibid.*
[113] BREITUNG, *supra* note 84, p. 681. See also HUMAN RIGHTS WATCH, 'They Took Me and Told Me Nothing: Female Genital Mutilation – A Human Rights Issue,' available at www.hrw.org/en/node/90862/section/7#_ftnref233.
[114] *Ibid.*
[115] WELLERSTEIN, *supra* note 15, p. 117; 'The Universal Declaration of Human Rights (Universal Declaration) which is the cornerstone of the modern human rights system, asserts that "[a]ll human beings are born free and equal in dignity and rights." It protects the right to personal security and the right not to be subjected to torture or to cruel, inhuman, or degrading treatment.'
[116] CEDAW, General Recommendation No. 12, 8th session, 1989, Violence Against Women; CEDAW, General Recommendation No. 19, 11th session, 1992, Violence against women. On violence against women also see Chapter 22 by Kate Rose-Sender.
[117] See Universal Declaration of Human Rights, G.A. Res. 217A (III), UN GAOR, 3rd Sess., Article 25, UN Doc. A/810, 1948 (hereinafter Universal Declaration); UN Declaration on the Elimination of Violence Against Women, G.A. Res. 48/104, UN GAOR, 48th Sess., Article 3(f), UN Doc. A/48/629, reprinted in 33 I.L.M., 1994, pp. 1049, 1052 (hereinafter Violence Against Women Declaration).
[118] Convention Against Torture and Other Cruel, Inhuman or Degrading Treatment or Punishment, G.A. Res. 46, UN GAOR, 39th Sess., Supp. No. 51, at 197, UN Doc. A/39/708 (1984) (hereinafter CATCID). To be covered by the Convention, torture must be inflicted by or "with the consent or acquiescence of a public official or other person acting in an official capacity." The failure of African countries to enforce existing laws prohibiting female

right to personal dignity,[119] the right to be free from discrimination,[120] and the rights of children.[121] Claiming as torture or degrading treatment that which most of society views as normal and beneficial because of culture, makes the freedom-from-torture approach unlikely to be much help in eradicating FC.[122] The rights-of-the-child approach also offers little success in this regard.[123] Most mothers circumcise their daughters because they believe in the procedure and want their daughters to have the social benefits and acceptance that come with FC.[124] Therefore, even though the Women's Convention enables women and girls, at least in theory, to contest FC, on grounds of gender equality and health, it might not help much in the international campaign to eradicate the practice.

USING MULTI-LEVEL APPROACHES TO ELIMINATE FC

With an arsenal of treaties, conventions, and resolutions, the international campaign against FC is well equipped doctrinally. However, the ambitious declarations in these documents can only be realized if they are effectively enforced. Lack of effective enforcement is the perennial obstacle to the realization and enjoyment of international legal rights.[125] With no implementation, women are forced to fight isolated battles against a practice that is still being allowed to continue. FC is considered to be quite different from other internationally recognized fundamental human rights violations, however, because there is no literal 'State action' involved.[126] Those fighting for changes must take into account the deeply felt beliefs of the people who practise FC, and

---

circumcision arguably satisfies CATCID's "acquiescence of a public official" requirement. BREITUNG, *supra* note 86, p. 682. See also Universal Declaration, Article 5.

[119] See International Covenant on Civil and Political Rights, opened for signature 16 December 1966, Article 9, 999 UNTS 171, 172 (entered into force 23 March 1976); Universal Declaration, *supra* note 117, Article 1.

[120] See Violence Against Women Declaration, *supra* note 60, Article 3(e), p. 1052. FC is rooted in discrimination against women. It is an instrument for socializing girls into prescribed roles within the family and community. It is therefore intimately linked to the unequal position of women in the political, social, [cultural] and economic structures of societies where it is practiced. See also WELLERSTEIN, *supra* note 15, p. 115; '[FC] is a ritual of purification that reinforces a woman's subordination by repressing her sexuality and controlling her reproductive functions.' The ritual is used to ensure a woman's chastity and reinforce her role as her husband's property, thus is one way men continue to derive power and control over women as a group.

[121] CRC, *supra* note 59.

[122] BREITUNG, *supra* note 84, p. 682.

[123] *Ibid.*, p. 679.

[124] *Ibid.*, p. 680.

[125] ERIKA SUSSMAN, 'Contending with Culture: An Analysis of the Female Genital Mutilation Act of 1996, *Cornell International Law Journal* (31 Cornell Int'l L.J. 193), 1998, p. 204.

[126] WELLERSTEIN, *supra* note 15, p. 114. Traditionally, international governing bodies and non-governmental organizations have focused on protesting human rights violations inflicted, sanctioned, or mandated directly by governments.

not just blindly campaign for enforcement of international and local legislation that criminalizes the practice. The issue should be addressed on all fronts by uniting the international community and uniformly declaring that FC violates fundamental human rights.[127]

States should not just provide specific legislation, but also give funding to enable communities to (1) devote significant amounts of attention to educating both men and women about the health hazards, dangers and horrors of the practice, (2) develop culturally sensitive outreach activities for victims and perpetrators of the ritual, and (3) involve governmental agencies and community-based organizations in the fight to abolish FC, through, *e.g.* introducing alternative recourses to the legislative prohibition of the practice, like spiritualization (circumcision through words) and clinicalization.[128] States should also provide 'public information campaign about the effect of the practice on children, and private counseling of parents whenever possible.'[129]

Preventive healthcare measures involving physician-led education campaigns and strict monitoring of the midwives and doctors performing FC could be integral to the successful eradication of the practice.[130] Information on why the practice is prevalent, the physical and psychological effects as well as religious requirements should be accessible to a broad range of people and disseminated on a wider scale.[131] 'Understanding the spread of the practice through this light will enable opponents of FC to start to make a difference.'[132] Communities in States that do not take any action to implement the laws should assemble in large numbers and exert pressure on their government leaders in order to implement low-cost education and health maintenance programmes and also help prevent medically unnecessary surgeries from occurring.[133]

It is also important to recognize the influence of societal and psychological pressures. Indeed, this is also so in Western States, where, due to overwhelming patriarchal influence and socialization, many women believe that they must undergo plastic surgery in order to gain social status and acceptance among their peers. This is the same acceptance the women in communities practicing FC seek. Thus, in both cases, the women are often unaware of the severe medical, physical and emotional harms associated with either procedure. These women usually become submissive to the procedures in hopes of being considered

---

[127] WELLERSTEIN, *supra* note 15, p. 103.
[128] See JESSICA A. PLATT, *Female Circumcision: Religious Practice v. Human Rights Violation*, available at www.org.law.rutgers.edu/publications/law-religion/articles/RJLR_3_1_5.pdf, p. 27. See also *Ibid.*
[129] TOUBIA, *supra* note 6, p. 234.
[130] DIMAURO, *supra* note 89, p. 343.
[131] TOUBIA, *supra* note 6, p. 232. See also Recommendation No.14 (a) (iv) which recommends introduction of educational and training programmes.
[132] CARDENAS, *supra* note 1, p. 311.
[133] DIMAURO, *supra* note 89, p. 344.

'normal' in their society.[134] 'Perhaps the way we convince a woman that she is feminine and beautiful regardless of her breast size is the same way we begin to change the belief that, to be a "real woman," one needs to be circumcised.'[135]

Implementation of the laws should also include aggregating local knowledge from the communities practicing FC and international technical and financial resources to create a multitude of programmes.[136] Critical stakeholders in elimination efforts include influential members of the community such as religious leaders, health professionals and teachers, as well as traditional midwives.[137] Traditional midwives who perform circumcision should be given information on the harmful consequences FC and the opportunity to acquire employable skills and alternative sources of income. Midwives who abandon the practice have a potentially powerfully constructive role to play in efforts to eliminate it.[138]

There is currently a network of organizations working with local African communities to stop FC.[139] They have begun to promote alternative methods to the FC practice. This is done at the local level to help change the community's consciousness. One of these changes is 'circumcision through words,' which encourages FC to occur spiritually rather than physically. 'Circumcision through words' grew out of the collaborated efforts of a Kenyan group, Maendeleo Ya Wanawake Organization (hereinafter MYWO), and the Program for Appropriate Technology in Health (hereinafter PATH) in an attempt to prevent the health complications associated with the practice of FC from occurring.[140] This includes a week-long programme of counseling, training and informing young women on the basic concepts of sexual and reproductive health and hygiene.[141] This method rejects the harmful practice of FC, while retaining and celebrating the rich African traditions that are both beneficial and central to the fabric of African life.[142] A similar ritual is being carried out in Uganda among the Sabiny tribe. The programme in this community is promoted by elders in the clan who formed the Elders Association in 1992.[143] Recently, another African women's empowerment group, Tostan, started working with communities that practice FC in The Gambia.[144] This organization provides information about basic rights

---

[134] CARDENAS, *supra* note: p. 292.
[135] *Ibid.*, p. 311.
[136] TOUBIA, *supra* note 6, p. 233.
[137] HUMAN RIGHTS WATCH, *supra* note 113.
[138] *Ibid.*
[139] RAHMAN and TOUBIA, *supra* note 60, p. 12.
[140] CESAR CHELALA, 'New Rite is Alternative to Female Circumcision', *San Francisco Chronicle*, 16 September 1998, available at www.articles.sfgate.com/1998-09-16/opinion/17730816_1_female-circumcision-bat-mitzvah-female-genital-mutilation (last visited 6 August 2010).
[141] PLATT, *supra* note 128, p. 27. See also CHELALA, *Ibid.*
[142] SANUMAN, *supra* note 25.
[143] CHELALA, *supra* note 140.
[144] LALLA-MAHARAJH, *supra* note 98. See also Tostan Community-led Development, available at www.tostan.org.

to health and freedom from harm. Through this knowledge, the communities themselves identify what no longer serves them. They also discover 'the stronger links between, for example, [FC] and tetanus'[145] – understanding that there are invisible germs that lead to an infection after an initial wound, which can lead to death.[146] This concept works with the ultimate respect for the community and addresses the issue at the root, thus, making sure that the changes made are sustainable and owned.[147] These alternative methods have hopes of success and are not resisted by the communities practicing FC because they offer an attractive alternative towards improving women's and girls' health as well as quality of life, rather than a blunt prohibition to a long-established cultural practice.

Another alternative that is very controversial is clinicalization of FC. The combination of trained physicians and advanced medical science and technology renders the practice of FC more sanitary, limiting adverse health consequences to women and children.[148] Some scholars argue that this fact diminishes the usefulness of a campaign that focuses solely on the health hazards and physical repercussions associated with FC.[149] The practice provides no medical benefits and leads to many adverse physical and psychological complications, for example infibulation, which then require the consultation of a physician.[150] The American Academy of Pediatrics (hereinafter AAP) revised a 1998 policy that condemned all forms of FC to allow doctors to 'offer the nick' to immigrant communities (this proposal was retracted).[151]

'Although [FC] is not what the human rights violation activists typically target, it should receive the same consideration as other violations of the fundamental rights to be free from bodily invasion and torture.'[152] Apart from human rights, the practice should be linked to other rights, like health, religion, women's economic development, education, family planning and child development.[153]

---

[145] *Ibid.*
[146] *Ibid.*
[147] *Ibid.*
[148] PLATT, *supra* note 128, p. 27.
[149] DIMAURO, *supra* note 89, p. 344. See also CARDENAS, *supra* note 1, p. 312.
[150] MARK GOULD, *Life after Female Genital Mutilation*, Guardian.co.uk, available at www.guardian.co.uk/society/2010/feb/17/reversing-female-genital-mutilation. Consultant gynaecologist Geetha Subramanian is on of only a handful of medical professionals in the United Kingdom to carry out FC reversals (deinfibulation). Dr. Subramanian sees women whose families originate in sub-Saharan Africa, Yemen, the United Arab Emirates, Malaysia and Indonesia.
[151] LYNN HARRIS, *Female Genital Mutilation in the US; No Compromise*, Violence Against Women, available at www.salon.com/life/feature/2010/06/02/fgm_genital_nick (last visited 1 July 2010). Doctors and officials at Harborview hospital in Seattle came up with another alternative, one substantially more specific than the AAP's proposal: a small cut to the clitoral hood, with no tissue excised, conducted under local anesthetic on children old enough to give consent. This proposal was never put in place due to reaction by anti-FC advocates, and the fact that it would be in violation of the Hippocratic oath. See also *Ibid.*
[152] WELLERSTEIN, *supra* note 15, p. 115.
[153] TOUBIA, *supra* note 6, p. 233.

7. CONCLUSION

Despite the number of legislative attempts to prohibit and alleviate the problem of FC, the practice continues in many States around the world. In order for this unhealthy practice to be stopped, the most plausible and effective solution to the conflict between the cultural practice of FC and women's and girls' health rights, is promoting an international understanding of the practice.[154] If women are to be considered as equal and responsible members of society, no aspect of their physical, psychological, or sexual integrity can be compromised.[155] A global action against FC cannot undertake to abolish this one violation of women's rights without placing it firmly within the context of efforts to address the social and economic injustice women face the world over.[156] 'A serious impediment to equality for women is the prevalence of culture and religion, which impact on societal values and make the existing legal framework ineffective.'[157] A concerted effort has to be made by States to combat this situation. The conditions necessary for women to claim their rights under the Women's Convention have to be created, by making policy makers aware of the obligations of the State under the Convention.[158] Greater efforts should also be made to highlight awareness of the Optional Protocol as a complaints mechanism and build trust in the rulings of CEDAW.[159] Some scholars have argued that CEDAW should have the power to take States before a permanent tribunal that has the ability to enforce remedies it suggests, thus sending a strong message to States that women's rights are inviolable and are protected by the weight of international law.[160]

Adopting laws is only one element in what has to be a comprehensive action programme if elimination of FC is to be effective. Criminalization of the practice and approaching it through punitive action against practitioners and family members may drive the practice underground.[161] CEDAW, among other treaty monitoring bodies, has highlighted the importance of educating communities and raising awareness about FC and other harmful practices.[162] The implementation efforts should integrate grassroots education efforts. The

---

[154] RAHMAN and TOUBIA, *supra* note 60, p.13.
[155] TOUBIA, *supra*, note 6, p. 235.
[156] TOUBIA, *supra* note 6, p. 235.
[157] Dairiam, *supra* note 93, p. 17.
[158] Ibid.
[159] MUDORCH, *supra* note 102, p. 27.
[160] OWJN, *supra* note 90. See also Kerri Ritz, 'Soft Enforcement: Inadequacies of Optional Protocol as a Remedy for the Convention on the Elimination of All Forms of Discrimination Against Women', *Suffolk Transnational Law Review* (25 Suffolk Transnat'l L. Rev. 191), 2001.
[161] HUMAN RIGHTS WATCH, *supra* note 113. See also World Health Organization (hereinafter WHO), Department of Women's Health, Health Systems and Community Health, 'Female Genital Mutilation, Programmes to Date: What Works and What Doesn't,' 1999, p. 14 available at www.giga-hamburg.de/content/iaa/archiv/fgm/FGM-Projektuebersicht.pdf.
[162] CEDAW, Recommendation No. 14.

campaign must gradually transform public opinion about the practice through widespread education.[163] The programmes should utilize the resources of local individuals from the communities practicing FC. They should also enlist leadership of people from the community, like healthcare providers, politicians and teachers.[164] Most importantly, there should be sustained and coordinated long-term commitment by the campaigners.[165] 'Research from [States] where [FC] is common shows that an approach addressing the underlying factors which perpetuate the practice and other violations of women's human rights, is essential.'[166] The programmes on elimination of FC should encourage the flow of information, as well as national and local debates involving both men and women, with the aim that communities which interconnect collectively abandon FC.

States should not simply give their assent to the need to protect and promote women's human rights in yet another piece of paper. To achieve something where FC is concerned, conferences should be 'more than just another occasion for fine rhetoric and conviviality.'[167] They must be a genuine catalyst for action and the swift delivery of real protection.

---

[163] SUSSMAN, *supra* note 125, p. 248.
[164] *Ibid.*
[165] *Ibid.*
[166] HUMAN RIGHTS WATCH, *supra* note 113.
[167] Amnesty International Document (ACT 77/01/95), available at www.amnesty.org/en/library/asset/ACT77/001/1995/en/d7c9b031-eb6b-11dd-b8d6-03683db9c805/act770011995en.html) (last visited 26 August 2010).

ARTICLE 13

States parties shall take all appropriate measures to eliminate discrimination against women in other areas of economic and social life in order to ensure, on a basis of equality of men and women, the same rights, in particular:

(a) The right to family benefits;
(b) The right to bank loans, mortgages and other forms of financial credit;
(c) The right to participate in recreational activities, sports and all aspects of cultural life.

CHAPTER 14
EQUALITY AND ECONOMIC AND SOCIAL LIFE INCLUDING IMPLICATIONS FOR THE EUROPEAN UNION

Dagmar SCHIEK and Jule MULDER

1. INTRODUCTION

Article 13 obliges States parties to take all appropriate measures to eliminate discrimination against women in other areas of economic and social life. It lists a few specific fields (family benefits, bank loans, mortgages and other forms of financial credit, and recreational activities, sports and cultural life), but this list is non-exhaustive. Accordingly, Article 13 also covers areas of economic and social life which are not explicitly mentioned. Article 13(a) and (b), which aim at supporting financial autonomy of women, should be seen in conjunction with Article 14 on rural women.[1] This provision stresses Signatory States' obligation to take special account of the situation of rural women. This special situation is *inter alia* characterized by them being active in the informal sector of the economy, and therefore face specific problems accessing family benefits and financial credits. In reading Articles 13 and 14 together, Signatory States are obliged to pay specific attention to potential exclusion of rural women from benefits and credits.

Article 13 focuses on State and non-State actors within the cultural and economic sphere alike, and is, as such, an important provision in order to achieve substantive equality within the public and the private sphere.[2] 'Access to economic resources, participation in labour force, and control over income'

---

[1] Jo LYNN SOUTHARD, 'Protection of Women Human Rights under the Convention on the Elimination of all Forms of Discrimination Against Women', *Pace University School of Law International Law Review*, 8(1), 1996, p. 57.

[2] On the substantial equality approach within the Convention see, for example: ALDA FACIO and MARTHA I. MORGAN, 'Equity or Equality for Women? Understanding CEDAW's Equality Principle', *Alabama Law Review*, 60, 2008–09, pp. 1133–70.

determine a woman's status within society.³ Hence, the Convention aims at the 'practical realization of the principle of equality between women and men'.⁴ Private organizations and companies, such as banks, which have *de facto* influence on the opportunities of women, deserve special attention. States parties are therefore not only obliged to treat women equally but also have to ensure that non-State actors respect the Convention, by appropriate national legislation.⁵

We will discuss the content of Article 13 within the broader context of the UN and also draw some comparisons with EU law, in order to establish whether the EU hinders its Member States to fulfil their Convention obligations.

2. BROADER CONTEXT OF ARTICLE 13 WITHIN THE UN

Within the broader context of the UN political agenda, the Millennium Development Goals (MDGs) deserve special attention. These are central to today's UN development policies, which again impacts on gender relations. The Millennium Goals have been criticized for not appropriately reflecting gender equality within development targets. However, once the Goals are considered through the lens of the Convention it becomes quite obvious, how the Convention can strengthen the MDGs by addressing gender inequality as one of the causes of poverty.⁶ This is obvious in relation to their aim to 'promote gender equality and empower women'.⁷ However, also specific goals can contribute to a contextual reading of Article 13 Women's Convention. This is true, especially for Goal 1a, which aims at the reduction by half the proportion of people living on less than a dollar a day.⁸ If interpreted in context with this goal, Article 13 Convention on the Elimination of all Forms of Discrimination Against Women should not only be understood within a feminist empowerment paradigm but also within a poverty alleviation paradigm:⁹ women are often the

---

3   VALENTINE M. MOGHADAM, 'Women in Societies', *International Social Science Journal*, 43, 1994, p. 101.
4   CEDAW/C/DEU/CO/6, Concluding observations of the Committee on the Elimination of Discrimination Against Women, Germany, [Committee on the Elimination of Discrimination against Women Forty-third session 19 January – 6 February 2009] 10 February 2009, para. 22.
5   AIDA GONZÁLEZ MARTINEZ, 'Human Rights of Women', *Washington University Journal of Law & Policy*, 5, 2001, p. 171.
6   CERI HAYES, 'Out of the margins: the MDGs Though a CEDAW lens', *Gender & Development*, 13(1), 2005, p. 67.
7   See Goal 3, available at: www.undp.org/mdg/goal3.shtml [accessed: 15 September 2010].
8   See Goal 1a, available at: www.undp.org/mdg/goal1.shtml [accessed: 15 September 2010].
9   In general on such paradigms in relation to micro-credits MINISTRY OF WOMEN AFFAIRS NEW ZEALAND, 'Microfinance and women in literature' available at: www.mwa.govt.nz/news-and-pubs/publications/work-and-enterprise/women-in-literature [accessed 15 September 2010].

main provider in the family and at the same time constitute more than 50% of the poorest population.[10] Therefore, it is very important to grant women access to family benefits and financial services in order to ensure their participation on an equal footing with men in economic life. Such access is often denied as a result of stereotypes and/or legal concepts which seem to imply that a woman can only be the head of the household if there is no husband or other male family member.[11] Such stereotypes do not only prevent women from their empowerment but also harm the general economic development of the country.[12] Accordingly, enforcing the Convention can contribute to achieving the aims of the International Covenant on Economic, Social and Cultural Rights (ICESCR), which also has potential for mutual reinforcement. Being not gender specific, the ICESCR seems to face less controversy in some Signatory States.[13] It can thus become a tool for promoting aims pursued by Article 13 Convention on the Elimination of All Forms of Discrimination against Women. This seems even more important as Article 13 itself has not enjoyed much attention in the past as the Committee on the Elimination of All forms of Discrimination Against Women (CEDAW) seems to focus on other aspects of the Convention. The ICESCR itself also guarantees the equal access to economic, social and cultural rights in Articles 2(2) and 3. The Covenant does not only include a formal test of equal treatment, but a 'sophisticated methodology'[14] in order to 'define discrimination as legislation or practice, which maintain or aggravate disadvantages of a subjugated group in society'.[15] Furthermore, Article 9 explicitly ensures the right to social security, including family benefits,[16] which has, in conjunction with Articles 2 and 3, to be available to men and women alike. Finally, the Covenant also recognizes the right to take part in the cultural life, in Article 15.

The ICESCR, just like the Convention on the Elimination of All Forms of Discrimination against Women, aims at substantive equality when it comes to equal access to social, economic and cultural rights.[17] It can thus be read as

---

[10] JANICE WOOD WETZEL, *The World of Women: in Pursuit of Human Rights*, Macmillan, Basingstoke, England, 1993, p. 88.
[11] LYNN SOUTHARD, footnote 1, p. 58.
[12] See the preamble of the Convention, para. 7. LYNN SOUTHARD, footnote 1, p. 25.
[13] KARIMA BENNOUNE, 'The International Covenant on Economic, Social and Cultural Rights as a tool for combating discrimination against women: general observations and a case study on Algeria', *International Social Science Journal*, 2005, p. 351.
[14] KARIMA BENNOUNE, footnote 13, p. 353.
[15] KATARINA FROSTELL and MARTINA SCHEININ, 'Women', in: Asbjørn Eide, Catarina Krause and Allan Rosas (eds.), *Social, Economic and Cultural Rights: a textbook*, Kluwer Law International, The Hague, 2001, p. 336.
[16] CESCR General Comment No. 19, (General Comments), *The Right to Social Security (Article 9)* Thirty-ninth session (5–23 November 2007) E/C.12/GC/19, 4 February 2008, paras. 12–21.
[17] CESCR General Comment No. 16, (General Comments): *The equal right of men and women to the enjoyment of all economic, social and cultural rights (Article 3)* Thirty-fourth session

demanding consideration for women's real life experience instead of regarding experiences of men as the general norm. In this way, it can be read to counteract indirect inequalities and *de facto* discrimination within its material scope.

Finally, Article 26 International Covenant on Civil and Political Rights (ICCPR) has also to be considered. Although the Covenant aims at civil and political rights, Article 26 is interpreted as a '"free standing" right to equality' which effect does not depend on the subject matter of the case and whether such is covered by the ICCPR.[18] Therefore the Human Rights Committee can decide cases on the basis of Article 26 ICCPR which also fall within the scope of Article 13 of the Convention on the Elimination of All Forms of Discrimination against Women.

3. ARTICLE 13 ANALYSED

Article 13 is split in three sections. Section a focuses on family benefits, which are mainly (but not exclusively) supplied by State actors, section b focuses on credits, loans, and credits which are mainly given out by non-State actors and private institutions such as banks or building societies and finally section c focuses on the participation in recreational activities such as sports and other aspects of cultural live, which again can be influenced by both, State and non-State actors. As the different sections cover different areas in the law and address different actors, they will be discussed separately.

3.1. ARTICLE 13(A) (FAMILY BENEFITS)

Article 13(a) guarantees equal access to family benefits. Family benefits are mainly supplied by the State but can also be supplied by non-State actors such as employers who offer additional maternity leave[19] or parental leave or grant family benefits in kind by offering access to a crèche.[20] Family benefits include

---

(25 April-13 May 2005) E/C.12/2005/4, 11 August 2005, paras. 7-9.

[18] See for example, *Broeks v The Netherlands*, Communication No. 172/1984 (9 April 1987), UN Doc. Supp. No. 40 (A/42/40), 129. See also *Netherlands, Communication* No. 182/1984 (9 April 1987), UN Doc. Supp. No. 40 (A/42/40) at 160 (1987), para. 14; JAVAID REHMAN, *International Human Rights Law*, 2nd ed., 2010, Essex, Pearson Education Limited, p. 110.

[19] On the issue of Biological Reproduction in the Context of the Convention: SHELLEY WRIGHT, 'Human Rights and Women's Rights: An Analysis of the United Nations Convention on the Elimination of All Forms of Discrimination Against Women', Kathleen E. Mahoney and Paul Mahoney Editors, *Human Rights in the twenty-first century: A global challenge*, Martinus Nijhoff, Dordrecht, 1993, p. 82.

[20] See also CESCR General Comment No. 16, (General Comments): *The equal right of men and women to the enjoyment of all economic, social and cultural rights (Article 3)* Thirty-fourth session (25 April-13 May 2005) E/C.12/2005/4, 11 August 2005, para. 26.

financial support for young mothers or young families, child benefits or even support to acquire a family home. As the Human Rights Committee pointed out, the States parties are not only obliged to distribute such benefits without any discrimination but also to remove any *de facto* discrimination which impedes individual access to these benefits. In doing so, they should devote special attention to women as one of those groups within society traditionally facing problems to access benefits. This means *inter alia* that gender inequality should be accounted for when designing benefit formulas. Therefore, States have to consider factors which lead directly or indirectly to discrimination, such as different average life expectation, wage inequality, informal economic activities, or child rearing periods.[21]

Problems with Article 13(a) arise, when family benefits are only granted to the head of the household, which is in many countries the husband.[22] Article 13 rejects such an assumption. It aims at the equal legal status of married men and women. Therefore, the Human Rights Committee argues that Article 26 ICCPR would be violated, when a married woman loses her standing in court to her husband once she is married,[23] which makes it impossible for her to sue in her own name. The Article, however, does not provide necessarily for a new or more flexible definition of the family. This is problematic as modern families neither always include father, mother, and child, nor are always in a situation where the father is the only, or the strongest, provider of the family.[24]

Access to family benefits can involve discrimination against women if these are made available to one person in the family only, although they are meant to be of use to the whole family. If this person is the acknowledged 'head of household' or 'breadwinner', often the decision is made on the level of income. In these cases, the benefit will often be payable to a male household member, as men's income all over the world tends to be higher than women's income. This would constitute a case of indirect discrimination. The breadwinner concept is therefore problematic within Article 13(a).

In *S.W.M. Broeks v The Netherlands*,[25] where Broeks claimed a violation of Article 26 ICCPR and Article 9 in conjunction with Articles 2 and 3 ICESCR, the Human Rights Committee had to deal with the concept of the breadwinner. Broeks argued that the reduction of her unemployment benefits, which she received after being dismissed, violated her right to equal treatment, as her benefits were discounted, because she was not the 'breadwinner' of the

---

[21] CESCR General Comment No. 19, (General Comments): *The Right to Social Security (Article 9)* Thirty-ninth session (5–23 November 2007) E/C.12/GC/19, 4 February 2008, paras. 30–4.
[22] WOOD WETZEL, footnote 10, p. 154.
[23] *Graciela Ato del Avellanal v Peru*, Communication No. 202/1986 (28 October 1988), UN Doc. Supp. No. 40 (A/44/40) at 196 (1988).
[24] This is criticised by LYNN SOUTHARD, footnote 1, p. 58.
[25] Communication No. 172/1984 (9 April 1987), UN Doc. Supp. No. 40 (A/42/40), p. 129.

household. The Human Rights Committee found in her favour and argued that the Dutch Unemployment Benefit Act violated the right to equal treatment granted by Article 26 ICCPR and could not be justified. Accordingly, the Dutch rule discriminated against women, because married women had to prove that they where the 'breadwinner' of the family, by showing that they earned over a certain proportion of the income, or that they lived permanently separated from their husbands, while married men did not face such an obligation. The Committee considered such a difference not reasonable and it could therefore not be justified.[26] The ICESCR-Committee did not discuss the concept of the 'breadwinner' itself, however, because it did not deal with the indirect discriminatory effect the concept can have, as the case constituted direct discrimination.

Access to family benefits can also be denied, because of the special status of a person. In Bulgaria, for example, a female university student raised a complaint of sex discrimination because students were excluded from child care benefits.[27] The court accepted the argument that this constituted sex discrimination contrary to the Convention on the Elimination of All forms of Discrimination Against Women which requires equality of women and men in the allocation of grants and other assistance for students.[28] While the equal access to student grants and scholarships is protected in Article 10 d of the same Convention, the case is also relevant to Article 13, because child benefit is clearly a family benefit. Withholding it to students may well have cumulative exclusionary effects. For example, it may be common for women to support their male partners during their studies. These women will often already be mothers once their partners have finished their education and can support their studies in turn.

Finally, the State might also implement legislation which has not a disparate impact on women in general but only on women with a specific ethnic origin. For example, detrimental effect for Romani women flowed from Slovak legislation denying maternity benefits to mothers leaving a new born in the medical facility without the permission of the treating physician. Romani women often shun the Slovak practice to hospitalize mother and newborn for more than a few hours in order to care for their other children. They would return for retrieving the new born once they are formally released from the hospital. The legislation is ill adapted to the customs of Roma and thus exerts

---

[26] *Broeks v The Netherlands*, Communication No. 172/1984 (9 April 1987), UN Doc. Supp. No. 40 (A/42/40), p. 129, para. 14. See also, REHMAN, footnote18, p. 531.
[27] Bulgarian Supreme Administrative Court, under administrative, file 5063/2003.
[28] GENOVEVA TISHEVA, 'Bulgaria', Susanne Burri and Dagmar Schiek Editors, *Multiple Discrimination in EU Law Opportunities for legal responses to intersectional gender discrimination*, European Commission, Brussels, 2009, available at: www.ec.europa.eu/social/BlobServlet?docId=3808&langId=en [accessed 25 September 2010], p. 34.

detrimental effects for Romani women.²⁹ Since the children usually live with their biological parents afterwards and the benefit intents to support families with a newborn child, an exception from Article 13 a) cannot be justified. The intersectional character of the discriminatory effect does not change the finding, since the States have to take special care, that minority groups are not excluded from family benefits.³⁰

Another example for intersectional discrimination which is relevant within Article 13 refers to withholding childcare services in minority languages which has been addressed under the Finish legislation. The lack of child care in minority languages work to the disproportional detriment of women with a minority background, as they often refrain to use the child care facilities, because they do not offer the appropriate language for their children. As a consequence, those women are *de facto* refused to access the family benefit provided in kind, as there is no appropriate product available to them³¹ which additionally has the effect that those women cannot engage in paid employment.

3.2. ARTICLE 13(B) (FINANCIAL CREDIT)

Article 13(b) CEDAW is mainly aimed at non-State actors such as banks, building societies or insurance companies but would also include government agencies and State programmes which support credit facilities for certain groups within society. Women often face discrimination when obtaining loans and credits from such organizations,³² which further aggravates their vulnerable position in society, their dependency on their husbands and families and their

---

[29] International Federation for Human Rights, 'Comments to the Fourth Periodical Report of the Slovak Republic on Performance of the Obligation Arising from the Convention on the Elimination of All Forms of Discrimination Against Women', 2008, available at: www2.ohchr.org/english/bodies/cedaw/docs/ngos/CFIDH_Slovakia_41.pdf [accessed 15 September 2010], pp. 12–3.

[30] CESCR General Comment No. 19, (General Comments): *The Right to Social Security (Article 9)* Thirty-ninth session (5–23 November 2007) E/C.12/GC/19, 4 February 2008, para. 35.

[31] CEDAW, 41ˢᵗ Session: Finland, combined 5ᵗʰ and 6ᵗʰ report, 9 July 2008, available at: www.ishr.ch/treaty-body-monitor/cedaw [accessed 25 September 2010]. See also: KEVÄT NOUSIAINEN, 'Minorities' Right to Day Care: Liberal tolerance or identity maintenance', in: Dagmar Schiek and Anna Lawson (eds.), *European Union Non-Discrimination Law and Intersectionality: Investigating the triangle or racial, gender and disability discrimination*, Ashgate, Farnham etc, forthcoming, chapter 9; KEVÄT NOUSIAINEN, 'Finland', in: Susanne Burri and Dagmar Schiek (eds.), *Multiple Discrimination in EU Law Opportunities for legal responses to intersectional gender discrimination*, European Commission, Brussels, 2009, available at: www.ec.europa.eu/social/BlobServlet?docId=3808&langId=en [accessed 25 September 2010], pp. 50–1.

[32] REHMAN, footnote 18, p. 531.

freedom to develop economically.[33] The equal access to credit does, however, not only apply to credits for economic development, but also to consumer credits.[34]

Article 13(b) obliges States to ensure, that private institutions do not discriminate against women within their services.[35] As the Convention aims at the *de facto* equality of men and women, the Article does not only ensure the formal access[36] to financial services but also substantively equal treatment in contract conditions. Therefore, women must not be denied access to credit, mortgages or other financial services, neither formally nor substantially, nor is it allowed to offer women credits at higher interest rates than men, to understate the value of any real estate women may possess for the purpose of securing credit or to impose additional conditions such as a male guarantor.[37] Moreover, the use of statistical data, such as the inclusion of actuarial factors, are problematic as they disadvantage women by generalization and/or have no causal (but only a statistical) connection to the assessed risk.[38]

There are a number of methods to uncover discrimination within the financial services. The American Federal Financial Examination Council, for example, considered three methods to identify discrimination within financial services; overt evidence of disparate treatment, comparative evidence of disparate treatment, and evidence of disparate impact.[39] Overt evidence refers to a situation where the lender openly uses the sex of the applicant as the reason for differential treatment, comparative discrimination refers to a situation where women as a group are treated differently in comparison to men without the existence of any legitimate explanation, and the third one refers to situations where gender-neutral rules have a disparate impact on women (*i.e.* disproportionately exclude women) without the existence of a justification such as a business necessity.[40]

---

[33] The United Nation Fourth World Conference on Women, *Platform for Action*, Beijing, 1995, available at: www.un.org/womenwatch/daw/beijing/platform/economy.htm [accessed 25 September 2010], para. 156.

[34] DAGMAR SCHIEK, *Differenzierte Gerechtigkeit? Diskriminierungsschutz und Vertragsrecht*, Nomos, Baden-Baden, 2000.

[35] See for a list of actions: The United Nation Fourth World Conference on Women, *Platform for Action*, Beijing, 1995, available at: www.un.org/womenwatch/daw/beijing/platform/economy.htm [accessed 25 September 2010], para. 165.

[36] As suggested by JAN SCHÜRNBRAND, 'Auswirkungen des Allgemeinen Gleichbehandlungsgesetzes auf das Recht der Bankgeschäfte', *BKR*, 2007, p. 308.

[37] JOY NGWAKWE, 'Realizing Women's Economic, Social, and Cultural Rights: Challenges and Strategies in Nigeria', *Canadian Journal of Women and the Law*, 14, 2002, p. 142, p. 148.

[38] SCHIEK, footnote 34, p. 217.

[39] Federal Financial Examination Council, 'Interagency Fair Lending Examination Procedure', 2009, available at: www.ffiec.gov/PDF/fairlend.pdf [accessed at: 24 September 2010], p. i.

[40] TIMOTHY SMEEDING, 'Do Credit Market Barriers Exits for Minorities and Women Entrepreneurs?', Center For Policy Research, Working Paper No. 74, 2005, available at: www-cpr.maxwell.syr.edu/cprwps/wps74abs.htm [accessed 22 September 2010], p. 2.

Discrimination within the financial market has many origins, and occurs for many different reasons. Lenders might be prejudicial against women and turn down their applications on the ground of that bias or use statistical evidence to prove that women have poor credit qualifications, although such characteristics cannot be observed by the applicant. Additionally, the existence of long term relationships between the borrower and the lender and the operation on the same location might influence the interest rates[41] and disadvantages people who lack such a network. Since women start their careers and businesses often later in life, as they often raise children in younger age, they will lack such a network more often than men.

Other influence might also matter. So it was observed that married women often face discrimination when they are in the childbearing age which can either result out of a general prejudicial attitude against women with (potential) family responsibilities or discrimination on the ground of marital status.[42] Moreover, women might apply for smaller amounts, which the banks do not offer to the same lower rates than bigger credits, women own less land which often denies them access to credit, or women might not even apply to credits as they are under the impression that their request will be denied.[43] Finally, as women all over the world earn less money than men, they are more likely to belong to the poorer part of the population. As such they do not only face discrimination because they are women but also social discrimination because, in many cases the poor pay more for credit.[44]

Article 13(b) has been criticized for ignoring the unequal distribution of capital, land ownership and income between the sexes. It has been suggested that this inequality is the root of women's difficulties to acquire credit at the same conditions as men. For example, if banks grant lower interest if a debtor can offer more valuable securities this may be detrimental for women owning fewer assets. The same can be said about other underlying factors which limit women's access to credit, such as poverty.[45] This is especially problematic because poverty seems to feminize.[46] In the light of the MDGs, Article 13(b) Women's Convention calls upon the States to address the underlying reasons why women often do not have access to credit. The micro-credit programmes, which are discussed below, were

---

[41] SMEEDING, footnote 40, pp. 20–2.
[42] HELEN F. LAND, 'Equal Credit Opportunity: Women and Mortgage Credit', *The American Economic Review*, 72(2), 1982, pp. 166–70.
[43] WOMEN'S ISSUES NETWORK OF BELIZE, 'Shadow Report presented to CEDAW IN relation to the 3rd and 4th Period State Party Report of Government of Belize', 2007, available at: www.winbelize.org/BelizeShadowReport_Final%5B1%5D.pdf [accessed: 14 September 2010], p. 30.
[44] See for detailed discussion and further references SCHIEK, footnote 34, p. 235.
[45] LYNN SOUTHARD, footnote 1, p. 58.
[46] WOOD WETZEL, footnote 10, p. 88; The United Nation Beijing Declaration and Platform for Action, 'Fourth World Conference on Women' available at: www.un.org/womenwatch/daw/beijing/platform/plat1.htm [accessed 1 September 2010], para. 17.

established as a means to address some of these problems. However, as will be shown, they are not without problems. Such programmes go beyond non-discrimination law itself by breaking with the traditional banking business, which tenders only credit to those who 'are able to live up to an andocentric definition of financial success'.[47]

The Signatory States have the positive obligation to ensure equal treatment within the financial services which means that the States have to ensure the equal legal status of women and men within financial services but also affect the structure of the financial business to an extent, that women have the same opportunities. Such measures should include provisions which encourage banks to include financial products in their portfolio which are of more interest or specially designed for women, exclude the use of statistical evidence to justify gender discrimination, or address the underlying reasons for gender discrimination. The Convention as a political instrument to promote gender equality also supports States to promote gender equality at all levels, whether legally or culturally. Consequently, Article 13(b) of the Convention could also be used to support the States' support of women within areas they have deficits, in order to ensure they can enjoy equal access to financial services. Such support could include special training for women, the access to the relevant information and the general circulation of the rights.[48]

Whether women actually face discrimination within financial services is difficult to determine, and depends very much on the kind of service and the national context it will be provided in.[49] Many different studies in different areas in the worlds come to very difficult results when asking whether women actually face discrimination within the financial market. This, however, does not mean that gender discrimination within financial services is only a problem in developing countries or countries with a strong influence of the Shari'a. Rather it is a worldwide issue, although reasons for the occurring discrimination may differ.

As a study on the Italian financial market suggests women pay substantially more for overdraft facilities than men, despite the fact that there is no evidence that women are riskier lenders than men, that their companies' credit histories differ, or that they use different types of banks.[50] According to the study, banks seem to consider women lenders as riskier than male borrowers and

---

[47] LYNN SOUTHARD, footnote 1, 1, p. 59.
[48] For example pointed out by ALBANIAN COALITION FOR THE PREPARATION OF ALTERNATIVE REPORTS (ACPAR), 'CEDAW Shadow Report on the Situation of Women and Girls in the Republic of Albania', Altin Hazizaj (ed.), available at: www2.ohchr.org/english/bodies/cedaw/docs/ngos/ACPAR_Albania46.pdf [accessed 14 September 2010], p. 49.
[49] There are plenty of studies which exist on that topic. See for example: SMEEDING, footnote 40; ALBERTO ALESINA and FRANCESCA LOTTI, 'Do Women Pay More for Credit? Evidence from Italy', 2008, available at: www.nber.org/papers/w14202 [accessed 15 September 2010]; LAND, footnote 42, pp. 166–70.
[50] ALESINA and LOTTI, footnote 49.

Chapter 14. Equality and Economic and Social Life Including Implications for the European Union

consequently a female borrower with a female guarantor seems to be the worst possible option. Furthermore, while the interest rate generally seems to depend on the existence of social capital and trust, this does not have an equalising effect, meaning that women still pay more for credit than men.[51] Such discrimination can be the result of two kinds of reasons. On the one hand, women may be considered riskier borrowers on the base of statistics, on the other hand creditors may be biased against women and therefore consider them a bigger risk. As the study points out, there is no evidence that women actually are riskier borrowers than men. On the contrary, at least in the developing countries studies suggest that women are often the more reliable borrowers.[52] Consequently, the general bias against women seems a more likely reason for unequal treatment. Such bias could be explained by the existence of 'traditional' gender roles within the society, where women are more often in charge of the household, only few women work in manager positions, including boards of banks.[53] The study from Italy shows, that women often suffer discrimination without any obvious or rational reason. Such discrimination is prohibited under Article 13 and the Signatory States are under an obligation to ensure equal treatment of men and women.

As pointed out in a report on Albania, women often do not apply for loans, because they are treated as having a supporting role in the business and/or because they do not own as much collateral capital. Furthermore, it seems a common practice that wives register their property under the name of their husbands which makes them lose the ownership[54] and consequently lose their securities which would make them more desirable for lending institutions.

As stated above, microcredit programmes, originally designed as an instrument to further economic development, can be seen as addressing some issues of female exclusion from credit. These programmes provide access to small credits to the very poor, enabling them to start self employed businesses, often within the 'informal' or 'non-monetised' economy.[55] These programmes are especially relevant within the context of Article 14 of the Convention. Frequently, banks consider rural women who are economically active within the agriculture sector as not eligible for credits under 'normal' conditions. In addition to offering access to small scale credits, these programmes may also allow for unconventional forms of securing the credit. As a micro-strategy,

---

51 ALESINA and LOTTI, footnote 49, pp. 12–7.
52 For an overview see: BEATRIZ ARMEDÁRIZ DE AGHION and JONATHAN MORDUCH, *The Economics of Microfinance*, MIT Press, Cambridge, 2005, p. 19; WOMEN'S ISSUES NETWORK OF BELIZE, footnote 43, p. 30.
53 ALESINA and LOTTI, footnote 49, pp. 2–8.
54 ACPAR, footnote 48, p. 49.
55 KRISTEN GHODSEE, 'Rethinking Development Templates: Women and Microcredit in Post-Socialist Southeastern Europe', *Anthropology of East Europe Review*, 2003, 21(2), available at: www.condor.depaul.edu/~rrotenbe/aeer/aeer21_2.html [accessed: 23 September 2010].

micro credit programmes are supposed to improve the living conditions of the poor and enable them to participate in the economic development.[56] Micro-credit programmes adopt bottom up approaches, which consider the special needs of poor people who could not participate in the economic life, if only a traditional top-down approach, which focuses on the modernisation of the economy as a whole, would be employed. While these programmes are more frequently found in developing countries, they also exist in the developed 'western' world.[57]

As such, micro-credit programmes are not limited to women, but they are used more often by women than by men. Accordingly, if the terms of 'micro credits' (such as interest rates) are more detrimental than for 'normal credits', this will often result in *de facto* discrimination of women. Furthermore, many projects aim especially at female first time loaners in order to give them the chance to generate an independent source of income and to take care of themselves and their families.[58] Therefore, they deserve some consideration under Article 13(b).

Despite all their benevolent aims, these programmes may actually have discriminatory effects. These may derive from disproportionally high effective credit rates, resulting from the combination of product 'fees' and the interest rates themselves. Moreover, some programmes seem to be supporting traditional family concepts.[59] For example, there are reports on such micro-credit schemes, which only offer credits to women if their husbands guarantee the loan, or even cases where the loans are paid out to the husbands who have no legal obligation under the contract.[60] Consequently, whether they are beneficial to women's social position depends very much on how they are generated.

Micro-credit programmes which are in line with Article 13(b) need to avoid such situation, where the credit is offered to women but only in a discriminatory manner. Furthermore, it is important, that the micro credits have no higher interest rates than 'normal credits'. Such a policy would establish statistical disadvantage to the detriment of women, and thus often qualify as indirect discrimination against women. Such disadvantage is not only found in the developing world but also in the 'West' where women often apply for smaller amounts than men. To avoid higher interest rates, the amalgamation of several

---

[56] GARY M. WOLLER and WARNER WOODWORTH, 'Microcredit and Third World Development Policy', *Political Studies Journal*, 2001, p. 265.
[57] GHODSEE, footnote 55.
[58] Microcredit Summit Website, available at: www.microcreditsummit.org/about/what_is_microcredit/ [accessed 26 September 2010].
[59] JUDE FERNANDO, 'Nongovernmental Organizations, Micro-Credit, and Empowerment of Women', *Annals of the American Academy of Political and Social Science*, 554, 1997, pp. 150–77; FRANCISCA ISI OMORODION, 'Rural Women's Experiences of Micro-Credit Schemes in Nigeria: Case Study of Asian Women', *Journal of Asian and African Studies*, 42 (6), 2007, p. 480.
[60] JOY NGWAKWE, footnote 37, p. 148.

small credits into pools which are then offered to a group of women seems sensible; as such pooled credits could easily be compared to other credits schemes and be offered under the same conditions.

3.3. ARTICLE 13(C) (RECREATIONAL ACTIVITIES, SPORTS, CULTURAL LIFE)

Finally Article 13(c) obliges the States parties to ensure equal access to recreational activities, sport and all aspects of cultural life. Article 13(c) Convention aims towards two directions. On the one hand the States parties have to ensure, that private organizations do not discriminate against women, on the other hand, States are not allowed to discriminate themselves. Therefore, States are obliged to fund 'male' and 'female' sport and cultural activities alike and ensure that women have *de facto* equal access to all kind of activities, whether considered to be 'typical male' or not. The Article requires overcoming 'institutional barriers and other obstacles, such as those based in cultural and religious traditions, which prevent women from fully participating in cultural life'.[61] Such cultural, recreational and sport activities include all kind of leisure activities, from membership in a (sport) club or alike to the access to bars.

Article 13(c) is also relevant in conjunction with Article 10(g) of the same Convention which aims at the elimination of discrimination within education and mentions active participation in sport and physical education. Similar to Article 10(g), Article 13(c) addresses the (physical) well being of women,[62] and breaking the 'cycle of learned and thought submission to discrimination'.[63] As such the general access to sport activities and the access to physical education is not easy to separate and should be seen two sides of one medal, since not all physical education takes place in State schools or educational centres but also involves many private Sport Clubs and it is not possible to distinguish between recreational activities and physical education. For example, the Munich *Bergwacht*, a private association (*Verein*) rejected membership applications by women because this would have opened to them the opportunity to be trained as mountain guides. This again would have enabled specific leisure activities adjusted to women's needs in the mountains.[64]

---

[61] CESCR General Comment No. 16, (General Comments): *The equal right of men and women to the enjoyment of all economic, social and cultural rights (Article 3)*, Thirty-fourth session (25 April- 13 May 2005) E/C.12/2005/4, 11 August 2005, para. 31.
[62] LYNN SOUTHARD, footnote 1, p. 47.
[63] KATARINA TOMAŠEVSKI, *Women and human rights*, Zed Books, London, 1993, p. 24.
[64] LG München, 9 September 1992, *NJW RR*, 1993, p. 890 – the court granted the claimant access to the association which held a monopoly in the region. See also SCHIEK, footnote 34, p. 270.

Furthermore, as Article 13(c) aims at all recreational activities, sports and all aspects of cultural life, States need to ensure that they balance their public spending appropriately and do not favour certain sports preferred by men, such as football, rugby or basketball. Moreover, women need to be given *de facto* access to the available leisure activities. This means, that there need to be options to combine leisure activities with supervision of children (*i.e.* green spaces) or that the State needs to make sure that religious or cultural taboos or the fear of male violence do not prevent women from accessing certain facilities, such as swimming pools or fitness studios, which could be prevented by offering women only times.[65]

Discrimination within sport activities can also occur within the international platform. The Olympic Games and with it the Olympic Committee still offer less disciplines for women than for men, or employ dressing rules which makes it impossible for women from certain cultural or religious backgrounds to participate. While the Olympic Committee as a private corporation, registered in Switzerland, is not directly bound by the Convention, its Member States are.[66] Consequently, the States parties are obliged to refrain from discrimination against women athletes through their National Olympic Committees as well as through the national sponsorship of the athletes.[67] Such discriminatory treatment is prohibited under Article 13(c).

4. EU LAW AND ARTICLE 13

Article 13 is also interesting because it is offers some inroads for controlling existing EU legislation for its discriminatory effects. The Convention is relevant for the EU law application because, although the EU itself is not a Signatory of the Convention, most Member States are, The EU Member States therefore are bound by the Convention when applying and implementing EU legislation. Furthermore, gender equality constitutes an expression of fundamental human rights[68] and is therefore part of the general principles of European Union law which are inspired by Member States legal traditions and international treaties the Member States are signatories to.[69] This inspirational quality gives the Convention on the Elimination of all Forms of Discrimination Against Women

---

[65] SCHIEK, footnote 34, pp. 262–71, NOUSIAINEN, 'Finland', footnote 31, p. 50.
[66] CHANTALLE FORGUES, 'A Global Hurdle: The Implementation of an International Nondiscrimination Norm Protection Women from Gender Discrimination in International Sports', *Boston University International Law Journal*, 18, 2000, p. 261.
[67] FORGUES, footnote 66, p. 247, pp. 267–8.
[68] ECJ C-50/96 *Deutsche Telekom AG v Lilli Schröder* [2000] ECR I-743 at 794; ECJ Case 149/77 *Defrenne v Sabena* [1978] ECR 1365 at p. 1378.
[69] ECJ Case 11/70 *Internationale Handelsgesellschaft mbH v Einfuhr- und Vorratsstelle für Getreide und Futtermittel* [1970] ECR 1125, para. 4; PAUL CRAIG and GRÁINNE DE BÚRCA, *EU law Text, Cases, and Materials*, 4th edition, 2008, Oxford University Press, Oxford, pp. 382–8;

the status of an interpretative guideline for EU law itself. Finally, Directive 2004/113/EC[70] on the access and supply of goods and services refers to the Convention on the Elimination of all Forms of Discrimination Against Women explicitly in its recitals.[71] Nevertheless, the Convention's full potential has not yet been realized in the EU.[72] Partly, EU legislation even seems in contravention to Article 13.

4.1. ARTICLE 13(A) (FAMILY BENEFITS)

The material scope of Article 13(a) is covered by EU directives on equal treatment in employment and occupation. The Recast Directive 2006/54/EC[73] prohibits unequal treatment of employees in these fields, partly in overlap with Article 157 Treaty on the Functioning of the European Union (TFEU, ex Article 141 EC), which prohibits unequal pay.[74] Family benefits provided for by employers may constitute pay, in which case they are covered by Article 157 TFEU. Family benefits such as parental leave over and above statutory obligations are covered by Directive 2006/54/EC. Regarding family benefits for self-employed women, new Directive 2010/41/EU[75] on equal treatment between men and women engaged in self-employed activity aims at the equal treatment within family benefits. While the application of these directives is not always satisfactory, there is no contradiction between their norms and Article 13(a) Convention on the Elimination of All Forms of Discrimination Against Women.

ECJ Case 4/73 *J. Nold, Kohlen- und Baustoffgroßhandlung v Commission of the European Community* [1974] ECR 491, para. 13.

[70] Council Directive of 13 December 2004 implementing the principle of equal treatment between men and women in the access to and supply of goods and services, OJ 2004, L373/37.

[71] Recital 2 of the Preamble.

[72] RIKKI HOLTMAAT and CHRISTA TOBLER, 'CEDAW and the European Union's Policy in the Field of Combating Gender Discrimination', *Maastricht Journal of European and Comparative law*, 12(4), 2005, pp. 399–400.

[73] Directive 2006/54/EC of the European Parliament and of the Council of 5 July 2006 on the implementation of the principle of equal treatment and equal opportunities and equal treatment of men and women in matters of employment and occupation (recast), OJ L 204/23.

[74] Article 157 TFEU employs a broad definition of pay. Article 2(e) Directive 2006/54/EC defines pay as 'the ordinary basic or minimum wage or salary and any other consideration, whether in cash or in kind, which the worker receives directly or indirectly, in respect of his/her employment from his/her employer'. See also CATHERINE BARNARD, *EC Employment Law*, 3rd edition, 2006, Oxford University Press, Oxford, pp. 341–3.

[75] Directive of the European Parliament and of the Council of 7 July 2010 on the application of the principle of equal treatment between men and women engaged in an activity in a self-employed capacity and repealing Council Directive 86/613/EEC, OJ L 180/1.

4.2. ARTICLE 13(B) AND (C) (FINANCIAL SERVICES AND RECREATIONAL AND CULTURAL ACTIVITIES)

The material scope of Article 13(b) and (c) CEDAW is covered by Directive 2004/113/EC as well as Directive 2000/43/EC. The former protects women from discrimination in the access to and supply of goods and services, including financial services and leisure activities. Directive 2000/43/EC[76] on racial discrimination also covers access to and supply of goods and services. Its recitals mention explicitly that this directive also is relevant in cases of discrimination against women at the intersection of race and gender. Both directives apply to the private and public sector alike.[77]

Directive 2004/113/EC may seem problematic in the light of Article 13(b) and (c) on the grounds of its narrow formulation and the wide exception granted in favour of providers of financial services.

4.2.1. Financial Services

Financial service providers have sought to escape the application of this directive on them by taking recourse to the narrow formulation of its scope of application. According to Article 3(1), discrimination is only prohibited for access to and provision of such services which are 'available to the public irrespectively of the person concerned'. This has been interpreted as covering only agreements which have no individual element at all, as they are the only ones which are concluded irrespectively of the person concerned. Accordingly, any agreement which is specially designed for the needs of a single costumer or a group of costumers or include credit checks would fall outside the scope of application.[78] Such a limited interpretation is, however, not convincing because loan, bank and mortgage agreements are mostly highly standardized and focus on the economic success of the offered financial product.[79] Furthermore, the systematic interpretation of the Directive also supports the inclusion of credit agreements, because Article 5 of Directive 2004/113/EC provides for various exceptions within insurance agreements. This provision does not expand the Directive's scope of application to insurance contracts, but rather presupposes that these contracts are covered by Directive 20004/113/EC. If, however, credit agreements

---

[76] Council Directive of 29 June 2000 implementing the principle of equal treatment between persons irrespective of racial or ethnic origin, OJ L180/22.
[77] See for example Article 3(1) 2004/113/EC.
[78] Accordingly, there would be a difference between the scope of 2006/113/EC and 2000/43/EC, as Article 1(h) 2000/43/EC does not mention that the products need to be available irrespectively of the person concerned but only that they need to be available to the public. Schürnbrand, footnote 36, pp. 305–9.
[79] Dagmar Schiek, '§19 AGG', in: Dagmar Schiek (ed.), *Allgemeine Gleichbehandlungsgesetz*, 2007, Sellier, München, p. 331.

do not fall under the scope because the agreements are not available irrespectively of the person concerned, the same would apply to insurance agreements. Therefore credit agreements are within the scope of the Directive, just like insurance agreements. This is the only interpretation which is compatible with the Convention on the Elimination of All Forms of Discrimination against Women, which is a further argument to support it.

Furthermore, with regard to Article 13(b), the Member States need to 'ensure that in all new [insurance] contracts [...] the use of the sex as a factor in the calculation of premiums and benefits [...] shall not result in a difference in individuals' premiums and benefits'.[80] Member States might, however, allow a 'proportional unequal treatment within insurance contracts if a risk assessment based on relevant and accurate actuarial and statistic data'[81] can justify it, as long as they are not related to pregnancy and maternity[82] and do not result in denying access totally.[83] Actuarial factors, which are based on statistical data, detect the average risk, and therefore are problematic as they may have discriminatory effects. For example, the average woman lives longer, and consequently often has to pay more for her private pension or life insurance, although the lifespan does not only depend on sex but also on other factors like life style.[84]

The use of statistical data in order to assess the risk of insurance and related financial services is not without problems. These actuarial techniques often have detrimental effects for women, without having any causal link to the risk assessed. Rather, the link is only a statistical one. Thus, women are penalized for mathematical chances which arise from the average behaviour of women rather than granted an individual risk assessment. The economic justification for such behaviour is of course that individual risk assessment is more costly. However, mere cost arguments have traditionally not been accepted as justification for direct discrimination under EU Law.[85] As regards Article 13 of the Convention, differentiating between women and men on the basis of statistical data in access to credit and other financial services would seem problematic. States parties would thus be under an obligation to ensure that economic actors under their jurisdiction do not engage in such practices. Accordingly, if States parties are bound by the Convention, they would be barred from using the exception.[86]

---

[80] Article 5 I 2006/113/EC.
[81] Article 5 II 2006/113/EC.
[82] Article 5 III 2006/113/EC. See also ERIKA SZYSZCZAK, 'Social Policy', *International and Comparative Law Quarterly*, 54(4), 2005, p. 984.
[83] DAGMAR SCHIEK, '§20 AGG', footnote 79, p. 340.
[84] EUGENIA CARACCIOLO DI TORELLA, 'The Goods and Services Directive: Limitations and Opportunities', *Feminist Legal Studies*, 13, 2005, pp. 343–345.
[85] SCHIEK, footnote 34, pp. 201–6 and pp. 210–7. For a detailed discussion see also AG Jacobs Case C-227/04P *Lindorfer v Council* [2007] ECR I-6767.
[86] This is especially important if the Article 5 2006/113/EC exception does not only apply to insurance contracts but also all kind of credit agreements, as suggested by SCHÜRNBRAND,

Recently, the Court of Justice of the European Union had to decide whether the use of actuarial and statistic data within insurances violates higher European Union law. In its judgement the Court seems to agree with the Advocate General's assessment that the exception allowing such data as justification potentially permits derogation from the equal treatment of men and women. Consequently it argued that, such exception therefore has to expire after an appropriate transition period, which it identified to be the 21st of December 2012; five years after the Directive had to be implemented.[87] The Court has thus not removed the incompatibility of the Directive and the Convention entirely. It has, however, ensured that it will not last very much longer.

4.2.2. Recreational Activities and Cultural Life

The Directive foresees some limitation of the equal treatment principle. For example, the Directive 'shall not preclude differences in treatment, if the provision of the goods and services exclusively or primarily to members of one sex is justified by a legitimate aim and the means of achieving that aim are appropriate and necessary'.[88] Consequently single sex saunas or clubs might still be acceptable. Although this exception most likely will be interpreted strictly it makes the rights granted under the directive less certain and gives the Commission the difficult task to monitor the implementation and respect the balanced approach which takes interests beside equality into consideration. The broad exception, however, bears the risk that direct discrimination can be justified.[89] Nevertheless, the limitation seems to be in line with Article 13(c), as long as there are single sex establishment or single sex time slots for both sexes and do not exclude women from visiting such establishments. Such arrangements could even enhance the accessibility for women. For example, many women might not go to swimming pools, because they fear male violence or their religious or cultural background prevents them from doing so. If the swimming pool, however, has a women only time slot, many women might find the pool more accessible. Article 13(c) would, however, not be fulfilled, if the separation of the establishments means less service for women or if the time slots make it *de facto* impossible for women to access such establishments.

---

footnote 36, p. 309. In a recent European case the Advocate General assessed that the exception would violate the general principle of equal treatment between men and women, as it is lied down in Article 21 and 23 of the Charter of Fundamental Rights of the European Union, but did not refer to the Convention explicitly; AG Kokott Case C-236/09 *Association Belge des Consommateurs Test Achats ASBL and Others* [2011] ECR-000, paras. 41–69.

[87] ECJ Case C-236/09 *Association Belge des Consommateurs Test Achats ASBL and Others* [2011] ECR 000, paras. 31–34.
[88] Article 4(4) 2003/113/EC.
[89] CARACCIOLO DI TORELLA, footnote 84, p. 343.

5. CONCLUSION

In conclusion, it seems regrettable that Article 13 has not enjoyed more thorough academic attention to date, and that CEDAW has not utilized this provision more frequently by highlighting problems that are ongoing in States all over the world. In order to achieve factual equality for women, it is crucial that the mission of this Article is fulfilled. Granting women substantively equal access to financial assets through family benefits and credit facilities is decisive for their opportunities to enjoy equally with men the chance to earn income that enables them to sustain themselves and their children. Equal access to recreational activities (including sports) and cultural life is vital for enjoying life on equal terms with men. In addition, achieving equal access to benefits and credit for women can be seen as a contribution to combating poverty, and thus a good strategy in any form of development policy.

However, violations of Article 13 are certainly not only to be found in developing countries. As our analysis of EU law has demonstrated, such violation seems to routinely occur in European States. It is thus to be hoped that CEDAW shifts some of its attention to enforcing Article 13. Furthermore, Article 13 can also be utilized in order to interpret EU law in such ways as to exclude contradiction with the Convention on the Elimination of all Forms of Discrimination Against Women. Furthermore, EU Member States should, in fulfilling their obligations as Members of the EU, avoid making use of such clauses that would entail contraventions to Article 13.

ARTICLE 14

1. States parties shall take into account the particular problems faced by rural women and the significant roles which rural women play in the economic survival of their families, including their work in the non-monetized sectors of the economy, and shall take all appropriate measures to ensure the application of the provisions of the present Convention to women in rural areas.
2. States parties shall take all appropriate measures to eliminate discrimination against women in rural areas in order to ensure, on a basis of equality of men and women, that they participate in and benefit from rural development and, in particular, shall ensure to such women the right:

   (a) To participate in the elaboration and implementation of development planning at all levels;
   (b) To have access to adequate health care facilities, including information, counseling and services in family planning;
   (c) To benefit directly from social security programmes;
   (d) To obtain all types of training and education, formal and non-formal, including that relating to functional literacy, as well as, *inter alia*, the benefit of all community and extension services, in order to increase their technical proficiency;
   (e) To organize self-help groups and co-operatives in order to obtain equal access to economic opportunities through employment or self employment;
   (f) To participate in all community activities;
   (g) To have access to agricultural credit and loans, marketing facilities, appropriate technology and equal treatment in land and agrarian reform as well as in land resettlement schemes;
   (h) To enjoy adequate living conditions, particularly in relation to housing, sanitation, electricity and water supply, transport and communications.

CHAPTER 15

RURAL WOMEN'S RIGHT TO LAND AND HOUSING IN TIMES OF URBANIZATION

Ingrid WESTENDORP

1. INTRODUCTION

Article 14 of the Women's Convention is unique because it is the only provision in an international human rights instrument that deals specifically with the rights of women living in rural areas. Only one of the 187 parties to the Convention[1] has made a reservation to Article 14.[2] The provision acknowledges rural women's particular problems and their importance in respect of the economic survival of their families. States parties are obliged to take appropriate measures to abolish discrimination against rural women and they should ensure that these women can participate in and enjoy rural development. Equal treatment in comparison to men – and with regard to certain elements in comparison to urban women – should be guaranteed as regards participation in development planning, access to health care, enjoyment of social security, education including technical skills, organization of self-help groups and cooperation in order to get access to remunerated employment, participation in community activities, access to credits and loans and equal treatment regarding land reform or land resettlement programmes, and, finally adequate living conditions. The last point is remarkable since an adequate standard of living including housing and access to services and

---

[1] In October 2011, 187 States had become parties to the Women's Convention.
[2] So far the only State that has made a reservation to Article 14 is France. The reservation reads:
1. The Government of the French Republic declares that article 14, paragraph 2(c), should be interpreted as guaranteeing that women who fulfil the conditions relating to family or employment required by French legislation for personal participation shall acquire their own rights within the framework of social security.
2. The Government of the French Republic declares that article 14, paragraph 2(h), of the Convention should not be interpreted as implying the actual provision, free of charge, of the services mentioned in that paragraph.

facilities is not included in any of the other parts of the Convention and therefore it is not specifically guaranteed for urban women.

In almost every country in the world, rural areas are the poorest and they are characterized by a lack of, or a shortage of all kinds of services and facilities. Typically, gender biased customs and traditions thrive in rural areas and there is little incentive to alter them for women's benefit. To make matters worse, the world is engaged in one of the greatest urbanization crisis ever at the moment which means that international and national attention is drawn to the cities, especially the metropolises and the many problems they have to cope with. The result is that rural women are getting more and more marginalized and consequently it becomes increasingly harder for them to survive in the country.

Article 14 is very broad and touches upon many topics that are relevant for rural women. In the framework of this Chapter it is impossible to deal with all of these aspects. The choice has been made to concentrate on paragraphs 2(g) and (h). Women's lack of land is one of the biggest problems because it has several important consequences connected to the right to food, adequate housing, women's decision-making power, access to credit and loans, and the possibility to become economically independent. Women's lack of land is particularly wry in view of the fact that in many States the majority of agricultural workers are female. The central question of this Chapter therefore is how the various barriers that stand in the way between rural women and their land rights can be overcome and what role CEDAW plays or could play in this regard.

In the second section the historical development of Article 14 will be explored. Section three will discuss the situation of rural women in comparison to women living in urban areas. Next, the focus will be on the barriers that rural women face in respect of their land and housing rights and the attention that CEDAW pays to these problems. In the last section possibilities for improving rural women's right to land will be explored.

2. HISTORICAL DEVELOPMENT OF ARTICLE 14

The idea of including a specific provision on rural women was suggested rather late in the drafting process. In the 1970s there was a growing pressure on the Commission on the Status of Women (CSW) – in particular from the Food and Agriculture Organization (FAO) – to pay specific attention to the plight of rural women. It was pointed out that the majority of women in the world live in rural areas,[3] and that their position not only differs from that of urban women, but

---

[3] LISA R. PRUITT, 'Deconstructing CEDAW's Article 14: Naming and Explaining Rural Difference', in: *William & Mary Journal of Women and the Law*, Vol. 17:347, January 2011, p. 352.

also – and more significantly – from that of rural men.⁴ Many rural women who work as agricultural labourers in the family business are not paid for it nor is their position in any way secured. They may not have any property rights over the land and their access to land may depend on their relationship with their husband and his family. Especially in Africa and Asia, a widow and an abandoned or divorced woman may find herself landless with nowhere to go because she has no formal claim on the land that she has worked on.⁵

During the discussions on the fifth draft in 1976, the representative from India proposed a text concerning the situation of rural women and this proposal was backed up by the delegates from Egypt, Indonesia, Iran, Pakistan, Thailand and the United States of America.⁶ The counter proposal by France and Hungary to refer to specific problems of rural women in other substantive provisions instead of in a separate provision was not accepted by the CSW and India's proposal became Article 14 with a few amendments.⁷

Paragraph 2(h) on adequate living conditions was not yet included in the original draft.⁸ When the text of this specific subparagraph was proposed by Bangladesh, Ghana, Guyana, India, Kenya, New Zealand, Sweden, and the United Kingdom it was met with approval.⁹ Only the Dutch representative remarked on the lack of such rights in the rest of the Convention and thus the exclusion of urban women. However, the Dutch proposal to include urban women in a subparagraph of Article 14 about economic and social rights did not meet with consent.¹⁰ The question remains why subsequently nobody suggested devoting a separate Article on an adequate standard of living for all women.

Article 14 seems to be of more importance for developing than for developed States since an overwhelming majority of 90% of the rural population in the world lives in developing countries.¹¹ However, also in Western States there is a

---

4   The position of rural women's first received attention during the World Food Conference in Rome in 1974 and again during the first World Conference on Women in Mexico in 1975. See J.E. BIESHEUVEL-VERMEIJDEN, 'Loon naar Werken' (*To get what is due*), in: A.W. Heringa, J. Hes, L. Lijnzaad (eds), *Het Vrouwenverdrag: een beeld van een verdrag... (The Women's Convention: a picture of a treaty...)*, Maklu Uitgevers, Antwerpen-Apeldoorn, 1994, pp. 202–203.
5   BINA AGARWAL, 'Gender and Land Rights Revisited: Exploring New Prospects via the State, Family and Market', *Journal of Agrarian Change*, Vol. 3, Nos. 1and 2, January and April 2003, pp. 190–191.
6   LARS ADAM REHOF, *Guide to the Travaux Préparatoires of the United Nations Convention on the Elimination of All Forms of Discrimination Against Women*, Martinus Nijhoff Publishers, Dordrecht/Boston/London, 1993, p. 153.
7   Ibid., p. 156.
8   PRUITT, 2011, p. 357.
9   REHOF, 1993, p. 157.
10 The representative of the Netherlands stated 'that the concept expressed in paragraph 2(h) should apply to all women and wanted to see an additional, similar provision in the article dealing with economic and social life. The Chairman said that if the provisions dealing with rural women also applied to urban women, this should be made clear somewhere in the general provisions of the convention.', REHOF, 1993, p. 161.
11 PRUITT, 2011, p. 354.

significant difference between the standard of living of the urban and rural population, and implementation of Article 14 would mean that women's chances to become economically independent would increase.[12]

Although CEDAW has not (yet) adopted a specific General Recommendation on Article 14, the position of rural women is explicitly or implicitly mentioned in several of the General Recommendations that have been adopted so far. In General Recommendation No. 16 CEDAW draws attention to the weak economic position of women workers in family enterprises.[13] In General Recommendation No. 19 States parties are reminded that in rural areas women are at risk of gender-based violence because of persistent discriminatory traditional attitudes in rural areas.[14] General Recommendation No. 21 is important for rural women because it deals with issues related to women's property rights, inheritance rights, access to land and resources, and legal capacity.[15] General Recommendation No. 24 dealing with Article 12, women and health, draws attention to the connection between this provision and the specific requirements of Articles 14(2)(b), access for rural women to health care facilities, and (h), adequate living conditions that are critical in order to prevent disease.[16] Finally, in General Recommendation No. 27 on older women, CEDAW makes explicit mention of the position of rural women in connection with their right to education, access to services and housing, agricultural loans and credit and participation in development planning processes.[17]

3. URBAN VS. RURAL

Interestingly, Article 14 not only deals with the bias between men and women, but also with the difference in treatment, opportunities and access to facilities and services between urban and rural women.[18] The gap between rural and urban women is likely to get wider in future since the last few decades are

---

[12] On the position of rural women in the Netherlands see: BIESHEUVEL-VERMEIJDEN, 1994, p. 212.
[13] CEDAW General Recommendation No. 16 (tenth session, 1991), Unpaid women workers in rural and urban family enterprises.
[14] CEDAW General Recommendation No. 19 (11th session, 1992), Violence against women, para. 21 reads: 'Rural women are at risk of gender-based violence because traditional attitudes regarding the subordinate role of women that persist in many rural communities. Girls from rural communities are at special risk of violence and sexual exploitation when they leave the rural community to seek employment in towns.'
[15] CEDAW General Recommendation No. 21 (13th session, 1994) Equality in marriage and family relations.
[16] CEDAW General Recommendation No. 24 (20th session, 1999) Article 12: Women and health, para. 28.
[17] CEDAW General Recommendation No. 27 (42nd session, 2010) Older women and protection of their human rights. See in particular paras 19, 24, 47, and 49.
[18] PRUITT, 2011, p. 359.

Chapter 15. Rural Women's Right to Land and Housing in Times of Urbanization

characterized by an enormous, unstoppable flow of people from rural to urban areas. As a consequence, there is a certain metro centricity in the world today.[19] States, but also international organizations such as UN Habitat, are worried about the exponential growth of cities and the inability – especially in developing States – to cope with the enormous influx in cities of destitute rural people who are looking for work and a place to live.[20] This trend is certainly worrisome since funds are limited and if attention is focused on cities, the standard of living in rural areas, and in particular for women, is bound to drop.

Adequate housing conditions are more important for women than for men.[21] Due to the gendered division of work, a woman's life, especially in rural areas, is centred about the house and the plot of land she may have access to.[22] Inadequate facilities and services such as a lack of electricity, safe water, sanitation, garbage collection, transportation, and hospitals, will make a woman's life more difficult and will limit her chances to be gainfully employed.

While piped water is accepted as natural in the developed world and there is no difference to speak of between rural and urban areas, the situation in developing States is quite different. While services and facilities are common in the cities of developing countries, the situation in rural areas lags far behind. In a study carried out by the World Bank in 2010 it was reported that still many girls and women have to travel – *i.e.* mostly walk – more than an hour every day to collect the water necessary for the household.[23]

It is not only clean water that may be lacking in rural areas. Also electricity and energy for cooking and heating may be absent which means that alternatives must be used. Possible options are generators and bottled gas, kerosene, LPG, coal and charcoal, wood, straw, thatch and dung.[24] The cheaper the alternative, the more time and energy women have to spend on collecting it.[25]

---

[19] In the last five decades, almost 800 million people moved from rural to urban areas. PRUITT, 2011, pp. 352–353.
[20] UN Habitat decided to launch a special campaign on the living conditions in big cities in 2010 under the motto: Better City, Better Life.
[21] Adequate housing is more than a roof over one's head. According to the Committee on Economic, Social and Cultural Rights (CESCR) it entails seven elements: security of tenure, habitability, affordability, accessibility, location, availability of building materials, cultural adequacy. CESCR General Comment No. 4 on Adequate Housing, para. 8.
[22] INGRID WESTENDORP, *Women and Housing: Gender Makes a Difference*, Intersentia, Antwerp-New York, 2007, p. 113.
[23] PRUITT, 2011, p. 385, citing World Bank Policy Research Working Paper No. 5302, 2010 available at: www.wds.worldbank.org/external/default/WDSContentServer/IW3P/IB/2010/05/10/000158349_20100510114112/Rendered/INDEX/WPS5302.txt.
[24] For about 2 billion people in the world wood, dung and crop residues are the only source of energy. Irene Dankelman, *Gender and Environment: Lessons to Learn*, UN doc. EGM/NATDIS/2001/OP.2, para. 2.2. Also Komives *e.a*, 2001, pp. 14–15.
[25] Due to deforestation and general degradation of the environment it is not so easy anymore to find fuel wood. That is why in many urban areas, wood has become almost as expensive as kerosene or gas, while in rural areas the collection of wood costs women an excessive amount of energy and time. In a study carried out by the ILO in several countries in Asia, Africa and

In addition to these two basic facilities, the absence or limited presence of transport, schools, hospitals and markets may make life very hard in the country side and the more people leave, the fewer of these services are offered.

On the other hand, the living conditions in urban areas, and then specifically in the slums, may also be dire and it is therefore regrettable that the Women's Convention does not contain a provision on adequate living conditions that includes urban women. A possible explanation why such a provision was not included may be that the presence of infrastructure, sanitation, electricity, water supply, transportation, garbage collection, markets, shops, schools and hospitals were taken for granted in urban areas when the Convention was drafted.[26] At the time, the number of metropolises in the world was limited and they were predominantly to be found in developed countries. Meanwhile, the situation has changed dramatically and women in slum areas may also lack all of the above mentioned services and facilities. Still, research shows that while the living conditions are far below human rights standards, opportunities present themselves in slums that cannot be found in rural areas.[27] At least there is a chance that the children of slum dwellers may have a better future, while the children of those who stay behind in the rural areas face a very bleak prospect indeed.

4. THE IMPORTANCE OF LAND

The right to land can be qualified as the most important property right since it may not only provide a livelihood and a place to reside, but it also empowers and it gives status. Generally speaking, however, women are faced with the situation that they have fewer land rights and less control over any land they may possess than men, which has direct repercussions on the realization of their human rights, especially their living conditions.[28] Subparagraph 14(2)(g) explicitly links rural life to agriculture and thus to land and women's significant role in the

---

Latin America, it was shown that women's tasks are heavily burdened with this constant energy quest. Cooking and collecting fuels are two of the most time-consuming activities for women who, on an average, work considerably longer hours every day (11–14 hrs) than men (8–10 hrs). Using dung as a cooking fuel is also time-consuming. If the family does not own cattle, women have to put time in collecting dung in public places. Furthermore, making dung-cakes may take about two hours a day. WHO report, 1994, pp.83–84 and 89–90.

[26] Pruitt, 2011, p. 383.
[27] See *e.g.* Doug Saunders, *De trek naar de stad (Arrival City)*, Alfred A. Knopf Canada, 2010; also Floris-Jan van Luyn, *Een stad van boeren: De grote trek in China (A city of farmers: the big drift to the city in China)*, Atlas, Amsterdam-Antwerpen, 2008.
[28] This is also recognized by UN organs. See for instance Sub-Commission resolution 1997/19 on Women and the right to adequate housing and to land and property, UN doc. E/CN.4/SUB.2/RES/1997/19 of 27 August 1997, and Sub-Commission resolution 1998/15 on Women and the right to land, property and adequate housing, UN doc. E/CN.4/SUB.2/RES/1998/15 of 21 August 1998.

production of food.[29] In developing States two-thirds of women work in agriculture, yet only an insignificant percentage of these women actually own land.[30]

In the next subsections, first attention will be paid to the barriers that make it difficult or impossible for women to obtain and control land. Next, the consequences of the lack of land will be described. Lastly, the attention that CEDAW pays to the implementation of Article 14 on the domestic level will be examined.

4.1. BARRIERS TO OBTAIN AND CONTROL LAND

Basically, an individual can obtain land in three different ways: it may be provided by the State, land may be inherited, or a person manages to accrue enough funds to buy or lease land on the market.[31] The barriers that women face in obtaining and controlling land may be legal, labour and/or financial market related, or customary. All barriers have in common that they are based on or affected by gender stereotypes.

To start with, legal discrimination may be found in land distribution or land resettlement schemes by States because these may be male-biased.[32] Many national legal frameworks are still founded on the traditional idea that the family is a unit consisting of a male breadwinner who needs to provide for his wife and children. As a logical consequence, when the State distributes land it will be in the form of individual titles – be it of ownership, usufruct rights, rent or lease – which are given to men as heads of their families as it is assumed that women's access to land is in that way included.[33] However, this is based on the presumption that resources are equally shared within a household, and that women are treated with respect and dignity.[34] Sometimes, when it is obvious that women are heads of household they are also given individual titles, but in

---

[29] Worldwide, 428 million women work in the agricultural sector. PRUITT, 2011, p. 380.
[30] It is difficult to find an exact percentage because studies contradict each other and most of them are focused on specific countries only. It is clear, however, that the percentage is bound to be very low. According to a study conducted by the UN Food and Agriculture Organization (FAO) worldwide not even 2% of land would be owned by women. Sustainable Development Department of the FAO, *Women and sustainable food security*, available at: www.fao.org/SD/FSdirect/FBdirect/FSP001.htm, accessed on 26 October 2011.
[31] BINA AGARWAL, 'Gender and Land Rights Revisited: Exploring New Prospects via the State, Family and Market', *Journal of Agrarian Change*, Vol. 3, Nos. 1and 2, January and April 2003, p. 185.
[32] AGARWAL, 2003, pp. 197–200.
[33] TADESSE ZENABAWORKE, 2003, pp. 73, 75, 76 for respectively, Latin America, Asia and Sub-Sahara Africa.
[34] A household, however, is not a unitary body, since important inequalities may exist within the household as regards the distribution of resources and decision-making. ZENABAWORKE, 2003, pp. 67–68 Also, AGARWAL, 2003, p. 200.

many cases women are not acknowledged as the main breadwinners and they do not get any land or a smaller plot than male heads of household.[35]

In a minority of States legal discrimination may be found in respect of inheritance laws that distinguish between male and female heirs especially where real estate such as land and housing is concerned. Wives and daughters may inherit nothing or just a small part of the inheritance again based on the traditional idea that men are the providers and therefore need money and assets, and that women remain at home to take care of the household and children and therefore are taken financially care of. Sometimes denying women inheritance rights to land is justified by the argument that it would cause fragmentation and thus would affect the agricultural output.[36] Obviously, these laws will only have consequences for those women who belong to families that actually own real estate and where there is something to share. For the very poor of this world discriminatory inheritance laws are of no consequence.[37] Many Governments are sympathetic to women's plight and have changed the law in such a way that daughters and wives may inherit real estate, albeit sometimes smaller shares than brothers and husbands.[38]

Due to the segregation in the labour market, most women who are gainfully employed are to be found in typical 'female' jobs that are less valued and less paid than 'male' jobs. Many women work part-time or in the informal sector in order to be able to combine their employment with their household duties. Worldwide, working women earn between 15% – 20% less income than working men and this includes countries where women have received an education that is equal to that of men.[39] A lower income entails less possibility to save enough money to buy land or housing. A low income combined with the lack of property makes it difficult for many women to access credit and loans, especially those provided by the traditional banking system which will demand collateral.[40] Alternative loan systems, such as micro-credits, are usually provided to set up small businesses and not to enable a person to buy land.[41]

---

[35] In Honduras, for example when widows and single women were allotted plots of land, these were of very poor quality. ZENABAWORKE, 2003, p. 73.

[36] Fragmentation can also occur when only males inherit. Moreover, there are possible solutions to avoid a loss of productivity. AGARWAL, 2003, p. 196.

[37] According to the World Bank 'extreme poverty' means having to survive on US$1.50 per day. This amount has to cover all expenses as regards food, housing, health care, education, and transportation. It is estimated that 1.4 billion people worldwide live in extreme poverty.

[38] UN doc. A/HRC/19/53, Report of the Special Rapporteur on adequate housing, Raquel Rolnik, 26 December 2011, paras 24–26. Also: AGARWAL, 2003, p. 203. It is well known that Islamic law provides that daughters and wives only receive half the share that sons and husbands receive. Hindu inheritance law particularly discriminates between male and female heirs as far as arable land is concerned.

[39] See Chapter 11 in this book by Anja Wiesbrock.

[40] PRUITT, 2011, p. 383.

[41] AGARWAL, 2003, pp. 217–218.

Customary practices have a great influence on women's right to land. States in which the land used to be in the hands of clans or other communities, the land was divided among the men because of the age-old idea that should women be given land, this land would be lost to the clan if the woman would marry a non-clan member. Strangely enough, however, male title-holders were not restricted in any way as regards their control over the land. As a result, many, particularly young men, sold their land to the highest bidder and moved away, thus discarding another age-old tradition that the heir provides for the widow and unmarried sisters, and sees to it that they can live on the clan land for the rest of their lives.[42]

Customs and traditions also affect legal inheritance rights. The most important and most wide-spread custom is that of patrilocal residence and village *exogamy* for married women.[43] Many societies live according to an unwritten rule that daughters have to marry outside of their own community or village. Marriage means that the ties with the blood relatives are severed and that the married woman will settle down in her husband's community or village.[44] It is therefore seen as a waste of family property to give daughters the share of the land they are legally entitled to. Married women will gain access to their husband's or his family's house and land. In most cases, however, they do not have a legal claim on any of the real estate; they just have user rights as long as the relationship will exist. Since married women realize that their access to their husband's and in-laws' property is far from secure,[45] and they fear that they may have to leave the marital home should the relationship end in any way, they more or less willingly give up their rights of inheritance, especially of land, in exchange for the goodwill and the security their brother(s) may offer.[46] Under these circumstances a good relationship with her brother may proof to be a woman's last resort. Her brother may welcome her back in the natal home when

---

[42] The effect was that widows and unmarried girls were left behind without a place to live or a source of income. AGARWAL, 2003, p. 191. Also FLORENCE BUTEGWA, 1994, pp. 497–500.

[43] Patrilocal residence and village exogamy means that after marriage a man will take his wife to live in his or his parents' home, while his sisters go to live with their respective husbands. It can in particular be found in Africa and in Asia. ROSIÓ CÓRDOVA PLAZA, 2000, p. 161. Also AGARWAL, 2003, p. 204.

[44] For parents this custom may entail that they cannot rely on their daughter's support in old age, making them all the more preferring their sons.

[45] This is particularly true for those women who are married under customary law and those who are involved in polygamous marriages. Especially when customary marriages and polygamy are illegal, these women have no legal claim whatsoever when they are sent away or when their husband dies.

[46] Some male relatives are hostile to the idea that daughters and sisters could share in the inheritance. They may intimidate and threaten them, or even use actual force to dissuade them from claiming their share. Some men resist the increased power of women who hold property and/or the fact that the women's share of the inheritance will be at the expense of their own. AGARWAL, 2003, p. 204, also AGARWAL, 1994, pp. 271–276.

she is divorced or widowed and thus provide her with a roof over her head and maybe even a plot of land to cultivate.[47]

Social constructions or prohibitions also prevent women from obtaining or controlling land. Only men may be regarded as the rightful claimants to land. In addition, only men may be perceived as being able to control land while women may not be accepted as independent farmers but instead are considered to be a farmers' help who needs instructions.[48] Sometimes, customs forbid a woman to do all the farming work, such a ploughing.[49]

In some societies a good reputation is a prerequisite for receiving a title to a plot of land and single mothers, divorcees and widows may not meet this requirement. Either their chastity is called into question or they are blamed for their husband's death.[50]

4.2. CONSEQUENCES OF LACK OF LAND

The consequence of denying property rights to women is that they are made totally dependent on men for their access to land and housing. Therefore, good relationships with men are of vital importance for women. This may result in submissiveness to fathers, husbands and in-laws, remaining in abusive relationships, but also in giving up claims of inheritance in favour of brothers.

Another important consequence of denying property rights is that women's political power and participation in decision-making is affected. Property rights, particularly to real estate, are closely linked to power and status.[51] In many rural societies having property rights automatically means being entitled to membership of local decision-making bodies.[52] Landless people, like most

---

[47] AGARWAL, *A field of one's own: Gender and land rights in South Asia*, Cambridge University Press, Cambridge, 1994, pp. 260–268.

[48] A striking example may be found in El Salvador where the agrarian law stipulates that to be entitled to a plot of land a person must be an agricultural producer, 16 years or older, and have the Salvadoran nationality. At first blush, these requirements seem to be totally gender neutral. However, according to cultural views a farmer is a man and a woman can never be more than a farmer's help. Consequently, the local committees that were in charge of allotting land, hardly ever selected women. ZENABAWORKE, 2003, p. 72. Also AGARWAL, 2003, p. 200 on India.

[49] AGARWAL, 2003, p. 200 and p. 205.

[50] ZENABAWORKE, 2003, p. 73.

[51] Having property rights, especially with respect to land, may entail prestige and power over others, while belonging to the 'have-nots' implies vulnerability and subordination. ROSIÓ CÓRDOVA PLAZA, 'Gender roles, inheritance patterns, and female access to land in an *ejidal* community in Veracruz, México', in: Annelies Zoomers and Gemma v.d. Haar (eds.), *Current Land Policy in Latin America: Regulating Land Tenure under Neo-liberalism*, Royal Tropical Institute, Amsterdam, 2000, p. 161. Also AGARWAL, 2003, p. 197.

[52] In Mexico, for instance, women used to have explicit land rights. Since the reform only recognized *ejido* members may decide about the future of the *ejido*. Since only one family member may be an *ejidatario*, it is customary that this is to be the male head of household. As

Chapter 15. Rural Women's Right to Land and Housing in Times of Urbanization

women, are excluded from decision-making. Even within families the possession of land enhances a woman's status and improves her bargaining powers.[53]

If women do not own or control the land they cultivate, this will have repercussions for the agricultural production. Research shows that farm workers put less time and energy in farm work and invest less in the land when they realize that their position is uncertain or that someone else will be in control of the produce.[54]

Access to land reduces the risk of poverty and hunger. Already a small plot of land can make a difference. If a plot is too small to produce enough food for the family, it can certainly contribute towards the family's livelihood and diversity of food. Moreover, land is not only useful for subsistence agriculture, but it also offers possibilities for other non-farm activities.[55]

As already mentioned above, lack of land may also mean that access to credit and loans is limited or denied altogether since most banks demand collateral. As a consequence many schemes to improve a woman's economic circumstances are quenched in an early stage because the necessary funding cannot be raised.[56]

4.3. CEDAW'S ATTENTION FOR LAND IN ARTICLE 14

In order to get an idea to what extent CEDAW addresses the implementation of land rights of rural women on the domestic level, CEDAW's comments on the situation in more than 30 States between 2006 and 2011 were examined.[57]

The issue of rural women was not raised in all Concluding Observations (COs) that were examined. No specific mention was made of Article 14 in the comments on Albania, Australia, Denmark, Germany, Indonesia, Israel, Liechtenstein, The Netherlands, Panama, Sweden, Tunisia, Ukraine, and the United Arab Emirates. It is not clear why these COs do not address Article 14 since it seems unlikely that

---

a result less than 20% of the *ejido* membership are women. CARMEN DIANA DEERE and MAGDALENA LEÓN, 2000, p. 86. In Ethiopia the Peasant Association is relatively powerful since it manages and implements the land reform in addition to its function as judicial tribunal. Since only heads of households are allowed to become a member, only 20 and 25% of the membership was female in the 90s. ZENABAWORKE, 2003, p. 82.

[53] AGARWAL, 2003, p. 197.
[54] AGARWAL, 2003, pp. 193 and 195.
[55] AGARWAL, 2003, pp. 194–195.
[56] AGARWAL, 2003, p. 194.
[57] The 34 States represent different cultural backgrounds and different stages of development; the year between brackets indicates the year in which the Concluding Observations were adopted by CEDAW: Albania (2010), Argentina (2010), Australia (2010), Bangladesh (2011), Belarus (2011), Botswana (2010), Burkina Faso (2010), China (2006), Cuba (2006), Denmark (2006), Egypt (2010), Fiji (2010), Germany (2009), India (2007), Indonesia (2007), Israel (2011), Kenya (2011), Liechtenstein (2011), Malawi (2010), Mexico (2006), The Netherlands (2010), Panama (2010), Papua New Guinea (2010), Russian Federation (2010), Rwanda (2009), South Africa (2011), Sri Lanka (2011), Sweden (2008), Tunisia (2010), Turkey (2010), Uganda (2010), Ukraine (2010), United Arab Emirates (2010), Uzbekistan (2010).

rural women would not be in a disadvantaged situation in these countries. For instance, in the case of the Netherlands the Dutch Government itself reported that compared to men rural women 'have a lower professional level, fewer permanent appointments, less opportunity for independent entrepreneurship, a bigger chance of working part-time and more frequent participation in non-qualifying education'.[58] While Dutch NGOs reported in the 2009 Dutch Shadow Report that although women in rural areas are disadvantaged, a clear policy in respect of improving rural women's position is lacking.[59]

As regards the COs in which Article 14 was addressed, CEDAW expressed concern about the situation of rural women.[60] In a few cases the remarks consisted only of a few lines in which it was pointed out that relevant information on rural women was lacking or insufficient and the State parties (SPs) concerned were requested to include relevant information in their next report.[61]

The issue of access to and right to land was not raised in all cases.[62] This was the most striking as regards Rwanda since in the CO CEDAW itself stated that most rural women work in agriculture.[63]

In the COs where land rights were mentioned, SPs were advised to improve their protection of women's right of inheritance and ownership of land.[64] In some States clear legislation is lacking or the legislation is discriminatory, while in others predominantly customs and social constructions prevent women from claiming their rightful share of the inheritance.

CEDAW explicitly called upon some SPs to change discriminatory customs and traditional practices in rural areas since these were seen as one of the main reasons why women cannot realize their land rights.[65]

The matter of discriminatory practices as regards access to credit was also raised, but only in respect to a limited number of SPs.[66]

On the whole, CEDAW's attention to Article 14 in the COs is rather scant. It is not clear why the Article is not addressed at all in some comments and it is even more curious why the issue of land rights is not raised even in respect to States

---

[58] UN doc. CEDAW/C/NLD/5, Fifth periodic report of the Netherlands, 24 November 2008, p. 93 (English version).

[59] Netwerk VN Vrouwenverdrag (Dutch CEDAW Network), *Women's Rights, Some Progress, Many Gaps*, Shadow Report by Dutch NGOs (2005–2008), November 2009, pp. 73–74.

[60] For instance, concern is expressed as regards the situation of rural women in Argentina, Bangladesh, Botswana, Burkina Faso, China, Cuba, Fiji, Kenya, Malawi, Mexico, Papua New Guinea, Russian Federation, Rwanda, South Africa, and Uganda.

[61] This was the case in respect of Egypt and the Russian Federation.

[62] Land rights were not raised in the COs on Argentina, Mexico, Rwanda and Turkey.

[63] UN doc. CEDAW/C/RWA/CO/6, Concluding Observations, Rwanda, 8 September 2009, para. 37.

[64] Inheritance laws or the lack of them were raised in respect of Bangladesh, Botswana, Burkina Faso, Fiji, India, Malawi, Papua New Guinea, South Africa, and Uganda.

[65] This was done in the case of Bangladesh, Botswana, Burkina Faso, China, Kenya, Malawi, South Africa, Sri Lanka, and Uganda.

[66] Botswana, Burkina Faso, Cuba, Fiji, India, Papua New Guinea, and Uzbekistan.

that are clearly agricultural or where the majority of women are rural women. The suggestions for improvement that are made by CEDAW remain very general and focus on the elimination of discriminatory laws and customs without giving concrete suggestions. Only in one of the COs that were examined – the one on Sri Lanka – the SP was advised to introduce a system of joint or co-ownership of land for couples. However, the fact that specifically *married* couples are mentioned in the CO opens the door for discriminatory attitudes toward couples who have not married officially but for instance in accordance with customary practices.[67]

However, there may be hope that CEDAWs attention to rural women will improve. In view of the upcoming 56th CSW session, CEDAW has recently issued a General Statement on rural women and has recommended States parties, the United Nations and all its programmes, funds and agencies to coordinate action to increase rural women's empowerment and enhance their contribution to agricultural productivity and their role in poverty and hunger eradication.[68]

5. RURAL WOMEN'S FUTURE

Several measures could be taken to enhance rural women's access to and right to land and housing.

Joint titling for couples is a possibility where the State is involved in land reform or resettlement schemes. Couples will obtain a plot of land and or a house in both their names. This is advantageous for women for many reasons, such as it reduces their risk of being evicted, it raises their status in the family, it enhances their independence particularly as regards decisions on how to use the land or how to spend the family's income, and it will give them collateral if they wish to obtain credit.[69]

However, there are also disadvantages as opposed to individual titles for women. Joint titling with the husband means that it becomes very difficult to leave him or to make individual choices. Individual titles to land for women give them opportunity to pool resources with other women and collectively invest and cultivate. Indeed, Agarwal sees it as one of the best opportunities for women to gain access to and rights to land if next to traditions of family owned land other constructions of collective ownership are introduced. Next to collectivities of women who all own a plot of land, she also envisages constructions in which it is possible that the group of women who actually invests and tills the land is bigger than the group that owns the land.[70]

---

[67] UN doc. CEDAW/C/LKACO/7, Concluding Observations, Sri Lanka, 4 February, 2011, para. 39.
[68] CEDAW, General Statement on Rural Women, adopted on 19 October 2011 during the 50th session of the Committee. See: www2.ohchr.org/english/bodies/cedaw/docs/statements/StatementRuralWomen.pdf, last consulted on 24 January 2012.
[69] AGARWAL, 2003, p. 190.
[70] AGARWAL, 2003, pp. 201–202 and p. 206.

Furthermore, schemes similar to the idea of the Grameen Bank in Bangladesh[71] could be initiated by public authorities and/or by NGOs with support from the State. Such schemes should focus on women's access to and right to land by enabling them to lease or buy land as a group.[72] Such organizations could focus in particular on those women who would normally have the least chance to access land such as widows, divorced and unmarried women.

It may also be an option that usufruct/user constructions for women are created on commonly owned, or State owned land. Especially in societies where female exogamy is the rule, residence in a certain village or region could entail that women get access to commonly/State owned land without being able to dispose of this land. If they move away because they get married, they should become entitled to similar access rights in the village or community of their husband. Alternatively, if they are forced to leave their husband's community – either because they are separated or divorced from their husband or because they are widowed – their access rights to their natal land should be re-established.[73]

Social constructions that are based on the idea that land and housing should be in the hands of men because they have to take care of the extended family's access to land should be publicly analyzed and modified in accordance with the changed circumstances. It should be shown that the reason why men were traditionally granted the rights over real estate was their obligation to provide access to land to their widowed mothers and sisters-in-law and their abandoned and unmarried sisters. Times have changed, however and since many male heirs no longer take this responsibility but instead use the land for their own family or sell it and leave for the city, the reasoning behind the custom is no longer valid.[74] Accordingly, the habit should be changed in such a way that male and female heirs profit equally from the inheritance.

The image of a capable farmer should be changed from a male image into a male and female image. Women have proved for centuries that they are – more than – competent to till the land and they should be regarded and respected as independent farmers and no longer as a farmer's help.

---

[71] Grameen Bank is based on the idea that groups of people commit themselves to working together and are eligible to receive loans together in order to set up income-generating activities. The aim of the Bank is to improve the lives of the very poor by enabling them to help themselves. People who borrow money from the Grameen Bank do not need collateral. For more information see: www.grameen-info.

[72] By way of an example Agarwal mentions the Deccan Development Society (DDS) that works in India. See: www.ddsindia.com/www.default.asp.

[73] A similar construction has been suggested in China where Article 30 of the 2002 Law on the Protection of Rights and Interests of Women explicitly protects rural women's access to land – both for agricultural and housing purposes – also in case she has been divorced or widowed. UN doc. CEDAW/C/CHN/6–6, 10 June 2004, p. 53 (English version). AGARWAL, 2003, mentions this possibility in the context of India where a pilot project was initiated in Gujarat; see p. 216.

[74] AGARWAL, 2003, pp. 191 and 194.

It seems obvious that rural women cannot stay and survive in rural areas if services and facilities are not improved or no longer maintained. International organs and States should be aware that the focus on urbanization entails the danger of neglect for rural areas. That is why it is very timely that the 56th session of the Commission on the Status of Women (CSW) will focus on rural women and their role in poverty and hunger eradication at the beginning of 2012.[75] Hopefully, this will be an incentive for other actors to undertake action.

6. CONCLUDING REMARKS

Rural women need land in order to survive and lead a dignified life but in many States both legal and customary rules inhibit them from accessing and possessing land and use the land to its full potential. There is no doubt that the inclusion of a specific provision on rural women in the Women's Convention has led to increased attention for the situation of this group of women. The mere fact that States parties have to report on rural women's circumstances enhances the possibility that policy makers and politicians think about the conditions in rural areas, and understand that rural women have to be enabled and supported in playing their role as regards poverty and hunger eradication because the development of their country will depend on it.

CEDAW's attention for Article 14 and specifically for women's land rights has been rather insignificant and general. It is time for change. CEDAW should become more actively involved and informed. Access to and right to land is not only a problem in a limited number of developing States. All SPs should be requested to investigate women's land rights in depth and make an inventory of the problems and needs that rural women encounter, particularly with regard to negative customary practices that deny them their land rights. States parties, and thus also women, would benefit if CEDAW would collect good examples and give concrete suggestions on how rural women's situation could be improved. Additional efforts are needed to ensure that rural women do not bear the brunt of urbanization.

---

[75] The 56th session of the CSW (27th February till 9th March 2012 in New York) will focus on the theme: 'The empowerment of rural women and their role in poverty and hunger eradication, development and current challenges'.

ARTICLE 15

1. States parties shall accord to women equality with men before the law.
2. States parties shall accord to women, in civil matters, a legal capacity identical to that of men and the same opportunities to exercise that capacity. In particular, they shall give women equal rights to conclude contracts and to administer property and shall treat them equally in all stages of procedure in courts and tribunals.
3. States parties agree that all contracts and all other private instruments of any kind with a legal effect which is directed at restricting the legal capacity of women shall be deemed null and void.
4. States parties shall accord to men and women the same rights with regard to the law relating to the movement of persons and the freedom to choose their residence and domicile.

CHAPTER 16
EQUALITY OF MEN AND WOMEN BEFORE THE LAW: TOWARDS A NEW DUTCH LAW ON NAMES

Tilly DRAAISMA

1. INTRODUCTION

The equality of men and women before the law had already been confirmed in various international conventions, among which the Charter of the United Nations of 1945, the Universal Declaration of Human Rights of 1948, the International Covenants on Human Rights of 1966 and the Declaration on the Elimination of Discrimination Against Women of 1967 before in 1979 the Convention on the Elimination of All Forms of Discrimination Against Women was adopted.

In this Chapter the historical context and the drafting history of Article15 are sketched, followed by an indication of the significance of the Article and a reference to a relevant General Recommendation of CEDAW. Then follows a commentary on the Article and in the last section of this Chapter the significance of Article15 in a concrete case is demonstrated: the (current) Dutch Law on Names. Is that law in accordance with Article15?

2. HISTORICAL CONTEXT

Article 15 did not bubble up from some mysterious well in 1979 but has a longer history. In this section some older texts in which the substance matter of the Article can already be found are outlined.

2.1. CHARTER OF THE UNITED NATIONS

The aims of the United Nations are stated in the Charter of the United Nations as being 'to achieve international co-operation [...] in promoting and encouraging respect for human rights and for fundamental freedoms for all without distinction as to race, sex, language or religion' (Article 1, paragraph 3), and 'the United Nations shall promote universal respect for, and observance of, human rights and fundamental freedoms for all without distinction as to race, sex, language, or religion' (Article 55, sub-paragraph c).

2.2. UNIVERSAL DECLARATION ON HUMAN RIGHTS

The Universal Declaration on Human Rights reaffirms 'the faith in fundamental human rights [...] and in the equal rights of men and women' and provides that 'All human beings are born free and equal in dignity and rights' (Article1). Furthermore, it is stated that 'Everyone is entitled to all the rights and freedoms set forth in the Declaration, without distinction of any kind, such as race, colour, sex, language, religion, political or other opinion, national or social origin, property, birth or other status' (Article 2, paragraph 1).

2.3. INTERNATIONAL COVENANTS ON HUMAN RIGHTS

In the International Covenants on Human Rights, the States parties to the Covenants 'undertake to guarantee that the rights enunciated [...] will be exercised without discrimination of any kind as to race, colour, sex, language, religion, political or other opinion, national or social origin, property, birth or other status' (Article 2, paragraph 2 of the International Covenant on Economic, Social and Cultural Rights), respectively 'undertake to respect and to ensure to all individuals within its territory and subject to its jurisdiction the rights recognized in the present Convention, without distinction of any kind, such as race, colour, sex, language, religion, political or other opinion, national or social origin, property, birth or other status' (Article2, paragraph 1 of the International Covenant on Civil and Political Rights). Furthermore, both conventions 'undertake to ensure the equal right of men and women to the enjoyment of all [...] rights set forth in the [present] Covenant' (Article 3 of both Covenants).

2.4. DECLARATION ON THE ELIMINATION OF DISCRIMINATION AGAINST WOMEN

The Declaration on the Elimination of Discrimination Against Women (GA Resolution 2263 (XXII)) states that Discrimination Against Women is fundamentally unjust and 'constitutes an offence against human dignity' (Article 1), and that the following should be accomplished:

- the abolishment of existing laws, customs regulations and practices which are discriminatory against women;
- the adequate establishment of legal protection of equal rights of men and women according to national constitutions and the ratification of international instruments of the United Nations and specialized agencies (Article 2);
- the education of the public opinion towards the eradication of prejudice; and
- the abolition of customary and all other practices which are based on the idea of the inferiority of women (Article 3).

3. DRAFTING HISTORY OF ARTICLE 15

It can be said that the Convention is an extension of the Declaration. However, in the years that had passed, attitudes towards women's issues had undergone major changes and the Convention became far more substantial than the Declaration. This process was also reflected in the negotiations. Although minor for Article 15 this negotiating process is sketched in this section.

3.1. THE DRAFT PROPOSALS OF THE WORKING GROUP OF THE COMMISSION ON THE STATUS OF WOMEN[1]

The original proposal for Article15 was contained in the draft proposal by the Working Group of the Commission on the Status of Women of 1974. It provided:
Paragraph 1. 'The States parties shall accord to women equality with men before the law'.
Paragraph 2. 'The States parties shall accord to women equal civil and legal capacity with men in all stages of procedure in courts and tribunals'.
Paragraph 3. 'The States parties agree that all contracts directed at restricting the legal capacity of women shall be deemed null and void'.

---

1 UN doc. E/CN.6/589 (E/5451), Report of the 25th session.

Paragraph 4. 'The States parties shall accord men and women the same rights with regard to the law on the movement of persons and the freedom to choose their residence'.

3.2. THE PROPOSAL OF THE COMMISSION ON THE STATUS OF WOMEN[2]

In 1976 the Commission on the Status of Women examined the proposal of the Working group at her 650th meeting. Many of the representatives expressed their acceptance of the original text, at that time renumbered as Article 14. Thus, paragraph 1 of the original text of the proposal of the Working Group was adopted without a vote.

Sweden submitted a revised proposal for paragraph 2 entailing the inclusion of equal rights to conclude contracts and administer property as until then much discrimination had occurred in this regard. Identical rights between men and women were now clearly stated. This concrete provision of the Article was adopted unanimously by the Commission and read:

Paragraph 2. 'The States parties shall accord to women a civil and legal capacity *identical to that of* men, *and to exercise that capacity. They shall in particular give them equal rights to conclude contracts and administer property and treat them equally* in all stages of procedure in courts and tribunals'.

The United Kingdom expressed reservations regarding paragraph 3. The wording was vague and could be interpreted extensively. Belgium proposed an addition, thereby further invalidating the restriction on the legal capacity of women. This proposal was adopted by the Commission by 22 votes to 0, with no abstentions. The revised proposal read:

Paragraph 3. 'The States parties agree that all contracts *and other legal instruments of any kind* directed at restricting the legal capacity of women shall be deemed null and void'.

Egypt, Iran and Indonesia expressed reservations against paragraph 4. The reasons were conflict with their national laws. Egypt explained that according to Egyptian law a wife's place of residence is her husband's place of residence. 'Domicile' was added to 'residence' and the new proposal read:

Paragraph 4. 'The States parties shall accord men and women the same rights with regard to the law on the movement of persons and the freedom to choose their residence *and domicile*'.

---

[2] UN doc. E/CN.6/608 (E/5909), Report of the 26th session and resumed 26th session (1976).

3.3. REVIEWS OF THE WORKING GROUP OF THE THIRD COMMITTEE[3]

The Working Group of the Third Committee reviewed the draft adopted by the Commission on the Status of Women at its 16th and 17th meetings in 1978.

Paragraph 1 as proposed by the Commission was adopted without revisions by the Committee.

For purposes of its legal system, Egypt wished to record its reservations against paragraph 2, but did not oppose the paragraph itself. Orally, the United Kingdom proposed a slightly revised text which became the official proposal and read: Paragraph 2. 'The States parties shall accord to women a civil and legal capacity identical to that of men, and *the same opportunities* to exercise that capacity. They shall in particular give them equal rights to conclude contracts and administer property and treat them equally in all stages of procedure in courts and tribunals'.

With regard to paragraph 3, Ecuador proposed the deletion of the phrase: 'and all other legal instruments of any kind'. The representative expressed recognition of the need to abolish all legal instruments in the domestic civil law system restricting legal capacities of women, but said that if this paragraph were adopted the legal provisions of many countries supporting the Convention would become invalid, thereby creating an unstable legal vacuum.

Representatives of other countries were in favour of leaving the text as it was. Some said that paragraph 3 was no more than a repetition of the concepts included in paragraph 2. But that paragraph relates to equal rights for men and women to conclude contracts and to administer property, while paragraph 3 relates to the idea that, when women enjoy this right, it may not be renounced, nor may their legal capacity be restricted. The Netherlands explained that agreements between husband and wife, for example if a wife is coerced to sign a check or if a wife cannot enter a contract without her husband's consent, would be invalid according to paragraph 3. Rumania emphasized the reality that the issue of equal legal capacities for men and women was not limited to 'contractual matters' but should also encompass 'transactional matters'. For this reason the phrase 'and all other legal instruments of any kind' was necessary to avoid a restrictive interpretation that could be derived from paragraph 2, now that this paragraph did not allude to 'transactional matters'. Orally, Belgium proposed to change Ecuador's revision, which proposal was adopted by the Working Group of the Third Committee. As a result the paragraph read as follows:

---

[3] UN docs. A/C.3/32/L.59 (UN docs. A/C.3/32/L.59, Summary of Deliberations by Working Group (Preamble to Article 9) (06.12.1977); A/C.3/33/L.47/Corr. 1,2 (Summary of Deliberations by Working Group (Arts. 10 to 16) (28.11.1978); A/C.3/34/14 (Summary of Deliberations by Working Group (Title, Preamble, Arts. 2, 6, 9, 17 to 24) (30.11.1979), and A/C.3/33/WG.1/CRP.10/Add.1 (Proposal by Ecuador (Arts. 14, 15, 19)) (10.11.1978).

Paragraph 3. 'The States parties agree that all contracts and *all* other *private* instruments of any kind *with a legal effect which is* directed at restricting the legal capacity of women shall be deemed null and void'.

Paragraph 4 was adopted by the Working Group of the Third Committee with no changes.

3.4. THE THIRD COMMITTEE[4]

In 1979 the Third Committee adopted the proposals by the Working Group for Article 15, paragraphs 1, 3 and 4. The phrasing of paragraph 2 altered only slightly. The paragraph now reads:

Paragraph 2. 'The States parties shall accord to women *in civil matters*, legal capacity identical to that of men, and the same opportunities to exercise that capacity. They shall in particular give them equal rights to conclude contracts and administer property and treat them equally in all stages of procedure in courts and tribunals'.

3.5. PLENARY MEETING OF THE GENERAL ASSEMBLY OF THE UNITED NATIONS[5]

At the plenary meeting of the General Assembly the text of the Third Committee was adopted without revision although numerous opinions were expressed as to paragraph wording, especially regarding paragraphs 2 and 3.

In conclusion it can be said that, although maybe not spectacular, during the negotiating process there still were some changes made, especially in paragraphs 2 and 3, between the first draft of the Working Group in 1974 and the final text in the Convention of 1979.

4. SIGNIFICANCE OF ARTICLE 15

Although the principle of equality of men and women before the law is apart from the above mentioned international texts also embodied in various national constitutions, substantial and extensive discrimination continues to exist between men and women.

The Convention on the Elimination of All Forms of Discrimination Against Women of 1979 therefore clearly states in the Preamble that 'Discrimination

---

[4] UN doc. A/34/830 etc., Report of the Secretary-General (Draft by Third Committee), 14–12–1979.
[5] Official Records of the General Assembly, 34th Session, Agenda item 75.

Against Women violates the principles of equality of rights and respect for human dignity' which makes Article 15 a more effective provision for the equality of men and women. This goes all the more now that Article 15 stands at the outset of Part IV of the Convention and can be assumed, comparable to the Preamble, to be a guideline for the interpretation of the Articles of that part of the Convention.

To realize more substantial and practical equality there are also obligations of the States parties to the Convention not only to ensure that their legislation and practices do not discriminate against women, but also to eliminate Discrimination Against Women by any person, organization or enterprise, and to modify or abolish discriminatory customs and practices (Arts. 2 and 5). Furthermore, the Convention contains a provision ensuring that 'the adoption [...] of temporary special measures aimed at accelerating *de facto* equality between men and women shall not be considered discrimination' (Article 4).

Art 15, paragraph 1 affirms the equality of men and women before the law. To guarantee the same rights to men and women both, Article15, paragraph 2 provides for an identical legal capacity for men and women in civil matters, allowing men and women to have the same opportunities to exercise that capacity and providing for equal rights for women to conclude contracts and administer property. This paragraph also provides for the equal treatment of men and women in all juridical proceedings. In paragraph 3, contracts and other instruments that restrict the legal capacity of women are to be deemed null and void, and in paragraph 4 men and women are accorded the same rights regarding free personal movement and choice of residence and domicile.

In principle, personal life is considered free from governmental interference. The guarantee of 'equality before the law' (Article15), read in conjunction with the meaning of Article 2, may however be considered as applying directly to the private sphere. The inclusion of the private sphere therefore is imperative for the realization of (more) substantive equality between men and women. Article 15 not merely, simply or abstractly, sets forth the principle of equality between men and women: it concretely refers to numerous aspects of discrimination, especially in personal life, and states clearly that in these matters discrimination has no place. For this reason, Article 15 may be more effective in promoting the equality of men and women than previous provisions in international conventions and declarations.

5. RECOMMENDATIONS BY CEDAW

In its Resolution 44/82 the General Assembly designated the year 1994 as the International Year of the Family. To mark this event, CEDAW adopted at its 13th session (1994) General Recommendation number 21 in which it analyzed three Articles in the Convention that have a special significance for the status of women in the family. Article 15 is among these Articles. CEDAW's comments on this provision read as follows:[6]

'[7.] When a woman cannot enter into a contract at all, or have access to financial credit, or can do so only with her husband's or a male relative's concurrence or guarantee, she is denied legal autonomy. Any such restriction prevents her from holding property as the sole owner and precludes her from the legal management of her own business or from entering into any other form of contract. Such restrictions seriously limit the woman's ability to provide for herself and her dependents.

[8.] A woman's right to bring litigation is limited in some countries by law or by her access to legal advice and her ability to seek redress from the courts. In others, her status as a witness or her evidence is accorded less respect or weight than that of a man. Such laws or customs limit the woman's right effectively to pursue or retain her equal share of property and diminish her standing as an independent, responsible and valued member of her community. When countries limit a woman's legal capacity by their laws, or permit individuals or institutions to do the same, they are denying women their rights to be equal with men and restricting women's ability to provide for themselves and their dependents.

[9.] Domicile is a concept in common law countries referring to the country in which a person intends to reside and to whose jurisdiction she will submit. Domicile is originally acquired by a child through its parents but, in adulthood, denotes the country in which a person normally resides and in which she intends to reside permanently. As in the case of nationality, the examination of States parties' reports demonstrates that a woman will not always be permitted at law to choose her own domicile. Domicile, like nationality, should be capable of change at will by an adult woman regardless of her marital status. Any restrictions on a woman's right to choose a domicile on the same basis as a man may limit her access to the courts in the country in which she lives or prevent her from entering and leaving a country freely and in her own right.

[10]. Migrant women who live and work temporarily in another country should be permitted the same rights as men to have their spouses, partners and children join them.'

Up till now CEDAW has not made any other comments or recommendation in regard of Article 15.

6. COMMENTARY

In Article 15 an obligation of 'equality before the law' is formulated. Interpreted in the spirit of the Preamble and the entire Convention this 'equality' not only refers to the abolition of discrimination in the law, but also to the eradication of each and

---

[6] CEDAW General Recommendation No. 21, Equality in Marriage and Family Relations, 13th session, 1994.

every form of discrimination in practice, in other words it aims at real, substantive equality. Not only does Article 2, sub-paragraph (d) provide for the refraining from discrimination by public authorities or institutions, but Article2 sub-paragraph (e) also provides for the elimination of discrimination by any person, organization or enterprise, and Article 2, sub-paragraph (f) provides for the abolition of discrimination through customs and practices. Accordingly 'equality before the law' in Article 15, paragraph 1 is a principal criterion that applies to private individuals, organizations and enterprises and is thought to be at the nucleus of respect for individual dignity. The right not to be discriminated against on the basis of sex is, as a fundamental human right, to be enjoyed by all women.

With regard to the 'protection of women', in consideration of such matters as physical characteristics and women's role in society, the Declaration on the Elimination of Discrimination Against Women took the stance that 'protection' should be granted. However the position under the Convention is that, as there is some risk that 'protection' of women invites discrimination, the protection of working conditions as regards matters other than pregnancy and procreation, should be reviewed (Article11, paragraph 3). Even with regard to child-rearing the Declaration on the Elimination of Discrimination Against Women was of the view that it was a women's responsibility, but the Convention maintains that 'the upbringing of children requires a sharing of responsibility between men and women and society as a whole'. In this way, the Convention introduces the rather new concept of abolishing stereotyped ideas on the roles of men and women. In other words, the Convention's notion is one of absolute equality between men and women. However, the Convention aims at equality of results and of outcome, which leaves open the possibility of exceptions to equality of treatment.

By approving temporary special measures for accelerating *de facto* equality (Article 4), the Convention does not adopt the negative position that national institutions should not practice discrimination. In other words, the Convention does not take the view of formal, negative equality, so the right to equality does not exclude the treatment to remedy an inequality. Rather the Convention takes the position of substantive, positive equality, whereby it is the essential right of the person who actually receives an unequal treatment, to demand that it will be corrected. Accordingly, the standards for reviewing the status of equality should not merely be rational based criteria, but strict scrutiny criteria and a meticulous reading brings me to the conclusion that no derogation of the strict ban on discrimination as formulated in Article 15 is allowed.

The result of this reading is that Article 15 leaves *no* room for a plea of discretionary powers. A striking example where a Government is confronted with the result of this reading is the case of the Dutch Law on Names. Notwithstanding that the discussions on this law are about Article 16 of the Convention (and not directly about Article 15) the reason for the problems are to be found in the strict interpretation of Article 15.

7. TOWARDS A NEW DUTCH LAW ON NAMES?

7.1. THE LAW UP TILL 1 JANUARY 1998

In 1988 the Dutch Supreme Court decided that the Dutch Law on Names was discriminatory and not in accordance with Article 26 of the International Covenant on Civil and Political Rights.[7]

After more than thirty years, the Law on Names has now been changed,[8] and in the second periodic report to the Committee on the Elimination of Discrimination Against Women the Netherlands summarized the new law as follows:[9]

> 'The Law on Names has undergone a major change. Children born in wedlock automatically took the name of their father until 1 January 1998. Since then, however, it has been possible to choose between the surnames of the father and mother. This applies to all children who by law have two parents whose names can be chosen. They include all children who have a family law relationship with their parents as a result of acknowledgement or adoption and children born during a marriage. The surnames of all children in a family must be the same. The choice made by the parents is provisional in that a child may decide on reaching the age of majority to change the surname that it obtained under the new law or the transitional provisions to the name of the other parent.
>
> If no choice is made, a child born in wedlock takes the name of the father and a child born out of wedlock the name of the mother. When the legislation was being drafted the question of what action should be taken if no choice is made was discussed at length. At one point it was suggested that lots should be drawn. Although drawing lots would be entirely neutral, it was thought inappropriate to decide the name of a child by lot. Ultimately, it was decided that a child born in wedlock should take the name of its father if no choice is made.
>
> A married woman or a formerly married woman is entitled to use her husband's surname instead of her maiden name or to place her husband's surname before her maiden name (Article 9, Book 1, Civil Code). In future, a married man or formerly married man will have the same right. In addition, the name of the spouse may be added after the person's own name. The new Article 9 will also apply to registered partners.'

---

[7] HR 23 September 1988, NJ 1989, 740 (Beukema-van Veen).
[8] TILLY DRAAISMA, *De stiefouder: stiefkind van het recht. Een onderzoek naar de juridische plaatsbepaling van de stiefouder*, VU Uitgeverij, Amsterdam, 2001, pp. 36–40.
[9] UN doc. CEDAW/C/Net/2, Second periodic reports of States parties, The Netherlands, 15 March 1999, p. 92 (English text).

7.2. COMMENTS BY THE COMMITTEE

In her report to the General Assembly of the twenty-fourth and twenty-fifth sessions of the Committee on the Elimination of Discrimination Against Women the Committee made the following comments:[10]

> '223. The Committee further expresses concern that the new Law on Names provides that, where the parents cannot reach an agreement as to the name of a child, the father has the ultimate decision. The Committee believes that this contravenes the basic principle of the Convention regarding equality, in particular Article 16 (g) thereof.
> 224. The Committee recommends that the Government review the Law on Names and amend it to comply with the Convention.'

7.3. THE FOURTH PERIODIC REPORT OF THE NETHERLANDS AND THE COMMITTEE'S COMMENTS

In the fourth periodic report the Government of the Netherlands again stated as follows:[11]

> 'On 1 January 1998 the law on names was amended in one important respect. Since that date, parents have been able to choose whether the child will take the father's or the mother's surname. Once this choice has been made, any subsequent children take the same surname. The choice of name may be made when the child is acknowledged, when a judicial declaration of paternity is issued, when an adoption order is made, or before or at the latest immediately following the birth of the child.
> A child born into a marriage between a man and a woman takes the father's name unless the couple explicitly chooses the mother's name. The same applies in the case of adoption by an opposite-sex couple. If the adoptive parents are unmarried, or are of the same sex and married to each other, the child keeps the surname he/she already has unless an explicit choice is made for the surname of one of the adoptive parents. A child who is adopted by, and thus enters into a family-law relationship with, the spouse, registered partner or other life partner of his/her parent, retains his/her surname unless an explicit choice is made for the surname of the spouse or partner. In the case of an acknowledgment or a judicial declaration of paternity, the child bears the mother's name unless an explicit choice is made for the father's surname at the time of the acknowledgment or judicial declaration. If the child is 16 or over at the moment of entering into a family-law relationship with both parents, he/she declares to the registrar of births, deaths and marriages – or in the case of a judicial declaration of paternity, to the court – which surname he/she wishes to take.'

---

[10] UN doc. A/56/38, Report of the Committee on the Elimination of Discrimination Against Women (24th and 25th session), 2001, paras. 223 and 224.
[11] UN doc. CEDAW/C/NLD/4, Fourth periodic report of States parties: Netherlands, 10 February 2005, p. 81.

The comment of the Committee is obvious:[12]

> '33. The Committee reiterates its concern that the Law on Names provides that, where the parents cannot reach an agreement as to the name of a child, the father has the ultimate decision, which contravenes the basic principle of the Convention regarding equality, in particular Article 16(g) thereof.
> 34. The Committee repeats its recommendation that the State party review the Law on Names and amend it to comply with the Convention.'

7.4. THE FIFTH REPORT OF THE NETHERLANDS

On 30th June 2008 the Government of the Netherlands issued the fifth periodic report in which the following remarks on the Law of surnames are made:[13]

> 'The Commission (*sic*, TD) has repeated its recommendation that the law on surnames be revised and brought in line with the principle of equality, and particularly Article 16 (g) of the Convention (conclusion 33 and recommendation 34).
> From this recommendation the Dutch government draws the conclusion that the Commission is under the impression that the current Dutch law on surnames entails that, if the parents cannot agree on the name of their child, the father will make the ultimate decision. However, this does not accurately describe the current Dutch legislation.
> The law stipulates that, in this case, a child born within marriage receives the name of the father. According to Dutch law the married parents will jointly declare – either before or on the occasion of the registration of the birth – whether their child will have the surname of the father or mother.
> If they choose the father's surname, this declaration is not necessary as, if the parents do not choose a name the Registrar of births, deaths and marriages will automatically allocate the father's surname to the child's birth certificate.
> In its recommendation to change the Dutch law on surnames on this point, the Commission does not give a further explanation that addresses the question of whether there is an objective and reasonable ground for the preference in Dutch law for the name of father in the event of a lack of consensus. In this context the government would like to point out that the European Court of Human Rights (ECHR) did pay express attention to this question and subsequently concluded that the legislation does not discriminate and therefore does not violate Article 8 j° 14 of the European Convention on Human Rights and fundamental Freedoms (ECHR 27 April 2000, *Bijleveld versus the Netherlands*, appl. no. 42973/98). The ECHR took

---

[12] UN doc. CEDAW/C/NLD/CO/4, Concluding Comments of the Committee on the Elimination of Discrimination Against Women: Netherlands, 2 February 2007, p. 6, paras. 33 and 34.

[13] UN doc. CEDAW/C/NLD/5, Fifth periodic report of States parties: Netherlands, 24 November 2008, paras. 77–78.

into account that States that are a party to the UN Women's Convention enjoy a broad margin of appreciation with respect to this subject, which is strongly determined by national traditions. The 2002 evaluation of the law on surnames that has been in effect since 1 January 1998 shows that there is a clear preference among the Dutch population for a system of choice in which children can have the father's or the mother's surname. Furthermore, it is in the interest of the child that, if the parents cannot reach consensus about the question of what surname the child should have, a surname is not withheld. Finally, if the parents are not married the child will have the mother's surname even if the father has acknowledged the child. If the unmarried parents want the child to have the surname of the father they will jointly have to declare this when the father acknowledges the child.'

The Bijleveld-case

It is interesting to elaborate on the above cited case the Dutch Government is referring to. As far as relevant for our subject the facts, observations and decisions of the European Court of Human rights were as follows. As to the facts:

Applicant is a Dutch national, born in 1958, and living in Leiden. She and her husband have two sons, born in 1988 and 1991 respectively, and two daughters, born in 1994 and 1997 respectively. Pursuant to the relevant rules of Dutch law, these children bear the surname of the applicant's husband. As the applicant and her husband wished their sons to bear the surname of their father and their daughter to bear the surname of the applicant, the applicant filed a request on 12 September 1994 to change the surname of her, at that time still unborn, daughter.

On 24 November 1994, the State Secretary of Justice rejected the applicant's request. The applicant's subsequent appeal to the Regional Court of The Hague was rejected on 23 May 1996. The applicant filed a further appeal with the Administrative Law Division of the Council of State which was rejected in his decision of 25 September 1997.

The applicant filed complaints with the ECHR on 23 March 1998 that the former Dutch rules on surnames constituted a flagrant violation of the principle of non-discrimination as well as an unlawful interference with her right to respect for her private and family life. She relied on Articles 8 and 14 of the European Convention on Human Rights as well as on Article 26 of the International Covenant on Civil and Political Rights and Articles 2 and 16 of the Convention on the Elimination of All Forms of Discrimination Against Women.

The applicant further submitted that also the (new) rules on surnames are not in conformity with Articles 8 and 14 of the Convention. She argued that it is not the legislator but those involved – *i.e.* the parents – who must have the opportunity to choose the surname of their children. However, having made that choice for the parents, the legislator continues to interfere with the right to respect for a person's private and family life by depriving those directly involved of the right to choose a name themselves. She argued that parents must have equal rights in choosing the surname for their children. Under the (new) rules, in case of a conflict between the parents, the child will automatically obtain the father's surname. As, for the purpose of passing on her surname to her children, a mother's right to choose is therefore restricted by the father's power of veto, the new rules are also contrary to Article 14 of the European Convention in conjunction with Article 8 in that it constitutes discrimination on the mere grounds of sex without any objective justification.

As to the Dutch Law on Names the European Court observes the following, as far as relevant for our subject. In the first place the Court observes that, under the terms of Article 19 of the European Convention, it is not competent to examine the applicant's complaints under the International Covenant on Civil and Political Rights and the Convention on the Elimination of All Forms of Discrimination Against Women.

Furthermore, the Court recalls that legal restrictions on the possibility of changing surnames may be justified in the public interest, that Contracting States enjoy a wide margin of appreciation in this legal area and that it is not the task of the Court to substitute itself for the competent domestic authorities in determining the most appropriate policy for regulating changes of surnames in a particular Contracting State, but rather to review under the Convention the decisions that those authorities have taken in the exercise of their power of appreciation. Than the Court notes that the current possibilities under Dutch law for parents to choose whether their children will bear either the surname of the father or of the mother and recalling the Contracting States' wide margin of appreciation in this legal area, she (the Court) cannot find, in the particular circumstances of the present case, that the refusal of the applicant's request to give a different surname to her daughter than the surname given to her sons constituted a lack of respect for her private and family life within the meaning of Article 8 of the Convention.

The Court then recalls that for the purposes of Article 14 of the European Convention, a difference in treatment is discriminatory if it has no objective or reasonable justification, that is, if it does not pursue a legitimate aim or if there is not a reasonable relationship of proportionality between the means employed and the aim sought to be realized. The Contracting States enjoy a certain margin of appreciation in assessing whether and to what extent differences in otherwise similar situations justify a different treatment in law. And furthermore the Court observes that as to the question whether the rules currently in force entail a difference in treatment based on sex, these rules left the starting point that children of married parents and children whose paternity has been recognized by the father automatically bear the surname of the father. After the amendment of the rules on surnames, parents may choose which of their respective surnames will be given to their children, albeit with the restriction that all of their children will bear the same surname. The children of married parents will automatically bear the surname of their father. They can, however, obtain the mother's surname where the parents have made a joint declaration to this effect. Furthermore, this rule applies to both male and female children. Therefore, the Court finds no indication of a difference in treatment based on sex in their respect.

As regards the position of the parents on this point, it is true that the possibility to pass on the mother's surname to children of a married couple is made subject to the making of a joint declaration of the parents and that, in case the parents disagree on this point, the rule that children automatically bear the father's surname applies. There is therefore a difference in treatment between men and women in that the possibility to pass on a mother's surname is made dependent on an explicit agreement between both parents, whereas the possibility to pass on the father's surname is not based on such an agreement. The question therefore arises whether there is an objective or reasonable justification for this difference in treatment.

Recalling the margin of appreciation of Contracting States as to the assessment whether and to what extent differences in otherwise similar situations justify a difference in treatment, the Court accepts that a Contracting State may regard as undesirable a situation in which the surname of a child would remain undetermined until both parents have reached an agreement on this point and, in order to prevent such a situation, establish an automatic rule which applies in the absence of such an agreement. It therefore considers that, as to the difference in treatment complained of in the present case, there is a reasonable relationship of proportionality between the means employed and the aim sought to be realized.

For the above reasons, the Court, unanimously, declared the application inadmissible.

7.5. THE COMMITTEE'S COMMENTS

In her comments on the fifth report the Committee is very short and clear:[14]

> '10. The Committee acknowledges the relatively short time between the adoption of the previous concluding observations and the examination of their implementation. It regrets, however, that some of the concerns it expressed and the recommendations it adopted after the consideration of the fourth periodic report of the Netherlands [...] in 2007 have been insufficiently addressed. These include, for instance [...], the

---

[14] UN doc. CEDAW/C/NLD/CO/5, Concluding Comments of the Committee on the Elimination of Discrimination Against Women: Netherlands, 5 February 2010, p. 3, paras. 10 and 11.

Law on Names which continues to contravene the basic principle of the Convention regarding equality [...].

11. The Committee urges the Netherlands to make every effort to address the previous recommendations that have not yet been fully implemented, as well as the concerns contained in the present concluding observations.'

7.6. CONCLUDING OBSERVATIONS

Some conclusions I draw from the above are, *inter alia*, that (1) the Committee again urges the Netherlands to re-evaluate her Law on Names.[15] The Convention on the Elimination of All Forms of Discrimination Against Women starts its Part IV with Article 15 as a general rule, the specific rules are to be found in Article 16. Against the background of the strict interpretation of Article 15 advocated above this call of the Committee could be expected. However, it would be advisable if the Committee would adopt a clear General Recommendation on the correct, strict interpretation of Article 15. That way it would be possible to anticipate further divergent interpretations. (2) It is questionable if the generally formulated *obiter dictum* of the European Court in its observations in the *Bijleveld-case* is tenable in future judicial proceedings before other national and international courts. There was *no* appeal on Article 15 and the European Court had no competence in that matter. It is advisable in future judicial proceedings to make a subsidiary appeal on Article 15. (3) The European Court explicitly states that it has no competence to examine complaints under the Convention on the Elimination of All Forms of Discrimination Against Women. The appeal of the Netherlands in its fifth report on the *Bijleveld-case* therefore is too hasty.

8. CONCLUSION

The Convention on the Elimination of All Forms of Discrimination Against Women is the most comprehensive single legal document that deals with the rights of women in all fields. It is considered a major pillar for the advancement of women, taken as a set of guidelines to help national governments in addressing women's issues including revising its current laws and legislation. The Convention is a treaty that builds on older developments and consolidates all matters concerning women's rights. As formulated in the Preamble of the Convention, the underlying theme of the Convention is, in short, that

---

[15] This is not the place to dwell on possible solutions. As a way out one could think about enlargement of the legal options to choose a (double-) name and/or the creation of an explicit access to court possibly with preceding compulsory judicial mediation.

Discrimination Against Women is unjust and that such injustice should be eliminated so that genuine equality between men and women can be attained.

A first stage in achieving equality between men and women is to abrogate discriminatory laws and systems. The next stage is to take concrete measures to realize *de facto* equality, and the final stage is to address the consciousness found at the root of discrimination. Assuming that these three stages form a way to achieve equality between men and women, the Convention is indeed significant in terms of having reached the third stage, by calling for a change in the stereotyped perception of the roles of men and women.

The principles formulated in the Preamble serve as a guideline for interpreting each Article of the Convention, and so the principles formulated in Article 15, which stand at the outset of part IV of the Convention, serve also as a guideline for the interpretation of that Article.

In this Chapter the historical context and the drafting history of Article15 was sketched, followed by an indication of the significance of the Article and a reference to a relevant General Recommendation of CEDAW. Then followed a commentary on the Article and in the last section of this Chapter the significance of Article15 in a concrete case was demonstrated: the (current) Dutch Law on Names.

The investigation has shown that (1) it would be advisable in future judicial proceedings to make a subsidiary appeal on Article15, and that (2) the current Dutch Law on Names is *not* in accordance with the provisions of the Convention.

ARTICLE 16

1. States parties shall take all appropriate measures to eliminate discrimination against women in all matters relating to marriage and family relations and in particular shall ensure, on a basis of equality of men and women:

    (a) The same right to enter into marriage;
    (b) The same right freely to choose a spouse and to enter into marriage only with their free and full consent;
    (c) The same rights and responsibilities during marriage and at its dissolution;
    (d) The same rights and responsibilities as parents, irrespective of their marital status, in matters relating to their children; in all cases the interests of the children shall be paramount;
    (e) The same rights to decide freely and responsibly on the number and spacing of their children and to have access to the information, education and means to enable them to exercise these rights;
    (f) The same rights and responsibilities with regard to guardianship, wardship, trusteeship and adoption of children, or similar institutions where these concepts exist in national legislation; in all cases the interests of the children shall be paramount;
    (g) The same personal rights as husband and wife, including the right to choose a family name, a profession and an occupation;
    (h) The same rights for both spouses in respect of the ownership, acquisition, management, administration, enjoyment and disposition of property, whether free of charge or for a valuable consideration.

2. The betrothal and the marriage of a child shall have no legal effect, and all necessary action, including legislation, shall be taken to specify a minimum age for marriage and to make the registration of marriages in an official registry compulsory.

CHAPTER 17
ARTICLE 16 OF THE WOMEN'S CONVENTION AND THE STATUS OF MUSLIM WOMEN AT DIVORCE

Pauline KRUINIGER

1. INTRODUCTION

Although divorce[1] – one of the varieties of dissolution of marriage – is a universal phenomenon, its forms and procedures are worldwide not uniform. Historically influenced, cultural and religious views on divorce which are dominant within individual States, have characterized their domestic divorce laws and practices. Hence, Islam and its legal system which forms part of *Shari'a*,[2] has set its stamp on contemporary divorce laws and practices of States with an Islamic background (hereinafter 'Islamic' States).[3]

---

[1] The wording 'divorce' is used in this contribution as the collective term for the most common types of dissolution of marriage by the act of the parties or by judicial process, which may also include the annulment of the marriage, unless it is stated otherwise.

[2] *Shari'a* literally means 'path to the watering place' and has to be understood as the way to good life ordained by Allah. Therefore it is considered to be of divine origin. It is the general normative system of Islam which regulates the life of Muslims in all of its aspects. Hence, it comprises rules of conduct of religious, social, moral, ethical and legal (only a small part) nature. *Shari'a* has been derived from the *Qur'an* (revelations by Allah to the Prophet Muhammad), and *Sunna* (tradition or example of the Prophet and his Companions which consists of their wordings, deeds and behaviour). The understanding and elaboration of these sources by means of *qiyas* (analogical reasoning) and *ijma* (consensus of Muslim scholars) resulted in a corpus of legal rules (*fiqh*); hence, *Shari'a* is broader than *fiqh* and *Shari'a* law or Islamic law is derived from and part of *Shari'a*. *Fiqh* in the meaning of legal science, comprises four Sunni schools of law, the Hanafi, Maliki, Shafi'i and Hanbali, and the Shia school of law with its sub schools. This subdivision is one of the reasons which explain why *the* or uniform Islamic law does not exist. Law based upon *Shari'a* will therefore be indicated as 'Islamic' law in this contribution. See *e.g.* J. SCHACHT, *An introduction to Islamic law*, Clarendon Press, Oxford, 1982, or M. KAMALI, *Shari'a law; an introduction*, Oneworld Publications, Oxford, 2008.

[3] The notion "'Islamic' State(s)" will be used in this contribution for pragmatic reasons in order to refer to States with an Islamic background *i.e.* States with legislation which incorporates, at least to some extent, Islamic laws and customs.

There seems to be a tension between the status of women in Islam and the status of women as defined under international human rights law.[4] As a matter of fact, women's rights appear to be the most controversial and the hottest debated issue in the discussion about the compatibility of Islam and human rights. The rights of women under Islam are religiously influenced, whereas human rights including women's rights depend on universal values in order to guarantee the full realization of these rights worldwide.[5] In this respect one may speak of a situation of legal diversity in women's rights.

Exemplary in this respect is that divorces which originate from 'Islamic' States (hereinafter 'Islamic' divorces),[6] are considered to infringe upon fundamental substantive and procedural rights of women. Especially the repudiation or *talaq*, originally the extra-judicial, unilateral dissolution of marriage at the exclusive discretion by the husband, is notorious. The repudiation violates the right of equal accessibility to dissolution of marriage by the spouses since women have – in principle – no right to repudiate.[7] It also infringes upon procedural rights such as the right to be called upon or the right to hear both sides as the presence of the wife at the pronouncement of the repudiation is not required nor can she defend herself otherwise. But the legal reality of divorce and its practices in 'Islamic' States is much more complex and diverse as it will be demonstrated in this contribution. On closer inspection it appears that *the* repudiation or *the* 'Islamic' divorce or even *the* Islamic law does not exists: depending on their origin in one of the various schools of law and depending on legal, judicial and legislative developments in the 'Islamic' states, huge differences among the legal institutions and laws of these states can be distinguished.

The most comprehensive and 'specialized' of the various human rights instruments which deal with combating the above mentioned violations by guaranteeing equal rights for men and women in society and in the family, is the Convention on the Elimination of All Forms of Discrimination Against Women (hereinafter the Women's Convention or the Convention).[8] Today, thirty-six out of the 186 States which have ratified or acceded to this legally binding,

---

[4] E. YAHYAOUI KRIVENKO, *Women, Islam and International Law*, Martinus Nijhoff Publishers, Leiden, 2009, p. 4.
[5] M. BADERIN, *International human rights and Islamic law*, Oxford University Press, Oxford, 2005, pp. 23–26.
[6] The notion "'Islamic' divorces" will be used in this contribution for pragmatic reasons in order to refer to divorces which originate from States with an Islamic background. It should be kept in mind that *the* 'Islamic' divorce does not exist; instead one should refer to a Moroccan divorce or a Pakistani repudiation etcetera.
[7] Unless the husband has delegated this right to his wife e.g. through a clause inserted in the marriage contract. This so-called delegated repudiation or *talaq al-tamlik/talaq al-tafwid* rarely occurs.
[8] Adopted by the General Assembly of the United Nations on 18 December 1979, G.A. Res. 34/180, U.N. GAOR, 34th Sess., Supp. No. 46, at 193, U.N. doc. A/34/46 (1979); entry into force on 3 September 1981. See for its electronic version: www.un.org/womenwatch/daw/cedaw/text/econvention.htm (last check at 17 September 2010).

international human rights treaty,[9] are 'Islamic' States.[10] The ideal of sex equality of the Women's Convention originate in and has to compete with prevailing views on the status of men and women which maintain the discrimination against women in society, despite the existence of anti-discrimination instruments.[11] These views are based on the idea of superiority of men and/or inferiority of women which can be found in and are affirmed by social, cultural and/or traditional patterns, practices and sometimes even laws, and result in stereotyped gender roles.[12] The views hamper the development of women and their participation in the political, social, economical, cultural and other fields of life.[13] Non- or insufficient participation of women in society form obstacles to the development of society as a whole.[14] Hence, the Women's Convention seeks to modify, combat and abolish such pernicious social, cultural and/or traditional patterns, practices and laws in order to further freedom of discrimination and full equality of women with men.[15]

Article 16 of the Women's Convention aims at guaranteeing equal rights for men and women in marriage and family relations. Article 16 paragraph 1 sub c of the Women's Convention (hereinafter Article 16 (1)(c)) more specifically stipulates the same rights and responsibilities for men and women at its dissolution. Other paragraphs of Article 16 as well as other Articles of the Convention are significant as well for the status of women at divorce as these stipulate rights which are closely connected to and indispensable for guaranteeing gender equality at divorce.

Article 16 of the Women's Convention in relation to the status of women at divorce in 'Islamic' States is therefore the focus of this contribution. The following emerging issues will be highlighted: what is the significance of this provision on gender equality at divorce – especially in view of equal accessibility to divorce and procedural rights – for Muslim women? Subsequently: what is a

---

[9] Status as at 17 September 2010, see at www.treaties.un.org/Pages/ViewDetails. aspx?src=TREATY&mtdsg_no=IV-8&chapter=4&lang=en#57.

[10] The exact number of 'Islamic' States depends on the criteria which have been used for the selection in order to define a State as 'Islamic'; in this Chapter States are meant 'with legislation which incorporates or at least reflects to some extent Islamic laws and customs', see E. YAHYAOUI KRIVENKO, 2009, *supra* note 4, p. 115.

[11] WINDE EVENHUIS AND ESTHER VAN EIJK, *Met recht een vrouw; het VN-Vrouwenverdrag toegelicht*, Greber Uitgever & Distributeur, Amsterdam, 2001, p. 9. YAHYAOUI KRIVENKO, 2009, *supra* note 4, p. 23.

[12] See paragraph 6 of the Preamble to the Women's Convention; See also General Recommendation no.
21, UN doc. A/49/38, 13th Session 1994, para. 3, available at www2.ohchr.org/english/bodies/cedaw/comments.htm (last check at 17 September 2010); See also H.B. Schöpp-Schilling, 'The nature and scope of the Convention', in: Hanna Beate Schöpp-Schilling and Cees Flinterman (eds.), *The Circle of Empowerment; Twenty-five Years of the UN Committee on the Elimination of Discrimination against Women*, The Feminist Press, New York, 2007, pp. 16 and 23.

[13] See paragraph 7 of the Preamble to the Women's Convention.

[14] *Idem*.

[15] SCHÖPP-SCHILLING, 2007, *supra* note 12, p. 23.

constructive approach towards implementation of this provision in Islamic States especially in view of the apparent legal diversity in women's rights? Should, and to what extent, religion and/or culture play a role in influencing women's rights?

In order to provide answers section two will clarify one side of the legal diversity picture: the context and contents of Article 16 Women's Convention. Section three will deal with the other side of that picture: the divorce laws and practices of two selected Islamic States, Morocco and Pakistan, which offer quite a contrasting spectrum in this regard. Section four will examine the attitude of these States towards the Women's Convention, *inter alia*, by means of reservations and/or declarations. In section five it will be advocated that for the optimal realization of non-discrimination and gender equality at divorce in 'Islamic' States an approach to the Convention from a culturally nuanced perspective should be pursued which enhances the position of women while at the same time fundamental Islamic values are being respected.

2. ARTICLE 16 WOMEN'S CONVENTION

2.1. ITS CONTEXT

For a better understanding of Article 16 its context – its relationship with (similar provisions in) other instruments, the meaning of the Women's Convention's core notions, and its relationship with other Articles within this Convention – should be discussed first.

The Women's Convention, an elaboration of the Declaration on the Elimination of Discrimination against Women,[16] can be considered as the 'specialized' sequel to other international human rights instruments.[17] These instruments, the Universal Declaration of Human Rights (hereinafter UDHR),[18] the International Covenant on Civil and Political Rights (hereinafter ICCPR),[19] and the International Covenant on Economic, Social and Cultural Rights (hereinafter ICESCR),[20] also stipulate equality of men and women and outlaw sex discrimination. The look-alikes of Article 16 (1)(c) of the Women's Convention which prescribe equal rights and responsibilities for the spouses at divorce, are the Articles 16 (1) UDHR and 23 (4) ICCPR. Article 16 specifies the

---

[16] Proclaimed by United Nations General Assembly Resolution 2263 (XXII) of 7 November 1967.
[17] SCHÖPP-SCHILLING, 2007, *supra* note 12, p. 10.
[18] Adopted by the General Assembly of the United Nations on 10 December 1948, GA res. 217 A (III) at the Palais de Chaillot in Paris.
[19] Adopted by the General Assembly of the United Nations on 16 December 1976, GA res. 21/2200 (XXI), entry into force on 23 March 1976.
[20] Adopted by the General Assembly of the United Nations on 16 December 1976 by GA res. 21/2200 (XXI), entry into force on 3 January 1976.

meaning of the norm of gender equality as stipulated in the latter look-alikes. But these other instruments and their provisions are gender neutral and aimed at formal equality of men and women. The Convention goes further: it aims to achieve non-discrimination *against* women in particular, and full – formal ánd *de facto* – gender equality in the public as well as in the *private* sphere.[21] For these purposes it recognizes 'the importance of culture and tradition in shaping the thinking and behaviour of men and women and the significant part they play in restricting the exercise of basic rights by women.'[22]

The core notions of discrimination and gender equality have specific meanings in the context of the Women's Convention. Article 1 of the Women's Convention includes a comprehensive definition of the concept of discrimination specifically as discrimination *against* women, which goes beyond the common view of discrimination.[23] Women often encounter combined, and thus multiple, forms of discrimination because they are women ánd belong to other groups based on ethnicity, status, age, religion, disability etcetera. Moreover, women are part of a male-dominated world in which the specific needs of women are often disregarded.

The Women's Convention addresses a multiform notion of (gender) equality. This notion not only covers equal treatment before the law or formal equality ánd equality in practice or substantive or *de facto* equality; it also covers equality of opportunities reached by removal of apparently neutral, but unjustifiable barriers, and equality of results or outcome.[24] All these notions are interdependent and interrelated in order to achieve full (gender) equality. In the context of the Convention equality is not synonymous with gender neutrality, but it appropriately takes gender into consideration. Fredman identifies this concept of equality as 'equality as transformation'.[25] The Convention thus not only prohibits discrimination, but also requires positive actions in order to bring about a change in the pernicious structures, patterns and practices underlying discrimination and inequality.

Hence, States parties have to take into account and to apply the framework provisions, the Articles 2 to 5, supplementary to any of the substantive Articles 6 to 16.[26] Article 2 stipulates that the appropriate measures to eliminate discrimination *against* women should not only be taken by the State, but also by private persons, organizations or enterprises. Article 3 prescribes that States

---

[21] SCHÖPP-SCHILLING, 2007, *supra* note 12, pp. 10, 17, 18; YAHYAOUI KRIVENKO, 2009, *supra* note 4, p. 26.
[22] CEDAW General Recommendation no. 21, *supra* note 12, para. 3.
[23] *Idem*. For the Articles of the Women's Convention which are mentioned in this contribution see Annex I to this book or the Women's Convention at www.un.org/womenwatch/daw/cedaw/text/econvention.htm (last check at 17 September 2010).
[24] As described by S. FREDMAN, 'Beyond the dichotomy of formal and substantive equality: towards a new definition of equal rights', I. Boerefijn et al.(eds.), *Temporary special measures*, Intersentia, Antwerpen, 2003, p. 111.
[25] FREDMAN, 2003, *ibid.*, pp. 115–118.
[26] SCHÖPP-SCHILLING, 2007, *supra* note 12, p. 17.

parties shall take 'all appropriate measures, including legislation' to improve the position of women in all fields of life so that they can fully exercise and enjoy the human rights and fundamental freedoms on the base of equality with men. Article 4 states that States parties shall be allowed to adopt temporary special measures, the so-called affirmative action, as correction mechanism to accelerate *de facto* equality; these measures are then considered not to be discriminatory in view of that purpose as long as they are effective. Furthermore, the Articles 2 and 5 especially deal with the detrimental effects of culture and tradition to women. Article 2 sub paragraph f requires that 'all appropriate measures' should be taken 'to modify or abolish existing laws, regulations, customs and practices which constitute discrimination against women'. Article 5 stipulates that States parties shall take all appropriate measures to combat stereotyped roles and traditional or cultural role patterns which are detrimental to women. Article 23 allows for the application of any other legal provision that is more conducive to gender equality than any legal provision in the Women's Convention. Article 24, finally, prescribes that States parties 'undertake to adopt all necessary measures at the national level aimed at achieving the full realization of the rights recognized in the present Convention'. The formulation of these Articles indicates that the States parties have the discretion to select the means for their implementation, although the Convention can also impose specific means.

Furthermore, Article 9 on the abolition of discrimination in nationality laws and regulations is of the utmost importance for women at divorce: the status of being a national or citizen of a State guarantees them facilities such as access to public benefits and a choice of residence.[27] Article 15 is of major significance to Article 16 as it stresses in strong terms the importance of equal legal autonomy for women. Article 15 prescribes that 'States parties shall accord to women equality with men before the law' and equal legal capacity and rights in civil matters, amongst other things, by treating them equally in court proceedings. Recognition of equal legal autonomy and an equal status as citizen is essential for women to enjoy and exercise all their other human rights.[28]

The Women's Convention and the later adopted Optional Protocol (hereinafter OP) thereto provide for various monitoring mechanisms that may be used by the Committee on the Elimination of All Forms of Discrimination Against Women (hereinafter CEDAW). The Reporting procedure of Article 18, in combination with CEDAW's ability to make Suggestions and General Recommendations as contained in Article 21 of the Convention, appear to be significant for the interpretation of the meaning of Article 16 (1)(c). Although Suggestions and General Recommendations are not legally binding, their strength is their power of persuasion. Two other procedures, which are contained

---

[27] CEDAW General Recommendation No. 21 on Article 9, *supra* note 12, in para. 6.
[28] SCHÖPP-SCHILLING, 2007, *supra* note 12, p. 24.

in the OP,²⁹ are the Communication procedure (Article 2) which allows individual women or groups of women to submit a complaint to CEDAW about an alleged violation of any of the rights set forth in the Convention by a State party under whose jurisdiction they are, and the Inquiry procedure (Article 8) which entails that on the basis of reliable information that has been received, the Committee may conduct an investigation on 'grave or systematic violations by a State party of rights set forth in the Convention'. As yet, neither of these two procedures has been used in relation to Article 16.

2.2. NATURE OF ARTICLE 16

Article 16 affirms gender equality in marriage and the family, and clarifies the meaning of gender equality during marriage and at its dissolution in its paragraphs, which is further elaborated in General Recommendation no. 21 by CEDAW. Hence, Article 16 regulates matters belonging to the so-called private sphere.

For a long time society and also international and human rights law have been characterized by a public/private sphere divide.³⁰ Because of their biological and social role women traditionally belong to the domestic or private sphere which originally, contrary to the public sphere of life, was not or less regulated by law. Accordingly, women have fewer rights, powers and resources. Their activities were treated as inferior, as the private sphere is the domain in which cultural norms, traditions and practices especially with regard to the alleged nature of women and their roles in the family and the society, are dominant. That is why several States parties are disinclined to grant women equal rights and they have shown their reluctance by formulating reservations to Article 16. However, on several occasions CEDAW has declared that the exercise and enjoyment of equal rights in the family by women is a prerequisite for the exercise and enjoyment of human rights in other areas of life by them. Hence, General Recommendation no. 21 stresses that as the activities of women in the domestic sphere 'are invaluable for the survival of society, there can be no justification for applying different and discriminatory laws or customs to them.'³¹ CEDAW continues by stating the following objective: whatever form the family takes, 'and whatever the legal system, religion, custom or tradition within the country, the treatment of women in the family both at law and in private must accord with the principles of equality and justice for all people, as Article 2 of the Convention requires.'³²

---

[29] Optional Protocol to the Women's Convention, adopted by the General Assembly of the UN on 6 October 1999 (A/RES/54/4) entry into force on 22 December 2000. The full text of the Optional Protocol can be found in Annex II to this book. For more information on the OP see Chapter 21 by Sille Jansen.
[30] General Recommendation No. 21, *supra* note 12, para. 11; SCHÖPP-SCHILLING, 2007, *supra* note 12, pp. 23–24; YAHYAOUI KRIVENKO, 2009, *supra* note 4, pp. 9, 16, 38, 128–129.
[31] CEDAW General Recommendation No. 21, *supra* note 12, para. 12.
[32] *Ibid.*, para. 13.

Hence, the full text of Article 16(1)(c) of the Women's Convention reads as follows:

1. States parties shall take all appropriate measures to eliminate discrimination against women in all matters relating to marriage and family relations and in particular shall ensure, on a basis of equality of men and women:
(c) The same rights and responsibilities during marriage and at its dissolution;

Nevertheless, CEDAW observes that many countries rely on, among other things, the application of religious or customary law with regard to rights and responsibilities of the spouses 'rather than by complying with the principles contained in the Convention'.[33] CEDAW concludes that 'these variations in law and practice' result in 'invariably restricting' women's 'rights to equal status and responsibility within marriage' which contravene the provisions of the Convention.[34] An unequal status of women in marriage will consequently affect the status of women at divorce. Article 16 and General Recommendation No. 21 therefore elaborate on specific issues which have been observed as problematic in view of the status of women in marriage and at divorce. Exemplary in this respect is that the Committee while specifying Article 16 (1)(h), advocates the necessity of an equal property share at the end of a marriage or *de facto* relationship, among other things, 'in view of the woman's practical ability to divorce her husband and to support herself' and dependent family members, 'and to live in dignity as an independent person.'[35] In this respect, financial as well as non-financial contributions to the property such as raising children and taking care of the household, tasks often performed by the wife, should be accorded the same weight.[36] CEDAW also stresses the importance of legal capacity for the status of women in the family as included in Article 15 Women's Convention, *inter alia*, to provide them with a full right to bring litigation before the courts.[37]

2.3. DECLARATIONS AND RESERVATIONS

Article 16, however, appears to be the most problematic provision of the Women's Convention for 'Islamic' States. In its General Recommendation No. 21 of 1994, CEDAW 'notes with alarm' the number of States parties which have, if not entered general reservations or declarations to the Convention, massively entered reservations to the whole or part of this provision, *inter alia* based on

---

[33] *Ibid.*, para. 17.
[34] *Idem.*
[35] *Idem.*
[36] *Ibid.*, para. 32.
[37] *Ibid.*, para. 8.

Shari'a.[38] The significance of the mechanism of the reservation is that it allows a State to ratify or accede to a treaty while not committing itself to observe the reserved provision(s). And although the Convention only allows States to enter reservations which are compatible with its object and purpose,[39] it appears that incompatible or impermissible reservations cannot effectively be precluded, but can only be affected by the heat of the constant pressure of the Committee to withdraw them. The next section provides for information about the divorce laws and practices of Morocco and Pakistan, *inter alia*, to enable gaining insight in their reactions to the Women's Convention in the form of reservations and declarations which is the subject of section four.

3. 'ISLAMIC' DIVORCE LAWS AND PRACTICES

3.1. 'ISLAMIC' LAW AND DIVORCE

Nowadays, most legal systems of 'Islamic' States are governed by secular legislation but in general with the exception of family law, which still remains based in *Shari'a*. Family law is usually the only area of law in *Shari'a* that has survived replacement by European codes during the colonial period and secularization of the 'Islamic' State after its independence. It thus represents the Islamic identity. Muslims consider the observance of 'Islamic' family law also as a matter of religious obligation. 'Islamic' family law therefore appears to be the battlefield where conservative forces and reformist groups struggle over the extent of supremacy of religious values in the law.

The area of 'Islamic' family law, although based in *Shari'a*, has nevertheless been subject of reforms by many Muslim legislators by means of various *Shari'a* principles and methods (of interpretation) such as the following. *Shari'a* mainly includes as far as the legal subject matter is concerned, substantive rules. Procedural rules for litigation are part of the authority of the administration to enact rules in case *Shari'a* does not provide for it, the so-called *siyasa*.[40] During the twentieth century *siyasa* proved to be a most powerful instrument for

---

[38] See for an overview of the status of ratifications of and declarations or reservations made to the Women's Convention the website of the United Nations Treaty Collection: www.treaties.un.org/Pages/ViewDetails.aspx?src=TREATY&mtdsg_no=IV-8&chapter=4&lang=en#57 (last check at 17 September 2010). See also General Recommendation No. 21, *supra* note 12, paras.41–44. Although it appears that in particular 'Islamic' States have made reservations and declarations, it goes beyond the scope of this contribution to discuss the topic more in general and extensively. See for more general information on reservations: YAHYAOUI KRIVENKO, 2009, *supra* note 4, pp. 75–113.

[39] Pursuant to Article 28 Women's Convention which is in line with Article 19(c) of the Vienna Convention on the Law of Treaties.

[40] M. BERGER, *Klassieke Sharia en Vernieuwing*, Amsterdam University Press, Amsterdam, 2006, pp. 15, 72–73.

Muslim legislators in order to reform family law and in particular divorce law through statutory interventions: procedural statutes of litigation were used in order to influence the character of the substantive rules.

In *Shari'a* mainly three types of divorce can be distinguished:[41] *talaq* or the extra-judicial, unilateral repudiation by the husband;[42] *khul^c* or the repudiation (*talaq*) by the husband on demand of the wife in exchange for a financial or another kind of compensation by her; and *talaq-al tatliq* (or *tatliq*), also called *talaq-al tafriq* (or *tafriq*), or the *divorce* by judicial process on a limited number of grounds mostly initiated by the wife.[43] However, the Hanbali and Shafi'i schools of law do in general not acknowledge *talaq-al tatliq/talaq-al tafriq* as a method to dissolve the marriage; instead *faskh*, to be understood as *annulment* of the marriage by the judge for irregularity in the marriage contract, specific diseases, or the violation of contractual clauses, is acknowledged. In Maliki and Hanafi law *faskh* as *annulment* of the marriage by the judge based upon irregularities in the marriage contract or violation of a contractual clause, occurs as well apart from the *talaq-al tatliq/talaq-al tafriq* as type of *divorce*. However, the terms *talaq-al tatliq/talaq-al tafriq* and *faskh* may apparently be used interchangeably both in popular usage as well as in some (contemporary) laws. *Talaq*, as well as the other forms of divorce, can be either revocable[44] or irrevocable.[45] The judicial annulment of the marriage, *faskh*, definitively ends the marriage. The duties and rights emanating from the marriage are terminated

---

[41] The information in this section has been based upon Y. LINANT DE BELLEFONDS, *Traité de Droit Musulman Comparé*, Mouton & Co, Paris/La Haye, 1965, pp. 303–480. This highly recommendable book deals, *inter alia*, with dissolution of marriage in the legal comparative perspective of the four Sunni schools of law in *Shari'a*.

[42] *Talaq* does not require neither the consent of the wife nor a statement of reasons for it by the husband. The husband can delegate his power to repudiate to an agent or to his wife (*talaq al-tamlik/talaq al-tafwid*). See PEARL AND MENSKI, *Muslim Family Law*, Sweet & Maxwell, London, 1998, pp. 280–283.

[43] Dependent upon the school of law the court-pronounced divorce is referred to as *talaq-al tatliq* (in Maliki law) or *talaq-al tafriq* (in Hanafi law). In Maliki law *talaq-al tatliq* has to be understood as the repudiation by the judge *on behalf of* the husband. The Maliki recognize the largest number of grounds: non-payment of maintenance, long and unjustified absence, specific diseases, harm and discord. The Hanafi recognize the least number: sexual defect or specific diseases of the husband; the exercise of the spouse's (wife's or husband's) option of puberty: the right of rescission of the marriage which has been concluded by the legal guardian on behalf of the minor spouse, on coming of age; and non- conversion of the non-Muslim husband married to a converted wife.

[44] In case of the revocable repudiation or divorce, the husband has the option to revoke his pronouncement during c'idda' (the waiting period) of the wife even without her consent, in order to resume marital relations. Usually the first and second repudiation of the same wife and the divorce on restorable grounds like non-maintenance, are revocable.

[45] In case of the irrevocable repudiation or divorce the husband cannot revoke his pronouncement; this is the case after the lapse of c'idda' of the first and second repudiation of the same wife; immediately after the third repudiation of the same wife; prior to consummation; and in case of khulc or talaq-al tatliq or talaq-al tafriq on certain causes which are not restorable.

either forthwith in case of the annulment of the marriage and the irrevocable repudiation or divorce, or after the lapse of the waiting period, or *'idda'*, in case of the revocable repudiation or divorce.[46] Depending on the type of the dissolution of marriage involved, (legal) consequences and provisions after divorce or dissolution, such as the waiting period, the right to maintenance, the right to the deferred dower, the financial consolation and the right to care for the child(-ren) may result from it.[47]

On closer inspection it appears that 'Islamic' divorces, and especially repudiations and divorces based on the repudiation like *talaq* and *khul^c*, regarding their form and procedure may considerably differ from State to State: one may thus speak of legal diversity within 'Islamic' divorce laws as the exposition of the Moroccan and Pakistani divorce laws below will demonstrate.

3.2. DIVORCE IN MOROCCO

3.2.1. Introduction

Moroccan family law, initially codified in the *Mudawanna* in 1958 and still based on the Maliki school of law, was reformed in 1993 and, rather radically, in 2004.[48] The latter reforms were, *inter alia*, aimed at impeding the use of *talaq* or polygamy by men by introducing procedural and financial obstacles, and thus at fortifying the position of women in the law and society. Also new forms of divorce and improvements of already existing forms which are favourable to women have therefore been introduced.[49] In order to further the acceptance and the implementation of these family law reforms the Moroccan king presented them as based on and compatible with the Islamic tradition and *Shari'a*.[50] Large information campaigns were launched to bring the Moroccan Family Code

---

[46] He can only remarry her after she has been duly married to and divorced from another man.
[47] Respectively *'idda'*, *nafaqa*, *mahr*, *mut^ca* and *hadhana*. These consequences/provisions are not further discussed in this contribution. However, it is important to realize that divorce and (financial) post-divorce provisions are intertwined: one's choice for divorce or for a specific type of divorce is influenced by the (non) existence of these provisions.
[48] The driving forces behind the reforms were the women's movement and the Moroccan kings. Since 2004 Mudawwana is referred to as Mudawwana al-Usra (hereinafter Moroccan Family Code or MFC 2004).
[49] See Combined third and fourth periodic report of Morocco, submitted on 18 September 2006, UN doc. CEDAW/C/MAR/4, paras.342, 373, 374 (available at www.unhchr.ch/tbs/doc.nsf/0/830f372a8592f49fc125729c0046f172/$FILE/N0656369.pdf; last check at 17 September 2010).
[50] See *e.g.* the speech of Mohamed VI to the parliament in October 2003 (at www.mincom.gov.ma), the Preamble of the Moroccan Family Code of 2004 (in 'Guide pratique du Code de la Famille', available at www.ejustice.gov.ma/justice/fr/documentation) and L. Buskens, 'Recent debates on family law reform in Morocco: Islamic law as politics in an emerging public sphere', *Islamic Law and Society*, 2003, 1, pp. 70–131.

(hereinafter MFC 2004) to the attention of society at large. The two controversial issues, polygamy and repudiation, have, however, not been abolished as this would really have been unacceptable for the conservative and religious opponents to the reforms.

Morocco acceded to the Women's Convention on 21 June 1993 accompanied with declarations and reservations concerning the Articles 2, 9, 15 and 16.[51] But it took until 2001 before the Convention was published in the *Official Gazette* in order to officially announce the accession and the Convention itself in Morocco.[52] The status of the Convention, as well as of other ratified international instruments *vis-à-vis* national law, however, is not clear.[53] And although the Government has expressed the intention to reconsider its reservations and to accede to the Optional Protocol in March 2006, these intentions have not been realized so far.[54]

The principle of equality between women and men as defined in the Women's Convention has neither been incorporated in the Constitution nor in all the domestic laws.[55] Nevertheless, in the preamble of the MFC 2004 and in its Article 51 the equality between men and women in and after marriage and in the family is stressed as well as that the spouses share joint responsibility for the family and have the same rights and duties.[56]

3.2.2. Divorce

In Morocco *talaq*, *khul^c* and *talaq-al tatliq* occur and nowadays all these modalities are subject to judicial intervention by specialized judges of the – also

---

[51] See status of Women's Convention at www.treaties.un.org/Pages/ViewDetails. aspx?src=TREATY&mtdsg_no=IV-8&chapter=4&lang=en#57.
[52] See *e.g.* Considerations CEDAW on initial report of Morocco, CEDAW/C/SR 312, 313 and 320, para 61, available at www2.ohchr.org/english/bodies/cedaw/docs/MoroccoCO16_en.pdf (last check at 17 September 2010) and the NGOs' shadow report to the third and fourth periodic report coordinated by the Association Démocratique des Femmes du Maroc (hereinafter ADFM), 2007, para 9, available at www2.ohchr.org/english/bodies/cedaw/cedaws40.htm (last check at 17 September 2010).
[53] Concluding Comments of CEDAW, 2008, UN doc. CEDAW/C/MAR/CO/4, paras.12 and 13, available at www2.ohchr.org/english/bodies/cedaw/docs/CEDAW.C.MAR.CO.4_en.pdf (last check at 17 September 2010).
[54] Combined third and fourth periodic report of Morocco 2006, *supra* note 49, para. 29. See also the NGOs' shadow report to the third and fourth periodic report coordinated by ADFM, 2007, *supra* note 52, paras.21–36. See for the status of the reservations and declarations made by Morocco: www.treaties.un.org/Pages/ViewDetails.aspx?src=TREATY&mtdsg_no=IV-8&chapter=4&lang=en#EndDec.
[55] NGOs' shadow report to the third and fourth periodic report coordinated by ADFM, 2007, *supra* note 52, paras.52 and 59.
[56] The preamble of the MFC 2004, *supra* note 50, and Articles 4 and 51 para. 3 of the MFC 2004. Also in: Combined third and fourth periodic report of Morocco 2006, *supra* note 49, paras.18, 95, 365.

in 2004 established – family justice divisions of the courts.[57] These judges can take provisional measures in order to protect women and children in all cases of divorce.[58] Registration of each type of divorce and its revocation in the birth certificates of both spouses by the Registrar is mandatory.[59] Moroccan law does not recognize the matrimonial regime of community of property, but spouses are allowed to make an agreement on the management and sharing of the assets acquired during the marriage.[60] At the dissolution the judge will take such an agreement into account or, at its non-existence, will divide the assets taking into account the efforts, activities and the financial burdens of each spouse.

Talaq has been subjected to a specific legal procedure which includes, *inter alia*, the personal attendance of both spouses and the payment of a deposit as guarantee for his financial obligations by the husband in order to obtain a judicial approval for the pronouncement of *talaq*.[61] The repudiation has thus been deprived of its unilateral character as it belongs no longer to the absolute discretion of the husband. For a better protection of the wife a revocation has to be recorded and the wife has to be informed beforehand; when she disagrees, she may petition for divorce on the grounds of irretrievable breakdown.[62] The wife has the right to repudiate herself if authorized to by her husband (*talaq al-tamlik* or *tamlik*), which results in an irrevocable divorce.[63]

Since 2004 two types of consensual divorce occur: the divorce by mutual consent not on or upon conditions,[64] and *khul*ᶜ.[65] Both types are subject to the same legal procedure as *talaq*,[66] but immediately result in an irrevocable

---

[57] The Family Court consists of three specialized judges per court.
See for an overview of Moroccan divorce law and its reforms in 2004: F. SAREHANE, 'Le nouveau code marocain de la famille', GP 2004, pp. 2–17; L. JORDENS-COTRAN, *Nieuw Marokkaans Familierecht en Nederlands IPR*, SDU uitgevers, Den-Haag, pp. 293–405. See Combined third and fourth periodic report of Morocco 2006, *supra* note 49, para. 372.

[58] Article 121 MFC 2004.

[59] Article 141 MCF 2004.

[60] Article 49 MFC 2004.

[61] The total procedure includes the call to appear before the court to both spouses; at least one compulsory reconciliation attempt; the approval of the pronouncement of the repudiation by the court conditional upon payment of a mandatory deposit by the husband; the witnessing, recording and registration of the repudiation by two cudul, notaries; the ratification of the act by the homologation judge, and a motivated decision of the talaq procedure and settled provisions, qarar moeallal by the court; see Articles 78–93 MFC.

[62] Articles 124 and 94 MFC. See Combined third and fourth periodic report of Morocco, 2006, *supra* note 49, para. 378.

[63] Articles 78 and 89 MFC.

[64] Article 114 MFC.

[65] Article 115–120 MFC. The first type rather indicates an ending of the marriage by a mutual, friendly agreement while the second one points at the initiative of the wife. See L. JORDENS-COTRAN, 2007, *supra* note 57, pp. 334–339; and Guide Pratique, *supra* note 50, at Article 114 MFC.

[66] JORDENS-COTRAN, 2007, *supra* note 57, p. 337 and S. RUTTEN, 'Verstotingen in de Marokkaanse rechtspraktijk', *Migrantenrecht*, 2003, pp. 220–235.

divorce.[67] Also here the law provides additional protection: when the spouses disagree upon the compensation for *khul^c*, the court may intervene to fix a fair compensation;[68] and when the wife persists in her request for *khul^c* while the husband refuses to consent, she is entitled to petition for divorce on the ground of irretrievable breakdown.[69]

The wife can petition for a judicial divorce, *talaq-al tatliq*, on a limited number of grounds at the fault of the husband: non-payment of maintenance, physical or mental harm, unjustified and long absence, the oath not to have intercourse (*ila'*), oath of abstinence (*hajr*), redhibitory defects, and since 2004, harm caused by non-compliance with one or more of the conditions in the marriage contract[70] and the revolutionary grounds of irretrievable breakdown of the marriage (hereinafter called: *shiqaq*).[71] The procedure before the Family Court includes, *inter alia*, the attendance of both spouses and (a) reconciliation attempt(s),[72] and has been restricted in time.[73] A judicial divorce, except for the divorce on the grounds of non-payment of maintenance and the oath of abstinence, results in an irrevocable divorce.[74]

Recent overviews of the Moroccan Ministry of Justice and NGOs clearly demonstrate a shift from the repudiation-based divorces towards the judicial divorce, especially in favour of *shiqaq* in the period 2004–2008. The relative proportions were 4:1 in 2004 and 1:1 in 2008.[75] Within the category of repudiation-based divorces, 59,12% of these are based upon the divorce on

---

[67] Article 123 MCF.
[68] Article 120 MFC.
[69] *Idem.*
[70] Articles 98–113 MCF. The wife has to provide evidence for the existence of the grounds.
[71] Articles 94–97 MCF. These grounds can be invoked by either spouse, or specifically by the wife in case of: 1. her refusal to consent to a polygamous marriage by her husband (Article 45 MCF); b. her refusal to consent to revocation of talaq (Article 124 MCF); c. husband's refusal to consent to khulc (Art. 120 MCF); d. her inability to prove harm as ground for divorce (Article 100 MCF). The spouse(s) have to allege the irretrievable breakdown of the marriage, they do not have to provide evidence of it.
[72] Articles 94–113 MCF. If the reconciliation fails, the judge will settle (temporary) provisions and eventually grant the divorce after other failing attempts to 'solve the problem' such as setting a term in which the husband can comply with his duties or laying an injunction upon him.
[73] Articles 97 and 113 MCF. The judge has to decide on the divorce within six months either after the request for divorce on the grounds of irretrievable breakdown or after the failure of the attempted reconciliation in the case of a request on other grounds. See also: combined third and fourth periodic report of Morocco, 2006, *supra* note 49, para. 377.
[74] Article 122 MCF.
[75] See the 2008 overview 'Activité des sections de la famille 2004–2008' of the Moroccan Ministry of Justice via www.adala.justice.gov.ma/FR/Statistiques/Statistiques.aspx. (last check at 17 September 2010). See also: Association Marocaine de lutte contre la violence à l'égard des femmes, *l'application du Code de la Famille: acquis & défis*, 2005; La ligue démocratique pour les droits des femmes, *rapport annuel sur l'application du code de la famille*, March 2005; La ligue démocratique pour les droits des femmes (LDDF), *rapport annuel sur l'application du code de la famille 2006*; BENRADI et al, *Le code de la famille, perceptions et pratique judiciaire*, Friedrich Ebert Stiftung 2007; Association Marocaine de

mutual consent and *khul^c* opposed to 40,10% of other forms of repudiation (revocable and before consummation) in 2008; only 0.46% of the cases concern *tamlik*.[76]

However, a number of constraints regarding the enforcement of the MFC have been observed. It appears that it is 'difficult to obtain a hearing' before the court and that 'petitioners have to wait for long periods for rulings on divorce and support cases' because of congestion of the courts.[77] Furthermore, the 'low number of courts in several areas in Morocco', the corruption of the judiciary, the reluctance by some judges to implement new provisions such as the *shiqaq*-procedure, 'an inadequate sensitization and training of persons responsible for enforcing' the MFC, the still persisting culture of discrimination against women, the insufficient role of the media in combating stereotypes 'as well as the illiteracy and poverty of litigants, especially women' and the weak spread of information among women have been mentioned as well.[78]

3.2.3. Assessment

In theory, Moroccan women have access to various modalities of divorce: to the delegated repudiation, the divorce on mutual consent, *khul^c* and to the judicial divorce. But their drawbacks are either the dependence on the husband or the difficulty to prove the grounds for divorce. These modalities, except for the divorce on mutual consent and *shiqaq*, do not totally counterbalance the strong effect of *talaq*. Although restricted by the court's approval, the husband's option of repudiation is not independently accessible to women, nor can its exercise except for the revocation, be influenced by them. Women cannot object to the repudiation itself. The independent and thus most important facility to divorce for women is *shiqaq*.[79] It can be concluded that, although men and women have equal access to divorce on this ground, women formally do not have equal access to divorce in general. Despite the 'growing diversity' of divorces under Moroccan law since 2004, men and women do not equally 'share' all the same modalities. In its concluding comments in 2008 CEDAW therefore urges Morocco 'to

---

lutte contre la violence à l'égard des femmes, *La perception du Code de la Famille et de son environnement social et professionnel*, 2007.

[76] See the 2008 overview of the Moroccan Ministry of Justice, *supra* note 75.
[77] Combined third and fourth periodic report of Morocco, 2006, *supra* note 49, para. 389.
[78] NGOs' shadow report to the third and fourth periodic report coordinated by ADFM, 2007, *supra* note 52, paras.200 and 201; and MRS. N. SKALLI, Implementing CEDAW: Third and Fourth Periodic Reports, Geneva, 24 January 2008, presentation at the fortieth session of CEDAW, Geneva, 24 January 2008, available at www2.ohchr.org/english/bodies/cedaw/docs/statement/40Morocco.ppt (last check at 17 September 2010).
[79] 'Independent' in the meaning of independent regarding the access to divorce, because in order to finally obtain a divorce it has to be certain that the dispute is unsolvable and that reconciliation is impossible.

eliminate any other discrimination against women remaining' in its Family Code which in my opinion refers, *inter alia*, to the elimination of *talaq*.[80]

As to the procedural position of women the *talaq*-based divorce-procedure concerning *talaq* and *khul*[c], should be distinguished from the *tatliq*-procedure. The former does not represent an adversarial procedure,[81] but is one which is monitored by a judge and in which women have several procedural rights in order to establish a divorce by repudiation under guarantees for women and children.[82] Although the position of women has improved because of the administrative requirements, it still remains fundamentally a type of divorce which is at the disposition of men, although his prerogative and exclusive discretion has been constrained by the mandatory judicial approval. Generally speaking, the second type (*talaq-al tatliq*) implies an adversarial procedure under supervision of a judge in which women have procedural rights in order to establish a divorce under guarantees. In the context of the *shiqaq*-procedure the procedural position of men and women is, technically speaking, equal. However, as to the divorce procedure on the other grounds, one has to take into account the drawback of this procedure which is the difficult position of women in respect of costs (and evidence related to the other grounds).

The overall conclusion is that the position of Moroccan women has improved since the family law reforms in 2004, although the gender equality principle has not been constitutionalized and the MFC still contains discriminatory provisions. Hence, the NGOs argue that a situation of 'legal schizophrenia' exists as the MFC promotes gender equality on the other hand.[83] Adding a facility of divorce in which both spouses have an equal position as to access and procedure, is formally not totally counterbalancing *talaq* which mere existence implies inequality. However, the existence of an independent facility of divorce and its procedure which guarantee certain procedural rights and rights to provisions for women (and children) rather mitigates the inequality. Furthermore, Moroccan's divorce practice is encouraging as it appears to indicate an increase in the equal treatment divorce modality, *shiqaq*, and a decrease in *talaq*. As Ms Skalli in her presentation of the last periodic reports of Morocco, has put it: Morocco so far has 'climbed a number of steps. But there are still many other steps to climb, to achieve equality between men and women'.[84] Constitutionalizing the gender equality principle and the primacy of international law, withdrawing the reservations and acceding to the Optional Protocol and establishing independent

---

[80] Concluding comments of CEDAW, 2008, *supra* note 53, para. 37.
[81] In other words: a defended action.
[82] In the form of financial and other provisions.
[83] NGOs' shadow report to the third and fourth periodic report coordinated by ADFM, 2007, *supra* note 52, para. 176.
[84] MRS. N. SKALLI, presentation of Third and Fourth Periodic Reports Morocco, *supra* note 78.

family courts as also suggested by the Moroccan Government,[85] may *inter alia*, improve the enforcement of the MFC and thus further this equality.

3.3. DIVORCE IN PAKISTAN

3.3.1. Introduction

Contrary to Morocco, the *entire* contemporary Pakistani legal system is infused with appeals to Islam and thus with *Shari'a*.[86] In the area of family law each religious community is governed by its own personal law, so Muslims by Muslim personal law.[87] Contemporary Pakistani, Muslim divorce law, however, is the composite of classical *Shari'a* divorce laws of different schools, amended by reformist statutes and case law, and moulded into a Common Law framework.

The enactment of the Muslim Family Laws Ordinance in 1961 (hereinafter called MFLO),[88] the first Pakistani reform of family law, was aimed at amelioration of the position of women, *inter alia*, through the restriction of the unilateral power of the husband regarding repudiation and the enlargement of the limited rights of women to judicial divorce.[89] Judicial activism also played a major role in reforming family law: through *ijthihad* a new form of *khul^c*,[90] a divorce at the demand of the wife *without* the consent of the husband by the court, was created.[91] Nevertheless, the Pakistani divorce laws still contain

---

[85] Combined third and fourth periodic report of Morocco, 2006, *supra* note 49, para. 389.

[86] Which can be historically explained: the aim is to strengthen the identity of Pakistan after the separation from India, as homeland for South-Asian Muslims, thus to Islamize its entire legal system through 'attempts to cleanse' the original Anglo-Mohammedan legal system of unacceptable colonial, customary and Hindu elements. See W. MENSKI, *Comparative law in a global context; the legal systems of Asia and Africa*, Cambridge University Press, Cambridge, 2006, pp. 365–379; M. LAU, *The role of Islam in the legal system of Pakistan*, Martinus Nijhoff Publishers, Leiden/Boston, 2006.

[87] Pursuant to West Pakistan Muslim Personal Law (*Shari'at*) Application Act 1962; Pakistani Muslims are far from being a homogeneous group: the predominant school of law is the Hanafi, but the Shia school is also represented. Muslims are therefore considered to be Hanafi unless the contrary has been proven. 97% of the Pakistani population is Muslim, see M.S. MAHMOOD, *Presentation of Pakistan's combined Initial, Second and Third Periodic Report*, Geneva, 22 May 2007, p. 2, available at www2.ohchr.org/english/bodies/cedaw/docs/statement/Pakistan38.pdf (last check at 17 September 2010).

[88] Act VIII of 1961, in force on 15 July 1961. The MFLO does not follow any school of law in particular. Ever since its promulgation (parts of) the Act has survived several attacks for being repugnant to Islam and thus being invalid, see for more details: D. PEARL, *A textbook on Muslim Personal Law*, Croom Helm, London, 1987 pp. 113–114; LAU, 2006, *supra* note 86, pp. 155–160; MENSKI, 2006, *supra* note 86, pp. 374–379.

[89] Sections 7 and 8 MFLO.

[90] *Ijtihad* is a method of legal reasoning by interpretation to derive new rules of law, see SCHACHT, *supra* note 2, p. 299.

[91] See *Mst. Balqis Fatima v Najm-ul-Ikram Qureshi*, PLD 1959 Lahore 566; *Khursid Bib v Muhammad Amin*, PLD 1967 Supreme Court 97. For more details see L. CARROLL, 'Qur'an

discriminatory provisions.[92] The Islamisation of the law in the 1970s had a detrimental effect on the rights of women. One of its results, the Offence of Zina (Enforcement of Hudood) Ordinance of 1979 which introduced severe penalties for committing adultery or fornication,[93] had a rather nasty side effect. Remarried women were charged with adultery (*zina*) after a claim by their ex-husbands that there had never been a divorce, since there had been no notification of *talaq* as prescribed in Section 7.1 MFLO. The judiciary reacted in a pragmatic manner to this abuse by recognizing repudiations as valid even without compliance with the notification procedure. This reaction was seen as affecting – some authors even use the word 'undermining' – the MFLO.[94] Lau, however, indicates that analysis of recent case law show that Section 7 is being upheld in purely family law, not criminal law, cases.[95] The Protection of Women (Criminal Laws Amendment) Act of 2006 was the legislative reaction as it diluted the effects of the Zina Ordinance of 1979 among other things by redefining '*zina*'. The process of Islamisation of law was restrained by the emergence of Islamic extremism in the 1990s which had a deterrent effect on this process.

At its accession to the Women's Convention on 12 April 1996, Pakistan made a general declaration and entered a reservation to Article 29 section 1 of the Convention.[96] The general reservation makes the compliance with the provisions of the Convention subject to the Articles of the Pakistani Constitution which requires that all Pakistani laws shall be in accordance with *Shari'a*.[97] To the concern of CEDAW and NGOs, Pakistan has not (yet) ratified the Optional

---

2:229: "A charter granted to the wife"? Judicial khul'in Pakistan', *Islamic Law and Society*, 1996, pp. 91–126.

[92] Concluding comments of CEDAW, 2007, CEDAW/C/PAK/CO/3, paras.16, 17, 44 and 45, available at www.daccess-dds-ny.un.org/doc/UNDOC/GEN/N07/376/08/PDF/N0737608.pdf?OpenElement (last check at 17 September 2010). See also the CEDAW shadow report on Pakistan endorsed of over 900 Human Rights Organizations, 'Discrimination lingers on ...', submitted on 15 February 2007, pp. 9, 15, 51, available at www.iwraw-ap.org/resources/pdf/Pakistan%20SR%20(NCJP).pdf (last check at 17 September 2010).

[93] Ordinance no. VII of 9 February 1979.

[94] See *e.g.* the case of *Noor Khan v Haq Nawaz* 1982 FSC 265 (Pearl 1987, *supra* note 88, pp. 112–113); *Bashiran v Mohammad Hussain* PLD 1988 SC 186 (S. Sardar Ali and R. Naz, 'Marriage, Dower and Divorce: Superior Courts and Case Law in Pakistan', in: F. Shaheed *et al*, *Shaping women's live*, Lahore, Shirkat Gah, 1998, pp. 126–127. The National Commission on the Status of Women has already recommended to repeal the Zina Ordinance in 2003. See M. Lau, 'Country Surveys: Pakistan', *Yearbook of Islamic and Middle-Eastern Law 2005/2006*, pp. 452–456 and pp. 471–472.

[95] M. Lau, 'Sharia and National Law in Pakistan', in: J.M. Otto, *Sharia Incorporated*, Leiden, Leiden University Press, 2010, p. 416.

[96] See for the status of the declaration and reservation made by Pakistan: www.treaties.un.org/Pages/ViewDetails.aspx?src=TREATY&mtdsg_no=IV-8&chapter=4&lang=en (last check at 17 September 2010).

[97] Article 2, chapter 3 and part IX of the Pakistani Constitution, available at www.pakistani.org/pakistan/constitution/ (last check at 17 September 2010).

Protocol.[98] Furthermore, the Convention is not directly applicable in domestic law.[99]

Various Articles in the Pakistani Constitution are dedicated to the principle of equality and non-discrimination, although it does not contain a (specific) definition of discrimination against women or equality as defined in the Convention and as strongly recommended by CEDAW and NGOs.[100] Article 25 which establishes equality before the law, disallows discrimination on the basis of sex and allows the State to make special provisions for the protection of women and children, and Article 35 which urges the State to protect the marriage, the family, the mother and the child, are core provisions in respect of this contribution. Nevertheless, Pakistani society is still imbued with pervasive patriarchal attitudes and deep-rooted traditional and cultural stereotypes regarding the roles of women and men in society and in the family.[101]

3.3.2. Divorce

Dissolution of marriage in Pakistan can be extrajudicially achieved by *talaq*, *mubara'at* or *khul*^{c} as well as by *khul*^{c} established in court (hereinafter called: judicial *khul*^{c}) or by judicial process, *faskh*.

Section 7 MFLO subjects *talaq* by the husband to procedural restraints: the mandatory notice in writing to the Chairman of the Union Council, a copy thereof to the wife and a reconciliation attempt.[102] If the reconciliation fails and/or *talaq* is not revoked by the husband, it becomes legally valid after 90 days from the day of notification pursuant to Section 7 (3) MFLO. However, according to Pearl and Menski, Pakistani case law reveals that the notice requirements and the reconciliation appear in practice not to be mandatory, but rather optional and desirable.[103] Consequently, the non-compliance with the notice requirement does, according to them, not entail the non-validity of *talaq* as it will still be valid and effective under *Shari'a* law 'either at once or after the 90 days stipulated

---

[98] Concluding comments of CEDAW, 2007, *supra* note 92, para. 48. See also the CEDAW shadow report on Pakistan 2007, *supra* note 92, pp. 6, 15.

[99] Combined initial, second and third periodic reports, submitted on 3 August 2005, UN doc. CEDAW/C/PAK/1-3, para. 28, available at www.daccess-dds-ny.un.org/doc/UNDOC/GEN/N05/454/37/PDF/N0545437.pdf?OpenElement (last check at 17 September 2010); CEDAW shadow report on Pakistan 2007, *supra* note 92, pp. 6, 7.

[100] Combined periodic reports Pakistan 2005, *supra* note 99, paras. 30, 52, 53, 465–468 and 491. Also: Concluding comments of CEDAW 2007, *supra* note 92, paras. 14 and 15; and: CEDAW shadow report on Pakistan 2007, *supra* note 92, pp. 11 and 15.

[101] M.S. Mahmood, Presentation of Pakistan's combined Periodic Report 2007, *supra* note 87, p. 2; Combined periodic reports Pakistan, 2005, *supra* note 99, paras. 49, 86, 87, 90. Concluding comments of the CEDAW 2007, *supra* note 92, paras. 28 and 29.

[102] Non-compliance with this provision is punishable with imprisonment up to one year or a fine of 5,000 Rupees (approximately 44 Euros), see Section 7 (2) MFLO.

[103] Pearl and Menski, 1998, *supra* note 42, pp. 372–373.

by the MFLO'.[104] But Lau underlines that the repudiation is considered invalid in case of non-compliance with the notification procedure; according to him this notification procedure is being upheld by courts in purely family law cases.[105] The objective of the MFLO to protect women against instantaneous, oral divorce by making all forms of divorce revocable, was undermined as the court held that a verbal, triple *talaq* was irrevocable and thus immediately effective.[106] Pursuant to Section 8 MFLO the provisions of Section 7 MFLO apply *mutatis mutandis* to *talaq al-tafwid* and to dissolutions otherwise than by *talaq* such as *khul^c* or *mubara'at*. Hence, the above-mentioned remarks on the optional notice requirement and reconciliation attempt may also apply to these forms of dissolution. Although the occurrence of *talaq al-tafwid*, the delegated *talaq*, is extremely rare,[107] it appears that most of the stipulations made in the marriage contract are, remarkably enough, unconditional. The latter has an equalizing effect to the access to divorce by the spouses.

The (extra-judicial) dissolution of marriage by mutual agreement occurs in two, irrevocable forms: *mubara'at* and *khul^c*.[108] The latter exists in two varieties: not only the traditional, extra-judicial form,[109] but also the under 3.3.1 mentioned judicial form.[110] The wife may be entitled to *khul^c* decreed by the court *without* consent of her husband under three conditions:[111] the refusal of consent to *khul^c* by the husband; the renouncement of the dower and/or other (financial) benefits by her; and the conviction of the judge 'that the limits of God will not be observed' – in other words that the couple cannot live a harmonious marital life as envisaged by Islam – if the marriage is not dissolved.[112] However,

---

[104] See *Kaneez Fatima v Wali Muhammad*, PLD 1993 SC 901. It entails a punishment at worst, but daily practice demonstrates that punishments occur rarely.

[105] LAU, 2010, *supra* note 95, p. 416.

[106] Section 7 (3) MFLO; *Zubeida Khatoon* 1996 MLD 1689.

[107] Section 8 MFLO. The percentage of delegated *talaq* in Pakistan is estimated to be less than one, due to circumstances such as: ignorance about its existence, the frequent non-registration of marriages, and a discouraging policy by some Nikah Registrars (official to register marriages) because they are against this concept, or deem it 'haram', prohibited, or un-Islamic or against social order (sometimes even the wordings of Clause 18 in the marriage contract are faulty as it is stated "in the form of khula"). See: M. MUNIR, 'Stipulations in a Muslim Marriage Contract with Special Reference to Talaq al-tafwid Provisions in Pakistan', *Yearbook of Islamic and Middle Eastern Law*, 2005–2006, pp. 248–254; also: CEDAW shadow report Pakistan 2007, *supra* note 92, p. 51.

[108] It is *khul^c* when the wife has an aversion towards her husband and initiates the dissolution; but when the aversion is mutual and the initiative has been taken by both husband and wife, it is mubara'at; see: *Ghulam Sakina v Umar Baksh*, PLD 1964 SC 456.

[109] PEARL AND MENSKI 'presume' that extra-judicial forms of *khul^c* regularly occur in Pakistani society, but that 'such cases are not officially reported anywhere because they require no court intervention', see Pearl and Menski, 1998, *supra* note 42, p. 315.

[110] By an amendment in 2005 the judicial *khul^c* has been statutorily laid down in the Family Courts Act 1964.

[111] See the two leading cases: *Mst. Balqis Fatima v. Najm-ul-Ikram Qureshi*, PLD 1959 Lahore 566; *Khursid Bib v Muhammad Amin*, PLD 1967 Supreme Court 97.

[112] PLD 1959 Lahore 566, p. 593; PLD 1967 Supreme Court 97, p. 121.

the judicial *khul^c* cannot be considered as the 'charter granted to the wife'.[113] It appears that the judicial *khul^c* is usually pleaded as an alternative remedy for divorce under the Dissolution of Muslim Marriages Act 1939 (DMMA) because of the difficulties of evidence regarding the ground(s) for divorce.[114] But in practice either the judicial *khul^c* (ánd the divorce) was not granted since the woman was found not to be entitled to it because of her failure to establish a ground for divorce,[115] or the judicial *khul^c* was granted and the wife had to renounce her financial rights although she should have been entitled to divorce under the DMMA.[116] The liability of the wife for compensation can, in any event, be seen as a drawback as it affects the already generally weak financial position of divorcing women since they have no right for alimony than during the waiting period.

Faskh is the least accessed form of dissolution by women, because of an inordinate delay in litigation *inter alia* because of the inadequate number of family courts, stringent evidence requirements, the high costs and the lesser social acceptance of invoking judicial interference, notwithstanding the advantage of retaining her financial rights.[117] Article 2 DMMA stipulates the following grounds for the dissolution: absence of the husband; negligence or failure to maintain the wife; long-lasting imprisonment, the husband's failure to perform his marital duties, his continuing impotence, his insanity or leprosy or venereal disease, cruel treatment of the wife,[118] the option of puberty,[119] and any

---

[113] CARROLL, 1996, *supra* note 91.
[114] The Dissolution of Muslim Marriages Act of 1939, Act VIII of 1939, in force on 17 March 1939. See CARROLL, 1996, *supra* note 91, pp. 113–119; SARDAR ALI and NAZ 1998, *supra* note 94, p. 130.
[115] See *e.g.: Bashiran Bibi v Bashir Ahmad*, PLD 1987 Lahore 375. But see *Shahid Javed v Sabba Jabeen* (1991 CLC 805) in which the court stresses the right of *khul^c* as an independent right to the wife: the mere fact that she is not able to establish any ground for divorce, does not prejudice her right to *khul^c*.
[116] See *e.g. Abdul Majid v Rizia Bibi*, PLD 1975 Lahore 766; *Bibi Anwar Khatoon v Gulab Shah*, PLD 1988 Karachi 602. But see e.g. *Mst Hakimzadi v Nawaz Ali*, PLD 1972 Karachi 540 in which the court granted a judicial *khul^c* to the wife, although it held that the wife had proved ill-treatment and false accusation of adultery, both grounds for divorce. See also the Lahore High Court in *Abdul Majid* and the Karachi High Court in *Bibi Anwar Khatoon* (*supra* note). But see the opposite in *Farida Khanum v Maqbul Ilahi* 1991 MLD 1531 in which case the High Court held that the wife did not have to renounce her financial rights since several grounds for divorce had been proved and accepted.
[117] Therefore, lawyers even discourage women from filing a petition for divorce purely under the DMMA; see S. WARRAICH and C. BELCHING, 'Confusion worse confounded: a critique of divorce law and legal practice in Pakistan', in: F. Shaheed *et al.* (eds.), *Shaping women's lives: laws, practices and strategies in Pakistan*, Lahore, Shirkat Gah, 1998, pp. 199–200.
[118] Article 2 subsection viii DMMA further specifies cruelty into physical and mental ill-treatment.
[119] The option of puberty offers the wife who was married by her father or guardian before the age of 16 (and her husband) the opportunity to repudiate her marriage before the age of 18 as long as the marriage has not been consummated.

other ground which is recognized as valid for the dissolution of marriages under Muslim law.

Special Family Courts adjudicate judicial forms of dissolution of marriage and other family cases.[120] However, apart from the already mentioned obstacles and as recognized by the Pakistani Government, women experience considerable other difficulties which discourage them to seek judicial redress: the court environment is 'not congenial for women litigants', but 'disrespectful, humiliating' and results in a social stigma upon them; a 'State system or institution to provide information and guidance to women about their rights and ways to seek judicial redress and provision of legal assistance' is lacking, but also illiteracy and a low education status, poverty and 'seclusion of women and restricted mobility' denies 'women access to information'; furthermore, the family laws lack provisions on the rights of women after divorce.[121]

3.3.3. Assessment

Pakistani women have, theoretically speaking, access to *talaq-al-tafwid*, *mubara'at*, the traditional *khul^c*, the judicial *khul^c* and *faskh*. The former three are only options insofar as the husband cooperates and if she renounces her financial rights in the case of *khul^c*. The latter is practically less feasible because of financial, evidential and social obstacles. The wife's main tool for divorce seems to be the judicial *khul^c*, but she has no absolute or 'independent' right to it, due to the control on the irretrievableness of the marriage by the court, and the financial penalty of the compensation which may constrain her access. The conclusion is that this restricted 'charter' does not equal *talaq* and that the spouses under Pakistani law, in principle, have no equal right of access to divorce. Equal access may only be realized by an unconditional *talaq-al-tawfid*. Practice has shown that its access is strongly restricted by ignorance, social unacceptability and opposition by authorities.

A distinction has to be made between the extrajudicial and the judicial divorce modalities in respect of the procedural rights of women. In respect of the divorce (procedures) which are based on *talaq* (*talaq*-based divorces) the wife has no procedural rights. The notification-requirement of Section 7 MFLO, if it is applied at all, provides women no other protection than knowledge of *talaq* and the avoidance of an instant and definite divorce. In this respect their position has slightly improved, but *talaq* still remains a type of divorce at the disposition of men, although the latter has been restricted by the administrative requirement of notification. The judicial *khul^c* represents a procedure under supervision of a judge, in which the wife has the right to be heard in order to

---

[120] The Family Courts Act 1964, as amended in 2002.
[121] Combined periodic reports Pakistan 2005, *supra* note 99, paras.31, 32, 47, 48, 51; CEDAW shadow report Pakistan 2007, *supra* note 92, pp. 8, 9, 14, 53.

enable the judge to decide upon the granting or not of *khul^c* and upon the compensation. *Faskh* implies an adversarial procedure under supervision of the judge, but the enforcement of the wife's procedural rights is complicated by long-lasting and thus expensive procedures and evidential and social problems.

The greatest problem, however, that obstructs women's access to divorce and her rights appears to be the non-uniform application of the law because of lacunae in it which 'leaves room for interpretations' based on the various sects of *Shari'a* law and custom.[122] Moreover, these frequently conflicting interpretations result in unstable case law. Thus women often are in a legal limbo between statutory and *Shari'a* law and it is often unclear which set of rules prevails. Exemplary in this respect is the notification-requirement for *talaq* under Section 7 MFLO. Its mandatory nature has been affected in case-law, paradoxically enough in order to protect women. Hence, it can be stated that the legislation has serious shortcomings and that the judiciary has an ambiguous attitude towards divorce and women's rights. Courts have (played), as demonstrated, a pivotal role in supporting women's rights while they also show a gender discriminatory and women's hostile attitude.

In conclusion it can be stated that the status of Pakistani women has evolved to a much lesser extent on the road to equality compared to the status of Moroccan women. 'Much more needs to be done in achieving gender equality according to CEDAW'.[123] The same recommendations as in the case of Morocco such as constitutionalizing the gender equality principle and the primacy of international law, withdrawing the declaration and reservation, acceding to the Optional Protocol, combating the pernicious stereotypes, illiteracy, poverty, facilitating the approach to courts etcetera, are even more relevant for Pakistan.

4. ATTITUDE OF 'ISLAMIC' STATES TOWARDS THE WOMEN'S CONVENTION

Parts of the Convention and especially its Article 16 turn out to be most sensitive for 'Islamic' States, which is expressed in numerous reservations and declarations in order to avoid its observance. It is often contended that the reservations and declarations made by 'Islamic' States are expressions of the clash between Islam and the universal, secular Women's Convention, are religious of character and are aimed at preserving Islamic laws and practices;[124] moreover, that 'Islamic'

---

[122] WARRAICH and BALCHIN, 1998, *supra* note 117, p. 181.
[123] M.S. MAHMOOD, Presentation of Pakistan's combined Periodic Report 2007, *supra* note 87, p. 16.
[124] A.G. HAMID, 'Reservations to CEDAW and the implementation of Islamic family law: issues and challenges', *Asian Journal of International Law*, 1, 2006, p. 121; YAHYAOUI KRIVENKO, 2009, *supra* note 4, p. 130.

States have the right to do so as exercise of religious freedom. The analysis of these reservations and declarations offers not only wonderful insights in the diversity of views on rights of women, but also in the real motives of the States involved to enter them.[125]

Pakistan's general declaration makes the compliance with the provisions of the Convention subject to the Articles of the Pakistani Constitution; the latter requires that all Pakistani laws shall be in accordance with *Shari'a*. In Morocco's reservation to Article 16, the full equality of men and women at divorce is considered to be incompatible with *Shari'a*. This is, according to the Moroccan Government, based on the view that *Shari'a* guarantees 'to each of the spouses rights and responsibilities within a framework of equilibrium and complementary in order to preserve the sacred bond of matrimony'.[126] The background of this view is that *Shari'a* confers the right of divorce on women only by decision of the judge because it is the husband who bears all the financial responsibilities for his spouse and family at, during and after the marriage while the wife does not have any financial obligations and has control of her own property.[127] This reservation to Article 16 should be read with the Moroccan declaration on Article 2 of the Women's Convention in which the Moroccan Government states that it 'express its readiness to apply the provisions of this Article provided that: [...] they do not conflict with the provisions of Islamic Shariah.'[128] Moreover, the Moroccan Government declares that: 'certain of the provisions contained in the Moroccan Code of Personal Status according women rights that differ from the rights conferred on men may not be infringed upon or abrogated because they derive primarily from the Islamic Shariah, which strives, among its other objectives, to strike a balance between the spouses in order to preserve the coherence of family life'.[129]

The Pakistani Government has explained the declaration as facilitating Pakistan's accession to the Convention by 'assuaging the concerns' of its opponents: 'Subjecting the implementation of the Convention to the Constitution of Pakistan was a sensible course of action'.[130] The fact that no direct reference to Islamic law was made in the declaration can be explained as the eagerness of Pakistan to improve its image in the International Community.[131] According to Morocco's representative the reservations were

---

[125] YAHYAOUI KRIVENKO, 2009, *ibid.*, pp. 75–76.
[126] See the full text of this reservation:
www.treaties.un.org/Pages/ViewDetails.aspx?src=TREATY&mtdsg_no=IV-8&chapter=4&lang=en#57 (last check at 17 September 2010).
[127] *Idem.*
[128] *Idem.*
[129] *Idem.*
[130] Combined initial, second and third periodic reports of Pakistan, 2005, *supra* note 99, paras.2 and 3.
[131] A.E. MAYER, 'Religious reservations to the Convention on the Elimination of All Forms of Discrimination against Women: What Do They Really Mean?', in: Howland (eds.), *Religious*

'the result of national consensus and were not simply a decision of the Government'; 'Pressure on the Government, therefore, would not change that situation.'[132] He defended the reservations mainly 'as being an anti-fundamentalist prophylactic'.[133] He stated that Islam was 'a lifestyle and an integral part of Morocco's culture and traditions' and 'a rampart against fundamentalism and terrorism' and that 'a basic concern of his country was religious fundamentalism which would seek to impose intolerance'.[134] The representative also made it appear as if the Moroccan Government was constrained in its attempts to repeal discriminatory laws not only by the threat of fundamentalism, but also by Morocco's limited sources and popular resistance to change the law.[135]

Nevertheless, CEDAW has urged the two Governments to withdraw the declaration and the reservations without delay as these go against the object and purpose of the Convention and prohibit the full implementation of the Convention in Morocco and Pakistan.[136] Whereas Yahyaoui Krivenko interprets these reservations as to be 'no more than indicators of areas of concern', Mayer wipes the floor with the explanations of both Governments.[137] She considers the declaration and the reservations invoking Islam 'as the products of skewed political processes'; according to her the reservations simply express the refusal of the States to comply with the Women's Convention while pleading the apparent religious grounds as excuses.[138] This implies the need for a political will to reform the Family Codes in order to comply with the Convention. Furthermore, Mayer contends that the reservations and declaration in Islamic law terms cannot be considered as exercises of the right to religious freedom, *inter alia*, as this right can only be invoked to protect the religious beliefs and practices of minorities and not of the majority as is the case with Islam being the (State) religion in 'Islamic' States; but also because the version of 'Islamic' law which is officially applied within a specific State does not necessarily represent

---

Fundamentalism and The Human Rights of Women, Palgrave, New York, 2001, p. 109; YAHYAOUI KRIVENKO, 2009, *supra* note 4, p. 166.

[132] Women's Anti-Discrimination Committee – Press Releases WOM/937 320th Meeting (AM) 20 January 1997, via www.un.org/News/Press/docs/1997/19970120.wom937.html (last check at 17 September 2010).

[133] A.E. MAYER, 2001, *supra* note 131, p. 107.

[134] Women's Anti-Discrimination Committee – Press Releases WOM/937 320th Meeting (AM) 20 January 1997, via www.un.org/News/Press/docs/1997/19970120.wom937.html (last check at 17 September 2010).

[135] A.E. MAYER, 'Internationalizing the conversation on women's rights: Arab countries face the CEDAW Committee', in: Y.Y. Haddad and B. Freyer Stowasser (ed.), *Islamic law and the challenges of modernity*, Walnut Creek (CA), Altamira Press, 2004, pp. 147–149, 155.

[136] Concluding Comments of CEDAW (Morocco), 2008, *supra* note 53, para. 15 and Concluding comments of CEDAW (Pakistan) 2007, *supra* note 92, para. 13.

[137] YAHYAOUI KRIVENKO, 2009, *supra* note 4, pp. 163 and 167; MAYER, 2001, *supra* note 131 and MAYER, 2004, *supra* note 135.

[138] MAYER, 2001, *supra* note 131, pp. 106 and 114.

the individual religious beliefs of the inhabitants in that State.[139] In reality, 'Islamic' States do not even invoke the right to religious freedom in order to justify their deviations from the Convention; and if they would do so, this right is not a license to overrule the equality rights of women. Mayer finally stresses that in reality – instead of a clash between 'Islamic beliefs' and the secular Women's Convention – there is 'a clash of views within Muslim societies over whether there is any Islamic authority for discriminatory laws and policies affecting women and over whether Islamic law should in any case be the governing standard.'[140]

Remarkably, both the Moroccan and the Pakistani Government portray their States as being supportive of equal rights for women and as being or at least as trying to be compliant with the Convention. The Pakistani report, for example, reads that the Pakistani divorce laws ensure the same rights and responsibilities for the spouses during marriage and at its dissolution, hence that the Pakistani divorce laws are in compliance with Article 16 of the Convention.[141] It declares the different types of divorce for men and women as 'a difference of terminology in the case of Muslims'.[142] Morocco's representative explained the unequal treatment of women and men as actually equitable because of the difference in nature of men and women.[143] Although they thus try to rationalize their departures from the Convention, they are also aware of their shortcomings as they refer to some of them in their reports.[144]

5. CONCLUDING COMMENTS AND PROSPECTS

In the introductory section two issues have been put forward: what is the significance of Article 16 Women's Convention on gender equality at divorce – especially in view of equal accessibility to divorce and procedural rights – for Muslim women? And subsequently: what is a constructive approach towards implementation of this provision in Islamic States especially in view of the

---

[139] *Idem*, p. 110.
[140] *Idem*. See for an elaboration on this view Mayer's article 'The reformulation of Islamic thought on gender rights and roles', in: S. Akbarzadeh and B. MacQueen (eds.), *Islam and Human Rights in Practice*, Routledge, London, 2008, pp. 12–32.
[141] Combined initial, second and third periodic reports of Pakistan, 2005, *supra* note 99, para. 494.
[142] *Idem*.
[143] Women's Anti-Discrimination Committee – Press Releases WOM/937 320th Meeting (AM) 20 January 1997, via www.un.org/News/Press/docs/1997/19970120.wom937.html (last check at 17 September 2010).
[144] See *e.g.* concluding Comments of CEDAW (Morocco), 2008, *supra* note 53, paras.388–391; and: Combined initial, second and third periodic reports (Pakistan), 2005, *supra* note 99, paras.31, 47–51, 86, 495.

apparent legal diversity in women's rights? Should, and to what extent, religion and/or culture play a role in influencing women's rights?

The overview of the Moroccan and Pakistani divorce laws and practices in section three clearly demonstrates the legal diversity within 'Islamic' divorce laws. 'Islamic' divorces, especially the repudiation-based types, considerably differ regarding their form and procedure from State to State depending on their origin in one of the schools of law and on legal, judicial and legislative developments in the States involved. Although equal rights at divorce are stipulated in Article 16 Women's Convention, Moroccan and Pakistani women do in principle not enjoy the right of equal accessibility to divorce as the spouses do not share the same divorce modalities except for the Moroccan *shiqaq*-procedure. However, the latter and the Pakistani unconditional *talaq-al-tawfid* if authorized by the husband, rather mitigate this inequality because of the mere existence of *talaq*. Moroccan women enjoy far better and more procedural rights than their Pakistani sisters since the Moroccan repudiation-based divorces are monitored by the court which guarantees specific (procedural) rights. By contrast, the only legal provision for the Pakistani, extrajudicial repudiation-based divorces (so not the judicial *khul^c*) which might provide for some minimal procedural guarantees, the notification procedure, has been deprived of its mandatory nature.

In order to further the road to equality for women at divorce the Women's Convention has proven to be of the utmost importance. Although these States have not (yet) constitutionalized the primacy of international law, the pressure exerting powers of the Women's Convention and its reporting procedure to CEDAW, being a type of soft law, should not be underestimated. The fact that both States are eager to create the image of being supportive of equal rights for women in the international community is the result of these powers. And this has significance in two, interrelating respects: it corrodes the legitimacy of the discriminating domestic divorce laws, as it becomes more and more difficult for these States to justify their application; and it indicates that their legal systems and practices already are in a transitional stage of reform and actual compliance with the Convention.[145] Moreover, these 'external' pressures are indispensable for and complementary to the domestic pressures for reforms towards equality of women by NGOs.

The reservations and declarations made by these States as perceived expressions of the contended clash between Islam and the universal, secular Women's Convention appear especially to be of a political character. The contended clash is first and foremost a clash of views within Muslim societies concerning the extent of supremacy of religious values in the law. The Women's Convention as such does not oppose to religious influences but for these which

---

[145] MAYER, 2004, *supra* note 135, pp. 133–134, 156.

are pernicious to gender equality and the rights of women and result in inferior stereotyped roles for women.

However, 'Islamic' divorce laws can, in principle, never totally comply with the Convention's requirement of full equality as it is at odds with the fundamental principle in 'Islamic' law that either spouse has his/her own modalities of divorce. Full equality would imply the elimination of Islamic influences. Hence, it is to be considered whether or not full equality or a formalistic type of equality should be pursued; of course not to the detriment of women. Instead it may be a better option to strive for substantive equality and equality of results which implies that either spouse has access to divorce in order to effectively obtain a divorce under procedural guarantees for both spouses. Under these conditions different modalities of divorce for men and women are not per se discriminatory. In order to realize such a balanced system of divorce modalities 'Islamic' States have to (further) reform their domestic divorce laws in accordance with Islamic methodologies. Morocco is exemplary in this respect as its Government – under pressure of NGOs and CEDAW – has thus accomplished an independent accessible, judicial divorce modality for either or both spouses and submitted the repudiation-based divorces to judicial monitoring in accordance with 'Islamic' law.

In order to further the implementation of Article 16 (1)(c) in 'Islamic' States I therefore advocate an approach to the Convention from a culturally nuanced perspective which enhances the position of women while at the same time fundamental Islamic values are being respected.

ARTICLE 17

1. For the purpose of considering the progress made in the implementation of the present Convention, there shall be established a Committee on the Elimination of Discrimination against Women (hereinafter referred to as the Committee) consisting, at the time of entry into force of the Convention, of eighteen and, after ratification of or accession to the Convention by the thirty-fifth State Party, of twenty-three experts of high moral standing and competence in the field covered by the Convention. The experts shall be elected by States parties from among their nationals and shall serve in their personal capacity, consideration being given to equitable geographical distribution and to the representation of the different forms of civilization as well as the principal legal systems.
2. The members of the Committee shall be elected by secret ballot from a list of persons nominated by States parties. Each State party may nominate one person from among its own nationals.
3. The initial election shall be held six months after the date of the entry into force of the present Convention. At least three months before the date of each election the Secretary-General of the United Nations shall address a letter to the States parties inviting them to submit their nominations within two months. The Secretary-General shall prepare a list in alphabetical order of all persons thus nominated, indicating the States parties which have nominated them, and shall submit it to the States parties.
4. Elections of the members of the Committee shall be held at a meeting of States parties convened by the Secretary-General at United Nations Headquarters. At that meeting, for which two thirds of the States parties shall constitute a quorum, the persons elected to the Committee shall be those nominees who obtain the largest number of votes and an absolute majority of the votes of the representatives of States parties present and voting.
5. The members of the Committee shall be elected for a term of four years. However, the terms of nine of the members elected at the first election shall expire at the end of two years; immediately after the first election the names of these nine members shall be chosen by lot by the Chairman of the Committee.
6. The election of the five additional members of the Committee shall be held in accordance with the provisions of paragraphs 2, 3 and 4 of this article, following the thirty-fifth ratification or accession. The terms of two of the additional members elected on this occasion shall expire at the end of two years, the names of these two members having been chosen by lot by the Chairman of the Committee.

7. For the filling of casual vacancies, the State Party whose expert has ceased to function as a member of the Committee shall appoint another expert from among its nationals, subject to the approval of the Committee.
8. The members of the Committee shall, with the approval of the General Assembly, receive emoluments from United Nations resources on such terms and conditions as the Assembly may decide, having regard to the importance of the Committee's responsibilities.
9. The Secretary-General of the United Nations shall provide the necessary staff and facilities for the effective performance of the functions of the Committee under the present Convention.

ARTICLE 18

1. States parties undertake to submit to the Secretary-General of the United Nations, for consideration by the Committee, a report on the legislative, judicial, administrative or other measures which they have adopted to give effect to the provisions of the present Convention and on the progress made in this respect:

    (a) Within one year after the entry into force for the State concerned;
    (b) Thereafter at least every four years and further whenever the Committee so requests.

2. Reports may indicate factors and difficulties affecting the degree of fulfilment of obligations under the present Convention.

ARTICLE 19

1. The Committee shall adopt its own rules of procedure.
2. The Committee shall elect its officers for a term of two years.

ARTICLE 20

1. The Committee shall normally meet for a period of not more than two weeks annually in order to consider the reports submitted in accordance with article 18 of the present Convention.
2. The meetings of the Committee shall normally be held at United Nations Headquarters or at any other convenient place as determined by the Committee.

ARTICLE 21

1. The Committee shall, through the Economic and Social Council, report annually to the General Assembly of the United Nations on its activities and may make suggestions and general recommendations based on the examination of reports and information received from the States parties. Such suggestions and general recommendations shall be included in the report of the Committee together with comments, if any, from States parties.
2. The Secretary-General of the United Nations shall transmit the reports of the Committee to the Commission on the Status of Women for its information.

ARTICLE 22

The specialized agencies shall be entitled to be represented at the consideration of the implementation of such provisions of the present Convention as fall within the scope of their activities. The Committee may invite the specialized agencies to submit reports on the implementation of the Convention in areas falling within the scope of their activities.

CHAPTER 18

CEDAW: A FULL HUMAN RIGHTS TREATY BODY?

Cees FLINTERMAN

1. INTRODUCTION

One of the many interesting features of the Women's Convention is that its text was negotiated within the context of the United Nations Commission on the Status of Women (CSW) whereas all other human rights treaties originate from the United Nations Commission on Human Rights (CHR). CSW is an intergovernmental body that was created by the Economic and Social Council (ECOSOC) of the United Nations at the same time (1946) as the CHR. The first draft of the Women's Convention was adopted by CSW meeting in Vienna, and then forwarded through ECOSOC to the United Nations General Assembly for final adoption. It is remarkable that also in the Third Committee of the General Assembly the draft text was further negotiated by government representatives who were concerned with women's issues and not necessarily with human rights problems.

This negotiating background has had a deep impact on CEDAW from its start in 1982. CEDAW was initially not seen as a full human rights treaty body. For a long time, for example, its annual sessions took place in Vienna, later New York, far away from Geneva where the other human rights treaty bodies have been meeting. Consequentially, CEDAW was not facilitated in its work by the United Nations Secretariat in Geneva, now the Office of the High Commissioner of Human Rights, but by the United Nations Division for the Advancement of Women (DAW) in Vienna, later New York.

That situation has almost completely been changed in the first decade of the new millennium: CEDAW is now having two sessions of three weeks in Geneva and one in New York, just like the Human Rights Committee (HRC) and it is facilitated by the Office of the High Commissioner for Human Rights. But, more importantly, CEDAW is now seen as a full human rights treaty body. In order to substantiate this point I will highlight a number of relevant developments within CEDAW over the years relying thereby also on my own experiences in the

Committee that I was privileged to serve for eight years (2003–2010). I will first focus on the membership of the Committee; then I will address the mandate of CEDAW which has been given such a dynamic interpretation by the Committee and which has been extended through the adoption of the Optional Protocol. Next the attention will be drawn to the working methods of the Committee, where CEDAW has played and is still playing a pioneering role. The next section will be devoted to the crucial role of NGOs, both women NGOs and human rights NGOs, in the activities of the Committee. In the final section, I will return to the main question raised in this Chapter which is whether CEDAW can be considered at the present time as a full human rights treaty body.

2. COMPOSITION OF CEDAW

Part V of the Women's Convention (Articles 17–22) contains a number of procedural provisions relating to CEDAW. They describe the nature of CEDAW, the characteristics of its members, their election through States parties, and the modalities of the election process in Article 17. The other articles refer to the obligation of States parties to submit reports (Article 18); the right of the Committee to adopt its own rules of procedure and to elect its own officers (Article 19); the Committee's working time (Article 20); the obligations of CEDAW to report to the General Assembly through the Commission on the Status of Women and ECOSOC (Article 21); and the role of United Nations specialized agencies in the reporting process (Article 22).

Article 17 provides that CEDAW is composed of 23 members whereas all other human rights treaty bodies usually have 18 members or less, such as the Committee Against Torture (CAT). Members must be of high moral standing and must have competence in the field, or better fields, covered by the Convention. Every two years, States parties elect or re-elect previous experts for a four year term by secret ballot from a list of candidates. Candidates are nominated by States parties. Usually there is quite some interest by States parties to nominate experts which has as a consequence that experts have to engage with the support of their governments in sometimes fierce election campaigns. The two times (2002 and 2006) that I was a candidate myself, there were 24 candidates for twelve places. Elections take place in the meeting of States parties. The Women's Convention encourages States parties to an equitable geographical distribution of the membership and to the representation of the different forms of civilization as well as the principal legal systems; it, however, does not prescribe a fixed distribution among the five regions that are (still) recognized within the United Nations. This has as a consequence that in practice it may happen that a particular region is 'underrepresented' in CEDAW, either because there were insufficient candidates from the region concerned, or because candidates from such a region were not adequately supported in their election

Chapter 18. CEDAW: A Full Human Rights Treaty Body?

campaigns by their governments or their governments had not enough to offer themselves in exchange for support of their candidates.

Once elected by the meeting of States parties, members are sitting in their private capacity as is stipulated in Article 17 para. 1. This is of crucial importance and at the same time in practice a matter of some concern. In CEDAW a number of its members had and have high governmental functions, such as ambassadors or high ranking civil servants. The question arises whether it is feasible for such members to be truly independent from their governments. One day such members may be engaged as members of CEDAW in the critical assessment of a report of a State party which has tense relations with the State of the member. In other situations, a State from which a member comes may have very outspoken policies on sensitive women's issues, such as abortion, homosexuality or divorce. For those members who have in their day-to-day life positions that are closely related to government, it is in such situations a challenge to be seen, particularly by the outside world, as truly independent. Having said that, I would like to stress that over the eight years of my membership of the Committee I have only in a very limited number of cases experienced some feelings of uneasiness about the true 'independence' of my colleagues. I have always been deeply impressed by the hard work for, and the genuine and deep commitment to the cause of the protection and promotion of women's human rights by my colleagues. My explanation for this is that most members in one way or another have suffered from gender discrimination themselves; almost all of them have played or are playing leading roles in the struggle for the elimination of discrimination against women in their own countries.

That brings me to another interesting point of CEDAW's composition: since 1982 women have dominated as members of CEDAW. In its 30 years of existence only four men have been CEDAW members, two Swedes, one Fin, and one Dutchman. I should immediately add that other human rights treaty bodies are generally male dominated except the Committee on the Rights of the Child. There is certainly an obligation on States parties to all human rights treaties to strive for a gender balance in the composition of treaty bodies. I would, however, hesitate to argue in favour of such a balance in the context of CEDAW although I truly believe that the achievement of gender equality is an issue which concerns both women and men. Given the tenacity of discrimination against women in all countries in the world, it is of great importance that women have a focal point within the United Nations system of protection and promotion of women's human rights, both in the political arena (CSW) and the quasi-legal field (CEDAW).

This is not to say that CEDAW is an exclusively legal body. I have always found it very important that the members of CEDAW come from all walks of life representing a large variety of professional disciplines, including law, history, literature, psychology, political science, sociology and medicine. This enables CEDAW to draw on the professional expertise and experience of its members with respect to a variety of life situations in which women find themselves and to discuss, discern, and evaluate the full potential of discriminatory actions against women under all Articles of the Women's Convention. It enables CEDAW to develop a holistic approach on gender issues and to give appropriate and pertinent recommendations – dealing both with legal and extra-legal dimensions of discrimination against women – to States parties after the examination of a State report. The extension of the mandate of CEDAW to the examination of individual complaints and the initiation of inquiries, as provided for in the Optional Protocol, may, however, require an increase in the number of members with an appropriate legal background.

3. MANDATE

The Women's Convention gave CEDAW only a limited mandate, which was surprising and in contrast with the International Convention on the Elimination of All Forms of Racial Discrimination (ICERD) which was adopted in 1965 and which provided for an individual communication procedure in its Article 14 which would, however, only become effective in the 1980s. Some efforts were made during the negotiations on including a complaint procedure in the Women's Convention but it soon became clear that those efforts would lead to a delay in the adoption of the text of the Convention and they were, therefore, dropped. It was only in the late nineties that the Women's Convention could be complemented with an Optional Protocol which would make CEDAW competent to deal with individual complaints and to initiate inquiries in those States that would ratify the Protocol;[1] so far 104 of the 187 States parties to the Women's Convention have taken this important step.[2]

Article 18 imposes an obligation on States parties to submit reports to CEDAW through the Secretary-General of the United Nations in which they have to cover the legislative, judicial and other measures that they have taken to implement their obligations under the Convention and to indicate the progress they have made in that respect. They may also indicate the factors and difficulties they are encountering in implementing the Convention. The first task of CEDAW in order to execute its mandate under Article 18 to examine State reports was to adopt its Rules of Procedure and a set of Reporting Guidelines which could assist States in the preparation of their reports. These Rules and Guidelines have been regularly revised and can be found on the website of the Office of the High Commissioner for Human Rights.[3]

---

[1] For more information on the Optional Protocol and CEDAW's jurisprudence see Chapter 21 by Sille Jansen in this book.
[2] This was the situation in February 2012.
[3] The website for CEDAW can be found at: 'www2.ohchr.org/english/bodies/cedaw/index.htm'.

Chapter 18. CEDAW: A Full Human Rights Treaty Body?

The reporting procedure, including the important role of NGOs and IGOs, has been described in detail at many other places. Here I would like to highlight some of my experiences in the framework of CEDAW over a period of eight years. During that period I have been involved in the examination of reports of more than 120 different States. That sounds impressive but in reality it means that of the total number of States that are parties to the Women's Convention I have only seen two thirds. This indicates that there is a problem of under-reporting and non-reporting. Many States parties do not implement their obligation to submit a report every four years; this has led CEDAW to the practice to allow States parties to submit so-called combined reports; in that manner the periodicity of the reporting obligation can be maintained nominally. Other States parties do not report at all; there are even States parties that have not yet submitted an initial report which is according to Article 18 due one year after the entry into force of the Convention for the State concerned. There is also a problem of over-reporting; those concern States parties that report in time, but in which there are in some cases no significant developments given the short time span between the last examination by the Committee of the earlier periodic report and the time of submission of the new report. CEDAW is trying to address these problems by encouraging under-reporting and non-reporting States parties to seek international assistance in the preparation of their reports.

But the problems surrounding the reporting obligation are much larger and face all treaty bodies. In the imaginary, ideal situation for example that all States parties to the Women's Convention would report in time, CEDAW would have to deal with around 46 reports per year. Presently it deals with eight State reports per session, which adds up to 24 reports per year. Given also the other aspects of the mandate of CEDAW (individual complaints, inquiries, general recommendations), it is clear that CEDAW simply lacks the time to deal with more reports than it presently does.

4. WORKING METHODS

Article 19 of the Women's Convention allows CEDAW to adopt its own rules of procedure and to elect its officers. Article 20 of the Women's Convention provides that CEDAW shall normally meet for a period of not more than two weeks (*sic*) and that its meetings shall normally be held at the United Nations Headquarters or any other convenient place as determined by the Committee. These Articles are a poor reflection of the present day reality in which CEDAW finds itself. CEDAW has, of course, adopted its Rules of Procedure and has adapted them every now and then over the past 30 years in the light of new developments such as the entry into force of the Optional Protocol. It is also electing its own officers every two years after elections of new members to the Committee by the meeting of States parties have taken place. But equally important is how CEDAW works in practice and what working methods have been adopted by the Committee to implement its mandate in the most effective and efficient manner. Below, I will give a few examples of the interesting and promising, sometimes pioneering, steps that CEDAW has taken in this respect.

I should, however, begin by pointing out that Article 20 has in practice been bypassed by the United Nations General Assembly. As from 2008, the General Assembly has allowed CEDAW to have three sessions of three weeks per year, two sessions in Geneva and one in New York. In earlier years the number of sessions had already been increased to two per year, both in New York. There is still an amendment to Article 20 pending to the effect that the meeting time of CEDAW will be increased, but this amendment has not yet received a sufficient number of ratifications by States parties. It seems, however, that also without a formal amendment, the situation of the 'discrimination' of CEDAW concerning its meeting time in comparison with other human rights treaty bodies has already been remedied by the General Assembly. Article 20 also seems to give the power to CEDAW to determine itself where it would like to meet. Practice has shown that financial considerations prevail and that it is the Secretary-General of the United Nations who decides where CEDAW meets.

The burden of work seems overwhelming for CEDAW, especially since the time that CEDAW has also been mandated to examine individual complaints and to initiate inquiries in accordance with the Optional Protocol. One way to cope with these tasks has been the introduction by CEDAW of a strict time management. During the examination of State reports CEDAW members are allowed to intervene only twice for not more than three minutes per intervention. It is certainly not easy to raise relevant questions in such a short time but it is doable, especially in light of the fact that on a big screen behind the Chair it is shown in capital letters that your time is up when you exceed your time. CEDAW is also using so-called task forces in the examination of State reports. Such task forces are composed of a limited number of members (5 to 8) who will take the lead in the dialogue with States parties in the framework of the examination of State reports; such task force members are given a little more time for their interventions (5 minutes), whereas other CEDAW members who do not belong to the task force, are restricted to 2 minutes. This time management device has certainly led to a more dynamic and fruitful dialogue with States parties.

Another example relates to the country rapporteurs who have been given a more prominent role. In the examination of State reports, one of the CEDAW members is given the role of country rapporteur. She or he is made responsible for the preparation of the dialogue with the State party concerned and for the drafting of the concluding comments after the dialogue has taken place. The draft of the concluding comments is presented to the plenary of CEDAW for final adoption. In the past, long hours were spent on the precise formulation of the concluding comments in plenary. Now the country rapporteur collects all amendments suggested by other members to her or his draft concluding comments in advance and she or he presents an amended draft to the plenary indicating which amendments have been included and which rejected. This has led to a much speedier adoption of the concluding comments and has created the necessary time for the plenary discussion of draft decisions on individual complaints and other matters, such as the discussions on general recommendations that are prepared by CEDAW.

More examples could be given of the serious way in which CEDAW addresses and implements its working methods. I already briefly referred to the procedure on concluding comments that has been devised by CEDAW; a similar procedure has been developed in the framework of the individual communications procedure. The issue of the constant improvement of its working methods is always high on the agenda of CEDAW. It was also the main item on the agenda of the three informal sessions of CEDAW (The Netherlands, Germany, and France) that I have attended during my time in CEDAW. Such informal sessions are financed by governments of States parties and are devoted primarily to issues of working methods and the discussion of pending or upcoming themes of general recommendations.

5. CEDAW AND NGOS

The Women's Convention does not refer to NGOs in Part V. In Article 22 it mentions specialized agencies which may be invited by CEDAW to submit reports on the implementation of the Convention in areas falling within the scope of their activities. CEDAW has always made great use of this; at the beginning of each CEDAW session specialized agencies are given the opportunity to inform CEDAW on the States whose reports will be examined during that session. More and more specialized agencies present their information in collective reports which are prepared by United Nations country teams working in the country concerned. Such information is of a vital character for CEDAW in preparing itself for the constructive dialogue with States parties. Likewise, United Nations country teams and individual specialized agencies are encouraged to utilize the concluding comments of CEDAW in their contacts with the government of the State party whose report has been examined by CEDAW.

Despite the silence of the Women's Convention, from the beginning NGOs have played an important, if not crucial role in the activities of the Committee. That is not surprising because the Women's Convention itself, and the consequent establishment of CEDAW, can be seen as the successful outcome of the commitment and dedication of women's organizations around the world. Over the years, CEDAW has strengthened its relationship with NGOs with the aim of enhancing the role of NGOs in the implementation by States parties at the domestic level. On the basis of my own experiences as member of CEDAW, I can only say that without the active involvement of NGOs, both women's and human rights NGOs, CEDAW could not have done its work with the same high quality outcome. I have always been deeply impressed by the commitment of such NGOs and the high expectations they have about the significance of the Women's Convention as a tool to improve the situation of women in their countries. One outstanding example of such an NGO is the International Women's Rights Action Watch Asia Pacific (IWRAW) which is based in Malaysia and which assists, despite its name, domestic women and human rights NGOs around the world in the preparation of so-called shadow or alternative reports. Equally important is the support that IWRAW gives to such domestic NGOs to address CEDAW at the beginning of each session and to provide further information to the members of CEDAW in lunch meetings and individual encounters. IWRAW is also assisting, where needed, domestic NGOs to see to it that the State party implements the recommendations by CEDAW after the examination of the State report.

In 2010 CEDAW adopted a statement in which it highlighted a number of aspects of its relationship with NGOs. In that statement it addresses *inter alia* the role of NGOs in the reporting process. CEDAW has always made it clear that it expects States parties to consult NGOs when preparing the State report and to make this report available to all sectors of civil society; at the same time, it stresses that the report has to be the report of the State party and that the role NGOs have played in providing information for the State report should never exclude the possibility of the submission by NGOs of an alternative or shadow report. NGOs are also encouraged to address CEDAW at the beginning of each session and to attend and observe the meetings of CEDAW during which the relevant State report is examined by CEDAW. It further encourages NGOs to provide information to the Committee in the framework of its follow-up procedure on concluding comments and on decisions on individual communications. There is no doubt that also in the context of the individual complaints procedure, NGOs have an important role to play by assisting women in the preparation of their complaints or by complaining on their behalf and in monitoring the implementation by States parties of the decisions taken by CEDAW on such complaints.

Finally, CEDAW has always recognized the essential contributions of NGOs to the enhancement of the outreach and awareness of the Convention and its Optional Protocol, its concluding comments, its general recommendations and its view and decisions. It further encourages NGOs to contribute to the translation of CEDAW's documents into local languages. NGOs in all countries have indeed been deeply involved in the organization of training seminars, awareness programmes and all sorts of other activities to give (domestic) life to the rather abstract provisions of the Women's Convention.

In this context one interesting recent development should be mentioned and that is the role of National Human Rights Institutes (NHRIs) which have been set up in many States around the world in accordance with the so-called Paris

Principles (1992) which stipulate that such NHRIs should be financed by the government but with effective guarantees for their independence. Such NHRIs play an important role at the national level between the government and NGOs. CEDAW, like other human rights treaty bodies, has created a special place for such NHRIs which are neither to be seen as government branches nor as NGOs. They may submit reports to CEDAW and present such reports orally at the beginning of each session in a separate time slot. NHRIs can also be of great importance in monitoring the implementation by the State party concerned of the concluding comments adopted by CEDAW in respect of that State. That is fully in line with the basic objective of the supervisory role of CEDAW as foreseen by the Women's Convention which is the strengthening of women's human rights at the domestic level.

6. CONCLUDING REMARKS

In the sections above I have highlighted a limited number of the relevant provisions of Part V of the Women's Convention which establish the supervisory structure. No reference has yet been made to Article 21 which empowers CEDAW to make suggestions and general recommendations based on the examination of reports and information received from States parties. CEDAW has made ample use of this power by adopting so far 28 General Recommendations in which it has further interpreted and substantiated the obligations of States parties under the Women's Convention and its various substantive provisions. It has also adopted an impressive number of suggestions and statements on a wide range of issues, including statements on concrete situations of concern, such as Afghanistan and Iraq, and a statement on the role of national parliaments in the implementation of the Convention.

Not everything could be said in this short Chapter about the role of CEDAW, but one conclusion is unmistakably clear: CEDAW has developed over the years into a full human rights treaty body. Its move from New York to Geneva confirms this development. Today, the Committee is considered a vital and essential part of the United Nations human rights treaty bodies system. Old challenges remain, such as the imperative need to make the Women's Convention a living reality in all parts of the world. New challenges present themselves such as how to achieve the objective of full substantive and formal equality of women and men together with other human rights treaty bodies, with political human rights organs, such as CSW and the Human Rights Council, and with the relevant parts of the United Nations Secretariat, such as United Nations Women; this objective can only be achieved with the full participation and involvement of all other stakeholders, such as States parties to the Women's Convention, women's and human rights NGOs and in particular individual women and men. I feel privileged to be directly involved in that struggle.

ARTICLE 24

States parties undertake to adopt all necessary measures at the national level aimed at achieving the full realization of the rights recognized in the present Convention.

CHAPTER 19
DUE DILIGENCE MANIA

Menno T. KAMMINGA

1. INTRODUCTION

Article 24 of the Women's Convention is a strongly worded provision. It obviously means that States parties to the Convention must do whatever is necessary to achieve a specific result, *i.e.* 'full realization of the rights recognized in the Convention.' In recent years a widely shared view has nevertheless emerged among experts on the Convention that the obligation to take 'all necessary measures', both in respect of abuses by State agents and by non-State actors, amounts to an obligation to exercise due diligence. Yakin Erktürk, the UN Special Rapporteur on violence against women, for example, has written that 'the concept of due diligence provides a yardstick to determine whether a State has met or failed to meet its obligations in combating violence against women.'[1] This short contribution tries to demonstrate that reliance on due diligence in such cases is both unnecessary and counterproductive.

The story of the emergence of the concept of due diligence in human rights discourse is familiar to any student of international human rights law. The concept first arose in 1988, in *Velásquez Rodríguez v. Honduras*, the very first dispute before the Inter-American Court of Human Rights. The case was about the disappearance of Manfredo Velásquez Rodríguez. There was no conclusive evidence that government agents had been responsible for his abduction. But the Court nevertheless found that his right to life had been breached by Honduras because of the Government's failure to adequately investigate his disappearance. The Court famously observed that:

> An illegal act which violates human rights and which is initially not directly imputable to a State (for example, because it is an act of a private person or because the person responsible has not been identified) can lead to international responsibility

---

[1] YAKIN ERKTÜRK, UN Special Rapporteur on violence against women, The Due Diligence Standard as a Tool for the Elimination of Violence against Women, 20 January 2006, UN doc. E/CN.4/2006/61, para. 14.

of the State, not because of the act itself, but because of the lack of due diligence to prevent the violation or to respond to it as required by the Convention.²

The Court did not provide an authority or explain why it had decided to rely on the notion of due diligence. It simply derived its finding from Article 1(1) of the American Convention on Human Rights according to which States parties undertake not only to 'respect' certain rights and freedoms but also to 'ensure' the free and full exercise of these rights and freedoms to persons within their jurisdiction. *Velásquez Rodríguez* was welcomed enthusiastically by the human rights movement. It became a *cause célèbre* that appeared in all the textbooks. The idea that States have a due diligence obligation to prevent and to respond to violations was also embraced by the UN human rights treaty bodies and by the United Nations itself.

CEDAW observed in its General Recommendation No. 19: 'Under general international law and specific human rights covenants, States may also be responsible for private acts if they fail to act with due diligence to prevent violations of rights or to investigate and punish acts of violence, and for providing compensation.'³

The Human Rights Committee was more lukewarm in its General Comment No. 31. It observed that under Article 2 of the International Covenant on Civil and Political Rights States Parties are obliged to take appropriate measures *or* to exercise due diligence to prevent, punish, investigate or redress the harm caused by private persons or entities (emphasis added).⁴ In other words, the Committee was careful not to replace the positive obligation to take appropriate measures by the due diligence test but left both options open.

Due diligence was also included in a series of international instruments concerning violence against women. Most recently, UN General Assembly Resolution 64/137 entitled Intensification of Efforts to Eliminate all Forms of Violence against Women, stressed that States '… must exercise due diligence to prevent, investigate and punish the perpetrators of violence against women and girls …'⁵ It is noteworthy that while CEDAW and the Human Rights Committee limited the obligation to exercise the due diligence standard to harm caused by non-State actors the General Assembly seems to suggest that it is a general obligation that also applies to abuses committed by State agents.

---

2   *Velásquez Rodríguez*, Inter-American Court of Human Rights, judgment of 29 July 1988, Annual Report of the IACtHR, 1988, p. 971. 28 ILM (1989) p. 326.
3   CEDAW, General Recommendation No. 19, Violence against Women, 1992, para. 9.
4   Human Rights Committee, General Comment No. 31, Nature of the General Legal Obligation Imposed on States Parties to the Covenant, 28 March 2004, para. 8.
5   UN General Assembly Resolution 64/137, 27 October 2009, preamble.

2. INTERNATIONAL LAW

In general international law, the standard of due diligence has a long history. It has traditionally been perceived as being part of the international minimum standard by which aliens must be treated. In the *Neer Claim* the General Claims Commission established by the United States and Mexico observed that:

> ... the treatment of an alien, in order to constitute an international delinquency should amount to an outrage, to bad faith, to willful neglect of duty, or to an insufficiency of governmental action so far short of international standards that every reasonable and impartial man would readily recognize its insufficiency.[6]

Due diligence in general international law therefore is a rather weak standard with a high threshold.[7] More recently, the International Court of Justice has begun relying on due diligence in a human rights case. In the *Bosnian Genocide case* it observed with regard to the obligation to prevent genocide under the Genocide Convention:

> ... it is clear that the obligation in question is one of conduct and not one of result, in the sense that a State cannot be under an obligation to succeed, whatever the circumstances, in preventing the commission of genocide: the obligation of States parties is rather to employ all means reasonably available to them, so as to prevent genocide so far as possible. A State does not incur responsibility simply because the desired result is not achieved; responsibility is however incurred if the State manifestly failed to take all measures to prevent genocide which were within its power, and which might have contributed to preventing the genocide. In this area the notion of 'due diligence', which calls for an assessment *in concreto*, is of critical importance. Various parameters operate when assessing whether a State has duly discharged the obligation concerned. The first, which varies greatly from one State to another, is clearly the capacity to influence effectively the action of persons likely to commit, or already committing, genocide.[8]

It follows that the obligation to exercise due diligence is determined by two aspects. First, it is an obligation of conduct or an obligation to make an effort. It is not an obligation to achieve a specified result.[9] Second, the obligation to exercise due diligence is an obligation to take 'reasonable measures'. What is

---

[6] L.F.H. Neer and Pauline Neer (United States) v. United Mexican States, 15 October 1926, 4 RIAA (1926) pp. 61–62.

[7] See also MALCOLM SHAW, *International Law*, Cambridge University Press, Cambridge, 5th ed., 2003, p. 735.

[8] International Court of Justice, *Case Concerning the Application of the Convention on the Prevention and Punishment of the Crime of Genocide*, judgment of 26 February 2007, para. 430.

[9] RICCARDO PISILLO-MAZZESCHI, 'Responsabilité de l'Etat pour violation des obligations positives relatives aux droits de l'homme', RCADI vol. 233 (2008) para. 13.

'reasonable' is context-specific and depends on the capacity of the State.[10] The State enjoys a certain amount of discretion (margin of appreciation) regarding the measures to be employed.

3. DOMESTIC LAW

In domestic law, the concept of due diligence or reasonable care also has a considerable history. Under the US Securities Act of 1933 it refers to the care a reasonable person should take before entering into a transaction.[11] In other words, a buyer is expected to keep her/his eyes open and ask critical questions otherwise (s)he loses her/his right to hold the seller liable for any defects to the product.

Reversely, exercising due diligence is the process by which exposure to liability may be reduced. 'Doing due diligence' is a well-established part of a company's risk management process. It is what an accountant does when checking the books of a company. Business loves due diligence because they know they are protected against liability if they have checked all the boxes. Legal advisers and insurance companies insist on it because they know from experience that the courts will exonerate them and their clients as long as they have done due diligence. Due diligence therefore is one of the essential tools of lawyers working in the legal departments of multinational enterprises.

It is thus not surprising that the International Chamber of Commerce and other corporate interest groups responded enthusiastically when John Ruggie, the UN Secretary-General's Special Representative on Business and Human Rights, suggested that the standard by which companies should be held accountable for human rights abuses was the standard of due diligence.[12] According to John Ruggie's school of thought, companies that conduct 'human rights due diligence' thereby immunize themselves from accusations of having committed human rights abuses and reduce their exposure to litigation.[13] In his latest report Ruggie himself has, however, been careful to point out that conducting human rights due diligence by itself should not 'automatically and fully' absolve a company from liability.[14]

---

[10] Monica Hakimi, 'State Bystander Responsibility', 21 EJIL (2010) p. 341, 372.
[11] Section 11 of the US Securities Act of 1933.
[12] Report of the Special Representative of the Secretary-General on the issue of human rights and transnational corporations and other business enterprises, John Ruggie, UN doc. A/HRC/8/5, 7 April 2008, paras 56–64.
[13] See for example, John F.Sherman, III and Amy Lehr, 'Human Rights Due Diligence: Is It Too Risky?' Corporate Social Responsibility Initiative Working Paper No. 55, John F. Kennedy School of Government, Harvard University, February 2010, p. 4.
[14] Report of the Special Representative of the Secretary-General on the issue of human rights and transnational corporations and other business enterprises, John Ruggie, UN doc. A/HRC/14/27, 9 April 2010, para. 86.

4. WOMEN'S RIGHTS

Unfortunately, the women's rights groups that embraced due diligence did not stop to reflect whether by adopting a concept derived from general international law and from business law they might be depriving themselves of the more stringent standards already developed by human rights treaty bodies. These include positive obligations and the obligation to respect, protect and fulfil. Why should States' obligations in the field of human rights be reduced to a mere due diligence obligation?

The content of the due diligence obligation moreover depends on the resources available to the State in question. It is understandable that States that are accused of having taking insufficient measures to prevent abuses by private actors on their territory defend themselves with the argument that they have exercised due diligence to prevent such abuses. It is difficult to understand, on the other hand, why human rights groups should insist that due diligence is the test by which the conduct of States should be judged.

Whether reliance on due diligence is to be applauded or not has benefited from remarkably little critical scholarly reflection.[15] In a recent textbook on international human rights law[16] six of the contributing authors (Chinkin, Clapham, Joseph, Megret, Otto and Rodley) refer apparently approvingly to the concept of due diligence. Only one (Rodley) acknowledges that obligations to exercise due diligence are obligations of conduct rather than obligations of result.

5. EUROPEAN COURT OF HUMAN RIGHTS

Interestingly, the European Court of Human Rights has used the concept of due diligence only sparingly. Instead, it has preferred to rely on the notion of positive obligations.[17] At the time of writing, 'due diligence' had appeared only six times in the dicta ('The Law') of the Court's Grand Chamber. In four of these cases the Court relied on due diligence to examine whether the State complained against had acted with sufficient speed in deportation proceedings.[18] In the two remaining cases due diligence was not invoked by the Court but by defendant States to bolster their argument that they had acted in compliance with the

---

[15] But see some of the contributions in CARIN BENNINGER-BUDEL (ed.), *Due Diligence and its Application to Protect Women from Violence*, Nijhoff, Leiden, 2008.

[16] DANIEL MOECKLI et al. (eds), *International Human Rights Law*, Oxford University Press, Oxford, 2010.

[17] For an analysis of the Court's reliance on positive obligations, see A.R. MOWBRAY, *The Development of Positive Obligations under the European Convention on Human Rights by the European Court of Human Rights*, Hart Publishing, Oxford, 2004.

[18] *Chahal v. United Kingdom*, *Slivenko v. Latvia*, *A. and others v. United Kingdom* and *Saadi v. United Kingdom*.

Convention.[19] This supports the observation made above that due diligence risks being invoked defensively to justify abusive conduct rather than offensively to increase human rights protection.

It is true that due diligence does appear in some chamber judgments concerning domestic violence. For example, in *Opuz v. Turkey* the Court held that Turkey had violated the applicant's right to life because the national authorities had not displayed due diligence to prevent violence against the applicant and her mother, in particular by pursuing criminal or other appropriate preventive measures against her violent husband.[20] But overwhelmingly, the Court prefers to rely on positive obligations in its judgments. Typical for the Court's approach are two cases: *Tahsin Acar v. Turkey* and *Rantsev v. Cyprus and Russia*.

Tahsin Acar v. Turkey was about facts very similar to *Velásquez Rodríguez*.[21] A man had disappeared after having been abducted by persons in an unmarked car. There was no conclusive evidence that the abduction had been carried out by government agents. Unlike the Inter-American Court, the European Court did not base its findings on due diligence. It concluded that Turkey had violated Article 2, not because there was evidence that it was responsible for his death but because it had failed to carry out an adequate and effective investigation into his disappearance. According to the Court the following elements were required for an investigation to meet this standard: the authorities must act of their own motion; investigations must be conducted by persons independent from those implicated in the matter; and the investigation must be capable of leading to the identification and punishment of the perpetrators. The Court pointed out that the latter obligation is 'not an obligation of result, but of means. The authorities must have taken the reasonable steps available to them to secure the evidence concerning the incident.'[22] According to the Court, the investigation must also be prompt and there must be a sufficient element of public scrutiny.

Rantsev v. Cyprus and Russia was about a Russian woman who died after having been trafficked from Russia to Cyprus. The Court concluded unanimously that under Article 4 of the Convention States parties are under a positive obligation to effectively prevent and investigate trafficking in persons.[23] The difference with the approach taken by the Inter-American Court in *Velásquez Rodríguez* is striking. By laying down the result that must be achieved (effective prevention and investigation) the Court did much more for the victims than if it would merely have held that States have to make a due diligence effort to achieve this result. The term 'due diligence' again does not appear in this judgment at all.

---

[19] *Kudla v. Poland* and *M.S.S. v. Belgium and Greece*.
[20] *Opuz v. Turkey*, European Court of Human Rights, judgment of 9 June 2009, para. 131.
[21] *Tahsin Acar v Turkey*, European Court of Human Rights (Grand Chamber), judgment of 8 April 2004.
[22] *Ibid.*, para. 223.
[23] *Rantsev v. Cyprus and Russia*, European Court of Human Rights, judgment of 7 January 2010.

6. CONCLUSIONS

In 1988, the Inter-American Court of Human Rights needed a yardstick by which it could hold Honduras responsible for an abuse perpetrated by unknown actors. Since it could not find such a yardstick in international human rights law it introduced a standard from general international law: Failure to act with due diligence. The Court held that a State party violates the American Convention on Human Rights if it fails to act with due diligence to prevent and respond to a violation. Such an approach made a lot of sense at a time when international human rights law was still in its infancy.

Since then, however, the case law of human rights treaty bodies has grown exponentially. The European Court of Human Rights in particular has increasingly developed standards by which States may be held responsible for having failed to prevent and repress abuses. The Court's steppingstone for this has been the notion of positive obligations. From this notion the Court has deduced that abuses must be *effectively* prevented and investigated. According to the case law, investigations must be able to act of their own motion; be conducted by persons independent from those implicated in the matter; and be capable of leading to the identification and punishment of the perpetrators. Investigations must also be prompt and there must be a sufficient element of public scrutiny.

Advocates of due diligence as a tool to promote women's rights should perhaps be reminded that they have not invented the concept. The due diligence standard has an established meaning in both general international law and domestic law. It is widely perceived as a weak standard, an obligation of conduct rather than an obligation of result. Its exercise is subject to available resources and to a margin of appreciation. For precisely these reasons, the obligation to act with due diligence is a standard that is well liked by governments and by companies. When accused of abuses they have learned to defend themselves by arguing that they have acted with all due diligence and therefore are not accountable.

Against this background, what could be the possible advantages of replacing the positive obligations mentioned above by a requirement to act with due diligence or to suggest that these obligations must be carried out with due diligence? In my view, there are only disadvantages. Because of the dubious content of the due diligence standard, putting a due diligence label on positive obligations actually calls into question and risks undermining those obligations. This scenario is especially problematic if the exercise of due diligence is made applicable not only to abuses by non-State actors but also by State agents.

Perhaps the genie is already out of the bottle. But if it is not it should be put back into it as soon as possible.

ARTICLE 28

1. The Secretary-General of the United Nations shall receive and circulate to all States the text of reservations made by States at the time of ratification or accession.
2. A reservation incompatible with the object and purpose of the present Convention shall not be permitted.
3. Reservations may be withdrawn at any time by notification to this effect addressed to the Secretary-General of the United Nations, who shall then inform all States thereof. Such notification shall take effect on the date on which it is received.

CHAPTER 20
RESERVATIONS TO THE WOMEN'S CONVENTION: A MUSLIM PROBLEM ILL-ADDRESSED?

Zoé LUCA

1. INTRODUCTION

As an instrument aimed at altering fundamental inequalities in societies, many if not all of which built on patriarchal values, the Women's Convention was always going to be controversial. This controversy is particularly evident in the number and types of reservations entered by States parties over the years.[1] The 'universality/integrity' debate was prominent during the drafting process and it has not abetted since.[2] States parties have been accused of compromising the integrity of the Convention by entering reservations that, to the Committee, other States and scholars, have been manifestly contrary to the object and purpose of the Convention. Over the years, as the Women's Convention has inched its way towards universal ratification, the landscape has been marred by States parties' apparent inability to accept their obligations. While the Women's Convention is not the only human rights treaty to have suffered the ailment of reservations, it has without a doubt been one of the most afflicted instruments. Today, as universal ratification is within arm's reach, it is appropriate to re-examine the issue of reservations and the Committee's response over the years. Within this discussion it is equally pertinent to focus in particular on States with a majority Muslim population, as it has been alleged that, as other

---

[1] For the purposes of this contribution, reservation is defined as a unilateral statement, however phrased or named, made by a State or international organization when signing, ratifying, formally confirming, accepting, approving or acceding to a treaty or by a State when making a notification of succession to a treaty, whereby the State or organization purports to exclude or to modify the legal effect of certain provisions of the treaty in their application to that State or to that international organization. See UN doc. A/65/10, *Report of the International Law Commission*, 3 May-4 June and 5 July-6 August 2010, para. 105.

[2] See REBECCA COOK, 'Reservations to the Convention of All Forms of Discrimination Against Women', *Virginia Journal of International Law*, 30, 1990, p. 644.

States begin to heed the Committee's calls for withdrawal of reservations, the issue will acquire an essentially Muslim character.[3]

Building on prior contributions by scholars, this Chapter is a modest attempt to assess CEDAW's efforts to narrow the scope and number of reservations to the Convention and whether, to quote one scholar, 'reservations have become an essentially Muslim problem'. To that end, the next section briefly addresses the background against which the discussion on reservations is set, touching on the drafting history, the sorts of reservations that have been entered by States upon ratification of the Convention and the current state of reservations. Thereafter, the practice of the Committee outside the reporting procedure is explained, demonstrating the evolving position taken by CEDAW and its endeavours to maintain the integrity of the Convention. In a third section, the practice, since 2004,[4] of States that are either Islamic republics or have a majority Muslim population is outlined, along with the response by CEDAW within the framework of its constructive dialogue with these States parties.

2. BACKGROUND

The drafting history of Article 28 of the Women's Convention, which regulates reservations to the treaty, has been well-documented.[5] The picture that emerges from the *travaux préparatoires* reveals the divergent positions of those States that felt that sufficient guidance was provided by the Vienna Convention on the Law of Treaties (hereinafter VCLT) and those that felt it desirable that a separate provision be inserted within the Convention. The text adopted in the end reflects

---

[3] HANNA BEATE SCHÖPP-SCHILLING, 'Reservations to the Convention on the Elimination Against Women: an unresolved issue or (no) new developments?', in: Ineta Ziemele (ed.), *Reservations to human rights treaties and the Vienna Convention regime: conflict, harmony or reconciliation*, Martinus Nijhoff, Leiden, 2004, p. 37.

[4] The practice of States prior to 2005 has been examined by others. See amongst others LIESBETH LIJNZAAD, *Reservations to UN-Human Rights Treaties: ratify and ruin?*, Martinus Nijhoff, Dordrecht, 1995, pp. 298 – 370; HANNA BEATE SCHÖPP-SCHILLING, 'Reservations to the Convention on the Elimination Against Women: an unresolved issue or (no) new developments?', in: Ineta Ziemele (ed.), *Reservations to human rights treaties and the Vienna Convention regime: conflict, harmony or reconciliation*, Martinus Nijhoff, Leiden, 2004, pp. 3 – 38; on the practice of States parties with a predominantly Muslim population see notably SHAHEEN SARDAR ALI, *Gender and Human Rights in Islam and international law. Equal before Allah, unequal before man?*, Kluwer Law International, The Hague/London/Boston, 2000.

[5] See for instance REBECCA COOK, 'Reservations to the Convention of All Forms of Discrimination Against Women', *Virginia Journal of International Law*, 30, 1990, pp. 673 – 678; LIESBETH LIJNZAAD, *Reservations to UN-Human Rights Treaties: ratify and ruin?*, Martinus Nijhoff, Dordrecht, 1995, p. 300; LARS ADAM REHOF, *Guide to the travaux préparatoires on the United Nations Convention on the Elimination of All Forms of Discrimination Against Women*, Martinus Nijhoff, Dordrecht, 1993, pp. 234 – 237.

the corresponding VCLT provision[6] and adopts the 'object and purpose' test, originally articulated by the International Court of Justice (ICJ) in the *Reservations to the Genocide Convention* case[7] and subsequently introduced in the VCLT, albeit taking a firmer stand on reservations incompatible with the object and purpose of the Convention than that taken in the VCLT. Indeed, while the VCLT provides that such reservations may not be formulated, the Women's Convention holds that they will not be permitted.[8]

Article 29, which regulates the dispute settlement mechanism, also deals with reservations in the sense that it explicitly allows States parties to declare that they do not consider themselves bound by the procedure contained in Article 29(1). While the latter is subject to a great number of reservations (no fewer than 41 States had entered reservations in respect of this provision by June 2011), it will not be dealt with in depth in this contribution as the focus is placed instead on reservations of a substantive nature.[9]

Reservations may only be formulated by a State at the stage of signing, ratifying, accepting, approving or acceding to a treaty.[10] While States parties may not formulate new reservations, they may, of course, withdraw them at any time.[11] Unlike provided for in Article 20(1) VCLT, the Women's Convention does not contain a provision requiring the explicit acceptance of a reservation by other States parties, nor is there an equivalent to Article 20 ICERD, as had been proposed by Denmark during the drafting process.[12]

---

[6] Article 19(c) VCLT provides that 'A State may, when signing, ratifying, accepting, approving or acceding to a treaty, formulate a reservation unless (...) in cases not falling under subparagraphs (a) and (b), the reservation is incompatible with the object and purpose of the treaty.'

[7] *Reservations to the Convention on the Prevention and Punishment of the Crime of Genocide*, Advisory Opinion of 28 May 1951, 1951 ICJ Reports 15.

[8] For a discussion on the implications of this difference in language see BELINDA CLARK, 'The Vienna Convention Reservations Regime and the Convention on Discrimination Against Women', *American Journal of International Law*, 85, 1991, p. 307.

[9] It could be argued that, as these reservations remove the opportunity to resolve disputes on other reservations with recourse to the ICJ, they do, in fact, impact heavily on States' obligations since the question of permissibility of reservations to substantive provisions cannot be dealt with in a judicial forum. However, as Schöpp-Schilling points out, the Article 29(1) mechanism has not been used even where States had not excluded its application. For the drafting history of Article 29, see LARS ADAM REHOF, *Guide to the travaux préparatoires on the United Nations Convention on the Elimination of All Forms of Discrimination Against Women*, Martinus Nijhoff, Dordrecht, 1993, pp. 238 – 239.

[10] Article 19(1) VCLT.

[11] Article 28(3), Women's Convention.

[12] Article 20 ICERD provides that '1. (...) Any State which objects to the reservation shall, within a period of ninety days from the date of the said communication, notify the Secretary-General that it does not accept it. 2. A reservation incompatible with the object and purpose of this Convention shall not be permitted, nor shall a reservation the effect of which would inhibit the operation of any of the bodies established by this Convention be allowed. A reservation shall be considered incompatible or inhibitive if at least two thirds of the States parties to this Convention object to it.'

Since it was opened for ratification on 1 March 1980, the Women's Convention has been subjected to an extraordinary number of reservations, leading some commentators to describe it as 'among the most heavily reserved of international human rights conventions'[13] and further entrenching the seemingly unbridgeable gap between universal ratification and the Convention's integrity.

2.1. TYPES OF RESERVATIONS

The reservations entered take different forms and, at this juncture, it is useful to provide a short description of the various types. Apart from permissible reservations to Article 29(1), States have also entered reservations that do not refer to a specific provision and that grant superior status to domestic law in the event of conflict with the provisions of the Convention. By way of illustration, upon ratification in 2006, Oman entered a reservation to '[a]ll provisions of the Convention not in accordance with the provisions of the Islamic Sharia and legislation in force in the Sultanate of Oman'. Finland's objection to this reservation concisely summarises the problems inherent in such a reservation:

> 'The Government of Finland notes that a reservation which consists of a general reference to religious or other national law without specifying its contents does not clearly define to other Parties to the Convention the extent to which the reserving State commits itself to the Convention and creates serious doubts as to the commitment of the receiving State to fulfil its obligations under the Convention. Such reservations are, furthermore, subject to the general principle of treaty interpretation according to which a party may not invoke the provisions of its domestic law as justification for a failure to perform its treaty obligations.'[14]

States have also entered generally-worded reservations to specific treaty provisions. Egypt's reservation to Article 2 is a case in point: 'The Arab Republic of Egypt is willing to comply with the content of this article, provided that such compliance does not run counter to the Islamic *Sharia*.' Such a reservation in reference to Article 2 is particularly problematic since that is the provision that

---

[13] REBECCA COOK, 'Reservations to the Convention of All Forms of Discrimination Against Women', *Virginia Journal of International Law*, 30, 1990, p. 644.

[14] The objection, in reaction to a reservation, that domestic law may not be invoked to justify a State's failure to perform a treaty does not find support with the International Law Commission. See the commentary to draft guideline 3.1.11 in UN doc. A/62/10, *Report of the International Law Commission*, 7 May-5 June and 9 July-10 August 2007, para. 154. On this question see also INEKE BOEREFIJN, 'Impact on the Law of Treaty Reservations', in: Menno Kamminga and Martin Scheinin (eds), *The impact of human rights law on general international*, Oxford University Press, Oxford, 2009, pp. 73 – 75.

'identifies the nature of the general legal obligations of States parties'.[15] Indeed, as explained below, CEDAW has identified this provision as being central to the object and purpose of the Convention. General reservations to any substantive Article give rise to concern since their exact scope and impact cannot be determined; a point that the Committee has made consistently.

Some States have entered specific reservations to clearly identified provisions, sometimes motivating their action with an explanation within the reports submitted to the Committee. While this does not necessarily entail that the reservation is compatible with the object and purpose of the Convention, and thus permissible, it does make the scope and effect of the reservation clearer.[16]

Finally, a number of States have entered unilateral statements under the label of declarations. Where these so-called declarations in fact exclude or alter the legal effect of the provisions of the Convention, they amount to reservations and are considered as such for the purposes of this contribution.[17] Those States that have entered declarations amounting to reservations include Tunisia, which declared that it would not act in conformity with the Women's Convention if it was contrary to Article 1 of its Constitution; Spain, in relation to succession to the throne; and Pakistan that declared its accession as subject to the provisions of its Constitution.

2.2. THE EVOLVING STATE OF RESERVATIONS

By the end of 1992, of the 120 States parties to the Convention, 81 States had ratified without entering reservations, while 27 States had 'made reservations to substantive provisions or other declarations'.[18] Between 1994 and 2004 sixteen

---

[15] UN DOC. CEDAW/C/2010/47/GC.2, *General Recommendation no. 28 on the core obligations of States parties under Article 2 of the Convention on the Elimination of All Forms of Discrimination Against Women*, 19 October 2010, para. 6.

[16] As is shown below, CEDAW has identified a number of provisions to which any sort of reservations must be considered incompatible with the object and purpose of the Convention, yet it has not always done so in a consistent manner. These provisions include Articles 2 and 16.

[17] This approach is consistent with the definition of reservation provided by the ILC in its draft guidelines and by the provisions of guideline 1.3, according to which 'the character of a unilateral statement as a reservation or an interpretive declaration is determined by the legal effect it purports to produce'. See UN doc. A/65/10, *Report of the International Law Commission*, 3 May-4 June and 5 July-6 August 2010, para. 105. The Committee has also adopted this approach, following Article 2(1)(d) VCLT. See UN doc. A/53/38/Rev. 1, *Report of the Committee on the Elimination of Discrimination Against Women*, 14 May 1998, Part Two, Chapter I, para. 4.

[18] LIESBETH LIJNZAAD, *Reservations to UN-Human Rights Treaties: ratify and ruin?*, Martinus Nijhoff, Dordrecht, 1995, p. 300; LARS ADAM REHOF, *Guide to the travaux préparatoires on the United Nations Convention on the Elimination of All Forms of Discrimination Against Women*, Martinus Nijhoff, Dordrecht, 1993, p. 304.

States ratified the Convention with reservations,[19] ten of which were States with a predominantly Muslim population, bringing the number of reserving States up to 57[20] out of a total number of States parties of 175. Six of these reserving States entered general reservations that referred to the primacy of their Constitution and/or Sharia Law over the provisions of the Convention,[21] in clear disregard to the Committee's call for reservations to be formulated in as specific a manner as possible. In addition to their general reservations, Lesotho, Liechtenstein, Malaysia and Saudi Arabia also entered reservations to substantive Articles (including Articles 2, 5, 7, 9 and 16). Some of the States that only formulated reservations to specific Articles did not motivate their decision, while others relied on Sharia law or on religious and personal laws (the latter being the case of Singapore).[22]

By October 2011, 187 States had ratified the Convention, fifty-six of which entered reservations and/or declarations that amount to reservations.[23] Of these, forty-one States have entered reservations and/or declarations to substantive Articles or that do not refer to a specific provision of the Convention. Twenty-two were States that are either Islamic republics or have a predominantly Muslim population.[24] Looking at the twelve new States parties since 2004,[25] only five ratified without entering reservations. These are Marshall Islands, Montenegro, Nauru, Swaziland and Kiribati. The remaining seven States all entered reservations to specific provisions,[26] with the exception of Brunei, Monaco and Oman which coupled their reservations to specific Articles with a general reservation that referred either to the Constitution/national legislation or Islam or both (as in the case of Oman). It should be highlighted that the Cook Islands, which had entered reservations to Articles 2(f), 5(a) and 11(2)(b), withdrew them all in 2007.

---

[19] These were Kuwait, Algeria, Bahrain, the Democratic Republic of Korea, Fiji, Lebanon, Lesotho, Liechtenstein, Malaysia, Mauritania, Niger, Pakistan, Saudi Arabia, Singapore, Switzerland and Syrian Arab Republic. See HANNA BEATE SCHÖPP-SCHILLING, 'Reservations to the Convention on the Elimination Against Women: an unresolved issue or (no) new developments?', in: Ineta Ziemele (ed.), *Reservations to human rights treaties and the Vienna Convention regime: conflict, harmony or reconciliation*, Martinus Nijhoff, Leiden, 2004, p. 30.

[20] This number includes ten States parties which entered reservations to Article 29(1) only.

[21] These are Lesotho, Liechtenstein, Malaysia, Mauritania, Pakistan and Saudi Arabia. See HANNA BEATE SCHÖPP-SCHILLING, 'Reservations to the Convention on the Elimination Against Women: an unresolved issue or (no) new developments?', in: Ineta Ziemele (ed.), *Reservations to human rights treaties and the Vienna Convention regime: conflict, harmony or reconciliation*, Martinus Nijhoff, Leiden, 2004, p. 30.

[22] *Ibid.*, p. 31.

[23] This number includes those States that have entered reservations to Article 29 (1) only. Please note that the declarations by Germany, Mexico and the Netherlands have not been included as they do not amount to reservations in the eyes of the author. The declaration by Pakistan is, however, considered a reservation for the purposes of this Chapter.

[24] Four other States with a predominantly Muslim population entered reservations to Article 29(1) alone. These are Ethiopia, Indonesia, Turkey, Yemen.

[25] These are Brunei, Cook Islands, Marshall Islands, Micronesia, Monaco, Montenegro, Nauru, Oman, Qatar, Swaziland, the United Arab Emirates and Kiribati.

[26] Note that the Cook Islands withdrew its reservation to Article 11(2)(b) in 2007.

While a majority of new ratifying States entered reservations, it is notable that only three entered reservations that did not refer to a specific provision. A narrow majority of States have therefore partially complied with the Committee's requests, though this may serve only as limited consolation since all these new States, with the exception of Brunei, have nevertheless entered reservations to Article 16. Today, twenty-seven States have entered reservations to Article 16 and seventeen to Article 2. Given States' persistence in formulating reservations that the Committee has explicitly indicated as impermissible, it is appropriate to turn to CEDAW's efforts in addressing the problem outside the reporting mechanism.

3. CEDAW'S RESPONSE OUTSIDE THE REPORTING MECHANISM

The Committee has not remained passive in the face of this trend. Indeed, CEDAW manifested its concern at an early stage when it requested the Treaty Section of the Office of Legal Affairs of the UN Secretariat to shed light on who had the competence to determine the compatibility of a reservation with the object and purpose of the Convention.[27] Outside its efforts within the reporting mechanism, which are examined in a subsequent section, CEDAW has taken additional steps, adopting its first general recommendation on reservations in 1987, in which it welcomed the decision of States parties to consider the question but refrained from elaborating a position on the incompatibility of (certain) reservations.[28] This was followed, in 1992, by General Recommendation No. 20, in which the Committee recommends that States parties, in preparation for the 1993 World Conference on Human Rights,

> '(a) Raise the question of the validity and the legal effect of reservations to the Convention in the context of reservations to other human rights treaties;
> (b) Reconsider such reservations with a view to strengthening the implementation of all human rights treaties;
> (c) Consider introducing a procedure on reservations to the Convention comparable with that of other human rights treaties'.

---

[27] The answer to this important question came in 1984 and provided that 'the functions of the Committee do not appear to include a determination of the incompatibility of reservations, although reservations undoubtedly affect the application of the Convention and the Committee might have to comment thereon in its reports in this context'. See UN doc. CEDAW/C/2001/II/4, *Ways and means of expediting the work of the Committee. Report of the Secretariat*, 30 May 2001, Annex VI.

[28] For an interesting insight into the reasons underlying the fact that it took five years for the Committee to adopt a general recommendation on reservations see ELIZABETH EVATT, 'Finding a voice for women's rights: the early years of CEDAW', *The George Washington International Law Review*, 3, 2002, pp. 535 – 539.

The Committee's efforts were rewarded when UN Member States included the issue of reservations in the Vienna Declaration and Programme of Action.[29] Yet fundamental questions remained unanswered. Thus the standards by which the compatibility of reservations should be assessed remained unaddressed, as did the question of who was competent to conduct such an assessment.

The Committee adopted a new approach when it devoted a number of paragraphs to the question of reservations in its General Recommendation No. 21 (1994) on Equality in marriage and family relations. The Committee takes a firm approach when it *requires* that States parties gradually work towards withdrawing their reservations. The Committee places emphasis on the alarming number of reservations to Article 16 and the number of combined reservations to Articles 2 and 16. It also highlights the inconsistency of those States that, having ratified without reservations, nonetheless maintain laws not in conformity with the Convention.[30] Through this General Recommendation, therefore, the Committee stresses the fundamental importance of certain provisions of the Convention, setting the stage for the future determination of the incompatibility of reservations to these Articles.

In the same year, the Committee decided to amend the reporting guidelines for States' reports by outlining specific requirements on reservations.[31] Of particular relevance is the Committee's unequivocal position on the incompatibility with the object and purpose of the Convention of reservations made in respect of Articles 2 and 3 or those reservations that are not entered to a specific Article, though it does not motivate this position.[32] It should be noted that the current reporting guidelines, which in effect replace all previous guidelines, do not contain such a specific statement on the incompatibility of reservations. Additionally, these guidelines do not refer to Article 3 but instead

---

[29] *World Conference on Human Rights: The Vienna Declaration and Programme for Action*, New York, 25 June 1993, 45, para. 5, and p. 55, para. 39.

[30] See para. 41 of General Recommendation No. 21 'The Committee has noted with alarm the number of States parties which have entered reservations to the whole or part of Article 16, especially when a reservation has also been entered to Article 2, claiming that compliance may conflict with a commonly held vision of the family based, *inter alia*, on cultural or religious beliefs or on the country's economic or political status'; and para. 45: 'The Committee noted, on the basis of its examination of initial and subsequent periodic reports, that in some States parties to the Convention that had ratified or acceded without reservation, certain laws, especially those dealing with family, do not actually conform to the provisions of the Convention'.

[31] See UN doc. A/50/38, *Report of the Committee on the Elimination of Discrimination Against Women*, 18 July 1996.

[32] *Ibid*, The Committee states: 'States parties that have entered general reservations which do not refer to a specific Article of the Convention or reservations to Articles 2 and 3 should make a particular effort to report on the effect and interpretation of those reservations. The Committee considers such reservations to be incompatible with the object and purpose of the Convention'.

to Articles 7, 9 and 16 (in addition to Article 2 and general reservations not in reference to a specific provision).[33]

The next major step came in 1998, when the Committee adopted a statement on reservations to the Convention. CEDAW takes its strongest stand to date, stating unambiguously that it considers Article 2 to be central to the objects and purpose of the Convention[34] and its view that reservations to Article 16 are impermissible.[35] While the Committee explicitly singles out Articles 2 and 16, it also makes implicit references to other provisions. This, in the eyes of a former Committee member, can be read as indicating 'that the Committee [has] moved, perhaps unwittingly and certainly not explicitly, to a position from which it might consider all reservations to substantive Articles to be incompatible with the object and purpose of the Convention and thus impermissible'.[36] As becomes evident from an examination of the Committee's treatment of reservations within its Concluding Comments, this has not been the path taken by CEDAW.

In the context of its participation in the Inter-Committee Meeting (ICM) and Meeting of Chairpersons of the Human Rights Treaty Bodies (MC), CEDAW has remained involved in the discussion on reservations. The Working Group on

---

[33] See UN doc. HRI/GEN/2/Rev.6, *Compilation of guidelines on the form and content of reports to be submitted by States parties to the international human rights treaties. Report of the Secretary-General*, 3 June 2009, Chapter 5, para. C.3. The paragraph states: 'General information on reservations and declarations should be included in the common core document in accordance with paragraph 40 (b) of the harmonized reporting guidelines. In addition, specific information in respect of reservations and declarations to the Convention should be included in the Convention-specific document submitted to the Committee in accordance with the present guidelines, the Committee's statements on reservations and, where applicable, the Committee's concluding observations. Any reservation to or declaration relating to any Article of the Convention by the State party should be explained and its continued maintenance clarified. States parties that have entered general reservations which do not refer to a specific Article, or which are directed at Articles 2 and/or 7, 9 and 16 should report on the interpretation and the effect of those reservations. States parties should provide information on any reservations or declarations they may have lodged with regard to similar obligations in other human rights treaties'.

[34] See UN doc. A/53/38/Rev. 1, *Report of the Committee on the Elimination of Discrimination Against Women*, 14 May 1998, Part Two, Chapter I, para. 16. The Committee states: 'The Committee holds the view that Article 2 is central to the objects and purpose of the Convention. States parties which ratify the Convention do so because they agree that discrimination against women in all its forms should be condemned and that the strategies set out in Article 2, subparagraphs (a) to (g), should be implemented by States parties to eliminate it.'.

[35] See *ibid*, para. 17. The Committee states: 'Neither traditional, religious or cultural practice nor incompatible domestic laws and policies can justify violations of the Convention. The Committee also remains convinced that reservations to Article 16, whether lodged for national, traditional, religious or cultural reasons, are incompatible with the Convention and therefore impermissible and should be reviewed and modified or withdrawn.'

[36] See HANNA BEATE SCHÖPP-SCHILLING, 'Reservations to the Convention on the Elimination Against Women: an unresolved issue or (no) new developments?', in: Ineta Ziemele (ed.), *Reservations to human rights treaties and the Vienna Convention regime: conflict, harmony or reconciliation*, Martinus Nijhoff, Leiden, 2004, p. 27.

Reservations, established pursuant to a request by the fourth ICM and the seventeenth MC,[37] held its first meeting on 8 and 9 June 2006 in Geneva. CEDAW was not represented at this meeting, during which the participants discussed the report, prepared by the Secretariat, on the practice of treaty bodies[38] and adopted some recommendations for the fifth ICM. At the Working Group's next meeting, on 14 and 15 December 2006, CEDAW summarised its handling of reservations through its two General Recommendations on the issue and its 1998 statement referred to above. Additionally, it highlighted its increasingly bold approach to reservations in its concluding comments.[39] This prompted members of the Working Group to note that CEDAW's position is indeed stronger than that of other Committees, since it explicitly underlines the incompatibility of some reservations. The Working Group went on to adopt a set of recommendations, building on those it had adopted at its first meeting. Of particular relevance is the Working Group's position on treaty bodies' competence to assess the validity of reservations which, as evidenced by the reactions to the Human Rights Committee's take on Trinidad and Tobago's reservation to the ICCPR, is a question that has been the subject of quite some controversy.[40] The Working Group, for its part, determined that 'treaty bodies are competent to assess the validity of reservations and, in the event, the implications of a finding of invalidity of a reservation, particularly in the examination of individual communications [...]'.[41] This, coupled with the Working Group's position on the consequences of an invalid reservation (the latter must be considered null and void and the State concerned thus remains a party to the Treaty without benefit of the reservation),[42] means that the treaty bodies as a whole, including CEDAW, have adopted an unequivocal position on reservations that are incompatible with the object and purpose of a given human rights treaty.

As this overview demonstrates, the Committee has evolved considerably from its timid first steps in the early 1980s to its current assertion of its competence to determine the impermissibility of certain reservations. It is to be commended for having taken proactive steps on the issue of reservations,

---

[37] See UN doc. A/60/278, *Effective implementation of international instruments on human rights, including reporting obligations under international instruments on human rights*, 19 August 2005, Annex, Part IX, para. VI.

[38] See UN doc. HRI/MC/2005/5, *The practice of human rights treaty bodies with respect to reservations to international human rights treaties*, 13 June 2005.

[39] See UN doc. HRI/MC/2007/5, *Report of the meeting of the working group on reservations*, 9 February 2005, para. 14.

[40] See INEKE BOEREFIJN, 'Impact on the Law of Treaty Reservations', in: Menno Kamminga and Martin Scheinin (eds), *The impact of human rights law on general international*, Oxford University Press, Oxford, 2009, pp. 87 – 92.

[41] See UN doc. HRI/MC/2007/5, *Report of the meeting of the working group on reservations*, 9 February 2005, para. 5.

[42] See *ibid.*, para. 16(7).

although it might be argued that, based on its conflicting guidelines, it has been inconsistent in indicating those Articles reservations to which would be deemed incompatible with the object and purpose of the Convention. Yet to what extent has the Committee's increasingly bold approach impacted on the practice of States with a predominantly Muslim population? Additionally, how has it attempted to grapple with the question within its constructive dialogue with these States parties and have its efforts been echoed by objecting States?

4. CEDAW AND MUSLIM STATES IN THE REPORTING MECHANISM

4.1. ASSESSING THE PRACTICE OF MUSLIM STATES SINCE 2004

Just over half of States with substantive reservations are Islamic republics or have a majority Muslim population. While non-Muslim States largely reserve to Articles 11 and 16,[43] four of them have entered reservations to Articles 2 and 9. Muslim States, on the other hand, overwhelmingly enter reservations to Articles 2, 9, 15 and 16. Eleven have entered reservations to Article 2, fourteen to Article 9, seven to Article 15 and a whopping nineteen to Article 16.

Muslim States are also the overwhelming culprits when it comes to entering general reservations that do not refer to a specific provision. Thus Brunei Darussalam, which ratified in 2006 and has yet to submit a report to the Committee, entered the following reservation upon ratification: 'The Government of Brunei Darussalam expresses its reservations regarding those provisions of the said Convention that may be contrary to the Constitution of Brunei Darussalam and to the beliefs and principles of Islam, the official religion of Brunei Darussalam (...)'. Others having made similar reservations referring to the Constitution and/or Islamic law include Mauritania, Malaysia, Libya, Oman, Pakistan, Saudi Arabia and Tunisia. In comparison, only two non-Muslim States have entered such general reservations, Spain and Monaco. In quantitative terms, therefore, Muslim countries dominate the reservations landscape overall and constitute the majority of those having entered expressly impermissible reservations (to Articles 2 and 16).

Of the sixteen reserving Muslim States that have submitted reports and have been reviewed since the beginning of 2005, half have indicated, in one way or the other, their willingness or intention to review and/or withdraw (some of) their reservations. Thus Bangladesh has stated that it is willing to consider withdrawing its reservations; Egypt has assured the Committee that efforts to

---

[43] A total of eleven non-Muslim States have entered reservations to Article 16 and seven to Article 11.

withdraw its reservation to Article 2 are underway (as the provision is not in conflict with Egypt's Constitution or legislation),[44] though it has explicitly stated that it is not willing to withdraw its reservations to Article 16(e) and (f), as 'doing so would diminish the rights of women under Islamic law and Egyptian law, which provide rights for wom[e]n and relieve women of responsibilities which men alone are required to bear';[45] Malaysia, having indicated its readiness to review its reservations to Articles 5(a) and 7(b) in 2006, withdrew those reservations along with that to Article 16(2) in July 2010. Yet it indicated in its last dialogue with CEDAW that it was not willing to similarly review its reservations to Articles 9(2) and 16(1) and (2).[46] The fact that it eventually removed its reservation to Article 16(2) in spite of its initial reluctance might be cause for optimism. Mauritania, for its part, has the intention to withdraw its general reservation (though it has yet to do so since its last report was examined in 2007); Niger is undertaking efforts with the aim of withdrawing; Tunisia has taken steps (and indeed removed similar reservations to the Convention on the Rights of the Child in 2008).[47] Bahrain and Morocco are also on board.

While these are highly positive developments, it should be noted that, until the reservations are indeed revised and/or withdrawn, nothing can be taken for granted. By way of example, the Maldives, which had indicated having begun the formal process of withdrawing some of the reservations during the examination of its initial report, have yet to remove said reservations (and reiterated their assurances to the Committee in 2007).[48] While the reservation to Article 7(a) was withdrawn in 2010, the Maldives maintain a reservation to Article 16. Additionally, other Muslim States are not as accommodating. Thus Saudi Arabia is of the view that its general reservation simply does not conflict with the Convention. The answer provided in response to the Committee's probe

---

[44] See UN doc. CEDAW/C/EGY/7, *Consideration of reports submitted by States parties under Article 18 of the Convention on the Elimination of All Forms of Discrimination Against Women. Combined sixth and seventh periodic reports of States parties. Egypt*, 5 September 2008, Part I, para. 2.2.

[45] See UN doc. CEDAW/C/EGY/7, *Consideration of reports submitted by States parties under Article 18 of the Convention on the Elimination of All Forms of Discrimination Against Women. Combined sixth and seventh periodic reports of States parties. Egypt*, 5 September 2008, Part III, para. 16.1.

[46] See UN doc. CEDAW/C/MYS/CO/2, *Concluding comments of the Committee on the Elimination of Discrimination Against Women: Malaysia*, 31 May 2006, para. 9.

[47] On 16 August, 2011, the Tunisian Council of Ministers adopted a draft decree lifting all specific reservations to the Convention (but not the general declaration). To the author's knowledge, at the time of writing, Tunisia had not yet formally removed its reservations. Thus for the purposes of this contribution, Tunisia's specific reservations are taken into account. For further information on the draft decree see Human Rights Watch, *Tunisia: Government Lifts Restrictions on Women's Rights Treaty*, 6 September 2011, available at www.hrw.org/news/2011/09/06/tunisia-government-lifts-restrictions-women-s-rights-treaty, last consulted on 14 October 2011.

[48] See UN doc. CEDAW/C/MDV/CO/3, *Concluding comments of the Committee on the Elimination of Discrimination against Women: Maldives*, 2 February 2007, para. 11.

for further details on the scope and impact of this reservation deserves particular attention. The State declares:

> 'The general reservation made by the Kingdom does not affect the core of the Convention or detract from its legal force before the judicial and executive authorities. It is merely a precautionary measure at a time when human rights concepts are developing rapidly as a result of interpretations following the entry into force of international human rights instruments such as the Convention. Not only might these interpretations sometimes go beyond the literal content of the provisions, but the interpretation might, itself, become a core principle in the opinion of some of the subcommittee's experts. The reservation is thus primarily a *precautionary measure against possible interpretations of the Convention* that might contradict legal provisions in force in the Kingdom. In any case, the government does not believe that the wording of its reservation interferes with its obligations under the Convention. This is clear from the Kingdom's report, which lays out the Sharia and legal provisions relating to women and shows clearly that *there is no contradiction between the main provisions that form the basis of the Convention and Islamic Sharia principles relating to women's rights.*'[49]

This lengthy quote illustrates the State's fear over the potential for interpretation of its obligations under the Convention. This might be in response to CEDAW's progressive approach in its interpretation but the result is that the prospects for withdrawal of the reservation are not bright (this in spite of the State's assurances that there are no contradictions between the provisions of the Convention and the principles of Sharia).

Lebanon is reluctant to review its reservation to Article 9(2), motivating its stance by referring to the politically sensitive nature of nationality law.[50] It is equally reluctant to withdraw its reservation to Article 16. The United Arab Emirates have simply undertaken no process of review. As part of the motivation behind the reservations, the UAE stated that the provisions of Article 2(f) conflict with those of the Islamic Sharia concerning inheritance; that the acquisition of nationality is an internal matter; and that it complies with the provisions of Article 16 in so far as it does not conflict with the principles of the provisions of the Islamic Sharia.[51] Clearly these are not elaborations or explanations for the reservations and there is no reason to believe that they will be withdrawn.

---

[49] See UN doc. CEDAW/C/SAU/Q/2/Add.1, *Responses to the list of issues and questions contained in document number CEDAW/C/SAU/Q/2, A.H. 1428 (A.D. 2007)*, 18 December 2007, para. 2 (emphasis added).

[50] See UN doc. CEDAW/C/LBN/3, *Consideration of reports submitted by States parties under Article 18 of the Convention on the Elimination of All Forms of Discrimination against Women. Third periodic report of States parties. Lebanon*, 7 July 2006, para. 3.

[51] See UN doc. CEDAW/C/ARE/Q/1/Add.1, *Responses to the list of issues and questions with regard to the consideration of the initial periodic report. United Arab Emirates*, 19 October 2009, para. 4.

Thus the picture is mixed. While some Muslim States appear, at least if taken at face value, to be ready to withdraw their problematic reservations (and indeed some have already done so to some extent), others appear to be digging their heels in the ground. Many do not spontaneously, in their reports, provide in-depth information on the scope and impact of their reservations and the Committee does not always receive satisfactory responses to its questions.

4.2. CEDAW'S REACTION WITHIN THE REPORTING MECHANISM

An examination of the Committee's treatment of reservations within the framework of its constructive dialogue with States also reveals a mixed picture, with inconsistencies apparent in CEDAW's concluding comments.

To begin with the list of written issues and questions to States' reports, the Committee has, since 2004, consistently addressed the question of reservations (unless, as in the cases of Bahrain's combined initial and second and Lebanon's third periodic reports, the reservations were already adequately addressed). Where States did not follow the guidelines for reporting, the Committee always requested clarification on the scope and impact of reservations and requested information on the progress made towards the removal of reservations. It occasionally asked the State party to indicate the timeframe for the full harmonization of its legislation with the Convention and consequent removal of reservations.[52] Thus the Committee has repeatedly prevented States parties from ignoring the important issue of reservations. While the reaction from the States has not always been satisfactory, as seen above, CEDAW has ensured the inclusion of reservations within its constructive dialogue, thereby maintaining the issue high on the agenda.

The Committee's consistency in its list of issues has not always been reflected in its Concluding Observations, however. While the recommendations made always involve the question of reservations when applicable, the manner in which these are addressed has differed considerably. Thus CEDAW has oscillated between urging the State party to 'complete as soon as possible the process of withdrawal [of its reservation]'[53] or 'recognize the negative impact of its nationality law [...], revise its nationality law and remove its reservation to

---

[52] See UN doc. CEDAW/C/TUN/Q/6, *List of issues and questions with regard to the consideration of periodic reports. Tunisia*, 29 March 2010, para. 3; and UN doc. CEDAW/C/BGD/Q/7, *List of issues and questions with regard to the consideration of periodic reports. Bangladesh*, 6 September 2010, para. 1.

[53] See UN doc. CEDAW/C/MRT/CO/1, *Concluding Comments of the Committee on the Elimination of Discrimination Against Women: Mauritania*, 11 June 2007, para. 10.

Article 9, paragraph 2'[54] and strongly encouraging 'to consider narrowing'[55] its reservations. On at least one occasion, the Committee has, for the same report, *requested* the State party to withdraw its reservation to Article 9(2) while merely urging it to *consider withdrawing* its general reservation.[56] CEDAW has also varied in its pronouncement on those reservations which it considers contrary to the object and purpose of the Convention. Thus in its examination of Niger's combined initial and second report in 2007 it brought attention to its view that reservations to Articles 2 and 16 are contrary to the object and purpose of the Convention while omitting to take a similar position with regards to Niger's reservation to Article 15(4). Yet in its list of concerns following examination of Bahrain's combined initial and second report, the Committee states that it considers reservations to Article 15(4), *inter alia*, as contrary to the object and purpose of the Convention. In 2010, at its 47th session, the Committee further perplexes when, upon examining Tunisia's period report, it expresses concern over reservations to Articles 9(2), 16(1)(c)(d)(f)(g) and (h) and 15(4) as it considers that 'some of these reservations are incompatible with the object and purpose of the Convention.' Yet at its 45th session, the Committee was of the opinion that Articles 2(f), 9, 15(2) and 16 were all central to the object and purpose of the Convention.[57]

It is not just these inconsistencies that weaken the Committee's position. Indeed, while often specifying, in its Concluding Comments, that it regards certain reservations as going against the object and purpose of the Convention, the Committee rarely, if ever, motivates its position. Thus pronouncements on the impermissibility of reservations are devoid of any legal substantiation – a trait hardly conducive to convincing States parties of their legal obligations.

The picture that emerges from an examination of CEDAW's Concluding Comments to Muslim State reports is thus confused. On the one hand, it is clear that reservations are high on the list of preoccupations for Committee members. Yet the language used to request or urge the removal of impermissible reservations varies in its forcefulness and the Committee has created confusion with regards to those reservations that it considers contrary to the object and purpose of the Convention (and thus impermissible).

---

[54] See UN doc. CEDAW/C/LBN/3, *Concluding Comments of the Committee on the Elimination of Discrimination Against Women: Lebanon*, 8 April 2008, para.43.

[55] See UN doc. CEDAW/C/ARE/CO/1, *Concluding Comments of the Committee on the Elimination of Discrimination Against Women: United Arab Emirates*, 5 February 2010, para. 17.

[56] See UN doc. CEDAW/C/SAU/CO/2, *Concluding Comments of the Committee on the Elimination of Discrimination Against Women: Saudi Arabia*, 8 April 2008, para. 10 and para. 28.

[57] See UN doc. CEDAW/C/ARE/CO/1, *Concluding Comments of the Committee on the Elimination of Discrimination Against Women: United Arab Emirates*, 5 February 2010, para. 16.

5. OBJECTIONS BY STATES PARTIES

Of the twenty-four States that have objected since the Convention was opened for ratification, only two are not members of the Council of Europe (CoE) – Mexico and Canada. The objections have covered different types of reservations, formulated by both Muslim and non-Muslim countries. A large number of States have objected to reservations entered in respect of Article 16 including, interestingly, France and Ireland which themselves maintain an impermissible reservation to that provision. Additionally, States have recalled the impermissibility of generally worded reservations to specific Articles and reservations so broadly formulated that they run against the object and purpose of the Convention.

It is striking that not a single Muslim country has objected to any reservation, permissible or not. Considering that sixteen Muslim States parties have either entered no reservation or have done so only with regards to Article 29(1), it is rather deplorable that none have taken the initiative to react and use this mechanism to shed light on their position regarding broadly formulated reservations or reservations to provisions that have been singled out repeatedly by the Committee (in particular Articles 2 and 16). While objections from all non-reserving States would indeed have been a welcome development, it is arguable that objections from Muslim countries to impermissible reservations would have contributed tremendously to the evolution of the debate. Thus while countries such as Turkey, Afghanistan (admittedly otherwise occupied at present), Azerbaijan, Djibouti, Eritrea, Ethiopia, Guinea, Indonesia and Nigeria, amongst other States, are to be commended for their lack of (substantive) reservations, they may also be singled out for criticism for failing to express themselves on the matter.

Yet CEDAW also holds part of the responsibility for failing to be consistent in its acknowledgement and praise of objections and for failing to encourage them. While the Committee, in its Concluding Comments, has at times commended a State's objections,[58] it has not done so in a uniform manner with all objecting States. Thus Belgium, which in 2007 objected to Brunei Darussalam's reservations, received no recognition for this when its report was examined one year later. The Committee, with a view to strengthening its position, ought not only have praised all objecting States but could have, in a forward-thinking manner, actively encouraged those States that have entered no (impermissible) reservations to object to reservations of a manifestly impermissible nature. To be fair, the Committee did address objections in its statement on reservations in 1998. It stated that '[s]ome States formally lodge objections to reservations to Articles 2 and 16. The Committee recognizes and appreciates the positive impact

---

[58] It has done so in the cases of Finland, Norway, Sweden, the Netherlands and Germany.

that the use of this procedure can have in encouraging States to withdraw or modify reservations [...] It is optimistic that more States parties will rigorously review and object to impermissible reservations to the Convention'.[59] Yet this only demonstrates CEDAW's awareness of the potential utility of objections. Why, then, did it choose not to harness this potential in a systematic manner?

It is true that objections have a limited impact and form part of a political game. Yet they serve the purpose of further strengthening the Committee's position as regards the impermissibility of certain reservations and shed light on States parties' interpretations of the Convention. Given the magnitude of the reservations issue, it is almost tragic that neither the Committee nor States parties have chosen to make more use of this tool.

6. CONCLUSIONS

The question of reservations to the Women's Convention manifested itself already during the drafting process, yet those around the negotiating table did not see fit to diverge from the Vienna Convention regime – a decision that, today, appears wholly misguided.[60] The Committee has made a valiant attempt at reigning in a galloping problem, and for that it must be applauded. It began addressing reservations early on and has encouraged States parties again and again to narrow and withdraw their reservations. For all its worth, however, this effort has been flawed and fluctuating. The Committee has created confusion as regards those provisions that it considers central to the object and purpose of the Convention and it has failed to contribute a consistent legal argument to motivate its position. Yet while this is undesirable, the responsibility for the state of reservations ultimately rests with reserving States – a majority of which, as had been feared in 2004, have turned out to be Muslim.

This gloomy reality does not mean that the Women's Convention has been stripped of its integrity, however. The proportion of reserving States has slowly diminished as universal ratification has inched closer. Additionally, a fair portion of reserving Muslim States has responded positively to CEDAW's constant push for withdrawal of reservations – and the Arab spring may yet prove to bring about radical changes.[61] CEDAW has now joined forces with the UN's other human rights monitoring bodies, presenting a united front on the question of competence for determining the impermissibility of reservations.

---

[59] See UN doc. A/53/38/Rev. 1, *Report of the Committee on the Elimination of Discrimination Against Women*, 14 May 1998, Part Two, Chapter I, para. 20.

[60] See LIESBETH LIJNZAAD, *Reservations to UN-Human Rights Treaties: ratify and ruin?*, Martinus Nijhoff, Dordrecht, 1995, p. 300.

[61] As has happened in the case of Tunisia. See footnote 47 above.

The Committee should continue its efforts within the reporting mechanism, perhaps paying more attention to the uniformity of its Concluding Comments. In addition, it would be advisable that a new General Recommendation on the question of reservations be elaborated, providing a solid legal base. Finally, when the time comes for the Committee to examine a case under the Optional Protocol that involves a provision to which the State concerned has made an impermissible reservation, the Committee must not shy away from making a bold statement.

CHAPTER 21
THE OPTIONAL PROTOCOL TO THE WOMEN'S CONVENTION: AN ASSESSMENT OF ITS EFFECTIVENESS IN PROTECTING WOMEN'S RIGHTS

Sille JANSEN

1. INTRODUCTION

The drafting of the Women's Convention was a major accomplishment. Its creation is recognition of the fact that general human rights treaties do not sufficiently address women's rights. Since its creation in 1979 the Women's Convention has been ratified by an overwhelming number of 187 States.[1] The Convention has, however, not escaped the scepticism that is generally felt where implementation of human rights treaties is concerned. As with many human rights treaties the only implementation mechanism of the Women's Convention remained a reporting system for many years.[2] This reporting mechanism placed the Committee on the Elimination of Discrimination against Women (CEDAW) in a passive position. CEDAW's ability to contribute to the implementation of the Women's Convention was limited to making recommendations based on reports.

This situation changed in the year 2000, when the Optional Protocol to the Women's Convention entered into force, adding two monitoring mechanisms to the reporting mechanism: the individual complaint procedure and the inquiry procedure.[3] The decisions of CEDAW under these procedures are, however, not legally binding. State parties are merely required to 'give due consideration to the

---

[1] See for a direct link to the list of ratifications: The United Nations website www.un.org/womenwatch/daw/cedaw/states.htm [situation April 2012].

[2] UN doc. A/RES/34/180, *Convention on the Elimination of All Forms of Discrimination against Women*, 18 December 1979, Article 18. Article 29 of the Women's Convention offers State parties to refer disputes on the interpretation of the Convention to the International Court of Justice. However, many States have made a reservation to this clause and it was never used until now.

[3] UN doc. A/RES/54/4, *Optional Protocol to the Convention on the Elimination of All Forms of Discrimination against Women*, 15 October 1999. The Optional Protocol currently has 104

views of the Committee' once it has presented its decision.⁴ Thus, the success of the complaints mechanism relies mainly on the good will of States to follow recommendations. The question rises whether the Optional Protocol is effectively implementing women's rights. To answer this question, the developments that made the Optional Protocol's monitoring mechanisms possible will be examined first. To assess the effectiveness of the individual complaints procedure and the inquiry procedure, the approach CEDAW has taken in the interpretation of complaints brought under these procedures will be assessed. Special attention will be paid to the follow up that States have given to the recommendations. In the conclusion, an indication of the effectiveness of the Optional Protocol with regard to the implementation of women's rights is made.

2. THE EVOLUTION OF THE PROCEDURES OF THE PROTOCOL

At the time of the drafting of the Women's Convention, there was no political will to insert implementation mechanisms besides the rather weak reporting procedure. States did negotiate on the question whether an additional implementation mechanism should be in place and if so, who would be allowed to monitor it.⁵ It was, however, a time in which implementation mechanisms for human rights were generally lacking. Some country delegates argued that it would be more useful to have a complaint procedure for crimes like apartheid and racial discrimination than a complaint procedure for discrimination against women, on the assumption that the former are more serious crimes.⁶ Thus, initially no procedure besides the reporting mechanism was included to protect the rights set forth in the Convention.

The idea that discrimination against women is not such a grave crime persisted.⁷ After the entering into force of the Women's Convention, however, it became more and more obvious that the tools available to CEDAW were not sufficient to guarantee the implementation of the Women's Convention. Some

---

parties. See for a direct link to the list of ratifications: The United Nations website www.un.org/womenwatch/daw/cedaw/protocol/sigop.htm [situation April 2012].

[4] UN doc. A/RES/54/4, *Optional Protocol to the Convention on the Elimination of All Forms of Discrimination against Women*, 15 October 1999, Article 7.4.

[5] A. BYRNES and J. CONNORS, 'Enforcing the Human Rights of Women: A Complaints Process for the Women's Convention?', *Brooklyn Journal of International Law*, Vol. 21, 1996, pp. 686.

[6] See for a short history, CEDAW website available at: www.un.org/womenwatch/daw/cedaw/protocol/history.htm [accessed 25 November 2010].

[7] For an assessment of the scope of violence against women see: UN General Assembly, *In-depth study on all forms of violence against women: report of the Secretary-General*, 6 July 2006, A/61/122/Add.1, available at: www.unhcr.org/refworld/docid/484e58702.html [accessed 18 August 2011].

States did hint in the direction of a complaints procedure, but it was only in the nineteen nineties that serious interest in such a procedure became apparent.[8]

The UN Commission on the Status of Women reviewed the mechanisms of implementation and reported that they were unsatisfactory, an observation to which the Secretary General of the United Nations agreed.[9] During the same period, a large NGO movement was calling strongly for the strengthening of the institutions which were overseeing the implementation of women's rights. This NGO advocacy campaign pushed the Commission on the Status of Women and the United Nations General Assembly (UNGA) forward and a certain momentum was created. In 1993, a Declaration and Programme of Action were adopted by the UNGA, which stated that the possibility of the right to petition should be examined by the Commission.[10]

In 1994, it was at the University of Limburg in Maastricht[11] that the first text for an Optional Protocol that would install an individual complaints procedure and an inquiry procedure was drafted.[12] There were no official government delegations present at the drafting; it was a meeting of an independent expert group consisting of international human rights lawyers.[13] In 1995, when the Commission on the Status of Women adopted a document which contained the elements that would be part of the Optional Protocol, it clearly reflected the Maastricht draft.[14] With the Maastricht draft, the process of adopting an individual complaints procedure accelerated. A women's rights momentum was created, with the Beijing 1995 Platform for Action as a catalyst. Reports and working groups were quickly established. These made it possible for the Optional Protocol to be adopted in its current form on October 6th 1999 by the United Nations General Assembly (even though it was still incomplete, according to some).[15] The Protocol was opened for signatures on human rights day, December 10th 1999. By December 22nd, the tenth instrument of ratification had already been received by the Secretariat, and the Protocol thereby entered into force.[16]

The Optional Protocol provides for two additional supervisory mechanisms. The first is the individual complaints procedure, set out in Article 2 of the

---

[8] Supra note 5 at p. 690.
[9] UN doc. E/CN.6/1991/10, *Examining Existing Mechanisms for Communications on the Status of Women: Report of the Secretary General*, 1991, paras. 136–156.
[10] Supra note 5 at p. 692.
[11] Nowadays this University is known as Maastricht University.
[12] Supra note 5 at p. 693.
[13] See for a short history, CEDAW website available at: www.un.org/womenwatch/daw/cedaw/protocol/history.htm [accessed 25 November 2010].
[14] UN doc. A/50/38, *Report of the Commission on the Elimination of Discrimination Against Women 14th Session*, 31 May 1995, pp. 2–5.
[15] F.G. ISA, 'The Optional Protocol for the Convention on the Elimination of all Forms of Discrimination Against Women: Strengthening the Protection Mechanisms of Women's Human Rights', 20 *Arizona Journal of International and Comparative Law* (2003), p. 309.
[16] UN doc. A/RES/54/4, *Optional Protocol to the Convention on the Elimination of All Forms of Discrimination against Women*, 15 October 1999, Article 16.

Protocol. The second procedure is an inquiry procedure, described in Article 8 of the Protocol, which authorizes CEDAW to start an investigation if it has received information which points at grave or systematic violation of the Women's Convention by a State party.

Complaints have been filed to CEDAW since the Protocol's adoption in 1999, but the first decision on an individual complaint was only made in 2003 and the first (and so far only) inquiry report was finalized in 2005. This delay between the entering into force of the Protocol and the first decision on an individual complaint can be explained by two factors. The first is that the Protocol does not work retroactively; this is relevant because it means individual complaints can only be made for violations which occurred after the Protocol entered into force for the State party. The second factor is that the often lengthy domestic remedies have to be exhausted before a complaint can be brought to the Committee (Article 2 of the Optional Protocol). As for the inquiry procedure, the first request to start an inquiry was submitted to CEDAW in 2002. The inquiry was finalized in 2005.

3. THE TERMS OF THE PROTOCOL AND ITS CASE LAW

3.1. THE INDIVIDUAL COMPLAINTS PROCEDURE

3.1.1. Introduction

CEDAW, vested with the authority to examine individual complaints, consists of twenty-three experts of 'high moral standing and competence in the field covered by the Convention.'[17] The requirements for the members of CEDAW was set up at the time the Convention was drafted, not taking into account the fact that an individual complaints procedure would come into existence. Although the decisions of CEDAW are not legally binding, the procedure is a legalistic one. And, whereas the procedure of the examination of the complaints is legal in its nature, no legal experience is required of those who examine and decide on the complaints. As a result, of the twenty-three experts on the Committee in 2010, only eight held a degree in law.[18] Only seven members of the Committee seem – based on the short biographies provided – to practice law on a daily basis. In its composition CEDAW resembles a highly educated jury rather than a bench of judges and it may therefore occur that the working group of five members that is selected to examine a complaint, may only consist of members with no

---

[17] UN doc. A/RES/34/180, *Convention on the Elimination of All Forms of Discrimination against Women*, 18 December 1979, Article 17.
[18] See for a list of members: The United Nations website www.un.org/womenwatch/daw/cedaw/members.htm [accessed 25 November 2010].

background in law. In view of the technical legal issues, such as admissibility, that the Committee has to consider this raises some concerns.

In the following sections, several aspects of CEDAW's case law will be examined; the admissibility of complaints, the justiciability of the rights of the Convention, the margin of discretion of the States and indirect discrimination, the due diligence obligations of States and the follow up given by States to decisions of CEDAW.

3.1.2. Admissibility

Rules with regard to admissibility are laid down in Article 4 of the Optional Protocol. Three of the admissibility criteria will be highlighted here. First, the requirement that domestic remedies must be exhausted has caused some uncertainty as it is not clear when the exception to this rule is applicable. The exception reads: 'unless the application of such remedies is unreasonably prolonged or unlikely to bring effective relief'. The threshold for this exception to inadmissibility seems – from decisions published so far – rather high. The second and third admissibility criteria concern the jurisdiction of the Committee *ratione materiae* and *ratione temporis*. The jurisdiction of the committee *ratione temporis* is limited to complaints concerning a violation of which the facts occurred prior to the entry into force of the Protocol for the State party concerned, 'unless those facts continued after that date'. Here again, it is the exception that causes some uncertainty. From the case analysis, it is not clear which criteria determine whether the facts continue after the date of entry into force, rather this seems to be determined on a case to case basis.

3.1.2.1. Exhaustion of Domestic Remedies

The case of *N.S.F. v United Kingdom of Great Britain and Northern Ireland*, concerned a woman and her two children who had fled from a violent ex-husband in Pakistan to the United Kingdom. Upon arrival, the woman's request for asylum was rejected. Her complaint to CEDAW was declared inadmissible because some of the local remedies which now had become near to impossible for her to access would become more accessible to her if she were to complain about gender discrimination, which she had failed to do. CEDAW concludes that the complaint should be referred back to the national level and that the complainant should indeed bring her complaints about gender discrimination forward in an application to the Home Office and in an application for judicial review. CEDAW will have the opportunity to re-examine the case should it come back after these procedures fail. These lengthy procedures could have been considered to be disregarded. Article 4 of the OP which states that remedies may be left aside if 'the application of such remedies is unreasonably prolonged or unlikely to bring effective relief' should not be a dead letter. It could take years before the case finally returns to CEDAW and the family will continue to live in uncertainty during this time. On the other hand, the requirement of exhaustion of domestic remedies is a necessary precaution that touches on the sovereignty of States. It has been well established by other international human rights bodies that States need to be given the opportunity to resolve complaints at the national level, and that they can only be subjected to international bodies once national mechanisms have been exhausted.[19]

3.1.2.2. Admissibility *Ratione Materiae*

It was the first-born daughter of the deceased Count of Bulnes who brought the case of *Cristina Muñoz-Vargas y Sainz de Vicuña v Spain*, which concerns the title of nobility.[20] The daughter does not agree that her brother has inherited the title of Count, since he is younger and would therefore only inherit the title because he is male. The case was declared inadmissible *ratione temporis*, but eight members issued a concurring opinion. While they agree that the complaint is inadmissible they state that it is not inadmissible *ratione temporis* but *ratione materiae*. Article 1 of the Women's Convention protects women against discrimination 'in the political, economic, social, cultural, civil or any other field'. The concurring opinion finds that a title of nobility is only of symbolic value and has 'no legal or material effect'. Denying the woman in question this title on the basis of her gender cannot be seen as a violation of the Women's Convention as it has no 'effect or purpose of impairing or nullifying the recognition, enjoyment or exercise by women on a basis of equality of men and women, of human rights and fundamental freedoms in all fields'. It is true that the Convention and the Optional Protocol are in existence to protect women from real discrimination and not for trivial inconveniences. Yet in our society today, social status and nobility title can have a real impact on a woman's or man's life. It is exactly in old structures like nobility that discrimination of women and the idea of inferiority of women is vested. Eliminating gender biases in these areas are thus not so insignificant that they can be ignored.

3.1.2.3. Admissibility *Ratione Temporis*

The first case considered by CEDAW, *B.J. v Germany*, concerns a classic example of our time.[21] A woman, B.J., marries a man to become a homemaker while her husband pursues his career. After some time, the couple divorces and the woman finds herself in an abominable financial situation. B.J. claims that the German

---

[19] See for example Human Rights Committee Communication Nos. 222/1987 *M. K. v France*, 1356/2005 *Antonio Parra Corral v Spain* and 1420/2005 *Eugene Linder v Finland*.

[20] UN doc. CEDAW/C/39/D/7/2005, *Cristina Muñoz-Vargas y Sainz de Vicuña v Spain*, 9 August 2007.

[21] UN doc. A/59/38, *Ms. B.J. v Germany*, 14 July 2004.

statutes which regulate divorce allow for gender-based discrimination in the area of the equalization of accrued gains and the equalization of pensions.

The complaint of Mrs B.J. was declared inadmissible on two grounds. First, CEDAW found that B.J. did not exhaust all domestic remedies available to her. Second, the Committee found that the facts had occurred before the entry into force of the OP in Germany and that they did not continue after this date. Interestingly, two members of the Committee, Krisztina Morvai and Meriem Belmihoub-Zerdani, disagreed on both accounts. These members claimed that the complaint concerned the still ongoing proceedings on the maintenance fee and was therefore not inadmissible *ratione temporis*. Focusing on the exhaustion of local remedies, the authors state that the exception to this rule, that one does not have to exhaust local remedies if 'the application of such remedies is unreasonably prolonged or unlikely to bring effective relief', should be applied. The five years that the ongoing proceedings had taken so far were unreasonably long since the procedure concerns a rather simple legal issue of maintenance. Furthermore, the dissenting opinion states that the courts 'should have determined and granted a decent maintenance for her a long time ago' and thus claims that 'for an older woman who raised three children and worked for the benefit of her spouse for three decades living in such uncertainty five years after the divorce is rightly considered to be unacceptable and a serious violation of her human rights in and of itself.'

It seems that in this first case, CEDAW used a prudent and rather legalistic approach. Whereas the dissenting opinion raises more sympathy with defenders of the rights in the Women's Convention it is also understandable why CEDAW took a cautious approach. CEDAW cannot manifest itself as an activist court. Being too audacious could endanger the potential amount of ratifications of the Protocol as well as its authoritative position. Nonetheless, the procedure was specifically created to give the Women's Convention teeth and CEDAW should not be afraid to use them when necessary.

In the previously mentioned case of *Cristina Muñoz-Vargas y Sainz de Vicuña v Spain* relating to the title of nobility, CEDAW decided to elaborate on the admissibility criterion *ratione temporis*. It did not do so before and in all likelihood realized that many complaints will have to be declared inadmissible *ratione temporis* if no further indications are given as to what point in time is relevant for the admissibility. 'The relevant fact', CEDAW states, 'is when the right to succession to the title of the author's father was vested in the author's brother. That date was on 3 October 1980 when the royal decree of succession was issued.'[22] It is not clear why CEDAW does not attribute relevance to the fact the possession of the title by the brother and thus the possible violation continued until after the OP was ratified by Spain. This is particularly of interest since in the case of *Rahime Kayhan v Turkey* CEDAW came to a different

---

[22] *Ibid.*, para. 11.5.

conclusion. In this case, a woman brought a complaint on the basis of gender discrimination for her wearing a head scarf.[23] CEDAW decided that the facts of the case started before the entry into force of the OP, but also continued after that had happened, stating that: 'The effects of the loss of her status continue still', thus referring to the exception in Article 4. The case was therefore not inadmissible *ratione temporis*. It is unclear why in this case the effects of the violation are considered to be continuing whereas in *B.J. v Germany* and *Cristina Muñoz-Vargas y Sainz de Vicuña v Spain* they were not.

The approach of CEDAW towards admissibility seems incoherent.[24] It seems that CEDAW has not yet come to a standard approach to determine whether a case is admissible *ratione temporis*. Especially the reasoning which determines whether the facts continue after the entry into force seems inconsistent. Although it may not be uncommon for a new complaints mechanism to need time to crystallize its approach, the lack of a systematic approach poses real risk to the credibility of the mechanism.

3.1.3. Justiciability and the Margin of Discretion

According to Article 2 of the OP, 'a violation of any of the rights set forth in the Convention' can be the subject of a complaint. Thus, all the rights in the Women's Convention are in principle justiciable. This is quite a progressive approach, since the Women's Convention encompasses many economic and social rights, such as the right to work, the right to education and the right to health. In view of the fact that all these rights are guaranteed from the perspective of non-discrimination and equality, justiciability is also limited to encompass these aspects, and does not regard economic and social rights as such. Distinguishing between civil and political rights and economic and social rights would undermine the long established doctrine of indivisibility of human rights.[25] Which is not to say that in practice such a distinction is absent; provisions in treaties concerning civil and political rights are more often justiciable than those concerning economic and social rights. The fact that the social and economic rights of the Women's Convention are considered to be equally justiciable is a distinctive feature that should be cherished.

A significant difference, however, still persists in the discretion States have to implement these rights, and a larger 'margin of discretion' seems applicable where economic and social rights are concerned. The concept of the 'margin of

---

[23] UN doc. CEDAW/C/34/D/8/2005, *Rahime Kayhan v Turkey*, 27 January 2006.

[24] See also: A. Byrnes and E. Bath, 'Violence against Women, the Obligation of Due Diligence, and the Optional Protocol to the Convention on the Elimination of All Forms of Discrimination against Women – Recent Developments', 8 (3) *Human Rights Law Review* (2008), pp. 517–533.

[25] M. Bijnsdorp, 'The Strength of the Optional Protocol to the United Nations Women's Convention', *Netherlands Quarterly of Human Rights*, Vol. 18, No. 3, August 2000, p. 338.

discretion' as it is called by CEDAW is directly derived from the concept of 'margin of appreciation' as explored by *e.g.* the European Court of Human Rights (ECHR). The ECHR leaves a wider margin of discretion in cases which concern social or economic rights and CEDAW seems to follow this approach. CEDAW has raised the issue of the margin of discretion specifically in the case of *Dung Thi Thuy Nguyen v The Netherlands*. In this case, it was decided that although Article 11 paragraph 2(b) of the Women's Convention holds the obligation to 'introduce maternity leave with pay or with comparable social benefits without loss of former employment, seniority or social allowances', there is a margin of discretion. The claim brought by Thi Thuy Nguyen concerned differential treatment in maternity leave benefits.[26] Thi Thuy Nguyen claimed that she was discriminated against on the basis of her gender, because she was not able to accumulate maternity leave benefits from two different types of jobs. According to CEDAW, Article 11 paragraph 2(b) does not entail the obligation that all income should be compensated so Thi Thuy Nguyen did not have to be compensated for both jobs. Here, the State parties have a margin of discretion, in which they can manoeuvre to fulfil the obligation of the Women's Convention. The Netherlands did not exceed this margin of discretion and thus a violation of the Women's Convention was not found by CEDAW.

Not all the Committee members agreed to this observation. Three members issued an individual dissenting opinion on the merits of the case. The conclusion they draw is that the legal framework on maternity leave in The Netherlands may not constitute direct discrimination of women, but it does constitute indirect discrimination.[27] This would be the case because it is mainly women who have two jobs, one as a part-time salaried worker and one as a part-time worker in their husband's firm.[28] It is in this situation that benefits may not always be accumulated and women find themselves more often in this situation. These dissenting members of the Committee recommend the State party to research whether indeed women are disproportionately affected by the non-accumulation of benefits and if so, to make appropriate adjustments.

The Netherlands has up till now not submitted a report on these recommendations. In its 2005 Country Report it is stated that the act concerned, the Invalidity Insurance (Self-Employment) Act, will be repealed. How the payment of benefits to self-employed women during pregnancy and maternity leave and adoption leave are to be arranged after the Act's repeal is still under consideration.[29]

---

[26] UN doc. CEDAW/C/36/D/3/2004, *Dung Thi Thuy Nguyen v The Netherlands*, 29 August 2006.
[27] UN doc. CEDAW/C/36/D/3/2004, *Dung Thi Thuy Nguyen v The Netherlands*, 29 August 2006, p. 15.
[28] This was also recognized by The Netherlands in its fourth country report to CEDAW, UN doc. CEDAW/C/NLD/4, 4th *periodic report of The Netherlands to the United Nations on the Elimination of All Forms of Discrimination against Women*, 10 February 2005.
[29] *Ibid.*, p. 64.

This case illustrates the fact that although no formal hierarchy between rights exists, CEDAW is quite hesitant to find a violation in this case where an economic right is concerned. The wide, in this case arguably over-stretched margin of discretion left to the State, indicates that economic rights in the Women's Convention are justiciable in theory but that the threshold to find a violation may be higher. The wide margin of discretion may, however, also be due to the fact that this case concerns indirect discrimination. Interestingly, the argument that the case would concern indirect discrimination is put forward for the first time by the dissenting members of CEDAW. Unfortunately, while these members recognize the facts as indirect discrimination they do not refer to the Articles under which indirect discrimination is prohibited in the Convention. Where indirect discrimination is concerned, the text of the Women's Convention itself is not self-evident and clarification on this issue by CEDAW would be helpful. In European Council Directives, indirect discrimination is defined to be in place if: 'an apparently neutral provision, criterion or practice would put persons having a particular religion or belief, a particular disability, a particular age, or a particular sexual orientation at a particular disadvantage compared with other persons.'[30] This definition is not reflected in Article 1 of the Women's Convention which defines 'discrimination against women' to be: 'any distinction, exclusion or restriction made on the basis of sex which has the effect or purpose of impairing or nullifying the recognition, enjoyment or exercise by women, irrespective of their marital status, on a basis of equality of men and women, of human rights and fundamental freedoms in the political, economic, social, cultural, civil or any other field.' Strictly interpreted, this means that there must be a distinction made on the basis of sex. If there is such a distinction, it is not necessary for it to have the purpose of discriminating against women to be discriminatory. Yet, a distinction is still necessary, whereas indirect discrimination may occur exactly in the case of seemingly neutral policies such as the Dutch Invalidity Insurance (Self-Employment) Act. The definition of discrimination against women in the Women's Convention is unfortunately formulated in such a way that doubt may arise whether indirect discrimination falls within its realm.

3.1.4. Interim Measures

Article 5 of the OP refers the possibility to CEDAW to take provisional measures, which can be taken if the State against which a complaint has been made is on the verge of causing 'irreparable harm', which is a rather serious condition. It means that CEDAW in such a situation has the competence to directly influence a State's domestic policy or actions, at least in the case at hand. It is remarkable

---

[30] Council Directive 2000/78/EC of 27 November 2000, *Establishing a general framework for equal treatment in employment and occupation*, Official Journal L 303, pp. 16–22.

that the rules of procedure stipulate that the interim measure is for the State party's 'urgent consideration'. To ask States to take a measure into 'urgent consideration' also means that the measure is not legally binding; an interim measure thus remains a request by CEDAW. While the possibility for CEDAW to request interim measures adds to its authority, the fact that these interim measures are not legally binding raises concerns. Even interim measures which are binding, such as those taken by the International Court of Justice are not always adhered to by States. In pre-final drafts of the OP, additional language spelling out the duty of State parties to comply with interim measures was drafted, *e.g.* 'the State party shall comply with the request'.[31] This language was later deleted because State parties supposedly have a general duty to comply with the Protocol (good faith) and need not to be reminded of this duty specifically in the Article on interim measures. In view of the human rights compliance records of most if not all States, it is naïve to believe that States need not to be told to comply with a request for an interim measure because they will already do so in accordance with good faith. It is more likely that this clause was deleted exactly because it would make the duties on the State parties too heavy, and creating an international obligation to comply with requests for interim measures. Taking away this obligation directly undermines the potential efficacy of the OP.

So far, CEDAW has ordered interim measures in two cases. In the case of *N.S.F. v United Kingdom of Great Britain and Northern Ireland* CEDAW requested the United Kingdom not to expel the woman whose case was under consideration by CEDAW. The United Kingdom abided by the request. In *A.T. v Hungary*, a victim of domestic violence is insufficiently protected by the State.[32] The victim requested for interim measures to be taken by the Hungarian government to protect her from her abusive husband. CEDAW submitted such a request to the State for its urgent consideration, 'asking the State party to provide immediate, appropriate and concrete preventive interim measures of protection to the author, as may be necessary, in order to avoid irreparable damage to her person'.[33] In response, Hungary supplied A.T. with legal counsel for the civil proceedings she was still involved in, but at no point in time, even after a repeated request, did Hungary provide A.T. and her children with shelter. This inadequate response is according to CEDAW caused by 'a lack of effective legal and other measures' being in place in Hungary; there is for example no possibility of issuing a restraint order in Hungarian law.[34] CEDAW seemed flustered by the situation and decided to not only make recommendations with regard to the case under consideration but also to issue more general

---

[31] UN doc. E/CN.6/1997/WG/L.1, Article 5, as researched in M. BIJNSDORP, 'The Strength of the Optional Protocol to the United Nations Women's Convention', *Netherlands Quarterly of Human Rights*, Vol. 18, No. 3, August 2000, pp. 329–355.
[32] UN doc. *CEDAW/C/32/D/2/2003, Ms. A.T. v Hungary*, 26 January 2005.
[33] *Ibid.*, para. 4.2.
[34] *Ibid.*, para. 9.5.

recommendations to be implemented to improve the all-over situation of women in Hungary. Hungary was required to report within six months on the actions taken to implement the recommendations. In the report provided by Hungary in 2000, Hungary states that for women 'the most dangerous milieu is the family, the most dangerous place is the home and the most likely perpetrator is the husband, life companion, ex-husband or ex-life companion.'[35] The report, issued three years prior to the submission of the case by A.T., then lists a number of laws and policies in place to protect women from domestic violence. Evidently, none of these policies were implemented in such a way that they protected A.T.

3.1.5. Due Diligence

In the case of *A.T. v Hungary* and in two other cases decided to date, CEDAW has determined that the State failed to fulfil its obligations towards its citizens. All three cases concern domestic violence. The claim made by the victim in *A.T. v Hungary* is that the State neglected its positive obligations by remaining passive and thus supported the abusive situation to remain in place.[36] It is clear that Hungary had not implemented General Recommendation No 19, which affirms a positive obligation on States: 'Under general international law and specific human rights covenants, States may also be responsible for private acts if they fail to act with due diligence to prevent violations of rights or to investigate and punish acts of violence, and for providing compensation.'[37] CEDAW maintains its vision expressed in General Recommendation No 19 and states in its decision that in the case of domestic violence, the State party has a positive obligation. This is an important decision for all women. It means that CEDAW is convinced that the State has a duty in this sphere that is often referred to as private, and in which many women suffer on a daily basis.[38] CEDAW takes a progressive hands-on approach with actual obligations for the State parties and shows it is willing to interpret the rights of the Convention in a way that gives them real content.[39]

---

[35] UN doc. CEDAW/C/Hun/4-5, 4*th* and 5*th* periodic report of Hungary to the United Nations on the Elimination of All Forms of Discrimination against Women, 19 September 2000.
[36] UN doc. *CEDAW/C/32/D/2/2003, Ms. A.T. v Hungary*, 26 January 2005, para. 3.1.
[37] UN doc. *CEDAW/C/32/D/2/2003, Ms. A.T. v Hungary*, 26 January 2005, para. 9.2.
[38] C. Garcia-Moreno, H.A.F.M. Jansen, M. Ellsberg, L. Heise, C.H. Watts, 'Prevalence of intimate partner violence: findings from the WHO multi-country study on women's health and domestic violence', *The Lancet*, Vol. 368, 2006, pp. 1260–1269. The reported lifetime prevalence of physical or sexual partner violence, or both, varied from 15% to 71%, with two sites having a prevalence of less than 25%, seven between 25% and 50%, and six between 50% and 75%. Between 4% and 54% of respondents reported physical or sexual partner violence, or both, in the past year.
[39] B. Sokhi-Bulley, 'The Optional Protocol to CEDAW: First Step', *Human Rights Law Review*, Vol. 6(1), 2006, p.152.

CEDAW maintains this view in two following cases against Austria. In the case of *Şahide Goekce (deceased) v Austria* the victim had suffered from domestic violence by her husband, who eventually shot her.[40] The Committee quotes in this case the same line as was quoted in the *A.T. v Hungary*, firmly establishing the due diligence obligation of the State party that involves positive obligations to protect women. In Austria, a comprehensive model to combat domestic violence is in place, but the actions of the State actors who are to give effect to this model did not fulfil the State's due diligence obligation. This is particularly the case on the day Şahide's life comes to its brutal end, 'Şahide Goekce called the emergency call service a few hours before she was killed, yet no patrol car was sent to the scene of the crime'.[41] Given the violent history of the husband's behaviour, the police should have been aware that this was an emergency situation. Prosecuting the murderer after the crime had happened was, according to the Committee, not enough to compensate for the failure to fulfil due diligence obligations earlier in the process.[42] The Committee finds a violation of the Articles for which the complaint was raised. The same decision is made that year in the case of *Fatma Yildirim (deceased) v Austria*. In this case the woman concerned was severely threatened by her husband many times, the authorities refused to take appropriate action and finally Fatma was stabbed to death by her husband. The Committee concludes that also in this case the State party did not fulfil its due diligence obligations. The arrest of Fatma's husband should, given the extremely dangerous circumstances of the case, not have been denied by the Public Prosecutor. In particular, Fatma's husband was dependent on his staying married for his resident permit. The divorce, as the authorities should have known, could have a dangerous effect on the soon to be ex-husband.

In the first case concerning a non-Western country, the Committee found that the Philippines had failed to fulfil its due diligence obligation to banish gender stereotypes and to instruct its judiciary accordingly.[43] This case concerns a woman who was raped. She underwent a medical examination within 24 hours after the assault and reported the case to the police within 48 hours. Yet, not only did it take the court 8 years to prosecute the accused, the court also acquitted him because the victim did not physically resist the sexual assault thereby reconfirming the myth that lack of physical resistance means consent. These and other misconceptions – such as the fact that the court found it unbelievable that a man in his sixties could ejaculate when the victim was resisting – let to the acquittal of the accused. The Committee commemorates the General Recommendation No. 19 in which it is stated that States should have laws in

---

[40] UN doc. CEDAW/C/39/D/5/2005, *Şahide Goekce (deceased) v Austria*, 6 August 2005.
[41] *Ibid.*, para. 12.1.3.
[42] A. Byrnes and E. Bath, 'Violence against Women, the Obligation of Due Diligence, and the Optional Protocol to the Convention on the Elimination of All Forms of Discrimination against Women – Recent Developments', 8(3) *Human Rights Law Review* (2008), p. 525.
[43] UN doc. CEDAW/C/46/D/18/2008, *Karen Tayag Vertido v The Philippines*, 1 September 2010.

place which adequately protect women from *e.g.* rape – which the Philippines failed to do by not making lack of consent an essential element of the definition of rape. Thus, the Philippines were found to have violated the Convention and were given specific instructions for follow up, including appropriate and regular training on General Recommendation No. 19, for judges, lawyers and law enforcement personnel.

3.1.6. Follow-up

Despite these detailed instructions of the Committee to violating States, it is not self-evident that these instructions will be followed. It is at this point where the non-binding character of the Optional Protocol may take its toll.

With regard to Hungary, it was specified above that the measures described in the country report of 2000 were highly insufficient. In Hungary's 2006 progress report, a rather vague reference is made to the case of 2003: 'Hungary ratified the Supplementary Protocol to the CEDAW Convention in 2001. The recommendations of the CEDAW have been translated into Hungarian and were published in the autumn of 2003. The issue is being disseminated to the widest possible range of users.'[44] Without referring to any recommendations given by the Committee, the report does mention measures which aim to address these recommendations. In 2004, a crisis centre was set up to help women who are suffering from violence in the family. This centre has a round-the-clock telephone and assistance service and can initiate instant action if necessary. In the first half of 2005, temporary shelter home projects have been started in seven regions of Hungary and in Budapest. In 2005, the Ministry of Youth, Family, Social Affairs and Equal Opportunity started an awareness raising campaign on violence in the family. It seems that, even though it did not report specifically on the implementation of the recommendations, Hungary has made some efforts to implement them.

Hungary was, however, also found in violation of the Convention in the case of *A.S. v Hungary*. This case concerns a Roma woman who needed a caesarean section. The doctors of the State hospital provided her with the caesarean section but also performed a sterilization that the woman in question did not consent to.[45] The Committee had already once before addressed the issue of sterilization in its General Recommendation No. 21, which stipulates the importance of adequately informing the woman about other contraceptive measures. In the case at hand, the woman was denied the right to specific information on sterilization and the Committee found that the State party has violated Article 10(h), Article 16 and Article 12, which oblige State parties to provide appropriate

---

[44] UN doc. CEDAW/C/HUN/6, 6*th* *Periodic Report of the Republic of Hungary to the United Nations on the Elimination of All Forms of Discrimination against Women*, 15 June 2006.
[45] UN doc. *CEDAW/C /36/D/4/2004, A.S. v Hungary*, 29 August 2006.

services in connection with pregnancy. CEDAW found that, besides the fact that the note the woman had to sign only had the Latin name for sterilization on it, it is very unlikely that in the 17 minutes between her arrival at the hospital in labour and the sterilization she was provided with appropriate information and counselling for her to take a well-considered and voluntary decision.

The Committee thus found violations of all the Articles put before it to be examined. It recommends the State party to appropriately compensate A.S. and also issues general recommendations. These general recommendations concern the implementation guarantees to prevent sterilizations without consent from happening again. No reference to these recommendations or any hints of implementation can be found in the most recent country report submitted by Hungary. Hungary has not yet appropriately compensated A.S., in fact no compensation has been given to A.S. whatsoever. CEDAW has reminded Hungary to take action, but so far this has remained to no avail. The fact that Hungary does not fulfil the recommendations set by the Committee indicates a real lack of effectiveness of the individual complaints procedure.

3.2. CONCLUSION

The Committee takes a restrictive approach to questions of admissibility. It has set out a strongly-fenced framework for questions of admissibility *ratione temporis*. This framework seems, however, not fully consistent which may make the outcome of the assessment by CEDAW quite unpredictable. The Committee has made it clear that it will not deal with complaints if local remedies have not been completely exhausted and there is still a chance of success on the national level. The Committee has taken a rather critical look at whether a complaint is admissible *ratione materiae.* In this regard the Committee will possibly not take an approach that would end discrimination of women (*e.g.* in the area inheritance of titles of nobility) but may instead take a legalistic approach.[46]

Having analysed the six cases which were decided on the merits, some observations can be made. First of all, the Committee is not afraid to use the powers vested in it and has its ability to request interim measures, and make specific and general recommendations. While assessing cases, the Committee has interpreted some Articles of the Convention to imply positive obligations on the States in case of domestic violence; a rather progressive approach. Positive obligations are not uncontroversial and it is a good sign that CEDAW is not afraid to use them, thus giving real content to the rights of the Convention. In other areas, the Committee is willing to leave a certain margin of discretion to

---

[46] A. BYRNES and E. BATH, 'Violence against Women, the Obligation of Due Diligence, and the Optional Protocol to the Convention on the Elimination of All Forms of Discrimination against Women – Recent Developments', 8(3) *Human Rights Law Review* (2008), p. 532.

State parties. With regard to social and economic rights, the Committee awards such a broad margin of discretion that serious doubt is casted on the real justiciability of these rights. Whereas such justiciability exists in theory, no violation will be found if States can manoeuvre in too wide a margin. The legalistic approach taken may pose problems for the justiciability of indirect discrimination as this is not prohibited by the Women's Convention explicitly.

4. THE INQUIRY PROCEDURE

The inquiry procedure is set out in Article 8 of the Optional Protocol: 'If the Committee receives reliable information indicating grave or systematic violations by a State party of rights set forth in the Convention, the Committee shall invite that State party to cooperate in the examination of the information and to this end to submit observations with regard to the information concerned.' So far, one such inquiry has taken place in Mexico.[47] Mexico ratified the Optional Protocol in March 2002, upon which, in October of that year two NGOs required CEDAW to start an inquiry procedure into the abduction, rape and murder of women in and around Ciudad Juárez, State of Chihuahua, Mexico. These NGOs also provided evidence on murders and the ongoing impunity of those responsible and the lack of due diligence amongst authorities. CEDAW decided to start a confidential inquiry and request Mexico to allow two experts to visit the region and provide them with assistance. Mexico committed to do so and in October 2003 a visit was made. The experts found that the crimes were sexual crimes and were committed against the victims because they were women and because they are poor. The crimes had been tolerated by the authorities with total indifference for the same reasons.[48] An intervention of international human rights bodies was thought to be essential for the Mexican authorities to recognize the gravity of the situation.[49] CEDAW concluded that the events around Ciudad Juárez are not isolated, but are 'systematic violations of women's rights founded in a culture of violence and discrimination that is based on women's alleged inferiority, a situation that has resulted in impunity.' The Committee issued a list of recommendations directed at the Mexican authorities aimed at improving investigations, preventing violence and generally to eliminate discrimination against women.

The observations of Mexico in response to these recommendations point to the correlation between the emancipation of women in the area of labour (more

---

[47] UN doc. CEDAW/C/2005/OP.8/Mexico, *Report on Mexico produced by the Committee on the Elimination of Discrimination against Women under Article 8 of the Optional Protocol to the Convention, and reply from the Government of Mexico*, 27 January 2005.
[48] *Ibid.*, p. 14.
[49] *Ibid.*, p. 40.

women accessing formal employment in the maquiladora industry) and the violence. Mexico states that 'the increase in working hours led to a series of negative effects on their family lives, including domestic violence.'[50] This initial statement, which could be interpreted as rather demeaning, and blaming women's labour emancipation for the violence, is followed by a factual representation and recognition of the problem. It becomes clear that of the 92 sexual offences registered from 1993 to 2003, sentences have been handed down in only 4 cases, a mere 4.34%.[51] In addition, measures that will be taken in the future as a response to CEDAW's recommendations are listed.

CONCLUSION

The impact of the inquiry procedure is hard to measure, not in the least because the situation in Ciudad Juárez has received a lot of attention internationally through other channels. International institutions such as the Inter-American Court of Human Rights as well as NGOs such as Amnesty International have brought the situation to the attention of the public. CEDAW can, however, based on the country reports submitted by Mexico, keep monitoring the situation and give follow up recommendations where necessary.

5. CONCLUSION

This Chapter has assessed the success of the implementation mechanisms of the Optional Protocol to the Women's Convention while examining the coming into existence of the Protocol, assessing the approach of CEDAW to individual complaints and the inquiry procedure and examining the follow up to CEDAW's recommendations.

With regard to the approach to individual complaints, admissibility decisions and decisions on the merits were analysed separately. It is clear that the Committee has been prudent in the area of admissibility. Addressing issues of admissibility too lightly will compromise the work of the Committee in the long run; it may have a negative impact on ratifications and good will of States already party to the Protocol. What is worrying, however, is the inconsistent approach of CEDAW to decisions of admissibility. Adjusting the requirements of membership of CEDAW to include legal experience and expertise could be a welcome measure. When looking into the merits of the cases, the Committee is eager to protect certain rights but shy to protect others; in particular social and economic rights. Fortunately, it does not hesitate to indicate areas, *e.g.* domestic violence,

---

[50] *Ibid.*, p. 50.
[51] *Ibid.*, p. 58.

in which positive obligations for States apply. CEDAW's approach to indirect discrimination remains uncertain; the fact that the Women's Convention itself does not adequately address this issue raises concerns. In general, it can be observed that all cases but one decided so far were brought against European States. Hopefully in time the proceedings will become of a more global character. The case against the Philippines is hopefully the first of many.

It is difficult to measure the impact of the inquiry procedure, as it has been used only once so far and the procedure was not isolated from other international efforts to address the situation in Ciudad Juárez. The follow up given to this report by CEDAW may lead to more diplomatic pressure on the Mexican Government to address the situation effectively.

With regard to the responses by States to the recommendations made by the Committee, the non-binding character of the Protocol takes its toll. The manner in which States deal with their follow-up obligation is lax. States have so far not reported to the Committee within six months after the recommendations were made. From the Country Reports it appears that in most cases some consideration and follow up is given to the recommendations of the Committee. CEDAW has a dialogue with States who are not appropriately addressing its recommendations. These dialogues concern both the recommendations made in the individual complaint procedure and the recommendations based on the Country Report. The follow-up to violations found by CEDAW in individual cases is at the same priority level as follow-up to general recommendations in connection with their country reports. Since the recommendations in the individual procedure are as non-binding as the general recommendations, it is not surprising that the implementation of these quasi-judicial decisions depends solely on diplomatic efforts and the goodwill of States. With regard to interim measures, the wording of the Protocol is not as strong as it could be. It must be remarked, however, that in one of the two cases in which CEDAW did request an interim measure, the State at hand complied with it.

Overall, the procedures of the Optional Protocol have not provided the sharp teeth needed to adequately protect the rights set forth in the Women's Convention. First, inconsistencies and ambiguities exist in CEDAW's approach to individual complaints. Second, the recommendations that flow from these cases are given neither priority nor urgency by most receiving States. Women, who come to the Committee as a last resort, see their States condemned and compensation awarded. Yet in many cases, no improvement is made and no compensation is received. The non-binding character of the decisions made by the Committee pushes the real implementation of these decisions in the realm of diplomacy. Not only is the goodwill of States highly unreliable, it also makes women whose rights have been violated depend on the willingness of that same violator to receive the redress they have been awarded.

CHAPTER 22
EMERGING FROM THE SHADOWS: VIOLENCE AGAINST WOMEN AND THE WOMEN'S CONVENTION

Kate Rose-Sender

1. INTRODUCTION

It is dangerous to be a woman. Violence against women (VAW) is as old as humanity and has been tolerated, accepted and clothed in the protective cloak of tradition or religion across societies. It takes many forms, including sexual, physical or emotional abuse by a partner or other family member, sexual harassment, exploitation and abuse by authority figures, trafficking, forced marriage, dowry related violence, female genital mutilation, honour killing and systematic sexual abuse as part of armed conflict. In a ten country study on women's health and domestic violence conducted by the World Health Organization:

- Between fifteen and seventy one percent of women reported physical or sexual abuse by a domestic partner;
- Twenty four percent of women in rural Peru, twenty eight percent of women in Tanzania, thirty percent of women in rural Bangladesh and forty percent of women in South Africa reported that their first sexual experience was not consensual;
- Between four and twelve percent of women reported being physically abused during pregnancy.[1]

Every year about 5,000 women are murdered in the name of honour. Trafficking in women and girls for purposes of sexual services and forced labour continues

---

[1] C. García-Moreno et al., *WHO multi-country study on women's health and domestic violence against women: initial results on prevalence, health outcomes and women's responses*, World Health Organization, Geneva, 2005.

to be a growing problem which often affects the most vulnerable.² An American female soldier in Iraq was more likely to be raped by a fellow soldier than killed by enemy fire.³ And, of course, forced and child marriages remain widely practiced in many countries in Asia, the Middle East and sub-Saharan Africa.

It is an often repeated proposition that at the time of the drafting of the Convention on the Elimination of All Forms of Discrimination Against Women (the Women's Convention) violence against women was considered an internal domestic problem and not on the international agenda. This may be true but, if so, it also reveals the need for both the Convention and the subsequent interpretation and application by its monitoring body, the Committee on the Elimination of Discrimination Against Women (CEDAW). This Chapter addresses the Women's Convention in formulation and function with regard to violence against women. It begins with a look at the history and drafting process. It then goes on to examine the role of civil society in awareness-raising before concluding with an assessment of the extent to which the Convention has succeeded in addressing the problem of violence.

2. FORMULATION – THE DRAFTING PROCESS

The initial drafting of the Women's Convention was delicately negotiated to support and not undermine women's rights. The aim was to create a treaty which would be acceptable to a sufficient number of States with a potential for effective implementation and enforcement but which was nonetheless nonthreatening to potential States parties.⁴ The Convention was meant to 'embrace all aspects of the life of women, that is, political and civil rights, social, economic and cultural rights, and also family rights. Such a single international instrument would be an effective legal basis for winning and defending the real equality of women with men in many countries of the world.'⁵

The recognition that women might well need extra protection and that, in practice, measures implemented for the general protection of human rights were not sufficient to protect women's rights⁶ led to the decision to draft a special convention addressing issues of equality for women, despite concerns about drafting a convention covering rights already addressed.⁷ It was this concern

---

2   *Ibid.*
3   N. GIBBS (quoting Representative Jane Harman), 'Sexual assaults on female solders: don't ask, don't tell', *Time*, (8 March 2010), electronically available at www.time.com/time/magazine/article/0,9171,1968110,00.html (last visited 19 July 2010).
4   See generally UN doc. E/CN.6/589, 14 January – 1 February 1974.
5   UN doc. E/CN/NGO/254, 11 January 1974, statement submitted by the Women's International Democratic Federation.
6   See *e.g.* UN doc. E/CN.6/W.1 Add.4 at 14.
7   *Ibid.*

which led to the decision to focus on equality and non discrimination rather than to create an instrument which addressed specific problems faced by women. This approach led the drafting committee to focus on what it identified as the general themes which represented the primary obstacle to full exercise of human rights for women.[8] Unfortunately, the recognition that violence against women is also a violation of human rights and does represent such an obstacle was not directly acknowledged or addressed by the Convention and was only later explicitly included through General Recommendations No. 12 and 19 of the Committee.[9] These Recommendations thus served to close what could have been a significant lacuna in the Convention.

Bodily integrity may not have been on the international agenda when the Women's Convention was drafted but it was part of the international human rights consciousness well before the 1970's women's rights movement made it an impossible issue to ignore.[10] While issues of bodily integrity and violence against women were not a part of the questionnaire on the Legal Status and Treatment of Women distributed to Member States by the Secretary General in 1950 on behalf of the Commission on the Status of Women,[11] a list of communications prepared by the Secretary General in 1954 for the Commission dealing 'with the principles relating to the promotion of women's rights' lists a communication from the St Joan's International Social and Political Alliance which urges the Commission to 'give careful consideration to any measures which have been taken by States with a view to abolishing customs which violate the physical integrity of women.' It should be noted that the Alliance, which was founded in 1911, has had consultative status with the Economic and Social Council since 1952, and was an active proponent of protection of women's rights from the inception of the discussions within the Council.[12]

In 1972, the Commission began the highly consultative process of drafting an international instrument to address the problem of discrimination against women. Commission Resolution 5(XXIV) of 24 February 1972 established a working group to 'begin work on the preparation of a new draft instrument or instruments.'[13] By 1974, draft articles were ready to be distributed to governments for discussion. Neither violence against women nor, more generally, bodily integrity, are part of this draft but bodily integrity was subsequently brought into the discussion by the member of the Commission on the Status of Women representing Belgium in 1976 during the evaluation of the prospective

---

[8] Ibid.
[9] CEDAW, General Recommendation No. 12, 8th session, 1989, Violence Against Women; CEDAW, General Recommendation No. 19, 11th session, 1992, Violence against women.
[10] J. JOACHIM, 'Shaping the human rights agenda: the case of violence', in: M.K. Meyer and E. Prügl (eds.), *Gender politics in global governance*, Rowman & Littlefield, 1999, p. 142.
[11] UN doc. E/CN/6/W.1.Add 4.
[12] UN doc. E/CN/CR.7, 1954.
[13] Ibid.

wording of Article 7 (subsequently Article 6). Article 7, as proposed by Belgium, read: 'Each State Party agrees to take all appropriate measures, including legislation, to combat all forms of traffic in women, exploitation of prostitution of women and attacks on the physical integrity of women.'[14]

In the summary record of the 638th meeting, the following exchange is recorded:

ARTICLE 7

40. Mrs Coene (Belgium) proposed that Article 7 should be supplemented by the addition of the phrase 'and attacks on the physical integrity of women', as proposed in the Belgian text appearing in document E/CN/.6/591/Add.1. It was true that while most countries disavowed and punished such practices, they nevertheless continued to form part of custom and tradition.

41. Begum Faridi (Pakistan) said that she would prefer the original text of Article 7. The Belgian amendment addressed itself to a further aspect of the problem, but it was not the only one. Accordingly, it was preferable to keep to the basic text.

42. Mrs Moller (Denmark) noted that the text of article 7 was not very clear. In order to bring it more into line with the World Plan of Action, she proposed that it should be reworded to read: 'State Parties agree to take all appropriate measures, including legislation, to combat prostitution and the illicit traffic in women.'

43. Ms Tyabji (India) supported the Danish proposal.

44. Mrs Hussein (Egypt) supported by Begum Faridi (Pakistan) felt that the insertion of the insertion of the term 'illicit' made the text more confused, since the traffic in women could in no event be considered as licit. Her delegation preferred Article 7 as it appeared in the draft convention.

45. Ms Tyabji (India), supported by Mrs Maka (Guinea) said that in view of the previous statements, she supported the original text of Article 7.

46. Mrs Salyo (Indonesia), supported by Mrs Gueye (Senegal) noted that no delegation had supported the amendment proposed by the Belgian delegation.

47. Mrs Coene (Belgium) withdrew the amendment to Article 7 submitted by her delegation.

---

[14] UN doc. E/CN/.6/591/Add.1.

What is noteworthy about this exchange is that it was not a representative of a State where custom or tradition might have made protection of women from a violation of their physical integrity problematic who derailed any further exploration of the subject, something which might have been anticipated on the grounds of an anticipated resistance. Rather, it was the representative of Denmark who diverted the discussion away from the proposed amendment as soon as the representative from Pakistan raised an objection. Pakistan's assertion that this was a 'further aspect of the problem' is vague and does not foreclose further discussion. One asks: What problem? Prostitution, trafficking, or the abuse of women? If attacks on physical integrity are a further aspect of a problem, could there have been further discussion regarding whether or not this should be addressed, either here or elsewhere in the convention? It was the representative of Denmark who 'changed the subject' and provided an avenue by which the apparently difficult subject of physical integrity could be avoided. This is interesting in light of what it may say about the attitude of the European or Western States with regard to the Islamic and developing world and its ability to meet international human rights standards when they concern women. As I discuss further, in section 3, subsequent clarifications by CEDAW have both made it evident that violations of physical integrity are to be read as violations of the Convention and that State parties should report thereon. Additionally, States parties seem not to have objected to this reporting requirement, indicating that direct inclusion in the Convention might not have been as problematic for some States as was feared. The final agreed text of the Convention, concluded in 1979, excluded any mention of physical integrity or violence against women and, as had been originally proposed by the working group, is headed 'Prostitution' simply saying: 'States Parties shall take all appropriate measures, including legislation, to suppress all forms of traffic in women and exploitation of prostitution of women.'

The representative of Denmark had diverted discussion by reference to the World Plan of Action and her desire to bring the Convention more closely into line with that instrument. But the plan itself, in the process of implementation, encountered the reality of daily violence against women in both the developed and developing world in the monitoring of trends in women's health status. A 1980 report on progress towards implementation of the Plan states: 'Most victims of rape and other sexual offenses are female, and most victims of domestic violence are women. Many women have not sought help because of fear of publicity and exposure, the feeling of guilt that they have been responsible for the attack and the feeling that police action would be futile.'[15] As implementation of the World Plan of Action was impeded by the problem of violations of the physical integrity of women, the Plan might well have been better served through the proposed Belgian Amendment. At the very least, the Belgian amendment

---

[15] UN doc. E/CN.6/637, 9 January 1980.

would have put violation of the physical integrity of women directly onto the international agenda. Instead, that was left to civil society, in good part through the World Conferences which were begun during the United Nations Decade for Women.

3. RAISING AWARENESS

Civil society had raised the issue of violations of physical integrity in 1954 and continued to do so through what became known as EVAW (End Violence Against Women), a broad domestic and international movement, directed at ending violence against women. From the beginning, it was international women's organizations which were responsible for the shift in focus with regard to violence against women and for finally getting it onto the United Nations Agenda.[16] As discussed above, these efforts can be traced back to the1950's but became internationally visible in 1970 with the promulgation of an agenda consisting of three main points: that gender violence is unjust and violates women's basic rights; that it is caused by structural inequities between men and women; and that States should be pressured into action through increased visibility for the issue.[17] This last strategy seems particularly important in light of the earlier attempts to bring the issue to the attention of the UN.

In general terms, women's rights were definitely on the agenda by the time of the 1975 Mexico City World Conference on Women. This first Conference was a result of the 1972 UN General Assembly proclamation making 1975 International Women's Year.[18] It was here, in Mexico City, that the World Plan of Action was established and the plan arose for the UN Decade for Women which was proclaimed five months later.[19] The Mexico City Conference ended with the identification of three broad goals of equality, development and peace, largely reflecting attempts to integrate women into the ongoing focus of the international community.[20]

Despite compelling evidence and the continuing efforts of some NGOs, bodily integrity was not perceived as one of those major themes with which the international community was willing to deal. The burden of keeping the issue of violence in the lives of women before the international community rested almost

---

[16] J. JOACHIM, 1999, p. 142.
[17] Ibid.
[18] In 1972, the General Assembly, in its Resolution 3010 (XXVII), proclaimed 1975 International Women's Year.
[19] The UN Decade for Women (1976–1985) sought to address the needs of women in what were then known as the first, second, and third worlds with a tripartite theme of equality, peace, and development by making recommendations for action at local, national, and international levels.
[20] Declaration of Mexico on the Equality of Women and Their Contribution to Development and Peace, 1975, United Nations E/CONF.66/34.

completely on civil society. The 1980 list of communications received by the Commission on the Status of Women with regard to International Instruments and National Standards[21] included seven communications received in 1979 regarding 'the sexual mutilation of females'. The International Council of Social Democratic Women sent the Commission a record of the discussions of their tenth Conference which had been devoted to the theme of Violence in Society. Their final resolution states:

> 'Because of the secondary role and unequal situation in society of women throughout history, women have suffered the effects of violence to a greater degree than men…we are subject to a kind of violence which deprive (sic) us of some of our rights as full human beings.'[22] This was true at a time when the majority of participants in the international dialogue were discussing the end of colonialism, détente, peace and security and terrorism. These discussions certainly also involved women's rights but, while many women continued to be bought and sold, confined to their homes, sexually mutilated, beaten, raped and otherwise violated, much of the international dialogue concerned 'the full and equitable political participation (for women) essential to essential action for peace.'[23]

By 1980, the year of the second World Conference on Women in Copenhagen, the Women's Convention had been adopted by the General Assembly and there was growing awareness of a gap between women's rights and their ability to exercise them. The Report of the World Conference of the United Nations Decade for Women: Equality, Development and Peace, Copenhagen, July 1980,[24] explicitly refers to violence against women, the first time the issue was acknowledged in a UN document. The Conference adopted a Resolution on 'battered women and violence in the family'.[25] The Legislative Measures section of the final report states: 'Legislation should also be enacted and implemented in order to prevent domestic and sexual violence against women. All appropriate measures, including legislative ones, should be taken to allow victims to be fairly treated in all criminal procedures.'[26]

At the third Conference, in Nairobi, in 1985, violence against women again made the agenda, if not yet as strongly or as broadly as it would within the following ten years. In its information note, the Division on the Advancement of Women (DAW) stated with regard to the Nairobi Conference:

> …violence against women truly emerged as a serious international concern. The Forward-looking Strategies adopted by the Conference linked the promotion and

---

[21] UN doc. E/CN.6/CR.25.
[22] Ibid., at 12–13.
[23] Ibid., at 59.
[24] UN doc. A/CONF.94/35 (80.IV.30).
[25] Ibid.
[26] Ibid.

maintenance of peace to the eradication of violence against women in both the public and private spheres. The Conference included violence as a major obstacle to the achievement of development, equality and peace, the three objectives of the Decade.

The review and appraisal of the achievements of the Decade for Women states in the section on Areas for Specific Action, subsection on Social Services:

> 231. Governments should undertake effective measures, including mobilizing community resources to identify, prevent and eliminate all violence, including family violence, against women and children and to provide shelter, support and reorientation services for abused women and children. These measures should notably be aimed at making women conscious that maltreatment is not an incurable phenomenon, but a blow to their physical and moral integrity, against which they have the right (and the duty) to fight, whether they are themselves the victims or the witnesses. Beyond these urgent protective measures for maltreated women and children, as well as repressive measures for the authors of this maltreatment, it would be proper to set in motion long-term supportive machineries of aid and guidance for maltreated women and children, as well as the people, often men, who maltreat them.[27]

Violence against women was finally on the international agenda but primarily as domestic violence with little attempt as of yet to address the problems of State condoned or sponsored violence or traditional practices. Additionally, the issue of how to address the problem was far from settled by vague statements which, while exhorting Governments to take effective measures, shifted a portion of the responsibility onto the women themselves.

Acting on a recommendation by the Commission on the Status of Women, the General Assembly adopted the first resolution on domestic violence in 1985.[28] The Resolution approaches the issue of domestic violence from the perspective of protection of vulnerable groups, that is women and children, and the preservation of the family, not from the point of view of the right of a woman to be free from violation of her physical integrity. Nevertheless, it does make clear that domestic violence is a problem that has to be addressed at both State and international levels. The 1985 Resolution called for specific action. As a result, the 1986 Expert Group Meeting on Violence in the Family, with special emphasis on its effects on women was convened. The Meeting produced 'concrete recommendations with regard to legal reform, police, prosecutor and health sector training, social and resource support for victims. It also made clear that domestic violence was a global phenomenon which was significantly underreported.'[29]

---

[27] Report of the World Conference to Review and Appraise the Achievements of the United Nations Decade for Women: Equality, Development and Peace, Nairobi, 15–26 July 1985.
[28] UN GA Res. 40/36.
[29] DAW Information Note.

The GA Resolution and the Experts Meeting were followed by an ECOSOC Resolution from the Commission on the Status of Women on Efforts to Eradicate Violence against Women within the Family and within Society. The ECOSOC Resolution expanded the focus from the domestic arena to society as a whole, declaring that the Council is '[c]ognizant of the fact that violence against women exists in various forms in everyday life in all kinds of societies and that concerted and continuous efforts are required for its eradication [...].' This was an important shift and one that was immediately reinforced by a 1989 United Nations publication which set out the many different ways that violence against women permeated their lives and was tolerated, or even condoned, by society, including the State. The book considered economic, social and political aspects as well as the ethnic, religious, and political conflicts which contribute to violence against women.[30] In so doing, it set out the full dimensions of the problem and the extent to which gender based violence, including violations of bodily integrity and physical and psychological intimidation, diminished women's ability fully to exercise their other basic human rights. Finally, as the DAW observes,

> 'with a growing understanding of the link between gender and violence, the approach to the issue within the United Nations shifted. First, it became clear that violence in the family was not the only form of violence against women. Second, the gender-based nature of violence against women and its linkage to subordination, inequality between women and men, and discrimination, led to its categorization as a matter of human rights.[31]

An issue of significant importance, initially ignored or avoided by the international community and considered to be an internal, domestic and cultural matter,[32] then recognized incrementally, was finally fully on the agenda.

Ironically, the recognition of the significant impact violence has in all its forms on women's lives met resistance at the Vienna Conference of 1993, when the UN Commission on Human Rights which had convened the conference insisted that violence was not a human rights issue for three reasons:

> '1. It occurs primarily in the private home of the family, in which international governmental organization have no right to interfere without a specific mandate;
> 2. It is perpetrated by private individuals rather than the state; and
> 3. It does not occur in gross patterns.'[33]

---

[30] Violence against Women in the Family, UN Office at Vienna Center for Social Development and Humanitarian Affairs, New York, United Nations 1989.
[31] DAW Information Note.
[32] J. JOACHIM, 1999, p. 142.
[33] Ibid., p. 153.

The perspective of the Commission represented a significant step backwards in that violence against women was once again being narrowly interpreted to fit within the family, making it possible to avoid custom, tradition, state action, or international responsibility for protection of rights. But, at the conference, '[t]he global campaign for women's human rights, undertaken by a loose coalition of women's human rights advocates from around the world, succeeded in making governments acknowledge that violence against women is a fundamental violation of their human rights.'[34] And, once the bell had been rung, it could not be unrung. In 1994, the General Assembly passed the Declaration on the Elimination of All Forms of Violence Against Women which unequivocally acknowledged that violence against women was an international issue.[35] That same year the Commission on Human Rights appointed a Special Rapporteur on Violence Against Women. And in 1995, in Beijing, the elimination of violence against women became a priority for the United Nations Development Fund for Women (UNIFEM), which was then appointed to administer the UN Trust Fund to End Violence against Women established in 1996 by General Assembly Resolution 50/166.[36] Violence against women in all its forms was finally irrevocably on the international agenda.

4. FUNCTION – THE WORK OF THE COMMITTEE

But, what of the Women's Convention? The Convention had been broadly drafted to attract as much support as possible. The exclusion of violence against women may have been a deliberate decision but it did not arise out of a lack of awareness of the problem. The Committee on the Elimination of Discrimination of Women (CEDAW) first met in 1982. A view of their activities with regard to violence against women is an interesting example of the extent to which a treaty monitoring body can utilize the accepted rules of interpretation to address the spirit as well as the words of the covenant. The 1969 Vienna Convention on the Law of Treaties states clearly that a treaty is be interpreted according to its plain meaning in light of the object and purpose.[37] The object and purpose of the Women's Convention is clear: to eliminate all forms of discrimination against women. As international acknowledgement grew of the extent to which violence in all its forms was directed at women to a disproportionate extent and hindered

---

[34] N. HEYZER, Working towards a world free from violence against women: UNIFEM's contribution, 6 *Gender and Development* 3 (1998), p.17 at 18.
[35] See H. CHARLESWORTH, 'The Declaration on the Elimination of All Forms of Violence Against Women', 'ASIL Insight', *AJIL* (1994) at 2.
[36] GA Res. A/Res/50/166, The role of the United Nations Development Fund for Women in eliminating violence against women, 16 February 1996.
[37] Article 31(1), Vienna Convention on the Law of Treaties, 23 May 1969, United Nations, *Treaty Series*, Vol. 1155, p. 331.

their ability to function in society on an equal footing with men, the Committee was able to interpret the treaty commitments to make it clear that what might have been a potential lacuna was in reality covered by implication in articles throughout the Convention.

The Women's Convention entered into force on the 3rd of September 1981 and has become the primary human rights instrument for the protection of women's rights.[38] Its monitoring body CEDAW was established in 1982 and is composed of 23 international experts on women's issues. It is the Committee's responsibility to monitor the progress of States parties to the Convention in implementing their commitments under the treaty. At each of its sessions, CEDAW reviews reports submitted by the States parties. These reports are due to the Committee within one year of ratification or accession, and every four years subsequently. CEDAW members then comment on the report and ask questions in order to obtain additional information as necessary.

The Committee has the power to make recommendations when it identifies a specific area which impacts treaty obligations and to which they would like to see States parties devote more attention in their reports. It was this ability that CEDAW chose to exercise at its eighth session in 1989, when it discussed the high incidence of violence against women in General Recommendation 12, where it recommended that States parties include information about this problem in their reports.[39] General Recommendation 12 identifies five specific Articles of the Convention, 2 (Policy Measures), 5 (Sex Role Stereotyping and Prejudice), 11 (Employment), 12 (Health), and 16 (Marriage and Family). CEDAW was in line with ECOSOC, and well ahead of the Human Rights Commission, in its awareness of the extent to which violence or the threat of violence affected aspects of women's lives well beyond the domestic sphere. At the Committee's tenth session 'it was decided to allocate part of the eleventh session to a discussion and study of article 6 and other articles of the convention relating to violence towards women and the sexual harassment and exploitation of women.'[40]

In 1992, the Committee took the matter a step further and adopted General Recommendation 19, which 'requires national reports to the Committee to include statistical data on the incidence of violence against women, information on the provision of services for victims, and legislative and other measures taken to protect women against violence in their everyday lives, such as harassment at the workplace, abuse in the family and sexual violence.'[41] General Recommendation No. 19 adds Article 1, which defines discrimination, to the list of articles which address gender based violence. It clarifies that: 'The definition

---

[38] H. CHARLESWORTH, 'ASIL Insight', *AJIL*, 1994, at 2.
[39] CEDAW, General Recommendation No. 12, 8th session, 1989, Violence Against Women.
[40] CEDAW, General Recommendation No. 19, 11th session, 1992, Violence Against women.
[41] www.un.org/womenwatch/daw/cedaw/history.htm *(last visited 16 July 2010).*

of discrimination includes gender based violence, that is, violence that is directed against a woman because she is a woman or that affects women disproportionately. It includes acts that inflict physical, mental or sexual harm or suffering, threats of such acts, coercion and other deprivations of liberty. Gender-based violence may breach specific provisions of the Convention, regardless of whether those provisions of the convention specifically mention violence.'[42] So, the Committee has taken violence against women all the way from dismissal as 'a further aspect of the problem' which the drafters decided not to include to the recognition that gender based violence 'impairs or nullifies the enjoyment by women of human rights and fundamental freedoms under general international law or under human right conventions'.[43] A paradigm shift had occurred. Gender based violence is now illegal in the majority of States.[44] The problem has not gone away. 'One out of three women in the world has been beaten, coerced into sex, or otherwise abused in her lifetime.'[45] But it is actively being addressed and CEDAW is a primary resource in that process.

And what has been the response of the Islamic world to this clarification of the content of international human rights standards when they concern women? If indeed the drafters were concerned about how acceptable an assertion of women's rights to be free from gender based violence would be to Islamic States or to States with a large Islamic population, what has been their response to General Recommendations Nos. 12 and 19? A superficial review of 39 States parties to the Women's Convention, which are either Islamic republics or have majority Islamic populations, reveals a pattern emerging from the reporting. These States, upon submitting their initial report, may not address violence against women or barely mention it. Subsequently, however, and in response to CEDAW's comments, all gradually begin addressing it in much more depth. The only glaring exceptions are the United Arab Emirates (submitted in 2008 and makes no mention at all) and Libya (which only mentions it to say that no traditional practices exist which constitute VAW).[46] Of course, as with any human rights reporting mechanism, we must be aware that sometimes an issue is really only mentioned to placate the Committee and, in such a case, it can be useful to look at the Concluding Observations to see the Committee's reaction and to see what was discussed in the oral presentation. What is important here is that the General Recommendations are being followed. States are reporting and the problem is out in the open, on the agenda and being addressed.

---

[42] Para. 6.
[43] Para. 7.
[44] See generally *Not a Minute More*, UNIFEM, New York, 2003.
[45] S.T. Fried, 'Violence against women', 6 *Health and Human Rights* 2 (2003), pp. 89 at 91.
[46] Note, however, that of the 39 States examined, four have not submitted reports at all. These are Afghanistan, Brunei Darussalam, Oman and Qatar.

5. SUMMARY AND CONCLUSIONS

Looking back at the drafting process it is unavoidable to ask: Could violence against women have been included in the Convention and should it have been? Tracing the growing awareness of the scope and impact of gender based violence, it becomes clear that 'only with efforts to eliminate violence against women [could] the Women's Convention fully achieve its purpose of eliminating all forms of discrimination against women.'[47] The Committee looked to the object and purpose of the Convention and found, running through it, a theme: the necessity for women to be able to freely exercise their rights without harm or fear of harm being perpetrated on them by virtue of their gender. The Women's Convention is fulfilling its purpose and, through the work of the Committee, has overcome the taboo that meant silent suffering for so many, finally to address fully violence against women.

---

[47] E. MISIAVEG, Important steps and instructive models in the fight to eliminate violence against women, 52 *Wash & Lee L. Rev.*, 1995, p. 1109 at 1119.

CHAPTER 23
THE IMPACT OF CORRUPTION UPON WOMEN'S RIGHTS: A NEGLECTED AREA?

Martine BOERSMA

1. INTRODUCTION

1.1. BACKGROUND

> *'I gave a bribe in Mulago when my mother was very ill and needed an x-ray. At first it looked complicated but when we started using money, everything was simplified. In every section I had to pay money. Finally the medicine was not available in Mulago and we were still directed to a specific pharmacy in Wandegeya which I believe belonged to the doctor who worked on my mother.'*[1]

The statement above was made by a man from Uganda, and clearly reveals the problem which the present contribution aims to address: corruption in the public sector, and its effects upon the lives of women. There is ample reason to believe that corrupt practices, such as bribery in public hospitals, impact disproportionately upon women's rights, especially because corruption hits the poor the hardest. Since the majority of the 1.5 billion people worldwide living on one dollar a day – or less – is female, women are already particularly disadvantaged by corruption.[2]

The specific consequences of corruption upon the lives of women are beginning to receive increased attention, although relatively little research has been done so far in this area. Most research related to gender and corruption

---

[1] NORDIC CONSULTING GROUP, *A Gender Analysis of Corruption – Forms, Effects and Eradication Strategies*, Study prepared for the Royal Danish Embassy in Uganda, September 2009, p. 29.

[2] This phenomenon is known as the 'feminization of poverty'. BIANCA SCHIMMEL and BIRGIT PECH, *Corruption and Gender: Approaches and Recommendations for Technical Assistance. Focal Theme: Corruption and Trafficking in Women*, Deutsche Gesellschaft für Technische Zusammenarbeit (GTZ), Eschborn, 2004, pp. 11–12.

focuses on the question whether or not women are less likely to engage in corrupt practices as compared to men.[3] This is explicitly not the approach of the current Chapter. Instead of viewing women as actual or possible performers of corrupt acts, their role as (potential) victims of corruption is examined.

Furthermore, until quite recently, corruption was mainly perceived as an economic and political problem, rather than as a human rights issue. However, this appears to be changing. A study conducted by the International Council for Human Rights Policy provides valuable insights into the relationship between corruption and human rights violations.[4] Moreover, the recent concluding observations of the UN human rights treaty bodies are paying more and more attention to the harmful effects of corruption upon human rights. The question rises, however, to what extent these observations take note of the gender dimension.

The goal of the present contribution is to bring together the available findings on the gender impact of corruption with the research done on the human rights dimension of corruption, in order to establish a women's rights perspective on corruption. Hence, the central research question to be answered is: *How does corruption impact upon women's rights, and what attention has been paid to this matter by the UN human rights treaty bodies in their concluding observations on State Reports?*

1.2. STRUCTURE AND METHODOLOGY

The research question posed above will be answered by adopting the following structure and methodology. Firstly, Section 2 describes what is actually meant by the notion of 'corruption', and discusses the various forms it can take. Secondly, Section 3 discusses different ways in which corruption specifically

---

[3] For research on this interesting topic, see, *inter alia*, DAVID DOLLAR, RAYMOND FISMAN and ROBERTA GATTI, 'Are Women Really The "Fairer" Sex? Corruption and Women in Government', *Journal of Economic Behaviour & Organization*, 46 (2001), pp. 423–429 arguing that women are less corrupt than men. On the contrary, see ANNE MARIE GOETZ, 'Political Cleaners: Women as the New Anti-Corruption Force?' *Development and Change*, 38 (2007), pp. 87–105 and HUNG-EN SUNG, 'Fairer Sex or Fairer System? Gender and Corruption Revisited', *Social Forces*, 82 (2003), p. 703–23 holding that this is not the case.

[4] INTERNATIONAL COUNCIL ON HUMAN RIGHTS POLICY, *Corruption and Human Rights: Making the Connection*, Geneva, 2009. In the context of the ICHRP project on corruption and human rights, several working papers were written, one of which deals with the impact of corruption upon women's rights in Ghana: NAMAWU ALHASSAN ALOLO, *Corruption, Human Rights and Gender: An Empirical Investigation Ghana*, Working Paper for the International Council on Human Rights Policy, Geneva 2007. Furthermore, see also MAGDALENA SEPÚLVEDA CARMONA and JULIO BACIO TERRACINO, 'Corruption and Human Rights: Making the Connection', in: Hans Nelen and Martine Boersma (eds.), *Corruption & Human Rights*, Intersentia, Antwerp, 2010, pp. 25–48. Moreover, a substantial part of the PhD dissertation of the author of the present Chapter 23 is devoted to the conceptualization of corrupt practices as violations of human rights.

Chapter 23. The Impact of Corruption upon Women's Rights: A Neglected Area?

impacts upon the lives of women. To this end, available literature and case studies, emanating from scholars, governmental institutions and NGOs have been used. These factual findings will subsequently be placed within the human rights discourse, and 'translated' into possible violations of women's rights, as enshrined in the ICCPR, the ICESCR, and the Women's Convention. From the outset it must be noted that in this respect, no claim to exhaustiveness is made. It goes well beyond the scope of the present work to identify *all* possible violations of women's rights brought about by corruption. Thirdly, Section 4 discusses the practice of the UN human rights treaty bodies, in order to determine to what extent attention has been paid in their concluding observations to the impact of corruption upon women's rights. Do these bodies sufficiently acknowledge the gender dimension of corruption? Finally, conclusions are drawn in Section 5, which also addresses a number of recommendations to human rights scholars and practitioners, and to the treaty bodies in particular.

2. DEFINING 'CORRUPTION'

2.1. PUBLIC VS. PRIVATE SECTOR CORRUPTION

The term 'corruption' is not easy to define. Many definitions were formulated over the years by scholars and organizations working in various disciplines. Unfortunately, not even the key treaty on corruption, *i.e.* the United Nations Convention Against Corruption of 2003 (hereafter: UNCAC), defines the notion. Hence, it is necessary to turn to other sources, such as anti-corruption NGO Transparency International, the World Bank, and scholarly work done on the topic.

Transparency International (hereafter: TI)[5] defines corruption as 'the misuse of *entrusted* power for private benefit' (emphasis added, MB). This definition contains three elements: (i) a misuse of power; (ii) a power that is entrusted; and (iii) a private benefit. Regarding the second element, TI does not distinguish between power that is entrusted in the public sector or in the private sector. In respect of the third element, the benefit, this does not necessarily have to accrue to the person in power; it is also possible that his or her family or friends are the ones profiting from the corrupt act.[6]

The World Bank is also a major player in the anti-corruption field. The Bank provides that corruption is 'the abuse of *public* office for private gain' (emphasis

---

[5] Transparency International, founded in 1993, is a prominent anti-corruption NGO with a Berlin-based Secretariat and many National Chapters worldwide. Its mission is 'to create change towards a world free of corruption'. See TI's website <www.transparency.org>, last consulted 5 July 2010.

[6] JEREMY POPE, *TI Source Book 2000. Confronting Corruption: The Elements of a National Integrity System*, Transparency International, Berlin, 2000, p. 1 footnote 2.

added, MB).⁷ This definition contains the same three elements as TI's definition, with one major difference: the World Bank's definition only covers corruption in the public sector, not corruption in the private sector.⁸

The difference in the definitions employed by the two organizations demonstrates the two main forms of corruption: public sector corruption and private sector corruption. Public sector corruption takes place within the public domain, involving State actors. Nevertheless, non-State actors can also be involved, for example when an individual or a corporation bribes a public official. Private sector corruption, however, occurs within and between non-State actors, such as corporations, NGOs and other private institutions.

Given the wide scope of TI's activities, it is understandable that this organization aims to cover a broad range of both public and private conduct.⁹ However, in academic literature a majority of scholars in the fields of law, political science, and economics focuses upon the public sector. This approach dates back to 1931 and since then, corruption is most frequently defined in terms of public sector conduct.¹⁰ The same holds true for many of the international and regional anti-corruption treaties that were concluded in recent years.

The present Chapter is also concerned with public sector corruption, since the State is the main actor in the human rights field. Therefore, the term 'corruption' refers to acts or omissions involving State actors, and will be understood as *'the abuse of public office for private or political gain'*. Moreover, since corruption may not only benefit the officeholder (or his or her family and friends) in the private sphere, but also or exclusively in his or her professional capacity (*e.g.* when the gains of corruption will accrue to the official's political party)¹¹ it is appropriate to extend the phrase 'for private gain' to 'for private or political gain'.

---

[7] WORLD BANK, 'Helping Countries Combat Corruption. The Role of the World Bank', <www1.worldbank.org/publicsector/anticorrupt/corruptn/corrptn.pdf>, last consulted 5 July 2010.

[8] Given the fact that basic social services such as health care and education are mainly provided by the public sector, it is likely that the effects of public sector corruption upon women are more harmful than the effects of private-to-private corruption (for example corrupt practices between corporations).

[9] In the past however, TI did employ a definition of corruption which was limited to the public sector only. Now, the NGO has broadened its working sphere by including private sector corruption as well.

[10] Corruption was defined by J.J SENTURIA, 'Corruption, Political', in: E.R.A. Seligman (ed.), *Encyclopaedia of the Social Sciences*, Macmillan, New York 1931, pp. 448–452.

[11] JOHN GARDINER, 'Defining Corruption', in: Arnold J. Heidenheimer and Michael Johnston (eds.), *Political Corruption: Concepts and Contexts*, Transaction, New Brunswick 2002, pp. 25–40 at 26.

2.2. GRAND VS. PETTY CORRUPTION

Apart from the public-private divide, it is – theoretically – possible to separate grand corruption from petty corruption. These terms do not refer to the scale of corruption or to the size of the resources involved, but to the level of authority where corrupt conduct takes place. Grand corruption, sometimes referred to as political corruption, takes place at the policy formulation end of politics, and involves public officials operating at the highest levels of the State. Petty corruption is also named bureaucratic corruption, administrative corruption, survival corruption, street-level or low corruption. It is committed at the implementation end of politics, where citizens meet public officials, for example in hospitals, schools, police stations, and court rooms.[12]

2.3. TAXONOMY

Following the formulation of a general definition of corruption, it is important to classify the phenomenon into different types of conduct. Fortunately, the UNCAC offers a good point of departure. Given the fact that currently 145 States are Party to this treaty, the definitions it contains are supported by a great number of countries.[13] The UNCAC (which does not distinguish between grand and petty corruption) lists five types of corruption: bribery, trading in influence, embezzlement, abuse of functions, and illicit enrichment.

2.3.1. Bribery

In popular expression, some scholarly works and some international and regional legal instruments, the notions corruption and bribery are used as synonyms. The offence of bribery indeed forms the 'hard core' of corruption. Nonetheless, most scholars hold the opinion that corruption covers much more than bribery, which is also reflected in the main anti-corruption treaties, such as the UNCAC, the Inter-American Convention Against Corruption and the African Union Convention on Preventing and Combating Corruption.

Bribery, also known as 'speed money', 'grease payments', 'kickbacks', 'baksheesh', 'sweeteners' or 'pay-offs', is a form of corruption which necessarily involves two parties, and therefore two forms of bribery can be distinguished. *Active bribery* is committed by the bribe-payer, the supply-side. Article 15 of the UNCAC defines it as 'the promise, offering or giving, to a public official, directly

---

[12] JENS CHR. ANDVIG et al., 'Corruption: A Review of Contemporary Research', *CMI Report, R 2001:7*, Chr. Michelsen Institute, Bergen 2001, pp. 10–12.

[13] <www.unodc.org/unodc/en/treaties/CAC/signatories.html>, Signatories to the UN Convention Against Corruption, last consulted 5 July 2010.

or indirectly, of an undue advantage, for the official him- or herself or another person or entity in order that the official act or refrain from acting in the exercise of his or her official duties'.

Passive bribery on the other hand is committed by the bribe-taker, the public official. The UNCAC provides that passive bribery is: 'the solicitation or acceptance by a public official, directly or indirectly, of an undue advantage, for the official him- or herself or another person or entity, in order that the official act or refrain from acting in the exercise of his or her official duties'.

One must keep in mind that bribes can be offered voluntarily by the supply-side. This is so-called *transactive corruption*, in which there is agreement between the bribe-payer and the bribe-taker, who benefit both. However, bribes can also be extorted by the public official concerned. In such a case, a citizen is confronted with the choice of either bribing or not getting the intended benefits, such as receiving medical care or education. This is known as *extortive corruption*, which leaves no other possibility for the bribing party than to pay the public official. In this situation, the public official commits passive bribery in a legal sense, while in reality it was the most active party.[14] It is appropriate to observe that extortive bribery might be necessary for public officials in order to obtain a decent income. In certain developing countries, medical personnel, school teachers, and police officers are substantially underpaid, which leaves them no other choice than collecting additional sources of income from bribes in order to provide a livelihood for their own families.

It should be noted that the 'currency' of bribery, *i.e.* that which is offered to, or demanded by, the public official, need not be monetary per se. More attention should be paid to the so-called 'body currency': sexual favours that are demanded from women, for example when they are unable to pay the bribes in cash.[15]

The counter-obligation which the bribe-taking public official has to meet can be either *according to law* or *against the law*. The former happens *e.g.* if, after payment of bribes, a person is given a benefit he or she is legally entitled to receive, such as proper hospital treatment or a fair hearing in a court case. By contrast, the latter happens if a person is not entitled to the benefit.

2.3.2. Trading in Influence

Like bribery, trading in influence consists of an active and a passive side as well. Article 18(a) of the UNCAC defines *active trading in influence* as 'the promise, offering or giving to a public official or any other person directly or indirectly, of

---

[14] SYED HUSSEIN ALATAS, *Corruption: Its Nature, Causes and Functions*, Avebury, Aldershot Brookfield, Vt., USA, 1990, p. 3.
[15] NORDIC CONSULTING GROUP, *A Gender Analysis of Corruption – Forms, Effects and Eradication Strategies*, p. 39.

an undue advantage in order that the public official or the person abuse his real or supposed influence with a view to obtaining from an administration or public authority an undue advantage for the original instigator of the act or for any other person'.

The other side of the coin, *passive trading in influence*, is described in Article 18(b) of the UNCAC as 'the solicitation or acceptance by a public official or any other person, directly or indirectly, of an undue advantage for himself or herself or for another person in order that the public official or the person abuse his or her real or supposed influence with a view to obtaining from an administration or public authority an undue advantage'.

2.3.3. Embezzlement

A third form of corruption is embezzlement. Frequently used synonyms are misappropriation, pillaging of State assets, diversion of property and simply theft. Unlike bribery and trading in influence, embezzlement does not necessarily include two parties, it is a form of 'auto corruption'.[16] Embezzlement can take many forms. The World Bank lists as examples: spontaneous privatization of State assets, theft of financial resources of the government, theft of cash from treasuries, extended advances to public officials which were never paid back and payments for fictitious ghost workers.[17]

The UNCAC provides a definition of embezzlement in Article 17: 'the embezzlement, misappropriation or other diversion by a public official for his or her benefit or the benefit of another person of entity, of any property, public or private funds or securities or any other thing of value entrusted to the public official by virtue of his or her position'.[18]

2.3.4. Abuse of Functions

Abuse of functions is defined in Article 19 of the UNCAC as 'the performance of or failure to perform an act, in violation of laws, by a public official in the discharge of his or her functions, for the purpose of obtaining an undue advantage for himself or herself or for another person or entity'. Hence, this is a rather broad category, under which many corrupt practices can be brought.

---

[16] ALATAS, *Corruption: Its Nature, Causes and Functions*, p. 2.
[17] WORLD BANK, 'Helping Countries Combat Corruption. The Role of the World Bank', p. 10.
[18] Embezzlement is also seen as an act of corruption by the Inter-American Convention Against Corruption (Article XI (1)(d)) and is included in the SADC Protocol (Article 3 (1)(d)) and in the African Union Convention on Preventing and Combating Corruption (Article 4 (1) (d)).

2.3.5. Illicit Enrichment

Illicit enrichment is, according to Article 20 of the UNCAC, 'a significant increase in the assets of a public official that he or she cannot reasonably explain in relation to his or her lawful income'.[19] This is quite a problematic concept. First, one could reasonably argue that an unexplainable increase in income does not constitute corruption in itself. The money could also come from other illegal sources. Second, even if it is assumed that the increase consists of means collected through acts of corruption, then 'illicit enrichment' is more likely to refer to the result of corruption, rather than to a specific type of corruption. Third, the concept reverses the burden of proof. The alleged corrupt public official has to demonstrate that the increase in income is caused by legal means. This can cause problems of incompatibility of national legislation. Moreover, it has been noted that the presumption of innocence might be at stake.[20] Despite these difficulties, the concept of illicit enrichment is included in the UNCAC, and will be considered a type of corruption.

3. CORRUPTION AS A WOMEN'S RIGHTS ISSUE

3.1. INTRODUCTION

Having established the content of the notion of 'corruption' and its various faces, the time has come to consider the gender dimension of this multi-faceted phenomenon. When discussing the impact of corruption upon the lives of women, the U4 Anti-Corruption Resource Centre[21] distinguishes between impact in the following areas: (i) access to decision-making power; (ii) protection of women's rights; and (iii) access to resources.[22] This three-tier framework will be taken as a starting point. For the purposes of clarity, the three categories will be named: the political dimension, the law enforcement dimension, and the socio-economic dimension.

---

[19] It is also codified in the African Union Convention (Article 4 (1) (g)) and in the Inter-American Convention Against Corruption (Article IX).

[20] PETER W. SCHROTH, 'The African Union Convention on Preventing and Combating Corruption', *Journal of African Law*, 49 (2005), pp. 24–38 at 27–30.

[21] The U4 Anti-Corruption Resource Centre (<www.u4.no>) is funded by seven bilateral donor agencies: DFID (UK), Norad (Norway), Sida (Sweden), CIDA (Canada), GTZ (Germany), MinBuZa (The Netherlands), and BTC (Belgium). U4 is operated by the Chr. Michelsen Institute (CMI) in Bergen, Norway, a private social science research institute working on issues of development and human rights (<www.cmi.no>). U4 closely cooperates with Transparency International.

[22] U4 ANTI-CORRUPTION RESOURCE CENTRE, 'State of Research on Gender and Corruption', *U4 Expert Answer* (24 June 2009), pp. 3–4.

Chapter 23. The Impact of Corruption upon Women's Rights: A Neglected Area?

What is important to note here, is the fact that corruption is a discriminatory practice per se, since public officials will favour those courses of action that are beneficial to themselves, regardless of the consequences for the public good, such as women's rights. Therefore, corruption is inherently incompatible with the fundamental principles of equality and non-discrimination.

3.2. THE POLITICAL DIMENSION: ACCESS TO DECISION-MAKING POWER

The first way in which corruption affects women is related to the fact that in several parts of the world there is an income and property gap between men and women, and an unequal right to inheritance. For this reason, women rely more heavily on financial schemes by the government. Corruption in such schemes, usually grand corruption at the governmental level, is therefore detrimental to women. Moreover, in corrupt political systems it is difficult for women to change their situation, because they generally cannot afford to bribe politicians in order to advance their interests.[23] Also, whenever women stand for public office, they might be unable to buy electoral votes or to bribe electoral officials, and thus they cannot compete with their male competitors, who do have the resources for vote-buying and bribery.[24]

The situation described above clearly impedes women's political rights. Rights of political participation are enshrined in Article 25 of the ICCPR, which includes the right to participate in public affairs, the right to vote, the right to stand for elective office, and the right of equal access to public service.[25] The Women's Convention lays down related provisions in Articles 7 and 8.[26] Under these provisions, State parties to the Convention should take serious efforts to remove corrupt practices in the field of political participation, so that women can fairly participate.

---

[23] *Ibid.* at p. 3.
[24] ALOLO, *Corruption, Human Rights and Gender: An Empirical Investigation Ghana* at para. 87 *et seq.*; U4 ANTI-CORRUPTION RESOURCE CENTRE, 'State of Research on Gender and Corruption', at p. 3.
[25] MANFRED NOWAK, *UN Covenant on Civil and Political Rights: CCPR Commentary*, Engel 2nd edition, Kehl 2005, pp. 563–596. and UN Doc. CCPR/C/21/Rev.1/Add.7, Human Rights Committee, *General Comment No. 25 on the right to participate in public affairs, voting rights and the right of equal access to public service (Article 25)*, Fifty-seventh session 12 July 1996.
[26] The text of Articles 7 and 8 of the Women's Convention can be found in Annex I to this book. On womens's political rights, also see Chapter 8 by Margreet de Boer.

3.3. THE LAW ENFORCEMENT DIMENSION: PROTECTION OF WOMEN'S RIGHTS

The second way in which corruption disproportionately harms women concerns the extent to which women can ensure and protect their rights within the law enforcement system (*i.e.* police and security forces, and the justice system).[27] Two specific areas will be discussed here: corruption in the justice system, and the problem of human trafficking.

3.3.1. *The Justice System*

In the justice sector, a worrisome practice is that of bribery of judges, prosecutors, and court officials. Cases will be decided on the basis of the bribe that has been given, rather than on the merits.[28] Given the fact that women are generally poorer than men, and can probably not afford to pay the bribe, this leads to an unequal situation, where cases will be decided in favour of men.[29] Moreover, in case women cannot pay bribes in cash, they might be tempted to pay bribes in kind, *i.e.* by means of offering sexual favours to judges.[30]

Another type of corruption that has been reported within the justice system is the embezzlement of court fines and of funds intended for court projects, *e.g.* the construction of new court buildings. Thus, fewer court facilities are available to process cases, resulting in delays and backlogs. For women, the consequences of this might be particularly severe, because court premises might not be physically accessible to them. Whenever women have to travel far in order to reach the nearest court, they might not be able to do so, for example because they have to take care of their families.[31]

From the human rights perspective, practices such as bribery and embezzlement in the judicial branch can violate women's right to equality before courts and tribunals and the right to a fair trial, as contained in Article 14(1) of the ICCPR.[32] Moreover, the Women's Convention sets out in Article 16 that

---

[27] U4 ANTI-CORRUPTION RESOURCE CENTRE, 'State of Research on Gender and Corruption', p. 3.

[28] For more on judicial corruption, see TRANSPARENCY INTERNATIONAL, *Global Corruption Report 2007: Corruption in Judicial Systems*, Cambridge University Press, Cambridge, 2007.

[29] INTERNATIONAL COUNCIL ON HUMAN RIGHTS POLICY, *Corruption and Human Rights: Making the Connection*, pp. 7–8; SCHIMMEL and PECH, *Corruption and Gender: Approaches and Recommendations for Technical Assistance. Focal Theme: Corruption and Trafficking in Women*, p. 13 *et seq*. ALOLO, *Corruption, Human Rights and Gender: An Empirical Investigation Ghana*, para. 82 *et seq*. NORDIC CONSULTING GROUP, *A Gender Analysis of Corruption – Forms, Effects and Eradication Strategies*, pp. 15–16.

[30] ALOLO, *Corruption, Human Rights and Gender: An Empirical Investigation Ghana*, para. 84.

[31] *Ibid.*, para. 83.

[32] See NOWAK, *UN Covenant on Civil and Political Rights: CCPR Commentary*, pp. 302–357; UN Doc. CCPR/C/GC/32 (2007), HUMAN RIGHTS COMMITTEE, *General Comment No. 32 on the*

women have certain rights related to marriage and family.[33] Judicial corruption renders these rights ineffective.

3.3.2. Human Trafficking

Another practice in which corruption leaves women particularly vulnerable is human trafficking.[34] Research demonstrates that corruption is a major causal factor in the occurrence of human trafficking. Moreover, 85 per cent of all trafficking victims are women.[35] Traffickers will only be able to proceed whenever corrupt public officials are involved. This involvement can consist of public officials who either turn a blind eye to the activities of traffickers, or facilitate these, because they will be given a bribe.[36]

In legal terms, trafficking is governed by the Protocol to Prevent, Suppress and Punish Trafficking in Persons, Especially Women and Children (hereafter: Trafficking Protocol), supplementing the UN Convention Against Transnational Organized Crime (UNCTOC), under which State parties have a number of obligations. However, the Protocol is not a human rights treaty.[37]

From a human rights perspective, trafficking can be brought under Article 8 of the ICCPR, which prohibits slavery, servitude, and forced or compulsory labour.[38] It has been noted that States have four obligations with regard to trafficking committed by non-State actors: (i) the obligation to prohibit

---

right to equality before courts and tribunals and to a fair trial (Article 14), Ninetieth session 23 August 2007.

[33] The text of Article 16 can be found in Annex I. For further reading on Article 16, see Chapter 17 by Pauline Kruiniger.

[34] Trafficking in persons is defined by Article 3(a) of the Trafficking Protocol as 'the recruitment, transportation, transfer, harbouring or receipt of persons, by means of the threat or use of force or other forms of coercion, of abduction, of fraud, of deception, of the abuse of power or of a position of vulnerability or of the giving or receiving of payments or benefits to achieve the consent of a person having control over another person, for the purpose of exploitation.'

[35] SCHIMMEL and PECH, *Corruption and Gender: Approaches and Recommendations for Technical Assistance. Focal Theme: Corruption and Trafficking in Women*, p. 16.

[36] SHELDON X. ZHANG and SAMUEL L. PINEDA, 'Corruption as a Causal Factor in Human Trafficking', in: Dina Siegel and Hans Nelen (eds.), *Organized Crime: Culture, Markets and Policies*, Springer Studies of Organized Crime 2008, pp. 41–55 at 45. For an overview of the various types of corrupt involvement of public officials in trafficking, see SCHIMMEL and PECH, *Corruption and Gender: Approaches and Recommendations for Technical Assistance. Focal Theme: Corruption and Trafficking in Women*, p. 17.

[37] JOAN FITZPATRICK, 'Trafficking as a Human Rights Violation: The Complex Intersection of Legal Frameworks for Conceptualizing and Combating Trafficking', *Michigan Journal of International Law*, 24 (2003), pp. 1143–1167 at 1151.

[38] The question rises under which paragraph of Article 8 of the ICCPR human trafficking can be brought. Nowak argues that human trafficking is a slavery-like practice (*i.e.* servitude under Article 8(2)): NOWAK, *UN Covenant on Civil and Political Rights: CCPR Commentary*, p. 200, para. 13. However, Scarpa argues that human trafficking can also be classified, under certain circumstances, as slavery under Article 8(1): SILVIA SCARPA, *Trafficking in Human Beings: Modern Slavery*, Oxford University Press, Oxford, 2008, p. 88.

trafficking and related acts; (ii) the obligation to investigate, prosecute, and punish traffickers with due diligence; (iii) the obligation to protect trafficking victims; and (iv) the obligation to address the causes and consequences of trafficking.[39] Moreover, the Women's Convention specifically mentions trafficking in Article 6, under which Parties to the Convention have to take all appropriate measures to suppress trafficking.[40] Hence, fighting corrupt practices also falls under the obligations of States.

3.4. THE SOCIO-ECONOMIC DIMENSION: ACCESS TO RESOURCES

The third affected area relates to the fact that women are, more than men, reliant upon social services provided by governments. The following will discuss the health and education sector as examples of areas where corruption is especially harmful to women, and can constitute violations of their human rights.

3.4.1. Health

The public health sector is particularly vulnerable to corruption.[41] Several forms of corruption can be observed, although the following overview is by no means exhaustive. First of all, bribery of doctors and nurses is highly problematic. Bribes have to be paid for a wide variety of goods and services: to obtain medical treatment at all; to receive a hospital bed; to receive the prescription of the right medication; and to receive medication that ought to be free.[42] Furthermore, it has been reported that medical personnel employed in public hospitals might open expensive private clinics, to which patients from the public hospitals are referred- at high costs. Also, hospital equipment and medicines from the public hospitals may be embezzled, among other things for use in private clinics.[43]

---

[39] Tom Obokata, *Trafficking in Human Beings from a Human Rights Perspective: Towards a Holistic Approach*, Martinus Nijhoff Publishers, International Studies in Human Rights Vol. 89, Leiden 2006, pp. 148–164.

[40] The text of Article 6 can be found in Annex I. In Chapter 7, Article 6 is examined by Marjolein van den Brink and Marjan Wijers.

[41] For more on corruption in the health sector, see Transparency International, *Global Corruption Report 2006: Corruption and Health*, Pluto Press, London – Ann Arbor, Michigan 2006; Taryn Vian, 'Health Care', in: Bertram I. Spector (ed.), *Fighting Corruption in Developing Countries: Strategies and Analysis*, Kumarian Press, Bloomfield, CT 2005, pp. 43–63.

[42] Alolo, *Corruption, Human Rights and Gender: An Empirical Investigation Ghana*, para. 71, 72, 73, 75, 76. Maaria Seppänen and Pekka Virtanen, *Corruption, Poverty and Gender. With Case Studies of Nicaragua and Tanzania*, Finland Ministry for Foreign Affairs, 2008, pp. 82–88.

[43] Alolo, *Corruption, Human Rights and Gender: An Empirical Investigation Ghana*, para. 74. Seppänen and Virtanen, *Corruption, Poverty and Gender. With Case Studies of Nicaragua and Tanzania*, p. 83.

Chapter 23. The Impact of Corruption upon Women's Rights: A Neglected Area?

There are several reasons why corruption in the health sector has more severe effects on women than on men. First of all, women are more likely to make use of public health facilities. Men might be able to rely on private health care, because of their higher incomes. Second, women are more often in need of medical care then men, due to their needs surrounding pregnancy and child delivery. Third, women usually have to take care of sick children and elderly relatives in need of medical care. Hence, women are confronted more often with the demand for bribes.[44]

Corrupt practices in the health sector can violate the right to health, as laid down, *inter alia*, in Article 12 of the ICESCR. It is generally accepted that this right consists of four elements: availability, accessibility, acceptability and quality (the so-called AAAQ-framework).[45] Corruption may violate each of these elements. For example, the accessibility dimension consists of four aspects: non-discrimination, physical access, economic access (affordability) and access to information.[46] Whenever bribes have to be paid for supposedly free medical care, this contravenes the aspect of non-discrimination: those who cannot afford to bribe, will be denied access to medical care. Also, the practice of having to pay bribes hinders women's economic access to the right to health. The same is true for the practice of opening expensive private clinics. Moreover, whenever bribes have to be paid to obtain the correct prescription for drugs, this means that without paying the bribe, the wrong drug would be prescribed. This violates the quality dimension of the right to health.[47]

The Women's Convention contains provisions on the right to health in Article 12(1), ordering States to take all appropriate measures to eliminate health care discrimination.[48] In the author's opinion, this provision encompasses the obligation of States to combat corruption in the health sector, in order to guarantee accessible health care for women, without bribery. Furthermore, under Article 12(2) States have to ensure appropriate services to women in relation to pregnancy and post-natal care. This provision's clear reference to free

---

[44] BRIGIT TOEBES, 'The Impact of Acts of Corruption on the Enjoyment of the Right to Health', Working Paper for the International Council on Human Rights Policy, Geneva 2007, para. 37. See also U4 ANTI-CORRUPTION RESOURCE CENTRE, 'Gender, Corruption and Health', *U4 Expert Answer* (10 August 2009); SEPPÄNEN and VIRTANEN, *Corruption, Poverty and Gender. With Case Studies of Nicaragua and Tanzania*, pp. 93–95. NORDIC CONSULTING GROUP, *A Gender Analysis of Corruption – Forms, Effects and Eradication Strategies*, pp. 14–15.

[45] UN Doc. E/C.12/2000/4, Committee on Economic, Social and Cultural Rights, *General Comment No. 14 on the right to the highest attainable standard of health*, Twenty-second session 11 August 2000, para. 12.

[46] General Comment No. 14, para. 12(b).

[47] A highly useful study on corruption and the right to health is BRIGIT TOEBES, 'Health Sector Corruption and Human Rights: A Case Study', in: Hans Nelen and Martine Boersma (eds.), *Corruption and Human Rights*, Intersentia, Antwerp, 2010. See also Toebes' working paper for the ICHRP.

[48] The text of Article 12 can be found in Annex I. In this book, Article 12 is examined in Chapter 12 by Nishara Mendis and Jennifer Sellin and in Chapter 13 by Phyllis Livaha.

services ought to mean that bribes cannot be demanded from pregnant women in order to receive medical treatment. Moreover, Article 14(b), which concerns rural women, also deserves to be mentioned.[49]

3.4.2. Education

Public education is another sector with a reportedly high amount of corruption.[50] Corruption in education can *inter alia* take the form of bribery. Bribes can be demanded for a variety of things, including for school admission and to pass examinations.[51] This practice is particularly harmful to school girls, since they might be forced to pay bribes by granting sexual favours. This is of course highly problematic, and contributes to the spread of HIV/AIDS. In case of unwanted pregnancies, there is also a high chance that girls will quit their education.[52] Also, whenever monetary bribes are required to obtain school admission, parents might be more willing to pay bribes for their male children than for their female children, since the education of boys is still considered to be more important in a number of countries.[53]

Furthermore, embezzlement of resources is a serious problem, both at the higher and the lower governmental levels. Funds intended for education may 'disappear', leading to a lack of school buildings and materials, or to substandard facilities.[54]

The right to education is laid down, *inter alia*, in Articles 13 and 14 of the ICESCR, and is said to have four interrelated and essential features (the AAAA

---

[49] Article 14(b) of the Women's Convention provides that: 'States Parties shall take all appropriate measures to eliminate discrimination against women in rural areas in order to ensure, on a basis of equality of men and women, that they participate in and benefit from rural development and, in particular, shall ensure to such women the right to have access to adequate health care facilities, including information, counselling and services in family planning.'

[50] For more on corruption in education, see: U4 ANTI-CORRUPTION RESOURCE CENTRE, 'Corruption in the Education Sector', *U4 Issue*, Chr. Michelsen Institute, Bergen, 2006; U4 ANTI-CORRUPTION RESOURCE CENTRE, 'Gender, Corruption and Education', *U4 Expert Answer* (14 July 2009).

[51] ALOLO, *Corruption, Human Rights and Gender: An Empirical Investigation Ghana*, p. 77. NORDIC CONSULTING GROUP, *A Gender Analysis of Corruption – Forms, Effects and Eradication Strategies*, p. 14. SEPPÄNEN and VIRTANEN, *Corruption, Poverty and Gender. With Case Studies of Nicaragua and Tanzania*, pp. 136–139.

[52] ALOLO, *Corruption, Human Rights and Gender: An Empirical Investigation Ghana*, para. 78 et seq.; NORDIC CONSULTING GROUP, *A Gender Analysis of Corruption – Forms, Effects and Eradication Strategies*, p. 14; SEPPÄNEN and VIRTANEN, *Corruption, Poverty and Gender. With Case Studies of Nicaragua and Tanzania*, pp. 138–139.

[53] ALOLO, *Corruption, Human Rights and Gender: An Empirical Investigation Ghana*, para. 81; SEPPÄNEN and VIRTANEN, *Corruption, Poverty and Gender. With Case Studies of Nicaragua and Tanzania*, p. 32.

[54] SEPPÄNEN and VIRTANEN, *Corruption, Poverty and Gender. With Case Studies of Nicaragua and Tanzania*, pp. 136–139.

or four-A framework): availability, accessibility, acceptability, and adaptability.[55] As with the right to health, corruption can violate each of these features. The availability feature is violated whenever embezzlement leads to the absence of teaching materials, *e.g.* by the diversion of funds for school books. Furthermore, the non-discrimination element of the feature of accessibility is clearly violated in case of bribery: those children whose parents cannot afford the bribes are given discriminatory treatment. Also, whenever bribes have to be paid for school admission this violates the affordability element, which is also part of the feature of accessibility.

In addition to Article 13 of the ICESCR, Article 10 of the Women's Convention deserves to be mentioned.[56] In the light of this provision, State parties should actively tackle corruption in the education sector, in order to eliminate discrimination against women.

4. PRACTICE OF THE UN TREATY BODIES

Now as the influence of corrupt conduct on women has been discussed, and placed within the human rights discourse, it is fascinating to examine whether the concluding observations of the human rights treaty bodies devote any attention to this matter. It should be noted that in general, the treaty bodies are taking the problem of corruption more and more into consideration when discussing State reports. But in which ways are women's rights discussed in the observations on corruption? A search through all concluding observations of the Human Rights Committee, the Committee on Economic, Social and Cultural Rights, the Committee on the Elimination of Racial Discrimination, the Committee Against Torture, the Committee on the Elimination of Discrimination Against Women, and the Committee on the Rights of the Child, reveals the following.[57]

---

[55] UN Doc. E/C.12/1999/10, Committee on Economic, Social and Cultural Rights, *General Comment No. 13 on the right to education (Art. 13)*, Twenty-first session, 1999, para. 6.
[56] The text of Article 10 is contained in Annex I. In Chapter 10 the right to education is discussed by Fons Coomans.
[57] The study of the concluding observations has been conducted on 19 February 2010 by making use of the online UNCOM database of the Netherlands Institute of Human Rights (SIM, Utrecht): <http://sim.law.uu.nl/sim/Dochome.nsf> which contains all concluding observations of the HRC, CESCR, CERD, CAT, CEDAW and CRC. All observations in which corruption was discussed have been examined, in order to determine whether the specific impact of corruption upon women was taken into consideration or not.

4.1. CEDAW

First and foremost, it is remarkable that CEDAW, the organ supervising State compliance with the rights enshrined in the Women's Convention, seems to pay little attention to the issue of corruption. As compared to the other treaty bodies, only very few concluding observations discuss the matter. Only the concluding observations on China (1999)[58] and Thailand (2006)[59] are relevant. The observations on China state:

> 'Notwithstanding the serious efforts of the Government to combat trafficking in women, the Committee expresses its concern about reports in some localities of corrupt officials who are involved or colluding in the trade in women, including through payments from prostitutes.'[60]

As a result,

> 'The Committee urges the Government to investigate reports of local officials' involvement in trafficking and the exploitation of prostitution, and to prosecute all persons engaged in such practices.'[61]

Furthermore, the concluding observations on Thailand note:

> 'While welcoming the efforts made by the State Party in granting Thai citizenship to 80 per cent of the hill tribe people and approving it for 140,000 displaced persons, the Committee remains concerned about the complexity of the procedure for obtaining citizenship by hill tribe women. It is also concerned that many refugee women do not enjoy legal status in the country.'[62]

For this reason,

> 'The Committee urges the State Party to adopt measures that will facilitate and accelerate the process for obtaining citizenship by hill tribe women, including by addressing any corrupt practices by public officials responsible for determining the citizenship of applicants. It also calls on the State Party to take steps that will ensure that refugee women can obtain legal status.'[63]

---

[58] UN Doc. A/54/38, *CEDAW concluding observations on China*, 5 February 1999, paras. 251–336.
[59] UN Doc. CEDAW/C/THA/CO/5, *CEDAW concluding observations on Thailand*, 3 February 2006.
[60] CEDAW concluding observations on China, para. 290.
[61] CEDAW concluding observations on China, para. 291.
[62] CEDAW concluding observations on Thailand, para. 37.
[63] CEDAW concluding observations on Thailand, para. 38.

Hence, CEDAW considers the dangers of corruption in respect of trafficking in Chinese women, and the possibility of obtaining Thai citizenship by hill tribe women. Other issues are not discussed.

4.2. OTHER TREATY BODIES

As noted above, one of the few instances where corruption was discussed by CEDAW, the topic of human trafficking was involved. Other treaty bodies have also discussed the role of corruption in relation to this practice. The Human Rights Committee has paid attention to it on a number of occasions, *i.e.* in its concluding observations on Cambodia (1999),[64] Albania (2004),[65] Brazil (2005),[66] and Bosnia and Herzegovina (2006).[67] Moreover, also the Committee on Economic, Social and Cultural Rights has discussed the matter, *i.e.* in its concluding observations on Serbia and Montenegro (2005).[68] The Committee on the Rights of the Child also raises the issue in its observations on Kazakhstan (2006)[69] and Kyrgyzstan (2007).[70]

Furthermore, the Committee on the Rights of the Child commented upon corruption in the education sector. The observations on Mozambique (2002) state:

> 'While noting the State party's significant efforts in this domain, including the construction or renovation of many primary schools in the 1990s, the provision of free school materials to children, increases in primary school enrolment rates, efforts to improve the access to education of girls and to train teachers, the fall in the repetition and drop-out rates, the Committee remains *concerned* that [...]
> (i) There is alledged corruption and sexual abuse and economic exploitation of pupils by professionals, including teachers, in the school system.'[71]

---

[64] UN Doc. CCPR/C/79/Add.108, *HRC concluding observations on Cambodia*, 27 July 1999, para. 16.

[65] UN Doc. CCPR/CO/82/ALB, *HRC concluding observations on Albania*, 2 December 2004, para. 15.

[66] UN Doc. CCPR/C/BRA/CO/2, *HRC concluding observations on Brazil*, 1 December 2005, para. 15.

[67] UN Doc. CCPR/C/BIH/CO/1, *HRC concluding observations on Bosnia and Herzegovina*, 22 November 2006, par. 16.

[68] UN Doc. E/C.12/1/Add.108, *CESCR concluding observations on Serbia and Montenegro*, 23 June 2005, para. 52.

[69] UN Doc. CRC/C/OPSC/KAZ/CO/1, *CRC concluding observations (Optional Protocol) on Kazakhstan* 17 March 2006, para. 23.

[70] UN Doc. CRC/C/OPSC/KGZ/CO/1, *CRC concluding observations (Optional Protocol) on Kyrgyzstan* 4 May 2007, para. 25–26.

[71] UN Doc. CRC/C/15/Add.172, *CRC concluding observations on Mozambique* 3 April 2002, para. 56.

Hence,

> 'Noting the State party's own recommendations in its initial report, the Committee *recommends* that the State party [...]
> (i) end practices of corruption and sexual exploitation of pupils in the educational system.'[72]

These are the only concluding observations in which both corruption ánd the impact of this practice upon women are discussed by the treaty bodies.

5. CONCLUSIONS AND RECOMMENDATIONS

Corruption, *i.e.* 'the abuse of public office for private or political gain', can take various forms. From the literature that has been examined, it appears that this phenomenon has a disproportionate impact upon women as compared to men, especially in three areas: the political dimension, the law enforcement dimension, and the socio-economic dimension. One of the overall causes of the fact that corruption is particularly harmful to women, is the given fact that women have generally less financial resources than men. Hence, they cannot afford to pay bribes to obtain certain public goods or services.

The impact of corruption upon women's lives can be translated into human rights language, and it can then be concluded that various corrupt practices, such as bribery, can constitute violations of women's civil, political, economic, and social rights, as enshrined in the ICCPR, the ICESCR and the Women's Convention. Examples are the right to political participation, the right to equality before courts and tribunals and the right to a fair trial, the right to health, and the right to education.

When examining the concluding observations of the UN human rights treaty bodies, it becomes apparent that – although attention is being paid to the influence of corruption upon the enjoyment of human rights – very little attention is devoted to the specific impact of corruption upon the rights of women. The only topic that is discussed more often than once is the practice of human trafficking and the role of corrupt public officials in facilitating it. Also, the Committee on the Rights of the Child spells out the problem of corruption in the education sector.

The treaty bodies should devote more attention to the particular effects of corruption upon women's rights. This recommendation is specifically addressed to CEDAW, which pays hardly any attention to corruption in its concluding observations. One of the reasons that can possibly account for this gap, is the fact that treaty bodies have to rely on NGO information that is provided to them.

---

[72] CRC concluding observations on Mozambique, para. 57.

Whenever anti-corruption NGOs do not supply the treaty bodies with country-specific information about corruption, it will be difficult for the treaty bodies to address the matter in the constructive dialogue and the resulting concluding observations. Hence, it is also recommended that NGOs such as Transparency International provide the treaty bodies with data about concrete situations of corruption.

Closer cooperation between human rights advocates and anti-corruption practitioners will thus be beneficial to the work of the treaty bodies, and can also help anti-corruption campaigners, since the use of human rights language adds strength to the anti-corruption debate, and can offer additional avenues to combat corruption, for example by making use of domestic human rights mechanisms.

Given the strong evidence that corruption is detrimental to the realization of the rights put forward in the Women's Convention, corruption & women's rights no longer deserves to be a neglected area, and should be seriously examined by both human rights ánd anti-corruption scholars and practitioners alike.

CHAPTER 24
THE IMPACT AND EFFECTIVENESS OF STATE REPORTING UNDER THE WOMEN'S CONVENTION
The Case of the Netherlands*

Jasper KROMMENDIJK

1. INTRODUCTION

The Committee on the Elimination of Discrimination Against Women (CEDAW) has already expressed its concern three times with respect to the existence of the reformed political party, SGP, which excluded women from membership until 2006 and still continues to exclude women from being eligible for election.[1] CEDAW also determined thrice that the Law on Names continues to contravene the basic principle of the Women's Convention regarding equality of men and women.[2] It is therefore not surprising that CEDAW concluded in its latest Concluding Observations (COs) that some of the concerns, including those just mentioned, have been insufficiently addressed by the Netherlands.[3]

---

* This contribution must be seen as only a partial and limited selection out of a more extensive Ph.D. research that focuses on State reporting under the six main UN human rights treaties (ICCPR, ICESCR, ICRC, ICAT, ICERD and the Women's Convention).

[1] The second and third report were jointly considered by CEDAW on 6 July 2001, the fourth report on 24 January 2007 and the most recent one on 27 January 2010. Concluding Observations of the Committee on the Elimination of Discrimination Against Women (paras. 185–231), A/56/38(SUPP), 20 July 2001, paras. 219–220. Concluding comments of the Committee on the Elimination of Discrimination against Women, UN doc. CEDAW/C/NLD/CO/4, 2 February 2007, paras. 25–26. Concluding observations of the Committee on the Elimination of Discrimination against Women, UN doc. CEDAW/C/NLD/CO/5, 5 February 2010, para. 10. On the SGP case also see Chapter 8 in this book by Margreet de Boer.

[2] CEDAW points in particular to Article 16 (g) of the Women's Convention. The Law on Names provides that, where the parents cannot reach an agreement as to the name of a child, the father has the ultimate decision. COs 2001, A/56/38(SUPP), para. 223–224. UN doc. CEDAW/C/NLD/CO/4, para. 33–34. UN doc. CEDAW/C/NLD/CO/5, para. 10. On the Law on Names also see Chapter 16 in this book by Tilly Draaisma.

[3] UN doc. CEDAW/C/NLD/CO/5, para. 10. Besides the recommendations to adopt or amend legislation to comply with the Women's Convention with respect to the political party SGP

Jasper Krommendijk

This warrants the question what the impact of the other COs has been and how the COs are complied with by the Netherlands.

In this Chapter it will be argued that the COs for the Netherlands have hardly had any impact[4] and that they are ineffective in terms of securing compliance.[5] Section 2 will outline the impact at the domestic level and the attention that has been paid by domestic actors, such as Parliament, the media and courts, next to discussing the visibility of the Women's Convention. The other sections will illustrate this conclusion by highlighting several important factors and reasons for the scarce attention paid at the domestic level and the fact that COs hardly ever lead to policy changes that are directly the result of CEDAW's recommendations. That is to say, Section 3 focuses on the State level and the attitude of the Government (officials) towards the process of State reporting, whereas Section 4 examines the factors related to CEDAW.[6] Section 5 concentrates on the divergence of views between CEDAW and the Dutch Government about the nature of the obligations under the Women's Convention.

2. IMPACT AND ATTENTION AT THE DOMESTIC LEVEL

This section will demonstrate that COs are hardly discussed, invoked or referred to in Parliament.[7] At the same time, COs are largely absent in legal practice and are hardly ever picked up by the press.

---

and the Law on Names, CEDAW is also concerned about, among other issues, the low presence of women in high ranking posts, the persistence of gender-role stereotypes, the fact that the policy on violence against women is couched in gender-neutral wording, disadvantages women face on the labour market and the insufficient number of places of childcare.

[4] Impact is understood as the extent to which COs are picked up, discussed and referred to by domestic actors, such as the executive Government, Parliament, NGOs and the media.

[5] With effectiveness I mean a change in policy and/or legislation that was made as a consequence of and with the intention to comply with those COs. The latter definition makes clear that the focus in this Chapter is on a causal relationship between the measures taken by the authorities and those recommended by CEDAW.

[6] In order to establish those attitudes and perceptions twelve interviews were held with (former) Government officials from five different Ministries involved in the process of State reporting. In order to protect the anonymity of my interview subjects, the names or identities of those Government officials will not be disclosed. Given the limited number of pages, the results of the interviews will mainly be discussed in general terms. References with a randomly generated series of numbers that were assigned to the interview are only used when necessary.

[7] Parliament refers to both the First and the Second Chamber.

2.1. GOVERNMENTAL INFORMING OF PARLIAMENT

Parliament is kept informed about the process of State reporting, although it is not engaged in the drawing up of the report itself.[8] This means that the periodic State reports, the List of Issues and the Answers of the Government thereto will be sent to Parliament by way of information and the same will happen with CEDAW's COs and the Government's reaction to the COs.[9] In 2001 and 2007, a General Meeting took place with the State Secretary or Minister responsible for emancipation affairs on the basis of the COs and the Government's reaction.[10] During both General Meetings, no motions were adopted by Parliament, thereby warranting the conclusion that those meetings served as a noncommittal exchange of ideas between the Government and Parliament.

What is more, those Meetings about the COs have turned out not to be the right place for discussing specific substantive policies. During the General Meeting about the fourth periodic report, the Minister responsible for emancipation affairs, for example, mentioned that the Minister of Justice would send the evaluation to Parliament and that this would be the appropriate moment to discuss the COs concerning the law abolishing the ban on brothels.[11] Nevertheless, both in the letter that was attached to the second evaluation and the reaction of the Government, the COs were not referred to.[12] As a result, the

---

[8] The preparation of the periodic State report has so far been coordinated by the Directorate Emancipation, part of the Ministry of Social Affairs and Employment until February 2007 and the Ministry of Education, Culture and Science. Parliament and NGOs are not engaged in the drawing up of the report itself or the responses to the List of Issues. NGOs write, separately to the State report, a shadow report. E-Quality published the shadow report to the second and third State report and the fourth and fifth shadow report were written on behalf of the Dutch CEDAW-Network. The Dutch section of the International Commission of Jurists (NCJM) also wrote a shadow report to the second and third State report and the fourth shadow report was also written on their behalf.

[9] Parliamentary Papers II 2001/02, szw0000825, 1 October 2001. Parliamentary Papers II 2006/07, 30420, nr. 46, 13 July 2007. Noteworthy is that the letter of 2001 is only two and a halve pages long and only marginally addresses some recommendations, whereas the letter concerning the fourth reporting cycle is 9 pages.

[10] The COs about the second and third periodic report were discussed during a General Meeting on 28 November 2001. Parliamentary Papers II 2001/02, 28009 nr. 7. The General Meeting about the COs about the fourth periodic report took place on 10 October 2007. Parliamentary Papers II 2007/08, 30420, nr. 98. In the remainder of this Chapter, 'the State Secretary' will be used to refer to the State Secretary of Social Affairs and Employment Verstand-Bogaert, responsible for emancipation in the cabinet Kok II, in office from 3 August 1998 until 22 July 2002. 'The Minister' will refer to the Minister of Education, Culture and Science, Plasterk, responsible for emancipation in the cabinet Balkenende IV, in office from 22 February 2007 until 20 February 2010.

[11] Parliamentary Papers II 2007/08, 30420, nr. 98, 8. Noteworthy is the fact that the evaluation itself was sent to Parliament already on 23 April 2007. Parliamentary Papers II 2006/07 25437, nr. 54. Only the reaction of the Government was sent after the General Meeting. See Parliamentary Papers 2007/08 28684, nr. 119, 6 November 2007.

[12] Parliamentary Papers II 2007/08, 28684, nr. 119, 6 November 2007.

discussion in Parliament about (the evaluation of) the prostitution policy did not address the concerns of CEDAW at all.

The Women's Convention is often only referred to in a general way as being a point of reference and a framework for emancipation.[13] Moreover, in recent years the Women's Convention (and also the obligation to report) has often been referred to only in the context of *international* emancipation policy.[14] This might suggest that reporting is not directly relevant for policy making at the national level. Empirical evidence seems to support this conclusion, because COs are not mentioned in the notes, memoranda and letters laying down the policy in the field of emancipation. Only in a limited number of cases did the Government refer to COs out of its own motion, besides the letters it has sent to Parliament with a reaction on all COs.[15]

2.2. NATIONAL REPORTS AND IN-DEPTH STUDIES

At the domestic level, national reports have been conducted on the implementation of the Women's Convention, as well as in-depth studies about

---

[13] This is especially the case for the most recent letters and notes laying down the emancipation policy. The letters and notes between 1997/98 and 2001/02 did discuss the Women's Convention in relation to specific policies.

[14] In the note on emancipation policy 2008–2011 there are only references to the Women's Convention under Chapter 4, international emancipation policy, besides one reference in the summary to the fact that the starting points of equality of sexes and equal treatment are anchored in, among other instruments, the Women's Convention. Parliamentary Papers II 2007/08, 30420, nr. 50.

[15] First of all, the 'evaluation of the Committee' was mentioned in the context of the '*tussenschoolse opvang*' (school childcare during the afternoon). Parliamentary Papers II 2003/04, 29769, nr. 1, 6. Secondly, a letter from the Minister of Social Affairs and Employment refers to the necessity in the context of State reporting about the implementation of the Women's Convention of registration of gender and data and analysis of the different forms culturally related violence disaggregated by gender. Parliamentary Papers II 2003/04, 29200 XV, nr. 37, 5. Thirdly, the enactment of the budget of the Ministry of Social Affairs and Employment mentions the CO about the position of black migrant and refugee women. Parliamentary Papers II 2003/04, 29200 XV, nr. 2, 113. Fourthly, in response to a question about the trials concerning the SGP, the Prime Minister referred to CEDAW. Parliamentary Papers II 2005/06, nr. 3, 162–176. Fifthly, in reply to an answer, the Minister of Finance stated that the last 'advice' of CEDAW on the occasion of the fourth State report, with specific recommendations, did not have any practical consequences for the policy of the Ministry of Finance. Parliamentary Papers II, 2007/08, 30420, nr. 113, 4. Sixthly, in the enactment of the budget of the Ministry of Justice, it is provided that the recommendation of CEDAW concerning the Law on Names will be involved in the advice of the Working Group. Parliamentary Papers II, 2009/10, 32123 VI, nr. 2, 211. Finally, the Plan of Action of domestic violence mentioned the United Nations who urged the Government to review the gender-neutral wording of the policy. See the attachment to Parliamentary Papers II, 2007/08, 28345, nr. 70, 8. In this Plan of Action, CEDAW's final report was referred to in the footnote, together with the report of the Special Rapporteur on Violence Against Women, Yakin Ertürk, about her mission to the Netherlands. For the latter report see UN doc. A/HRC/4/34/Add.4, 7 February 2007.

thematic parts of the Convention.¹⁶ The Government has explicitly acknowledged that the first national report resulted in a higher visibility of the Women's Convention in terms of its meaning for the legal order and social and political developments and consequently a higher priority on the political agenda.¹⁷ In addition, the second national report referred to and discussed several of the COs to the combined second and third Dutch report, whereas in-depth studies examined CEDAW's General Recommendations and the COs of several States in relation to a topic in order to determine content, scope and significance of certain provisions of the Women's Convention. Therefore, those reports and studies do not only contribute to the visibility of the Women's Convention in general, but could also add to the impact of COs.¹⁸

It is important to point out that the national reports and in-depth studies were largely concentrated in the period between February 1998 and January 2004. After this period no in-depth studies were conducted anymore, except for a third national report that did not cover the (entire) Women's Convention, but

---

16 This is the result of a proposal to amend the Act on the approbation of the Convention that obliges the Minister to send a report to Parliament about the implementation of the Convention in the Netherlands every four years. In 1997 the first national report of the Commission Groenman was issued, which contained 65 recommendations. *Het Vrouwenverdrag in Nederland anno 1997. Verslag van de commissie voor de eerste nationale rapportage over de implementatie in Nederland van het Internationaal Verdrag tegen Discriminatie van Vrouwen* (February 1997). On the occasion of this report, a conference was held in Nijmegen on 17 October 1997 during which several priorities were established. See Parliamentary Papers II 1997/98, 25893, nr. 2. The second national report contained a thematic part about the position of migrant and refugee women (*Het VN-Vrouwenverdrag in relatie tot de positie van vreemdelingenvrouwen in het Nederlandse vreemdelingenrecht en vreemdelingenbeleid* (Adviescommissie voor vreemdelingenzaken, Den Haag, December 2003)) as well as a general part examining the implementation of the entire Convention (MARIANNE H. MARCHAND, *Emancipatie op een zijspoor?; tweede nationale rapportage inzake de implementatie van het VN-Vrouwenverdrag* (Belle van Zuylen Instituut, Universiteit van Amsterdam, February 2003)). For the thematic part of the second national report of the Advisory Committee on Migration Affairs (ACZV) see the annex to Parliamentary Papers II 2002/03, just030524, 10 June 2003. For the general part see the annex to Parliamentary Papers II 2003/04, szw0400002, 22 December 2003. In addition, five in-depth studies were conducted about the Convention in the Dutch legal order, the significance of Article 12 of the Convention to the Netherlands, the effect of the Convention on the legal position of pregnant women and young mothers, the implications of the Convention for the Netherlands concerning the prevention and elimination of violence against women and Article 5 of the Convention: www.rijksoverheid.nl/onderwerpen/vrouwenemancipatie/beleid-internationaal/verenigde-naties.
17 Parliamentary Papers II 1997/98, 25893, nr. 2, 2.
18 The commentaries of the CWI, E-quality and the CEDAW-Network about the reaction of the Government to the second national report, for example, mention and cite the critique and COs of CEDAW. Consequently, the COs about exit-programmes for prostitutes, the SGP and national machinery were touched upon during the General Meeting about the combined second and third report of CEDAW. Parliamentary Papers II 2003/04, 27061, nr. 23. Also the recommendation concerning statistics and information about violence was addressed in the thematic part of the second national report and also referred to in a letter of the Government concerning domestic violence. Parliamentary Papers II 2003/04, 29200 XV, nr. 37, 5.

only focused on distinction in education in relation to Articles 5 and 10 of the Convention.[19]

2.3. PARLIAMENTARY SCRUTINY

Parliamentarians never introduced a motion addressing or giving effect to COs.[20] Only in one instance have COs been mentioned in the proposal for amendment of the Law on Names. In the Explanatory Memorandum it was highlighted that the Netherlands had been given 'a rap on the knuckles' by CEDAW, but without explicitly reproducing the CO.[21] The role of Parliament in relation to CEDAW is thus rather limited. This has also been acknowledged by government officials. This is because the real political debate takes place on the basis of notes and letters laying down the emancipation policy. Because Parliament, and especially the Second Chamber, is seen as forming part of the 'core business' for the civil service, this limited attention by Parliament has an influence on the importance that government officials attach to CEDAW and the process of State reporting.[22] As long as politicians and Members of Parliament hardly use or invoke the Women's Convention and CEDAW, government officials will also refrain from doing so, because the civil service serves the politicians.

In general, the total number of references to the COs in the context of specific policy areas outside the Meetings about the report of CEDAW is 0, 1 or 2 times a year.[23] Those instances were mainly related to the COs in those fundamental areas where CEDAW found a violation (SGP) or determined that the law contravened the Convention (Law on Names), respectively three and four

---

[19] Karin Hoogeveen, Anke van Kampen and Frank Strudulski, *Rapportage ongezien onderscheid in het onderwijs* (Sardes, December 2006) included as an attachment to Parliamentary Papers II 2007/08, 30420, nr. 47. Remarkable is the fact that the Women's Convention is only mentioned 9 times in this report, and only in the first chapter laying out the background to the report. In the remaining 82 pages the Convention is not touched upon, nor does the reaction of the Government address the Convention. Parliamentary Papers II 2007/08, DE/2008/8871, 21 March 2008.

[20] Nonetheless, the *Women's Convention* was explicitly mentioned in five motions of Parliament.

[21] As will be explained below in the context of the Parliamentary Question raised in an earlier instance, the Proposal refers to a study concluding that the Law is not in conformity with the Women's Convention. Legislative proposal of Van der Laan Democrats 1966 (D66). Parliamentary Papers II 2005/06, nr. 29353, nr. 18, 4.

[22] According to those officials, the process of State reporting is seen as too distant from the primary – national – process. In comparison, the EU is more part of the core business also given the awareness of the official and political leadership. As a result, European comparisons among peers have more impact. Interview 44. If the Second Chamber would 'push' more, then the Government could really do something with the COs. Interview 91.

[23] In this context, the General Meeting in Parliament about the report and COs of CEDAW is not counted. 2009/10 (1), 2008/09 (1), 2007/08 (2), 2006/07 (1), 2005/06 (2), 2004/05 (1), 2003/04 (2), 2002/03 (0), 2001/02 (2).

times.²⁴ It might be because of their principled character that those COs had the highest impact and were picked up most frequently by Parliament and also the press. In two instances, there were references to the concerns and/or the COs in written Parliamentary questions. Interestingly, the starting point and necessary condition for those questions was a study or report that put the issue (high) on the political agenda.²⁵ Noteworthy is the number of questions raised by Bussemaker of the Labour Party (PvdA). Between 8 June 1999 and 25 September 2002, she put forward a Parliamentary question in which the Convention was referred to eleven times. This warrants the conclusion that the attention of Parliament for the Women's Convention and thus the extent to which COs are picked up, depend to a large extent upon the interests of individual Parliamentarians.

Interestingly, the vast majority of Parliamentary questions were raised in the Parliamentary years 1999/00–2002/03.²⁶ Hence, the visibility of the Women's Convention was higher in this period. As we have seen, it was in this period that nearly all national reports and in-depth studies were conducted. Illustrative is

---

24 Other policy areas in which the COs were referred to relate to the national machinery and NGOs, the fight against violence against women, sexual violence as grounds for asylum, the income requirement for family reunification and the prostitution policy. See respectively Parliamentary Papers II 2003/04, TK 25–1697–1698. Parliamentary Papers II 2003/04, 27061, nr. 23, 3–4 and 7. Parliamentary Papers II 2006/07, 30925, nr. 7, 8. Parliamentary Papers II 2007/08, 30573, nr. 7, 9. and Parliamentary Papers II 2009/10, 32211, nr. 5, 4.

25 On 25 January 2002, Bussemaker and Albayrak, Labour Party (PvdA) raised a question concerning the position of au-pairs and on 24 March 2005 a question by Van der Laan, Democrats 1966 (D66) with respect to the Law on Names. The starting point of the first question was a report of the University of Tilburg that was presented on 17 January 2002, although this report itself does not refer to the Women's Convention nor CEDAW or the COs. RALPH REEDE, *Positie van au-pairs uit landen buiten de Europese Unie in Nederland* (Wetenschapswinkel Katholieke Universiteit, Tilburg 2002). The question about au-pairs from countries outside the EU referred to 'criticism' of CEDAW and the remarks of the State Secretary before CEDAW, besides the concern of the Clara Wichmann Institute. Parliamentary Papers II, 2001/02, nr. 708. Also the question about the Law on Names was raised as a result of a report of the University of Utrecht of January 2005, which was presented to Van der Laan on 21 March 2005 during a symposium. See references to the report MARGRIET BRAAM, 'Vaders wil, geen wet meer' (University of Utrecht, January 2005) in the first paragraph of the Parliamentary question, Parliamentary Papers II 2004/05, nr, 1499. The Parliamentary question mentions the fact that the Netherlands is given a rap on the knuckles by CEDAW.

26 I searched for '*Vrouwenverdrag*' (Women's Convention) (30 results) and '*Verdrag*' (Treaty) AND '*discriminatie*' (discrimination) AND '*vrouwen*' (women) (25 results) in the period of 1–1–1995 until 9–6–2010 in Parlando in 'Kamervragen Eerste en Tweede Kamer'. The results are: 2009/10 (2), 2008/09 (2), 2007/08 (1), 2006/07 (1), 2005/06 (2), 2004/05 (2), 2003/04 (0), 2002/03 (3), 2001/02 (3), 2000/01 (4), 1999/00 (4), 1998/99 (1), 1997–98 (3) and 1996/97 (2). The difference is even greater if one considers the number of cases in which the Convention was mentioned by the Parliamentarian in the question itself, and not in the answer by the Government and if the questions are excluded that deal with foreign policy or the human rights situation in another country. 2009/10 (1), 2008/09 (0), 2007/08 (0), 2006/07 (0), 2005/06 (2), 2004/05 (2), 2003/04 (0), 2002/03 (2), 2001/02 (3), 2000/01 (3), 1999/00 (4), 1998/99 (0), 1997–98 (3) and 1996/97 (1).

also that Parliament did discuss the substantive content of the second State report in May 1999[27] and the shadow reports to the second and third report in February 2001.[28] In addition, the five motions and a legislative proposal concerning inheritance of noble titles, in which the Women's Convention was explicitly mentioned, were proposed in more or less the same period.[29] The majority of those five motions and the proposal were, *inter alia*, a reaction to national reports, the in-depth studies or shadow reports.

It is important to highlight in this context that the attention paid by Parliament and the Government to national reports and in-depth studies is more frequent and extensive in comparison with COs.[30] This could possibly be attributed to the fact that those national reports are more visible, thorough and contain a more comprehensive analysis and have a better understanding of the national context, given the fact that they are written by nationals. In addition, those reports are written in Dutch, whereas CEDAW's final report including the COs is not translated into Dutch.

An important mediating factor for Parliament's attention is NGO lobbying. The commentaries, opinions and advices of NGOs are often explicitly mentioned or reacted upon by Parliamentarians during General Meetings or in letters and notes of the Government.[31] This means that those NGOs are important for

---

[27] Parliamentary Papers II 1998/99, 26206, nr. 10.

[28] Parliamentary Papers II 2000/01, 27061, nr. 12.

[29] One motion of Tonkens, the Green Party (GL) and Stuurman (PvdA) concerned the obligation for every ministry to conduct one emancipation effect report every year. This motion referred to the second national report as a starting point. Parliamentary Papers II 2003/04, 27061, nr. 24. Another motion was proposed by de Wit (SP) for a country-wide helpdesk the protection of women, also without a valid residence permit. This motion was a reaction to the fourth in-depth study about domestic violence. There was also a motion proposed by Visser-van Doorn, Christian Democrats (CDA), Schimmel (D66), Bussemaker (PvdA) and Van Gent (GL) in the context of the combination of employment and care which referred to the shadow report to the second and third periodic report. Parliamentary Papers II 2000/01, 27061, nr. 12. The other two motions dealt with the amount of money for the information point aimed at an improved implementation of the Convention and extra financial resources for the protection of women that are the victims of violence. Parliamentary Papers II 2000/01, 27411, nr. 9. Parliamentary Papers II 1999/00, 19637, nr. 514. The legislative proposal by Van Wijmen and Ross-van Dorp (CDA)was about the inheritance of noble titles through female line. In the Explanatory Memorandum attention is paid explicitly to international treaties, especially the Women's Convention, whereby the critique of the first national report on the direct discrimination in legislation about nobility is explicitly mentioned. Parliamentary Papers II 2000/01, 27074, nr. 5.

[30] For the extensive reactions to the first and second national report, respectively 59 and 68 pages, see Parliamentary Papers II 1997/98, 25893, nr. 2 and the annex to Parliamentary Papers II 2003/04, szw0400002, 22 December 2003. See also the 62 detailed and specific questions concerning the substantive recommendations of the third in-depth study and the reaction of the Government thereto. Parliamentary Papers II 1998/99, 25893, nr. 6, 1–10.

[31] In its commentary about the reaction of the Government on the COs to the fourth report, the CEDAW-Network focused specifically on the status and direct applicability of Convention, emancipation effect reports, coordination emancipation policy and mainstreaming, report Antilles, structure of reporting and subsidies NGOs. Those same issues came back in during

'translating' COs to the domestic context and making Parliamentarians aware of those COs. The instrumental role of NGOs was also noted by several government officials. This is logical because the process of State reporting in itself is rather distant and invisible, because, as we shall see, it is hardly covered in the press and the Government does not have COs or State reports translated into Dutch. Parliament thus has to rely upon information of other sources, mainly NGOs.

2.4. MEDIA COVERAGE

The discussion in Parliament mentioned above about the critical comments in the shadow report to the second and third report was the result of an article in a newspaper.[32] This makes it clear that media coverage is an important factor contributing to the attention Parliament will pay to the CO. The attention of and the extent to which the dialogue with CEDAW and the subsequent COs were picked up by the press has decreased over time.[33] Whereas the shadow report and the COs concerning the second and third report were picked up by the

---

the General Meeting about the fourth report given the requests for separate notes about the division of responsibility and coordination and the status of the Convention. Parliamentary Papers II 2007/08, 30420, nr. 98, 61 and 65. For the comments of the CEDAW-Network, see www.steo.nl/vvnl/nieuws/2007/reactienetwerkkabinetsreactie.pdf (Last visited 9 June 2010). Another notable example is the question of the Socialist Party (SP) in the context of the prostitution policy referring to the COs reflecting the comments of the NGO *Vrouw en Recht* (Woman and Law) (VVR). Parliamentary Papers II 2009/10, 32211, nr. 5, 4. For the letter see www.vrouwenrecht.nl/opinie/vvr/brief_prostitutiewet1dec2009 (Last visited 9 June 2010). See also the references of Members of Parliament to the letter of the CEDAW-Network with questions about the implementation of the Women's Convention during the General Meetings of 7 and 12 November 2007, Parliamentary Papers II 2007/08, 30420, nrs. 97 and 106.

[32] See the references of Visser-van Doorn (CDA) and Bussemaker (PvdA) to the newspaper article '*Emancipatie is doorgeschoten*' (Emancipation has gone too far) in the discussion in Parliament on 5 February 2001 about issues related to the combination of work and care, paid leave and indirect discrimination. Parliamentary Papers II 2000/01, 27061, nr. 12, 3. One government official also emphasised that COs would have more influence if reported upon in the newspapers. Interview 91. Another government official noted the lack of attention. Interview 44.

[33] The analysis of the impact of the COs and the Women's Convention on the media focused on the printed press. Use was made of the Lexis Nexis newspaper search engine that provides access to five of the major countrywide newspapers *De Volkskrant*, *NRC Handelsblad*, *Trouw*, *Het Parool* and *AD/Algemeen Dagblad*. Unfortunately, this search engine does not provide access to the biggest newspaper *De Telegraaf* and the newspaper with a reformed character, *Nederlands Dagblad*, which is especially of interest because of the SGP. On 9 June 2010 a search was conducted on '*Vrouwenverdrag*' (Women's Convention) for the period 1 September 1994 and 9 June 2010 (163 results). Additionally, a search was performed with the terms '*Verdrag*' (Treaty) AND '*Vrouwen*' (Women) AND '*discriminatie*' (discrimination) AND NOT '*Vrouwenverdrag*' (Women's Convention) for the period 1 September 1994 and 9 June 2010 (180 results), whereby the articles were screened for their relevance and duplication. The total number of references to COs and/or critique and concern of CEDAW: 2009/10 (0),

media and rather extensively covered,³⁴ no attention was paid to the conclusions of CEDAW concerning the fourth and fifth reports. Illustrative of this scarce attention to CEDAW is the increase in the number of articles about the political party SGP in relation to the Women's Convention after 2005/06 due to the several Court decisions. Nonetheless, only in 1 of those 69 articles, a reference was made to CEDAW as well.³⁵ National reports and in-depth studies did receive relatively more attention by the press.³⁶

2.5. COURTS AND LEGAL PRACTICE

The Women's Convention is also largely absent in legal practice. Courts have only touched upon the Convention 30 times since December 1999.³⁷ Seven cases concern the political party SGP and eight others address immigration and asylum matters. In comparison, the European Convention on Human Rights

---

2008/09 (0), 2007/08 (0), 2006/07 (2), 2005/06 (1), 2004/05 (3), 2003/04 (2), 2002/03 (3), 2001/02 (11), 2000/01 (2).

34   FRANK RENOUR, *'Emancipatie schiet haar doel voorbij'* (Emancipation overshoots the mark), *Algemeen Dagblad*, 30 January 2001, 1. HERMAN STAAL, *'Emanciperen via VN'* (Emancipation by way of UN), *NRC Handelsblad*, 1 February 2001, 2. In addition, 14 articles about the exclusion of women from membership by the political party SGP referred to CEDAW's combined second and third report, whereby it was stated that CEDAW 'lectured the Government', 'rapped the Government over the knuckles', 'called the Government to order' or appealed or condemned the situation as to the existence of the political party. Eight out of those fourteen articles appeared in the Parliamentary year 2001/02, three in 2001/02, two in 2003/04 and one in 2005/06. Attention in the press was also paid to the critique of CEDAW concerning victims of domestic violence and the Law on Names. 'VN: SGP discrimineert', *Algemeen Dagblad*, 1 October 2001, 1, 'Minister Donner bekijkt praktische uitwerking; "het naamrecht is anno 2005 niet geëmancipeerd"' (Minister Donner examines the practical result; "the Law on Names in 2005 is not emancipated"), *Het Parool*, 22 April 2005, 6, 'Dubbele achternaam moet kunnen' (A double surname should be possible), *de Volkskrant*, 22 April 2005, 3, 'Dubbele achternaam kind' (Double surname child), *Trouw*, 22 April 2005, 4, 2001/02 (1) and 2004/05 (3).
35   MARIJN KRUK, *'Inperking van de islam treft ook andere religies'* (Restriction of Islam will also affect other religions), *Trouw*, 17 November 2005, 5.
36   That is to say, three articles appeared in the press about the first national report, one on the front page. AUKJE VAN ROESSEL, 'Ina Brouwer in een mijnenveld' (Ina Brouwer in a mine field), *de Volkskrant*, 21 March 1998, 1. BARBARA BERGER, *'De horzel steekt niet meer'* (The hornet does not sting anymore), *Trouw*, 12 April 1997, 2. 'Vrouwen in Nederland nog steeds achterop' (Women in the Netherlands are still behind), *Het Parool*, 19 March 1997, 1 and 2. For the in-depth study about Article 12, see MARJET GUNNING, *'Eigen bijdrage huisarts treft vrouw zwaar'* (Women are hit hard because they have to pay part of the general practitioner's bill themselves), *Trouw*, 2 July 1996. The study about domestic violence: *'Opvanghuizen weigeren hulp aan illegale vrouwen'* (Shelters refuse to help illegal women), *De Volkskrant*, 18 January 2000, 9.
37   I searched for *'Vrouwenverdrag'* (Women's Convention), 'CEDAW', *'Verdrag inzake de Uitbanning van alle Vormen van Discriminatie van Vrouwen'* (Convention on the Elimination of All Forms of Discrimination Against Women) and *'Vrouwenrechtenverdrag'* (Women's Rights Convention) in the online database www.rechtspraak.nl (12 April 2010). The database was created in December 1999.

was dealt with by courts over 11,000 times, whereas the European Court of Human Rights (ECtHR) itself was cited on more than 2250 occasions.[38]

CEDAW's COs were only explicitly mentioned four times. Two of those four cases related to the SGP.[39] The most recent example is the advice of the Solicitor General to the Supreme Court in the case of the SGP, which not only mentioned but also reproduced the COs of 2001 entirely.[40] Nevertheless, the Supreme Court itself did not refer to CEDAW or the COs in its judgement.[41] Earlier, the Court of Justice did refer to CEDAW's 'judgment' by way of confirming its own conclusion.[42] The decisions of the Council of State and the court in first instance about the SGP did, however, not mention the COs in their judgements.[43]

Apart from the SGP case, Dutch courts have hardly scrutinised the Women's Convention on its merits. Often, the Women's Convention is only cited together with other Conventions, such as the ECHR, and Article 1 of the Constitution.[44]

---

[38] I searched for 'EVRM' (European Convention on Human Rights) (11536 results) and 'EHRM' (European Court of Human Rights) (2,578 results) in the online database www.rechtspraak.nl (29 April 2010).

[39] In another case about the Law on Names there was a reference to academic literature in which the recommendation of Committee 2001 is discussed in the 'bibliography' of the conclusion of the Solicitor General of the Supreme Court. See the bibliography in the conclusion by Mr. F.F. Langemeijer LJN: AU9239, Supreme Court, R05/068HR. The other reference was done by a court to the concerns of CEDAW of 2001 about the position of prostitutes without a valid residence permit and the request to start monitor immediately the effects of the lifting of the ban on brothels. LJN: AE4749, Court Amsterdam, 013/020857-2.

[40] See sections 1.4 and 2.20 and 2.21 of the conclusion by Mr. F.F. Langemeijer, LJN: BK4547, Supreme Court, 08/01354. It is remarkable that the Solicitor General did not refer to the most recent COs of 2007.

[41] The Supreme Court ruled that the fact that a political party excludes women from being eligible for election cannot be accepted in the light of the prohibition of discrimination and Article 7 of the Convention in specific. According to the Court the State is obliged to take effective measures to address this situation. LJN: BK4547, Supreme Court, 08/01354, sections 4.5.5 and 4.6.1 and 4.6.2.

[42] LJN: BC0619, Court of Justice, 05/1725, section 5.10. Janse and Tigchelaar point to the fact that contrary to the judgement of the Court 's Gravenshage in which the (General) Recommendations of CEDAW were central, the consideration of CEDAW played a less prominent role in the ruling of the Court of Justice. Only after having concluded on the basis of other sources that the State violated Article 7 of the Convention, the Court referred to the 'judgement' of CEDAW as an additional argument. See LJN: AU2088, Court 's Gravenshage, HA ZA 03/3395. RONALD JANSE EN JET TIGCHELAAR, 'Het vrouwenrechtencomité: niet bekend en niet geacht?' in: N. Doornbos, N. Huls and W. van Rossum (eds), *Rechtspraak van buiten* (Deventer 2010), 306–316, 310–311.

[43] LJN: BB9493, Council of State, 200609224/1, LJN: AZ53, LJN: AZ5393, Court 's Gravenshage, AWB 06/2696, AU2091, Court 's Gravenshage, HA ZA 03/3396 and AU2088, Court 's Gravenshage, HA ZA 03/3395. Nevertheless, in the latter, the Court dealt extensively with CEDAW's General Recommendations.

[44] In the case about the preventive breast cancer screening for women older than 75 years, the claimants invoked Article 1 of the Constitution, Article 14 ECHR, Article 26 ICCPR, Articles 1 and 2 of the Women's Convention and Article 2 ICESCR. See LJN: BL3061, Court 's Gravenshage, 105.007.421/01 and LJN: BB6695, Court 's Gravenshage, KG 07/1099. In a case about self-employment tax deduction, Article 26 ICCPR, Article 14 ECHR and Article 2 of the Women's Convention were relied upon. LJN: BF7316, Supreme Court, 43992, LJN:

The courts also disagreed whether certain provisions of the Convention would have direct effect. In the SGP cases, the courts awarded direct effect to Article 7.[45] At other times, courts expressed their doubts as to the direct effect.[46] That is to say, in the case about maternity benefits for self-employed women the court considered Article 11, paragraph 3, sub b to be 'an instruction norm', because this provision does not include a direct and unambiguous regulation which would indicate that the State has a margin of appreciation.[47]

3. FACTORS AT THE STATE LEVEL

In this section, the attitude of the Government towards the process of State reporting will be addressed. The underlying assumption is that the incentives to comply with COs particularly depend on the perception of government officials of the process of State reporting and CEDAW in terms of its legitimacy, authority, persuasiveness and usefulness.[48] For this reason, several interviews

---

BA8832, Court of Justice Amsterdam, P06/00242 and LJN: AX2230, Court Haarlem, 05/4098. In the case about the Law on Names, Article 7 sub 1 ICRC and Articles 8 and 14 ECHR were appealed to. LJN: AU9239, Supreme Court, R05/068HR. In another case, the claimants invoked Article 11, sub 1 ICESR, CRC and the Women's Convention. LJN: AA6959, Court 's Gravenshage AWB 00/8599 VRWET. Article 1 of the Constitution, Article 6 ECHR and Articles 1, 3 and 13 of the Women's Convention were referred to in LJN: AE4383, Supreme Court, 1344. In the case about an asylum seeker who had exhausted all legal remedies, Article 8 ECHR, European Social Charter, Article 12 Women's Convention and Articles 9 and 24 ICRC were relied upon. LJN: BM0846, Court Utrecht, SBR 10/867 WMO.

[45] LJN: BK4547, Supreme Court, 08/01354, section 4.4. The Supreme Court also ruled that Article 7 does not offer the State a margin of appreciation (section 4.5.1). LJN: BC0619, Court of Justice 's Gravenshage, 05/1725, LJN: AU2088, sections 4.1 – 4.7. Court 's-Gravenhage. LJN: AU2088, Court 's-Gravenhage, HA ZA 03/3395, section 3.15. Also the Council of State ruled that Article 7 paragraph c constitutes a provision that is binding on all persons ('een ieder verbindende bepaling') in the sense of Article 94 of the Constitution. LJN:BB 9493 Council of State, 200609224/1.

[46] See the doubts expressed by the court concerning the direct effect of the Convention in general. The court determined that in any case, no duty on the part of the authorities could be derived from either the Women's Convention or the ICRC to afford shelter and support to everyone who enters the Netherlands. LJN: AB0942, Court Amsterdam, WB 00/4289. Also see LJN: AA6681, Court 's Gravenshage AWB 98/7896. In both cases the claimants did not invoke a specific provision of the Convention.

[47] Accordingly, the provision does not constitute a provision that is binding on all persons. LJN: BB0334, Court 's Gravenshage 257427/ HA ZA 06–170. Also see two cases of the Central Appeals Tribunal concerning Article 11 in relation to maternity benefits and social security. LJN: AH8706, Central Appeals Tribunal, 00/3437 WAZ and LJN: AA4301, Central Appeals Tribunal, 98/2020 NABW.

[48] The rationale for considering these theories and focus on the attitudes of key stakeholders in the context of State reporting is exactly because treaty monitoring bodies lack instruments to enforce and coerce compliance with the COs. This means that the effectiveness is mainly contingent upon other 'mechanisms', such as persuasion and learning. Hakimi argued in relation to the experience of the United States before the treaty monitoring bodies in recent years that it is unlikely that States accept as law the norms advanced by actors and

were conducted with government officials who were/are involved in the process of State reporting.[49] Those government officials primarily regard State reporting as ensuing from the obligation to report under the Women's Convention and in terms of accounting for one's actions, instead of an opportunity to learn, whereby the Government is willing to implement COs.[50] This section will explain why this is the case.

First of all, the idea prevails that the Netherlands is fulfilling its obligations under the Women's Convention.[51] During the General Meeting about the fourth periodic report, the Minister remarked that the Women's Convention obliges legislation and policy to eradicate discrimination against women and asks for 'appropriate measures' to promote women's development. In his opinion, the Netherlands fulfils this obligation.[52] The Minister therefore did not agree with the conclusion that the Netherlands failed the test or was given a clip round the ear, because in contrast with other States, the Netherlands 'did not break the regulations'. This self-satisfied attitude was also explicitly mentioned by several government officials.

In addition, COs are seen as 'advices' or mere 'opinions', whereby it is made clear that the political appraisal is ultimately made in the Netherlands.[53] During the General Meeting about the combined second and third report, the State Secretary emphasized that neither COs nor the Women's Convention need to be viewed as a timetable.[54] Several government officials also highlighted that 'we'

---

institutions, such as the treaty bodies, if they consider them illegitimate or merely aspirational. MONICA HAKIMI, 'Secondary human rights law', *Yale journal of international law* 34 (2009), 596–604.

[49] See *supra* note 7.

[50] The interviews with government officials have made it clear that officials attach importance to the process of State reporting and that there is a genuine commitment to report, which is considered – at least potentially – to be useful. Nevertheless, one government official stated that most departments see reporting as 'doing the chores' and he emphasized the lack of willingness to fundamentally change something. Interview 13. One official also stressed that reporting is merely an obligation entailing hardly any need for action in terms of an agenda for the future. Interview 44.

[51] In reply to a question of Stuurman (PvdA) whether the Netherlands is fulfilling the obligations arising from the Convention, the Minister of Social Affairs and Employment, Aart Jan de Geus, answered that the Government is indeed fulfilling its obligations, although he acknowledged that the second national report is critical. Parliamentary Papers 2003/04, 27061, nr. 23, 3–4 and 7.

[52] Parliamentary Papers II 2007/08, 30420, nr. 98, 6. The fact that the Netherlands is fulfilling the obligation to realize the rights for citizens under the Women's Convention was repeated in the letter of 5 November 2007. Parliamentary Papers II 2007/08, 30420, nr. 65.

[53] Parliamentary Papers II 2007/08, 30420, nr. 98, 7–8.

[54] The State Secretary used the word '*spoorboekje*' (railway timetable). According to the State Secretary, the Women's Convention aims to improve women's rights and governments have a certain margin to give an interpretation themselves meaning that the objectives of the Convention could be pursued differently. Similarly, during the General Meeting about the fourth periodic report, the Minister recognized that CEDAW's 'advices' are taken seriously, but that this does not mean that all the advices and comments will be adopted one-on-one.

have our own vision and 'they' (CEDAW) their interpretation. In this context, it was argued that CEDAW's remarks could easily be disregarded given their legally non-binding character.

This attitude towards State reporting and the COs is reflected in the explicit rejection of several COs. The most notable examples are the COs dealing with fundamental issues, such as those about the political party SGP and the Law on Names.[55] With respect to the SGP, the Government argued that in spite of CEDAW's conclusion, the Government is of the opinion that the current legislation meets the obligations of Article 7 of the Women's Convention.[56]

Similarly, the Government has made it clear that it did not share CEDAW's opinion that the Law on Names contravenes the Women's Convention.[57] As elaborated upon earlier, a Parliamentarian proposed an amendment to the Law on Names on the points that CEDAW expressed its concerns. In its opinion to this proposal, the Council of State has stated that CEDAW reproduced the Law on Names incorrectly.[58] In addition, the Council of State remarked in its opinion that CEDAW did not provide a further explanation as to the question whether an objective and reasonable ground exists concerning the preference in the Dutch Law for the name of the father when parents cannot reach an agreement as to the name of a child. It also referred to the 'margin of appreciation' States are entitled to under the Women's Convention and the fact that this subject is defined by national traditions and that there exists a clear preference of the Dutch population.[59] On the occasion of the advice the then

---

[55] It is remarkable that the COs that were (explicitly) rejected were the most specific and clear ones. Not only is the language stronger ('is a violation' and 'contravenes the basic principle of the Convention'), but it is only with respect to its findings in those *substantive* areas of concern that CEDAW refers to specific Articles of the Women's Convention.

[56] Parliamentary Papers II 2001/02, szw0000961, 2. Fourth periodic report of States parties, UN doc. CEDAW/C/NLD/4, 10 February 2005, 47–48. In his letter to Parliament with a reaction to the comments of CEDAW to the fourth report, the Minister explicitly rejected CEDAW's recommendation to consider withdrawing the appeal, because he considered the matter to be very principal so as to make appeal obvious, because several fundamental rights and the relationship between the legislature and the judiciary are at stake. Noteworthy is that the State solicitor even held during the appeal that the Convention does not have direct effect. This is contrary to paragraph 26 (and 11 and 12) of the COs to acknowledge the direct effect of the Women's Convention in the domestic legal order. See section 1.9, LJN: BC0619, Court of Justice 's-Gravenhage, 05/1725, 5 December 2007.

[57] Parliamentary Papers II 2001/02, szw0000961, 3. It was even argued that, although CEDAW is of the opinion that it should be regulated differently, the political appraisal is made in the Netherlands. Parliamentary Papers II 2007/08, 30420, nr. 98, 7–8.

[58] Parliamentary Papers II, 2005/06, 29353, nr. 20, 3. That is to say, if the parents cannot reach an agreement as to the name of a child, the child will automatically receive the name of the father instead of, as CEDAW states, the father having the ultimate decision.

[59] Parliamentary Papers II, 2005/06, 29353, nr. 20, 3. The Council put forward that the ECHR did pay attention to this question and concluded that discrimination is out of the question. The Council of State advised that the amendment should also go into this question for the assessment of the conformity of the current Law with Article 16 (g) of the Women's Convention.

Minister of Justice, Piet Hein Donner, consequently argued that he had doubts about whether CEDAW rightly established a conflict.[60]

In other instances, the Government has shown – more implicitly – that it did not understand or fully agree with CEDAW's concern and the measures recommended in the COs.[61] Illustrative is the remark of the State Secretary during the discussion of the fifth report that the Netherlands tries to do everything it can, and that it sometimes changes policies but that at other times the situation in the Netherlands is so specific 'that it is as it is'.[62]

Given the Government's own assessment of its compliance with the Women's Convention, it comes as no surprise that the Government sees the dialogue with CEDAW as a 'defence of the report' or a 'country-examination', whereby the main objective is to give 'a good answer' to the critical questions of CEDAW.[63] This means that the discussion of the State report with CEDAW hardly ever takes the form of a 'constructive dialogue'. During the discussion of the fifth State report, for example, there was hardly any self-criticism. Nor did the delegation express difficulties or problems or was CEDAW asked for suggestions. One government official pointed to the tension between the wish of CEDAW to have a constructive dialogue and substantive talks with experts, on the one hand, and the wish to speak with a politician, on the other hand. The latter unavoidably takes the form of a defence and a disguised discussion with Parliament. Other government officials pointed to the high number of questions leading to the 'dishing out of answers' instead of a real discussion.

Another important factor for the impact and effectiveness of the process of State reporting, not directly related to the attitude of the Government, is the strength of the national machinery and the knowledge of government officials. The Netherlands Emancipation Review Committee (Review Committee) concluded that the interdepartmental supporting structure has functioned insufficiently since 2001.[64] Similarly, a (comparative) study concluded that the national machinery has weakened since the nineties. The study, furthermore, pointed to the loss of the coordination function of the central policy unit, given

---

[60] Parliamentary Papers II, 2005/06, 29353, nr. 20, 4.
[61] See for example, the efforts that CEDAW urged the Government to take in paragraph 210 to provide training and education to prostitutes. The Government made it clear that the Dutch policy is targeted at fighting excrescences in prostitution and not prostitution as such. Other examples are the use of quotas, the responsibility of the European part of the Kingdom for the Netherlands Antilles and Aruba and the status of the Convention in the domestic legal system.
[62] For the purpose of this research, the discussion of the fifth State report during the 45th session was attended.
[63] Parliamentary Papers II 2006/07, 30420, nr. 24. Parliamentary Papers II 2007/08, 30420 nr. 61, 7. Parliamentary Papers II 2008/09, 30420, nr. 136, Parliamentary Papers II 2009/10, 30420 nr. 141.
[64] Visitatie Commissie Emancipatie, 'Coördinatie van emancipatiebeleid en gender mainstreaming bij de rijksoverheid', docs.minszw.nl/pdf/35/2007/35_2007_3_10317.pdf (last visited 11 June 2010), 11–12.

the fact that the function of the Direction Emancipation had been reduced to eight core policy areas.[65] This is also reflected in the limited control and pressure exercised by the Direction in relation to the follow-up and implementation of the COs vis-à-vis the responsible line Ministries, besides the letter of the Government with a reaction to all COs.[66]

The Review Committee has also concluded that there was a lack of gender expertise and knowledge among government officials about international obligations, including the Women's Convention.[67] An additional difficulty in this context is that emancipation of women in general is not regarded as a priority issue.[68] According to the Review Committee, the understanding that the necessity of having an emancipation policy and gender mainstreaming also results from international obligations is lacking.[69] Illustrative is the report of the Netherlands Government in the context of the 15th anniversary of the Beijing Declaration providing that the Government has 'no special actions aimed at human rights at (sic) women'.[70] An indication or explanation for this might be that various Ministries had been approached with requests for contributions to reports whereby the context was insufficiently clear and the deadlines too short.[71]

---

[65] J.V. OUTSHOORN, 'Insituties voor emancipatiebeleid: Nederland in een international context', docs.minszw.nl/pdf/129/2007/129_2007_3_10318.pdf (last visited 11 June 2010) and VISITATIE COMMISSIE EMANCIPATIE, 'Coördinatie van emancipatiebeleid en gender mainstreaming bij de rijksoverheid', docs.minszw.nl/pdf/35/2007/35_2007_3_10317.pdf (last visited 11 June 2010), 7–8.

[66] This issue was brought up by several government officials. See also the concern of CEDAW in UN doc. CEDAW/C/NLD/CO/5, para. 14.

[67] VISITATIE COMMISSIE EMANCIPATIE, 'Een beetje beter is niet goed genoeg. Emancipatiebeleid en gender mainstreaming bij de rijksoverheid. Eindrapportage visitaties 2005–2006' (2007), docs.minszw.nl/pdf/129/2007/129_2007_3_10315.pdf (last visited 11 June 2010), 28 and 33.

[68] Interview 87. There is a lack of interest among the official and political leadership. Interview 63. Interview 44.

[69] VISITATIE COMMISSIE EMANCIPATIE, 'Dat moet echt beter. Emancipatiebeleid en gender mainstreaming bij de rijksoverheid in 2005. Voorlopig beeld', 10. This report can be found in the attachment to Parliamentary Papers II 2005/06, 30420, nr. 3. Also see MARGREET DE BOER, 'Onwil of spraakverwarring? Of wat er moeilijk is aan het implementeren van het VN-Vrouwenverdrag', Tijdschrift voor genderstudies 4 (2008), 47–53, 48–49.According to De Boer, the Government shows insufficiently that the Convention includes human rights instead of only policy objectives. During the discussion of the second and third report, the Government itself stated that the it was 'by no means satisfied' that the Women's Convention was known well enough. Summary record, CEDAW/C/SR.512, 6 July 2001, para. 14.

[70] Report of the Netherlands Government to the UNECE for the preparation of regional review and appraisals in the context of the 15th anniversary of the adoption of the Beijing Declaration and Platform for Action in 2010 (The Hague, March 2009), www.unece.org/gender/documents/Beijing+15/Netherlands.pdf (Last visited 23 March 2010).

[71] VISITATIE COMMISSIE EMANCIPATIE, 'Coördinatie van emancipatiebeleid en gender mainstreaming bij de rijksoverheid', docs.minszw.nl/pdf/35/2007/35_2007_3_10317.pdf (last visited 11 June 2010), 20.

4. FACTORS RELATED TO CEDAW

In the previous section, several factors at the State level explaining the limited impact and effectiveness have been discussed. In this section, the focus will be on the functioning of CEDAW. There is, however, a clear interrelationship between the factors at the State level and those related to CEDAW, because the attitude and ideas of government officials about the process of State reporting and CEDAW are directly shaped by their experience with CEDAW.

First of all, government officials have lamented the fact that several of CEDAW's questions were rather basic and/or showed a limited knowledge about the national context. There was also a question by the Chinese delegate about isolation problems among elderly rural women as a consequence of a lack of public transport and community involvement.[72] This example was given by almost all government officials as an example of how the own mind frame and background and cultural differences of the several experts can be clearly heard in the questions, thereby showing a lack of understanding and knowledge about the Dutch context.[73] Other questions and remarks showed that not all experts were that well prepared, which was noted by government officials as well.[74] Although those rather small errors are completely understandable given the fact that expert members of CEDAW fulfil their work voluntarily without any remuneration, often next to full-time jobs, they might, nonetheless, have a negative consequence for the authoritativeness and the usefulness as perceived by the State.[75]

As a result of the limited possibility and time for experts to prepare themselves, they have to rely on the information provided by NGOs in their shadow reports. Officials criticise that CEDAW easily takes over the criticism of

---

[72] See Summary record of the 917th meeting, UN doc. CEDAW/C/SR.917, 18 March 2010, para. 34. The State Secretary responded by saying that 'I do not know whether you have visited our country', because it is two hours from border to border. She also stated that this is not the biggest problem the Netherlands is currently facing.

[73] They also pointed to the limited capacity of experts to acquaint themselves with all the subtleties of all the countries being reviewed, given their full time jobs besides the work as an expert.

[74] During the fifth dialogue, one expert remarked that ethnic and minority women are not visible in political functions, although Appendix 9 to the State report contains data and statistics about ethnic minority women in politics showing that this is not entirely the case. One government delegate referred in her response to a question of an expert to a study about gender-related violence that had been sent to CEDAW, but that had apparently not been read by the members of CEDAW. There was also a question about whether the Government is considering withdrawing declarations or reservations, while the Netherlands does not have reservations at all. Another expert referred to Suriname.

[75] That is to say, mainly instinctive. Interview 42. Also the fact that CEDAW sometimes is perceived as droning on and being too negative has a detrimental effect on its authority. Interview 33.

NGOs without question.[76] The problem with this is that NGOs often represent only one audience and at the same time lose sight of the economic reality as a result of which their criticism is seen as one-sided or only partially true. Conversely, the Government has to consider and weigh several interests which necessitate nuance and different point of views. This is insufficiently taken into account by CEDAW, which is seen by some government officials as holding 'a single issue campaign' by only adopting an empowerment and emancipation perspective, without considering that the reality is often more unmanageable. That is to say, CEDAW does not consider budgetary implications, economic interests, clashes with democracy and other fundamental rights and the legal dimensions, such as European Union Law.

A related issue is the alleged lack of independence. CEDAW is seen by some government officials as not always objective and political, also given internal discussions concerning sexual and reproductive health and lesbian, gay, bisexual and transgender rights. This means that several members are conservative and against certain – for the Netherlands at least natural – human rights.[77] Another point of concern is the fact that CEDAW only has two male members. It is perceived that the stature of CEDAW would improve if there would be more male experts, because there is a risk that CEDAW is seen as a biased club of feminist lawyers.[78]

Another factor explaining the limited impact and effectiveness that boils down to the usefulness is the specificity and determinacy of COs. Several COs are very broad and unspecific. This is especially the case with the COs about measures in the socio-economic field related to the labour market participation of women and the position of immigrant, refugee and minority women.[79] Those COs are rather undetermined and aspirational referring to 'greater efforts', 'additional programmes', 'sufficient childcare places', 'relevant follow-up steps', and the increase, intensifying or strengthening of efforts.[80] It is remarkable that one paragraph often includes multiple and diverse measures that CEDAW urges or recommends the Government to take, while each measure on its own is already rather broad and unspecific. Given the fact that the measures prescribed are general and do not outline a specific course of action, it is unclear what kind of measures CEDAW has in mind and how the State could intensify its efforts.

---

[76] The result of the fact that CEDAW seems to attach more value to the information of NGOs, little is done with the dialogue and the information from the Government. Interview 13.
[77] According to one government official, this does not do CEDAW any good. Interview 79.
[78] Interview 53.
[79] COs 2001, A/56/38(SUPP), paras. 203–206, 213–214 and 216–218. UN doc. CEDAW/C/NLD/CO/4, paras. 17–18, 27–30.
[80] For example, paragraph 204 recommended the review of legislation, but it was not indicated in what way legislation needed to be reviewed. Paragraph 206 referred to rather general notion such as measures to eliminate discrimination against immigrant, refugee and minority women, both in society at large and within their communities and the promotion of the human rights of women over discriminatory cultural practices. COs 2001, A/56/38(SUPP).

As a result, it might be uncertain what the contribution and the usefulness of the COs is. Officials also noted the long time span between the submission of the report and the List of Issues, both dealing with a period long before, while a lot of new developments have taken place in the meantime. As a consequence, the usefulness and impact is diminished as well.[81] Even when measures have been taken in line with COs, one could question whether this was the result of the COs. This also because, according to government officials, COs often coincide with the measures already in place.[82]

5. DIFFERING VIEWS ABOUT THE NATURE OF THE OBLIGATIONS

As has been made clear in the previous section, the Government sometimes rejects COs. This disagreement is essentially the result of the divergence of views about the nature of the obligations under the Women's Convention between the Government and CEDAW also in light of other international obligations. This is another important reason for the limited impact and effectiveness of the process of State reporting and COs.

Whereas CEDAW interprets the Women's Convention broadly and progressively, the State has a more restrictive view about the obligations under the Women's Convention.[83] This divergence is for example reflected in the discussion about the status and the direct effect of the Women's Convention.[84] According to the Government, the Women's Convention contains rather obligations of conduct than obligations of result, since the Convention is not giving an unambiguous framework because of the different national contexts in which it needs to be implemented.[85]

---

[81] In this regard it is interesting to note that the fifth report of the national rapporteur on human trafficking refers to the fourth State report and acknowledges that there is a great time lapse between the period about which is being reported and the moment of consideration of the report by CEDAW. Parliamentary Papers II 2006/07, 28638, nr. 32, 12 July 2007, 39–40.

[82] Nevertheless, it was noted by those officials that COs could support and strengthen policy that is being developed. What was made clear as well was that measures were often taken not because of the Women's Convention or the COs, but because the measures were seen as desirable and natural in themselves.

[83] See for example Feride Acar, former Chair of CEDAW, stating that CEDAW is 'famous for integrating progressive standards into its interpretation of the Convention' and that the views expressed by experts during the constructive dialogue 'bear testimony to a remarkably bold interpretation of the Convention'. FERIDE ACAR, 'Thoughts on the Committee's past, hopes for its future', in: C. Flinterman and B. Schöpp-Schilling (eds.), *The circle of empowerment: twenty-five years of the UN Committee on the Elimination of Discrimination Against Women* (New York: The Feminist Press at the City University of New York, 2007), 340–345, 342.

[84] UN doc. CEDAW/C/NLD/CO/4, para. 11 and 12. CEDAW/C/NLD/CO/5, 8, 12 and 13. See *supra* notes 46–48.

[85] Rather, the obligation of efforts needs to be translated in an obligation of result at the national level. Parliamentary Papers II 1997/98, 25893, nr. 5, 6.

A related issue is the disagreement about the form of equality that should be achieved on the basis of the Women's Convention, being it merely *de iure* or also *de facto*. The Government, for instance, has rejected the recommendation about the accessibility of elderly women to pensions and health care, because those facilities are at least formally equally accessible.[86] Another example of this is the reasoning that the obligation in Article 5 of the Convention has been fulfilled, because the Equal Treatment (Full-time and Part-time Workers) Act avoids any reference to full-time or part-time employees.[87] Similarly, the Government deems gender neutral wording of policy the correct starting point, for example in the context of domestic violence, human trafficking or the integration courses.[88]

This divergence of views also boils down to how one views the role and functions of the State in society vis-à-vis individual responsibilities and the extent to which other fundamental rights and freedoms and multiformity as such should be respected, given the potential clash that exists between State action and the freedom of expression, religion and education.[89] The Government, for example, does not seem to favour temporary special measures for specific (vulnerable) groups of women and minorities, at least not in the sense of the Women's Convention.[90] Furthermore, the Government considers that the

---

[86] Parliamentary Papers II 2001/02, szw0000961, 1.

[87] Fourth periodic report of States parties, UN doc. CEDAW/C/NLD/4, 10 February 2005, 62.

[88] See UN doc. CEDAW/C/NLD/CO/4, para. 19. See also the report of the Visitatie Commissie Emancipatie, 'Emancipatiebeleid en gender mainstreaming bij het Ministerie van Justitie. Eindrapportage visitatie 2005–2006' static.ikregeer.nl/pdf/BLG11190.pdf (last visited 11 June 2010), 7. A similar reasoning is applied in relation to integration courses in response to the concern of CEDAW in paragraph 27. The Government states that it 'feels that the Integration Act does not result in discrimination against women', because the mandatory requirement of integration courses applies to for all foreign nationals who want to live in the Netherlands permanently, irrespective of whether they are men or women. Fifth periodic report of States parties, UN doc. CEDAW/C/NLD/5, 24 November 2008, 27. This means that the Government does not consider whether this policy might disproportionately affect women.

[89] The first national report points to the fact that State action aimed at influencing the mentality of people in the context of gender ideology and stereotyping might conflict with respect for multiformity and the freedom of expression, religion and education. Besides, a possible disagreement about the desirably of authorities to steer and influence society, the report also refers to the doubts about the potential of the authorities. 'Het Vrouwenverdrag in Nederland anno 1997. Verslag van de commissie voor de eerste nationale rapportage over de implementatie in Nederland van het Internationaal Verdrag tegen Discriminatie van Vrouwen' (February 1997), www.rijksoverheid.nl/onderwerpen/vrouwenemancipatie/documenten-en-publicaties/rapporten/2004/10/15/het-vrouwenverdrag-in-nederland-anno-1997.html, 52–53.

[90] COs 2001, A/56/38(SUPP), para. 218. UN doc. CEDAW/C/NLD/CO/4, para. 18 and 19. UN doc. CEDAW/C/NLD/CO/5, paras. 22 and 23. During the discussion of the second and third report, the State Secretary explained that affirmative action plans had been tried in the Netherlands and had not yielded results. Summary record, UN doc. CEDAW/C/SR.512, 6 July 2001, para. 51. During the review of the fourth report, the Government said that it was against legal quotas for women holding public office or political positions because positions in the Ministry were filled on the basis of qualifications, irrespective of gender. Summary

improvement of the disadvantaged position of women belonging to ethnic minorities is 'their own responsibility to an important extent'.[91] Another example of how the role of the State could clash with the freedom of individuals is visible in the debate on whether or not a high number of women employed in part-time jobs is undesirable. According to the former Minister of Social Affairs and Employment, De Geus, it is not undesirable, because the freedom to choose whether or not to work should also be respected.[92]

These divergent views often boil down to conflicting obligations under international and European law, encompassing different standards of equality.[93] As we have seen, the Government often refers to other international obligations or jurisprudence of other international courts in order to justify non-compliance with COs.[94] For example, with respect to the Law on Names, the Government pointed to the ECtHR that ruled in a case against the Netherlands that the difference in treatment is reasonable and proportional.[95] In the context of the CO about the discrimination part-time workers are facing in relation to overtime, the Government mentioned the ruling of the European Court of Justice (ECJ) that 'it was not discriminatory to deny overtime pay to a part-time worker.'[96] Similarly, jurisprudence of the ECJ has curtailed the possible forms of preferential treatment.[97] As a consequence of those conflicting treaty obligations, an appraisal of interests has to take place. The Government regards

---

record of the 767th meeting (Chamber B), UN doc. CEDAW/C/SR.767(B), 5 March 2007, paras. 6 and 45. The Government did speak about 'the special temporary measures introduced by the Government to achieve equal representation in senior management positions were often reflected in such measures adopted at the company level.' Summary record of the 768th meeting (Chamber B), UN doc. CEDAW/C/SR.768(B), 2 February 2007, para. 15. It is, however, unclear which special temporary measures the Government refers to, since the fourth report does not mention them.

[91] Fourth periodic report of States parties, UN doc. CEDAW/C/NLD/4, 10 February 2005, 23. It also held that the focus of emancipation policy must shift from legislation to encouraging initiatives by women and girls themselves.

[92] Summary record of the 767th meeting (Chamber B), UN doc. CEDAW/C/SR.767(B), 5 March 2007, para. 7. In response to critical reactions of members of Parliament about the abandoning of the objective of men having a share in care tasks of 40% by 2010, Minister Plasterk remarked that he thinks that the Government should not determine that men should wash more socks. See the reactions of Van Gent (GL) and Van der Burg Parliamentary Papers II 2007/08, 30420, nr. 98, 3–4. According to him, women should get the freedom to develop themselves completely equal in all forms, instead of the Government saying that men should contribute 35% instead of 30% to care tasks. Parliamentary Papers II 2007/08, 30420, nr. 97, 23.

[93] RIKKI HOLTMAAT and CHRISTA TOBLER, 'CEDAW and the European Union's policy in the field of combating gender discrimination', *Maastricht Journal of European and Comparative Law* 12 (4) (2005), 399–425.

[94] During the discussion of the fourth report it was stated that the B-9 arrangement was in line with European Union guidelines for residence permits for victims who cooperated with the authorities.

[95] ECHR 27 April 2000, nr. 42 973/98 (Bijleveld vs. the Netherlands).

[96] Summary record, UN doc. CEDAW/C/SR.512, 6 July 2001, para. 47. COs 2001, A/56/38(SUPP), para. 214.

[97] Parliamentary Papers II 2004/05, 28770, nr. 11, 4.

the State as the most appropriate entity to do so. The Government has clarified this in the Memorandum of Answer in the context of the legislative approval of the Women's Convention by stating that the Women's Convention does not provide provisions concerning the delineation of the working of the non-discrimination principle vis-à-vis other fundamental rights and freedoms. As a result, every State should make this delineation itself with a view to other UN human rights treaties.[98] This is also possible given the broad provision in the Women's Convention, referring to 'all appropriate measures', which makes different interpretations of the Women's Convention feasible.[99]

6. CONCLUSION

This contribution found that the limited level of compliance and thus the effectiveness of State reporting under the Women's Convention for the Netherlands can be explained, first and foremost, by the limited impact and lack of attention paid by domestic actors. Above all, an active involvement of Parliament and media coverage are crucial for the attention paid and importance attached by government (officials) to the process of State reporting, which is essential for compliance with COs. From this perspective it is encouraging that CEDAW recently launched several initiatives to enhance the effectiveness, the aim of which is to increase the involvement of actors at the national level, such as NGOs and Parliament, in relation to the follow-up of COs.[100] In addition, a follow-up procedure was put into place.[101]

Nonetheless, it is still to be seen what the results of those initiatives will be, at least for the Netherlands. In light of the second main conclusion of this Chapter, the effects will not be world-shattering, because the biggest obstacle for compliance with COs are the not so positive attitudes and ideas of government officials about the usefulness, legitimacy, authority and persuasiveness of the

---

[98] See the quote of Schuurmans and Jordens 74-lb Zwolle, 1992, 1372 in MATTHIJS DE BLOIS, 'De mannenpartij en het Vrouwenverdrag', *Nemesis* 6 (2002), 169–179, 178.

[99] Verslag van de workshops van het Symposium 'Handen en voeten aan het Vrouwenverdrag', Rijksuniversiteit Limburg, 4 November 1994, *Nemesis 1* (1995), 19–22, 21–22.

[100] 'Statement by the Committee on the Elimination of Discrimination Against Women on its relationship with non-governmental organizations' adopted during the 45th session (18 January – 5 February 2010), www2.ohchr.org/english/bodies/cedaw/docs/statements/NGO.pdf. See the statement 'National Parliaments and the Convention on the Elimination of All Forms of Discrimination Against Women' adopted during the 45th session, www2.ohchr.org/english/bodies/cedaw/docs/statements/Parliamentarians.pdf (last visited 15 June 2010). Also see the – standard – paragraph in the COs inviting the Government to encourage Parliament 'to take necessary steps with regard to the implementation' of the COs. UN doc. CEDAW/C/NLD/CO/5, para. 9.

[101] CEDAW requests the State to submit a follow op report, within two years, about 'the steps undertaken to implement the recommendations contained in paragraphs 27 and 29.' UN doc. CEDAW/C/NLD/CO/5, para. 52.

process of State reporting and CEDAW. The perception of government officials is reinforced by the functioning and working of CEDAW and the fact that there exists a fundamental divergence in views regarding the nature of the obligations under the Women's Convention between the Government and CEDAW. This has as a result that COs are hardly complied with and hardly ever lead to changes in policy and/or legislation.

One might wonder whether the results only hold true for the Netherlands or apply to other States as well. The limited academic research conducted so far as well as the concept paper of the High Commissioner proposing a unified Standing treaty body hint at a larger generalizability of the findings.[102] This would imply that the limited impact and compliance with COs of CEDAW and the other UN human right treaty bodies is endemic in the *current* system of treaty monitoring and supervision. This also begs the question whether this means that this limited follow-up of COs is inherent in the system or susceptible to change and if so, whether changes should take place within the existing system or whether the system as a whole needs to be reformed.

---

[102] *Concept paper on the High Commissioner's proposal* for a unified Standing treaty body, UN doc. HRI/MC/2006/2, 22 March 2006, paras. 20–28. See especially paragraph 26 in which it is provided that: 'governments frequently pay insufficient attention to the recommendations adopted by the treaty bodies, and lack of awareness or knowledge among national constituencies about the monitoring procedures and their recommendations, renders these invisible at the national level.' For a general study about the impact of UN human rights treaties in twenty different countries that reaches a rather similar conclusion while pointing to comparable factors, see CHRISTOF HEYNS and FRANS VILJOEN, 'The impact of United Nations human rights treaties on the domestic level', *Human rights quarterly* 23 (2001), 483–535. For (critical) reviews of the level of compliance with the Women's Convention in relation to CEDAW see: VEDNA JIVAN and CHRISTINE FORSTER, 'Challenging conventions: in pursuit of greater legislative compliance with CEDAW in the Pacific', *Melbourne journal of international law* 10 (2009), 655–690. ANGELA M. BANKS, 'CEDAW, compliance and custom: human rights enforcement in Sub-Saharan Africa', *Fordham international law journal* 32 (2009), 781–845.

MAASTRICHT SERIES IN HUMAN RIGHTS

The *Maastricht Centre for Human Rights* supervises research in the field of human rights conducted at Maastricht University's Faculty of Law. This research is interdisciplinary, with a particular focus on public international law, criminal law and social sciences. The titles in the Series contribute to a better understanding of different aspects of human rights *sensu lato*.

Published titles within the Series:

1. Ineke Boerefijn, Fons Coomans, Jenny Goldschmidt, Rikki Holtmaat and Ria Wolleswinkel (eds.), *Temporary Special Measures. Accelerating de facto Equality of Women under Article 4(1) UN Convention on the Elimination of All Forms of Discrimination against Women* (2003)
   ISBN 90-5095-359-X
2. Fons Coomans and Menno T. Kamminga (eds.), *Extraterritorial Application of Human Rights Treaties* (2004)
   ISBN 90-5095-394-8
3. Koen De Feyter and Felipe Gómez Isa (eds.), *Privatisation and Human Rights in the Age of Globalisation* (2005)
   ISBN 90-5095-422-7
4. Ingrid Westendorp and Ria Wolleswinkel (eds.), *Violence in the domestic sphere* (2005)
   ISBN 90-5095-526-6
5. Fons Coomans (ed.), *Justiciability of Economic and Social Rights* (2006)
   ISBN 978-90-5095-582-9
6. Jan C.M. Willems (ed.), *Developmental and Autonomy Rights of Children: Empowering Children, Caregivers and Communities. 2nd revised edition* (2007)
   ISBN 978-90-5095-726-7
7. Alette Smeulers and Roelof Haveman (eds.), *Supranational Criminology: Towards a Criminology of International Crimes* (2008)
   ISBN 978-90-5095-791-5
8. Hans van Crombrugge, Wouter Vandenhole and Jan C.M. Willems (eds.), *Shared Pedagogical Responsibility* (2008)
   ISBN 978-90-5095-813-4
9. Hildegard Schneider and Peter Van den Bossche (eds.), *Protection of Cultural Diversity from a European and International Perspective* (2008)
   ISBN 978-90-5095-864-6

10. Fons Coomans, Fred Grünfeld and Menno T. Kamminga (eds.), *Methods of Human Rights Research* (2009)
    ISBN 978-90-5095-879-0
11. Jan CM Willems (ed.), *Children's Rights and Human Development. A Multidisciplinary Reader* (2010)
    ISBN 978-94-000-0032-2
12. Martine Boersma and Hans Nelen (eds.), *Corruption & Human Rights: Interdisciplinary Perspectives* (2010)
    ISBN 978-94-000-0085-8
13. Hans Nelen and Jacques Claessen (eds.), *Beyond the Death Penalty* (2012)
    ISBN 978-1-78068-060-6
14. Fons Coomans and Rolf Künneman (eds.), *Cases and Concepts on extraterritorial Obligations in the Area of Economic, Social and Cultural Rights* (2012)
    ISBN 978-94-000-0046-9
15. Chen Weidong and Taru Spronken (eds.), *Three Approaches to Combating Torture in China* (2012)
    ISBN 978-1-78068-088-0